Lecture Notes in Computer Science   **10977**

Commenced Publication in 1973
Founding and Former Series Editors:
Gerhard Goos, Juris Hartmanis, and Jan van Leeuwen

Editorial Board

David Hutchison
   Lancaster University, Lancaster, UK
Takeo Kanade
   Carnegie Mellon University, Pittsburgh, PA, USA
Josef Kittler
   University of Surrey, Guildford, UK
Jon M. Kleinberg
   Cornell University, Ithaca, NY, USA
Friedemann Mattern
   ETH Zurich, Zurich, Switzerland
John C. Mitchell
   Stanford University, Stanford, CA, USA
Moni Naor
   Weizmann Institute of Science, Rehovot, Israel
C. Pandu Rangan
   Indian Institute of Technology Madras, Chennai, India
Bernhard Steffen
   TU Dortmund University, Dortmund, Germany
Demetri Terzopoulos
   University of California, Los Angeles, CA, USA
Doug Tygar
   University of California, Berkeley, CA, USA
Gerhard Weikum
   Max Planck Institute for Informatics, Saarbrücken, Germany

More information about this series at http://www.springer.com/series/7407

Cezar Câmpeanu (Ed.)

Implementation and Application of Automata

23rd International Conference, CIAA 2018
Charlottetown, PE, Canada, July 30 – August 2, 2018
Proceedings

 Springer

Editor
Cezar Câmpeanu (iD)
University of Prince Edward Island
Charlottetown, PE
Canada

ISSN 0302-9743   ISSN 1611-3349 (electronic)
Lecture Notes in Computer Science
ISBN 978-3-319-94811-9   ISBN 978-3-319-94812-6 (eBook)
https://doi.org/10.1007/978-3-319-94812-6

Library of Congress Control Number: 2018947440

LNCS Sublibrary: SL1 – Theoretical Computer Science and General Issues

Printed on acid-free paper

This Springer imprint is published by the registered company Springer International Publishing AG
part of Springer Nature
The registered company address is: Gewerbestrasse 11, 6330 Cham, Switzerland

Preface

This volume contains the papers presented at the 23rd International Conference on Implementation and Application of Automata (CIAA 2018) organized by the School of Mathematical and Computational Science, University of Prince Edward Island, during July 30 – August 2, 2018, in Charlottetown, Prince Edward Island, Canada. The CIAA conference series is a major international venue for the dissemination of new results in the implementation, application, and theory of automata.

There were 39 submissions from 19 different counties: Algeria, Bulgaria, Canada, China, France, Finland, France, Germany, India, Israel, Italy, Japan, Pakistan, Poland, Russia, Singapore, Slovakia, South Africa, South Korea, Sweden, and the USA. Each submission was reviewed by at least three reviewers and thoroughly discussed by the Program Committee (PC). The committee decided to accept 23 papers for oral presentation and publication in this volume. The program also includes four invited talks by Anne Condon, Stavros Konstantinidis, Andreas Malcher, and Jacques Sakarovitch.

The previous 22 conferences were held in various locations all around the globe: Paris (2017), Seoul (2016), Umeå (2015), Giessen (2014), Halifax (2013), Porto (2012), Blois (2011), Winnipeg (2010), Sydney (2009), San Francisco (2008), Prague (2007), Taipei (2006), Nice (2005), Kingston (2004), Santa Barbara (2003), Tours (2002), Pretoria (2001), London Ontario (2000), Potsdam (WIA 1999), Rouen (WIA 1998), and London Ontario (WIA 1997 and WIA 1996). Like its predecessors, the theme of CIAA 2018 was the implementation of automata and applications in related fields. The topics of the presented papers include state complexity of automata, implementations of automata and experiments, enhanced regular expressions, and complexity analysis.

I would like to thank to the members of the PC and the external reviewers for their help in selecting the papers. I am very grateful to all invited speakers, authors of submitted papers, and participants who made CIAA 2018 possible. I also note that the work of the PC and the preparation of the proceedings were greatly simplified by the EasyChair conference system.

I also appreciate the help of the editorial staff at Springer in producing this book, in particular to Alfred Hofmann, Anna Kramer, and their Computer Science Editorial team, for their guidance and help during the process of publishing this volume and for supporting the event through publication in the LNCS series.

Finally, I am grateful to the conference sponsors: the University of Prince Edward Island (the President, the Vice President of Academics and Research, the Dean of Science, and the Associate Dean of School of Mathematical and Computational

Science), and the Atlantic Association for Research in the Mathematical Sciences (AARMS) for their generous financial support, and Meetings & Conventions PEI for their continuous logistic support.

We all look forward to seeing you at CIAA 2019 in Kosice, Slovakia!

May 2018   Cezar Câmpeanu

Organization

Program Committee

Francine Blanchet-Sadri	The University of North Carolina at Chapel Hill, USA
Cezar Câmpeanu (Chair)	University of Prince Edward Island, Canada
Arnaud Carayol	CNRS, LIGM, Université Paris Est, France
Jean-Marc Champarnaud	LITIS, University of Rouen, France
Salimur Choudhury	Algoma University, Canada
Jan Daciuk	Gdańsk University of Technology, Poland
Dora Giammarresi	University of Rome Tor Vergata, Italy
Yo-Sub Han	Yonsei University, Japan
Markus Holzer	Institut für Informatik, Universität Giessen, Germany
Oscar Ibarra	University of California, Santa Barbara, USA
Galina Jiraskova	Slovak Academy of Sciences, Slovakia
Juhani Karhumäki	University of Turku, Finland
Sylvain Lombardy	LaBRI, CNRS, Institut Polytechnique de Bordeaux, France
Carlo Mereghetti	University of Milan, Italy
Frantisek Mraz	Charles University, Prague, Czech Republic
Cyril Nicaud	LIGM Universitè Paris Est, France
Alexander Okhotin	St. Petersburg State University
Giovanni Pighizzini	University of Milan, Italy
Daniel Reidenbach	Loughborough University, UK
Rogério Reis	University of Porto, Portugal
Kai Salomaa	Queen's University, Canada
Shinnosuke Seki	University of Electro-Communications, Japan
Klaus Sutner	Carnegie Mellon University, USA
Mikhail Volkov	Ural State University, Russia
Bruce Watson	Stellenbosch University, South Africa
Abuzer Yakaryilmaz	University of Latvia, Latvia
Hsu-Chun Yen	National Taiwan University, Taiwan

Additional Reviewers

Becker, Tim	De La Higuera, Colin
Beier, Simon	Francis, Nadime
Carpentieri, Bruno	Freydenberger, Dominik D.
Cherubini, Alessandra	Gauwin, Olivier
Cho, Da-Jung	Guingne, Franck
Conrad, Tim	Gutierrez, Abraham
Dassow, Jürgen	Haque, Sardar

Jugé, Vincent
Kapoutsis, Christos
Kari, Jarkko
Kim, Hwee
Ko, Sang-Ki
Kosolobov, Dmitry
Kufleitner, Manfred
Loff, Bruno
Madonia, Maria
Maletti, Andreas
McQuillan, Ian
Mercas, Robert
Nicart, Florent
Ouardi, Faissal

Pribavkina, Elena
Ravikumar, Balasubramanian
Reinhardt, Klaus
Ryzhikov, Andrew
Schabanel, Nicolas
Schmitz, Sylvain
Serre, Olivier
Smith, Taylor
Strauss, Tinus
Sutner, Klaus
Szykuła, Marek
Talbot, Jean-Marc
Tamm, Hellis
Zheng, Shenggen

Contents

X   Contents

On Design and Analysis of Chemical Reaction Network Algorithms

Anne Condon$^{(\boxtimes)}$

The Department of Computer Science,
University of British Columbia, Vancouver, Canada
condon@cs.ubc.ca

The fields of DNA computing, molecular programming and DNA nanotechnology offer exciting new possibilities for organizing and manipulating matter at the nanoscale, and prompt us to think about computation in creative new ways. Molecules reacting in a test tube change state, and counts of molecules can in principle be used to simulate counter machines, all in a highly distributed, asynchronous and stochastic manner. In this talk I'll give some background on models of molecular programming, focusing on Stochastic Chemical Reaction Networks, and describe some beautiful results and open problems pertaining to this model of computing.

Stochastic Chemical Reaction Networks (CRNs) have traditionally been used to model the dynamics of interacting molecules in a well-mixed solution [1], particularly when the counts of some molecular species is low, in which case mass action kinetics is not a good model. More recently, stochastic CRNs have become a popular model for describing molecular programs - programs that can be executed in a test tube or other wet environment [2,3]. Reactions are the basic instructions of these programs, acting on molecules in a well-mixed solution. CRNs are closely related to population protocols among resource-limited agents in distributed networks [4], as well as models of gene regulatory networks, infectious diseases and voting processes [5–8].

Stable Function Computation by CRNs. In one model of predicate computation by CRNs proposed by Angluin et al. [9,10], inputs are represented by initial counts of certain molecular species in a well-mixed solution of fixed volume. Chen et al. [11] studied function computation in essentially the same model. For example, if the solution contains n_1 copies of species X_1 and n_2 copies of species X_2, then the two reactions of Fig. 1(a) eventually produce a number of Y's equal to $n_1 + n_2$, while the single reaction of Fig. 1(b) produces a number of Y's equal to the min of the counts of X_1 and X_2, and the reactions of Fig. 1(c) produce the max of the counts. (Assume that the rate constant associated with each reaction is 1, although these assertions are true regardless of the rate constant.)

The evolution of a "computation" by a CRN can be described as a sequence of configurations, where each configuration is a vector of counts of molecular species and the initial configuration describes initial species counts. There is an underlying probabilistic model, consistent with the principles of chemical reactions (under fixed environmental conditions such as temperature), that determines the rates and relative likelihoods of reactions as a function of molecular

© Springer International Publishing AG, part of Springer Nature 2018
C. Câmpeanu (Ed.): CIAA 2018, LNCS 10977, pp. 1–3, 2018.
https://doi.org/10.1007/978-3-319-94812-6_1

$$\begin{array}{ccc}
X_1 \to Y & X_1 + X_2 \to Y & X_1 \to Y + Z_1 \\
X_2 \to Y & & X_2 \to Y + Z_2 \\
& & Z_1 + Z_2 \to Y' \\
& & Y + Y' \to Z \\
\text{(a)} & \text{(b)} & \text{(c)}
\end{array}$$

Fig. 1. Simple CRNs for stably computing the (a) sum, (b) min and (c) max of the counts of two molecular species X_1 and X_2. The output is represented by the number of copies of species Y. The CRN of part (c) integrates the CRN of part (a) with a slight variant of part (b), thereby computing the max as the sum minus the min.

species counts, reaction rate constants, and the volume of the enclosing solution. From this probabilistic model, notions of correctness (perhaps allowing for a small probability of error) as well as efficiency (depending on reaction rates, which in turn depend on rate constants and counts of molecular reactants) can be formulated.

All of the CRNs of Fig. 1 compute their functions *stably* [9–11]: on any computation, a configuration is eventually reached with probability 1 in which the counts of output species are consistent with the function being computed, and once reached, the counts never change subsequently. The class of functions that can be stably computed by CRNs is exactly the semi-linear functions [10,11].

Stable Function Composition. A basic question is: given two CRNs that stably compute two functions f and g, when is it possible to compose the CRNs in order to compute the composition $g \circ f$? Stable composition is certainly possible when the CRN that computes f is *output-oblivious* - that is, no output species is a reactant in any reaction of the CRN. Not all semi-linear functions are output-oblivious. We will show that the max function and generalizations are not output-oblivious, and present a characterization of which semilinear functions can be stably computed by output-oblivious CRNs.

CRNs with Error: Approximate Majority. The Approximate Majority problem is as follows: in a mixture of two types of species where the gap between the counts of the majority and minority species is above some threshold, which species is in the majority? CRNs that solve Approximate Majority with low error probability have been well studied but have been difficult to analyze [12]. We'll describe a simple way to analyze CRNs for Approximate Majority [13], as well as several variants, e.g., when reaction rates are uncertain or when some molecules are Byzantine. These CRNs are described in Fig. 2 which is from Condon et al. [13]. Key to our approach is to first analyze a very simple CRN for Approximate Majority involving tri-molecular reactions, i.e., reactions with three reactants. We can show that well-studied bi-molecular CRNs for Approximate Majority essentially emulate the tri-molecular protocol, and also that the same analysis principles can be used to prove correctness and efficiency of multi-valued consensus.

$$X+Y \xrightarrow{1/2} X+B \quad (0'\text{x})$$

$$X+Y \to B+B \quad (0') \qquad X+Y \xrightarrow{1/2} Y+B \quad (0'\text{y})$$

$$X+X+Y \to X+X+X \quad (1) \qquad X+B \to X+X \quad (1') \qquad X+B \to X+X \quad (1')$$

$$X+Y+Y \to Y+Y+Y \quad (2) \qquad Y+B \to Y+Y \quad (2') \qquad Y+B \to Y+Y \quad (2')$$

(a) Tri-molecular CRN.   (b) Double-B CRN.   (c) Single-B CRN.

Fig. 2. A tri-molecular and two bi-molecular chemical reaction networks (CRNs) for Approximate Majority. Reactions (0'x) and (1'y) of Single-B have rate constant $1/2$ while all other reactions have rate constant 1.

References

1. Gillespie, D.T.: Exact stochastic simulation of coupled chemical reactions. J. Phys. Chem. **81**, 2340–2361 (1977)
2. Cook, M., Soloveichik, D., Winfree, E., Bruck, J.: Programmability of chemical reaction networks. In: Condon, A., Harel, D., Kok, J., Salomaa, A., Winfree, E. (eds.) Algorithmic Bioprocesses, pp. 543–584. Springer, Heidelberg (2009). https://doi.org/10.1007/978-3-540-88869-7_27
3. Soloveichik, D., Cook, M., Winfree, E., Bruck, J.: Computation with finite stochastic chemical reaction networks. Nat. Comput. **7**(4), 615–633 (2008)
4. Angluin, D., Aspnes, J., Diamadi, Z., Fischer, M.J., Peralta, R.: Computation in networks of passively mobile finite-state sensors. Distrib. Comput. **18**(4), 235–253 (2006)
5. Bower, J.M., Bolouri, H.: Computational Modeling of Genetic and Biochemical Networks. MIT Press, Cambridge (2004)
6. Cruise, J., Ganesh, A.: Probabilistic consensus via polling and majority rules. Queueing Syst. **78**(2), 99–120 (2014)
7. Perron, E., Vasudevan, D., Vojnovic, M.: Using three states for binary consensus on complete graphs. In Proceedings of the 28th IEEE Conference on Computer Communications (INFOCOM), pp. 2527–2535. (2009)
8. Moussaïd, M., Kämmer, J.E., Analytis, P.P., Neth, H.: Social influence and the collective dynamics of opinion formation. PLoS ONE **8**(11), e78433 (2013)
9. Angluin, D., Aspnes, J., Diamadi, Z., Fischer, M., Peralta, R.: Computation in networks of passively mobile finite-state sensors. Distrib. Comput. **18**(4), 235–253 (2006)
10. Angluin, D., Aspnes, J., Eisentat, D.: Stably computable predicates are semi-linear. In: Proceedings of the Twenty-Fifth Annual ACM Symposium on Principles of Distributed Computing, pp. 292–299. ACM (2006)
11. Chen, H., Doty, D., Soloveichik, D.: Deterministic function computation with chemical reaction networks. Nat. Comput. **13**(4), 517–534 (2014)
12. Angluin, D., Aspnes, J., Eisenstat, D.: A simple population protocol for fast robust approximate majority. Distrib. Comput. **21**(?), 87–102 (2008)
13. Condon, A., Hajiaghayi, M., Kirkpatrick, D., Maňuch, J.: Simplifying analyses of chemical reaction networks for approximate majority. In: Brijder, R., Qian, L. (eds.) DNA 2017. LNCS, vol. 10467, pp. 188–209. Springer, Cham (2017). https://doi.org/10.1007/978-3-319-66799-7_13

Regular Expressions and Transducers over Alphabet-Invariant and User-Defined Labels

Stavros Konstantinidis[1]([⊠]), Nelma Moreira[2], Rogério Reis[2], and Joshua Young[1]

[1] Saint Mary's University, Halifax, NS, Canada
s.konstantinidis@smu.ca, jyo04@hotmail.com
[2] CMUP & DCC, Faculdade de Ciências da Universidade do Porto, Rua do Campo Alegre, 4169-007 Porto, Portugal
{nam,rvr}@dcc.fc.up.pt

Abstract. We are interested in regular expressions and transducers that represent word relations in an alphabet-invariant way—for example, the set of all word pairs u, v where v is a prefix of u independently of what the alphabet is. Current software systems of formal language objects do not have a mechanism to define such objects. We define transducers in which transition labels involve what we call set specifications, some of which are alphabet invariant. In fact, we consider automata-type objects, called labelled graphs, where each transition label can be any string, as long as that string represents a subset of a certain monoid. Then, the behaviour of the labelled graph is a subset of that monoid. We do the same for regular expressions. We obtain extensions of known algorithmic constructions on ordinary regular expressions and transducers, including partial derivative based methods, at the broad level of labelled graphs such that the computational efficiency of the extended constructions is not sacrificed. Then, for regular expressions with set specs we obtain a direct partial derivative method for membership. For transducers with set specs we obtain further algorithms that can be applied to questions about independent regular languages, in particular the witness version of the property satisfaction question.

Keywords: Alphabet-invariant transducers · Regular expressions Partial derivatives · Algorithms · Monoids

1 Introduction

We are interested in 2D regular expressions and transducers over alphabets whose cardinality is not fixed, or whose alphabet is even unknown. In particular,

Research supported by NSERC (Canada) and by FCT project UID/MAT/00144/ 2013 (Portugal). Reference [16] is a detailed version of this paper.

assume that the alphabet is $\Gamma = \{0, 1, \ldots, n-1\}$ and consider the 2D regular expression

$$\left(0/0 + \cdots + (n-1)/(n-1)\right)^* \left(0/e + \cdots + (n-1)/e\right)^*,$$

where e is the symbol for the empty string. This 2D regular expression has $O(n)$ symbols and describes the prefix relation: all word pairs (u, v) such that v is a prefix of u. Similarly, consider the transducer in Fig. 1, which has $O(n^2)$ transitions. Current software systems of formal language objects require users to enter all these transitions in order to define and process the transducer. We want to be able to use special labels in transducers such as those in the transducer $\hat{t}_{\mathrm{sub2}}$ in Fig. 2. In that figure, the label $(\forall/=)$ represents the set $\{(a, a) \mid a \in \Gamma\}$ and the label $(\forall/\forall\neq)$ represents the set $\{(a, a') \mid a, a' \in \Gamma, a \neq a'\}$. Moreover that transducer has only a fixed number of 5 transitions. Similarly, using these special labels, the above 2D regular expression can be written as $(\forall/=)^*(\forall/e)^*$. Note that the new regular expression as well as the new transducer in Fig. 2 are *alphabet invariant* as they contain no symbol of the intended alphabet Γ—precise definitions are provided in the next sections.

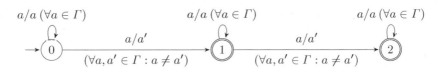

Fig. 1. The transducer realizes the relation of all (u, v) such that $u \neq v$ and the Hamming distance of u, v is at most 2.

We also want to be able to define algorithms that work *directly* on regular expressions and transducers with special labels, without of course having to expand these labels to ordinary ones. Thus, for example, we would like to have an efficient algorithm that computes whether a pair (u, v) of words is in the relation realized by the transducer in Fig. 2, and an efficient algorithm to compute the composition of two transducers with special labels.

We start off with the broad concept of a set B of labels, called *label set*, where each label $\beta \in B$ is simply a string that represents a subset $\mathcal{I}(\beta)$ of a monoid M. Then we define type B automata (called *labelled graphs*) in which every transition label is in B. Similarly we consider type B regular expressions whose base objects (again called *labels*) are elements of B and represent monoid subsets. Our first set of results apply to any user-defined set B and monoid M. Then, we consider further results specific to the cases of (i) 1D regular expressions and automata (monoid $M = \Gamma^*$), (ii) 2D regular expressions and transducers (monoid $M = \Gamma^* \times \Gamma^*$) with special labels (called *set specs*). We note that a concept of label set similar to the one defined here is considered in [12]. In particular, [12] considers label sets with weights, and the objectives of that work are different from the ones here.

We emphasize that we do not attempt to define regular expressions and automata outside of monoids; rather we use monoid-based regular expressions and automata as a foundation such that (i) one can define such objects with alphabet invariant labels or with a priori unknown label sets B, as long as each of the labels represents a subset of a known monoid; (ii) many known algorithms and constructions on monoid-based regular expressions and automata are extended to work directly and as efficiently on certain type B objects.

We also mention the framework of symbolic automata and transducers of [23, 24]. In that framework, a transition label is a logic predicate describing a set of domain elements (characters). The semantics of that framework is very broad and includes the semantics of label sets in this work. As such, the main algorithmic results in [23, 24] do not include time complexity estimates. Moreover, outside of the logic predicates there is no provision to allow for user-defined labels and related algorithms working directly on these labels.

The paper is organized as follows. The next section makes some assumptions about *alphabets* Γ of non-fixed size. Section 3 defines two specific label sets: the set of *set specs*, in which each element represents a subset of Γ or the empty string, and the set of *pairing specs* that is used for transducer-type labelled graphs. Some of these label sets can be *alphabet invariant*. Section 4 discusses the general concept of a *label set* B, which has a behaviour $\mathcal{I}$ and refers to a monoid mon B; that is, $\mathcal{I}(\beta)$ is a subset of mon B for any label $\beta \in B$. Section 5 defines type B labelled graphs $\hat{g}$ and their behaviours $\mathcal{I}(\hat{g})$. When B is the set of pairing specs then $\hat{g}$ is a transducer-type graph and realizes a word relation. Section 6 defines regular expressions $\mathbf{r}$ over any label set B and their behaviour $\mathcal{I}(\mathbf{r})$, and establishes the equivalence of type B graphs and type B regular expressions (Theorem 1) as well as the partial derivative automaton corresponding to $\mathbf{r}$ via the concept of linear form of $\mathbf{r}$ (Theorem 3). Then, for a regular expression $\mathbf{r}$ over set specs it presents the partial derivative machinery for deciding directly if a word is in $\mathcal{L}(\mathbf{r})$ (Lemma 11). Section 7 considers the possibility of defining 'higher level' versions of product constructions that work on automata/transducers over known monoids. To this end, we consider the concept of *polymorphic operation* '$\odot$' that is partially defined between two elements of some labels sets B, B', returning an element of some label set C, and also partially defined on the elements of the monoids mon B and mon B', returning an element of the monoid mon C. In this case, if $\odot$ is known to work on automata/transducers over mon B, mon B' then it would also work on type B, B' graphs (Theorem 4). Section 8 presents some basic algorithms on automata with set specs and transducers with set specs. Section 9 defines the composition of two transducers with set specs such that the complexity of this operation is consistent with the case of ordinary transducers (Theorem 5). Section 10 considers the questions of whether a transducer with set specs realizes an identity and whether it realizes a function. It is shown that both questions can be answered with a time complexity consistent with that in the case of ordinary transducers (Theorems 6 and 7). Section 11 shows that, like ordinary transducers, transducers with set specs that define independent language properties can be processed directly (without expanding them) and efficiently to answer the witness version of the property satisfaction question for regular languages (Corollary 2 and Example 12). Finally, the last section contains a few concluding remarks and directions for future research.

2 Terminology and Alphabets of Non-fixed Size

The set of positive integers is denoted by $\mathbb{N}$. Then, $\mathbb{N}_0 = \mathbb{N} \cup \{0\}$. Let S be a set. We denote the *cardinality* of S by $|S|$ and the set of all subsets of S by 2^S. To indicate that ϕ is a *partial mapping* of a set S into a set T we shall use the notation $\phi : S \dashrightarrow T$. We shall write $\phi(s) = \bot$ to indicate that ϕ is not defined on $s \in S$.

An *alphabet space* Ω is an infinite and totally ordered set whose elements are called *symbols*. We shall assume that Ω is fixed and contains the digits $0, 1, \ldots, 9$, which are ordered as usual, as well as the *special symbols*

$$\forall \quad \exists \quad \not\exists \quad = \quad \neq \quad / \quad e \quad \oplus \quad \oslash$$

We shall denote by '<' the total order of Ω. As usual we use the term *string* or *word* to refer to any finite sequence of symbols. The *empty string* is denoted by ε. For any string w we say that w is *sorted* if the symbols contained in w occur in the left to right direction according to the total order of Ω. For example, the word 012 is sorted, but 021 is not sorted. For any set of symbols S, we use the notation wo(S) = the sorted word consisting of the symbols in S. For example, if $S = \{0, 1, 2\}$, then wo$(S) = 012$ and wo$(\{2, 0\}) = 02$.

Let $g \in \Omega$ and w be a string. The expression $|w|_g$ denotes the number of occurrences of g in w, and the expression alph w denotes the set $\{g \in \Omega : |w|_g > 0\}$, that is, the set of symbols that occur in w. For example,

$$\text{alph}\,(1122010) = \{0, 1, 2\}.$$

An *alphabet* is any finite nonempty subset of Ω. In the following definitions we consider an alphabet Γ, called the alphabet of *reference*, and we assume that Γ *contains at least two symbols and no special symbols*.

Algorithmic Convention About Alphabet Symbols. We shall consider algorithms on automata and transducers where the alphabets Γ involved are not of fixed size and, therefore, $|\Gamma| \to \infty$; thus, the alphabet size $|\Gamma|$ is accounted for in time complexity estimates. Moreover, we assume that each Γ-symbol is of size $O(1)$. This approach is also used in related literature (e.g., [1]), where it is assumed implicitly that the cost of comparing two Γ-symbols is $O(1)$.

In the algorithms presented below, we need operations that require to access only a part of Γ or some information about Γ such as $|\Gamma|$. We assume that Γ has been preprocessed such that the value of $|\Gamma|$ is available and is $O(\log |\Gamma|)$ bits long and the *minimum symbol* $\min \Gamma$ of Γ is also available. In particular, we assume that we have available a *sorted array* ARR_Γ consisting of all Γ-symbols. While this is a convenient assumption, if in fact it is not applicable then one can make the array from Γ in time $O\big(|\Gamma| \log |\Gamma|\big)$. Then, the minimum symbol of Γ is simply $\text{ARR}_\Gamma[0]$. Moreover, we have available an *algorithm* notIn(w), which returns a symbol in Γ that is not in alph w, where w is a *sorted word* in Γ^* with $0 < |w| < |\Gamma|$. Next we explain that the desired algorithm

notIn(w) can be made to work in time $O(|w|)$.

The algorithm notIn(w) works by using an index i, initially $i = 0$, and incrementing i until $\mathrm{ARR}_\Gamma[i] \neq w[i]$, in which case the algorithm returns $\mathrm{ARR}_\Gamma[i]$.

3   Set Specifications and Pairing Specifications

Here we define expressions, called set specs, that are used to represent subsets of the alphabet Γ or the empty string. These can be used as labels in automata-type objects (labelled graphs) and regular expressions defined in subsequent sections.

Definition 1. *A* set specification, *or* set spec *for short, is any string of one of the four forms*

$$e \qquad \forall \qquad \exists w \qquad \nexists w$$

where w is any sorted nonempty string containing no repeated symbols and no special symbols. The set of set specs is denoted by SSP.

Let $F, \exists u, \nexists u, \exists v, \nexists v$ be any set specs with $F \neq e$. We define the partial operation $\cap: \mathrm{SSP} \times \mathrm{SSP} \dashrightarrow \mathrm{SSP}$ *as follows.*

$e \cap e = e, \quad e \cap F = F \cap e = \bot$
$\forall \cap F = F \cap \forall = F$
$\exists u \cap \exists v = \exists \,\mathrm{wo}\,(\,\mathrm{alph}\,u \cap \mathrm{alph}\,v), \quad \textit{if}\,(\,\mathrm{alph}\,u \cap \mathrm{alph}\,v) \neq \emptyset$
$\exists u \cap \exists v = \bot, \quad \textit{if}\,(\,\mathrm{alph}\,u \cap \mathrm{alph}\,v) = \emptyset$
$\nexists u \cap \nexists v = \nexists \,\mathrm{wo}\,(\,\mathrm{alph}\,u \cup \mathrm{alph}\,v)$
$\exists u \cap \nexists v = \exists \,\mathrm{wo}\,(\,\mathrm{alph}\,u \setminus \mathrm{alph}\,v), \quad \textit{if}\,(\,\mathrm{alph}\,u \setminus \mathrm{alph}\,v) \neq \emptyset$
$\exists u \cap \nexists v = \bot, \quad \textit{if}\,(\,\mathrm{alph}\,u \setminus \mathrm{alph}\,v) = \emptyset$
$\nexists u \cap \exists v = \exists v \cap \nexists u$

Example 1. As any set spec X is a string, it has a length $|X|$. We have that $|\forall| = 1$ and $|\exists w| = 1 + |w|$. Also,

$$\exists 035 \cap \exists 1358 = \exists 35, \quad \nexists 035 \cap \exists 1358 = \exists 18, \quad \nexists 035 \cap \nexists 1358 = \nexists 01358.$$

Lemma 1. *For any given set specs G and F, $G \cap F$ can be computed in time $O(|G| + |F|)$.*

Definition 2. *Let Γ be an alphabet of reference. We say that a set spec F* respects Γ, *if the following restrictions hold when F is of the form $\exists w$ or $\nexists w$:*

$$w \in \Gamma^* \text{ and } 0 < |w| < |\Gamma|.$$

In this case, the language $\mathcal{L}(F)$ *of F (with respect to Γ) is the subset of $\Gamma \cup \{\varepsilon\}$ defined as follows:*

$$\mathcal{L}(e) = \{\varepsilon\}, \qquad \mathcal{L}(\forall) = \Gamma, \qquad \mathcal{L}(\exists w) = \mathrm{alph}\,w, \qquad \mathcal{L}(\nexists w) = \Gamma \setminus \mathrm{alph}\,w.$$

The set of set specs that respect Γ is denoted as follows

$$\mathrm{SSP}[\Gamma] = \{\alpha \in \mathrm{SSP} \mid \alpha \text{ respects } \Gamma\}.$$

Remark 1. In the above definition, the requirement $|w| < |\Gamma|$ implies that there is at least one Γ-symbol that does not occur in w. Thus, to represent Γ we must use $\forall$ as opposed to the longer set spec $\exists\,\mathrm{wo}(\Gamma)$.

Lemma 2. *Let Γ be an alphabet of reference and let $F \neq e$ be a set spec respecting Γ. The following statements hold true.*

1. *For given $g \in \Gamma$, testing whether $g \in \mathcal{L}(F)$ can be done in time $O(\log |F|)$.*
2. *For given $g \in \Gamma$, testing whether $\mathcal{L}(F) \setminus \{g\} = \emptyset$ can be done in time $O(|F|)$.*
3. *For any fixed $k \in \mathbb{N}$, testing whether $|\mathcal{L}(F)| \geq k$ can be done in time $O(|F| + \log |\Gamma|)$, assuming the number $|\Gamma|$ is given as input along with F.*
4. *Testing whether $|\mathcal{L}(F)| = 1$ and, in this case, computing the single element of $\mathcal{L}(F)$ can be done in time $O(|F|)$.*
5. *Computing an element of $\mathcal{L}(F)$ can be done in time $O(|F|)$.*
6. *If $|\mathcal{L}(F)| \geq 2$ then computing two different $\mathcal{L}(F)$-elements can be done in time $O(|F|)$.*

Now we define expressions for describing certain finite relations that are subsets of $(\Gamma \cup \{\varepsilon\}) \times (\Gamma \cup \{\varepsilon\})$.

Definition 3. *A* pairing specification, *or* pairing spec *for short, is a string of the form*

$$e/e \qquad e/G \qquad F/e \qquad F/G \qquad F/= \qquad F/G\neq \qquad (1)$$

where F, G are set specs with $F, G \neq e$. The set of pairing specs is denoted by PSP. *The* inverse p^{-1} *of a pairing spec p is defined as follows depending on the possible forms of p displayed in (1):*

$$(e/e)^{-1} = (e/e), \qquad (e/G)^{-1} = (G/e), \quad (F/e)^{-1} = (e/F),$$
$$(F/G)^{-1} = (G/F), \quad (F/=)^{-1} = (F/=), \quad (F/G\neq)^{-1} = (G/F\neq).$$

Example 2. As a pairing spec p is a string, it has a length $|\mathsf{p}|$. We have that $|\forall/e| = 3$ and $|\exists u/\nexists v| = 3 + |u| + |v|$. Also, $(\forall/e)^{-1} = (e/\forall)$ and $(\exists u/\forall\neq)^{-1} = (\forall/\exists u\neq)$.

Definition 4. *A pairing spec is called* alphabet invariant *if it contains no set spec of the form $\exists w, \nexists w$. The set of alphabet invariant pairing specs is denoted by* $\mathrm{PSP}^{\mathrm{invar}}$.

Definition 5. *Let Γ be an alphabet of reference and let p be a pairing spec. We say that p* respects Γ, *if any set spec occurring in p respects Γ. The set of pairing specs that respect Γ is denoted as follows*

$$\mathrm{PSP}[\Gamma] = \{\mathsf{p} \in \mathrm{PSP} : \mathsf{p} \text{ respects } \Gamma\}.$$

The relation $\mathcal{R}(\mathsf{p})$ *described by p (with respect to Γ) is the subset of $\Gamma^* \times \Gamma^*$ defined as follows.*

$$\mathcal{R}(e/e) = \{(\varepsilon, \varepsilon)\}; \quad \mathcal{R}(e/G) = \{(\varepsilon, y) \mid y \in \mathcal{L}(G)\};$$

$$\mathcal{R}(F/e) = \{(x, \varepsilon) \mid x \in \mathcal{L}(F)\}; \quad \mathcal{R}(F/G) = \{(x, y) \mid x \in \mathcal{L}(F), y \in \mathcal{L}(G)\};$$
$$\mathcal{R}(F/\!=) = \{(x, x) \mid x \in \mathcal{L}(F)\};$$
$$\mathcal{R}(F/G\!\neq) = \{(x, y) \mid x \in \mathcal{L}(F), y \in \mathcal{L}(G), x \neq y\}.$$

Remark 2. All the alphabet invariant pairing specs are

$$e/e \qquad e/\forall \qquad \forall/e \qquad \forall/\forall \qquad \forall/\!= \qquad \forall/\forall\neq$$

Any alphabet invariant pairing spec p respects all alphabets of reference Γ, as p contains no set specs of the form $\exists w$ or $\not\exists w$.

4   Label Sets and Their Behaviours

We are interested in automata-type objects (labelled graphs) $\hat{g}$ in which every transition label β represents a subset $\mathcal{I}(\beta)$ of some monoid M. These subsets are the behaviours of the labels and are used to define the behaviour of $\hat{g}$ as a subset of M—see next section for labelled graphs. We shall use the notation

ε_M for the neutral element of the monoid M.

If S, S' are any two subsets of M then, as usual, we define

$$SS' = \{mm' \mid m \in S,\, m' \in S'\} \quad \text{and} \quad S^i = S^{i-1}S \quad \text{and} \quad S^* = \cup_{i=0}^{\infty} S^i,$$

where $S^0 = \{\varepsilon_M\}$ and the monoid operation is denoted by simply concatenating elements. We shall only consider *finitely generated* monoids M where each $m \in M$ has a unique *canonical* (string) representation $\underline{m}$. Then, we write $\underline{M} = \{\underline{m} \mid m \in M\}$.

Example 3. We shall consider two standard monoids. First, the free monoid Γ^* (or Σ^*) whose neutral element is ε. The canonical representation of a nonempty word w is w itself and that of ε is e: $\underline{\varepsilon} = e$. Second, the monoid $\Sigma^* \times \Delta^*$ (or $\Gamma^* \times \Gamma^*$) whose neutral element is $(\varepsilon, \varepsilon)$. The canonical representation of a word pair (u, v) is $\underline{u}/\underline{v}$. In particular, $\underline{(\varepsilon, \varepsilon)} = e/e$.

A *label set* B is a nonempty set of nonempty strings (over Ω). A *label behaviour* is a mapping $\mathcal{I} : B \to 2^M$, where M is a monoid. Thus, the behaviour $\mathcal{I}(\beta)$ of a label $\beta \in B$ is a subset of M. We shall consider label sets B with *fixed behaviours*, so we shall

denote by mon B the *monoid of B* via its fixed behaviour.

Notational Convention. We shall make the *convention* that for any label sets B_1, B_2 with fixed behaviours $\mathcal{I}_1, \mathcal{I}_2$, we have:

if mon $B_1 = $ mon B_2 then $\mathcal{I}_1(\beta) = \mathcal{I}_2(\beta)$, for all $\beta \in B_1 \cap B_2$.

With this convention we can simply use a single behaviour notation $\mathcal{I}$ for all label sets with the same behaviour monoid, that is, we shall use $\mathcal{I}$ for any B_1, B_2 with mon $B_1 = $ mon B_2. This convention is applied in the example below: we use $\mathcal{L}$ for the behaviour of both the label sets Σ_e and SSP$[\Gamma]$.

Example 4. We shall use some of the following label sets and their fixed label behaviours.

1. $\Sigma_e = \Sigma \cup \{e\}$ with behaviour $\mathcal{L} : \Sigma_e \to 2^{\Sigma^*}$ such that $\mathcal{L}(g) = \{g\}$, if $g \in \Sigma$, and $\mathcal{L}(e) = \{\varepsilon\}$. Thus, mon $\Sigma_e = \Sigma^*$.
2. Σ with behaviour $\mathcal{L} : \Sigma \to 2^{\Sigma^*}$ such that $\mathcal{L}(g) = \{g\}$, for $g \in \Sigma$. Thus, mon $\Sigma = \Sigma^*$.
3. SSP$[\Gamma]$ with behaviour $\mathcal{L} : \text{SSP}[\Gamma] \to 2^{\Gamma^*}$, as specified in Definition 2. Thus, mon SSP$[\Gamma] = \Gamma^*$.
4. REG Σ = REG Σ_e = all regular expressions over Σ with behaviour $\mathcal{L} :$ REG $\Sigma \to 2^{\Sigma^*}$ such that $\mathcal{L}(r)$ is the language of the regular expression r. Thus, mon (REG Σ) = Σ^*.
5. $[\Sigma_e, \Delta_e] = \{x/y \mid x \in \Sigma_e, y \in \Delta_e\}$ with behaviour $\mathcal{R} : [\Sigma_e, \Delta_e] \to 2^{\Sigma^* \times \Delta^*}$ such that $\mathcal{R}(e/e) = \{(\varepsilon, \varepsilon)\}, \mathcal{R}(x/e) = \{(x, \varepsilon)\}, \mathcal{R}(e/y) = \{(\varepsilon, y)\}, \mathcal{R}(x/y) = \{(x, y)\}$, for any $x \in \Sigma$ and $y \in \Delta$. Thus, mon $[\Sigma_e, \Delta_e] = \Sigma^* \times \Delta^*$.
6. PSP$[\Gamma]$ with behaviour $\mathcal{R} : \text{PSP}[\Gamma] \to 2^{\Gamma^* \times \Gamma^*}$ as specified in Definition 5. Thus, mon PSP$[\Gamma] = \Gamma^* \times \Gamma^*$.
7. PSP^{invar} with behaviour $\mathcal{R}_\perp : \text{PSP}^{\text{invar}} \to \{\emptyset\}$. Thus, $\mathcal{I}(\beta) = \emptyset$, for any $\beta \in \text{PSP}^{\text{invar}}$.
8. If B_1, B_2 are label sets with behaviours $\mathcal{I}_1, \mathcal{I}_2$, respectively, then $[B_1, B_2]$ is the label set $\{\beta_1/\beta_2 \mid \beta_1 \in B_1, \beta_2 \in B_2\}$ with behaviour and monoid such that $\mathcal{I}(\beta_1/\beta_2) = \mathcal{I}_1(\beta_1) \times \mathcal{I}_2(\beta_2)$ and mon $[B_1, B_2]$ = mon $B_1 \times$ mon B_2.
9. [REG Σ, REG Δ] with behaviour $\mathcal{R}$ in the monoid $\Sigma^* \times \Delta^*$ such that $\mathcal{R}(\mathbf{r}/\mathbf{s}) = \mathcal{L}(\mathbf{r}) \times \mathcal{L}(\mathbf{s})$, for any $\mathbf{r} \in$ REG Σ and $\mathbf{s} \in$ REG Δ.

For any monoid of interest M, $\underline{M}$ is a label set such that

$$\text{mon } \underline{M} = M \quad \text{and} \quad \mathcal{I}(\underline{m}) = \{m\}.$$

Thus for example, as mon PSP$[\Gamma]$ = mon $\underline{\Gamma^* \times \Gamma^*} = \Gamma^* \times \Gamma^*$ and the behaviour of PSP is denoted by $\mathcal{R}$, we have $\mathcal{R}(\underline{(0,1)}) = \mathcal{R}(0/1) = \{(0,1)\} = \mathcal{R}(\exists 0/\exists 1)$.

Remark 3. We shall not attempt to define the set of all labels. We limit ourselves to those of interest in this paper. Of course one can define new label sets X at will, depending on the application; and in doing so, one would also define concepts related to those label sets, such as the mon X.

5 Labelled Graphs, Automata, Transducers

Let B be a label set with behaviour $\mathcal{I}$. A *type B graph* is a quintuple

$$\ddot{g} = (Q, B, \delta, I, F)$$

such that Q is a nonempty set whose elements are called *states*; $I \subseteq Q$ is the nonempty set of initial, or start states; $F \subseteq Q$ is the set of final states; δ is a set, called the set of *edges* or *transitions*, consisting of triples (p, β, q) such that

$p, q \in Q$ and β is a nonempty string of Ω-symbols; the set of *labels* Labels$(\hat{g}) =$ $\{\beta \mid (p, \beta, q) \in \delta\}$ is a subset of B.

We shall use the term *labelled graph* to mean a type B graph as defined above, for some label set B. The labelled graph is called *finite* if Q and δ are both finite. *Unless otherwise specified, a labelled graph, or type B graph, will be assumed to be finite.*

As a label β is a string, the length $|\beta|$ is well-defined. Then, the *size* $|e|$ of an edge $e = (p, \beta, q)$ is the quantity $1 + |\beta|$ and the size of δ is $\|\delta\| = \sum_{e \in \delta} |e|$. Then the *graph size* of $\hat{g}$ is the $|\hat{g}| = |Q| + \|\delta\|$. A *path* P of $\hat{g}$ is a sequence of consecutive transitions, that is, $P = \langle q_{i-1}, \beta_i, q_i \rangle_{i=1}^{\ell}$ such that each (q_{i-1}, β_i, q_i) is in δ. The path P is called *accepting*, if $q_0 \in I$ and $q_\ell \in F$. If $\ell = 0$ then P is empty and it is an accepting path if $I \cap F \neq \emptyset$. A state is called *isolated*, if it does not occur in any transition of $\hat{g}$. A state is called *useful*, if it occurs in some accepting path. Note that any state in $I \cap F$ is useful and can be isolated. The labelled graph $\hat{g}$ is called *trim*, if

every state of $\hat{g}$ is useful, and $\hat{g}$ has at most one isolated state in $I \cap F$.

Definition 6. *Let* $\hat{g} = (Q, B, \delta, I, F)$ *be a labelled graph, for some label set B with behaviour $\mathcal{I}$. We define the* behaviour $\mathcal{I}(\hat{g})$ *of $\hat{g}$ as the set of all $m \in$ mon B such that there is an accepting path $\langle q_{i-1}, \beta_i, q_i \rangle_{i=1}^{\ell}$ of $\hat{g}$ with*

$$m \in \mathcal{I}(\beta_1) \cdots \mathcal{I}(\beta_\ell).$$

The expansion $\exp \hat{g}$ *of $\hat{g}$ is the labelled graph* $(Q, \underline{\mathrm{mon}\ B}, \delta_{\exp}, I, F)$ *such that*

$$\delta_{\exp} = \{(p, \underline{m}, q) \mid \exists\, (p, \beta, q) \in \delta : m \in \mathcal{I}(\beta)\}.$$

In some cases it is useful to modify $\hat{g}$ by adding the transition $(q, \varepsilon_{\underline{\mathrm{mon}\ B}}, q)$ (a self loop) for each state q of $\hat{g}$. The resulting labelled graph is denoted by $\hat{g}^\varepsilon$.

Remark 4. The above definition remains valid with no change if the labelled graph, or its expansion, is not finite. The expansion graph of $\hat{g}$ can have infinitely many transitions—for example if $\hat{g}$ is of type REG Σ.

Lemma 3. *For each type B graph $\hat{g} = (Q, B, \delta, I, F)$, we have that*

$$\mathcal{I}(\hat{g}) = \mathcal{I}(\exp \hat{g}) \quad and \quad \mathcal{I}(\hat{g}) = \mathcal{I}(\hat{g}^\varepsilon).$$

Definition 7. *Let* Σ, Δ, Γ *be alphabets.*

1. *A* nondeterministic finite automaton *with empty transitions, or* ε-NFA *for short, is a labelled graph* $\hat{a} = (Q, \Sigma_e, \delta, I, F)$. *If* Labels$(\hat{a}) \subseteq \Sigma$ *then $\hat{a}$ is called an* NFA. *The* language $\mathcal{L}(\hat{a})$ *accepted by $\hat{a}$ is the behaviour of $\hat{a}$ with respect to the label set Σ_e.*
2. *An* automaton with set specs *is a labelled graph* $\hat{b} = (Q, \mathrm{SSP}[\Gamma], \delta, I, F)$. *The* language $\mathcal{L}(\hat{b})$ *accepted by $\hat{b}$ is the behaviour of $\hat{b}$ with respect to* $\mathrm{SSP}[\Gamma]$.
3. *A* transducer *(in standard form) is a labelled graph* $\hat{t} = (Q, [\Sigma_e, \Delta_e], \delta, I, F)$. *The* relation $\mathcal{R}(\hat{t})$ *realized by $\hat{t}$ is the behaviour of $\hat{t}$ with respect to* $[\Sigma_e, \Delta_e]$.

4. *A* transducer with set specs *is a labelled graph* $\hat{s} = (Q, \text{PSP}[\Gamma], \delta, I, F)$. *The relation* $\mathcal{R}(\hat{s})$ *realized by* $\hat{s}$ *is the behaviour of* $\hat{s}$ *with respect to* $\text{PSP}[\Gamma]$.
5. *An* alphabet invariant transducer *is a labelled graph* $\hat{i} = (Q, \text{PSP}^{\text{invar}}, \delta, I, F)$. *If* Γ *is an alphabet then the* Γ-*version of* $\hat{i}$ *is the transducer with set specs* $\hat{i}[\Gamma] = (Q, \text{PSP}[\Gamma], \delta, I, F)$.

Remark 5. The above definitions about automata and transducers are equivalent to the standard ones. The only slight deviation is that, instead of using the empty word ε in transition labels, here we use the empty word symbol $\boldsymbol{e}$. This has two advantages: (i) it allows us to make a uniform presentation of definitions and results and (ii) it is consistent with the use of a symbol for the empty word in regular expressions. As usual about transducers $\hat{t}$, we denote by $\hat{t}(w)$ the *set of outputs of* $\hat{t}$ on input w, that is,

$$\hat{t}(w) = \{u \mid (w, u) \in \mathcal{R}(\hat{t})\}.$$

Moreover, for any language L, we have that $\hat{t}(L) = \cup_{w \in L}\hat{t}(w)$.

Lemma 4. *If* $\hat{b}$ *is an automaton with set specs then* $\exp\hat{b}$ *is an* ε-*NFA. If* $\hat{s}$ *is a transducer with set specs then* $\exp\hat{s}$ *is a transducer (in standard form).*

Convention. Let $\Phi(\hat{u})$ be any statement about the behaviour of an automaton or transducer $\hat{u}$. If $\hat{v}$ is an automaton or transducer with set specs then we make the convention that the statement $\Phi(\hat{v})$ means $\Phi(\exp\hat{v})$. For example, "$\hat{s}$ is an input-altering transducer" means that "$\exp\hat{s}$ is an input-altering transducer"—a transducer $\hat{t}$ is *input-altering* if $u \in \hat{t}(w)$ implies $u \neq w$, or equivalently $(w, w) \notin \mathcal{R}(\hat{t})$, for any word w.

Example 5. The transducers in Fig. 2 are alphabet invariant. Both transducers are much more succinct compared to their expanded Γ-versions, as $|\Gamma| \to \infty$:

$$|\exp\hat{t}_{\text{sub2}}[\Gamma]| = O(|\Gamma|^2) \quad \text{and} \quad |\exp\hat{t}_{\text{px}}[\Gamma]| = O(|\Gamma|).$$

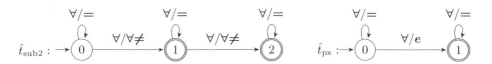

Fig. 2. The left transducer realizes the relation of all (u, v) such that $u \neq v$ and the Hamming distance of u, v is at most 2. The right transducer realizes the relation of all (u, v) such that v is a proper prefix of u.

Following [25], if $\hat{t} = (Q, [\Sigma_e, \Delta_e], \delta, I, F)$ is a transducer then $\hat{t}^{-1}$ is the transducer $(Q, [\Delta_e, \Sigma_e], \delta', I, F)$, where $\delta' = \{(p, y/x, q) \mid (p, x/y, q) \in \delta\}$, such that $\mathcal{R}(\hat{t}^{-1}) = \mathcal{R}(\hat{t})^{-1}$.

Lemma 5. *For each transducer* $\hat{s}$ *with set specs we have that* $\mathcal{R}(\hat{s}^{-1}) = \mathcal{R}(\hat{s})^{-1}$ *and* $\exp(\hat{s}^{-1}) = (\exp\hat{s})^{-1}$.

6   Regular Expressions over Label Sets

We extend the definitions of regular and 2D regular expressions to include set specs and pairing specs, respectively. We start off with a definition that would work with any label set (called set of atomic formulas in [20]).

Definition 8. *Let B be a label set with behaviour $\mathcal{I}$ such that no $\beta \in B$ contains the special symbol $\oslash$. The set $\mathrm{REG}\,B$ of* type B regular expressions *is the set of strings consisting of the 1-symbol string $\oslash$ and the strings in the set Z that is defined inductively as follows.*

- *$\varepsilon_{\mathrm{mon}\,B}$ is in Z, and every $\beta \in B$ is in Z.*
- *If $\mathbf{r}, \mathbf{s} \in Z$ then $(\mathbf{r} + \mathbf{s}), (\mathbf{r} \cdot \mathbf{s}), (\mathbf{r}^*)$ are in Z.*

The behaviour $\mathcal{I}(\mathbf{r})$ of a type B regular expression $\mathbf{r}$ is defined inductively as follows.

- *$\mathcal{I}(\oslash) = \emptyset$ and $\mathcal{I}(\varepsilon_{\mathrm{mon}\,B}) = \varepsilon_{\mathrm{mon}\,B}$;*
- *$\mathcal{I}(\beta)$ is the subset of $\mathrm{mon}\,B$ already defined by the behaviour $\mathcal{I}$ on B;*
- *$\mathcal{I}(\mathbf{r} + \mathbf{s}) = \mathcal{I}(\mathbf{r}) \cup \mathcal{I}(\mathbf{s}); \quad \mathcal{I}(\mathbf{r} \cdot \mathbf{s}) = \mathcal{I}(\mathbf{r})\mathcal{I}(\mathbf{s}); \quad \mathcal{I}(\mathbf{r}^*) = \mathcal{I}(\mathbf{r})^*.$*

Example 6. Let Σ, Δ be alphabets. Using Σ as a label set, we have that $\mathrm{REG}\,\Sigma$ is the set of ordinary regular expressions over Σ. For the label set $[\Sigma_e, \Delta_e]$, we have that $\mathrm{REG}[\Sigma_e, \Delta_e]$ is the set of rational expressions over $\Sigma^* \times \Delta^*$ in the sense of [20].

Example 7. Consider the UNIX utility `tr`. For any strings u, v of length $\ell > 0$, the command `tr` u v can be 'simulated' by the following regular expression of type PSP[ASCII]

$$\left((\nexists u/{=}) + (\exists u[0]/\exists v[0]) + \cdots + (\exists u[\ell - 1]/v[\ell - 1]) \right)^*$$

where ASCII is the alphabet of standard ASCII characters. Similarly, the command `tr` $-$`d` u can be 'simulated' by the type PSP[ASCII] regular expression $(\exists u/e + \nexists u/{=})^*$.

The Thompson method, [22], of converting an ordinary regular expression over Σ—a type Σ_e regular expression in the present terminology—to an ε-NFA can be extended without complications to work with type B regular expressions, for any label set B. Similarly, the state elimination method of automata, [6], can be extended to labelled graphs of any type B.

Theorem 1. *Let B be a label set with behaviour $\mathcal{I}$. For each type B regular expression $\mathbf{r}$, there is a type B graph $\hat{g}(\mathbf{r})$ such that*

$$\mathcal{I}(\mathbf{r}) = \mathcal{I}(\hat{g}(\mathbf{r})) \quad \text{and} \quad |\hat{g}(\mathbf{r})| = O(|\mathbf{r}|).$$

Conversely, for each type B graph $\hat{g}$ there is a type B regular expression $\mathbf{r}$ such that $\mathcal{I}(\hat{g}) = \mathcal{I}(\mathbf{r})$.

Derivatives based methods for the manipulation of regular expressions have been widely studied [2,5,7,8,10,17,18]. In recent years, partial derivative automata were defined and characterised for several kinds of expressions. Not only they are in general more succinct than other equivalent constructions but also for several operators they are easily defined (e.g. for intersection [3] or tuples [11]). The partial derivative automaton of a regular expression over Σ^* was introduced independently by Mirkin [18] and Antimirov [2]. Champarnaud and Ziadi [9] proved that the two formulations are equivalent. Lombardy and Sakarovitch [17] generalised these constructions to weighted regular expressions, and recently Demaille [11] defined derivative automata for multitape weighted regular expressions.

Here we define the partial derivative automaton for a regular expressions of a type B. Given a finite set S of expressions we define its behaviour as $\mathcal{I}(S) = \bigcup_{\mathbf{s} \in S} \mathcal{I}(\mathbf{s})$. We say that two regular expressions $\mathbf{r}, \mathbf{s}$ of a type B are *equivalent*, $\mathbf{r} \sim \mathbf{s}$, if $\mathcal{I}(\mathbf{r}) = \mathcal{I}(\mathbf{s})$. Let the *set of labels* of an expression $\mathbf{r}$ be the set $\mathsf{SS}(\mathbf{r}) = \{ \beta \mid \beta \in B \text{ and } \beta \text{ occurs in } \mathbf{r} \}$. The *size* of an expressions $\mathbf{r}$ is $\|\mathbf{r}\| = |\mathsf{SS}(\mathbf{r})|$; it can be inductively defined as follows:

$$\| \oslash \| = 0, \quad \|\varepsilon_{\text{mon } B}\| = 0, \quad \|\beta\| = 1$$
$$\|\mathbf{r} + \mathbf{s}\| = \|\mathbf{r}\| + \|\mathbf{s}\|$$
$$\|\mathbf{rs}\| = \|\mathbf{r}\| + \|\mathbf{s}\|$$
$$\|\mathbf{r}^*\| = \|\mathbf{r}\|.$$

We define the *constant part* $\mathsf{c} : \text{REG } B \to \{\varepsilon_{\text{mon } B}, \oslash\}$ by $\mathsf{c}(\mathbf{r}) = \varepsilon_{\text{mon } B}$ if $\varepsilon_{\text{mon } B} \in \mathcal{I}(\mathbf{r})$, and $\mathsf{c}(\mathbf{r}) = \oslash$ otherwise. This function is extended to sets of expressions by $\mathsf{c}(S) = \varepsilon_{\text{mon } B}$ if and only if exists $\mathbf{r} \in S$ such that $\mathsf{c}(\mathbf{r}) = \varepsilon_{\text{mon } B}$.

The *linear form* of a regular expression $\mathbf{r}$, $\mathsf{n}(\mathbf{r})$, is given by the following inductive definition:

$$\mathsf{n}(\oslash) = \mathsf{n}(\varepsilon_{\text{mon } B}) = \emptyset,$$
$$\mathsf{n}(\beta) = \{(\beta, \varepsilon_{\text{mon } B})\},$$
$$\mathsf{n}(\mathbf{r} + \mathbf{r}') = \mathsf{n}(\mathbf{r}) \cup \mathsf{n}(\mathbf{r}'),$$
$$\mathsf{n}(\mathbf{rr}') = \begin{cases} \mathsf{n}(\mathbf{r})\mathbf{r}' \cup \mathsf{n}(\mathbf{r}') & \text{if } \mathsf{c}(\mathbf{r}) = \varepsilon_{\text{mon } B}, \\ \mathsf{n}(\mathbf{r})\mathbf{r}' & \text{otherwise}, \end{cases}$$
$$\mathsf{n}(\mathbf{r}^*) = \mathsf{n}(\mathbf{r})\mathbf{r}^*,$$

where for any $S \subseteq B \times \text{REG } B$, we define $S\varepsilon_{\text{mon } B} = \varepsilon_{\text{mon } B}S = S$, $S\oslash = \oslash S = \oslash$, and $S\mathbf{s} = \{ (\beta, \mathbf{rs}) \mid (\beta, \mathbf{r}) \in S \}$ if $\mathbf{s} \neq \varepsilon_{\text{mon } B}$ (and analogously for $\mathbf{s}S$). Let $\mathcal{I}(\mathsf{n}(\mathbf{r})) = \bigcup_{(\beta, \mathbf{s}) \in \mathsf{n}(\mathbf{r})} \mathcal{I}(\beta)\mathcal{I}(\mathbf{s})$.

Lemma 6. *For all* $\mathbf{r} \in \text{REG } B$, $\mathbf{r} \sim \mathsf{c}(\mathbf{r}) \cup \mathsf{n}(\mathbf{r})$.

Proof. The proof is trivial proceeding by induction on $\mathbf{r}$.   □

For a regular expression $\mathbf{r}$ and $\beta \in \mathsf{SS}(\mathbf{r})$, the *set of partial derivatives* of $\mathbf{r}$ w.r.t. β is

$$\hat{\partial}_\beta(\mathbf{r}) = \{ \mathbf{s} \mid (\beta, \mathbf{s}) \in \mathsf{n}(\mathbf{r}) \}.$$

It is clear that we can iteratively compute the linear form of an expression $\mathbf{s} \in \hat{\partial}_\beta(\mathbf{r})$, for $\beta \in \mathsf{SS}(\mathbf{r})$. The set of all the resulting expressions is denoted by $\pi(\mathbf{r})$, and $\mathsf{PD}(\mathbf{r}) = \pi(\mathbf{r}) \cup \{\mathbf{r}\}$ is the set of partial derivatives of $\mathbf{r}$.

The *partial derivative graph* of $\mathbf{r}$ is the labeled graph

$$\hat{a}_{\mathrm{PD}}(\mathbf{r}) = \big(\mathsf{PD}(\mathbf{r}), B, \delta_{\mathrm{PD}}, \{\mathbf{r}\}, F\big),$$

where $F = \{\, \mathbf{r}_1 \in \mathsf{PD}(\mathbf{r}) \mid \mathsf{c}(\mathbf{r}_1) = \varepsilon_{\mathrm{mon}\,B} \,\}$, $\delta_{\mathrm{PD}} = \varphi(\mathbf{r}) \cup \mathsf{F}(\mathbf{r})$ with $\varphi(\mathbf{r}) = \{(\mathbf{r}, \beta, \mathbf{r}') \mid (\beta, \mathbf{r}') \in \mathsf{n}(\mathbf{r})\}$ and $\mathsf{F}(\mathbf{r}) = \{\, (\mathbf{r}_1, \beta, \mathbf{r}_2) \mid \mathbf{r}_1 \in \pi(\mathbf{r}) \wedge \beta \in \mathsf{SS}[\mathbf{r}] \wedge \mathbf{r}_2 \in \hat{\partial}_\beta(\mathbf{r}_1) \,\}$.

The following lemma generalizes from ordinary regular expressions [5,9,18], and shows that the set of (strict) partial derivatives is finite.

Lemma 7. π *satisfies the following:*

$$\begin{aligned}
\pi(\oslash) = \pi(\varepsilon_{\mathrm{mon}\,B}) &= \emptyset, & \pi(\mathbf{r}_1 + \mathbf{r}_2) &= \pi(\mathbf{r}_1) \cup \pi(\mathbf{r}_2), \\
\pi(\beta) &= \{\varepsilon_{\mathrm{mon}\,B}\}, & \pi(\mathbf{r}_1 \mathbf{r}_2) &= \pi(\mathbf{r}_1)\mathbf{r}_2 \cup \pi(\mathbf{r}_2), \\
\pi(\mathbf{r}^*) &= \pi(\mathbf{r})\mathbf{r}^*.
\end{aligned}$$

Theorem 2. *We have that* $|\pi(\mathbf{r})| \le \|\mathbf{r}\|$ *and* $|\mathsf{PD}(r)| \le \|r\| + 1$.

Proof. Direct consequence of Lemma 7 using induction on $\mathbf{r}$. ☐

The proof of the following result is analogous to the ones for ordinary regular expressions [2,18].

Theorem 3. $\mathcal{I}(\hat{a}_{\mathrm{PD}}(\mathbf{r})) = \mathcal{I}(\mathbf{r})$.

A direct algorithm to decide if an element of mon B belongs to $\mathcal{I}(\mathbf{r})$ depends on the behaviour $\mathcal{I}$ of the particular label set B.

6.1   Regular Expressions with Set Specifications

Here we consider regular expressions of type $\mathsf{SSP}[\Sigma]$ whose fixed behaviours are languages over the alphabet Σ. We want a direct algorithm to decide if a word belongs to the language represented by the expression. Given $L_1, L_2 \subseteq \Sigma^*$ and $x \in \Sigma$, the *quotient* of a language[1] w.r.t x satisfies the following relations

$$\begin{aligned}
x^{-1}(L_1 \cup L_2) &= x^{-1}L_1 \cup x^{-1}L_2, \quad x^{-1}L_1^* = (x^{-1}L_1)L_1^*, \\
x^{-1}(L_1\,L_2) &= (x^{-1}L_1)L_2 \text{ if } \varepsilon \notin L_1 \ \text{ or } \ (x^{-1}L_1)L_2 \cup x^{-1}L_2 \text{ if } \varepsilon \in L_1.
\end{aligned}$$

Quotients can be extended to words and languages: $\varepsilon^{-1}L = L$, $(wx)^{-1}L = x^{-1}(w^{-1}L)$ and $L_1{}^{-1}L = \bigcup_{w \in L_1} w^{-1}L$. If $L_1 \subseteq L_2 \subseteq \Sigma^*$ then $L_1{}^{-1}L \subseteq L_2{}^{-1}L$ and $L^{-1}L_1 \subseteq L^{-1}L_2$.

---

[1] It is customary to use $x^{-1}L$ for denoting quotients; this should not be confused with the inverse p^{-1} of a pairing spec.

Given two set specifications $F, G \in \mathrm{SSP}[\Sigma] \setminus \{e\}$ we extend the notion of partial derivative to the set of partial derivatives of F w.r.t G with possible $F \neq G$, by

$$\partial_F(G) = \begin{cases} \{e\} & \text{if } F \cap G \neq \bot, \\ \emptyset & \text{otherwise.} \end{cases}$$

and $\partial_F(\mathbf{r}) = \hat{\partial}_F(\mathbf{r})$ for all other cases of $\mathbf{r}$.

The set of partial derivatives of $\mathbf{r} \in \mathrm{REG\,SSP}[\Sigma]$ w.r.t. a word $x \in (\mathrm{SSP}[\Sigma] \setminus \{e\})^\star$ is inductively defined by $\partial_\varepsilon(\mathbf{r}) = \{\mathbf{r}\}$ and $\partial_{xF}(\mathbf{r}) = \partial_F(\partial_x(\mathbf{r}))$, where, given a set $S \subseteq \mathrm{REG\,SSP}[\Sigma]$, $\partial_F(S) = \bigcup_{\mathbf{r} \in S} \partial_F(\mathbf{r})$. Moreover one has $\mathcal{L}(\partial_x(\mathbf{r})) = \bigcup_{\mathbf{r}_1 \in \partial_x(\mathbf{r})} \mathcal{L}(\mathbf{r}_1)$.

Lemma 8. *For two set specifications $F, G \in \mathrm{SSP}[\Sigma]$, $\mathcal{L}(F)^{-1}\mathcal{L}(G) = \{\varepsilon\}$ if $F \cap G \neq \bot$, and $\mathcal{L}(F)^{-1}\mathcal{L}(G) = \emptyset$ otherwise.*

For instance, if $\exists w \cap \not\exists u \neq \bot$ then

$$\mathcal{L}(\exists w)^{-1}\mathcal{L}(\not\exists u) = \bigcup_{x \in \mathrm{alph}\, w} x^{-1}(\Sigma \setminus \mathrm{alph}\, u) = \{\varepsilon\}.$$

Lemma 9. *For all $\mathbf{r} \in \mathrm{REG\,SSP}[\Sigma]$ and $F \in \mathrm{SSP}[\Sigma]$, $\mathcal{L}(F)^{-1}\mathcal{L}(\mathbf{r}) = \mathcal{L}(\partial_F(\mathbf{r}))$.*

Proof. For $\mathbf{r} = \emptyset$ and $\mathbf{r} = e$ it is obvious. For $\mathbf{r} = G$ the result follows from Lemma 8. In fact, if $\mathcal{L}(F)^{-1}\mathcal{L}(G) = \{\varepsilon\}$ then $\partial_F(G) = \{e\}$ and thus $\mathcal{L}(\partial_F(\mathbf{r})) = \{\varepsilon\}$; otherwise if $\mathcal{L}(F)^{-1}\mathcal{L}(G) = \emptyset$ then $\partial_F(G) = \emptyset$, and also $\mathcal{L}(\partial_F(\mathbf{r})) = \emptyset$. The remaining cases follow by induction as with ordinary regular expressions. □

Lemma 10. *For all $g \in (\mathrm{SSP}[\Sigma] \setminus \{e\})^*$, $\mathcal{L}(g)^{-1}\mathcal{L}(\mathbf{r}) = \mathcal{L}(\partial_g(\mathbf{r}))$.*

Proof. By induction on $|g|$ using Lemma 9. □

Lemma 11. *For all $w \in \Sigma^*$, the following propositions are equivalent:*

1. $w \in \mathcal{L}(\mathbf{r})$
2. $w = x_1 \cdots x_n$ and there exists $s(w) = F_1 \cdots F_n$ with $F_i \in \mathrm{SS}(\mathbf{r})$, $\exists x_i \cap F_i \neq \bot$ and $c(\partial_{s(w)}(\mathbf{r})) = \varepsilon$.

7   Label Operations and the Product Construction

We shall consider partial operations $\odot$ on label sets B, B' such that, when defined, the product $\beta \odot \beta'$ of two labels belongs to a certain label set C. Moreover, we shall assume that $\odot$ is also a partial operation on mon B, mon B' such that, when defined, the product $m \odot m'$ of two monoid elements belongs to mon C. We shall call $\odot$ a *polymorphic* operation (in analogy to polymorphic operations in programming languages) when $\mathcal{I}(\beta \odot \beta') = \mathcal{I}_1(\beta) \odot \mathcal{I}_1(\beta')$ where $\mathcal{I}_1, \mathcal{I}_2, \mathcal{I}$ are the behaviours of B, B', C. This concept shall allow us to also use $\odot$ as the name of the product construction on labelled graphs that respects the behaviours of the two graphs.

Example 8. We shall consider the following monoidal operations, which are better known when applied to subsets of the monoid.

- $\cap : \Sigma^* \times \Sigma^* \dashrightarrow \Sigma^*$ such that $u \cap v = u$ if $u = v$; else, $u \cap v = \bot$. Of course, for any two languages $K, L \subseteq \Sigma^*$, $K \cap L$ is the usual intersection of K, L.
- $\circ : (\Sigma_1^* \times \Delta^*) \times (\Delta^* \times \Sigma_2^*) \dashrightarrow (\Sigma_1^* \times \Sigma_2^*)$ such that $(u, v) \circ (w, z) = (u, z)$ if $v = w$; else, $(u, v) \circ (w, z) = \bot$. For any two relations R, S, $R \circ S$ is the usual composition of R, S.
- $\downarrow : (\Sigma^* \times \Delta^*) \times \Sigma^* \dashrightarrow (\Sigma^* \times \Delta^*)$ such that $(u, v) \downarrow w = (u, v)$ if $u = w$; else, $(u, v) \downarrow w = \bot$. For a relation R and language L,

$$R \downarrow L = R \cap (L \times \Delta^*). \tag{2}$$

- $\uparrow : (\Sigma^* \times \Delta^*) \times \Sigma^* \dashrightarrow (\Sigma^* \times \Delta^*)$ such that $(u, v) \uparrow w = (u, v)$ if $v = w$; else, $(u, v) \downarrow w = \bot$. For a relation R and language L,

$$R \uparrow L = R \cap (\Sigma^* \times L). \tag{3}$$

Definition 9. *Let B, B', C be label sets with behaviours $\mathcal{I}_1, \mathcal{I}_2, \mathcal{I}$, respectively. A polymorphic operation $\odot$ over B, B', C, denoted as "$\odot : B \times B' \Rightarrow C$", is defined as follows.*

- *It is a partial mapping:* $\odot : B \times B' \dashrightarrow C$.
- *It is a partial mapping:* $\odot : \mathrm{mon}\, B \times \mathrm{mon}\, B' \dashrightarrow \mathrm{mon}\, C$.
- *For all $\beta \in B$ and $\beta' \in B'$ we have*

$$\mathcal{I}(\beta \odot \beta') = \mathcal{I}_1(\beta) \odot \mathcal{I}_2(\beta'),$$

where we assume that $\mathcal{I}(\beta \odot \beta') = \emptyset$, if $\beta \odot \beta' = \bot$; and we have used the notation $S \odot S' = \{m \odot m' \mid m \in S, m' \in S', m \odot m' \neq \bot\}$. for any $S \subseteq \mathrm{mon}\, B$ and $S' \subseteq \mathrm{mon}\, B'$.

Example 9. The following polymorphic operations are based on label sets of standard automata and transducers using the monoidal operations in Example 8.

- "$\cap : \Sigma_e \times \Sigma_e \Rightarrow \Sigma_e$" is defined by
  - the partial operation $\cap : \Sigma_e \times \Sigma_e \dashrightarrow \Sigma_e$ such that $x \cap y = x$, if $x = y$, else $x \cap y = \bot$; and
  - the partial operation $\cap : \Sigma^* \times \Sigma^* \dashrightarrow \Sigma^*$.
  Obviously, $\mathcal{L}(x \cap y) = \mathcal{L}(x) \cap \mathcal{L}(y)$.
- "$\circ : [\Sigma_e, \Delta_e] \times [\Delta_e, \Sigma'_e] \Rightarrow [\Sigma_e, \Sigma'_e]$" is defined by
  - the operation $\circ : [\Sigma_e, \Delta_e] \times [\Delta_e, \Sigma'_e] \dashrightarrow [\Sigma_e, \Sigma'_e]$ such that $(x/y_1) \circ (y_2/z) = (x/z)$ if $y_1 = y_2$, else $(x/y_1) \circ (y_2/z) = \bot$; and
  - the operation $\circ : (\Sigma^* \times \Delta^*) \times (\Delta^* \times \Sigma'^*) \dashrightarrow (\Sigma^* \times \Sigma'^*)$.
  Obviously, $\mathcal{R}((x, y_1) \circ (y_2, z)) = \mathcal{R}((x, y_1)) \circ \mathcal{R}((y_2, z))$.
- "$\downarrow : [\Sigma_e, \Delta_e] \times \Sigma_e \Rightarrow [\Sigma_e, \Delta_e]$" is defined by
  - the operation $\downarrow : [\Sigma_e, \Delta_e] \times \Sigma_e \dashrightarrow [\Sigma_e, \Delta_e]$ such that $(x/y) \downarrow z = (x/y)$ if $x = z$, else $(x/y) \downarrow z = \bot$; and
  - the operation $\downarrow : (\Sigma^* \times \Delta^*) \times \Sigma^* \dashrightarrow (\Sigma^* \times \Delta^*)$.

Obviously, $\mathcal{R}((x/y) \downarrow z) = \mathcal{R}(x/y) \downarrow \mathcal{L}(z)$.

- "$\uparrow\colon [\Sigma_e, \Delta_e] \times \Delta_e \Rightarrow [\Sigma_e, \Delta_e]$" is defined by
  - the operation $\uparrow\colon [\Sigma_e, \Delta_e] \times \Delta_e \dashrightarrow [\Sigma_e, \Delta_e]$ such that $(x/y) \uparrow z = (x/y)$ if $y = z$, else $(x/y) \uparrow z = \bot$; and
  - the operation $\uparrow\colon (\Sigma^* \times \Delta^*) \times \Sigma^* \dashrightarrow (\Sigma^* \times \Delta^*)$.

Obviously, $\mathcal{R}((x/y) \uparrow z) = \mathcal{R}(x/y) \uparrow \mathcal{L}(z)$.

Example 10. The following polymorphic operations are based on label sets of automata and transducers with set specs.

- "$\cap\ :\ \mathrm{SSP}[\Gamma] \times \mathrm{SSP}[\Gamma] \Rightarrow \mathrm{SSP}[\Gamma]$" is defined by the partial operation $\cap\ :\ \mathrm{SSP}[\Gamma] \times \mathrm{SSP}[\Gamma] \dashrightarrow \mathrm{SSP}[\Gamma]$, according to Definition 1, and the partial operation $\cap\ :\ \Gamma^* \times \Gamma^* \dashrightarrow \Gamma^*$. For any $B, F \in \mathrm{SSP}[\Gamma]$, we have $\mathcal{L}(B \cap F) = \mathcal{L}(B) \cap \mathcal{L}(F)$.
- "$\downarrow\colon \mathrm{PSP}[\Gamma] \times \Gamma_e \Rightarrow \mathrm{PSP}[\Gamma]$" is defined as follows. First, by the partial operation $\downarrow\colon \mathrm{PSP}[\Gamma] \times \Gamma_e \dashrightarrow \mathrm{PSP}[\Gamma]$ such that

$$\mathsf{p} \downarrow x = \begin{cases} e/\operatorname{right} \mathsf{p}, & \text{if } x = e \text{ and left } \mathsf{p} = e; \\ \exists x/\operatorname{right} \mathsf{p}, & \text{if } x, \text{left } \mathsf{p} \neq e \text{ and } x \in \mathcal{L}(\text{left } \mathsf{p}); \\ \bot, & \text{otherwise.} \end{cases}$$

Second, by the partial operation $\downarrow\colon (\Sigma^* \times \Delta^*) \times \Sigma^* \dashrightarrow (\Sigma^* \times \Delta^*)$. We have that $\mathcal{R}(\mathsf{p} \downarrow x) = \mathcal{R}(\mathsf{p}) \downarrow \mathcal{L}(x)$. Moreover we have that $\mathsf{p} \downarrow x$ can be computed from p and x in time $O(|\mathsf{p}|)$.

- "$\uparrow\colon \mathrm{PSP}[\Gamma] \times \Delta_e \Rightarrow \mathrm{PSP}[\Gamma]$" is defined as follows. First, by the partial operation $\uparrow\colon \mathrm{PSP}[\Gamma] \times \Delta_e \dashrightarrow \mathrm{PSP}[\Gamma]$ such that $\mathsf{p} \uparrow x = (\mathsf{p}^{-1} \downarrow x)^{-1}$. Second, by the partial operation $\uparrow\colon (\Sigma^* \times \Delta^*) \times \Delta^* \dashrightarrow (\Sigma^* \times \Delta^*)$. We have that $\mathcal{R}(\mathsf{p} \uparrow x) = \mathcal{R}(\mathsf{p}) \uparrow \mathcal{L}(x)$. Moreover we have that $\mathsf{p} \uparrow x$ can be computed from p and x in time $O(|\mathsf{p}|)$.

Further below, in Sect. 9, we define the polymorphic operation '$\circ$' between pairing specs.

Definition 10. *Let $\hat{g} = (Q, B, \delta, I, F)$ and $\hat{g}' = (Q', B', \delta', I', F')$ be type B and B', respectively, graphs and let "$\odot : B \times B' \Rightarrow C$" be a polymorphic operation. The* product *$\hat{g} \odot \hat{g}'$ is the type C graph*

$$\big(P, C, \delta \odot \delta', I \times I', F \times F'\big)$$

defined as follows. First make the following two possible modifications on $\hat{g}, \hat{g}'$: if there is a label β in $\hat{g}$ such that $\varepsilon_{\mathrm{mon}\,B} \in \mathcal{I}(\beta)$ then modify $\hat{g}$ to $\hat{g}'^\varepsilon$; and if there is a label β' in $\hat{g}'$ (before being modified) such that $\varepsilon_{\mathrm{mon}\,B'} \in \mathcal{I}(\beta')$ then modify $\hat{g}'$ to $\hat{g}'^\varepsilon$. In any case, use the same names $\hat{g}$ and $\hat{g}'$ independently of whether they were modified. Then P and $\delta \odot \delta'$ are defined inductively as follows:

1. $I \times I' \subseteq P$.
2. *If $(p, p') \in P$ and there are $(p, \beta, q) \in \delta$ and $(p', \beta', q') \in \delta'$ with $\beta \odot \beta' \neq \bot$ then $(q, q') \in P$ and $\big((p, p'), \beta \odot \beta', (q, q')\big) \in \delta \odot \delta'$.*

Example 11. Here we recall three known examples of product constructions involving automata and transducers.

1. For two ε-NFAs $\hat{a}, \hat{a}'$, using the polymorphic operation "$\cap : \Sigma_e \times \Sigma_e \Rightarrow \Sigma_e$", the product construction produces the ε-NFA $\hat{a} \cap \hat{a}'$ such that $\mathcal{L}(\hat{a} \cap \hat{a}') = \mathcal{L}(\hat{a}) \cap \mathcal{L}(\hat{a}')$. Note that if $\hat{a}, \hat{a}'$ are NFAs then also $\hat{a} \cap \hat{a}'$ is an NFA.
2. For two transducers $\hat{t}, \hat{t}'$, using the polymorphic operation "$\circ : [\Sigma_e, \Delta_e] \times [\Delta_e, \Sigma_e'] \Rightarrow [\Sigma_e, \Sigma_e']$", the product construction produces the transducer $\hat{t} \circ \hat{t}'$ such that $\mathcal{R}(\hat{t} \circ \hat{t}') = \mathcal{R}(\hat{t}) \circ \mathcal{R}(\hat{t}')$.
3. For a transducer $\hat{t}$ and an ε-NFA $\hat{a}$, using the polymorphic operation "$\downarrow : [\Sigma_e, \Delta_e] \times \Sigma_e \Rightarrow [\Sigma_e, \Delta_e]$", the product construction produces the transducer $\hat{t} \downarrow \hat{a}$ such that $\mathcal{R}(\hat{t} \downarrow \hat{a}) = \mathcal{R}(\hat{t}) \downarrow \mathcal{L}(\hat{a})$. Similarly, using the polymorphic operation "$\uparrow : [\Sigma_e, \Delta_e] \times \Delta_e \Rightarrow [\Sigma_e, \Delta_e]$", the product construction produces the transducer $\hat{t} \uparrow \hat{a}$ such that $\mathcal{R}(\hat{t} \uparrow \hat{a}) = \mathcal{R}(\hat{t}) \uparrow \mathcal{L}(\hat{a})$. These product constructions were used in [14] to answer algorithmic questions about independent languages—see Sect. 11.

Lemma 12. *The following statements hold true about the product graph $\hat{g} \odot \hat{g}' = (P, C, \delta \odot \delta', I \times I', F \times F')$ of two trim labelled graphs $\hat{g}, \hat{g}'$ as defined in Definition 10.*

1. $|P| = O(|\delta||\delta'|)$ *and* $|\delta \odot \delta'| \leq |\delta||\delta'|$.
2. *If the value $\beta \odot \beta'$ can be computed from the labels β and β' in time, and is of size, $O(|\beta| + |\beta'|)$, then $\|\delta \odot \delta'\|$ is of magnitude $O(|\delta|\|\delta'\| + |\delta'|\|\delta\|)$ and $\delta \odot \delta'$ can be computed within time of the same order of magnitude.*

Theorem 4. *If "$\odot : B \times B' \Rightarrow C$" is a polymorphic operation and $\hat{g}, \hat{g}'$ are type B, B', respectively, graphs then $\hat{g} \odot \hat{g}'$ is a type C graph such that*

$$\mathcal{I}(\hat{g} \odot \hat{g}') = \mathcal{I}(\exp \hat{g} \odot \exp \hat{g}').$$

How to Apply the Above Theorem. We can apply the theorem when we have a known product construction $\odot$ on labelled graphs $\hat{u}, \hat{u}'$ over monoids M, M' (see Example 11) and we wish to apply a 'higher level' version of $\odot$; that is, apply $\odot$ on labelled graphs $\hat{g}, \hat{g}'$ with behaviours in the monoids M, M'. This would avoid expanding $\hat{g}$ and $\hat{g}'$. We apply the theorem in Lemma 13.2, in Theorem 5 and in Corollary 1.

8   Automata and Transducers with Set Specifications

Here we present some basic algorithms on automata and transducers with set specs. These can be applied to answer the satisfaction question about independent languages (see Sect. 11).

Lemma 13. *Let $\hat{b} = (Q, \mathrm{SSP}[\Gamma], \delta, I, F)$ and $\hat{b}' = (Q', \mathrm{SSP}[\Gamma], \delta', I', F')$ be trim automata with set specs and let w be a string.*

1. *There is a $O(|\hat{b}|)$ algorithm* nonEmptyW($\hat{b}$) *returning either a word in $\mathcal{L}(\hat{b})$, or* None *if $\mathcal{L}(\hat{b}) = \emptyset$. The decision version of this algorithm,* emptyP($\hat{b}$), *simply returns whether $\mathcal{L}(\hat{b})$ is empty.*
2. *There is a $O(|\Gamma| + |\delta|\|\delta'\| + |\delta'|\|\delta\|)$ algorithm returning the automaton with set specs $\hat{b} \cap \hat{b}'$ such that $\mathcal{L}(\hat{b} \cap \hat{b}') = \mathcal{L}(\hat{b}) \cap \mathcal{L}(\hat{b}')$.*
3. *There is a $O(|w|\|\hat{b}|)$ algorithm returning whether $w \in \mathcal{L}(\hat{b})$.*

Proof. (Partial) For the <u>second</u> statement, we compute the product $\hat{b} \cap \hat{b}'$. As the value $\beta \cap \beta'$ of two labels can be computed in linear time, Lemma 12 implies that $\hat{b} \cap \hat{b}'$ can be computed in time $O(|\Gamma| + |\delta|\|\delta'\| + |\delta'|\|\delta\|)$. Now we have

$$\mathcal{L}(\hat{b} \cap \hat{b}') = \mathcal{L}(\exp \hat{b} \cap \exp \hat{b}') \tag{4}$$

$$= \mathcal{L}(\exp \hat{b}) \cap \mathcal{L}(\exp \hat{b}') \tag{5}$$

$$= \mathcal{L}(\hat{b}) \cap \mathcal{L}(\hat{b}') \tag{6}$$

Equation (4) follows from the fact that "$\cap : \mathrm{SSP}[\Gamma] \times \mathrm{SSP}[\Gamma] \Rightarrow \mathrm{SSP}[\Gamma]$" is a polymorphic operation—see Theorem 4 and Example 10. Equation (5) follows from the fact that each $\exp \hat{b}, \exp \hat{b}'$ is an ε-NFA and the operation $\cap$ is well-defined on these objects—see Lemma 4 and Example 11. For the <u>third</u> statement, one makes an automaton with set specs $\hat{b}_w$ accepting $\{w\}$, then computes $\hat{a} = \hat{b}_w \cap \hat{b}$, and then uses emptyP($\hat{a}$) to get the desired answer.

Lemma 14. *Let, $\hat{s} = (Q, \mathrm{PSP}[\Gamma], \delta, I, F)$ be a trim transducer with set specs and let $\hat{a} = (Q', \Gamma_e, \delta', I', F')$ be a trim ε-NFA, and let (u, v) be a pair of words.*

1. *There is a $O(|\hat{s}|)$ algorithm* nonEmptyW($\hat{s}$) *returning either a word pair in $\mathcal{R}(\hat{s})$, or* None *if $\mathcal{R}(\hat{s}) = \emptyset$. The decision version of this algorithm,* emptyP($\hat{s}$), *simply returns whether $\mathcal{R}(\hat{s})$ is empty.*
2. *There is a $O(|\Gamma| + |\delta|\|\delta'\| + |\delta'|\|\delta\|)$ algorithm returning the transducer with set specs $\hat{s} \downarrow \hat{a}$ such that $\mathcal{R}(\hat{s} \downarrow \hat{a}) = \mathcal{R}(\hat{s}) \downarrow \mathcal{L}(\hat{a})$.*
3. *There is a $O(|u|\|v\|\|\hat{s}|)$ algorithm returning whether $(u, v) \in \mathcal{R}(\hat{s})$.*

9   Composition of Transducers with Set Specifications

Next we are interested in defining the composition $p_1 \circ p_2$ of two pairing specs in a way that $\mathcal{R}(p_1) \circ \mathcal{R}(p_2)$ is equal to $\mathcal{R}(p_1 \circ p_2)$. It turns out that, for a particular subcase about the structure of p_1, p_2, the operation $p_1 \circ p_2$ can produce two or three pairing specs. To account for this, we define a new label set:

$\mathrm{PSP}_+[\Gamma]$ consists of strings $p_1 \oplus \cdots \oplus p_\ell$,

where $\ell \in \mathbb{N}$ and each $p_i \in \mathrm{PSP}[\Gamma]$. Moreover we have the (fixed) label behaviour $\mathcal{R} : \mathrm{PSP}_+[\Gamma] \to 2^{\Gamma^* \times \Gamma^*}$ such that

$$\mathcal{R}(p_1 \oplus \cdots \oplus p_\ell) = \mathcal{R}(p_1) \cup \cdots \cup \mathcal{R}(p_\ell).$$

Definition 11. *Let Γ be an alphabet of reference. The partial operation*

$$\circ : \mathrm{PSP}[\Gamma] \times \mathrm{PSP}[\Gamma] \dashrightarrow \mathrm{PSP}_+[\Gamma]$$

is defined between any two pairing specs p_1, p_2 *respecting* Γ *as follows.*

$$p_1 \circ p_2 = \bot, \quad \text{if } \mathcal{L}(\mathrm{rset}\, p_1) \cap \mathcal{L}(\mathrm{left}\, p_2) = \emptyset.$$

Now we assume that the above condition is not true and we consider the structure of p_1 *and* p_2 *according to Definition 3(1) using* A, B, F, G, W, X, Y, Z *as set specs, where* $A, B, F, G \neq e$—*thus, we assume below that* $\mathcal{L}(B) \cap \mathcal{L}(F) \neq \emptyset$ *and* $\mathcal{L}(X) \cap \mathcal{L}(Y) \neq \emptyset$.

$$(W/X) \circ (Y/Z) = W/Z \qquad (W/B) \circ (F/=) = W/B \cap F$$

$$(W/B) \circ (F/G\neq) = \begin{cases} W/G, & \text{if } |\mathcal{L}(B \cap F)| \geq 2 \\ W/\,G \cap \not\exists b, & \text{if } \mathcal{L}(B \cap F) = \{b\} \text{ and } \mathcal{L}(G) \setminus \{b\} \neq \emptyset \\ \bot, & \text{otherwise.} \end{cases}$$

$$(B/=) \circ (F/Z) = B \cap F/Z \qquad (B/=) \circ (F/=) = B \cap F/=$$

$$(B/=) \circ (F/G\neq) = \begin{cases} \bot, & \text{if } \mathcal{L}(G) = \mathcal{L}(B \cap F) = \{g\} \\ B \cap F/G\neq, & \text{otherwise.} \end{cases}$$

$$(A/B\neq) \circ (F/Z) = \begin{cases} A/Z, & \text{if } |\mathcal{L}(B \cap F)| \geq 2 \\ A \cap \not\exists b/Z, & \text{if } \mathcal{L}(B \cap F) = \{b\} \text{ and } \mathcal{L}(A) \setminus \{b\} \neq \emptyset \\ \bot & \text{otherwise.} \end{cases}$$

$$(A/B\neq) \circ (F/=) = \begin{cases} \bot, & \text{if } \mathcal{L}(A) = \mathcal{L}(B \cap F) = \{a\} \\ A/B \cap F\neq, & \text{otherwise.} \end{cases}$$

$$(A/B\neq) \circ (F/G\neq) = \begin{cases} A/G, & \text{if } |\mathcal{L}(B \cap F)| \geq 3 \\ A \cap \not\exists b/G \cap \not\exists b, & \text{if } \mathcal{L}(B \cap F) = \{b\} \text{ and } \mathcal{L}(A) \setminus \{b\} \\ & \qquad \neq \emptyset \text{ and } \mathcal{L}(G) \setminus \{b\} \neq \emptyset \\ \boldsymbol{D}, & \text{if } \mathcal{L}(B \cap F) = \{b_1, b_2\} \\ \bot, & \text{otherwise.} \end{cases}$$

where $\boldsymbol{D}$ consists of up to three $\oplus$-terms as follows: $\boldsymbol{D}$ includes $A \cap \not\exists b_1 b_2/G$, if $\mathcal{L}(A) \setminus \{b_1, b_2\} \neq \emptyset$; $\boldsymbol{D}$ includes $\exists b_1/G \cap \not\exists b_2$, if $b_1 \in \mathcal{L}(A)$ and $\mathcal{L}(G) \setminus \{b_2\} \neq \emptyset$; $\boldsymbol{D}$ includes $\exists b_2/G \cap \not\exists b_1$, if $b_2 \in \mathcal{L}(A)$ and $\mathcal{L}(G) \setminus \{b_1\} \neq \emptyset$; $\boldsymbol{D} = \bot$ if none of the previous three conditions is true.

Remark 6. In the above definition, we have omitted cases where $p_1 \circ p_2$ is obviously undefined. For example, as $F/=$ and $F/G\neq$ are only defined when $F, G \neq e$, we omit the case $(W/e) \circ (F/=)$.

Remark 7. If we allowed $\bot$ to be a pairing spec, then the set $\mathrm{PSP}[\Gamma]$ with the composition operation '$\circ$' would be 'nearly' a semigroup: the subcase

"$(A/B{\neq}) \circ (F/G{\neq})$ with $\mathcal{L}(B \cap F) = \{b_1, b_2\}$" in the above definition is the only one where the result of the composition is not necessarily a single pairing spec. For example, let the alphabet Γ be $\{0, 1, 2\}$ and $A = \exists 01$, $B = F = \exists 12$, and $G = \exists 012$. Then,

$$\mathcal{R}(A/B{\neq}) \circ \mathcal{R}(F/G{\neq}) = \{(0,0), (0,1), (0,2), (1,0), (1,1)\},$$

which is equal to $\mathcal{R}(\{\exists 0/\exists 012, \exists 1/\exists 01\})$. This relation is not equal to $\mathcal{R}(\mathsf{p})$, for any pairing spec p.

Lemma 15. *The relation* $\mathcal{R}(\mathsf{p}_1 \circ \mathsf{p}_2)$ *is equal to* $\mathcal{R}(\mathsf{p}_1) \circ \mathcal{R}(\mathsf{p}_2)$, *for any pairing specs* $\mathsf{p}_1, \mathsf{p}_2$ *respecting* Γ.

Remark 8. The polymorphic operation "$\circ : \mathrm{PSP}[\Gamma] \times \mathrm{PSP}[\Gamma] \Rightarrow \mathrm{PSP}_+[\Gamma]$" is well-defined by the partial operations $\circ$ in Definition 11 and in Example 8.

Definition 12. *Let* $\hat{t} = (Q, \mathrm{PSP}[\Gamma], \delta, I, F)$ *and* $\hat{s} = (Q', \mathrm{PSP}[\Gamma], \delta', I', F')$ *be transducers with set specs. The transducer* $\hat{t} \circledcirc \hat{s}$ *with set specs is defined as follows. First compute the transducer* $\hat{t} \circ \hat{s}$ *with labels in* $\mathrm{PSP}_+[\Gamma]$. *Then,* $\hat{t} \circledcirc \hat{s}$ *results when each transition* $(p, \mathsf{p}_1 \oplus \cdots \oplus \mathsf{p}_\ell, q)$ *of* $\hat{t} \circ \hat{s}$, *with* $\ell > 1$, *is replaced with the* ℓ *transitions* (p, p_i, q).

Theorem 5. *For any two trim transducers* $\hat{t} = (Q, \mathrm{PSP}[\Gamma], \delta, I, F)$ *and* $\hat{s} = (Q', \mathrm{PSP}[\Gamma], \delta', I', F')$ *with set specs,* $\hat{t} \circledcirc \hat{s}$ *can be computed in time* $O(|\Gamma| + |\delta|\|\delta'\| + |\delta'|\|\delta\|)$. *Moreover,* $\mathcal{R}(\hat{t} \circledcirc \hat{s}) = \mathcal{R}(\hat{t}) \circ \mathcal{R}(\hat{s})$.

10   Transducer Identity and Functionality

The question of whether a given transducer is functional is of central importance in the theory of rational relations [19]. Also important is the question of whether a given transducer $\hat{t}$ realizes an *identity*, that is, whether $\hat{t}(w) = \{w\}$, when $|\hat{t}(w)| > 0$. In [1], the authors present an algorithm $\mathtt{identityP}(\hat{t})$ that works in time $O(|\delta| + |Q||\Delta|)$ and tells whether $\hat{t} = (Q, \Sigma, \Delta, \delta, I, F)$ realizes an identity. Here we have that

$$\text{for trim}\, \hat{t},\; \mathtt{identityP}(\hat{t}) \text{ works in time } O(|\delta||\Delta|). \qquad (7)$$

The algorithm $\mathtt{functionalityP}(\hat{s})$ deciding functionality of a transducer $\hat{t} = (Q, \Gamma, \delta, I, F)$ first constructs the *square transducer* $\hat{u}$, [4], in which the set of transitions $\delta_{\hat{u}}$ consists of tuples $((p, p'), y/y', (q, q'))$ such that $(p, x/y, q)$ and $(p', x/y', q')$ are any transitions in $\hat{t}^\varepsilon$. Then, it follows that $\hat{t}$ is functional if and only if $\hat{u}$ realizes an identity. Note that $\hat{u}$ has $O(|\delta|^2)$ transitions and its graph size is $O(|\hat{t}|^2)$. Thus, we have that

$$\text{for trim}\, \hat{t},\; \mathtt{functionalityP}(\hat{t}) \text{ works in time } O(|\delta|^2|\Delta|). \qquad (8)$$

Theorem 6. *The question of whether a trim transducer* $\hat{s} = (Q, \mathrm{PSP}[\Gamma], \delta, I, F)$ *with set specs realizes an identity can be answered in time* $O(|\delta||\Gamma|)$.

Remark 9. Consider the trim transducer $\hat{s}$ with set specs in Theorem 6. Of course one can test whether it realizes an identity by simply using identityP(exp $\hat{s}$), which would work in time $O(|\delta_{\mathrm{exp}}||\Gamma|)$ according to (7). This time complexity is clearly higher than the time $O(|\delta||\Gamma|)$ in the above theorem when $|\delta_{\mathrm{exp}}|$ is of order $|\delta||\Gamma|$ or $|\delta||\Gamma|^2$ (for example if $\hat{s}$ involves labels $\forall/=$ or $\forall/\forall$).

Theorem 7. *The question of whether a trim transducer $\hat{s} = (Q, \mathrm{PSP}[\Gamma], \delta, I, F)$ with set specs is functional can be answered in time $O(|\delta|^2|\Gamma|)$.*

Remark 10. Consider the trim transducer $\hat{s}$ with set specs in Theorem 7. Of course one can simply use functionalityP(exp $\hat{s}$) to test whether $\hat{s}$ is functional, which would work in time $O(|\delta_{\mathrm{exp}}|^2|\Gamma|)$ according to (8). This time complexity is clearly higher than the time $O(|\delta|^2|\Gamma|)$ in the above theorem when $|\delta_{\mathrm{exp}}|$ is of order $|\delta||\Gamma|$ or $|\delta||\Gamma|^2$ (for example if $\hat{s}$ involves labels $\forall/=$ or $\forall/\forall$).

11   Transducers and Independent Languages

Let $\hat{t}$ be a transducer. A language L is called $\hat{t}$-*independent*, [21], if

$$u, v \in L \text{ and } v \in \hat{t}(u) \quad \text{implies} \quad u = v. \tag{9}$$

If $\hat{t}$ is input-altering then, [15], the above condition is equivalent to

$$\hat{t}(L) \cap L = \emptyset. \tag{10}$$

The *property described* by $\hat{t}$ is the set of all $\hat{t}$-independent languages. Main examples of such properties are code-related properties. For example, the transducer $\hat{t}_{\mathrm{sub2}}$ describes all the 1-substitution error-detecting languages and $\hat{t}_{\mathrm{px}}$ describes all prefix codes. The *property satisfaction* question is whether, for given transducer $\hat{t}$ and regular language L, the language L is $\hat{t}$-independent. The *witness* version of this question is to compute a pair (u, v) of different L-words (if exists) violating condition (9).

Remark 11. The witness version of the property satisfaction question for input-altering transducers $\hat{s}$ (see Eq. (10)) can be answered in time $O(|\hat{s}| \cdot |\hat{a}|^2)$, where $\hat{a}$ is the given ε-NFA accepting L (see [15]). This can be done using the function call nonEmptyW($\hat{s} \downarrow \hat{a} \uparrow \hat{a}$). Further below we show that the same question can be answered even when $\hat{s}$ has set specs, and this could lead to time savings.

Corollary 1. *Let $\hat{s} = (Q, \mathrm{PSP}[\Gamma], \delta, I, F)$ be a transducer with set specs and let $\hat{b} = (Q', \Gamma_e, \delta', I', F')$ be an ε-NFA. Each transducer $\hat{s} \downarrow \hat{b}$ and $\hat{s} \uparrow \hat{b}$ can be computed in time $O(|\Gamma| + |\delta|\|\delta'\| + |\delta'|\|\delta\|)$. Moreover, we have that*

$$\mathcal{R}(\hat{s} \downarrow \hat{b}) = \mathcal{R}(\hat{s}) \downarrow \mathcal{L}(\hat{b}) \quad \text{and} \quad \mathcal{R}(\hat{s} \uparrow \hat{b}) = \mathcal{R}(\hat{s}) \uparrow \mathcal{L}(\hat{b}).$$

Corollary 2. *Consider the witness version of the property satisfaction question for input-altering transducers $\hat{s}$. The question can be answered in time $O(|\hat{s}| \cdot |\hat{a}|^2)$ even when the transducer $\hat{s}$ involved has set specs.*

Example 12. We can apply the above corollary to the transducer $\hat{t}_{\mathrm{sub2}}[\Gamma]$ of Example 5, where Γ is the alphabet of $\hat{b}$, so that we can decide whether a regular language is 1-substitution error-detecting in time $O(|\hat{b}|^2)$. On the other hand, if we used the ordinary transducer $\exp \hat{t}_{\mathrm{sub2}}[\Gamma]$ to decide the question, the required time would be $O(|\Gamma|^2 \cdot |\hat{b}|^2)$.

12   Concluding Remarks

Regular expressions and transducers over pairing specs allow us to describe many independence properties in a simple, alphabet invariant, way and such that these alphabet invariant objects can be processed as efficiently as their ordinary (alphabet dependent) counterparts. This is possible due to the efficiency of basic algorithms on these objects presented here. A direction for further research is to investigate how algorithms not considered here can be extended to regular expressions and transducers over pairing specs; for example, algorithms involving transducers that realize synchronous relations.

Algorithms on *deterministic* machines with set specs might not work as efficiently as their alphabet dependent counterparts. For example the question of whether $w \in \mathcal{L}(\hat{b})$, for given word w and DFA $\hat{b}$ with set specs, is probably not decidable efficiently within time $O(|w|)$. Despite this, it might be of interest to investigate this question further.

Label sets can have any format as long as one provides their behaviour. For example, a label can be a string representation of a FAdo automaton, [13], whose behaviour of course is a regular language. At this broad level, we were able to generalize a few results like the product construction and the partial derivative automaton. A research direction is to investigate whether more results can be obtained at this level, or even for label sets satisfying some constraint. For example, whether membership, or other decision problems, can be decided using partial derivatives for regular expressions involving labels other than set and pairing specs[2].

References

1. Allauzen, C., Mohri, M.: Efficient algorithms for testing the twins property. J. Autom. Lang. Comb. **8**(2), 117–144 (2003)
2. Antimirov, V.M.: Partial derivatives of regular expressions and finite automaton constructions. Theor. Comput. Sci. **155**(2), 291–319 (1996)
3. Bastos, R., Broda, S., Machiavelo, A., Moreira, N., Reis, R.: On the average complexity of partial derivative automata for semi-extended expressions. J. Autom. Lang. Comb. **22**(1–3), 5–28 (2017)

---

[2] While we have not obtained in this work the partial derivatives corresponding to a regular expression involving pairing specs, it is our immediate plan to do so—see [16].

4. Béal, M.-P., Carton, O., Prieur, C., Sakarovitch, J.: Squaring transducers: an efficient procedure for deciding functionality and sequentiality. Theor. Comput. Sci. **292**(1), 45–63 (2003)
5. Broda, S., Machiavelo, A., Moreira, N., Reis, R.: On the average state complexity of partial derivative automata: an analytic combinatorics approach. Int. J. Found. Comput. Sci. **22**(7), 1593–1606 (2011). MR2865339
6. Brzozowski, J.A., McCluskey, E.J.: Signal flow graph techniques for sequential circuit state diagrams. IEEE Trans. Electron. Comput. **12**, 67–76 (1963)
7. Brzozowski, J.: Derivatives of regular expressions. J. Assoc. Comput. Mach. **11**, 481–494 (1964)
8. Caron, P., Champarnaud, J.-M., Mignot, L.: Partial derivatives of an extended regular expression. In: Dediu, A.-H., Inenaga, S., Martín-Vide, C. (eds.) LATA 2011. LNCS, vol. 6638, pp. 179–191. Springer, Heidelberg (2011). https://doi.org/10.1007/978-3-642-21254-3_13
9. Champarnaud, J.M., Ziadi, D.: From Mirkin's prebases to Antimirov's word partial derivatives. Fundam. Inf. **45**(3), 195–205 (2001)
10. Champarnaud, J.M., Ziadi, D.: Canonical derivatives, partial derivatives and finite automaton constructions. Theor. Comput. Sci. **289**, 137–163 (2002)
11. Demaille, A.: Derived-term automata of multitape rational expressions. In: Han, Y.-S., Salomaa, K. (eds.) CIAA 2016. LNCS, vol. 9705, pp. 51–63. Springer, Cham (2016). https://doi.org/10.1007/978-3-319-40946-7_5
12. Demaille, A., Duret-Lutz, A., Lombardy, S., Saiu, L., Sakarovitch, J.: A type system for weighted automata and rational expressions. In: Holzer, M., Kutrib, M. (eds.) CIAA 2014. LNCS, vol. 8587, pp. 162–175. Springer, Cham (2014). https://doi.org/10.1007/978-3-319-08846-4_12
13. FAdo: Tools for formal languages manipulation. http://fado.dcc.fc.up.pt/. Accessed Apr 2018
14. Konstantinidis, S.: Transducers and the properties of error-detection, error-correction and finite-delay decodability. J. Univ. Comput. Sci. **8**, 278–291 (2002)
15. Konstantinidis, S.: Applications of transducers in independent languages, word distances, codes. In: Pighizzini, G., Câmpeanu, C. (eds.) DCFS 2017. LNCS, vol. 10316, pp. 45–62. Springer, Cham (2017). https://doi.org/10.1007/978-3-319-60252-3_4
16. Konstantinidis, S. Moreira, N., Reis, R., Young, J.: Regular expressions and transducers over alphabet-invariant and user-defined labels. arXiv.org, arXiv:1805.01829 (2018)
17. Lombardy, S., Sakarovitch, J.: Derivatives of rational expressions with multiplicity. Theor. Comput. Sci. **332**(1–3), 141–177 (2005)
18. Mirkin, B.G.: An algorithm for constructing a base in a language of regular expressions. Eng. Cybern. **5**, 51–57 (1966)
19. Sakarovitch, J.: Elements of Automata Theory. Cambridge University Press, Berlin (2009)
20. Sakarovitch, J.: Automata and rational expressions. arXiv.org, arXiv:1502.03573 (2015)
21. Shyr, H.J., Thierrin, G.: Codes and binary relations. In: Malliavin, M.P. (ed.) Séminaire d'Algèbre Paul Dubreil Paris 1975–1976 (29ème Année). LNM, vol. 586, pp. 180–188. Springer, Heidelberg (1977). https://doi.org/10.1007/BFb0087133
22. Thompson, K.: Regular expression search algorithm. Commun. ACM (CACM) **11**, 419–422 (1968)

23. Veanes, M.: Applications of symbolic finite automata. In: Konstantinidis, S. (ed.) CIAA 2013. LNCS, vol. 7982, pp. 16–23. Springer, Heidelberg (2013). https://doi. org/10.1007/978-3-642-39274-0_3

24. Veanes, M., Hooimeijer, P., Livshits, B., Molnar, D., Bjorner, N.: Symbolic finite state transducers: algorithms and applications. In: Field, J., Hicks, M. (eds.) Proceedings of the 39th ACM SIGPLAN-SIGACT Symposium on Principles of Programming Languages, POPL 2012, pp. 137–150 (2012)

25. Sheng, Y.: Regular languages. In: Rozenberg, G., Salomaa, A. (eds.) Handbook of Formal Languages, vol. I, pp. 41–110. Springer, Heidelberg (1997). https://doi. org/10.1007/978-3-642-59136-5_2

Boosting Pushdown and Queue Machines by Preprocessing

Martin Kutrib, Andreas Malcher$^{(\boxtimes)}$, and Matthias Wendlandt

Institut für Informatik, Universität Giessen, Arndtstr. 2, 35392 Giessen, Germany
{kutrib,andreas.malcher,matthias.wendlandt}@informatik.uni-giessen.de

Abstract. Motivated by preprocessing devices occurring for example in the context of syntactic parsers or HTML sanitization, we study pairs of finite state transducers and deterministic machines such as pushdown automata or queue automata as language accepting devices, where the original input is translated by a finite state transducer to an input of the deterministic machine which eventually accepts or rejects the preprocessed input. As deterministic machines we study input-driven machines as well as reversible machines equipped with a pushdown store or a queue store. It turns out that the preprocessing boosts on the one hand the computational power of the machines in all four cases, but on the other hand preserves and adds some positive closure properties as well as decidable problems. Thus, the preprocessing extends the computational power moderately by retaining most of the nice properties of the original machine.

1 Introduction

The syntactical analysis of a computer program, a web page, or an XML document is typically done after the lexical analysis in which the correct formatting of the input is verified, comments are removed, the spelling of the commands is checked, and the sequence of input symbols is translated into a list of tokens. This preprocessing of the input is typically done by a finite state transducer and the output is subsequently processed by a more powerful machine such as, for example, a pushdown automaton. Further examples where the input is preprocessed and afterwards processed by other devices are HTML sanitization and embedded SQL. As a generalization of preprocessing one may have, for example, cascades of preprocessors $P_1, P_2, \ldots, P_n$, where the output of P_i is the input for the next preprocessor P_{i+1}. Cascades of finite state transducers have been used, for example, in [8] for extracting information from natural language texts.

In terms of formal languages, machines processing preprocessed input can be formulated as follows. Let T be some transducer such as, for example, a finite state transducer or a pushdown transducer (see, e.g., [1]), and M be some accepting machine such as, for example, a finite automaton or a pushdown automaton. Then, for such a pair (M, T), we are interested in the set of words w such that $T(w)$ is accepted by M. From a language theoretic perspective it is an immediate question which language classes can be accepted by such composed devices.

© Springer International Publishing AG, part of Springer Nature 2018
C. Câmpeanu (Ed.): CIAA 2018, LNCS 10977, pp. 28–40, 2018.
https://doi.org/10.1007/978-3-319-94812-6_3

Clearly, the answer depends on the power of both components. If T is a finite state transducer and M is a finite automaton, nothing more than regular languages can be described by (M, T), since a finite automaton can be constructed that simultaneously simulates T on the input given and M on the output produced by T. Similarly, if T is a finite state transducer and M is a pushdown automaton, nothing more than the context-free languages can be described. On the other hand, if T is a nondeterministic pushdown transducer and M is a pushdown automaton, then it is possible to construct for any recursively enumerable language L some pair (M, T) accepting L. For the language classes in between these both extremes there are interesting results given in [7]. For example, it is shown that a pair (M, T) of a deterministic pushdown transducer T combined with a deterministic pushdown automaton M can accept the non-context-free language $\{ wcw \mid w \in \{a, b\}^* \}$. Moreover, cascades of deterministic pushdown transducers are studied and a strict hierarchy with respect to the number of transducers is obtained. If we confine ourselves with the combination of finite state transducers and pushdown automata, then the combination of a nondeterministic finite state transducer with a deterministic or nondeterministic pushdown automaton as well as of a deterministic finite state transducer with a nondeterministic pushdown automaton gives nothing more than the context-free languages. Finally, the combination of a deterministic finite state transducer and a deterministic pushdown automaton gives the deterministic context-free languages. Thus, we can summarize that, roughly speaking, the preprocessing by finite state transducers leads to the classes inside the context-free languages, whereas the preprocessing by pushdown transducers leads to language classes beyond the context-free languages. So far, we have not put any restriction on the automata except the property of working deterministically or nondeterministically. It is therefore an obvious approach to consider restricted pushdown automata and to investigate whether the restrictions can be compensated by the preprocessing.

In this paper, we will basically consider two restricted versions of deterministic pushdown automata, namely, input-driven pushdown automata and reversible pushdown automata. Both variants are in addition real-time deterministic pushdown automata, whose corresponding language class is known to be a proper subset of the deterministic context-free languages. Input-driven pushdown automata are ordinary pushdown automata where the actions on the pushdown store are dictated by the input symbols. This variant of pushdown automata has been introduced in 1980 by Mehlhorn in [16] and further investigations have been done in 1985 by von Braunmühl and Verbeek in [5]. The early results comprise the equivalence of nondeterministic and deterministic models and the proof that the membership problem is solvable in logarithmic space. The model has been revisited in 2004 in [2] where, for example, descriptional complexity aspects for the determinization are investigated as well as closure properties and decidability questions which turned out to be similar to those of finite automata. More results on the model may be found in the survey [17].

The second model we are going to investigate in more detail in connection with a preprocessing transducer are reversible pushdown automata which have been introduced in [10] and are basically pushdown automata which are forward and backward deterministic. This means that every configuration has a unique successor configuration and a unique predecessor configuration. Reversible computations are information preserving computations and are mainly motivated by the physical observation that a loss of information results in heat dissipation [15]. For reversible pushdown automata it is known that they accept a language class that lies properly in between the regular languages and the real-time deterministic context-free languages, they share with deterministic pushdown automata the closure under complementation and inverse homomorphism, whereas the closure under union and intersection with regular languages gets lost, and they still have an undecidable inclusion problem.

It turns out that in both cases the preprocessing by weak deterministic finite state transducers leads to language classes that properly contain the original language class, but on the other hand is properly contained in the deterministic context-free languages as well. Thus, the preprocessing boosts the power of the original automata moderately. In addition, some closure properties as well as positive decidability results are preserved as well.

If we replace the data structure of a pushdown store by a queue, we obtain for the above-discussed cases input-driven queue automata [11] and reversible queue automata [13]. Again, we may ask what happens when the input is preprocessed by finite state transducers. Interestingly, we can apply similar methods as are done for pushdown automata and we obtain again language classes that properly contain the original language class, but on the other hand are properly contained in the general language classes. Thus, the preprocessing boosts also in this case the power of the original automata moderately and preserves some closure properties as well as positive decidability results.

2   Definitions and Preliminaries

Let Σ^* denote the set of all words over the finite alphabet Σ. The *empty word* is denoted by λ, and $\Sigma^+ = \Sigma^* \setminus \{\lambda\}$. The *reversal* of a word w is denoted by w^R. For the *length* of w we write $|w|$. We use $\subseteq$ for *inclusions* and $\subset$ for *strict inclusions*.

In this paper, the preprocessing of the input will be done by *one-way finite state transducers* which are basically finite automata with the ability to emit symbols. We consider here essentially *deterministic* finite state transducers (DFST) which are formally defined as a system $T = \langle Q, \Sigma, \Delta, q_0, \delta \rangle$, where Q is the set of *internal states*, Σ is the set of *input symbols*, Δ is the set of *output symbols*, q_0 is the initial state, and δ is the *transition function* mapping from $Q \times \Sigma$ to $Q \times \Delta^*$. By $T(w) \in \Delta^*$ we denote the output computed by T on input $w \in \Sigma^*$.

Since we are interested in weak preprocessing devices, we will consider *length-preserving* deterministic finite state transducers, also known as Mealy machines, where the transition function is restricted to be a mapping from $Q \times \Sigma$ to $Q \times \Delta$. Moreover, we will put the additional restriction on the transition function to be *injective* and obtain injective DFSTs (injective Mealy machines).

Let M be an automaton such as, for example, a finite automaton, pushdown automaton, or queue automaton, and T be a transducer such as, for example, a finite state transducer or a pushdown transducer. Furthermore, the output alphabet of T is the input alphabet of M. Then, the language accepted by the pair (M, T) is $L(M, T) = \{ w \in \Sigma^* \mid T(w) \in L(M) \}$.

3   Boosting Input-Driven Machines

A conventional deterministic pushdown automaton (DPDA) is an input-driven pushdown automaton (IDPDA), if the next input symbol defines the next action on the pushdown store. To this end, the input alphabet Σ is divided into three disjunct sets Σ_N, Σ_D, and Σ_R, where a symbol from Σ_N implies a state change only without changing the pushdown store, a symbol from Σ_D implies a state change and the pushing of a symbol, and a symbol from Σ_R implies a state change and the popping of a symbol. This partition of the input alphabet is also called *signature*.

Input-driven pushdown automata have properties which are similar to those of finite automata. For example, it is shown in [5] that the language classes accepted by nondeterministic and deterministic models coincide. Considering the usually studied closure properties it has been shown in [2] that IDPDAs (like finite automata) are closed under the Boolean operations, concatenation, iteration, and reversal. It should be noted that the results for union, intersection, and concatenation only hold in general if the underlying automata have *compatible* signatures, that is, if they possess an identical pushdown behavior on their input symbols. In contrast to finite automata, it is known that IDPDAs are not closed under homomorphism and inverse homomorphism. With regard to decidability questions, inclusion is decidable in case of compatible signatures in contrast to the undecidability of inclusion for arbitrary DPDAs. Together with known positively decidable questions for arbitrary DPDAs, we obtain that the questions of emptiness, finiteness, equivalence, and inclusion are all decidable for IDPDAs, which is true for finite automata as well. Obviously, every language accepted by an IDPDA is a real-time deterministic context-free language. On the other hand, it is easy to see that the language class accepted by IDPDAs is also a proper subset of the real-time deterministic context-free languages. For example, the languages $L_1 = \{ a^n \$ a^n \mid n \geq 1 \}$ and $L_2 = \{ a^n b^{2n} \mid n \geq 1 \}$ are not accepted by any input-driven pushdown automaton. On the other hand, the marginally changed languages $L_1' = \{ a^n \$ b^n \mid n \geq 1 \}$ and $L_2' = \{ a^n (bc)^n \mid n \geq 1 \}$ are accepted by IDPDAs. For L_1' every a induces a push-operation, every b induces a pop-operation, and a \$ leaves the pushdown store unchanged. Similarly, for L_2' every a induces a push-operation, every b induces a pop-operation, and a c leaves the pushdown store unchanged. Obviously, L_1' can be obtained from L_1 by a simple finite state transduction which translates all a's before the \$ to a's, and all a's after the \$ to b's. Similarly, L_2' can be obtained from L_2 by translating every a to a and every b alternately to b and c. In both cases we can observe that the preprocessing of the input by a deterministic finite state transducer, which is in addition injective and length-preserving, helps to enlarge the class of languages accepted.

In the following, we will study *tinput-driven* pushdown automata (TDPDA) which are pairs (M, T), where T is an injective and length-preserving DFST and M is an IDPDA. TDPDAs have been introduced in [14] and in the sequel we will summarize basic results on their computational capacity, closure properties, and decidability questions.

By choosing a DFST that realizes the identity it is clear that every IDPDA can be simulated by a TDPDA. Furthermore, as discussed above, language L_1 is an example of a deterministic context-free language that is not accepted by any IDPDA, but accepted by a TDPDA. Thus, TDPDAs can be more powerful than IDPDAs. On the other hand, every TDPDA can be simulated by a real-time DPDA. The basic idea is to compute the output of the DFST internally so that the IDPDA can directly be simulated. Since every IDPDA works in real time, the resulting DPDA works in real time as well. Finally, it is possible to show that the real-time deterministic context-free language $\{ a^n b^{n+m} a^m \mid n, m \geq 1 \}$ cannot be accepted by any TDPDA. Hence, we obtain the following proper hierarchy.

Theorem 1. $\mathscr{L}(IDPDA) \subset \mathscr{L}(TDPDA) \subset \mathscr{L}(rt\text{-}DPDA)$.

It is a nice feature of IDPDAs that their nondeterministic and deterministic variants coincide which in addition deepens the analogy to finite automata. Thus, it is an obvious question whether a similar result can be shown for TDPDAs. Since a TDPDA consists of two components, each of which may work deterministically or nondeterministically, we are concerned with four cases. We denote by $\text{TDPDA}_{x,y}$ with $x, y \in \{n, d\}$ a TDPDA whose transducer works in mode x and whose pushdown automaton works in mode y. Since determinization is possible for IDPDAs, we obtain that the classes $\text{TDPDA}_{d,n}$ and $\text{TDPDA}_{d,d}$ as well as $\text{TDPDA}_{n,n}$ and $\text{TDPDA}_{n,d}$ coincide. On the other hand, language $\{ a^n b^{n+m} a^m \mid n, m \geq 1 \}$ cannot be accepted by any $\text{TDPDA}_{d,d}$, but is accepted by a $\text{TDPDA}_{n,d}$. Hence, we have the following hierarchy.

Theorem 2.

$$\mathscr{L}(TDPDA_{d,d}) = \mathscr{L}(TDPDA_{d,n}) \subset \mathscr{L}(TDPDA_{n,n}) = \mathscr{L}(TDPDA_{n,d}).$$

For the rest of the section where we will discuss closure properties and decidability questions we confine ourselves to considering $\text{TDPDA}_{d,d}$s only. When studying binary language operations such as union, intersection, or concatenation for IDPDAs and TDPDAs it is essential that the signatures of the corresponding IDPDAs are compatible. For IDPDAs the closure under union, intersection, and concatenation is shown in [2], but the compatibility of the signatures has to be provided. If this condition is not fulfilled, the closure results may get lost. Consider, for example, the languages $\{ a^n b^n c^m \mid n, m \geq 1 \}$ and

$\{\, a^n b^m c^m \mid n, m \geq 1 \,\}$ which each can be accepted by an IDPDA. However, both signatures are not compatible and the intersection of both languages gives the non-context-free language $\{\, a^n b^n c^n \mid n \geq 1 \,\}$. In case of binary language operations for TDPDAs we additionally have to require that both transducers realize the same transduction. Then, similar to the proofs for IDPDAs, the closure under the Boolean operations can be shown. Additionally, a detailed construction shows the closure under inverse homomorphism for TDPDAs which is in contrast to IDPDAs.

Theorem 3. *Let* (M, T) *and* (M', T) *be two TDPDAs with compatible signatures. Then, TDPDAs accepting the intersection* $L(M, T) \cap L(M', T)$, *the union* $L(M, T) \cup L(M', T)$, *the complement* $\overline{L(M, T)}$, *and the inverse homomorphic image* $h^{-1}(L(M, T))$ *for some homomorphism* h *can effectively be constructed.*

On the other hand, one can prove the non-closure under iteration, reversal, length-preserving homomorphism, and concatenation. The latter non-closure result interestingly holds even if both signatures are compatible and both transducers are identical: we consider language $L = \{\, a^n b^n \mid n \geq 1 \,\} \cup \{\, b^n a^n \mid n \geq 1 \,\}$ which is accepted by some TDPDA since a DFST can translate L to language $\{\, a^n b^n \mid n \geq 1 \,\} \cup \{\, c^n d^n \mid n \geq 1 \,\}$ which is clearly accepted by some IDPDA. However, if TDPDAs were closed under concatenation, then $L \cdot L \cap a^+ b^+ a^+ = \{\, a^n b^{n+m} a^m \mid n, m \geq 1 \,\}$ could be accepted by some TDPDA which is a contradiction. The remaining non-closure results can basically be shown by utilizing again the fact that $\{\, a^n b^{n+m} a^m \mid n, m \geq 1 \,\}$ is not accepted by any TDPDA. The closure properties are summarized in Table 1.

Table 1. Closure properties of the language families discussed. Symbols $\cup_c$, $\cap_c$, and $\cdot_c$ denote union, intersection, and concatenation with compatible signatures. Such operations are not defined for DFAs and DPDAs and are marked with '—'.

	—	$\cup$	$\cap$	$\cup_c$	$\cap_c$	$\cdot$	$\cdot_c$	$*$	$h_{l.p.}$	h^{-1}	REV
REG	Yes	Yes	Yes	—	—	Yes	—	Yes	Yes	Yes	Yes
$\mathscr{L}$(IDPDA)	Yes	No	No	Yes	Yes	No	Yes	Yes	No	No	Yes
$\mathscr{L}$(TDPDA)	Yes	No	No	Yes	Yes	No	No	No	No	Yes	No
$\mathscr{L}$(rt-DPDA)	Yes	No	No	—	—	No	—	No	No	Yes	No

Since the questions of emptiness, finiteness, infiniteness, universality, and regularity are decidable for DPDAs, all questions are decidable for TDPDAs as well. However, the question of inclusion is undecidable for DPDAs, but decidable for IDPDAs. Thus, the question arises whether or not inclusion is decidable for two TDPDAs (M, T) and (M', T). Since the inclusion of the languages $L(M, T) \subseteq L(M', T)$ is equivalent to $L(M, T) \cap \overline{L(M, T)} = \emptyset$ and we know that TDPDAs are closed under complementation and intersection and the emptiness problem for TDPDAs is decidable, we obtain that the inclusion problem is decidable under the condition that the signatures of the given TDPDAs are compatible. Moreover, the latter assumption is in fact necessary, since it is shown in [14] that the inclusion problem becomes undecidable in case of incompatible signatures even for IDPDAs with the additional restriction on their pushdown store to be a counter only.

Let us now replace the data structure of a pushdown store by a queue store. In this way, we obtain *input-driven queue automata* (IDQA) introduced in [11] and *tinput-driven queue automata* studied in [12]. Here, every IDQA has a signature $(\Sigma_N, \Sigma_D, \Sigma_R)$, where a symbol from Σ_N leaves the queue store unchanged, a symbol from Σ_D enters a symbol to the queue store, and a symbol from Σ_D removes a symbol from the queue store. Interestingly, for TDQAs we can apply similar ideas and methods as for TDPDAs which lead to similar results as for the pushdown variants.

Similar to our discussion for TDPDAs, both languages $L_1 = \{\, a^n \$ a^n \mid n \geq 1 \,\}$ and $L_2 = \{\, a^n b^{2n} \mid n \geq 1 \,\}$ are not accepted by any IDQA, whereas their preprocessed variants $L_1' = \{\, a^n \$ b^n \mid n \geq 1 \,\}$ and $L_2' = \{\, a^n (bc)^n \mid n \geq 1 \,\}$ are easily accepted by TDQAs. Hence, TDQAs may be more powerful than IDQAs. On the other hand, every TDQA can be simulated by some real-time deterministic queue automaton (rt-DQA) and it can be shown that the language $\{\, a^n b^{n+m} a^m \mid n, m \geq 1 \,\}$ already used is not accepted by any TDQA as well. Hence, we obtain the following hierarchy.

Theorem 4. $\mathscr{L}(IDQA) \subset \mathscr{L}(TDQA) \subset \mathscr{L}(rt\text{-}DQA)$.

Considering deterministic and nondeterministic variants of the underlying transducer T and the underlying IDQA M of a TDQA (M, T) leads again to four cases. For TDPDAs it is known that the underlying IDPDA can always be determinized which leads to two classes depending on whether the underlying finite state transducer is deterministic or nondeterministic. This is no longer true for TDQAs, since it can be shown that language

$$\{\, a^n \$ h(w_1) \$ h(w_2) \$ \cdots \$ h(w_m) \mid m, n \geq 1, w_k \in \{a, b\}^n, 1 \leq k \leq m,$$
$$\text{and there exist } 1 \leq i < j \leq m \text{ so that } w_i = w_j \,\},$$

where h is the homomorphism that maps a to $\#a$ and b to $\#b$, is accepted by some $\text{TDQA}_{d,n}$, but not by any $\text{TDQA}_{d,d}$. On the other hand, each $\text{TDQA}_{n,n}$ can be converted to an equivalent $\text{TDQA}_{n,d}$. Here, the basic idea is to shift the nondeterminism of the IDQA to the transducer. This means basically that the transducer additionally guesses the nondeterministic moves of the IDQA and outputs these guesses as suitable symbols which in turn can be processed by an IDQA in a deterministic way. Finally, it is possible to separate the language classes induced by $\text{TDQA}_{d,n}$s and $\text{TDQA}_{n,n}$s using the union of the languages $\{\, u\$v\#_1 u \mid u, v \in \{a, b\}^* \,\}$ and $\{\, u\$v\#_2 v \mid u, v \in \{a, b\}^* \,\}$. Altogether, these results lead to the following hierarchy.

Theorem 5. $\mathscr{L}(TDQA_{d,d}) \subset \mathscr{L}(TDQA_{d,n}) \subset \mathscr{L}(TDQA_{n,n}) = \mathscr{L}(TDQA_{n,d})$.

Under the condition of compatible signatures it is again possible to show the closure under the Boolean operations. However, the closure under union and intersection may get lost if the signatures are no longer compatible. For example, the languages $\{ ba^n ca^n b \mid n \geq 0 \}$ and $\{ ba^n ba^m ca^m b \mid m, n \geq 0 \}$ are each accepted by some TDQA with different signatures, but it is shown in [6] that their union is not even accepted by any real-time DQA.

Theorem 6. *Let (M, T) and (M', T) be two TDQAs with compatible signatures. Then, TDQAs accepting the intersection $L(M, T) \cap L(M', T)$, the union $L(M, T) \cup L(M', T)$, and the complement $\overline{L(M, T)}$ can effectively be constructed.*

Interestingly, the reversal of the union of the above languages is accepted by some TDQA, which shows the non-closure under reversal. Further non-closure results are known for concatenation, iteration, and length-preserving homomorphism. These proofs are basically identical to that for TDPDAs, since the proofs refer to the fact that language $\{ a^n b^{n+m} a^m \mid n, m \geq 1 \}$ is not accepted by any TDPDA, which is true for any TDQA as well. The closure properties are summarized in Table 2. Since it is known that the questions of emptiness, finiteness, universality, inclusion, equivalence, regularity, and context-freeness are undecidable for IDQAs [11], it is clear that all questions are undecidable for TDQAs as well. However, when considering the restricted variant of k-turn deterministic queue automata (DQA$_k$), which means that in every computation at most k changes between increasing and decreasing the queue store may take place for some fixed integer k, then the questions of emptiness, finite, and universality become decidable [11]. These decidability results can be extended to hold for IDQA$_k$s and TDQA$_k$s as well. Furthermore, exploiting again the closure under the Boolean operations in case of compatible signatures and the decidability of emptiness, it can be shown that inclusion and equivalence is decidable for TDQA$_k$s with compatible signatures.

Table 2. Closure properties of the language families discussed. Symbols $\cup_c$ and $\cap_c$ denote union and intersection with compatible signatures. Such operations are not defined for DFAs and DQAs and are marked with '—'.

	—	$\cup$	$\cap$	$\cup_c$	$\cap_c$	$\cdot$	$*$	$h_{l.p.}$	REV
REG	Yes	Yes	Yes	—	—	Yes	Yes	Yes	Yes
$\mathscr{L}$(IDQA)	Yes	No	No	Yes	Yes	No	No	No	No
$\mathscr{L}$(TDQA)	Yes	No	No	Yes	Yes	No	No	No	No
$\mathscr{L}$(rt-DQA)	Yes	No	No	—	—	No	No	No	No

Theorem 7. *Let $k \geq 0$ be a constant and (M, T) as well as (M', T) be k-turn TDQA with compatible signatures. Then, emptiness, finiteness, and universality of $L(M, T)$ is decidable. Furthermore, the inclusion and the equivalence of $L(M, T)$ and $L(M', T)$ is decidable as well.*

Finally, we remark that the decidability of inclusion is no longer true for $IDQA_k$s in case of incompatible signatures which holds for $TDQA_k$s as well, whereas it is an open problem whether or not the equivalence problem is decidable for $IDQA_k$s or $TDQA_k$s in case of incompatible signatures. If we come back to general TDQAs, then it is known that inclusion and equivalence is undecidable even if compatible signatures are considered.

We can summarize so far that the preprocessing of the input in case of input-driven automata with pushdown or queue store boosts their computational power, but at the same time preserves the nice features of input-driven automata such as the closure under Boolean operations as well as the decidability of inclusion and equivalence in case of compatible signatures.

4   Boosting Reversible Machines

Reversible pushdown automata (REV-PDA) are conventional DPDAs that in addition to their transition function δ possess a reverse transition function $\delta^{\leftarrow}$ such that a configuration c' is reached from configuration c by applying δ if and only if c is reached from c' by applying $\delta^{\leftarrow}$. REV-PDAs have been introduced in [10] and it is shown there, for example, that REV-PDAs can be assumed to work in real time and induce a language class that is a proper subset of the real-time deterministic context-free languages which is witnessed by the language $L = \{\, a^n b^n \mid n \geq 1 \,\}$. The gap between reversible and irreversible context-free languages is very small, since the slightly changed language $L' = \{\, a^n c b^{n-1} \mid n \geq 1 \,\}$ is accepted by a REV-PDA. Again as observed for IDPDAs, language L' can be obtained from L by preprocessing the input by an injective and length-preserving deterministic finite state transducer. Hence, we will consider in the following *transducer reversible pushdown automata* (T-REV-PDA) which are pairs (M, T), where T is an injective and length-preserving DFST and M is a REV-PDA. Similarly, if M is a reversible finite automaton or a reversible queue automaton [13] (REV-QA), we obtain *transducer reversible finite automata* (T-REV-FA) as well as *transducer reversible queue automata* (T-REV-QA). All these models have been introduced in [3,4] and we will in the sequel summarize known results with respect to their computational capacity and closure properties. Since general DQAs may perform arbitrarily many λ-steps, which is necessary to show their computational universality, we limit for REV-QAs and T-REV-QAs the maximal number of consecutive λ-steps to a fixed number. Moreover, it can be shown for both models that they can be converted to equivalent REV-QAs and T-REV-QAs, respectively, that work in real time. It should also be noted that in a first definition the DFSTs had to be reversible as well. However, it is possible to cede this condition (as well as the condition of being injective), since it can be shown that both conditions can be recovered by the pair of transducer and automaton so that the same language classes are accepted not depending on the reversibility or injectivity of the given preprocessing transducer.

Concerning the computational capacity we can state that the preprocessing boosts the computational power of all three variants. For T-REV-FAs the equality with the regular languages can be established. As discussed above, a T-REV-PDA can accept the irreversible deterministic context-free language $\{\,a^n b^n \mid n \geq 1\,\}$, and language $\{\,a^m b^n \$w\#w \mid m, n \geq 0, w \in \{a, b\}^*\,\}$ is accepted by some T-REV-QA, but is not accepted by any REV-QA. On the other hand, by computing the output of the DFST internally and simulating the automaton directly on the output, every T-REV-PDA can be simulated by a real-time DPDA as well as every T-REV-QA can be simulated by a real-time DQA. The inclusions of both corresponding language classes are proper which is witnessed by the two languages

$$\{\,w\$w^R \mid w \in \{a, b\}^*\,\} \cup \{\,w\$c^n \mid w \in \{a, b\}^* \text{ and } |w| = n\,\} \text{ and}$$
$$\{\,w_1\$w_1\#w_2\$w_2 \mid w_1, w_2 \in \{a, b\}^*\,\} \cup \{\,w_1\$c^{|w_1|}\#w_2\$w_2 \mid w_1, w_2 \in \{a, b\}^*\,\}.$$

Hence, we have the following hierarchies.

Theorem 8. – $\mathscr{L}(\textit{T-REV-FA}) = REG$,
 – $\mathscr{L}(\textit{T-REV-FA}) \subset \mathscr{L}(\textit{REV-PDA}) \subset \mathscr{L}(\textit{T-REV-PDA}) \subset \mathscr{L}(\textit{rt-DPDA})$, and
 – $\mathscr{L}(\textit{T-REV-FA}) \subset \mathscr{L}(\textit{REV-QA}) \subset \mathscr{L}(\textit{T-REV-QA}) \subset \mathscr{L}(\textit{rt-DQA})$.

So far, we have required that the preprocessing transducer of our devices is deterministic and length-preserving. It has been discussed above that the reversibility and injectivity can be ceded without changing the language classes. This immediately raises the question what happens when both conditions are weakened. We will not discuss nondeterministic transducers here, since we want to stick with reversible models which are deterministic by definition. Interestingly, the condition to be length-preserving can be ceded as well without changing the corresponding language classes which means that the preprocessing transducer may be an arbitrary general finite state transducer. The basic idea of the construction is that such a general transducer T is converted to a length-preserving transducer T' that emits symbols which are identified with the words emitted by T. Then, the automaton M' has to work on this compressed alphabet which means that reading one symbol emitted by T' implies to simulate several steps of the original automaton M, which in turn means that M' must be able to handle compressed symbols over the pushdown alphabet and queue alphabet, respectively. However, this can be achieved for REV-PDAs as well as for REV-QAs by detailed constructions.

Theorem 9. *The family $\mathscr{L}(\textit{T-REV-PDA})$ is equal to the family of languages accepted by pairs of general DFSTs and REV-PDAs. The family $\mathscr{L}(\textit{T-REV-QA})$ is equal to the family of languages accepted by pairs of general DFSTs and REV-QAs.*

Finally, we discuss the closure properties of the families $\mathscr{L}(\text{T-REV-PDA})$ and $\mathscr{L}(\text{T-REV-QA})$ which are summarized in Table 3. We start with the complementation operation for which the positive closure can be shown. The traditional

Table 3. Closure properties of the language classes induced by transducer reversible automata.

	$-$	$\cup$	$\cap$	UR	$\cap$R	$\cdot$	$*$	$h_{l.p.}$	h^{-1}	REV
REG	Yes	Yes	Yes	Yes	Yes	Yes	Yes	Yes	Yes	Yes
$\mathscr{L}$(REV-PDA)	Yes	No	No	No	No	No	No	No	Yes	No
$\mathscr{L}$(T-REV-PDA)	Yes	No	No	Yes	Yes	No	No	No	Yes	No
$\mathscr{L}$(rt-DPDA)	Yes	No	No	Yes	Yes	No	No	No	Yes	No
$\mathscr{L}$(REV-QA)	Yes	No	No	No	No	No	No	No	Yes	No
$\mathscr{L}$(T-REV-QA)	Yes	No	No	Yes	Yes	No	No	No	Yes	No
$\mathscr{L}$(rt-DQA)	Yes	No	No	Yes	Yes	No	No	No	Yes	No

approach to show closure under complementation is to interchange accepting and non-accepting states. However, as in the construction for DPDAs [9] one has to ensure that the complete input is read and that no infinite loop on empty input is ever entered. The latter problem does neither occur for T-REV-PDAs nor for T-REV-QAs since both models can be assumed to work in real time. The former problem can be overcome by introducing a new sink state to which all undefined transitions are redirected and, to preserve reversibility, to log the predecessor of the sink state and the remaining input symbols on the pushdown store and queue store, respectively. For the closure under inverse homomorphism we can apply the fact shown in Theorem 9. In detail, it shown that the inverse homomorphic image can be represented by a pair of a general DFST and a REV-PDA or a REV-QA, respectively. Finally, we can use the DFST of a T-REV-PDA (T-REV-QA) for the reversible simulation of a regular language. Then, a standard construction using the Cartesian product shows the closure under union and intersection with regular languages. We note that REV-PDAs as well as REV-QAs are not closed under both operations in general. One has additionally to ensure that the given regular languages are reversible.

Theorem 10. *Let (M,T) be a T-REV-PDA (resp. T-REV-QA) and R a regular language. Then, a T-REV-PDA (resp. T-REV-QA) accepting the intersection $L(M,T) \cap R$, the union $L(M,T) \cup R$, the complement $\overline{L(M,T)}$, and the inverse homomorphic image $h^{-1}(L(M,T))$ for some homomorphism h can effectively be constructed.*

The families $\mathscr{L}$(T-REV-PDA) and $\mathscr{L}$(T-REV-QA) are not closed under intersection in general. Here, basically the proofs known for DPDAs and rt-DQAs apply. Due to the closure under complementation, both families cannot be closed under union as well. To show the non-closure under concatenation, iteration, reversal, and length-preserving homomorphism one can utilize some languages already used in the corresponding proofs for REV-PDAs, DPDAs, REV-QAs, and rt-DQAs. In all cases, the assumption that $\mathscr{L}$(T-REV-PDA) or $\mathscr{L}$(T-REV-QA) is closed under one operation leads to a language that is no longer acceptable by a DPDA or a rt-DQA, respectively.

Theorem 11. *The families $\mathscr{L}(T\text{-}REV\text{-}PDA)$ and $\mathscr{L}(T\text{-}REV\text{-}QA)$ are neither closed under union, intersection, concatenation, iteration, reversal, nor under length-preserving homomorphism.*

We can summarize that the preprocessing of the input also in case of reversible automata with pushdown or queue store boosts their computational power, preserves the positive closure results of the reversible automata, and adds the closure under union and intersection with regular languages.

References

1. Aho, A.V., Ullman, J.D.: The Theory of Parsing, Translation, and Compiling. Vol. I: Parsing. Prentice-Hall Inc., Englewood Cliffs (1972)
2. Alur, R., Madhusudan, P.: Visibly pushdown languages. In: Babai, L. (ed.) Symposium on Theory of Computing (STOC 2004), pp. 202–211. ACM (2004)
3. Axelsen, H.B., Kutrib, M., Malcher, A., Wendlandt, M.: Boosting reversible pushdown machines by preprocessing. In: Devitt, S., Lanese, I. (eds.) RC 2016. LNCS, vol. 9720, pp. 89–104. Springer, Cham (2016). https://doi.org/10.1007/978-3-319-40578-0_6
4. Axelsen, H.B., Kutrib, M., Malcher, A., Wendlandt, M.: Boosting reversible pushdown and queue machines by preprocessing (2018, Submitted to a journal)
5. von Braunmühl, B., Verbeek, R.: Input-driven languages are recognized in $\log n$ space. In: Karpinski, M., van Leeuwen, J. (eds.) Topics in the Theory of Computation, Mathematics Studies, vol. 102, pp. 1–19. North-Holland, Amsterdam (1985)
6. Cherubini, A., Citrini, C., Crespi-Reghizzi, S., Mandrioli, D.: QRT FIFO automata, breadth-first grammars and their relations. Theor. Comput. Sci. **85**, 171–203 (1991)
7. Citrini, C., Crespi-Reghizzi, S., Mandrioli, D.: On deterministic multi-pass analysis. SIAM J. Comput. **15**(3), 668–693 (1986)
8. Friburger, N., Maurel, D.: Finite-state transducer cascades to extract named entities in texts. Theor. Comput. Sci. **313**(1), 93–104 (2004)
9. Harrison, M.A.: Introduction to Formal Language Theory. Addison-Wesley, Reading (1978)
10. Kutrib, M., Malcher, A.: Reversible pushdown automata. J. Comput. Syst. Sci. **78**(6), 1814–1827 (2012)
11. Kutrib, M., Malcher, A., Mereghetti, C., Palano, B., Wendlandt, M.: Deterministic input-driven queue automata: finite turns, decidability, and closure properties. Theor. Comput. Sci. **578**, 58–71 (2015)
12. Kutrib, M., Malcher, A., Wendlandt, M.: Input-driven queue automata with internal transductions. In: Dediu, A.-H., Janoušek, J., Martín-Vide, C., Truthe, B. (eds.) LATA 2016. LNCS, vol. 9618, pp. 156–167. Springer, Cham (2016). https://doi.org/10.1007/978-3-319-30000-9_12
13. Kutrib, M., Malcher, A., Wendlandt, M.: Reversible queue automata. Fundam. Inform. **148**(3–4), 341–368 (2016)
14. Kutrib, M., Malcher, A., Wendlandt, M.: Tinput-driven pushdown, counter, and stack automata. Fundam. Inform. **155**(1–2), 59–88 (2017)
15. Landauer, R.: Irreversibility and heat generation in the computing process. IBM J. Res. Dev. **5**, 183–191 (1961)

16. Mehlhorn, K.: Pebbling mountain ranges and its application to DCFL-recognition. In: de Bakker, J., van Leeuwen, J. (eds.) ICALP 1980. LNCS, vol. 85, pp. 422–435. Springer, Heidelberg (1980). https://doi.org/10.1007/3-540-10003-2_89
17. Okhotin, A., Salomaa, K.: Complexity of input-driven pushdown automata. SIGACT News **45**(2), 47–67 (2014)

The Validity of Weighted Automata

Sylvain Lombardy[1] and Jacques Sakarovitch[2(✉)]

[1] LaBRI - UMR 5800 - Bordeaux INP - Bordeaux University - CNRS,
Bordeaux, France
[2] IRIF - UMR 8243 - CNRS/Paris Diderot University and Telecom ParisTech,
Paris, France
sakarovitch@enst.fr

Extended Abstract
(adapted from the introduction of [14])

This invited talk presents the work conducted on the problems that arise when dealing with weighted automata containing ε-transitions: how to define the behaviour of such automata in which the presence of ε-circuits results in infinite summations, and second how to eliminate the ε-transitions in an automaton whose behaviour has been recognised to be well-defined. The origin of this work is the implementation, in the AWALI platform [19], of an ε-transition removal algorithm for automata with weight in $\mathbb{Q}$ or $\mathbb{R}$, a case that had never been treated before in the rich literature on the subject of ε-transition removal algorithms (*cf.* [16] for a survey). The results of this work have been published in [14].

The equivalence between non-deterministic finite automata (NFA) and non-deterministic finite automata with ε-transitions (ε-NFA) is a basic result in the theory of finite automata (*e.g.* in [10]). Besides the proof that ε-transitions do not increase the power of the computation model, this equivalence allows simple constructions; hence the interest in the *construction* of NFA from ε-NFA which amounts to the computation of the *transitive closure* of the graph of ε-transitions, more or less intertwined with the construction of the NFA itself.

Automata with weights taken in semirings have been considered since the beginning of the 60's and the recent investigations on quantitative evaluation of systems make them of current interest. Removal of ε-transitions is of equal importance for weighted automata as for Boolean ones, but even the definition of the behaviour of a weighted automaton with ε-transitions is not so obvious: if the graph of ε-transitions contains a circuit, then the sum of the weights along the paths following this circuit may well be not defined, as for instance in the automaton $\mathcal{Q}_1$ of Fig. 1(a). For that reason, some of the most mathematically oriented works on automata, such as [1] or [12], have ruled out the possibility of having circuits of ε-transitions in automata, either explicitly with the hypothesis of *cycle-free* automata, or implicitly by considering the *discrete topology* on the weight semiring. As a result, the automaton $\mathcal{Q}_2$ of Fig. 1(b) is also considered as an illegitimate object. Yet, the natural topology on $\mathbb{Q}$ or $\mathbb{R}$ should allow to consider that such weighted automata with circuits of ε-transitions may be *valid*.

J. Sakarovitch Joint work with S. Lombardy.

© Springer International Publishing AG, part of Springer Nature 2018
C. Câmpeanu (Ed.): CIAA 2018, LNCS 10977, pp. 41–45, 2018.
https://doi.org/10.1007/978-3-319-94812-6_4

(a) $\mathcal{Q}_1$ (b) $\mathcal{Q}_2$

Fig. 1. A non-valid automaton $\mathcal{Q}_1$, and $\mathcal{Q}_2$ that should be considered valid

The definition of the behaviour of weighted automata with ε-transitions requires a theoretical framework in which it is possible to define *infinite sums*, at least some particular ones. It appears indeed that these infinite sums are created by the paths along a circuit (as in the loops in Fig. 1) and may be expressed by the star operator.

A first approach to solving the issue of infinite sums, which we call *the axiomatic approach*, is the setting of a framework in which the star operator is always defined — making the previous evaluation always possible — and satisfies a number of axioms that guarantee the behaviour be well-defined and the evaluation correct. This yields on one hand the notions of *complete*, and *continuous*, semirings (*cf.* [2,4,7,11]), and on the other the notion of *Conway* and *partial Conway semirings* (*cf.* [2,3,9]). The weighted automata we want to deal with, such as probabilistic or distance automata, are natural computational models, while their weight semirings (*e.g.* $\mathbb{Q}$, $\mathbb{R}$ or $\mathbb{Z}$min) are neither complete nor continuous nor partial Conway semirings. In order to address these cases, we have made the choice in our previous work ([17,18]) of a *topological approach* to infinite sums and to the notion of *summability* of infinite families.

A natural definition for a *valid* automaton is then that the family of all computations be summable, that is, that for every word w the family of weights of paths with label w be summable. One may be more cautious, and require that for every pair of states the family of weights of paths between these states and with label w be summable. This definition, taken in [17,18], yields a consistent theory; it however conceals the weakness of *not being effective* as it says nothing on how one can compute or decide that an infinite family is summable. As noted above, the evaluation of infinite sums is made through the star operator, which implies *block summations*. And then, computations are likely to meet two pitfalls, different, and almost opposite:

1. A subfamily of a summable family is not necessarily summable, and an evaluation may fail on what is considered as a 'valid' automaton. Such a situation occurs with the automaton $\mathcal{T}_2$ of Fig. 2(a) whose weights are in $\mathbb{N}_\infty$, the semiring $\mathbb{N} \cup +\infty$ equipped with the discrete topology, where an infinite sum is defined if, and only if, almost all terms are 0, or at least one term is $+\infty$. The sum of the weights of paths in this automaton is therefore defined, but the evaluation of this sum through the star operator may require to compute the star of 1 which is not defined.
2. On the other side, it is well-known that block summations may give values to non summable families. Automaton $\mathcal{Q}_3$ of Fig. 2(b) yields an example of such

a phenomenon. Weights of $\mathcal{Q}_3$ are in $\mathbb{Q}$ where, for every x in $]-1;1[$, the star of x is defined and is equal to $(1-x)^{-1}$. The usual formula for the evaluation of the computations labelled by ε gives $\left(\frac{-1}{2} + \frac{1}{2}\left(\frac{-1}{2}\right)^* \frac{1}{2}\right)^* = \frac{3}{5}$ but a direct computation on the *transition matrix* M yields $M^2 = -M$ which shows that computations grouped by length are not summable.

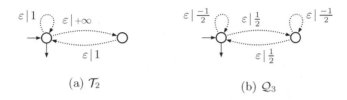

(a) $\mathcal{T}_2$ (b) $\mathcal{Q}_3$

Fig. 2. The two pitfalls of the ε-removal computations

We therefore take a *stronger definition of validity*: we will say that a weighted automaton is *valid* if the sum of weighted labels of *every rational set of paths* is well-defined. This definition has several outcomes. It insures first that in any kind of semirings, any (reasonable) ε-removal algorithm will succeed on every valid weighted automaton and turn it into an equivalent proper automaton. Second, this definition is not as restrictive as it may appear. It rules out tricky examples in awkward semirings (such as $\mathbb{N}_\infty$) but coincides with the former definition in all cases of usual semirings. It encompasses the cases treated with the axiomatic approach where indeed the decision of validity is trivial. Finally, this definition provides a framework in which the closure algorithm yields a decision procedure for the validity of automata in the cases we wanted to treat. All in all, this definition of validity is more complex than the other ones but fulfills our goals without narrowing its domain of application.

A byproduct of this definition of validity is the stability and consistency with natural transformations of automata: a subautomaton of a valid automaton is valid and so is a *covering* (kind of unfolding) of a valid automaton. The validity of automata is also consistent with that of rational expressions, provided the transformation of the latter into the former does not artificially introduce ε-transitions. This last condition brings to light a weakness of Thompson's construction compared to the other classical ones.

After the definition of validity, the next step is the computation of the behaviour of an automaton, which amounts to describing algorithms for ε-transition removal. It begins with the study of the relationships between the validity of an automaton and the starability of its transition matrix. In the axiomatic approach, the behaviour of an automaton is defined by the star of the transition matrix and the problem is to set up conditions that guarantee its starability. The topological approach goes in the opposite direction and an automaton which is not valid may well have a starable transition matrix. It is proved that under the condition that an automaton is valid, its transition matrix is starable and the classical formulas can be applied to compute the star. This leads to a first family of algorithms that have been abundantly described in the literature ([13,15,16]).

Another family of algorithms, hardly less classical, is based on the iteration of elementary operations of suppression of ε-transitions. The *correctness* comes from the correctness of each elementary operation, but the *termination* of the algorithm has to be carefully checked.

The final task is to address the problem of deciding the validity of an automaton. The success of an algorithm on a given automaton is not a sufficient condition for the automaton be valid. There is no general and uniform answer to the problem and that the existence, and the details, of a solution will depend on the properties of the weight semiring. It is for instance classical that the only valid automata with weights in $\mathbb{N}$ or $\mathbb{Z}$ are those with no circuits of ε-transitions, a decidable property. The opposite case, that is, the one in which every automaton is valid, and which meets the class of *rationally additive semirings* of [8], is also characterised.

The cases in-between, that is, semirings such that some, but not all, automata with circuits of ε-transitions are valid, is a new area of reasearch. In this work, it is established that the validity of $\mathbb{K}$-automata is decidable — decided by the success of the algorithm quoted above — when $\mathbb{K}$ is a *topological (partially) ordered positive* semiring (TOPS) with the property that the domain of the star operator is downward closed. This class of semirings contains for instance $\mathbb{Q}_+$, $\mathbb{R}_+$, $\mathbb{Z}$min (and all the tropical semirings). Moreover, in starable TOPS — such as for instance the semiring Rat A^* of rational languages over A^* — every weighted automaton is valid and this class contains the *continuous* semirings (*cf.* [5]).

With a last step, the decidability problem for $\mathbb{Q}$- or $\mathbb{R}$-automata is reduced to the one for automata with weights in TOPS by considering the *absolute value* of such automata. The initial goal of solving the problem of ε-transition removal algorithm for $\mathbb{Q}$- or $\mathbb{R}$-automata is then reached: we have both the theoretical justification and the algorithm that allows to transform the automaton $\mathcal{Q}_4$ of Fig. 3(a) into the automaton $\mathcal{Q}_5$ of Fig. 3(b).

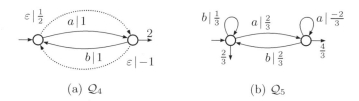

(a) $\mathcal{Q}_4$ (b) $\mathcal{Q}_5$

Fig. 3. A transformation which needs theoretical foundation

As a last remark, it can be mentioned that, for sake of simplicity, the only automata considered in this work are the weighted automata over free monoids, but the same definitions, constructions and results hold for automata over *graded monoids* (that is, monoids with a *length*), and thus in particular for *transducers*.

This work fills the *effectivity* gap that was left open by our definition of valid automata in [17,18]. In general, the success of any ε-removal algorithm may never insure the validity of an automaton. In order to reach a decidability procedure, we have been led to a strong definition of validity, which implies stability under automata transformations that are paths preserving. The algorithms described in this work are *implemented* in AWALI [19].

References

1. Berstel, J., Reutenauer, C.: Noncommutative Rational Series with Applications. Cambridge University Press, Cambridge (2011)
2. Bloom, S.L., Ésik, Z.: Iteration Theories. Springer, Heidelberg (1993). https://doi.org/10.1007/978-3-642-78034-9
3. Bloom, S.L., Ésik, Z., Kuich, W.: Partial Conway and iteration semirings. Fundam. Inform. **86**, 19–40 (2008)
4. Conway, J.H.: Regular Algebra and Finite Machines. Chapman and Hall, London (1971)
5. Droste, M., Kuich, W.: Semirings and formal power series. In: Droste et al. [6], pp. 3–28
6. Droste, M., Kuich, W., Vogler, H. (eds.): Handbook of Weighted Automata. Springer, Heidelberg (2009). https://doi.org/10.1007/978-3-642-01492-5
7. Eilenberg, S.: Automata, Languages and Machines, vol. A. Academic Press, New York (1974)
8. Ésik, Z., Kuich, W.: Locally closed semirings. Monatshefte für Mathematik **137**, 21–29 (2002)
9. Ésik, Z., Kuich, W.: Finite automata. In: Droste et al. [6], pp. 69–104
10. Hopcroft, J.E., Motwani, R., Ullman, J.D.: Introduction to Automata Theory, Languages and Computation, 3rd edn. Addison-Wesley, Boston (2006)
11. Kuich, W.: Automata and languages generalized to ω-continuous semirings. Theoret. Comput. Sci. **79**, 137–150 (1991)
12. Kuich, W., Salomaa, A.: Semirings, Automata, Languages. Springer, Heidelberg (1986). https://doi.org/10.1007/978-3-642-69959-7
13. Lehmann, D.J.: Algebraic structure for transitive closure. Theoret. Comput. Sci. **4**, 59–76 (1977)
14. Lombardy, S., Sakarovitch, J.: The validity of weighted automata. Int. J. Algebra Comput. **23**(4), 863–914 (2013)
15. Mohri, M.: Generic ε-removal and input ε-normalization algorithms for weighted transducers. Int. J. Found. Comput. Sci. **13**, 129–143 (2002)
16. Mohri, M.: Weighted automata algorithms. In: Droste et al. [6], pp. 213–254
17. Sakarovitch, J.: Elements of Automata Theory. Cambridge University Press, Cambridge (2009). corrected English translation of Éléments de théorie des automates, Vuibert, Paris (2003)
18. Sakarovitch, J.: Rational and recognisable power series. In: Droste et al. [6], pp. 105–174
19. Awali: Another Weighted Automata LIbrary. vaucanson-project.org/AWALI

Algorithms for Weighted Finite Automata with Failure Transitions

Cyril Allauzen$^{(\boxtimes)}$ and Michael D. Riley

Google, New York, NY, USA
allauzen@google.com, riley@google.com

Abstract. In this paper we extend several weighted finite automata (WFA) algorithms to automata with failure transitions (φ-WFAs). Failure transitions, which are taken only when no immediate match is possible at a given state, are used to compactly represent automata and have many applications. Efficient algorithms to intersect two φ-WFAs, to remove failure transitions, to trim, and to compute (over $\mathbb{R}_+$) the shortest distance in a φ-WFA are presented.

1 Introduction

Weighted finite automata are used in many applications including speech recognition [19], speech synthesis [11], machine translation [13], computational biology [10], image processing [2], and optical character recognition [7]. Such applications often have strict time and memory requirements, so efficient representations and algorithms are paramount. We examine one useful technique, the use of *failure transitions*, to represent automata compactly. A failure transition is taken only when no immediate match to the input is possible at a given state. In this paper, we will present efficient algorithms to combine, optimize and search weighted automata with failure transitions.

Aho and Corasick [1] introduce failure transitions in the context of efficient string matching from a finite set of strings input. Mohri [16] shows how to use failure transitions in string matching from finite automata input. Several authors explore constructing deterministic failure automata from arbitrary deterministic finite automata (*DFA*) for space optimization [6,15,22].

Automata with failure transitions, initially introduced for string matching problems, have found wider use including compactly representing language, pronunciation, transliteration and semantic models [3,8,12,14,20,21,27].

Mohri [18] gives a concise presentation of various fundamental weighted automata algorithms, many generalizations of classical algorithms to the weighted case. These algorithms include intersection, epsilon removal and shortest distance. Our goal here is to present similar algorithms for weighted automata with failure transitions.

This paper is organized as follows. In Sect. 2 we introduce the automata classes and related notation used here. In Sect. 3 we present the algorithms for automata with failure transitions. In Sect. 4 offer discussion and include mention of a related open-source software library.

© Springer International Publishing AG, part of Springer Nature 2018
C. Câmpeanu (Ed.): CIAA 2018, LNCS 10977, pp. 46–58, 2018.
https://doi.org/10.1007/978-3-319-94812-6_5

2   Preliminaries

2.1   Semirings

A *semiring* $K = (\mathbb{K}, \oplus, \otimes, \overline{0}, \overline{1})$ consists of a set $\mathbb{K}$ together with an associative and commutative operation $\oplus$ and an associative operation $\otimes$, with identities $\overline{0}$ and $\overline{1}$, respectively, such that $\otimes$ distributes over $\oplus$, and $\overline{0} \otimes x = x \otimes \overline{0} = \overline{0}$. A semiring is *commutative* if the $\otimes$ operation is also commutative.

Let K be a semiring equipped with a *metric* Δ.[1] A *family* $\{x_i\}_{i \in I}$ of elements in $\mathbb{K}$ is *summable* to $x \in \mathbb{K}$ if $\forall \eta > 0$ there is a $J_\eta \subset I$ such that

$$\Delta\Big(\bigoplus_{i \in L} x_i, x\Big) \leq \eta \tag{1}$$

for all finite L with $J_\eta \subseteq L \subset I$ [25].

2.2   Weighted Automata

A *weighted finite automaton* (*WFA*) $A = (\Sigma, Q, E, i, F, \rho)$ over a semiring K is given by a finite alphabet Σ, a finite set of states Q, a finite set of transitions $E \subseteq Q \times \Sigma \times \mathbb{K} \times Q$, an initial state $i \in Q$, a set of final states $F \subseteq Q$, and a *final weight function* $\rho: F \to \mathbb{K}$.

A transition $e = (p[e], \ell[e], w[e], n[e]) \in E$ represents a move from the *source* or *previous* state $p[e]$ to the *destination* or *next* state $n[e]$ with the *label* $\ell[e]$ and *weight* $w[e]$. The transitions with source state q are denoted by $E[q]$.

Transitions e_1 and e_2 are *consecutive* if $n[e_i] = p[e_{i+1}]$. A path $\pi = e_1 \cdots e_n \in E^*$ is a finite sequence of consecutive transitions. The source state of a path we denote by $p[\pi]$ and the destination state by $n[\pi]$. The label of a path is the concatenation of its transition labels: $\ell[\pi] = \ell[e_1] \cdots \ell[e_n]$. The weight of a path is obtained by $\otimes$-multiplying its transition weights: $w[\pi] = w[e_1] \otimes \cdots \otimes w[e_n]$. For a non-empty path, the i-th transition is denoted by π_i.

$P(q, q')$ denotes the set of all paths in A from q to q'. We extend this to sets in the obvious way: $P(q, R)$ denotes the set of all paths q to $q' \in R$ and so forth.

A path π is successful if it is in $P(i, F)$ and in that case the automaton is said to accept the input string $\alpha = \ell[\pi]$. The weight of $\alpha \in \Sigma^*$ assigned by the automaton is:

$$A(\alpha) = \bigoplus_{\pi \in P(i,F): \ell[\pi]=\alpha} w[\pi]\rho(n[\pi]). \tag{2}$$

2.3   Weighted Automata with ϵ or φ Transitions

A *weighted finite automaton with ϵ-transitions* (ϵ-*WFA*) $A_\epsilon = (\Sigma, Q, E_\epsilon, i, F, \rho)$ is a WFA extended to allow a transition to have an empty label denoted by ϵ: $E_\epsilon \subseteq Q \times (\Sigma \cup \{\epsilon\}) \times \mathbb{K} \times Q$. A *weighted finite automaton with failure transitions*

---

[1] A metric $\Delta : \mathbb{K} \times \mathbb{K} \to \mathbb{R}_+$ satisfies (1) $\Delta(x,y) = \Delta(y,x)$, (2) $\Delta(x,y) = 0$ iff $x = y$, and (3) $\Delta(x,y) \leq \Delta(x,z) + \Delta(y,z)$ for all $x, y, z \in \mathbb{K}$.

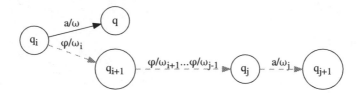

Fig. 1. The (dashed red) path $e_i = (q_i, \varphi, \omega_i, q_{i+1})$ to $e_j = (q_j, a, \omega_j, q_{j+1})$ is disallowed since a can be read already on $e = (q_i, a, \omega, q)$. (Color figure online)

(φ-*WFA*) $A_\varphi = (\Sigma, Q, E_\varphi, i, F, \rho)$ is a WFA extended to allow a transition to have a special *failure* label denoted by φ: $E_\varphi \subseteq Q \times (\Sigma \cup \{\varphi\}) \times \mathbb{K} \times Q$.

Neither ϵ and φ transitions add to a path label; they consume no input as their labels are identity elements of string concatenation for their respective automata. An ϵ-transition places no restriction on a path; it is a 'free' move. A failure transition, however, is followed only when the input can not be read immediately.

Specifically, a path $e_1 \cdots e_n$ in a φ-WFA is *disallowed* if it contains a subpath $e_i \cdots e_j$ such that $\ell[e_k] = \varphi$ for $i \leq k < j$ and there is another transition $e \in E$ such that $p[e_i] = p[e]$ and $\ell[e_j] = \ell[e] \in \Sigma$ (see Fig. 1). Since the label $a = l[e_j]$ can be read on e, we do not follow the failure transitions to read it on e_j as well.

We use $P^*(q, q') \subseteq P(q, q')$ to denote the set of (not dis-) allowed paths from q to q' in a φ-WFA. This again extends to sets in the obvious way. A path π is successful in a φ-WFA if $\pi \in P^*(i, F)$ and $\ell[\pi_{|\pi|}] \neq \varphi$ and only in that case is the input string $\alpha = \ell[\pi]$ accepted.[2]

The weight of $\alpha \in \Sigma^*$ assigned by the automaton is:

$$A_\varphi(\alpha) = \bigoplus_{\pi \in P^*(i,F):\, \ell[\pi]=\alpha,\, \ell[\pi_{|\pi|}]\neq\varphi} w[\pi]\rho(n[\pi]). \qquad (3)$$

For these automata, we will assume there are no ϵ- or φ-labeled cycles. When there is at most one exiting failure transition per state we call the automaton φ-deterministic. We will also assume the φ-WFAs in this paper are φ-deterministic.

Two automata are *equivalent* if they accept the same strings with the same weights. Any weighted finite automaton is trivially also a φ-WFA. In the next section we describe how to remove the failure transitions from a φ-WFA to produce an equivalent φ-free WFA. As with ϵ-transitions, φ-transitions do not extend the set of weighted languages, rational power series, representable by WFAs [5].

---

[2] The condition that a successful path cannot end in a φ-labeled transition simplifies the presentation without loss of generality since there is an equivalent φ-WFA with the final weights propagated to the φ sources.

φ-INTERSECTION(A_1, A_2)

1   $i \leftarrow (i_1, i_2)$
2   $Q \leftarrow S \leftarrow \{i\}$
3   **while** $S \neq \emptyset$ **do**
4      $(q_1, q_2) \leftarrow$ HEAD(S)
5   DEQUEUE(S)
6   **for each** $e_1 \in E_1[q_1]$ **do**
7   **if** $\ell[e_1] \neq \varphi$ **then**
8   **for** $e_2 \in E_2^*(q_2)$ s.t. $\ell[e_1] = \ell[e_2]$ **do**
9   ADD$((q_1, q_2), \ell[e_1], w[e_1] \otimes w[e_2], (n[e_1], n[e_2]))$
10   **else**
11   ADD$((q_1, q_2), \varphi, w[e_1], (n[e_1], q_2))$
12   **if** $q_1 \in F_1$ and $q_2 \in F_2$ **then**
13           $F \leftarrow F \cup \{(q_1, q_2)\}$
14           $\rho(q_1, q_2) \leftarrow \rho_1(q_1) \otimes \rho_2(q_2)$
15   **return** A

ADD(q, l, w, q')

1   **if** $q' \notin Q$ **then**
2      $Q \leftarrow Q \cup \{q'\}$
3   ENQUEUE(S, q')
4      $E \leftarrow E \cup \{(q, l, w, q')\}$

Fig. 2. Pseudocode of the intersection algorithm with failure transitions.

2.4 φ-Removed Automata

Given a φ-WFA $A - (\Sigma, Q, E, i, F, \rho)$, let the φ-removed transitions leaving q be defined as:

$$E^*[q] = \Big\{(q, a, \omega, q') : \quad \pi \in P^*(q, Q), a = \ell[\pi] = \ell[\pi_{|\pi|}] \in \Sigma, q' = n[\pi],$$

$$\omega = \bigoplus_{\pi' \in P^*(q,q'): a=\ell[\pi']=\ell[\pi'_{|\pi'|}], q'=n[\pi']} w[\pi']\Big\}$$

This is a set of (possibly new) transitions (q, a, ω, q'), one for each source state q and destination state q' of one or more a-labeled paths with optional leading failure transitions. The weight is the $\oplus$-sum of all such paths between those state pairs and with that label.

Then define the φ-removed WFA as $(\Sigma, Q, \cup_{q \in Q} E^*[q], i, F, \rho)$.

3   Algorithms

In this section we wish to extend some common WFA algorithms to the case where failure transitions are present.

3.1   Intersection

Computing the intersection of two WFAs is a fundamental operation and one of the most useful. For example, the application of an n-gram language model to an unweighted string (or more general unweighted automaton) is accomplished by intersection [3]. We extend intersection to φ-WFAs as follows:

Let K be a commutative semiring and let $A_1 = (\Sigma, Q_1, E_1, i_i, F_1, \rho_1)$ and $A_2 = (\Sigma, Q_2, E_2, i_2, F_2, \rho_2)$ be two φ-WFAs over the same alphabet. The intersection of A_1 and A_2 is a φ-WFA denoted by $A_1 \cap A_2$ and specified for all x by:

$$(A_1 \cap A_2)(x) = A_1(x) \otimes A_2(x). \tag{4}$$

Leaving aside φ-transitions, the following rule specifies how to compute a transition of $A_1 \cap A_2$ from transitions of A_1 and A_2 with matching labels: (q_1, a, ω_1, q_1') and (q_2, a, w_2, q_2') results in $((q_1, q_2), a, w_1 \otimes w_2, (q_1', q_2'))$. A simple algorithm to compute the intersection of two such automata, following the above rule, is given in [16].

The idea for extending the intersection algorithm when one or both automata have failure transitions is to output failure transitions where appropriate otherwise follow the failure transitions when matching. Figure 2 gives the pseudocode for computing $A = A_1 \cap A_2 = (\Sigma, Q, E, i, F, \rho)$ in this case.

E and F are assumed initialized to the empty set and grown as needed. The algorithm uses a queue S with arbitrary discipline to hold the state pairs yet to be examined. The state set Q is initially the pair of initial states (lines 1–2). Each time through the loop in lines 3–14, a new pair of states (q_1, q_2) is extracted from S (lines 4–5). Each non-φ-transition e_1 leaving q_1 is matched with φ-removed transitions e_2 leaving q_2 (lines 7–8). A transition is created with the matching label from (q_1, q_2) to $(n[e_1], n[e_2])$ with weight computed by $\otimes$-multiplying the weights of the matching transitions. A transition is also created for each φ-transition e_1 leaving q_1 from (q_1, q_2) to $(n[e_1], q_2)$ with weight $w[e_1]$ (lines 10–11). If q_1 and q_2 are final, the pair (q_1, q_2) is final with final weight computed by $\otimes$-multiplying the component final weights (lines 12–14).

If there are no failure transitions in A_1, this algorithm is simply the WFA intersection of A_1 with the φ-removed A_2 (lines 7–9). Failure transitions in A_1, however, appear in the output; they delay failure matching on that side (lines 10–11) similar to epsilon processing in ϵ-WFAs [16]. The choice of which automaton is used in line 6 can be generalized to be state-dependent. For example, one could use the automaton at line 6 for which $|E_i(q_i)|$ is less.

The worst-case time complexity of the algorithm is in $O(|E_1||Q_2|(m_2 + l_2 \log d_2))$, where d_i is the maximum out-degree, m_i is the maximum label multiplicity[3] and l_i the maximum length of a φ-labeled path at a state in A_i (assuming line 8 is implemented as a binary search).

3.2 φ-Removal

An algorithm to φ-remove a WFA A over alphabet Σ to produce an equivalent WFA is shown in Fig. 3. The pseudocode uses the algorithm of Fig. 2 to intersect the input with a φ-free WFA that accepts Σ^*. The intersection algorithm only outputs failure transitions from its first argument, as previously noted, and there are none. Intersection with Σ^* produces an equivalent result.

---

[3] Label multiplicity at state q is the maximum number of outgoing transitions in q sharing the same label.

φ-REMOVAL(A)

  1   $E_0 \leftarrow \{(i_0, a, \overline{1}, i_0) : a \in \Sigma\}$
  2   $\rho_0(i_0) \leftarrow \overline{1}$
  3   $A_0 \leftarrow (\Sigma, \{i_0\}, E_0, i_0, \{i_0\}, \rho_0)$
  4   **return** φ-INTERSECTION(A_0, A)

Fig. 3. Pseudocode of the φ-removal algorithm

φ-TRIM(A)

  1   $Acc, \Sigma_\perp \leftarrow \varphi$-ACCESSIBLE($A$)
  2   $CoAcc \leftarrow \varphi$-COACCESSIBLE(A)
  3   $E \leftarrow \{e \in E \mid \ell[e] \notin \Sigma_\perp[p[e]]\}$
  4   $Q' \leftarrow \phi,\ E' \leftarrow \phi$
  5   **if** $i \in F$ **then**
  6     $Q' \leftarrow Q' \cup \{i\}$
  7   **for** each $e \in E$ **do**
  8   **if** USEFUL(e) **then**
  9       $E' \leftarrow E' \cup \{e\}$
 10      $Q' \leftarrow Q' \cup \{p[e], n[e]\}$
 11   **return** $(\Sigma, Q', E', i, F \cap Q', \rho)$

USEFUL(e)

  1   **if** $Acc[p[e]] =$ UNDISCOVERED **then**
  2   **return** FALSE
  3   **if** $CoAcc[n[e]] \neq$ UNDISCOVERED **then**
  4   **return** TRUE
  5   **if** $(p[e], \varphi, \beta, q') \in E$ **then**
  6   **for** each $e' \in E^*[q']$ s.t. $\ell[e'] = \ell[e]$ **do**
  7   **if** $CoAcc[n[e']] \neq$ UNDISCOVERED **then**
  8   **return** TRUE
  9   **return** FALSE

Fig. 4. Pseudocode to trim a φ-WFA.

3.3 Trimming

Trimming removes states and transitions from an automaton that are useless. These could arise, for example, as the by-product of an intersection algorithm. In a WFA, a state or transition is useless if it is not on a successful path or equivalently, it is not both *accessible* and *coaccessible*. A state is accessible if it can be discovered in a visitation (e.g., depth-first) from the initial state [9]. Similarly, coaccessibility can be determined in a visitation in the reverse direction from the final states [9].

For a φ-WFA we must keep each state and transition that is on a successful path or equivalently if it is both φ-*accessible* from the initial state and φ-*coaccessible* to a final state. A state q is φ-accessible if $P^*(i, q)$ is not empty. φ-*accessible* transitions and φ-*coaccessible* states and transitions are similarly defined. Unlike a WFA we may also need to retain a state or transition in order to disallow a path in a φ-WFA. For example in Fig. 7 the a-labeled transition leaving state q and its destination state are needed, regardless if on a successful path, to disallow reading φa from q to q''.

Figure 4 gives the pseudocode to φ-trim a φ-WFA A. First the φ-*accessible* and φ-*coaccessible* states are found (lines 1–2). The set of disallowed labels at a state $\Sigma_\perp$, i.e. those that are not the label of a transition leaving q that is on a φ-accessible path, is also computed at this time. See below for their implementations. The disallowed transitions are then filtered out (line 3).

φ-ACCESSIBLE(A) φ-DISCOVER(n, q, N)

1   **for** each $q \in Q$ **do**   1   **if** $Acc[n] =$ UNDISCOVERED **then**
2       $Acc[q] \leftarrow$ UNDISCOVERED   2 $\Sigma_\perp[n] \leftarrow \Sigma_\perp[q] \cup \{l[e] \in \Sigma \mid e \in N\}$
3   $Acc[i] \leftarrow$ DISCOVERED   3   **else**
4   $S \leftarrow \{i\}$ 4 $\Sigma_\perp[n] \leftarrow \Sigma_\perp[n] \cap (\Sigma_\perp[q] \cup \{l[e] \in \Sigma \mid e \in N\})$
5   **while** $S \neq \emptyset$ **do**
6       $q \leftarrow$ HEAD(S)
7   DEQUEUE(S)
8       $N \leftarrow \{e \in E[q]$ s.t. $\ell[e] \notin \Sigma_\perp[q]$ and $Acc[n[e]] \notin \{$DISCOVERED, VISITED$\}\}$
9   **for** each $e \in N$ **do**
10   **if** $\ell[e] \neq \varphi$ **then**
11              $\Sigma_\perp[n[e]] \leftarrow \phi$
12              $Acc[n[e]] \leftarrow$ DISCOVERED
13   **else**
14   φ-DISCOVER($n[e], q, N$)
15              $Acc[n[e]] \leftarrow \varphi$-DISCOVERED
16   **if** $n[e] \notin S$ **then**
17   ENQUEUE($S, n[e]$)
18   **if** $Acc[q] =$ DISCOVERED **then**
19          $Acc[q] \leftarrow$ VISITED
20   **else**
21          $Acc[q] \leftarrow \varphi$-VISITED
22 **return** $Acc, \Sigma_\perp$

Fig. 5. Pseudocode to determine which states are φ-accessible and which labels are disallowed at a state.

The automaton is then examined for useful transitions and any found are retained in the result (lines 4–11). A transition is useful if its source state is φ-accessible and its destination is φ-coaccessible (lines 1–4) or if it is needed to forbid a path (lines 5–8).

Figure 5 gives the pseudocode for computing φ-accessibility. The algorithm uses an arbitrary queue S containing the states to be processed. Each time through the loop in lines 5–21, a new state q is extracted from S (lines 6–7). Each transition e leaving q that is not already *discovered*, *visited* or has a disallowed label is considered in turn (lines 8–9). If it is a non-φ-transition, then its destination state is marked as discovered and cleared of any previously disallowed labels (lines 10–12). Otherwise, it is a φ-transition and its destination state is marked as φ-*discovered* (line 14–15).

In this φ-discovered case, the disallowed labels at q together with the transition labels leaving q become the disallowed labels at $n[q]$ if just discovered (lines 1–2). Otherwise, the existing set is filtered by the disallowed labels at q and any newly allowed transition labels leaving q (lines 3–4).

Once a transition is processed, its destination state $n[q]$ is enqueued if needed (lines 16–17). Once all the transitions leaving q are processed, state q is marked as visited or φ-*visited* if previously discovered or φ-*discovered* (lines 18–21).

φ-coaccessibility on the φ-accessible component of A can be computed with a standard coaccessibility computation if restricted to paths that are φ-accessible, as previously found, and that do not end in a φ-labeled transition. The time complexity of trimming is dominated by the computation of φ-accessibility, which is in $O(l(|E| + (C_S + \log d)|Q|))$ where d is the maximum out-degree, l is the maximum length of a φ-labeled path in A, and C_S is the maximum cost of a queue operation for S.

3.4   Shortest Distance

Shortest-distance algorithms play a central role in applications on weighted automata requiring searching, counting, normalization or approximation [3,20,23,27]. In these applications, the tropical semiring $(\mathbb{R}_+\cup\{\infty\}, \min, +, \infty, 0)$ and the positive real semiring $\mathcal{R}_+ = (\mathbb{R}_+, +, \times, 0, 1)$ are among the most widely used.

Shortest Distance on WFAs and ϵ-WFAs. The *shortest distance* from the initial state i to state q in a WFA A over semiring K is defined as:

$$\delta[q] = \bigoplus_{\pi \in P(i,q)} w[\pi] \tag{5}$$

when well-defined and in $\mathbb{K}$ [17]. Mohri presented an algorithm to compute this shortest distance that is often much more efficient than alternatives such as Floyd-Warshall [17]. The pseudocode is shown in Fig. 6. We show his extended version where $\mathbb{K}$ is equipped with a metric Δ and an ϵ threshold.

The algorithm is a generalization of classical shortest distance algorithms over the tropical semiring[4] to more general semirings [9]. The algorithm uses a queue S to extract states (line 7) whose transitions e are *relaxed* to update $d[n[e]]$ (lines 11–13), the estimate of the shortest distance to that state. Unlike the classical algorithms, a second array $r[q]$ is maintained (lines 9, 14) that ensures that the weights added to $d[q]$ from paths in $P(i,q)$ are applied only once, important for the non-idempotent case (i.e. when $a \oplus a \neq a$). See [17] for the detailed proofs.

Mohri proved exact computation of $\delta[q]$ (with $\Delta(x,y) = 1_{x\neq y}$ and $\epsilon = 1$ for any queue S) when the input is acyclic, is over a k-closed semiring, or is k-closed for A.[5] For other semirings such as $\mathcal{R}_+$, it is an approximation algorithm controlled by ϵ. We prove convergence and correctness for $\mathcal{R}_+$ below.

Theorem 1. *Let A be a WFA over $\mathcal{R}_+$ equipped with the usual metric $\Delta(x,y) = |x - y|$. Assume the family of path weights $\{w[\pi]\}_{\pi \in P(i,q)}$ defining $\delta[q]$ is summable for all $q \in Q$. Then* SHORTESTDISTANCE*(A, S, ϵ) terminates for any queue S and any $\epsilon > 0$. Further for any $\eta > 0$, there is an $\epsilon > 0$ such that at termination $\Delta(d[q], \delta[q]) \leq \eta$ for any $q \in Q$.*

---

[4] Such as Dijkstra or Bellman-Ford with the appropriate queue disciplines on S.

[5] Semiring K is k-closed if for all a in $\mathbb{K}$, $\bigoplus_{i=0}^{k+1} a^i = \bigoplus_{i=0}^{k} a^i$. It is k-closed for A if the weight a of each cycle in A verifies $\bigoplus_{n=0}^{k+1} a^n = \bigoplus_{n=0}^{k} a^n$. The tropical semiring is 0-closed [17].

To prove this theorem, we first introduce a lemma. As in [17], define finite $D(q) \subseteq P(i, q)$, $q \in Q$ as the set of all paths whose weight have been added so far to $d[q]$ at some time in the execution of the program.

SHORTESTDISTANCE(A, S, ϵ)
1 **for** each $q \in Q$ **do**
2      $d[q] \leftarrow r[q] \leftarrow \bar{0}$
3    $d[i] \leftarrow r[i] \leftarrow \bar{1}$
4    $S \leftarrow \{i\}$
5   **while** $S \neq \emptyset$ **do**
6        $q \leftarrow$ HEAD(S)
7   DEQUEUE(S)
8        $r' \leftarrow r[q]$
9        $r[q] \leftarrow \bar{0}$
10   **for** each $e \in E[q]$ **do**
11           $d' \leftarrow d[n[e]] \oplus (r' \otimes w[e])$
12   **if** $\Delta(d[n[e]], d') \geq \epsilon$ **then**
13               $d[n[e]] \leftarrow d'$
14               $r[n[e]] \leftarrow r[n[e]] \oplus (r' \otimes w[e])$
15   **if** $n[e] \notin S$ **then**
16   ENQUEUE($S, n[e]$)
17       $d[i] \leftarrow \bar{1}$
18   **return** d

ENQUEUE(S_ϵ, q)
1 **if** $q \in Q$ **then**
2   ENQUEUE(S, q)
3 **else**
4      $e \leftarrow (q - |Q|), \varphi, \beta, q') \in E$
5   ENQUEUE($S_{\text{fifo}}[n[e]], q$)

HEAD(S_ϵ)
1 $q \leftarrow$ HEAD(S)
2 **if** $S_{\text{fifo}}[q] \neq \phi$ **then**
3   **return** HEAD($S_{\text{fifo}}[q]$)
4 **else**
5   **return** q

DEQUEUE(S_ϵ)
1 $q \leftarrow$ HEAD(S)
2 **if** $S_{\text{fifo}}[q] \neq \phi$ **then**
3   DEQUEUE($S_{\text{fifo}}[q]$)
4 **else**
5   DEQUEUE(S)

φ-SHORTESTDISTANCE(A, S, ϵ)
1 **return** SHORTESTDISTANCE($A_\epsilon, S_\epsilon, \epsilon$)

Fig. 6. Shortest-distance algorithm without [17] and with failure transitions.

Lemma 1. *For any path $\pi \in P(i, q)$, there is a $\theta_\pi > 0$ such that π is in $D(n[\pi])$ after some point in the execution of the algorithm provided the algorithm is run with $\epsilon \leq \theta_\pi$ and it terminates.*

Proof. If $|\pi| = 0$, then $\pi \in D(i)$ with $\theta_\pi = 1$ by line 3. If $|\pi| > 0$, let $\pi = \tau e$, $e \in E$ and assume, by induction, $\tau \in D(n[\tau])$ for all $\epsilon \leq \theta_\tau$. Let $\theta_\pi = \min\{\theta_\tau, w[\pi]\}$. State $n[\tau]$ was enqueued since $\tau \in D(n[\tau])$. When it is dequeued, which must happen since the algorithm is assumed to terminate, line 11 will succeed for π. This follows since $\Delta(d[n[e]], d[n[e]] \oplus (r' \otimes w[e])) = |r'w[e]| \geq |(w[\tau] + x) w[e]| \geq w[\pi] \geq \theta_\pi$, where x represents the weight of any other paths added to r'. Thus π is added to $D(n[\pi])$ at line 12 for all $\epsilon \leq \theta_\pi$.

Proof (Theorem 1). Termination: The $d[q]$ form a monotone increasing sequence of partial sums $d_1, d_2, \ldots$ during the execution of the program and are bounded above by $\delta(q)$. This ensures the condition in line 11 succeeds only finitely many times.

Convergence to $\delta[q]$: Select finite $J_\eta(q)$ to satisfy Eq. 1 for the summable family $\{w[\pi]\}_{\pi \in P(i,q)}$ for $\eta > 0$. By Lemma 1 there is a $\theta_q = \min_{\pi \in J_\eta(q)} \theta_\pi$ such that $J_\eta(q) \subseteq D(q)$ and by Eq. 1

$$\Delta\left(\bigoplus_{\pi \in D(q)} w[\pi], \delta[q] \right) \leq \eta$$

provided $\epsilon \leq \theta_q$. But $d[q] = \bigoplus_{\pi \in D(q)} w[\pi]$ as shown in [17]. So if we select ϵ as $\min_{q \in Q} \theta_q$, we prove the theorem. $\square$

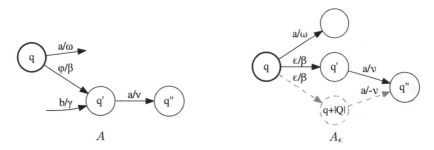

Fig. 7. Failure transitions in A are replaced by ϵ-transitions in A_ϵ. To compensate for the formerly disallowed paths, new (dashed red) negatively-weighted paths are added. (Color figure online)

The time complexity of the algorithm is in $O(N_\epsilon(|E| + C_S|Q|))$ where N_ϵ is the maximum number of times a state can be enqueued given the threshold ϵ and C_S is the maximum cost of a queue operation for S [17].

Since the transition labels play no role in the definitions and results of this section, they apply equally to ϵ-WFAs. In the next section, the labels matter. **Shortest Distance on φ-WFAs.** We define the *shortest distance* from the initial state i to state q in a φ-WFA as:

$$\delta[q] = \bigoplus_{\pi \in P^*(i,q)} w[\pi] \tag{6}$$

when well-defined and in $\mathbb{K}$.

We present an algorithm for the positive real semiring $\mathcal{R}_+$, an important case in applications. To do so, we will transform φ-WFA A on $\mathcal{R}_+$ to an equivalent ϵ-WFA A_ϵ on $\mathcal{R} = (\mathbb{R}, +, *, 0, 1)$. We can then use the SHORTESTDISTANCE algorithm in Fig. 6, suitably adapted.

Given a φ-WFA $A = (\Sigma, Q, E, i, F, \rho)$ with $Q = \{1, \ldots, |Q|\}$ define $Q_\epsilon = \{1, \ldots, 2|Q|\}$ and

$$E_\epsilon = \{(q, a, \omega, q') \in E : a \in \Sigma\} \cup$$
$$\{(q, \epsilon, \beta, q') : (q, \varphi, \beta, q') \in E\} \cup \{(q, \epsilon, \beta, q + |Q|) : (q, \varphi, \beta, q') \in E\} \cup$$
$$\{(q + |Q|, a, -\nu, q'') : (q, \varphi, \beta, q')(q', a, \nu, q'') \in P(q, q''), a \in \Sigma\}.$$

Then let the ϵ-WFA be $A_\epsilon = (\Sigma, Q_\epsilon, E_\epsilon, i, F, \rho)$. Each failure transition in A is relabeled with an ϵ in A_ϵ, allowing previously disallowed paths. To compensate for this, each disallowed consecutive φ- and a-labeled transition pair in A also has a corresponding negatively-weighted consecutive φ- and a-labeled transition pair in A_ϵ that cancels it (see Fig. 7) [20,23].

If A is acyclic, the family of path weights defining $\delta[q]$ is summable in A_ϵ since finite and SHORTESTDISTANCE can be applied. The cyclic case requires more care; the presence of negative weights means that the partial sums may diverge or converge to something other than $\delta[q]$ depending on the ordering of the summands (cf. the Reimann Rearrangement Theorem [24]). We will select a queue discipline for the new states in A_ϵ to ensure the correct behavior. The idea is to have the negatively-weighted terms be immediately cancelled by their positively-weighted counterparts in the running of the algorithm (cf. [26]). Figure 6 shows the pseudocode for the queue and the general shortest distance algorithm with failure transitions.

The queue S_ϵ enqueues states in Q in the arbitrary subqueue S (lines 1–2). New states $q + |Q|$, $q \in Q$ are enqueued in a FIFO subqueue array $S_{\text{fifo}}[q']$ indexed by the φ-successor state q' of q (lines 3–5). S_ϵ ensures that any new state is dequeued from the subqueue array (lines 2–3) just before its index state (lines 4–5). In this way, the positive and negative weights of the disallowed a transitions will immediately cancel in $d[q'']$ at relaxation (see Fig. 7).[6]

The complexity is the same as in the φ-free case since $|Q_\epsilon| = 2|Q|$, $|E_\epsilon| < 2|E|$ and $C_{S_\epsilon} \in O(C_S)$.

4   Discussion

The intersection algorithm presented ensures φ-determinism in the result with φ-deterministic input. Mohri and Yang [20] describe an alternative algorithm that adds φ-non-determinism but avoids the φ-removal $E_2^*[q_2]$.

The proof of Theorem 1 takes advantage of rather specific (complete, monotonic, total) order properties of $\mathbb{R}$ rather than more general metric properties.[7] Can this shortest distance algorithm be extended to further semirings? It is easy to see that if the algorithm is correct with semirings K_1 and K_2 having metrics Δ_1 and Δ_2, then $K_1 \times K_2$ having the square metric $\Delta(x,y) = \max(\Delta_1(x,y), \Delta_2(x,y))$ is also correct.

These algorithms have been implemented as part of SFST, an open-source C++ library for normalizing, sampling, combining, and approximating stochastic finite-state transducers [4].

---

[6] We could also add logic so that when line 12 of the shortest distance algorithm is executed for a disallowed transition then it is also always executed for any negative compensating transition in case $|r[q + |Q|]\nu| < \epsilon < |r[q']\nu|$. This however is an unneeded precaution since with small enough ϵ any discrepancy is insignificant compared to the floating-point precision of $d[q'']$.

[7] The real numbers can be defined axiomatically as a field with a complete, monotonic total order [24].

References

1. Aho, A.V., Corasick, M.J.: Efficient string matching: an aid to bibliographic search. Commun. ACM **18**(6), 333–340 (1975)
2. Albert, J., Kari, J.: Digital image compression. In: Droste, M., Kuich, W., Vogler, H. (eds.) Handbook of Weighted Automata. Monographs in Theoretical Computer Science. An EATCS Series, pp. 453–479. Springer, Heidelberg (2009). https://doi.org/10.1007/978-3-642-01492-5_11
3. Allauzen, C., Mohri, M., Roark, B.: Generalized algorithms for constructing language models. In: Proceedings of ACL, pp. 40–47 (2003)
4. Allauzen, C., Riley, M.: SFST: Stochastic FST Library (2017). http://sfst.opengrm.org
5. Berstel, J., Reutenauer, C.: Rational Series and Their Languages. Springer, Heidelberg (1988)
6. Björklund, H., Björklund, J., Zechner, N.: Compact representation of finite automata with failure transitions. Technical report, UMINF 13.11, Umeå University (2013)
7. Breuel, T.M.: The OCRopus open source OCR system. In: Proceedings of IS&T/SPIE 20th Annual Symposium (2008)
8. Chen, S., Goodman, J.: An empirical study of smoothing techniques for language modeling. Technical report, TR-10-98, Harvard University (1998)
9. Cormen, T., Leiserson, C., Rivest, R.: Introduction to Algorithms. MITP (1992)
10. Durbin, R., Eddy, S.R., Krogh, A., Mitchison, G.J.: Biological Sequence Analysis: Probabilistic Models of Proteins and Nucleic Acids. Cambridge University Press, London (1998)
11. Ebden, P., Sproat, R.: The Kestrel TTS text normalization system. Nat. Lang. Eng. **21**(3), 333–353 (2015)
12. Hellsten, L., Roark, B., Goyal, P., Allauzen, C., Beaufays, F., Ouyang, T., Riley, M., Rybach, D.: Transliterated mobile keyboard input via weighted finite-state transducers. In: FSMNLP 2017, pp. 10–19 (2017)
13. Iglesias, G., Allauzen, C., Byrne, W., de Gispert, A., Riley, M.: Hierarchical phrase-based translation representations. In: EMNLP 2011, pp. 1373–1383 (2011)
14. Katz, S.M.: Estimation of probabilities from sparse data for the language model component of a speech recogniser. IEEE Trans. Acoust. Speech Signal Process. **35**(3), 400–401 (1987)
15. Kourie, D.G., Watson, B.W., Cleophas, L.G., Venter, F.: Failure deterministic finite automata. In: Stringology, pp. 28–41 (2012)
16. Mohri, M.: String-matching with automata. Nord. J. Comput. **4**(2), 217–231 (1997)
17. Mohri, M.: Semiring frameworks and algorithms for shortest-distance problems. J. Automata Lang. Comb. **7**(3), 321–350 (2002)
18. Mohri, M.: Weighted automata algorithms. In: Droste, M., Kuich, W., Vogler, H. (eds.) Handbook of Weighted Automata. Monographs in Theoretical Computer Science. An EATCS Series, pp. 213–254. Springer, Heidelberg (2009). https://doi.org/10.1007/978-3-642-01492-5_6
19. Mohri, M., Pereira, F., Riley, M.: Speech recognition with weighted finite-state transducers. In: Benesty, J., Sondhi, M.M., Huang, Y.A. (eds.) Springer Handbook of Speech Processing. SH, pp. 559–584. Springer, Heidelberg (2008). https://doi.org/10.1007/978-3-540-49127-9_28
20. Mohri, M., Yang, S.: Competing with automata-based expert sequences. In: Proceedings of AISTATS (2018)

21. Novak, J.R., Minematsu, N., Hirose, K.: Failure transitions for joint n-gram models and G2P conversion. In: INTERSPEECH, pp. 1821–1825 (2013)
22. Nxumalo, M., Kourie, D.G., Cleophas, L., Watson, B.W.: An assessment of algorithms for deriving failure deterministic finite automata. S. Afr. Comput. J. **29**(1), 43–68 (2017)
23. Roark, B., Allauzen, C., Riley, M.: Smoothed marginal distribution constraints for language modeling. In: ACL 2013, vol. 1, pp. 43–52 (2013)
24. Rudin, W.: Principles of Mathematical Analysis, vol. 3. McGraw-Hill, New York (1964)
25. Sakarovich, J.: Rational and recognizable power series. In: Droste, M., Kuich, W., Vogler, H. (eds.) Handbook of Weighted Automata. Monographs in Theoretical Computer Science. An EATCS Series, pp. 105–174. Springer, Heidelberg (2009). https://doi.org/10.1007/978-3-642-01492-5_4
26. Schaefer, P.: Sum-preserving rearrangements of infinite series. Am. Math. Monthly **88**(1), 33–40 (1981)
27. Velikovich, L.: Semantic model for fast tagging of word lattices. In: 2016 IEEE Spoken Language Technology Workshop (SLT), pp. 398–405. IEEE (2016)

The Bottom-Up Position Tree Automaton and Its Compact Version

Samira Attou[1], Ludovic Mignot[2(✉)], and Djelloul Ziadi[2]

[1] Faculty of Mathematics, RECITS Laboratory, USTHB,
BP 32, El Alia, 16111 Bab Ezzouar, Algiers, Algeria
`sattou@usthb.dz`
[2] Groupe de Recherche Rouennais en Informatique Fondamentale,
Université de Rouen Normandie,
Avenue de l'Université, 76801 Saint-Étienne-du-Rouvray, France
{`ludovic.mignot,djelloul.ziadi`}`@univ-rouen.fr`

Abstract. The conversion of a given regular tree expression into a tree automaton has been widely studied. However, classical interpretations are based upon a Top-Down interpretation of tree automata. In this paper, we propose a new construction based on Gluskov's one using a Bottom-Up interpretation. One of the main goals of this technique is to consider as a next step the links with deterministic recognizers, consideration that cannot be performed with classical Top-Down approaches. Furthermore, we exhibit a method to factorize transitions of tree automata and show that this technique is particularly interesting for the Glushkov constructions, by considering natural factorizations due to the structure of regular expression.

1 Introduction

Automata are recognizers used in various domains of applications especially in computer science, *e.g.* to represent (non necessarily finite) languages, or to solve the membership test, *i.e.* to verify whether a given element belongs to a language or not. Regular expressions are compact representations for these recognizers. Indeed, in the case where elements are words, it is well known that each regular expression can be transformed into a finite state machine recognizing the language it defines. Several methods have been proposed to realize this conversion. As an example, Glushkov [6] (and independently Mc-Naughton and Yamada [9]) showed how to construct a non deterministic finite automaton with $n + 1$ states where n represents the number of letters of a given regular expression. The main idea of the construction is to define some particular sets named First, Follow and Last that are computed with respect to the occurrences of the symbols that appear in the expression.

These so-called Glushkov automata (or position automata) are finite state machines that have been deeply studied. They have been structurally characterized by Caron and Ziadi [4], allowing us to invert the Glushkov computation

C. Câmpeanu (Ed.): CIAA 2018, LNCS 10977, pp. 59–70, 2018.
https://doi.org/10.1007/978-3-319-94812-6_6

by constructing an expression with n symbols from a Glushkov automaton with $n + 1$ states. They have been considered too in the theoretical notion of one-unambiguity by Bruggemann-Klein and Wood [3], characterizing regular languages recognized by a deterministic Glushkov automaton, or with practical thoughts, like expression updating [2]. Finally, it is also related to combinatorial research topics. As an example, Nicaud [12] proved that the average number of transitions of Glushkov automata is linear.

The Glushkov construction was extended to tree automata [8,11], using a Top-Down interpretation of tree expressions. This interpretation can be problematic while considering determinism. Indeed, it is a folklore that there exist regular tree languages that cannot be recognized by Top-Down deterministic tree automata. Extensions of one-ambiguity are therefore incompatible with this approach.

In this paper, we propose a new approach based on the construction of Glushkov in a Bottom-Up interpretation. We also define a compressed version of tree automata in order to factorize the transitions, and we show how to apply it directly over the Glushkov computation using natural factorizations due to the structure of the expressions. The paper is structured as follows: in Sect. 2, we recall some properties related to regular tree expressions; we also introduce some basics definitions. We define, in Sect. 3, the position functions used for the construction of the Bottom-Up position tree automaton. Section 4 indicates the way that we construct the Bottom-Up position tree automaton with a linear number of states using the functions shown in Sect. 3. In Sect. 5, we propose the notion of compressed automaton and show how to reduce the size of the position automaton computed in the previous section.

2   Preliminaries

Let us first introduce some notations and preliminary definitions. For a boolean condition ψ, we denote by $(E \mid \psi)$ E if ψ is satisfied, $\emptyset$ otherwise. Let $\Sigma = (\Sigma_n)_{n \geq 0}$ be a finite ranked alphabet. A *tree* t over Σ is inductively defined by $t = f(t_1, \ldots, t_k)$ where $f \in \Sigma_k$ and $t_1, \ldots, t_k$ are k trees over Σ. The relation "s is a subtree of t" is denoted by $s \prec t$ for any two trees s and t. We denote by $\mathrm{root}(t)$ the root symbol of the tree t, *i.e.*

$$\mathrm{root}(f(t_1, \ldots, t_k)) = f. \tag{1}$$

The *predecessors* of a symbol f in a tree t are the symbols that appear directly above it. We denote by $\mathrm{father}(t, f)$, for a tree t and a symbol f the pairs

$$\mathrm{father}(t, f) = \{(g, i) \in \Sigma_l \times \mathbb{N} \mid \exists g(s_1, \ldots, s_l) \prec t, \mathrm{root}(s_i) = f\}. \tag{2}$$

These couples link the predecessors of f and the indices of the subtrees in t that f is the root of. Let us consider a tree $t = g(t_1, \ldots, t_k)$ and a symbol f. By definition of the structure of a tree, a predecessor of f in t is a predecessor of f

in a subtree t_i of t, or g if f is a root of a subtree t_i of t. Consequently:

$$\text{father}(t, f) = \bigcup_{i \leq n} \text{father}(t_i, f) \cup \{(g, i) \mid f \in \text{root}(t_i)\}. \tag{3}$$

We denote by T_Σ the set of trees over Σ. A tree language L is a subset of T_Σ.

For any 0-ary symbol c, let $t \cdot_c L$ denote the tree language constituted of the trees obtained by substitution of any symbol c of t by a tree of L. By a linear extension, we denote by $L \cdot_c L' = \{t \cdot_c L' \mid t \in L\}$. For an integer n, the n-th substitution ^{c,n} of a language L is the language $L^{c,n}$ recursively defined by

$$L^{c,n} = \begin{cases} \{c\}, & \text{if } n = 0, \\ L \cdot_c L^{c,n-1} & \text{otherwise.} \end{cases}$$

Finally, we denote by $L(E_1^{*c})$ the language $\bigcup_{k \geq 0} L(E_1)^{c,k}$.

An *automaton* over Σ is a 4-tuple $A = (\bar{Q}, \Sigma, Q_F, \delta)$ where Q is a set of states, $Q_F \subseteq Q$ is the set of final states, and $\delta \subset \bigcup_{k \geq 0}(Q^k \times \Sigma_k \times Q)$ is the set of transitions, which can be seen as the function from $Q^k \times \Sigma_k$ to 2^Q defined by

$$(q_1, \ldots, q_k, f, q) \in \delta \Leftrightarrow q \in \delta(q_1, \ldots, q_k, f).$$

It can be linearly extended as the function from $(2^Q)^k \times \Sigma_k$ to 2^Q defined by

$$\delta(Q_1, \ldots, Q_n, f) = \bigcup_{(q_1, \ldots, q_n) \in Q_1 \times \cdots Q_n} \delta(q_1, \ldots, q_n, f). \tag{4}$$

Finally, we also consider the function Δ from T_Σ to 2^Q defined by

$$\Delta(f(t_1, \ldots, t_n)) = \delta(\Delta(t_1), \ldots, \Delta(t_n), f).$$

Using these definitions, the language recognized by the automaton A is the language $\{t \in T_\Sigma \mid \Delta(t) \cap Q_F \neq \emptyset\}$.

A *regular expression* E over the alphabet Σ is inductively defined by:

$$E = f(E_1, \ldots, E_k), \qquad\qquad E = E_1 + E_2,$$
$$E = E_1 \cdot_c E_2, \qquad\qquad\qquad E = E_1^{*c},$$

where $k \in \mathbb{N}$, $c \in \Sigma_0$, $f \in \Sigma_k$ and $E_1, \ldots, E_k$ are any k regular expressions over Σ. In what follows, we consider expressions where the subexpression $E_1 \cdot_c E_2$ only appears when c appears in the expression E_1. The *language denoted* by E is the language $L(E)$ inductively defined by

$$L(f(E_1, \ldots, E_k)) = \{f(t_1, \ldots, t_k) \mid t_j \in L(E_j), j \leq k\},$$
$$L(E_1 + E_2) = L(E_1) \cup L(E_2),$$
$$L(E_1 \cdot_c E_2) = L(E_1) \cdot_c L(E_2),$$
$$L(E_1^{*c}) = L(E_1)^{*c},$$

with $k \in \mathbb{N}$, $c \in \Sigma_0$, $f \in \Sigma_k$ and $E_1, \ldots, E_k$ any k regular expressions over Σ.

A regular expression E is *linear* if each symbol Σ_n with $n \neq 0$ occurs at most once in E. Note that the symbols of rank 0 may appear more than once. We denote by $\overline{E}$ the linearized form of E, which is the expression E where any occurrence of a symbol is indexed by its position in the expression. The set of indexed symbols, called *positions*, is denoted by $\mathrm{Pos}(\overline{E})$. We also consider the *delinearization* mapping h sending a linearized expression over its original unindexed version.

Let ϕ be a function between two alphabets Σ and Σ' such that ϕ sends Σ_n to Σ'_n for any integer n. By a well-known adjunction, this function is extended to an *alphabetical morphism* from $T(\Sigma)$ to $T(\Sigma')$ by setting $\phi(f(t_1, \ldots, t_n)) = \phi(f)(\phi(t_1), \ldots, \phi(t_n))$. As an example, one can consider the delinearization morphism h that sends an indexed alphabet to its unindexed version. Given a language L, we denote by $\phi(L)$ the set $\{\phi(t) \mid t \in L\}$. The *image by ϕ* of an automaton $A = (\Sigma, Q, Q_F, \delta)$ is the automaton $\phi(A) = (\Sigma', Q, Q_F, \delta')$ where

$$\delta' = \{(q_1, \ldots, q_n, \phi(f), q) \mid (q_1, \ldots, q_n, f, q) \in \delta\}.$$

By a trivial induction over the structure of the trees, it can be shown that

$$\phi(L(A)) = L(\phi(A)). \tag{5}$$

3   Position Functions

In this section, we define the position functions that are considered in the construction of the Bottom-Up automaton in the next sections. We show how to compute them and how they characterize the trees in the language denoted by a given expression.

Let E be a linear expression over a ranked alphabet Σ and f be a symbol $\in \Sigma_k$. The set $\mathrm{Root}(E)$, subset of Σ, contains the roots of the trees in $L(E)$, *i.e.*

$$\mathrm{Root}(E) = \{\mathrm{root}(t) \mid t \in L(E)\}. \tag{6}$$

The set $\mathrm{Father}(E, f)$, subset of $\Sigma \times \mathbb{N}$, contains a couple (g, i) if there exists a tree in $L(E)$ with a node labeled by g the i-th child of is a node labeled by f:

$$\mathrm{Father}(E, f) = \bigcup_{t \in L(E)} \mathrm{father}(t, f). \tag{7}$$

Example 1. Let us consider the ranked alphabet defined by $\Sigma_2 = \{f\}$, $\Sigma_1 = \{g\}$, and $\Sigma_0 = \{a, b\}$. Let E and $\overline{E}$ be the expressions defined by

$$E = (f(a, a) + g(b))^{*_a} \cdot_b f(g(a), b), \quad \overline{E} = (f_1(a, a) + g_2(b))^{*_a} \cdot_b f_3(g_4(a), b).$$

Hence,

$$\text{Root}(\overline{E}) = \{a, f_1, g_2\},$$

$$\text{Father}(\overline{E}, f_1) = \{(f_1, 1), (f_1, 2)\}, \quad \text{Father}(\overline{E}, a) = \{(f_1, 1), (f_1, 2), (g_4, 1)\},$$

$$\text{Father}(\overline{E}, g_2) = \{(f_1, 1), (f_1, 2)\}, \quad \text{Father}(\overline{E}, b) = \{(f_3, 2)\},$$

$$\text{Father}(\overline{E}, f_3) = \{(g_2, 1)\}, \quad \text{Father}(\overline{E}, g_4) = \{f_3, 1\}.$$

Let us show how to inductively compute these functions.

Lemma 1. *Let E be a linear expression over a ranked alphabet Σ. The set $\text{Root}(E)$ is inductively computed as follows:*

$$\text{Root}(f(E_1, ..., E_n)) = \{f\},$$

$$\text{Root}(E_1 + E_2) = \text{Root}(E_1) \cup \text{Root}(E_2),$$

$$\text{Root}(E_1 \cdot_c E_2) = \begin{cases} \text{Root}(E_1) \setminus \{c\} \cup \text{Root}(E_2) & \text{if } c \in L(E_1), \\ \text{Root}(E_1) & \text{otherwise,} \end{cases}$$

$$\text{Root}(E_1^{*c}) = \text{Root}(E_1) \cup \{c\},$$

where $E_1, \ldots, E_n$ are n regular expressions over Σ, f is a symbol in Σ_n and c is a symbol in Σ_0.

Lemma 2. *Let E be a linear expression and f be a symbol in Σ_k. The set $\text{Father}(E, f)$ is inductively computed as follows:*

$$\text{Father}(g(E_1, ..., E_n), f) = \bigcup_{i \leq n} \text{Father}(E_i, f) \cup \{(g, i) \mid f \in \text{Root}(E_i)\},$$

$$\text{Father}(E_1 + E_2, f) = \text{Father}(E_1, f) \cup \text{Father}(E_2, f),$$

$$\text{Father}(E_1 \cdot_c E_2, f) = (\text{Father}(E_1, f) \mid f \neq c) \cup \text{Father}(E_2, f)$$
$$\cup \, (\text{Father}(E_1, c) \mid f \in \text{Root}(E_2))$$

$$\text{Father}(E_1^{*c}, f) = \text{Father}(E_1, f) \cup (\text{Father}(E_1, c) \mid f \in \text{Root}(E_1)),$$

where $E_1, \ldots, E_n$ are n regular expressions over Σ, g is a symbol in Σ_n and c is a symbol in Σ_0.

Proof (partial). Let us consider the following cases.

(1) Let us consider a tree $t = t_1 \cdot_c L(E_2)$ with $t_1 \in L(E_1)$. By definition, t equals t_1 where the occurrences of c have been replaced by some trees t_2 in $L(E_2)$. Two cases may occur. **(a)** If $c \neq f$, then a predecessor of the symbol f in t can be a predecessor of the symbol f in a tree t_2 in $L(E_2)$, a predecessor of the symbol f in t_1, or a predecessor of c in t_1 if an occurrence of c in t_1 has been replaced by a tree t_2 in $L(E_2)$ the root of which is f. **(b)** If $c = f$, since the occurrences of c have been replaced by some trees t_2 of $L(E_2)$, a predecessor of the symbol c in t can be a predecessor of the symbol c in a tree t_2 in $L(E_2)$, or a predecessor of c in t_1 if an occurrence of c has been replaced by itself (and therefore if it appears in $L(E_2)$). In both of these two cases, we conclude using Eqs. (3) and (6).

(2) By definition, $L(E_1^{*_c}) = \bigcup_{k \geq 0} L(E_1)^{c,k}$. Therefore, a tree t in $L(E_1^{*_c})$ is either c or a tree t_1 in $L(E_1)$ where the occurrences of c have been replaced by some trees t_2 in $L(E_1)^{c,k}$ for some integer k. Let us then proceed by recursion over k. If $k = 1$, a predecessor of f in t is a predecessor of f in t_1, a predecessor of f in a tree t_2 in $L(E_1)^{c,1}$ or a predecessor of c in t_1 if an occurrence of c in t_1 was substituted by a tree t_2 in $L(E_1)^{c,1}$ the root of which is f, $i.e.$

$$\text{Father}(E_1^{c,2}, f) = \text{Father}(E_1, f) \cup (\text{Father}(E_1, c) \mid f \in \text{Root}(E_1)).$$

By recursion over k and with the same reasoning, each recursion step adds Father(E_1, f) to the result of the previous step, and therefore

$$\text{Father}(E_1^{c,k}, f) = \text{Father}(E_1, f) \cup (\text{Father}(E_1, c) \mid f \in \text{Root}(E_1)).$$

$\square$

Let us now show how these functions characterize, for a tree t, the membership of t in the language denoted by an expression.

Definition 1. *Let E be a linear expression over a ranked alphabet Σ and t be a tree in $T(\Sigma)$. The property $P(t)$ is the property defined by*

$$\forall s = f(t_1, \ldots, t_n) \prec t, \forall i \leq n, (f, i) \in \text{Father}(E, \text{root}(t_i)).$$

Proposition 1. *Let E be a linear expression over a ranked alphabet Σ and t be a tree in $T(\Sigma)$. Then **(1)** t is in $L(E)$ if and only if **(2)** root(t) is in $\text{Root}(E)$ and $P(t)$ is satisfied.*

Proof (partial). Let us first notice that the proposition $1 \Rightarrow 2$ is direct by definition of Root and Father. Let us show the second implication by induction over the structure of E. Hence, let us suppose that root(t) is in Root(E) and $P(t)$ is satisfied.

(1) Let us consider the case when $E = E_1 \cdot_c E_2$. Let us first suppose that root(t) is in Root(E_2). Then c is in $L(E_1)$ and $P(t)$ is equivalent to

$$\forall s = f(t_1, \ldots, t_n) \prec t, \forall i \leq n, (f, i) \in \text{Father}(E_2, \text{root}(t_i)).$$

By induction hypothesis t is in $L(E_2)$ and therefore in $L(E)$.

Let us suppose now that root(t) is in Root(E_1). Since E is linear, let us consider the subtrees t_2 of t with only symbols of E_2 and a symbol of E_1 as a predecessor in t. Since $P(t)$ holds, according to induction hypothesis and Lemma 2, each of these trees belongs to $L(E_2)$. Hence t belongs to $t_1 \cdot_c L(E_2)$ where t_1 is equal to t where the previously defined t_2 trees are replaced by c. Once again, since $P(t)$ holds and since root(t) is in Root(E_1), t_1 belongs to $L(E_1)$.

In these two cases, t belongs to $L(E)$.

(2) Let us consider the case when $E = E_1^{*c}$. Let us proceed by induction over the structure of t. If $t = c$, the proposition holds from Lemmas 1 and 2. Following Lemma 2, each predecessor of a symbol f in t is a predecessor of f in E_1 (case **1**) or a predecessor of c in E_1 (case **2**). If all the predecessors of the symbols satisfy the case **1**, then by induction hypothesis t belongs to $L(E_1)$ and therefore to $L(E)$. Otherwise, we can consider (similarly to the catenation product case) the smallest subtrees t_2 of t the root of which admits a predecessor in t which is a predecessor of c in E_1. By induction hypothesis, these trees belong to $L(E_1)$. And consequently t belongs to $t' \cdots L(E_1)$ where t' is equal to t where the subtrees t_2 have been substituted by c. Once again, by induction hypothesis, t' belongs to $L(E_1^{*c})$. As a direct consequence, t belongs to $L(E)$. □

4 Bottom-Up Position Automaton

In this section, we show how to compute a Bottom-Up automaton with a linear number of states from the position functions previously defined.

Definition 2. *The* Bottom-Up position automaton $\mathcal{P}_E$ *of a linear expression* E *over a ranked alphabet* Σ *is the automaton* $(\Sigma, \mathrm{Pos}(E), \mathrm{Root}(E), \delta)$ *defined by:*

$$((f_1, \ldots, f_n), g, g) \subset \delta \Leftrightarrow \forall i \leq n, (g, i) \in \mathrm{Father}(E, f_i).$$

Example 2. The Bottom-Up position automaton $(\mathrm{Pos}(\overline{E}), \mathrm{Pos}(\overline{E}), \mathrm{Root}(\overline{E}), \delta)$ of the expression $\overline{E}$ defined in Example 1 is defined as follows:

$$\mathrm{Pos}(E) = \{a, b, f_1, g_2, f_3, g_4\}, \mathrm{Root}(\overline{E}) = \{a, f_1, g_2\},$$
$$\delta = \{(a, a), (b, b), ((a, a), f_1, f_1), ((a, f_1), f_1, f_1), ((a, g_2), f_1, f_1), ((f_1, a), f_1, f_1),$$
$$((f_1, f_1), f_1, f_1), ((f_1, g_2), f_1, f_1), ((g_2, a), f_1, f_1), ((g_2, f_1), f_1, f_1),$$
$$((g_2, g_2), f_1, f_1), (f_3, g_2, g_2), ((b, g_4), f_3, f_3), (a, g_4, g_4)\}$$

Let us now show that the position automaton of E recognizes $L(E)$.

Lemma 3. *Let* $\mathcal{P}_E = (\Sigma, Q, Q_F, \delta)$ *be the Bottom-Up position automaton of a linear expression* E *over a ranked alphabet* Σ, t *be a tree in* T_Σ *and* f *be a symbol in* $\mathrm{Pos}(E)$. *Then* **(1)** $f \in \Delta(t)$ *if and only if* **(2)** $\mathrm{root}(t) = f \wedge P(t)$.

Proof. Let us proceed by induction over the structure of $t = f(t_1, \ldots, t_n)$. By definition, $\Delta(t) = \delta(\Delta(t_1), \ldots, \Delta(t_n), f)$. For any state f_i in Δ_i, it holds from the induction hypothesis that

$$f_i \in \Delta(t_i) \Leftrightarrow \mathrm{root}(t_i) = f_i \wedge P(t_i). \tag{*}$$

Then, suppose that **(1)** holds (*i.e.* $f \in \Delta(t)$). Equivalently, there exists by definition of $\mathcal{P}_E$ a transition $((f_1, \ldots, f_n), f, f)$ in δ such that f_i is in $\Delta(t_i)$ for any integer $i \leq n$. Consequently, f is the root of t. Moreover, from the equivalence stated in Eq. (*), $\mathrm{root}(t_i) = f_i$ and $P(t_i)$ holds for any integer $i \leq n$. Finally and equivalently, $P(t)$ holds as a consequence of Eq. (3). The reciprocal condition can be proved similarly since only equivalences are considered. □

As a direct consequence of Lemma 3 and Proposition 1.

Proposition 2. *The Bottom-Up position automaton of a linear expression E recognizes* $L(E)$.

The Bottom-Up position automaton of a (not necessarily linear) expression E can be obtained by first computing the Bottom-Up position automaton of its linearized expression $\overline{E}$ and then by applying the alphabetical morphism h. As a direct consequence of Eq. (5).

Proposition 3. *The Bottom-Up position automaton of an expression E recognizes* $L(E)$.

5   Compressed Bottom-Up Position Automaton

In this section, we show that the structure of an expression allows us to factorize the transitions of a tree automaton by only considering the values of the Father function. The basic idea of the factorizations is to consider the cartesian product of sets. Imagine that a tree automaton contains four binary transitions (q_1, q_1, f, q_3), (q_1, q_2, f, q_3), (q_2, q_1, f, q_3) and (q_2, q_2, f, q_3). These four transitions can be factorized as a *compressed transition* $(\{q_1, q_2\}, \{q_1, q_2\}, f, q_3)$ using set of states instead of sets. The behavior of the original automaton can be simulated by considering the cartesian product of the origin states of the transition.

We first show how to encode such a notion of compressed automaton and how it can be used in order to solve the membership test.

Definition 3. *A* compressed tree automaton *over a ranked alphabet* Σ *is a 4-tuple* (Σ, Q, Q_F, δ) *where* Q *is a set of states,* $Q_F \subset Q$ *is the set of* final *states,* $\delta \subset (2^Q)^n \times \Sigma_n \times 2^Q$ *is the set of* compressed transitions *that can be seen as a function from* $(2^Q)^k \times \Sigma_k$ *to* 2^Q *defined by*

$$(Q_1, \ldots, Q_k, f, q) \in \delta \Leftrightarrow q \in \delta(Q_1, \ldots, Q_k, f).$$

Example 3. Let us consider the compressed automaton $A = (\Sigma, Q, Q_F, \delta)$ shown in Fig. 1. Its transitions are

$$\delta = \{(\{1, 2, 5\}, \{3, 4\}, f, 1), (\{2, 3, 5\}, \{4, 6\}, f, 2),$$
$$(\{1, 2\}, \{3\}, f, 5), (\{6\}, g, 4), (\{6\}, g, 5), (a, 6), (a, 4), (b, 3)\}.$$

The transition function δ can be restricted to a function from $Q^n \times \Sigma_n$ to 2^Q (*e.g.* in order to simulate the behavior of an uncompressed automaton) by considering for a tuple $(q_1, \ldots, q_k)$ of states and a symbol f in Σ_k all the "active" transitions $(Q_1, \ldots, Q_k, f, q)$, that are the transitions where q_i is in Q_i for $i \leq k$. More formally, for any states $(q_1, \ldots, q_k)$ in Q^k, for any symbol f in Σ_k,

$$\delta(q_1, \ldots, q_k, f) = \bigcup_{\substack{(Q_1, \ldots, Q_k, f, q) \in \delta, \\ \forall i \leq k, q_i \in Q_i}} \{q\}. \tag{8}$$

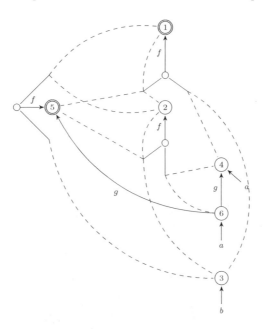

Fig. 1. The compressed automaton A.

The transition set δ can be extended to a function Δ from $T(\Sigma)$ to 2^Q by inductively considering, for a tree $f(t_1, \ldots, t_k)$ the "active" transitions $(Q_1, \ldots, Q_k, f, q)$ once a subtree is read, that is when $\Delta(q_i)$ and Q_i admits a common state for $i \leq k$. More formally, for any tree $t = f(t_1, \ldots, t_k)$ in $T(\Sigma)$,

$$\Delta(t) = \bigcup_{\substack{(Q_1,\ldots,Q_k,f,q)\in\delta, \\ \forall i \leq k, \Delta(t_i)\cap Q_i \neq \emptyset}} \{q\}.$$

As a direct consequence of the two previous equations,

$$\Delta(f(t_1, \ldots, t_n)) = \bigcup_{(q_1,\ldots,q_n)\in\Delta(t_1)\times\cdots\times\Delta(t_n)} \delta(q_1, \ldots, q_n, f). \tag{9}$$

The *language recognized by* a compressed automaton $A = (\Sigma, Q, Q_F, \delta)$ is the subset $L(A)$ of $T(\Sigma)$ defined by

$$L(A) = \{t \in T(\Sigma) \mid \Delta(t) \cap Q_F \neq \emptyset\}.$$

Example 4. Let us consider the automaton of Fig. 1 and let us show that the tree $t = f(f(b, a), g(a))$ belongs to $L(A)$. In order to do so, let us compute $\Delta(t')$ for each subtree t' of t. First, by definition,

$$\Delta(a) = \{4, 6\}, \qquad\qquad \Delta(b) = \{3\}.$$

Since the only transition in δ labeled by f containing 3 in its first origin set and 4 or 6 in its second is the transition $(\{2,3,5\},\{4,6\},f,2)$,

$$\Delta(f(b,a)) = \{2\}.$$

Since the two transitions labeled by g are $(\{6\},g,4)$ and $(\{6\},g,5)$,

$$\Delta(g(a)) = \{4,5\}.$$

Finally, there are two transitions labeled by f containing 2 in their first origin and 4 or 5 in its second: $(\{2,3,5\},\{4,6\},f,2)$ and $(\{1,2,5\},\{3,4\},f,1)$. Therefore

$$\Delta(f(f(b,a),g(a))) = \{1,2\}.$$

Finally, since 1 is a final state, $t \in L(A)$.

Let ϕ be an alphabetical morphism between two alphabets Σ and Σ'. The *image by* ϕ of a compressed automaton $A = (\Sigma, Q, Q_F, \delta)$ is the compressed automaton $\phi(A) = (\Sigma', Q, Q_F, \delta')$ where

$$\delta' = \{(Q_1, \ldots, Q_n, \phi(f), q) \mid (Q_1, \ldots, Q_n, f, q) \in \delta\}.$$

By a trivial induction over the structure of the trees, it can be shown that

$$L(\phi(A)) = \phi(L(A)). \tag{10}$$

Due to their inductive structure, regular expressions are naturally factorizing the structure of transitions of a Glushkov automaton. Let us now define the compressed position automaton of an expression.

Definition 4. *The* compressed Bottom-Up position automaton $\mathcal{C}(E)$ *of a linear expression E is the automaton* $(\Sigma, \mathrm{Pos}(E), \mathrm{Root}(E), \delta)$ *defined by*

$$\delta = \{(Q_1, \ldots, Q_k, f, \{f\}) \mid Q_i = \{g \mid (f,i) \in \mathrm{Father}(E,g)\}\}.$$

Example 5. Let us consider the expression $\overline{E}$ defined in Example 1. The compressed automaton of $\overline{E}$ is represented at Fig. 2.

As a direct consequence of Definition 4 and of Eq. (8),

Lemma 4. *Let E be a linear expression over a ranked alphabet Σ. Let $\mathcal{C}(E) = (\Sigma, Q, Q_F, \delta)$. Then, for any states $(q_1, \ldots, q_n)$ in Q^n, for any symbol f in Σ_k,*

$$\delta(q_1, \ldots, q_n, f) = \{f\} \Leftrightarrow \forall i \le n, (f,i) \in \mathrm{Father}(E, q_i).$$

Consequently, considering Definition 2, Lemma 4 and Eq. (9),

Proposition 4. *Let E be a linear expression over a ranked alphabet Σ. Let $\mathcal{P}_E = (\_,\_,\_,\delta)$ and $\mathcal{C}(E) = (\_,\_,\_,\delta')$. For any tree t in $T(\Sigma)$,*

$$\Delta(t) = \Delta'(t).$$

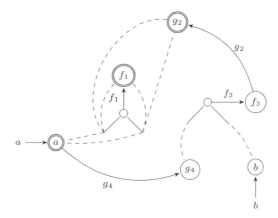

Fig. 2. The compressed automata of the expression $(f_1(a,a) + g_2(b))^{*_a} \cdot_b f_3(g_4(a), b)$.

Since the Bottom-Up position automaton of a linear expression E and its compressed version have the same states and the same final states,

Corollary 1. *The Glushkov automaton of an expression and its compact version recognize the same language.*

The compressed Bottom-Up position automaton of a (not necessarily linear) expression E can be obtained by first computing the compressed Bottom-Up position automaton of its linearized expression $\overline{E}$ and then by applying the alphabetical morphism h. Therefore, considering Eq. (10),

Proposition 5. *The compressed Bottom-Up position automaton of a regular expression E recognizes $L(E)$.*

6   Web Application

The computation of the position functions and the Glushkov constructions have been implemented in a web application (made in Haskell, compiled into Javascript using the REFLEX PLATFORM, represented with VIZ.JS) in order to help the reader to manipulate the notions. From a regular expression, it computes the classical Top-Down Glushkov defined in [8], and both the normal and the compressed versions of the Glushkov Bottom-Up automaton.

This web application can be found here [10]. As an example, the expression $(f(a,a) + g(b))^{*_a} \cdot_b f(g(a), b)$ of Example 1 can be defined from the literal input `(f(a,a)+g(b))*a.bf(g(a),b)`.

7   Conclusion and Perspectives

In this paper, we have shown how to compute the Bottom-Up position automaton associated with a regular expression. This construction is relatively similar to the classical one defined over a word expression [6]. We have also proposed a reduced version, the compressed Bottom-Up position automaton, that can be easily defined for word expressions too.

Since this construction is related to the classical one, one can wonder if all the studies involving Glushkov word automata can be extended to tree ones ([2–4,12]). The classical Glushkov construction was also studied *via* its morphic links with other well-known constructions. The next step of our study is to extend Antimirov partial derivatives [1] in a Bottom-Up way too (in a different way from [7]), using the Bottom-Up quotient defined in [5].

References

1. Antimirov, V.M.: Partial derivatives of regular expressions and finite automaton constructions. Theor. Comput. Sci. **155**(2), 291–319 (1996)
2. Bouchou, B., Duarte, D., Alves, M.H.F., Laurent, D., Musicante, M.A.: Schema evolution for XML: a consistency-preserving approach. In: Fiala, J., Koubek, V., Kratochvíl, J. (eds.) MFCS 2004. LNCS, vol. 3153, pp. 876–888. Springer, Heidelberg (2004). https://doi.org/10.1007/978-3-540-28629-5_69
3. Brüggemann-Klein, A., Wood, D.: One-unambiguous regular languages. Inf. Comput. **140**(2), 229–253 (1998)
4. Caron, P., Ziadi, D.: Characterization of Glushkov automata. Theor. Comput. Sci. **233**(1–2), 75–90 (2000)
5. Champarnaud, J., Mignot, L., Sebti, N.O., Ziadi, D.: Bottom-up quotients for tree languages. J. Autom. Lang. Comb. **22**(4), 243–269 (2017)
6. Glushkov, V.M.: The abstract theory of automata. Russ. Math. Surv. **16**, 1–53 (1961)
7. Kuske, D., Meinecke, I.: Construction of tree automata from regular expressions. RAIRO Theor. Inf. Appli. **45**(3), 347–370 (2011)
8. Laugerotte, É., Sebti, N.O., Ziadi, D.: From regular tree expression to position tree automaton. In: Dediu, A.-H., Martín-Vide, C., Truthe, B. (eds.) LATA 2013. LNCS, vol. 7810, pp. 395–406. Springer, Heidelberg (2013). https://doi.org/10.1007/978-3-642-37064-9_35
9. McNaughton, R.F., Yamada, H.: Regular expressions and state graphs for automata. IEEE Trans. Electron. Comput. **9**, 39–57 (1960)
10. Mignot, L.: Application: Glushkov tree automata. http://ludovicmignot.free.fr/programmes/glushkovBotUp/index.html. Accessed 27 Feb 2018
11. Mignot, L., Sebti, N.O., Ziadi, D.: Tree automata constructions from regular expressions: a comparative study. Fundam. Inform. **156**(1), 69–94 (2017)
12. Nicaud, C.: On the average size of Glushkov's automata. In: Dediu, A.H., Ionescu, A.M., Martín-Vide, C. (eds.) LATA 2009. LNCS, vol. 5457, pp. 626–637. Springer, Heidelberg (2009). https://doi.org/10.1007/978-3-642-00982-2_53

A New Hierarchy for Automaton Semigroups

Laurent Bartholdi[1,2], Thibault Godin[3], Ines Klimann[4],
and Matthieu Picantin[4(✉)]

[1] École Normale Supérieure, Paris, France
laurent.bartholdi@ens.fr
[2] Georg-August-Universität zu Göttingen, Göttingen, Germany
[3] University of Turku, Turku, Finland
thibault.godin@utu.fi
[4] IRIF, UMR 8243 CNRS & Université Paris Diderot, Paris, France
{klimann,picantin}@irif.fr

Abstract. We define a new strict and computable hierarchy for the family of automaton semigroups, which reflects the various asymptotic behaviors of the state-activity growth. This hierarchy extends that given by Sidki for automaton groups, and also gives new insights into the latter. Its exponential part coincides with a notion of entropy for some associated automata.

We prove that the ORDER PROBLEM is decidable when the state-activity is bounded. The ORDER PROBLEM remains open for the next level of this hierarchy, that is, when the state-activity is linear. Gillibert showed that it is undecidable in the whole family.

The former results are implemented and will be available in the GAP package FR developed by the first author.

Keywords: Automaton · Semigroup · Entropy · Hierarchy
Decision problem

1 Introduction

The family of automaton groups and semigroups has provided a wide playground to various algorithmic problems in computational (semi)group theory [1–6,8–11]. While many undecidable questions in the world of (semi)groups remain undecidable for this family, the underlying Mealy automata provide a combinatorial leverage to solve the WORD PROBLEM for this family, and various other problems in some important subfamilies. Recall that a Mealy automaton is a letter-to-letter, complete, deterministic transducer with same input and output alphabet, so each of its states induces a transformation from the set of words over its alphabet into itself. Composing these Mealy transformations leads to so-called

T. Godin—supported by the Academy of Finland grant 296018.

automaton (semi)groups, and the WORD PROBLEM can be solved using a classical technique of minimization.

The ORDER PROBLEM is one of the current challenging problems in computational (semi)group theory. On the one hand, it was proven to be undecidable for automaton semigroups by Gillibert [8]. On the other hand, Sidki introduced a polynomial hierarchy for invertible Mealy transformations in [19] and, with Bondarenko et al. in [6], solved the ORDER PROBLEM for its lowest level (bounded invertible automata).

Our main contributions in this paper are the following: an activity-based hierarchy for possibly non-invertible Mealy transformations (Sect. 3), extending Sidki's construction [19] to non-necessarily-invertible transformations; and a study of the algorithmic properties in the lowest level of the hierarchy, namely transducers with bounded activity. We prove:

Theorem (see Sect. 5). *The* ORDER PROBLEM *is decidable for bounded Mealy transformations; namely, there is an algorithm that, given a bounded initial Mealy automaton, decides whether the transformation τ that it defines has infinite order, and if not finds the minimal $r > s$ such that $\tau^r = \tau^s$.*

Our strategy of proof follows closely that of Sidki's [19] and Bondarenko, Bondarenko et al. [6], with some crucial differences. On the one hand, a naive count of the number of non-trivial states of a transformation does not yield a useful invariant, nor a hierarchy stable under multiplication; on the other hand, the structure of cyclic semigroups ($\langle a \mid a^m = a^{m+n} \rangle$ has index m and period n) is more complex than that of cyclic groups ($\langle a \mid a^m \rangle$ has order m).

2   Notions from Automata and Graph Theory

This section gathers some basics about automata, especially some links between automata, Mealy automata, automaton semigroups, and finite-state transformations. We refer the reader to handbooks for graph theory [15], automata theory [16], and automaton (semi)groups [5].

A *non-deterministic finite-state automaton* (**NFA** for short) is given by a directed graph with finite vertex set Q, a set of edges Δ labeled by an alphabet Σ, and two distinguished subsets of vertices $I \subseteq Q$ and $F \subseteq Q$. The vertices of the graph are called *states* of the automaton and its edges are called *transitions*. The elements of I and F are called respectively *initial* and *final* states. A transition from the state p to the state q with label x is denoted by $p \xrightarrow{x} q$.

A **NFA** is *deterministic*—**DFA** for short—(*resp. complete*) if for each state q and each letter x, there exists at most (*resp.* at least) one transition from q with label x. Given a word $\mathbf{w} = w_1 w_2 \cdots w_n \in \Sigma^*$ (where the w_i are letters), a *run with label* $\mathbf{w}$ in an automaton (**NFA** or **DFA**) is a sequence of consecutive transitions

$$q_1 \xrightarrow{w_1} q_2 \xrightarrow{w_2} q_3 \rightarrow \cdots \rightarrow q_n \xrightarrow{w_n} q_{n+1} .$$

Such a run is *successful* whenever q_1 is an initial state and q_{n+1} a final state. A word in Σ^* is *recognized* by an automaton if it is the label of at least one successful run. The *language* recognized by an automaton is the set of words it recognizes. A **DFA** is *coaccessible* if each state belongs to some run ending at a final state.

Let $\mathcal{A}$ be a **NFA** with stateset Q. The Rabin–Scott powerset construction [14] returns, in a nutshell, the (co)accessible **DFA**—denoted by det $(\mathcal{A})$—with states corresponding to subsets of Q, whose initial state is the subset of all initial states of $\mathcal{A}$ and whose final states are the subsets containing at least on final state of $\mathcal{A}$; its transition labeled by x from a state $S \subseteq 2^Q$ leads to the state $\{q \,|\, \exists p \in S, p \xrightarrow{x} q \text{ in } \mathcal{A}\}$. Notice that the size of the resulting **DFA** might therefore be exponential in the size of the original **NFA**.

The *language* of a **NFA** is the subset of Σ^* consisting in the words recognized by it. Given a language $L \subseteq \Sigma^*$, its *entropy* is

$$h(L) = \lim_{\ell \to \infty} \frac{1}{\ell} \log \# \left(L \cap \Sigma^\ell \right).$$

This quantity appears in various situations, in particular for subshifts [13] and finite-state automata [7]. We shall see how to compute it with matrices.

To a **NFA** $\mathcal{A}$, associate its *transition matrix* $A = \{A_{i,j}\}_{i,j} \in \mathbb{N}^{n \times n}$ where $A_{i,j}$ is the number of transitions from i to j. Let furthermore $v \in \mathbb{N}^n$ be the row vector with '1' at all positions in I and $w \in \mathbb{N}^n$ be the column vector with '1' at all positions in F. Then $vA^\ell w$ is the number of successful runs in $\mathcal{A}$ of length ℓ. Assuming furthermore that $\mathcal{A}$ is deterministic, $vA^\ell w$ is the cardinality of $L \cap \Sigma^\ell$. Since the transition matrix of an automaton $\mathcal{A}$ is non-negative, it admits a positive real eigenvalue of maximal absolute value, which is called its Perron-Frobenius eigenvalue and is written $\lambda(\mathcal{A})$. Assuming therefore that $\mathcal{A}$ is coaccessible, we get

Proposition 2.1. [18, Theorem 1.2] *Let $\mathcal{A}$ be a coaccessible **DFA** recognizing the language L. Then we have $h(L) = \log \lambda(\mathcal{A})$.*

2.1 Mealy Transducers

A *Mealy automaton* is a **DFA** over an alphabet of the form $\Sigma \times \Sigma$. If an edge's label is (x, y), one calls x the *input* and y the *output*, and denotes the transition by $p \xrightarrow{x|y} q$. Such a Mealy automaton $\mathcal{M}$ is assumed to be complete and deterministic in its inputs: for every state p and letter x, there exists exactly one transition from p with input letter x. We denote by x^p its corresponding output letter and by $p@x$ its target state, so we have

$$\boxed{p} \xrightarrow{\quad x|x^p \quad} \boxed{p@x}$$

In this way, states act on letters and letters on states. Such actions can be composed in the following way: let $\mathbf{q} \in Q^*$, $p \in Q$, $\mathbf{u} \in \Sigma^*$, and $x \in \Sigma$, we have

$$x^{\mathbf{q}p} = (x^{\mathbf{q}})^p \quad \text{and} \quad p@(\mathbf{u}x) = (p@\mathbf{u})@x \,.$$

We extend recursively the actions of states on letters and of letters on states (see below left). Compositions can be more easily understood via an alternative representation by a *cross-diagram* [1] (below right).

For all $x \in \Sigma$, $\mathbf{u} \in \Sigma^*$, $p \in Q$, $\mathbf{q} \in Q^*$, we have:

$$(\mathbf{u}x)^{\mathbf{q}} = \mathbf{u}^{\mathbf{q}} x^{\mathbf{q}@\mathbf{u}}$$

and

$$(\mathbf{q}p)@\mathbf{u} = \mathbf{q}@\mathbf{u} \cdot p@\mathbf{u}^{\mathbf{q}}.$$

$$
\begin{array}{ccc}
& \mathbf{q} & & p & \\
\mathbf{u} & \xrightarrow{} & \mathbf{u}^{\mathbf{q}} & \xrightarrow{} & \mathbf{u}^{\mathbf{q}p} \\
& \mathbf{q}@\mathbf{u} & & p@\mathbf{u}^{\mathbf{q}} & \\
x & \xrightarrow{} & x^{\mathbf{q}@\mathbf{u}} & & \\
& \mathbf{q}@\mathbf{u}x & &
\end{array}
$$

The mappings defined above are length-preserving and prefix-preserving. Note that in particular the image of the empty word is itself.

From an algebraic point of view, the composition gives a semigroup structure to the set of transformations $\mathbf{u} \mapsto \mathbf{u}^{\mathbf{q}}$ for $\mathbf{q} \in Q^*$. This semigroup is called *the semigroup generated by $\mathcal{M}$* and denoted by $\langle \mathcal{M} \rangle_+$. An *automaton semigroup* is a semigroup which can be generated by a Mealy automaton. Any element of such an automaton semigroup induces a so-called *finite-state* transformation.

Conversely, for any transformation t of Σ^* and any word $\mathbf{u} \in \Sigma^*$, we denote by $\mathbf{u}^t$ the image of $\mathbf{u}$ by t, and by $t@\mathbf{u}$ the unique transformation s of Σ^* satisfying $(\mathbf{u}\mathbf{v})^t = \mathbf{u}^t \mathbf{v}^s$ for any $\mathbf{v} \in \Sigma^*$. Whenever $Q(t) = \{t@\mathbf{u} : \mathbf{u} \in \Sigma^*\}$ is finite, t is said to be *finite-state* and admits a unique (minimal) *associated Mealy automaton* $\mathcal{M}_t$ with stateset $Q(t)$.

We also use the following convenient notation to define a finite-state transformation t: for each $u \in Q(t)$, we write an equation (traditionally called *wreath recursion* in the algebraic theory of automata) of the following form

$$u = (u@x_1, \ldots, u@x_{|\Sigma|})\sigma_u,$$

where $\sigma_u = [x_1{}^u, \ldots, x_{|\Sigma|}{}^u]$ denotes the transformation on Σ induced by u.

We consider the semigroup $\mathrm{FEnd}(\Sigma^*)$ of those finite-state transformations of Σ^*.

Example 2.2. The transformation $t_0 = (\mathbb{1}, t_0)[2,2]$ belongs to $\mathrm{FEnd}(\{1,2\}^*)$ with $Q(t_0) = \{\mathbb{1}, t_0\}$. See Examples 4.4 and 5.3 for further details about t_0.

Example 2.3. The transformation $p = (q, r)$ with $q = (r, \mathbb{1})$ and $r = (r, r)[2,2]$ also belongs to $\mathrm{FEnd}(\{1,2\}^*)$ with $Q(p) = \{\mathbb{1}, p, q, r\}$. See Fig. 1a for $\mathcal{M}_p$.

3   An Activity-Based Hierarchy for FEnd(Σ^*)

In this section we define a suitable notion of activity for finite-state transformations, together with two norms, from which we build a new hierarchy. We will prove its strictness and its computability in Sect. 4.

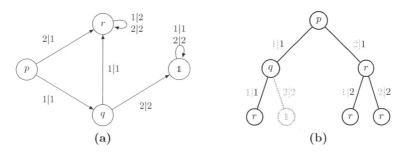

Fig. 1. (a) An example of a transformation p with $\alpha_p(1) = 1$ and $\alpha_p(2) = 2$. (b) The transformation p induces 3 nontrivial transformations on level 2: the leftmost one is associated with the output 11, the middle right one with 12 and the rightmost one with 12, hence nontrivial transformations can be reached by runs with only two different output words.

For any element $t \in \mathrm{FEnd}(\Sigma^*)$, we define its *activity* (see Fig. 1) as

$$\alpha_t : n \longmapsto \#\{\mathbf{v} \in \Sigma^n : \exists \mathbf{u} \in \Sigma^n,\ t@\mathbf{u} \neq \mathbb{1} \text{ and } \mathbf{u}^t = \mathbf{v}\}.$$

We next define two norms on $\mathrm{FEnd}(\Sigma^*)$. When α_t has polynomial growth, namely when the set $D = \{d : \lim_{n\to\infty} \frac{\alpha_t(n)}{n^d} = 0\}$ is nonempty, then we define $\|t\|_\mathrm{p} = \min D - 1$. Otherwise, the value of $\lim_{n\to\infty} \frac{\log \alpha_t(n)}{n}$ is denoted by $\|t\|_\mathrm{e}$. We then define the following classes of finite-state transformations:

$$\mathrm{SPol}(d) = \{\, t \in \mathrm{FEnd}(\Sigma^*) : \|t\|_\mathrm{p} \leq d \,\}$$
$$\text{and } \mathrm{SExp}(\lambda) = \{\, t \in \mathrm{FEnd}(\Sigma^*) : \|t\|_\mathrm{e} \leq \lambda \,\}.$$

We shall see in Theorem 3.3 that these yield a strict and computable hierarchy for $\mathrm{FEnd}(\Sigma^*)$. The following basic lemma is crucial:

Lemma 3.1. *For each $n \geq 0$, the map $t \mapsto \alpha_t(n)$ is subadditive.*

Proof: Assume $s, t \in \mathrm{FEnd}(\Sigma^*)$. For any $\mathbf{u} \in \Sigma^n$ with $(st)@\mathbf{u} \neq \mathbb{1}$, we have either $s@\mathbf{u} \neq \mathbb{1}$ or $t@\mathbf{u}^s \neq \mathbb{1}$. We deduce $\alpha_{st}(n) \leq \alpha_s(n) + \alpha_t(n)$ for each $n \geq 0$.

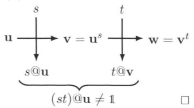

$\square$

We deduce that $\|.\|_\mathrm{p}$ and $\|.\|_\mathrm{e}$ are respectively $+-$ and max-subadditive.

Proposition 3.2. *Let Σ be an alphabet. For every integer $d \geq -1$, $\mathrm{SPol}(d)$ is a subsemigroup of $\mathrm{FEnd}(\Sigma^*)$. So is $\mathrm{SExp}(\lambda)$ for every $0 \leq \lambda \leq \#\Sigma$.*

As an easy corollary of Proposition 3.2, the subadditivity property allows us to compute the hierarchy class of any given Mealy automaton by considering only its generators.

Theorem 3.3. *Let Σ be an alphabet. The elements of the semigroup* $\mathrm{FEnd}(\Sigma^*)$ *can be graded according to the following strict hierarchy: for any* $d_1, d_2 \in \mathbb{Z}$ *with* $-1 < d_1 < d_2$ *and any* $\lambda_1, \lambda_2 \in \mathbb{R}$ *with* $0 < \lambda_1 < \lambda_2 < \#\Sigma$, *we have:*

$$\mathrm{SPol}(-1) \subsetneq \cdots \subsetneq \mathrm{SPol}(d_1) \subsetneq \cdots \subsetneq \mathrm{SPol}(d_2) \subsetneq \cdots \subsetneq \mathrm{SExp}(0)$$
$$\subsetneq \mathrm{SExp}(\lambda_1) \subsetneq \cdots \subsetneq \mathrm{SExp}(\lambda_2) \subsetneq \cdots \subsetneq \mathrm{SExp}(\#\Sigma) \,.$$

The proof of the previous result is postponed to the end of Sect. 4 on page 8. Sidki defined in [19] the activity of a finite-state automorphism $t \in \mathrm{FAut}(\Sigma^*)$ as

$$\theta_t : n \longmapsto \#\{\mathbf{u} \in \Sigma^n : t@\mathbf{u} \neq \mathbb{1}\},$$

and the corresponding classes $\mathrm{Pol}(d)$. Using this notion of activity θ for transformations leads inevitably to an impasse: the associated classes with fixed degree polynomial θ-activity would be not closed under composition. However it is straightforward that our new notion of activity α coincides with Sidki's activity θ in the case of automorphisms.

The class $\mathrm{SExp}(0)$ coincides with the infinite union $\bigcup_{d \geq -1} \mathrm{SPol}(d)$, whose corresponding automorphisms class is denoted by $\mathrm{Pol}(\infty)$ in [19].

4   Structural Characterization of the Activity Norm

From [6], we know that the finite-state automorphisms which have polynomial activity are exactly those whose underlying automaton does not contain entangled cycles (except on the trivial state). Moreover, the degree of the polynomial is given by the longest chain of cycles in the automaton. The first claim remains true for transformations, but things are a bit more involved for the second one (see Example 4.4).

To any minimal Mealy automaton $\mathcal{M}$ with stateset Q and alphabet Σ, we associate its *pruned output* automaton $\mathcal{M}^{\mathrm{out}}$ defined as the **NFA** with stateset $Q \smallsetminus \{\mathbb{1}\}$ (all states being final) and alphabet Σ, and whose transitions are given, for $p, q \in Q \smallsetminus \{\mathbb{1}\}$, by

$$p \xrightarrow{\;y\;} q \in \mathcal{M}^{\mathrm{out}} \quad \Longleftrightarrow \quad p \xrightarrow{\;x|y\;} q \in \mathcal{M}.$$

According to context, we shall identify a transformation $t \in \mathrm{FEnd}(\Sigma^*)$, the state of $\mathcal{M}_t$, and the corresponding state of $\mathcal{M}_t^{\mathrm{out}}$.

Lemma 4.1. *The activity of a transformation* $t \in \mathrm{FEnd}(\Sigma^*)$ *is the number of paths starting from t in the (non-complete) deterministic automaton* $\det(\mathcal{M}_t^{\mathrm{out}})$ *constructed via the Rabin–Scott construction.*

Proof. Let $t \in \mathrm{FEnd}(\Sigma^*)$ with $\mathcal{M}_t$ its associated automaton. Let us count the words $\mathbf{v} \in \Sigma^n$ for which there is a word $\mathbf{u} \in \Sigma^n$ with $t@\mathbf{u} \neq \mathbb{1}$ and $\mathbf{u}^t = \mathbf{v}$. For $n = 1$, $\alpha_t(1)$ is exactly the number of different outputs from the state t that do not lead to a trivial state of $\mathcal{M}_t$. Now for $\mathbf{v} \in \Sigma^n$, if $\mathcal{E}$ denotes the set of those states accessible from t by reading $\mathbf{v}$ (this corresponds to the Rabin–Scott powerset construction) in $\mathcal{M}_t^{\mathrm{out}}$, the number of ways to extend $\mathbf{v}$ without getting into a trivial state in $\mathcal{M}_t$ corresponds to the number of outputs of the state $\mathcal{E}$ in $\det\left(\mathcal{M}_t^{\mathrm{out}}\right)$, whence the result.   □

Whether the activity of a given $t \in \mathrm{FEnd}(\Sigma^*)$ is polynomial or exponential can be decided by only looking at the cycle structure of $\mathcal{M}_t^{\mathrm{out}}$. Any cycle considered throughout this paper is simple: no repetitions of vertices or edges are allowed. Two cycles are *coreachable* if there exists a path from any of them to the other one. A chain of cycles is a sequence of cycles such that each cycle is reachable from its predecessor.

Proposition 4.2. *A transformation $t \in \mathrm{FEnd}(\Sigma^*)$ has exponential activity if and only if it can reach two coreachable cycles with distinct labels in $\mathcal{M}_t^{\mathrm{out}}$.*

Proof. ($\Leftarrow$) Assume that t can reach a state $s \in \mathcal{M}_t^{\mathrm{out}}$ that lies on two cycles with distinct labels. There exist a word $\mathbf{u} \in \Sigma^*$ satisfying $t@\mathbf{u} = s$ and two words $\mathbf{v}, \mathbf{w} \in \Sigma^*$ satisfying $s@\mathbf{v} = s = s@\mathbf{w}$ and $\mathbf{v}^s \neq \mathbf{w}^s$. We obtain $\alpha_t(\ell) \geq \#\{\mathbf{x}^t \mid \mathbf{x} \in \mathbf{u}(\mathbf{v} + \mathbf{w})^* \cap \Sigma^\ell\}$ for $\ell \geq 0$. Therefore α_t grows exponentially. ($\Rightarrow$) Assume that t has exponential activity and cannot reach two coreachable cycles in $\mathcal{M}_t^{\mathrm{out}}$. By Lemma 4.1, there exist a subset $\mathcal{E} \subset Q$ and three words $\mathbf{u}, \mathbf{v}, \mathbf{w} \in \Sigma^*$ such that $\mathcal{E}$ is the set of nontrivial states accessible from t reading $\mathbf{u}$ and the paths labeled by $\mathbf{v}$ and $\mathbf{w}$ are cycles starting from $\mathcal{E}$ in $\mathcal{M}_t^{\mathrm{out}}$. It means that $\mathbf{v}$ and $\mathbf{w}$ are also cycles starting from t in $\mathcal{M}_t$, contradiction.   □

Using the subadditivity of the activity (see Lemma 3.1), we get for the polynomial activities:

Corollary 4.3. *Let $\mathcal{M}$ be a Mealy automaton. The transformations of $\langle \mathcal{M} \rangle_+$ are all of polynomial activity if and only if there are no coreachable cycles in the automaton $\det\left(\mathcal{M}^{\mathrm{out}}\right)$. Moreover the degree of the (polynomial) activity corresponds to the longest chain of cycles in $\det\left(\mathcal{M}^{\mathrm{out}}\right)$ minus 1.*

Example 4.4. Consider the transformation $t_0 = (\mathbb{1}, t_0)[2, 2]$ from Example 2.2, its square t_0^2, and the associated automata $\mathcal{M}_{t_0^2}$ and $\det\left(\mathcal{M}_{t_0^2}^{\mathrm{out}}\right)$:

Note that, before determinization, two disjoint cycles are accessible from the state t_0^2. In the determinized version, $\{t_0\}$ and $\{t_0^2\}$ both access to only one cycle, and we conclude $\{t_0, t_0^2\} \subset \mathrm{SPol}(0)$. By Proposition 3.2, we actually knew the full inclusion $\langle t_0 \rangle_+ \subset \mathrm{SPol}(0)$.

Defining further $t_k = (t_{k-1}, t_k)[2 - (k \bmod 2), 2 - (k \bmod 2)] \in \mathrm{FEnd}(\{1, 2\}^*)$, we obtain the family with $t_k \in \mathrm{SPol}(k) \setminus \mathrm{SPol}(k - 1)$ for $k > 0$, that witnesses the strictness of the polynomial part of the hierarchy from Theorem 3.3.

Using Proposition 2.1, we obtain an explicit formula for the norm $\| \cdot \|_e$:

Proposition 4.5. *Let t be a finite-state transformation with associated Mealy automaton $\mathcal{M}_t$. The norm $\|t\|_e$ is the logarithm of the Perron eigenvalue of the transition matrix of* $\det(\mathcal{M}_t^{\mathrm{out}})$:

$$\|t\|_e = \log \lambda(\det(\mathcal{M}_t^{\mathrm{out}})) \,.$$

Proof. By Lemma 4.1, the activity of t counts the number of paths in $\det(\mathcal{M}_t^{\mathrm{out}})$. Since all its states are final, this automaton is coaccessible and the cardinality of the language accepted when putting t as the initial state is exactly the activity of t. Therefore by Proposition 2.1, we have

$$\|t\|_e = \lim_{\ell \to \infty} \frac{\log \alpha_t(\ell)}{\ell} = \lim_{\ell \to \infty} \frac{1}{\ell} \log \sum_{t'=1}^{n} (A^\ell)_{t,t'} = h(L) = \log \lambda(\det(\mathcal{M}_t^{\mathrm{out}})),$$

with $A = (A_{i,j})_{i,j}$ the adjacency matrix of $\det(\mathcal{M}_t^{\mathrm{out}})$. □

Proof of Theorem 3.3. The strictness for the polynomial part is obtained from Example 4.4. Now, as the norm $\|.\|_e$ is the logarithm of the maximal eigenvalue of a matrix with integer coefficients, the classes $\mathrm{SExp}(\lambda)$ increase only when e^λ is an algebraic integer that is the largest zero of its minimal polynomial, *i.e.*, a root of a Perron number. Furthermore, each of these numbers is the norm of some finite-state transformation, see [12, Theorem 3] for a proof. It is also known that Perron numbers are dense in $[1, \infty)$, which gives us the strictness for the exponential part: $\lambda_1 < \lambda_2$ implies $\mathrm{SExp}(\lambda_1) \subsetneq \mathrm{SExp}(\lambda_2)$.

Finally, the growth rate can be computed with any precision $0 < \delta < 1$ in time $\Theta(-\log(\delta n))$, where n is the number of states of the automaton [17]. □

Example 4.6. Consider the transformations $r = (s,r)[1,1]$ and $s = (\mathbb{1},r)$ with common associated automata $\mathcal{M}$ (on the left) and $\det(\mathcal{M}^{\mathrm{out}})$ (on the right):

We find that $\alpha_r(n)$ and $\alpha_s(n+1)$ correspond to the n-th Fibonacci number. We deduce $\|r\|_e = \|s\|_e = \log \varphi$ where φ is the golden ratio, hence $r,s \in \mathrm{SExp}(\log \varphi)$.

5   The Orbit Signalizer Graph and the Order Problem

This section is devoted to the ORDER PROBLEM: can one decide whether a given element generates a finite semigroup? The latter is known to be undecidable for general automaton semigroups [8] and decidable for $\mathrm{Pol}(0)$ [6]. We give a general construction that associates a graph to a transformation of Σ^*, and show that, if finite, this graph lets us compute the index and period of the transformation. We show that this graph is finite for elements from SPol(0), and solve the ORDER PROBLEM in this manner.

Let Σ be an alphabet. We define the *orbit signalizer graph* Φ for $\mathrm{FEnd}(\Sigma^*)$ as the following (infinite) graph. The vertices are the pairs of elements in $\mathrm{FEnd}(\Sigma^*)$. For each letter $x \in \Sigma$, there is an arrow from the source (s, t) with label $(x : m, \ell)$ where m and ℓ are the minimal integers (with $\ell > 0$) satisfying

$$x^{st^{m+\ell}} = x^{st^m},$$

and with target $(r@x, t^\ell @ x^r)$ for $r = st^m$. The parameters m and ℓ correspond respectively to the *index* and to the *period* of the orbit of x under the action of st^ω, see Fig. 2.

In what follows, the intuition is roughly to generalize Fig. 2, by considering a path π instead of the letter x: such a construction leads also to a pan graph, whose handle has length between i_t^- and i_t^+, and whose cycle has length p_t. The main challenge here is to be able to keep the construction finite, when possible.

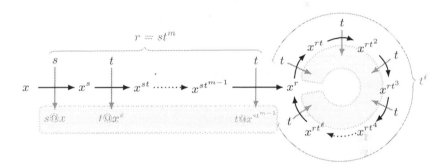

Fig. 2. The cross-diagram associated with the orbit of some letter $x \in \Sigma$ under the action of st^ω. The index m and period ℓ will complete the label of the x-arrow away from the vertex (s, t) in the graph Φ. Each of the two gray zones indicates an entry of the corresponding target vertex $(r@x, t^\ell @ x^r)$ with $r = st^m$.

The *inf-index-cost*, *sup-index-cost*, and the *period-cost* of a given walk π on Φ

$$\pi : (s, t) \xrightarrow{x_1 : m_1, \ell_1} \cdots \xrightarrow{x_{|\pi|} : m_{|\pi|}, \ell_{|\pi|}} (s', t')$$

are respectively defined by

$$i^-(\pi) = \sum_{1 \leq k \leq |\pi|} \left((1 - \delta_{m_k, 0}) \left((m_k - 1) \left(\prod_{1 \leq j < k} \ell_j \right) + 1 \right) \right),$$

$$i^+(\pi) = \sum_{1 \leq k \leq |\pi|} \left(\prod_{1 \leq j < k} \ell_j \right) m_k, \quad \text{and} \quad p(\pi) = \prod_{1 \leq i \leq |\pi|} \ell_i .$$

For any $t \in \mathrm{FEnd}(\Sigma^*)$, we define the *orbit signalizer graph* $\Phi(t)$ as the subgraph of Φ accessible from the source vertex $(\mathbb{1}, t)$. The *inf-index-cost*, *sup-index-cost*, and the *period-cost* of $t \in \mathrm{FEnd}(\Sigma^*)$ are then respectively defined by

$$i_t^- = \max_{\pi \text{ on } \Phi(t)} i^-(\pi), \qquad i_t^+ = \max_{\pi \text{ on } \Phi(t)} i^+(\pi), \qquad \text{and} \qquad p_t = \operatorname*{lcm}_{\pi \text{ on } \Phi(t)} p(\pi) .$$

Proposition 5.1. *The semigroup generated by an element* $t \in \mathrm{FEnd}(\Sigma^*)$ *is finite if and only if its index-costs* $i_t^\pm$ *and its period-cost* p_t *are finite. In that case, we have* $\langle t \rangle_+ = \langle t : t^{i_t} = t^{i_t + p_t} \rangle_+$ *for some index* i_t *with* $i_t^- \leq i_t \leq i_t^+$.

Proof. Let $\Sigma = \{x_1, \dots, x_{|\Sigma|}\}$. Let (s_0, t_0) be a vertex in Φ and (s_k, t_k) its successor vertex with arrow $x_k : m_k, \ell_k$ for $1 \leq k \leq |\Sigma|$.

(i_0, p_0) $\quad \boxed{(s_0, t_0)}$

$x_1 : m_1, \ell_1 \longrightarrow \boxed{(s_1, t_1)} \quad (i_1, p_1)$

$\vdots$

$x_{|\Sigma|} : m_{|\Sigma|}, \ell_{|\Sigma|} \longrightarrow \boxed{(s_{|\Sigma|}, t_{|\Sigma|})} \ (i_{|\Sigma|}, p_{|\Sigma|})$

For $0 \leq k \leq |\Sigma|$, let $(i_k, p_k) \in \{\omega, 0, 1, 2, \dots\} \times \{\omega, 1, 2, 3 \dots\}$ denote the possible minimal pair of ordinals (with $p_k > 0$) satisfying

$$s_k t_k^{i_k} = s_k t_k^{i_k + p_k} .$$

Whenever there is at least one successor with $(i_k, p_k) = (\omega, \omega)$, (s_0, t_0) satisfies also $(i_0, p_0) = (\omega, \omega)$, and so does any of its predecessors. Otherwise, we claim

$$\max_{1 \leq k \leq |\Sigma|} \left(m_k + \max(0, \ell_k(i_k - 1) + 1) \right) \leq i_0 \leq \max_{1 \leq k \leq |\Sigma|} (m_k + \ell_k i_k)$$

and

$$p_0 = \operatorname*{lcm}_{1 \leq k \leq |\Sigma|} \ell_k p_k.$$

Indeed, for $1 \leq k \leq |\Sigma|$ and for any $u \in \Sigma^*$, we have

$$y_k v = (x_k u)^{s_0 t_0^{m_k + \ell_k i_k}} = (y_k v)^{t_0^{\ell_k p_k}}$$

with $y_k = x_k^{s_0 t_0^{m_k}}$ and $v = u^{s_k t_k^{i_k + p_k}}$, as illustrated by the cross-diagram:

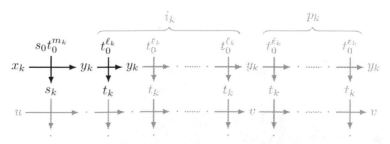

We conclude using an induction on the length of the paths.   □

Theorem 5.2. *The* ORDER PROBLEM *is decidable for any* $t \in \mathrm{FEnd}(\Sigma^*)$ *with a finite orbit signalizer graph* $\Phi(t)$.

Proof. Since $\Phi(t)$ is a graph with outdegree $\|\Sigma\| > 0$ by construction, its finiteness implies the existence of cycles. Consider the simple cycles (there is only a finite number of these). One can compute the index-costs $i^-(\kappa)$ and $i^+(\kappa)$ and the period-cost $p(\kappa)$ of each such cycle κ. Whenever $i^-(\kappa) > 0$ or $p(\kappa) > 1$ for some cycle κ, then t has infinite order, and finite order otherwise.   □

Example 5.3. The transformations $s = (s, \mathbb{1})[2, 2]$ and $t_0 = (\mathbb{1}, t_0)[2, 2]$ (on the left) admit respective graphs $\Phi(s)$ and $\Phi(t_0)$ (on the right):

According to Proposition 5.1, they generate the finite monoid $\langle\, s : s^2 = s \,\rangle_+$ and the free monoid $\langle\, t_0 : \quad \rangle_+$.

Example 5.4. The transformation $b = (a, \mathbb{1}, b)[2, 3, 1]$ from $\mathrm{SPol}(1) \smallsetminus \mathrm{SPol}(0)$ with $a = (\mathbb{1}, \mathbb{1}, a)[1, 1, 2]$ admits the finite graph $\Phi(b)$ displayed on Fig. 3, in which we can read that both ab and ba have period 1, and that b has thus period $p_b = 3$. According to Proposition 5.1 again, the index of b satisfies $4 \le i_b \le 9$, and can be explicitly computed as $i_b = 8$.

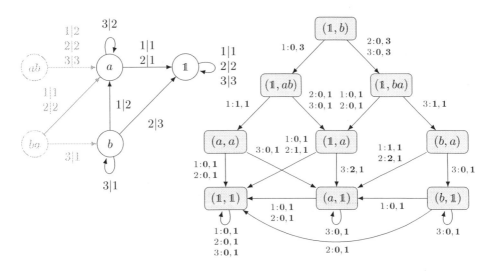

Fig. 3. The Mealy automaton $\mathcal{M}_b$ and the graph $\Phi(b)$ from Example 5.4.

Proposition 5.5. *Every bounded finite-state transformation $t \in \mathrm{SPol}(0)$ admits a finite orbit signalizer graph $\Phi(t)$.*

Proof. The activity α_t of $t \in \mathrm{SPol}(0)$ is uniformly bounded by some constant C:

$$\#\{\mathbf{v} \in \Sigma^n : \exists \mathbf{u} \in \Sigma^n,\ t@\mathbf{u} \neq \mathbb{1} \text{ and } \mathbf{u}^t = \mathbf{v}\} \leq C \quad \text{for} \quad n \geq 0 .$$

Now the vertices of the graph $\Phi(t)$ are those pairs (r, s) with $rs = t^K@\mathbf{u}$, where K is the greatest integer such that the images $\mathbf{u}^{t^i}$ for $i < K$ are pairwise different. Hence rs is the product of at most C nontrivial elements. Moreover these elements $t^i@\mathbf{u}$ for $i < K$ lie in a finite set, as t is a finite-state transformation, hence the vertices belong to a finite set. We conclude that the graph $\Phi(t)$ is finite. $\square$

Corollary 5.6. *The ORDER PROBLEM is decidable for $\mathrm{SPol}(0)$.*

References

1. Akhavi, A., Klimann, I., Lombardy, S., Mairesse, J., Picantin, M.: The finiteness problem for automaton semigroups. Internat. J. Alg. Comput. **22**(6), 1–26 (2012)
2. Bartholdi, L.: Algorithmic decidability of engel's property for automaton groups. In: Kulikov, A.S., Woeginger, G.J. (eds.) CSR 2016. LNCS, vol. 9691, pp. 29–40. Springer, Cham (2016). https://doi.org/10.1007/978-3-319-34171-2_3
3. Bartholdi, L.: FR-GAP package "Computations with functionally recursive groups", Version 2.4.3 http://www.gap-system.org/Packages/fr.html (2017)
4. Bartholdi, L., Mitrofanov, I.: The word and order problems for self-similar and automata groups arXiv:1710.10109 (2017)
5. Bartholdi, L., Silva, P.V.: Groups defined by automata. In: Pin, J.-É. (ed.) Handbook AutoMathA arXiv:1012.1531 (2018, to appear)
6. Bondarenko, I., Bondarenko, N., Sidki, S., Zapata, F.: On the conjugacy problem for finite-state automorphisms. Groups Geom. Dyn. **7**(2), 323–355 (2013)
7. Chomsky, N., Miller, G.A.: Finite state languages. Inf. Control **1**(2), 91–112 (1958)
8. Gillibert, P.: The finiteness problem for automaton semigroups is undecidable. Internat. J. Alg. Comput. **24**(1), 1–9 (2014)
9. Gillibert, P.: An automaton group with undecidable order and Engel problems. J. Algebra **497**, 363–392 (2018)
10. Godin, T., Klimann, I.: On bireversible Mealy automata and the Burnside problem. Theor. Comput. Sci. **707**, 24–35 (2018)
11. Klimann, I., Mairesse, J., Picantin, M.: Implementing computations in automaton (Semi)groups. In: Moreira, N., Reis, R. (eds.) CIAA 2012. LNCS, vol. 7381, pp. 240–252. Springer, Heidelberg (2012). https://doi.org/10.1007/978-3-642-31606-7_21
12. Lind, D.A.: The entropies of topological markov shifts and a related class of algebraic integers. Ergodic Theor. Dyn. Syst. **4**(2), 283–300 (1984)
13. Lind, D.A., Marcus, B.: An Introduction to Symbolic Dynamics and Coding. Cambridge University Press, New York (1995)
14. Rabin, M.O., Scott, D.: Finite automata and their decision problems. IBM J. Res. Develop. **3**(2), 114–125 (1959)
15. Rigo, M.: Advanced Graph Theory and Combinatorics. Wiley, Hoboken (2016)

16. Sakarovitch, J.: Elements of Automata Theory. Cambridge University Press, Cambridge (2009)
17. Shur, A.M.: Combinatorial complexity of regular languages. In: Hirsch, E.A., Razborov, A.A., Semenov, A., Slissenko, A. (eds.) CSR 2008. LNCS, vol. 5010, pp. 289–301. Springer, Heidelberg (2008). https://doi.org/10.1007/978-3-540-79709-8_30
18. Shur, A.M.: Comparing complexity functions of a language and its extendable part. RAIRO-Theor. Inf. Appl. **42**(3), 647–655 (2008)
19. Sidki, S.: Automorphisms of one-rooted trees: growth, circuit structure, and acyclicity. J. Math. Sci. **100**(1), 1925–1943 (2000)

Synchronizing Random Almost-Group Automata

Mikhail V. Berlinkov[1]([✉]) and Cyril Nicaud[2]

[1] Institute of Natural Sciences and Mathematics, Ural Federal University,
Ekaterinburg 620062, Russia
m.berlinkov@gmail.com
[2] LIGM, Université Paris-Est and CNRS,
5 bd Descartes, Champs-sur-Marne, 77454 Marne-la-Valléee Cedex 2, France
cyril.nicaud@u-pem.fr

Abstract. In this paper we address the question of synchronizing random automata in the critical settings of almost-group automata. Group automata are automata where all letters act as permutations on the set of states, and they are not synchronizing (unless they have one state). In almost-group automata, one of the letters acts as a permutation on $n-1$ states, and the others as permutations. We prove that this small change is enough for automata to become synchronizing with high probability. More precisely, we establish that the probability that a strongly connected almost-group automaton is not synchronizing is $\frac{2^{k-1}-1}{n^{2(k-1)}}(1+o(1))$, for a k-letter alphabet.

1 Introduction

A deterministic automaton is called *synchronizing* when there exists a word that brings every state to the same state. If it exists, such a word is called *reset* or *synchronizing*.

Synchronizing automata serve as natural models of error-resistant systems because a reset word allows to turn a system into a known state, thus reestablishing the control over the system. For instance, prefix code decoders can be represented by automata. If an automaton corresponding to a decoder is synchronizing, then decoding a reset word, after an error appeared in the process, would recover the correct decoding process.

There has been a lot of research done on synchronizing automata since pioneering works of Černý [3]. Two questions that attract major interest here are whether an automaton is synchronizing and what is the length of shortest reset words if the answer to the first question is 'yes'? These questions are also studied

This work is supported by the French National Agency through ANR-10-LABX-58, Russian Foundation for Basic Research, grant no. 16-01-00795, and the Competitiveness Enhancement Program of Ural Federal University. A major part of the research was conducted during the scientific collaboration under the Metchnikov program arranged by French Embassy in Russia.

C. Câmpeanu (Ed.): CIAA 2018, LNCS 10977, pp. 84–96, 2018.
https://doi.org/10.1007/978-3-319-94812-6_8

from different perspectives such as algorithmic, general statements etc. and in variety of settings, e.g. for particular classes of automata, random settings, *etc.* The reader is referred to the survey of Volkov [10] for a brief introduction to the theory of synchronizing automata.

One of the most studied direction of research in this field is the long-standing conjecture of Černý, which states that if an automaton is synchronizing, then it admits a reset word of length at most $(n-1)^2$, where n is the number of states of the automaton. This bound is best possible, as shown by Černý. However, despite many efforts, only cubic upper bounds have been obtained so far [7,8].

It is the probabilistic settings that interest us in this article. During the attempts to tackle the conjecture of Černý, lots of experiments have been done, showing that random automata seem to be synchronizing with high probability, and that their reset words seem to be quite small in expectation. This was proved quite recently in a series of articles:

– Skvortsov and Zaks [11] obtained some results for large alphabets (where the number of letters grows with n);
– Berlinkov [2] proved that the probability that a random automaton is not synchronizing is in $\mathcal{O}(n^{-k/2})$, where k is the number of letters, for any $k \geq 2$ (this bound is tight for $k = 2$);
– Nicaud [6] proved that with high probability a random automaton admits a reset word of length $\mathcal{O}(n \log^3 n)$, for $k \geq 2$ (but with less precise error terms than in [2]).

All these results hold for the *uniform distribution* on the set of deterministic and complete automata with n states on an alphabet of size k, where all automata have the same probability. And it is, indeed, the first probability distribution to study. The reader is referred to the survey [5] for more information about random deterministic automata.

In this article we study a distribution on a restricted set of deterministic automata, the *almost-group automata*, which will be defined later in this introduction. In order to motivate our choice, we first need to outline the main features of the uniform distribution on deterministic automata and how they were used in the proofs of the articles cited above.

In a deterministic and complete automaton, one can consider each letter as a map from the set of states Q to itself, which is called its *action*. The action of a given letter in a uniform random automaton is a uniform random mapping from Q to Q. Properties of uniform random mappings have been long studied and most of their typical[1] statistics are well known. The *functional graph* proved to be a useful tool to describe a mapping; it is the directed graph of vertex set Q, built from a mapping $f : Q \to Q$ by adding an edge $i \to j$ whenever $j = f(i)$. Such a graph can be decomposed as a set of cycles of trees. Vertices that are in

---

[1] In all the informal statements of this article, *typical* means *with high probability* as the size of the object (cardinality of the set, number of states of the automaton, ...) tends to infinity.

a cycle consists of elements $q \in Q$ such that $f^\ell(q) = q$ for some positive ℓ. They are called *cyclic vertices*.

The expected number of cyclic vertices in a uniform random mapping on a set of size n is in $\Theta(\sqrt{n})$. This is used in [6] and [2] to obtain the synchronization of most automata. The intuitive idea is that after reading a^n, the set of states already shrinks to a much smaller set, in a uniform random automaton; this gives enough leverage, combined with the action of the other letters, to fully synchronize a typical automaton.

In a nutshell, uniform random automata are made of uniform random mappings, and each uniform random mapping is already likely to synchronize most of the states, due to their inherent typical properties. At this point, it seems natural to look for "harder" random instances with regard to synchronization, and it was a common question asked when the authors presented their works.

In this article, to prevent easy synchronization from the separate action of the letter, we propose to study what we call *almost-group automata*, where the action of each letter is a permutation, except for one of them which has only one non-cyclic vertex. An example of such an automaton is depicted on Fig. 1.

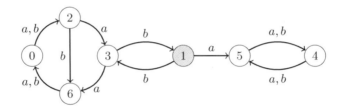

Fig. 1. An almost-group automaton with 7 states. The action of b is a permutation. The action of a is not, as 1 has no preimage by a; but if state 1 is removed, a acts as a permutation on the remaining states.

Since a group automaton with more than one state cannot be synchronizing, almost-group automata can be seen as the automata with the maximum number of cyclic states (considering all its letters) that can be synchronizing. The question we investigate in this article is the following.

Question: For the uniform distribution, what is the probability that a strongly connected almost-group automaton is synchronizing?

For this question, we consider automata with n states on a k-letter alphabet, with $k \geq 2$, and try to answer asymptotically as n tends to infinity. We prove that such an automaton is synchronizing with probability that tends to 1. We also provide a precise asymptotic estimation of the probability that it is not synchronizing. In other words, one can state our result as follows: group automata are always non-synchronizing when there are at least two states, but if one allows just one letter to act not bijectively for just one state, then the automaton is synchronizing with high probability. This suggests that from a probabilistic point of view, it is very difficult to achieve non-synchronization.

This article starts with recalling some basic definitions and notations in Sect. 2. Then some interesting properties of this set of automata regarding synchronization are described in Sect. 3. Finally, we rely on this properties and some elementary counting techniques to establish our result in Sect. 4.

2   Basic Definitions and Notations

Automata and Synchronization. Throughout the article, we consider automata on a fixed k-letter alphabet $A = \{a_0, \ldots, a_{k-1}\}$. Since we are only interested in synchronizing properties, we only focus on the transition structure of automata: we do not specify initial nor final states, and will never actually consider recognized languages in the sequel. From now on a *deterministic and complete automaton* (DFA) $\mathcal{A}$ on the alphabet A is just a pair $(Q, \cdot)$, where Q is a non-empty finite set of *states* and $\cdot$, the *transition mapping*, is a mapping from $Q \times A$ to Q, where the image of $(q, a) \in Q \times A$ is denoted $q \cdot a$. It is inductively extended to a mapping from $Q \times A^*$ to Q by setting $q \cdot \varepsilon = q$ and $q \cdot ua = (q \cdot u) \cdot a$, for any word $u \in A^*$ and any letter $a \in A$, where ε denote the empty word.

Let $\mathcal{A} = (Q, \cdot)$ be a DFA. A word $u \in A^*$ is a *synchronizing word* or a *reset word* if for every $q, q' \in Q$, $q \cdot u = q' \cdot u$. An automaton is *synchronizing* if it admits a synchronizing word. A subset of states $S \subseteq Q$ is *synchronized* by a word $u \in A^*$ if $|S \cdot u| = 1$.

Observe that if an automaton contains two or more terminal strongly connected components[2], then it is not synchronizing. Moreover if it has only one terminal strongly connected component S, then it is synchronizing if and only if S is synchronized by some word u. For this reason, most works on synchronization focus on strongly connected automata, and this paper is no exception.

Almost-Group Automata. Let $\mathcal{S}_n$ be the set of all permutations of $E_n = \{0, \ldots, n-1\}$. A *cyclic point* of a mapping f is an element x such that $f^\ell(x) = x$ for some positive ℓ. An *almost-permutation* of E_n is a mapping from E_n to itself with exactly $n-1$ cyclic points; its unique non-cyclic point is called *dangling point* (or *dangling state* later on, when we use this notion for automata). Equivalently, an almost-permutation is a mapping that acts as a permutation on a subset of size $n - 1$ of E_n and that is not a permutation. Let $\mathcal{S}'_n$ denote the set of almost-permutations on E_n.

An *almost-group automaton* is a DFA such that one letter act as an almost-permutation and all others as permutations. An example of such an automaton is given in Fig. 1. For counting reasons, we need to normalize the automata, and define $\mathcal{G}_{n,k}$ as the set of all almost-group automata on the alphabet $\{a_0, \ldots, a_{k-1}\}$ whose state set is E_n and such that a_0 is the almost-permutation letter.

Probabilities. In this article, we equip non-empty finite sets with the uniform distribution, where all elements have same probability. The sets under consideration are often sequences of sets, such as $\mathcal{S}_n$; by abuse of notation, we say that

---

[2] A strongly connected component S is terminal when $S \cdot u \subseteq S$ for every $u \in A^*$.

a property *hold with high probability* for $\mathcal{S}_n$ when the probability that it holds, which is defined for every n, tends to 1 as n tends to infinity.

3 Synchronization of Almost-Group Automata

In this section we introduce the main tools that we use to describe the structure of synchronizing and of non-synchronizing almost-group automata.

The notion of a *stable pair*, introduced by Kari [4], has proved to be fruitful mostly by Trahtman, who managed to use it for solving the famous *Road Coloring Problem* [9]. We make use of this definition in our proof as well, along with some ideas coming from [9].

A pair of states $\{p, q\}$ is called *stable*, if for every word u there is a word v such that $p \cdot uv = q \cdot uv$. The *stability* relation given by the set of stable pairs joined with a diagonal set $\{(p, p) \mid p \in Q\}$ is invariant under the actions of the letters and complete whenever $\mathcal{A}$ is synchronizing. The definition on pairs is sound as stability is a symmetric binary relation. It is also transitive whence it is an equivalence relation on Q which is a congruence, i.e. invariant under the actions of the letters.

Notice also, that an automaton is synchronizing if and only if its stability relation is complete, that is, all pairs are stable. Because of that, if an automaton is not synchronizing and admits a stable pair, then one can consider a non-trivial factorization of the automaton by the stability relation. So, we aim at characterizing stable pairs in a strongly-connected non-synchronizing almost-permutation automaton, in order to show there is a slim chance for such a factorization to appear when switching to probabilities.

For this purpose, we need the definition of a *deadlock*, which is a pair that cannot be merged into one state by any word (somehow opposite to the notion of stable pair). A subset $S \subseteq Q$ is called an F-clique of $\mathcal{A}$ if it is a set of maximum size such that each pair of states from S is a deadlock. It follows from the definition that all F-cliques have same size and that the image of F-clique by a letter or a word is also an F-clique.

Let us reformulate [9, Lemma 2] for our purposes and present a proof for self-completeness.

Lemma 1. *If S and T are two F-cliques such that $S \setminus T = \{p\}$ and $T \setminus S = \{q\}$, for some states p and q, then $\{p, q\}$ is a stable pair.*

Proof. By contradiction, suppose there is a word u such that $\{p \cdot u, q \cdot u\}$ is a deadlock. Then $(S \cup T) \cdot u$ is an F-clique because all its pairs are deadlocks. Since $p \cdot u \neq q \cdot u$, we have $|S \cup T| = |S| + 1 > |S|$ contradicting maximality of S. □

Lemma 2. *Each strongly-connected almost-group automaton $\mathcal{A} \in \mathcal{G}_{n,k}$ with at least two states, admits a stable pair containing the dangling state that is synchronized by a_0.*

Proof. If $\mathcal{A}$ is synchronizing, then we are done because all pairs are stable. In the opposite case, there must be an F-clique F_1 of size at least two.

Let p_0 be the dangling state (which is not permuted by a_0) and let d be the product of all cycle lengths of a_0. Since $\mathcal{A}$ is strongly-connected there is a word u such that $p_0 \in F_1 \cdot u$. By the property of F-cliques, $F_2 = F_1 \cdot u$ and $F_3 = F_2 \cdot a_0^d$ are F-cliques too. Notice that p_0 is the only state which does not belong to the cycles of a_0 and all the cycle states remains intact under the action a_0^d, by construction of d. Hence $F_2 \setminus F_3 = \{p_0\}$ and $F_3 \setminus F_2 = \{p_0 \cdot a_0^d\}$. Hence, by Lemma 1, $\{p_0, p_0 \cdot a_0^d\}$ is a stable pair. This concludes the proof since $p_0 \cdot a_0 = p_0 \cdot a_0^{d+1}$. $\qquad\Box$

To characterize elements of $\mathcal{G}_{n,k}$ that are not synchronizing, we build their *factor automata*, which is defined as follows. Let $\mathcal{A}$ be a DFA with stability relation ρ. Let $\mathcal{C} = \{C_1, \ldots, C_\ell\}$ denote its classes for ρ. The *factor automaton* of $\mathcal{A}$, denoted by $\mathcal{A}/\rho$, is the automaton of set of states $\mathcal{C}$ with transition function defined by $C_i \cdot a = C_j$ in $\mathcal{A}/\rho$ if and only if $C_i \cdot a \subseteq C_j$ in $\mathcal{A}$. Or equivalently, if and only if there exists $q \in C_i$ such that $q \cdot a \in C_j$ in $\mathcal{A}$.

Lemma 3. *If $\mathcal{A} \in \mathcal{G}_{n,k}$ is strongly-connected, then its factor automaton $\mathcal{A}/\rho$ is a strongly-connected permutation automaton.*

Proof. Strong-connectivity follows directly from the definition. If one of the letters was not a permutation on the factor automaton, then there would be a stable class S in $\mathcal{A}$ which has no incoming transition by this letter. It would follow that there is no incoming transition to every state of S in $\mathcal{A}$ either. However, this may happen only for the letter a_0 and the (unique) dangling state p_0 by this letter. Due to Lemma 2, the dangling state p_0 must belong to a stable pair whence there is another state in S: this contradicts that p_0 is the only state with no incoming transition by a_0. $\qquad\Box$

Lemma 4. *Let $\mathcal{A} \in \mathcal{G}_{n,k}$ and let D be the stable class of $\mathcal{A}$ that contains the dangling state p_0. Then the set of stable classes can be divided into two disjoint, but possibly empty, subsets $\mathcal{B}$ and $\mathcal{S}$ such that*

- *$D \in \mathcal{B}$ and $|B| = |D|$ for every $B \in \mathcal{B}$;*
- *$|S| = |D| - 1$ for every $S \in \mathcal{S}$;*
- *The a_0-cycle of $\mathcal{A}/\rho$ that contains D only contains elements of $\mathcal{S}$ besides D;*
- *Every other cycle in $\mathcal{A}/\rho$ lies entirely in either $\mathcal{B}$ or $\mathcal{S}$.*

Proof. Since stable pairs are mapped to stable pairs, the image of a stable class by any letter must be included in a stable class. Recall that by Lemma 3 all letters in $\mathcal{A}/\rho$ act as permutations on the stable classes. Our proof consists in examining the different cycles of the group automaton $\mathcal{A}/\rho$. Let us consider any cycle of a letter a in $\mathcal{A}/\rho$, made of the stable classes $C_0, C_1, \ldots, C_{r-1}$ with $C_j \cdot a \subseteq C_{j+1 \pmod{r}}$, for any $j \in \{0, \ldots r-1\}$.

If $a \neq a_0$ then the letter a acts as a permutation in $\mathcal{A}$, and for each j, we have $|C_j| \leq |C_{j+1 \pmod{r}}|$, since a does not merge pairs of states. Therefore,

$$|C_0| \leq |C_1| \cdots \leq |C_{r-1}| \leq |C_0|.$$

As a direct consequence, all $|C_j|$ have same cardinality.

If $a = a_0$, then observe that the same argument can be used when one removes the dangling state p_0 and its outgoing transition by a_0: the action of a_0 on $Q \setminus \{p_0\}$ becomes a well-defined permutation. Henceforth, if this cycle does not degenerate to a simple loop consisting of only D, then all the other elements of the cycle are stable classes of size $|D| - 1$. And this is the only place where changes of size may happen in $\mathcal{A}/\rho$. The lemma follows from the strong-connectivity of $\mathcal{A}/\rho$.   □

Notice that an almost-group automaton is non-synchronizing if and only if it has at least two stable classes. The following theorem is a consequence of this fact and of Lemma 4.

Theorem 1. *A strongly-connected almost-group automaton $\mathcal{A}$ is non-synchronizing if and only if its partitioning described in Lemma 4 is such that $|\mathcal{B} \cup \mathcal{S}| > 1$.*

4   Counting Non-synchronizing Almost-Group Automata

In this section, we use counting arguments to establish our main result: a precise estimation of the asymptotic number of strongly connected almost-group automata that are not synchronizing.

Recall that our working alphabet is $A = \{a_0, \ldots, a_{k-1}\}$, that $E_n = \{0, \ldots, n-1\}$ and that $\mathcal{G}_{n,k}$ is the set of almost-group automata on A with set of states E_n. Our first counting lemma is immediate.

Lemma 5. *For any $n \geq 1$, there are exactly $(n-1)n!$ almost-permutations of E_n. The number of elements of $\mathcal{G}_{n,k}$ is therefore equal to $(n-1)n!^k$.*

Proof. An almost-permutation of E_n is characterized by its element with no preimage x_0, the way it permutes $E_n \setminus \{x_0\}$ and the image of x_0 in $E_n \setminus \{x_0\}$. Since there are n choices for x_0, $(n-1)!$ ways to permute the other elements and $n-1$ choices for the image of x_0, the result follows.   □

4.1   Strong-Connectivity

Our computations below focus on strong-connectivity. We shall need an estimation of the number of strongly connected group automata and almost-group automata. The proofs of the following lemmas are kind of folklore and thus presented only in the extended version [1] due to a space limit.

Lemma 6. *There are at most $n(n-1)!^k(1+o(1))$ group automata with set of states E_n that are not strongly-connected. Henceforth, there are $n!^k(1+o(n^{1-k}))$ strongly-connected group automata.*

Lemma 7. *The number of not strongly-connected almost-group automata is at most $2(n-1)n(n-1)!^k(1+o(1))$. Henceforth, almost-group automata are strongly connected with high probability: there are $(n-1)n!^k(1+o(n^{1-k}))$ strongly connected elements in $\mathcal{G}_{n,k}$.*

4.2   Non-synchronizing Almost-Group Automata: A Lower Bound

In this section we give a lower bound on the number of strongly connected elements of $\mathcal{G}_{n,k}$ that are not synchronizing. In order to do so, we build a sufficiently large family of automata of that kind. The construction of this family is intuitively driven by the structure given in Lemma 4 but the formal details of the construction can be done without mentioning this structure.

For $n \geq 3$, let $\mathcal{F}_{n,k}$ be the subset of $\mathcal{G}_{n,k}$, made of the almost-group automata on A with set of states E_n such that:

1. there exists a state p that is not the dangling state p_0 such that for every letter $a \neq a_0$, either $p \cdot a = p_0$ and $p_0 \cdot a = p$, or $p \cdot a = p$ and $p_0 \cdot a = p_0$;
2. for at least one letter $a \neq a_0$, we have $p \cdot a = p_0$ and $p_0 \cdot a = p$;
3. there exists a state $q \in Q' = E_n \setminus \{p, p_0\}$ such that the action of a_0 on $Q \setminus \{p_0\}$ is a permutation with q being the image of p;
4. the image of the dangling state by a_0 is $p_0 \cdot a_0 = q$.
5. let q' be the preimage of p by a_0; if one removes the states p and p_0 and set $q' \cdot a_0 = q$, then the resulting automaton is a strongly connected group automaton;

The structure of such an automaton is depicted on Fig. 2. Clearly from the definition, an element of $\mathcal{F}_{n,k}$ is a strongly connected almost group automaton with the dangling state p_0.

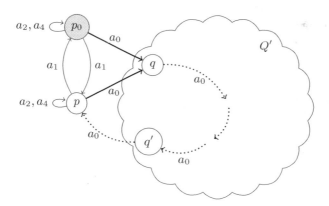

Fig. 2. The shape of an element of $\mathcal{F}_{n,k}$, with the dangling state p_0.

Lemma 8. *For every $n \geq 3$, every automaton of $\mathcal{F}_{n,k}$ is not synchronizing.*

Proof. First observe that $\{p_0, p\}$ is the only pair that can be synchronized by reading just a letter, which has to be a_0. The preimage of $\{p_0, p\}$ is either $\{p_0, p\}$ for $a \neq a_0$ or a singleton $\{q'\}$ otherwise. Hence, no other pair can be mapped to $\{p_0, p\}$ and thus be synchronized by more that one letter.   □

Lemma 9. *There are* $(2^{k-1} - 1)n(n-1)(n-2)(n-2)!^k(1 + o(n^{1-k}))$ *elements in* $\mathcal{F}_{n,k}$*. Thus there are at least that many strongly connected non-synchronizing almost-group automata.*

Proof. From the definition of $\mathcal{F}_{n,k}$, we observe that there are $n(n-1)(n-2)$ ways to choose p_0, p and q. Once it is done, we choose any strongly connected group automaton $\mathcal{A}'$ with $n-2$ states in $E_N \setminus \{p_0, p\}$; there are $(n-2)!^k(1 + o(n^{1-k}))$ ways to do that according to Lemma 6. We then change the transition from the preimage q' of q by a_0 by setting $q' \cdot a_0 = p$. We set $p \cdot a_0 = p_0 \cdot a_0 = q$. Finally we choose the actions of the letters $a \in A \setminus \{a_0\}$ on $\{p_0, p\}$ in one of the $2^{k-1} - 1$ possible ways, as at least one of them is not the identity. This concludes the proof, since all the elements of $\mathcal{F}_{n,k}$ are built exactly once this way.   □

Observe that using the definitions of Lemma 4, an element of $\mathcal{F}_{n,k}$ consists of exactly one stable class $\{p_0, p\}$ in $\mathcal{B}$ and $n-2$ stable classes of size 1 in $\mathcal{S}$.

4.3   Non-synchronizing Almost-Group Automata: An Upper Bound

In this section, we upper bound the number of non-synchronizing strongly-connected elements of $\mathcal{G}_{n,k}$ using the characterization of Lemma 4. In the sequel, we freely use the notations used in this lemma (the sets D, $\mathcal{B}$, $\mathcal{S}$, ...).

Let $b \geq 1$, $s \geq 0$ and $\ell \geq 1$ be three non-negative integers such that $(\ell + 1)b + \ell s = n$. Let $\mathcal{G}_{n,k}(b, s, \ell)$ denote the subset of $\mathcal{G}_{n,k}$ made of the automata such that $|\mathcal{B}| = b$, $|\mathcal{S}| = s$ and $|D| = \ell + 1$.

Lemma 10. *The number of non-synchronizing strongly-connected elements of* $\mathcal{G}_{n,k}(b, s, \ell)$ *is at most*

$$\begin{cases} n!(n-2)!^{k-1}(n-2)(2^{k-1}-1) & \text{if } b = 1, \ s = n-2, \ \text{and } \ell = 1, \\ n! \max(1, s)\ell\big(b!s!(\ell+1)!^b\ell!^s\big)^{k-1} & \text{otherwise.} \end{cases}$$

Proof. Our proof consists in counting the number of ways to build, step by step, an element of $\mathcal{G}_{n,k}(b, s, \ell)$.

Firstly, by elementary computations, one can easily verify that the number of ways to split E_n into b subsets of size $\ell + 1$ and s subsets of size ℓ is exactly

$$\frac{n!}{(\ell+1)!^b \ell!^s b! s!}. \tag{1}$$

Secondly, let us count the number of ways to define the transitions at the level of the factor automaton, i.e. between stable classes, as follows:

- Choose a permutation on $\mathcal{B}$ in $b!$ ways and on $\mathcal{S}$ in $s!$ ways for each of the $k - 1$ letters $a \neq a_0$.
- Choose which stable class of $\mathcal{B}$ is the class D, i.e. the one containing the dangling state p_0, amongst the b possibilities.
- Choose a permutation for a_0 on the $b - 1$ classes $\mathcal{B} \setminus \{D\}$ in $(b-1)!$ ways.

– If $s \neq 0$, choose one of the $s!$ permutations of $\mathcal{S}$ for the action of a_0 on these classes, then alter the action of a_0 the following way: choose the image D' of D by a_0 in $\mathcal{S}$ in s ways, then insert it in the a_0-cycle: if D'' is the former preimage of D', then now $D \cdot a_0 = D'$ and $D'' \cdot a_0 = D$ in $\mathcal{A}/\rho$.
– If $s = 0$, then set $D \cdot a_0 = D$ in $\mathcal{A}/\rho$.

In total, the number of ways to define the transitions of the factor automaton $\mathcal{A}/\rho$, once the stable classes are chosen is

$$(b!s!)^{k-1}b(b-1)! \max(1,s)s! = b!^k s!^k \max(1,s). \tag{2}$$

Now, we need to define transitions between stable classes for all letters. For all letters but a_0, there are b injective transitions between stable classes of size $\ell+1$ and s injective transitions between stable classes of size ℓ, that is, there are at most $(\ell+1)!^b \ell!^s$ ways to define them for each of the $k-1$ letters. This is an upper bound, as some choices may result in an automaton that is, for instance, not strongly connected. We refine this bound for the case $\ell = 1, b = 1, s = n-2$: one of the letters must swap the states in the single 2-element class in $\mathcal{B}$ for strong connectivity, so we count just one choice instead of 2 (for $(\ell+1)!$) to define this letter on this component, that is, we consider only $2^{k-1} - 1$ ways to define all permutations on $\mathcal{B}$ in this case, instead of the $((\ell+1)!^b)^{k-1}$ upper bound in the general case (this refinement is used to match our lower bound).

For the action of a_0, we additionally choose the dangling state $p_0 \in D$ in $\ell+1$ ways and its image in $D \cdot a_0$ in ℓ ways: there are ℓ choices in the case where $D \cdot a_0 = D$, since $p_0 \cdot a_0 \neq p_0$, and also when $D \cdot a_0 \neq D$, since $D \cdot a_0 \in \mathcal{S}$ in this case, according to Lemma 4. Then, it remains to define the injective transitions between the $\mathcal{B} \setminus \{D\}$ blocks in $(\ell+1)!^{b-1}$ ways, and the $s+1$ injective transitions between the $\mathcal{S} \cup \{D'\}$ blocks in $\ell!^{s+1}$ ways, where $D' = D \setminus \{p_0\}$.

Thus, the number of ways to define the transitions between stable classes is at most $((\ell+1)!^b \ell!^s)^{k-1} \ell(\ell+1)(\ell+1)!^{b-1} \ell!^{s+1} = \ell(\ell+1)(\ell+1)!^{bk} \ell!^{sk}$, in the general case, and $2(2^{k-1} - 1)$ in the case $\ell = 1, b = 1, s = n-2$.

Putting together (1), (2) and this last counting result yield the lemma. □

Lemma 11. *The number of non-synchronizing strongly-connected almost-group automata in $\mathcal{G}_{n,k}$ is at most $n(2^{k-1} - 1)n!(n-2)!^{k-1}(1 + o(1/n))$.*

Proof. By Lemma 9 and Theorem 1, the number of non-synchronizing strongly-connected almost-group automata in $\mathcal{G}_{n,k}$ is at most

$$n! \sum_{\ell=1}^{\lfloor n/2 \rfloor} \sum_{\{b,s \,|\, b(\ell+1)+s\ell=n\}} N_{\ell,b,s}, \tag{3}$$

where $b \geq 1$, $s \geq 0$, and $b+s \geq 2$, and where $N_{\ell,b,s}$ is defined by

$$N_{\ell,b,s} = \begin{cases} \max(1,s)\ell(b!s!(\ell+1)!^b \ell!^s)^{k-1}, & \text{for } (\ell,b,s) \neq (1,1,n-2) \\ (n-2)!^{k-1}(n-2)(2^{k-1}-1), & \text{for } (\ell,b,s) = (1,1,n-2). \end{cases} \tag{4}$$

To finish the proof, it will be sufficient to prove that the sum in (3) is asymptotically equivalent to the term $N_{1,1,n-2}$ since $n!N_{1,1,n-2}$ is asymptotically equivalent to the expression stated in Lemma 11.

To prove this, let us consider the following fraction for $(\ell, b, s) \neq (1, 1, n-2)$:

$$\frac{N_{1,1,n-2}}{N_{\ell,b,s}} = \frac{n-2}{\max(1,s)\ell} \frac{(n-2)!^{k-1}(2^{k-1}-1)}{(b!s!(\ell+1)!^b\ell!^s)^{k-1}} \geq \left(\frac{(n-2)!}{b!s!(\ell+1)!^b\ell!^s}\right)^{k-1}, \quad (5)$$

where we used that $n - 2 = s\ell + b(\ell + 1) - 2 \geq s\ell$, as b and ℓ are positive; thus $n - 2 \geq \max(1,s)\ell$ if $s > 0$; but it also holds if $s = 0$ since $b + s \geq 2$.

Observe that, for positive ℓ and m we have

$$\frac{(bm)!}{m!^b} = \left(\frac{1 \cdot 2 \cdots m}{1 \cdot 2 \cdots m}\right)\left(\frac{(m+1)(m+2)\cdots 2m}{1 \cdot 2 \cdots m}\right)\cdots\left(\frac{((b-1)m+1)\cdots bm}{1 \cdot 2 \cdots m}\right)$$
$$\geq 1^m \cdot 2^m \cdots b^m = b!^m$$

Hence, for $m = \ell + 1$, we have $\frac{(b(\ell+1))!}{(\ell+1)!^b} \geq b!^{\ell+1}$. Similarly, one can get that

$$\frac{n!}{(b(\ell+1))!} \frac{1}{\ell!^s} \geq \left(\frac{(b+s)!}{b!}\right)^{\ell}. \quad (6)$$

Let $M_{\ell,b,s} = \frac{(n-2)!}{b!s!(\ell+1)!^b\ell!^s}$, the expression in brackets of (5). This quantity can be bounded from below as follows.

$$M_{\ell,b,s} = \frac{1}{n(n-1)b!s!} \frac{(b(\ell+1))!}{(\ell+1)!^b} \frac{n!}{(b(\ell+1))!\ell!^s} \quad (7)$$
$$\geq \frac{b!^{\ell+1}}{n(n-1)b!s!}\left(\frac{(b+s)!}{b!}\right)^{\ell} \geq \frac{(b+s)!^{\ell}}{n^2 s!}. \quad (8)$$

Recall that we want to prove that $M_{\ell,b,s}$ is sufficiently large, so that $N_{1,1,n-2}$ is really larger than $N_{\ell,b,s}$. Notice that there are at most quadratic in n number of combinations (ℓ, b, s) satisfying $b(\ell+1) + s\ell = n$, as for any values $1 \leq b, \ell < n$ there is at most one suitable value of s. Therefore, cubic lower bound on $M_{\ell,b,s}$ is enough in general. We distinguish two cases:
▷ If $\ell \geq 2$, then $M_{\ell,b,s} \geq n^{-2}(b+s)!^{\ell-1}$. If $b+s \geq \ln n$, this expression is greater than $\Theta(n^3)$ by Stirling formula. Otherwise, because $b(\ell+1) + s\ell = n$, we have $\ell \geq \frac{n}{\ln n} - 1$ and as $b + s \geq 2$ the same $\Theta(n^3)$ lower bound holds.
▷ If $\ell = 1$, then $s = n - 2b$ and $M_{\ell,b,s} \geq \frac{(n-b)!}{n^2(n-2b)!}$. Clearly, this expression decreases as b increases; for $b = 3$ it is greater than $\Theta(n)$ (and there is only one such term) and for $b > 3$ it is greater than $\Theta(n^3)$. If $b = 1$, then $s = n - 2$ and this is the term $N_{1,1,n-2}$. The only remaining case is when $b = 2$, $\ell = 1$, and $s = n - 4$. For this case by (5), we get

$$\frac{N_{1,1,n-2}}{N_{\ell,b,s}} \geq \left(\frac{(n-2)!}{b!s!(\ell+1)!^b\ell!^s}\right)^{k-1} = \left(\frac{(n-2)!}{8(n-4)!}\right)^{k-1} = \Theta(n^{2(k-1)}). \quad (9)$$

Thus, we proved that the sum (3) is indeed asymptotically equal to the term $N_{1,1,n-2}$ multiplied by $n!$. □

4.4   Main Result and Conclusions

Now, we are ready to prove our main result on the asymptotic number of strongly connected elements of $\mathcal{G}_{n,k}$ that are not synchronizing.

Theorem 2. *The probability that a random strongly connected almost-group automaton with n states and $k \geq 2$ letters is not synchronizing is equal to*

$$(2^{k-1} - 1)n^{-2(k-1)}\left(1 + o(1)\right).\tag{10}$$

In particular, random strongly connected almost-group automata are synchronizing with high probability as n tends to infinity.

Proof. Lemmas 9 and 11 give lower and upper bounds on the number of strongly-connected non-synchronizing almost-group automata, which are both equal to $(2^{k-1} - 1)n^3(n-2)!^k(1 + o(1/n))$. We conclude the proof using the estimation on the number of strongly-connected almost-group automata given in Lemma 7. □

Thus we obtained a precise asymptotic on the probability for strongly-connected almost group automata of being synchronizable for any alphabet size. Apart from generalizing this result, it would be natural, as in [2], to design an algorithm which would test on synchronization a given random strongly-connected almost-group automaton in optimal average time.

We are thankful to anonymous referees whose comments helped to improve the presentation of the results.

References

1. Belinkov, M., Nicaud, C.: Synchronizing random almost-group automata (2018). https://arxiv.org/abs/1805.02154
2. Berlinkov, M.V.: On the probability of being synchronizable. In: Govindarajan, S., Maheshwari, A. (eds.) CALDAM 2016. LNCS, vol. 9602, pp. 73–84. Springer, Cham (2016). https://doi.org/10.1007/978-3-319-29221-2_7
3. Černý, J.: Poznámka k homogénnym eksperimentom s konečnými automatami. Matem.-fyzik. Časopis Slovenskej Akadémie Vied **14**(3), 208–216 (1964)
4. Kari, J.: Synchronization and stability of finite automata. J. UCS **8**(2), 270–277 (2002). https://doi.org/10.3217/jucs-008-02-0270
5. Nicaud, C.: Random deterministic automata. Math. Found. of Comp. Sci. **2014**, 5–23 (2014). https://doi.org/10.1007/978-3-662-44522-8_2
6. Nicaud, C.: Fast synchronization of random automata. In: APPROX/RANDOM 2016. Leibniz International Proceedings in Informatics (LIPIcs), vol. 60, pp. 43:1–43:12 (2016)
7. Pin, J.E.: On two combinatorial problems arising from automata theory. In: Proceedings of the International Colloquium on Graph Theory and Combinatorics, vol. 75, pp. 535–548 (1983)
8. Szykula, M.: Improving the upper bound on the length of the shortest reset word. In: 35th Symposium on Theoretical Aspects of Computer Science (STACS 2018). LIPIcs, vol. 96, pp. 56:1–56:13 (2018)

9. Trahtman, A.: The road coloring problem. Israel J. Math. **172**(1), 51–60 (2009). https://doi.org/10.1007/s11856-009-0062-5
10. Volkov, M.V.: Synchronizing automata and the Černý conjecture. In: Martín-Vide, C., Otto, F., Fernau, H. (eds.) LATA 2008. LNCS, vol. 5196, pp. 11–27. Springer, Heidelberg (2008). https://doi.org/10.1007/978-3-540-88282-4_4
11. Zaks, Y., Skvortsov, E.: Synchronizing random automata. Discrete Math. Theor. Comput. Sci. **12**(4) (2010)

A Comparison of Two N-Best Extraction Methods for Weighted Tree Automata

Johanna Björklund, Frank Drewes, and Anna Jonsson[✉]

Department of Computing Science, Umeå University, Umeå, Sweden
{johanna,drewes,aj}@cs.umu.se

Abstract. We conduct a comparative study of two state-of-the-art algorithms for extracting the N best trees from a weighted tree automaton (wta). The algorithms are BEST TREES, which uses a priority queue to structure the search space, and FILTERED RUNS, which is based on an algorithm by Huang and Chiang that extracts N best runs, implemented as part of the Tiburon wta toolkit. The experiments are run on four data sets, each consisting of a sequence of wtas of increasing sizes. Our conclusion is that BEST TREES can be recommended when the input wtas exhibit a high or unpredictable degree of nondeterminism, whereas FILTERED RUNS is the better option when the input wtas are large but essentially deterministic.

1 Introduction

Data-driven language processing involves as a rule weighted language models. Rather than providing a definite answer as to whether a sentence belongs to a target language, these return a probability or a fitness score. This reflects the inherently ambiguous nature of human language and is convenient for statistical machine learning, but it often complicates downstream processing. When the output of a machine translation system is not limited to a small set of possible translations, but is a weighted device ranking the universe of all possible outputs, efficient algorithms are needed to find the highest-scoring solutions. This problem is known as the N-best problem. The input is a weighted automaton M and a natural number N, and task is to find N best-ranking elements with respect to M. The difficulty of the problem, and indeed whether there is a unique or several interchangeable solutions, largely depends on the type of automata at hand and the domain from which weights are taken.

We consider the N-best problem for weighted tree automata [3,4], which are useful in natural language processing, owing to their capability to rank parse trees of context-free languages. This makes them useful for syntax-based forms of processing, as demonstrated in, e.g., machine translation and program verification. Weighted tree automata [2] are typically defined over algebras that have at least as much structure as a semiring, but semifields or even fields are often used. The weight of a computation (called a run) of an automaton on an input tree is the semiring product of the weights of the rules applied, and the weight

© Springer International Publishing AG, part of Springer Nature 2018
C. Câmpeanu (Ed.): CIAA 2018, LNCS 10977, pp. 97–108, 2018.
https://doi.org/10.1007/978-3-319-94812-6_9

of the tree is the semiring sum of the weights of all runs on this tree. We restrict ourselves to the so-called tropical semiring, which means that the weight of a run is the (ordinary) sum of the weights of the applied rules and the weight of a tree is the minimum of the weights of its runs.

Our main contribution is an empirical evaluation of two N-best algorithms for weighted tree automata (wta) M over the tropical semiring. Both algorithms represent the state of the art, but operate in quite different ways. The first of these is an indirect method based on an N-best runs (or derivations) algorithm proposed by Huang and Chiang [5] and implemented in the wta toolkit Tiburon [7]. The algorithm computes N best runs in time $O(mN \log N)$, where m is the number of transitions of the wta. This can be used to compute N best trees by generating a list of N' best runs of M, for some large enough $N' \geq N$. These runs are evaluated to the corresponding trees and duplicates are discarded to obtain a list of N best trees. Henceforth, we refer to this method by FILTERED RUNS. FILTERED RUNS thus takes a heuristic approach in the sense that an unlucky user may request too large or small a number of best runs, either wasting time or not gathering enough runs to find N unique best trees.

The second algorithm that we evaluate is BEST TREES [1], a generalisation of an N-best algorithm for string automata [8]. Intuitively, BEST TREES implements a breadth-first search, while making extensive use of pruning to avoid a combinatorial explosion. The running time of BEST TREES is $O(N^2 \cdot (mn \log N + n^3))$ [1, slightly simplified], where m and n are the number of transitions and states of the input wta. Hence, the algorithm is less efficient than the pure N-best runs algorithm by Huang and Chiang, even though both are polynomial. However, BEST TREES is guaranteed to produce exactly the desired number of trees without the need to discard duplicates, whereas FILTERED RUNS may require the enumeration of a large number of runs. The latter can happen if the input wtas exhibit a high degree of nondeterminism, i.e. if the number of distinct trees among the N best runs grows slowly (logarithmically in the worst case) with increasing N. FILTERED RUNS is thus expected to run faster even on large wtas if there is no or very little nondeterminism, while the asymptotic advantage of BEST TREES should become apparent as the degree of nondeterminism increases. We perform empirical evaluations in order to (a) confirm this expected behaviour and (b) get an idea about how the algorithms compare on different kinds of wta and varying amounts of nondeterminism.

To study this in a setting where the type, size, and amount of nondeterminism of input wtas can be varied in a controlled way, we run our experiments on a range of synthesized wtas designed for this purpose rather than using "real life" wtas. While the results mostly confirm the theoretical expectations, they show that the precise behaviour is not as simple as the theoretical worst case analysis suggests. In particular, the running time of FILTERED RUNS depends on aspects other than the pure amount of nondeterminism, such as the order in which the transition rules of the input wta are given.

2   Preliminaries

We write $\mathbb{N}$ for the set of nonnegative integers, $\mathbb{N}_+$ for $\mathbb{N} \setminus \{0\}$, and $\mathbb{R}_+$ for the set of non-negative reals; $\mathbb{N}^\infty$ and $\mathbb{R}_+^\infty$ denote $\mathbb{N} \cup \{\infty\}$ and $\mathbb{R}_+ \cup \{\infty\}$, respectively. For $n \in \mathbb{N}$, $[n] = \{i \in \mathbb{N} \mid 1 \leq i \leq n\}$. Thus, in particular, $[0] = \emptyset$ and $[\infty] = \mathbb{N}$. The cardinality of a (countable) set S is written $|S|$, and the powerset of S is denoted by $pow(S)$. The n-fold Cartesian product of a set S with itself is denoted by S^n. As usual, the set of all finite sequences over S is denoted by S^*, and the empty sequence by λ.

For a set A, an A-labelled *tree* is a partial function $t \colon \mathbb{N}_+^* \to A$ whose domain $dom(t)$ is a finite non-empty set that is prefix-closed and closed to the left: whenever $vi \in dom(t)$ for some $v \in \mathbb{N}_+^*$ and $i \in \mathbb{N}_+$, it holds that $v \in dom(t)$ (prefix-closedness) and $vj \in dom(t)$ for all $1 \leq j \leq i$ (closedness to the left). The size of t is $|t| = |dom(t)|$. An element v of $dom(t)$ is called a *node of t*, and $|\{i \in \mathbb{N}_+ \mid vi \in dom(t)\}|$ is the *rank of v*. The *subtree* of $t \in T_\Sigma$ rooted at v is the tree t/v defined by $dom(t/v) = \{u \in \mathbb{N}_+^* \mid vu \in dom(t)\}$ and $t/v(u) = t(vu)$ for every $u \in \mathbb{N}_+^*$. If $t(\lambda) = f$ and $t/i = t_i$ for all $i \in [k]$, where k is the rank of λ in t, then we denote t by $f[t_1, \ldots, t_k]$, which may be identified with f if $k = 0$.

A *ranked alphabet* is a disjoint union of finite sets of symbols, $\Sigma = \bigcup_{k \in \mathbb{N}} \Sigma_{(k)}$. For $f \in \Sigma$, the $k \in \mathbb{N}$ such that $f \in \Sigma_{(k)}$ is the *rank* of f, denoted by $rank(f)$. The set T_Σ of ranked trees over Σ consists of all Σ-labelled trees t in which the rank of every node $v \in dom(t)$ equals the rank of $t(v)$. For a set T of trees we denote by $\Sigma(T)$ the set of trees which have a symbol from Σ in their root, with direct subtrees in T, i.e., $\{f[t_1, \ldots, t_k] \mid k \in \mathbb{N}, f \in \Sigma_{(k)}, \text{ and } t_1, \ldots, t_k \in T\}$.

In the following, let $\square \notin \Sigma$ be a special symbol of rank 0. The set of *contexts over Σ* is the set C_Σ of trees $c \in T_{\Sigma \cup \{\square\}}$ containing exactly one node $v \in dom(c)$ with $c(v) = \square$. The *substitution* of another tree t into c results in the tree $c[\![t]\!]$ given by $dom(c[\![t]\!]) = dom(c) \cup \{vu \mid u \in dom(t)\}$ and

$$c[\![t]\!](w) = \begin{cases} c(w) & \text{if } w \in dom(c) \setminus \{v\}, \text{ and} \\ t(u) & \text{if } w = vu \text{ for some } u \in dom(t) \end{cases}$$

for all $w \in dom(c[\![t]\!])$.

Recall that the domain of the *tropical semiring* is $\mathbb{R}_+^\infty$, with min serving as addition and real-valued addition as multiplication. A *weighted tree language* over the tropical semiring is a mapping $L \colon T_\Sigma \to \mathbb{R}_+^\infty$, where Σ is a ranked alphabet. Such languages can be specified by a *weighted tree automaton with final states* (wta). A wta is a system $M = (Q, \Sigma, R, Q_\mathrm{f})$ consisting of

- a finite set Q of symbols of rank 0 called *states*;
- a ranked alphabet Σ of *input symbols* disjoint with Q;
- a finite set R of *transition rules* $f[q_1, \ldots, q_k] \xrightarrow{w} q$, where $q, q_1, \ldots, q_k \in Q$, $f \in \Sigma_{(k)}$, and $w \in \mathbb{R}_+$; and
- a set $Q_\mathrm{f} \subseteq Q$ of *final states*.

A transition rule $r \colon f[q_1, \ldots, q_k] \xrightarrow{w} q$ will also be viewed as a symbol of rank k, so that R becomes a ranked alphabet. In addition, we view every state $q \in Q$

as a symbol of rank 0. We define the set $runs_M^q \subseteq T_{R \cup Q}$ of q-*runs of* M, their resulting trees $result_M(\rho)$, and their weights $wt_M(\rho)$ (for $\rho \in runs_M^q$) inductively, as follows:

1. For every state $q \in Q$, $q \in runs_M^q$ with $result_M(q) = q$ and $wt_M(q) = 0$.
2. For every $r\colon f[q_1, \ldots, q_k] \xrightarrow{w} q$ in R and all $\rho_1 \in runs_M^{q_1}, \ldots, \rho_k \in runs_M^{q_k}$, $\rho = r[\rho_1, \ldots, \rho_k] \in runs_M^q$ with $result_M(\rho) = f[result_M(\rho_1), \ldots, result_M(\rho_k)]$, and $wt_M(\rho) = w + \sum_{i \in [k]} wt_M(\rho_i)$.

The set of *accepting* runs is $runs_M = \{runs_M^q \mid q \in F\}$.

Now, the weighted tree language $M\colon T_\Sigma \to \mathbb{R}_+^\infty$ *recognised by* M is given by

$$M(t) = \min\{wt_M(\rho) \mid \rho \in runs_M^q \text{ is accepting and } result_M(\rho) = t\}$$

for all $t \in T_\Sigma$ (where, by convention, $\min \emptyset = \infty$). In other words, $M(t)$ is the minimal weight of an accepting run of t. Note that we, by a slight abuse of notation, denote by M both the wta and the weighted tree language it computes.

For a wta M and an $N \in \mathbb{N}^\infty$ as input, the *N-best runs problem* is the problem to compute a sequence of N accepting runs of minimal weight according to M. More precisely, an algorithm solving the problem outputs a sequence $\rho_1, \rho_2, \ldots$ of N pairwise distinct accepting runs such that there are no $i \in [N]$ and $\rho \in runs_M \setminus \{\rho_1, \ldots, \rho_i\}$ with $wt_M(\rho) < wt_M(\rho_i)$. (If the total number N' of accepting runs is smaller than N, the algorithm only outputs N' runs.)

Similarly, the *N-best trees problem* asks to compute pairwise distinct trees $t_1, t_2, \ldots$ in T_Σ of minimal weight, i.e., such that there are no $i \in [N]$ and $t \in T_\Sigma \setminus \{t_1, \ldots, t_i\}$ with $M(t) < M(t_i)$.

3   Previous Work

The difference between the two N-best problems is that, in the nondeterministic case, distinct runs may result in the same tree. The wta toolkit Tiburon provides an implementation of the N-best runs algorithm by Huang and Chiang [5]. This yields an obvious procedure for solving the N-best trees problem: one simply computes N' best runs $\rho_1, \rho_2, \ldots$ for large enough N', and outputs those $result_M(\rho_i)$ for which $result_M(\rho_i) \notin \{result_M(\rho_1), \ldots, result_M(\rho_{i-1})\}$. This procedure is guaranteed to produce the desired result because any given tree has at most an exponential number of runs, which means that the next tree will be encountered after at most exponentially many steps. (If there are no more accepting runs one can simply continue to enumerate arbitrary ones of the remaining trees, whose weight will by definition be ∞.)

The N-best trees algorithm developed in [1] avoids the detour via N' best runs. We now give a short summary of the reasoning that leads to this algorithm. Let the size parameters of the input wta M be the following:

– m is the number $|R|$ of transition rules of M,
– n is the number of states, and

– r is the maximum rank of symbols.

The algorithm explores its search space by maintaining a priority queue K of trees that are candidates of output trees. The trees in the queue mark the frontier of the search space, the priority being determined primarily by the minimal value of $M(c[\![t]\!])$, where c ranges over all possible contexts. To determine this value, note that the definition of $M(t)$ works also for trees $t \in T_{\Sigma \cup Q}$. In particular, t can be of the form $c[\![q]\!]$, where c is a context and $q \in Q$. This is useful because of the following. For a run of the form $\rho[\![\rho']\!]$ where $\rho' \in runs_M^q$ we clearly have $wt_M(\rho[\![\rho']\!]) = wt_M(\rho) + wt_M(\rho')$. Hence, if we denote by M^q the wta obtained from M by replacing its set of final states by $\{q\}$, then

$$M(c[\![t]\!]) = \min_{q \in Q} \left(M(c[\![q]\!]) + M^q(t) \right)$$

for all contexts c and all trees t.

As $M(c[\![p]\!])$ is independent of t, a context c that minimises it can be calculated in advance. Such a context c, which we call a *cheapest context*[1] of q and which is henceforth denoted by c_q, is thus a cheapest context into which a subtree t can be embedded in order to reach a final state, once the state q has been reached at the root of t. As was shown in [1], a family $(c_q)_{q \in Q}$ of cheapest contexts can efficiently be computed given M.

To solve the N-best trees problem, when looking at a tree t in the frontier of our search space we are, intuitively, interested in the tree $c[\![t]\!]$ that has the least possible weight. The smaller this weight is, the higher should the priority of t be. Clearly, when comparing trees with regard to this, c can be assumed to be one of the cheapest contexts c_p. Thus, our aim has to be to determine the state q that minimises the weight of $c_q[\![t]\!]$. We call such a state an *optimal state* for t, and denote it by $opt(t)$ (breaking ties arbitrarily). In the algorithm, optimal states can efficiently be computed in an incremental way as trees are assembled from subtrees, provided that a small amount of bookkeeping information is stored along with each tree.

Now, the N-best trees algorithm maintains data structures T and K, where

– T is a set of trees that have already been processed and
– K is a priority queue of trees in $\Sigma(T)$, the frontier of the search space.

The queue K initially contains the trees in Σ_0. Its priority order $<_K$ is defined by $t <_K t' \iff \Delta(t) < \Delta(t')$, where $\Delta(s) = M(c_{opt(s)}[\![s]\!])$ for all $s \in T_\Sigma$.

We reproduce the pseudocode of the base algorithm from [1] in Algorithm 1. As discussed in detail in [1], the set of trees enqueued in line 13 can be pruned because for every state q at most N trees for which q is an optimal state may ever become relevant. An additional optimisation was used in the implementation used for the experiments of this paper: once the algorithm has outputted $i \leq N$ trees, it suffices to keep $N - i$ rather than N trees in K for each optimal state. Hence, the queue shrinks as progress is made. While this does not affect the asymptotic running time, it does yield a significant improvement in practise.

---

[1] In [1] the term *smallest completion* was used.

Algorithm 1. Compute $N \in \mathbb{N}^\infty$ trees of minimal weight according to a wta M

1: **procedures** BEST TREES(M, N)
2:    compute cheapest contexts for all states
3:    $T \leftarrow \emptyset; K \leftarrow \emptyset$
4:    enqueue(K, Σ_0)
5:    $i \leftarrow 0$
6:    **while** $i < N \wedge K$ is nonempty **do**
7:        $t \leftarrow$ dequeue(K)
8:        $T \leftarrow T \cup \{t\}$
9:        **if** $M(t) = \Delta(t)$ **then**
10:            output(t)
11:            $i \leftarrow i + 1$
12:        **end if**
13:        enqueue($K, expand(T, t)$)
14:    **end while**
15: **end procedures**

---

4   Experiments

In this section, we experimentally verify the time complexity of BEST TREES, and then compare its performance with the indirect method FILTERED RUNS.

It is easy to construct worst-case scenarios in which BEST TREES works exponentially faster than FILTERED RUNS. For example, let $\Sigma = \Sigma_{(0)} \cup \Sigma_{(1)}$ with $\Sigma_{(0)} = \{a\}$ and $\Sigma_{(1)} = \{f\}$, and consider the wta M with two states q_1, q_2, and the rules $a \xrightarrow{0} q_i$ and $f[q_i] \xrightarrow{1} q_j$ for all $i, j \in [2]$, where q_1 is final. Then $M(t) = |t|$ for every tree $t \in T_\Sigma$ and thus BEST TREES simply enumerates trees by size. However, each tree t has $2^{|t|}$ accepting runs, all of weight $|t|$, and thus FILTERED RUNS needs to generate $2^{|t|} - 1$ best runs to discover t.

In the following, we conduct experiments on synthesized sets of wtas which, rather than triggering this kind of worst-case behaviour, are designed to shed light on particular aspects of the algorithms in less extreme (and thus perhaps practically more relevant) cases. An annotated collection containing all of these wta sets is available on the project web page[2], along with the measured running times for each wta. Due to space restrictions, we limit ourselves for the present to brief descriptions of the data.

The experiments were run on a computer with 8 Intel i7 processors, each at a speed of 3.6 GHz and with 16 GB memory allocated for the JVM. The efficiency results are based on repeated experimentation, and each reported running time is a mean value of five runs. As both BEST TREES and FILTERED RUNS are deterministic algorithms, the existing (but relatively low) variance in the running times is due to variations in the execution environment, e.g., overall system load. All plots show the running times in milliseconds as a function of N or wta size, which is why we exclude the y axis labels from the figures.

---

[2] http://people.cs.umu.se/aj/besttrees_experiments/.

4.1 Data

Below follows a short presentation of the wta sets used in this paper. Each set consists of a sequence of language-equivalent wtas of increasing sizes. The relatively small wta sizes are due to the limitations of Tiburon: increasing the number of states causes out-of-memory errors when adding more nondeterminism.

BASIC EXAMPLE. A sequence of 20 wtas, starting with the example wta in [1]. Each subsequent automaton was derived from its predecessor by mirroring an existing run for some tree t by the addition of new states and rules resulting in an alternative run on t. Thus, the numbers of states and transition rules increase at the same rate, which allows us to check the running time as a function of the number of states and rules on the one hand, and of N on the other hand. The amount of nondeterminism, however, does not significantly increase as only t gets one more accepting run.

DIFFERENT WEIGHTS. A sequence of 16 wtas over a, b of rank 0 and 0, resp., and states $q_1, \ldots, q_4$, in which all of the transition rules have different weights. All states are final. The transition rules have the weight of the index of their target state. The weight of transition rule $b[q_i, q_j] \rightarrow q_k$ is $ijk/100$, where ijk is interpreted as a number in decimal notation. The ℓ-th wta ($\ell \in [16]$) consists of the first 4ℓ of these rules if ordered according to decreasing weight. As a consequence, the degree of nondeterminism is moderate throughout, but is changing as the wta sizes grow, as the later rules result in the best runs. In particular, the degree of nondeterminism of the final wta including all transition rules is low because only the rules $a \rightarrow q_1$ and $b[q_1, q_1] \rightarrow q_1$ result in cheapest runs.

MODIFIED DIFFERENT WEIGHTS. Similar to DIFFERENT WEIGHTS, but transition rules on b are added in a different order, starting with $b[q_1, q_1] \rightarrow q_1$ (see the project web page (see footnote 1) for details). Hence, the best runs in all 16 wtas are those which assign q_1 to all nodes, which means that the degree of nondeterminism is small and grows moderately with growing wta sizes.

EQUAL WEIGHTS. The wta set EQUAL WEIGHTS is also similar to the set DIFFERENT WEIGHTS, but the weights are equal (all 0) apart from the rules on a, which have weight 4. Thus, this example has the highest possible degree of nondeterminism.

4.2 Running Time of BEST TREES

Let us first compare the measured running times of BEST TREES with the theoretical bound $O(N^2 \cdot (mn \log N + n^3))$ derived in [1].[3]

A somewhat unexpected outcome of our experiments was that our implementation of the computation of the cheapest contexts in line 2 of Algorithm 1, which makes use of an algorithm by Knuth [6], turned out to be slightly less efficient

---

[3] For the sake of clarity, the expression is slightly simplified. In particular, the maximum rank r of symbols is taken to be constant, as it is typically small in practise.

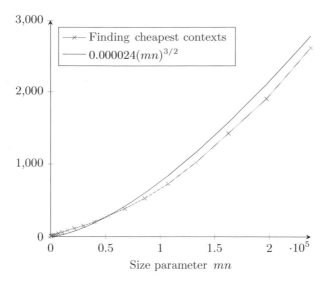

Fig. 1. Running time of finding the cheapest contexts for wtas of increasing size in the set BASIC EXAMPLE.

than the theoretical upper bound $O(mn \log n)$. Plotted against the parameter mn, $O(mn \log n)$ should basically become linear when finding the cheapest contexts for BASIC EXAMPLE. As can be seen in Fig. 1, the practical running time appears to instead be proportional to $(mn)^{3/2}$ on this type of input automata. Further experiments revealed that when m was increased while n was kept constant (suggesting a running time of $\Theta(m)$), we instead acquired figures resembling $\Theta(m^2)$ very closely. Optimising the computation of the cheapest contexts could therefore give a certain gain when N is small, but since the computation time is independent of N, its influence vanishes as N grows. Due to this not being optimised, we from here on disregard the time for finding the cheapest contexts when presenting running times for BEST TREES. This, however, only affects the runs on BASIC EXAMPLE significantly.

The numbers of rules and states increase at a similar rate in the wta sequence BASIC EXAMPLE; this behaviour allows us to vary the two parameters N and mn. Based on the theoretical upper bounds, the running times should be in $O(N^2 \log N)$ and $O((mn)^{3/2})$ (the latter because of the term n^3 in the theoretical estimation, which equals $(mn)^{3/2}$ for $m = n$). This is confirmed by our results, which are visualised in Fig. 2a for increasing N, and in Fig. 2b for increasing mn. As may be expected, these running times are slightly better than the theoretical worst-case estimations.

As N varies, the theoretical worst-case running time of $O(N^2 \log N)$ is only reached when the priority queue used by the algorithm is at its maximal length throughout most of the execution. Simply put, this only happens when most trees can reach most states. In practise, the running time is therefor likely to be lower. This is for instance the case for the BASIC EXAMPLE test set.

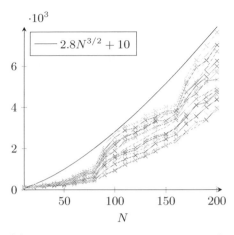

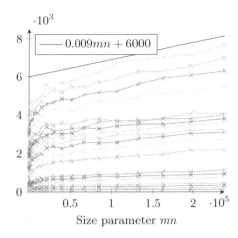

(a) Running time depending on N; the multiple lines represent the increasingly large wtas of BASIC EXAMPLE.

(b) Running time depending on the size of wtas; the multiple lines represent $N \in \{10, 20, ..., 200\}$.

Fig. 2. Running time of BEST TREES on the BASIC EXAMPLE set.

Here, the algorithm exhibits the behaviour shown in Fig. 2a, which is roughly proportional to $N^{3/2}$.

The waviness of the plot is explained by the pattern of the language recognised by the input wtas: it only contains trees with an even number of symbols of rank 0. By there only being a binary symbol in addition to the rank 0 symbols, all of the trees in the language have an odd number of binary symbols. When all of the trees with $2i - 1$ binary symbols have been found, the next accepted tree is amongst the trees with $2i + 1$ binary symbols. However, all of the possibilities for $2i$ binary symbols have to be processed as well since a rule application adds at most one binary symbol to the resulting tree. Thus, the jumps in the plot represent going from finding the trees with $2i - 1$ binary symbols to finding the trees with $2i + 1$ binary symbols.

The measured running time as a function of the size of wtas is also lower than the theoretical upper bound $O((mn)^{3/2})$ in this example, namely linear.

4.3   Comparison of BEST TREES and FILTERED RUNS

In these experiments, we used Tiburon v.1.0. We ran Tiburon on the input wta to get d_N runs where d_N is the smallest number of runs that produces N distinct trees. The number d_N was found manually for each combination of input wta and value of N. Then, the list of runs was filtered using a Python script such that only the N best trees remained. The filtering was done by going through the list top-down and collecting only the unseen trees (by comparing each to the previously collected ones) until N trees were gathered. The time spent on filtering is included in the reported running times but negligible compared to the running time of Tiburon.

Figure 3 shows how the running times of FILTERED RUNS and BEST TREES compare on the two extreme example sets. Even though BEST TREES is polynomial on BASIC EXAMPLE (as confirmed above), it is much less efficient than FILTERED RUNS, which can be explained with the insignificant degree of nondeterminism of the wtas in BASIC EXAMPLE. Turning to EQUAL WEIGHTS instead, the situation changes: as seen in Fig. 3b, BEST TREES remains polynomial whereas FILTERED RUNS appears to exhibit the expected exponential behaviour as it is sensitive to the high (and growing) degree of nondeterminism in EQUAL WEIGHTS.

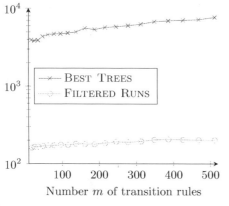 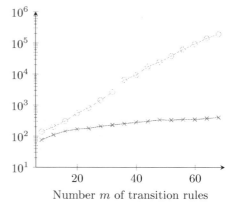

(a) Comparison of BEST TREES and FILTERED RUNS when run on the BASIC EXAMPLE wta set for $N = 200$.

(b) Comparison of BEST TREES and FILTERED RUNS when run on the EQUAL WEIGHTS wta set for $N = 30$.

Fig. 3. BEST TREES and FILTERED RUNS when run on BASIC EXAMPLE and EQUAL WEIGHTS for fixed N.

The results for the less extreme sets DIFFERENT WEIGHTS and MODIFIED DIFFERENT WEIGHTS are shown in Fig. 4. On the former, the running time of FILTERED RUNS is quite erratic, which can be explained with the changing degree of nondeterminism. In particular, the running time drops towards the end because the degree of nondeterminism does. Because of the low, and slowly but steadily growing degree of nondeterminism of MODIFIED DIFFERENT WEIGHTS, FILTERED RUNS runs faster on this set and the behaviour is much smoother as wta sizes increase.

4.4   Discussion

An obvious advantage of BEST TREES is that its argument N is simply the number of best trees desired. In contrast, using FILTERED RUNS with the current

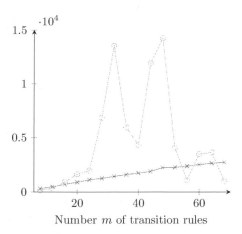
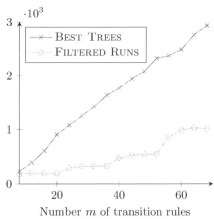

(a) Comparison of BEST TREES and FILTERED RUNS when run on the DIFFERENT WEIGHTS wta set.

(b) Comparison of BEST TREES and FILTERED RUNS when run on the MODIFIED DIFFERENT WEIGHTS wta set.

Fig. 4. BEST TREES and FILTERED RUNS when run on DIFFERENT WEIGHTS and MODIFIED DIFFERENT WEIGHTS for $N = 100$.

interface of Tiburon makes it necessary to guess the number d_N of runs needed to produce sufficiently many best runs. To avoid a trial and error procedure, one would have to compute an appropriate – and thus exponentially large – upper bound N' on d_N from N, resulting in a running time that is guaranteed to be exponentially less efficient than BEST TREES even in cases where the actual d_N equals N. However, note that this is not an intrinsic weakness of FILTERED RUNS because the best runs algorithm of [5] allows for a lazy implementation that outputs runs one by one upon request. It should thus not be difficult to modify the Tiburon implementation so as to allow for $N' = \infty$, resulting in an infinite (lazy) list of runs that can be inspected in FILTERED RUNS to extract any number of best trees. The more serious limitation of FILTERED RUNS is that its running time is directly related to the number N' of best runs required, which is difficult to predict. The running times reported in our experiments are therefore indicative of how many runs had to be computed for each value of N.

Overall, BEST TREES shows a more predictable and smoother behaviour than FILTERED RUNS, allowing us to predict its time consumption more reliably if the structure of input wtas is not well known (see Fig. 4a).

During the experiments, the memory usage of Tiburon became too high when running it on the nondeterministic wta sets for $N > 10$, forcing us to increase the memory allocated for the JVM from 2–4 GB to 16 GB. In contrast, BEST TREES did not encounter such problems and thus seems to use less memory.

5   Conclusion

We have experimentally validated the running time of BEST TREES, the N-best algorithm for wtas proposed in [1], and the practical results were in line with the theoretical predictions. We then continued to compare BEST TREES with FILTERED RUNS. Whereas BEST TREES can be said to take a direct approach, FILTERED RUNS is indirect in the sense that it computes a large number of best runs, and then discards those that duplicate previously outputted trees.

As it is easy to create "artificial" examples that make FILTERED RUNS exponentially less efficient than BEST TREES, we used more benign input automata in our experiments. The experimental results confirm that the degree of nondeterminism has a decisive influence on the relative efficiency of both methods. The greater simplicity of FILTERED RUNS makes it preferable if the degree of nondeterminism is low and the input wtas are large. Conversely, if the degree of nondeterminism is high in comparison to the size of the wta, BEST TREES is the more efficient algorithm.

Another, more general, advantage of BEST TREES is that it provides guarantees, and that it avoids unpredictable behaviour such as the one seen in Fig. 4a, which may be important in applications where the structure of the input automata is varied or unclear. Using the currently available implementation provided by Tiburon, one can also add that it is inconvenient to be forced to guess the number of runs needed to get N distinct trees.

References

1. Björklund, J., Drewes, F., Zechner, N.: Efficient enumeration of weighted tree languages over the tropical semiring. J. Comput. Syst. Sci. (2017)
2. Fülöp, Z., Vogler, H.: Weighted tree automata and tree transducers. In: Droste, M., Kuich, W., Vogler, H. (eds.) Handbook of Weighted Automata. Monographs in Theoretical Computer Science. An EATCS Series. Springer, Heidelberg (2009). https://doi.org/10.1007/978-3-642-01492-5_9
3. Gécseg, F., Steinby, M.: Tree Automata. Akadémiai Kiadó (1984). https://arxiv.org/abs/1509.06233
4. Gécseg, F., Steinby, M.: Tree languages. In: Rozenberg, G., Salomaa, A. (eds.) Handbook of Formal Languages, vol. 3, Chap. 1, pp. 1–68. Springer, Heidelberg (1997). https://doi.org/10.1007/978-3-642-59126-6_1
5. Huang, L., Chiang, D.: Better k-best parsing. In: Proceedings of the Conference on Parsing Technology 2005, pp. 53–64. Association for Computational Linguistics (2005)
6. Knuth, D.E.: A generalization of Dijkstra's algorithm. Inf. Process. Lett. **6**, 1–5 (1977)
7. May, J., Knight, K.: Tiburon: a weighted tree automata toolkit. In: Ibarra, O.H., Yen, H.-C. (eds.) CIAA 2006. LNCS, vol. 4094, pp. 102–113. Springer, Heidelberg (2006). https://doi.org/10.1007/11812128_11
8. Mohri, M., Riley, M.: An efficient algorithm for the n-best-strings problem. In: Proceedings of the Conference on Spoken Language Processing (2002)

State Complexity of Overlap Assembly

Janusz A. Brzozowski[1], Lila Kari[1], Bai Li[1], and Marek Szykuła[2(✉)]

[1] David R. Cheriton School of Computer Science,
University of Waterloo, Waterloo, ON N2L 3G1, Canada
{brzozo,lila}@uwaterloo.ca, bai.li.2005@gmail.com
[2] Institute of Computer Science, University of Wrocław,
Joliot-Curie 15, 50-383 Wrocław, Poland
msz@cs.uni.wroc.pl

Abstract. The *state complexity* of a regular language L_m is the number m of states in a minimal deterministic finite automaton (DFA) accepting L_m. The state complexity of a regularity-preserving binary operation on regular languages is defined as the maximal state complexity of the result of the operation where the two operands range over all languages of state complexities $\leq m$ and $\leq n$, respectively. We find a tight upper bound on the state complexity of the binary operation *overlap assembly* on regular languages. This operation was introduced by Csuhaj-Varjú, Petre, and Vaszil to model the process of self-assembly of two linear DNA strands into a longer DNA strand, provided that their ends "overlap". We prove that the state complexity of the overlap assembly of languages L_m and L_n, where $m \geq 2$ and $n \geq 1$, is at most $2(m-1)3^{n-1} + 2^n$. Moreover, for $m \geq 2$ and $n \geq 3$ there exist languages L_m and L_n over an alphabet of size n whose overlap assembly meets the upper bound and this bound cannot be met with smaller alphabets.

Keywords: Overlap assembly · Regular language · State complexity
Tight upper bound

1 Introduction

The *state complexity* of a regular language is the number of states in a minimal deterministic finite automaton (DFA) accepting the language. The state complexity of a regularity-preserving binary operation on regular languages is the maximal state complexity of the result of the operation when the operands range over all languages of state complexities $\leq m$ and $\leq n$; it is a function of m and n. State complexity was introduced by Maslov [14] in 1970, but his short paper was relatively unknown for many years. A more complete study of state complexity was presented by Yu et al. [15] in 1994. Since the publication

This work was supported by the Natural Sciences and Engineering Research Council of Canada under grants No. OGP0000871 and R2824A01, and by the National Science Centre, Poland, under project number 2014/15/B/ST6/00615.

C. Câmpeanu (Ed.): CIAA 2018, LNCS 10977, pp. 109–120, 2018.
https://doi.org/10.1007/978-3-319-94812-6_10

of [15], many authors have written on this subject; for an extensive bibliography see the recent surveys [1,8]. In particular, the state complexities of the so-called basic operations, namely Boolean operations, concatenation, star and reversal in various subclasses of the class of regular languages have been studied [1].

We consider the state complexity of a biologically inspired binary word and language operation called *overlap assembly*. Formally, overlap assembly is a binary operation which, when applied to two input words xy and yz (where y is their nonempty *overlap*), produces the output xyz. As a formal language operation, overlap assembly was introduced by Csuhaj-Varjú et al. [4] under the name "self-assembly", and studied by Enaganti et al. [6,7]. A particular case of overlap assembly, called *chop operation*, where the overlap consists of a single letter, was studied in, e.g., [10]. Other similar operations have been studied in the literature, such as the *short concatenation* [3], which uses only the maximum-length (possibly empty) overlap y between operands, the Latin product of words [9] where the overlap consists of only one letter, and the operation $\bigotimes$ which imposes the restriction that the non-overlapping part xz is not empty [12]. Overlap assembly can also be considered as a particular case of semantic shuffle on trajectories with trajectory $0^*\sigma^+1^*$ [5] or as a generalization of the operation $\bigodot_N$ from [5] which imposes the length of the overlap to be $\geq N$.

In this paper we investigate the state complexity of overlap assembly as a binary operation on regular languages. Section 2 describes the biological motivation of overlap assembly. Section 3 introduces our notation, and describes an NFA that accepts the results of overlap assembly of two regular languages, given by their accepting DFAs. In Sect. 4 we prove that the state complexity of the overlap assembly of languages L_m and L_n, where $m \geq 2$ and $n \geq 1$, is at most $2(m-1)3^{n-1}+2^n$. Moreover, for $m \geq 2$ and $n \geq 3$ there exist languages L_m and L_n over an alphabet of size n whose overlap assembly meets the upper bound and, in addition, this bound cannot be met with smaller alphabets.

2   Overlap Assembly

The bio-operation of overlap assembly was intended to model the procedure whereby short DNA single strands can be concatenated (assembled) together into longer strands under the action of the enzyme DNA polymerase, provided they have ends that "overlap". Recall that DNA single strands are oriented words from the DNA alphabet $\Delta = \{A, C, G, T\}$, where one end of a strand is labeled by $5'$ and the other by $3'$, and two DNA single strands of opposite orientation, that are Watson-Crick (W/C) complementary, bind to each other to form a DNA double-strand. The W/C complementarity of DNA strands has been traditionally modeled [11,13] as an antimorphic involution $\theta \colon \Delta^* \longrightarrow \Delta^*$, that is, an involution on Δ (θ^2 is the identity on Δ) extended to an antimorphism on Δ^*, whereby $\theta(uv) = \theta(v)\theta(u)$ for all $u, v \in \Delta^*$. In this formalism, the W/C complement of a DNA strand $u \in \Delta^+$ is $\theta(u)$.

Using the convention that a word x over the DNA alphabet represents the DNA single strand x in the $5'$ to $3'$ direction (usually depicted as the top strand of a double DNA strand), the *overlap assembly* of a strand uv with a strand $\theta(w)\theta(v)$ is illustrated in Fig. 1.

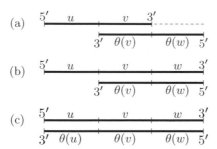

Fig. 1. (a) The two input DNA single-strands, uv and $\theta(w)\theta(v)$ bind to each other through their complementary segments v and $\theta(v)$, forming a partially double-stranded DNA complex. (b) DNA polymerase extends the $3'$ end of the strand uv. (c) DNA polymerase extends the $3'$ end of the other strand. The resulting DNA double strand is considered to be the output of the *overlap assembly* of the two input single strands.

Assuming that all involved DNA strands are initially double-stranded, that is, whenever the strand x is available, its W/C complement $\theta(x)$ is also available, this model was further simplified [4] as follows: Given words x, y over an alphabet Σ, the *overlap assembly of x with y* is defined as:

$$x \odot y = \{z \in \Sigma^+ \mid \exists u, w \in \Sigma^*, \exists v \in \Sigma^+ : x = uv, y = vw, z = uvw\}.$$

This can be naturally generalized to languages: Given languages L_m and L_n of state complexities m and n, respectively, the overlap assembly of L_m and L_n is defined as: $L_m \odot L_n = \{z \mid z = x \odot y, x \in L_m, y \in L_n\}$.

3   An ε-NFA for Overlap Assembly

A *deterministic finite automaton (DFA)* is a quintuple $\mathcal{D} = (Q, \Sigma, \delta, q_0, F)$, where Q is a finite non-empty set of *states*, Σ is a finite non-empty *alphabet*, $\delta: Q \times \Sigma \to Q$ is the *transition function*, $q_0 \in Q$ is the *initial* state, and $F \subseteq Q$ is the set of *final* states. We extend δ to functions $\delta: Q \times \Sigma^* \to Q$ and $\delta: 2^Q \times \Sigma^* \to 2^Q$ as usual. A DFA $\mathcal{D}$ *accepts* a word $w \in \Sigma^*$ if $\delta(q_0, w) \in F$. The language accepted by $\mathcal{D}$ is denoted by $L(\mathcal{D})$. If q is a state of $\mathcal{D}$, then the language $L_q(\mathcal{D})$ of q is the language accepted by the DFA $(Q, \Sigma, \delta, q, F)$. A state is *empty* (or *dead* or a *sink state*) if its language is empty. Two states p and q of $\mathcal{D}$ are *equivalent* if $L_p(\mathcal{D}) = L_q(\mathcal{D})$. A state q is *reachable* if there exists $w \in \Sigma^*$ such that $\delta(q_0, w) = q$. A DFA $\mathcal{D}$ is *minimal* if it has the smallest number of states and the smallest alphabet among all DFAs accepting $L(\mathcal{D})$. It is well known that a DFA is minimal if it uses the smallest alphabet, all of its states are reachable, and no two states are equivalent.

A *nondeterministic finite automaton (NFA)* is a quintuple $\mathcal{N} = (R, \Sigma, \eta, I, F)$, where R, Σ, and F are as Q, Σ, and F in a DFA respectively, $\eta: R \times \Sigma \to 2^R$, and $I \subseteq R$ is the *set of initial states*. Each triple (p, a, q) with $p, q \in R$, $a \in \Sigma$ is a *transition* if $q \in \eta(p, a)$. A sequence $((p_0, a_0, q_0), (p_1, a_1, q_1), \ldots, (p_{k-1}, a_{k-1}, q_{k-1}))$ of transitions, where $p_{i+1} = q_i$ for $i = 0, \ldots, k - 2$ is a *path* in $\mathcal{N}$. The word $a_0 a_1 \cdots a_{k-1}$ is the word *spelled* by the path. A word w is *accepted* by $\mathcal{N}$ if there exists a path with $p_0 \in I$ and $q_{k-1} \in F$ that spells w. If $q \in \eta(p, a)$ we also use the notation $p \xrightarrow{a} q$. We extend this notation also to words, and write $p \xrightarrow{w} q$ for $w \in \Sigma^*$. An *ε-NFA* is an NFA in which transitions under the empty word ε are also permitted.

Given any two DFAs, we construct an ε-NFA that recognizes the overlap assembly of the languages accepted by the DFAs. This proves constructively that the family of regular languages is closed under overlap assembly.

Let $\mathcal{D}_m = (Q_m, \Sigma, \delta_m, 0, F)$ and $\mathcal{D}'_n = (Q'_n, \Sigma, \delta'_n, 0', F')$ be two DFAs with $\mathcal{D}_m$ recognizing L_m and $\mathcal{D}'_n$ recognizing L'_n, where $F = \{f_1, \ldots, f_h\}$ and $F' = \{f'_1, \ldots, f'_{h'}\}$. Let $Q_m = \{0, \ldots, m - 1\}$, $Q'_n = \{0', \ldots, (n - 1)'\}$ and let 0 and $0'$ be the initial states. We claim that the NFA $\mathcal{N}$, constructed as shown below, accepts the result of the overlap assembly of L_m and L'_n.

The NFA is defined as $\mathcal{N} = (R, \Sigma, \eta, \{r_0\}, F_\mathcal{N})$ where the set of states is $R = (Q_m \cup \{t\}) \times (Q'_n \cup \{s'\})$ with s', t new symbols not occurring in $Q_m \cup Q'_n$, the initial state is $r_0 = (0, s')$, and the set of final states is $F_\mathcal{N} = \{(t, q') \mid q' \in F'\}$. Intuitively, the NFA simulates reading the word first by $\mathcal{D}_m$, then by both $\mathcal{D}_m$ and $\mathcal{D}'_n$, and then by $\mathcal{D}'_n$. Hence the states in R contain a state of $\mathcal{D}_m$ and a state of $\mathcal{D}'_n$. The states with s' indicate that $\mathcal{D}'_n$ has not yet read any letter, while the states with t indicate that $\mathcal{D}_m$ has finished the reading. The set of transitions η is defined below. The informal explanations at the right of transition definitions assume two operands $uv \in L_m$ and $vw \in L'_n$ respectively. The word $z = uvw$ belongs to their overlap assembly.

i $\{(q_i, s') \xrightarrow{a} (q_j, s') \mid q_i \xrightarrow{a} q_j \in \delta_m\}$; read u.

ii $\{(q_i, s') \xrightarrow{a} (q_j, q'_k) \mid q_i \xrightarrow{a} q_j \in \delta_m, \ 0' \xrightarrow{a} q'_k \in \delta'_n\}$; read the first letter of v.

iii $\{(q_i, q'_k) \xrightarrow{a} (q_j, q'_\ell) \mid q_i \xrightarrow{a} q_j \in \delta_m, \ q'_k \xrightarrow{a} q'_\ell \in \delta'_n\}$; read the remainder of v.

iv $\{(f_i, q'_k) \xrightarrow{\varepsilon} (t, q'_k) \mid f_i \in F, \ q'_k \in Q'_n\}$; v has been read.

v $\{(t, q'_k) \xrightarrow{a} (t, q'_\ell) \mid q'_k \xrightarrow{a} q'_\ell \in \delta'_n\}$; these rules read w.

Figure 2 shows the construction of an NFA, denoted by $\mathcal{N}'$, for two particular two-state DFAs $\mathcal{D}_2$ and $\mathcal{D}'_2$ accepting the languages $L(\mathcal{D}_2)$ (all words over $\{a, b\}^*$ that have an odd number of as) and $L(\mathcal{D}'_2)$ (all words over $\{a, b\}^*$ that end in the letter a). Note that the overlap assembly of $L(\mathcal{D}_2)$ and $L(\mathcal{D}'_2)$ is $L(\mathcal{D}'_2)$.

In the automaton $\mathcal{N}'$ of Fig. 2, states $(0, s')$ and $(1, s')$ in the first row of the figure behave as specified in Rule (i), using the transitions of $\mathcal{D}_2$. Rule (ii) moves the states from the first row to the second row of the figure. In the second row the transitions are those of the direct product of $\mathcal{D}_2$ and $\mathcal{D}'_2$, as directed by Rule (iii). Note that neither Rule (i) nor Rule (ii) can be used again since s' does not appear as a component of any state after Rule (iii) is used. When $\mathcal{N}'$ is in a state where the first component is 1, which is a final state of $\mathcal{D}_2$, $\mathcal{N}'$ can

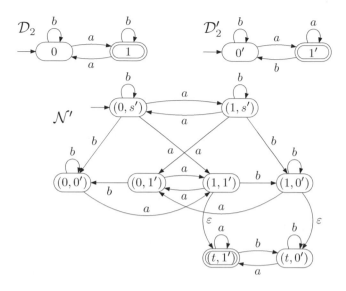

Fig. 2. An example of an NFA $\mathcal{N}'$ that accepts the overlap assembly of the languages accepted by the DFAs $\mathcal{D}_2$ and $\mathcal{D}'_2$.

move to the next row following Rule (iv), and change the first component of the state to t. Note that Rule (iii) cannot be used again since t appears as the first component of every state after Rule (iv) is used. Finally, $\mathcal{N}'$ moves to the third row and follows the transitions of $\mathcal{D}'_2$. Note that Rule (iv) cannot be used again because of t. While the NFA $\mathcal{N}'$ has eight states, converting it to a DFA and minimizing this DFA results in D'_2. The NFA $\mathcal{N}'$ accepts the overlap assembly of $L(D_2)$ and $L(D'_2)$. In general, the following result holds:

Proposition 1. *Let L_m and L'_n be two regular languages accepted by the DFAs defined above, and let the NFA $\mathcal{N}$ be the automaton constructed as above. NFA $\mathcal{N}$ has the following properties:*

1. *If $uv \in L_m$ and $vw \in L'_n$, then $r_0 \xrightarrow{uvw} r_f$ in $\mathcal{N}$ where $r_f \in F_{\mathcal{N}}$.*
2. *If $r_0 \xrightarrow{z} r_f$ in $\mathcal{N}$, then there exist $u, w \in \Sigma^*$, $v \in \Sigma^+$ such that $z = uvw$, where $uv \in L_m$ and $vw \in L'_n$.*
3. *$\mathcal{N}$ accepts $L_m \odot L'_n$.*

Proof. 1. For the first claim, let $v = ax$, where $a \in \Sigma$. If $uv \in L_m$ then $0 \xrightarrow{uax} f_i$, for some $f_i \in F$ in $\mathcal{D}_m$. So there exist q_i and q_j in Q_m such that $0 \xrightarrow{u} q_i \xrightarrow{a} q_j \xrightarrow{x} f_i$ in $\mathcal{D}_m$. Similarly, if $vw \in L_n$, then there exist q'_k and q'_ℓ in Q'_n such that $0' \xrightarrow{a} q'_k \xrightarrow{x} q'_\ell \xrightarrow{w} f'_j$, for some $f'_j \in F'$ in $\mathcal{D}'_n$.

By construction we have in $\mathcal{N}$:

$$(0, s') \underset{(i)}{\xrightarrow{u}} (q_i, s') \underset{(ii)}{\xrightarrow{a}} (q_j, q'_k) \underset{(iii)}{\xrightarrow{x}} (f_i, q'_\ell) \underset{(iv)}{\xrightarrow{\varepsilon}} (t, q'_\ell) \underset{(v)}{\xrightarrow{w}} (t, f'_j),$$

which proves our first claim.

2. Suppose that $r_0 \xrightarrow{z} r_f$ in $\mathcal{N}$, where $r_f \in F_{\mathcal{N}}$. By the construction of $\mathcal{N}$, such a path must proceed by i applications of rule (i), one application of rule (ii), j applications of rule (iii), one ε-transition via rule (iv), and k applications of rule (v), where $i, j, k \geq 0$. Thus there exist u, v, and w in Σ^* such that $z = uvw$, $|u| = i$, $|v| = j + 1$, and $|w| = k$. Owing to the construction of $\mathcal{N}$, there must exist derivations $0 \xrightarrow{uv} f_i$ in $\mathcal{D}_m$ and $0' \xrightarrow{vw} f'_j$ in $\mathcal{D}'_n$, which means $uv \in L_m$ and $vw \in L'_n$.

3. If $x \in L_m$ and $y \in L'_n$, then by (1), for every u, v, w where $x = uv$ and $y = vw$, uvw is recognized by $\mathcal{N}$; so $L_m \odot L_n \subseteq L(\mathcal{N})$. Conversely, if a word z is recognized by $\mathcal{N}$, then by (2), $z = uvw$ for some u, v, w where $uv \in L_m$ and $vw \in L_n$; so $L(\mathcal{N}) \subseteq L_m \odot L_n$. Hence $L(\mathcal{N}) = L_m \odot L_n$. □

4   Tight Upper Bound for Overlap Assembly

To establish the state complexity of overlap assembly we need to determinize the ε-NFA $\mathcal{N} = (R, \Sigma, \eta, r_0, F_{\mathcal{N}})$ defined in Sect. 3, and then minimize the resulting DFA. The first step is to find an upper bound on the number of subsets S of the set R of states of $\mathcal{N}$. We begin by characterizing the reachable subsets of R. They will all have the form

$$S = \{(q, s')\} \cup (\{q\} \times S') \cup (\{t\} \times T'), \tag{1}$$

where $q \in Q_m$, $T' \subseteq S' \subseteq Q'_n$ if $q \notin F$, $T' = S' \subseteq Q'_n$ if $q \in F$, and S' is non-empty unless $S = \{(0, s')\}$. We call q the *selector* of S, subset $S' \setminus \{0'\}$ is its *core*, and subset T' is its *subcore*.

We illustrate this using the NFA of Fig. 2. The initial subset is $\{(0, s')\}$; this has form (1) with $S' = T' = \emptyset$. From this initial subset we reach by b the subset $\{(0, s'), (0, 0')\} = \{0, s'\} \cup (\{0\} \times \{0'\})$; here $T' = \emptyset$ and $S' = \{0'\}$. By a we reach $\{(1, s')\} \cup \{(1, 1')\} \cup \{(t, 1')\} = \{(1, s')\} \cup (\{1\} \times \{1'\}) \cup (\{t\} \times \{1'\})$; here $S' = T' = \{1'\}$.

We now proceed to prove the claim about form (1).

Lemma 1. *Let $m \geq 2$, $n \geq 1$, and let $\mathcal{D}$ be the DFA obtained by determinization of the NFA for the overlap assembly $L_m \odot L_n$. Every reachable subset of $\mathcal{D}$ is of the form (1). Moreover, if $q \notin F$, then S cannot be distinguished from $S \cup \{(q, 0')\}$.*

Proof. First we show that every reachable subset $S \subseteq R$ is of the desired form. We will prove this claim by induction. The initial subset $\{(0, s')\}$ has this form. Suppose that S has this form, consider a letter $a \in \Sigma$, and the subset $U = \eta(S, a)$. Observe that $(\delta_m(q, a), s')$ is the only pair in U containing s', because of the transitions (i) and because $\mathcal{D}_m$ is deterministic. Also, every state (q, p'), where $p' \in Q'_n \cup \{s'\}$, is mapped to a state $(\delta_m(q, a), r') \in \{\delta_m(q, a)\} \times Q'_n$ by the transitions (ii) and (iii). Finally, the states in $\{t\} \times T'$ are mapped only to states from $\{t\} \times Q'_n$ by the transitions (iv) and (v).

Note that subsets S with $S' = \emptyset$ are not reachable, unless S is the initial subset $\{(0, s')\}$.

We show that if $S = \{(q, s')\} \cup (\{q\} \times S') \cup (\{t\} \times T')$ is reachable, then $T' \subseteq S'$. Let $r' \in T'$. Then there exists a word xy such that:

$$(0, s) \xrightarrow{x} (q_1, p') \xrightarrow{\varepsilon} (t, p') \xrightarrow{y} (t, r'),$$

where $q_1 \in F$. We also have: $(q_1, p') \xrightarrow{y} (q_2, r')$. Thus $(q_2, r') \in S$, and so $r' \in S'$.

We observe that if $q \in F$, then by ε-transitions (transitions (iv)), every state $(q, r') \in S$ is mapped to (t, r'), thus $T' = S'$, which concludes the characterization of reachable subsets.

Finally, we show that if $q \notin F$, then S cannot be distinguished from $S \cup \{(q, 0')\}$. Indeed, let $a \in \Sigma$ be any letter. Then $\eta((q, 0'), a) = \eta((q, s'), a)$ because the transitions (iii) and (ii) coincide. Since $(q, s') \in S$, we have $\eta(S, a) = \eta(S \cup \{(q, 0')\}, a)$. □

From Lemma 1 two reachable subsets with a different selector, or a different core, or a different subcore are potentially distinguishable. If two reachable subsets have the same selector, core, and subcore, then they can differ only by state $(q, 0')$ if the selector q is not in F; thus they cannot be distinguished. If two reachable subsets have the same selector q that is in F, then they cannot differ just by $(q, 0')$, as by ϵ-transitions from $(q, 0')$ we immediately obtain $(t, 0')$.

Theorem 1. *For $m \geq 2$ and $n \geq 1$, the state complexity of $L_m \odot L_n$ is at most*

$$2(m - 1)3^{n-1} + 2^n.$$

Proof. Using Lemma 1, we count the number of potentially reachable and distinguishable subsets $S = \{(q, s')\} \cup (\{q\} \times S') \cup (\{t\} \times T')$.

Reachable Subsets: For every state $q \in Q_m$, we count the number of potentially reachable subsets with selector q. There are 2 cases:

- If q is non-final, we can choose any non-empty set $S' \subseteq Q'_n$ of cardinality k and any subset T' of S'. The number of ways of doing this is $\sum_{k=1}^{n} \binom{n}{k} 2^k$.
- If q is final, again we choose any non-empty set S', but now $T' = S'$ is fixed. The number of ways of doing this is $2^n - 1$.

There is also the initial subset $\{(0, s')\}$ which contributes 1 to the sum. In total, this yields:

$$(m - |F|) \cdot \left(\sum_{k=1}^{n} \binom{n}{k} 2^k \right) + |F| \cdot (2^n - 1) + 1.$$

Distinguishable Subsets: The above formula gives the number of potentially reachable subsets, but overestimates the state complexity because not all subsets are distinguishable. Recall that by Lemma 1 if the selector q is not in F, then S cannot be distinguished from $S \cup \{(q, 0')\}$. Thus we do not need to count subsets S without $0'$, as $S \cup \{(q, 0')\}$ is potentially reachable and always equivalent to S. Hence, for a given $q \in Q_m \setminus F$ we choose S' to be any subset of Q'_n that contains $0'$, and again let T' be any subset of S'. This can be done in $\sum_{k=1}^{n} \binom{n-1}{k-1} 2^k$ ways.

Thus the total number of potentially reachable and distinguishable subsets is at most

$$(m - |F|) \cdot \left(\sum_{k=1}^{n} \binom{n-1}{k-1} 2^k \right) + |F| \cdot (2^n - 1) + 1.$$

By algebra, we have $\sum_{k=1}^{n} \binom{n-1}{k-1} 2^k = 2 \cdot 3^{n-1}$, which is greater than $2^n - 1$; so this formula is maximized when $|F| = 1$, and we conclude that the maximum state complexity of overlap assembly is $2(m-1)3^{n-1} + 2^n$.   □

Theorem 2. *At least n letters are required to meet the bound from Theorem 1.*

Proof. Let $q \in F$ be a final state of $\mathcal{D}_m$. For each $p' \in Q'_n$ we consider the subset $T_{p'} = \{(q, s'), (q, p'), (t, p')\}$. If the upper bound is met, then, in particular, all subsets S with $q \in F$ must be reachable in view of Lemma 1. These subsets were counted in the upper bound, and there are no other subsets of reachable form that could be equivalent to them when the upper bound is met. Hence, in particular all subsets $T_{p'}$ must be reachable.

Suppose that $T_{p'}$ is reachable by a word $w_{p'}a_{p'}$, for some letter $a_{p'}$. Note that (q, p') is the only one of the three states in $T_{p'}$ that can be reached by transitions (ii) of the NFA. Consider $\eta(r_0, w_{p'})$; it must contain (r, s') for some $r \in Q_m$, because by Lemma 1 every reachable subset has exactly one such pair. Thus, (r, s') must be mapped by transitions (ii) induced by $a_{p'}$ to (q, p'). Therefore, $\delta'_n(0', a_{p'}) = p'$, which proves that $a_{p'}$ are different for every p'.   □

We define the witness DFAs for $m, n \geq 2$. Let $\Sigma = \{a_0, \ldots, a_{n-1}\}$.

Let $\mathcal{W}_m = (Q_m, \Sigma, \delta_m, 0, F)$ be defined as follows: $F = \{0\}$; $a_i \colon \mathbf{1}_m$ for $i \in \{0, 2, \ldots, n-1\}$, where $\mathbf{1}_m$ is the identity transformation on Q_m; $a_1 \colon (0, 1, \ldots, m-1)$ is a cyclic permutation of Q_m.

Let $\mathcal{W}'_n = (Q'_n, \Sigma, \delta'_n, 0', F')$ be defined as follows: $F = \{(n-1)'\}$; $a_0 \colon (Q'_n \to 0')$ maps all the states of Q'_n to $0'$; $a_i \colon (1', 2', 3', \ldots, (i-1)', 0', i', \ldots, (n-1)')$ for $i \in \{1, \ldots, n-1\}$. Here a_i permutes the states of Q'_n, mapping $1'$ to $2'$, $2'$ to $3'$, etc., then $(i-1)'$ to $0'$, $0'$ to i', and then i' to $(i+1)'$, etc., and $(n-1)'$ to $1'$.

The transitions of these DFAs with $m = 3$ and $n = 4$ states are illustrated in Fig. 3. Let L_m and L'_n be the languages of $\mathcal{W}_m$ and $\mathcal{W}'_n$, respectively.

By a *cyclic shift* of a core subset $S' \subseteq \{1', \ldots, (n-1)'\}$ we understand any subset obtained by shifting the states along the cycle $(1', \ldots, (n-1)')$, i positions clockwise, i.e., the subset $\{(((p - 1 + i) \bmod (n-1)) + 1)' \mid p' \in S'\}$ for any $i \geq 0$. The *next* and *previous* cyclic shifts correspond to $i = 1$ and $i = n-2$, respectively.

The transitions of letters $a_1, a_2, \ldots, a_{n-1}$ produce next cyclic shifts of the states in $\{1', \ldots, (n-1)'\}$, with the exception that state $0'$ replaces one of the states in the cycle. The idea behind the witness is that we can add an arbitrary state to the core using these letters and produce arbitrary cyclic shifts as well, as will be shown later. Letter a_0 plays an important role of reset, which is necessary to reach small subsets. The main difficulty is that a_1 shares both roles of producing cyclic shifts and switching the selector.

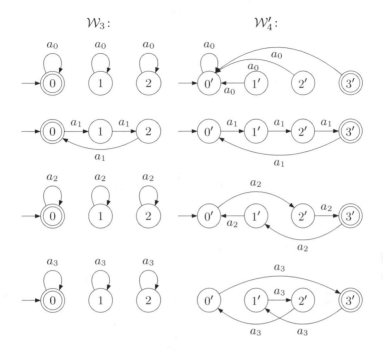

Fig. 3. The action of the letters in $\mathcal{W}_3$ and $\mathcal{W}'_4$.

Theorem 3. *For $m \geq 2$ and $n \geq 3$, $L_m \odot L'_n$ meets the upper bound.*

Proof. Reachability: It is enough to show that all subsets S from Lemma 1 are reachable, with the exception that if $q \notin F$ then it suffices to show reachability of either $S \setminus \{(q, 0')\}$ or $S \cup \{(q, 0')\}$.

• First we show that for all subsets $S = \{(q, s')\} \cup (\{q\} \times S')$, where $q \in Q_m \setminus \{0\}$ and $\emptyset \neq S' \subseteq Q'_n \setminus \{0'\}$, either $S \setminus \{(q, 0')\}$ or $S \cup \{(q, 0')\}$ is reachable. These subsets have core S' and an empty subcore.

We prove this by induction on the size $|S'|$ of the core. For $|S'| = 0$, apply $a_1^q a_0$ to $(0, s')$; this yields $\{(q, s'), (q, 0')\}$.

Consider $|S'| = 1$. If $q = 1$, then we just use a_1, which yields $\{(1, s'), (1, 1')\}$. To meet the other subsets $\{(1, s'), (1, p')\}$ for $p \geq 2$, from $\{(1, s'), (1, 1')\}$ we use $a_0 a_p$. For $q \geq 2$, we use $a_1^{q-1} a_0 a_1$, which yields $\{(q, s'), (q, 1')\}$. Then to meet the other subsets $\{(q, s'), (q, p')\}$ for $p \geq 2$, from $\{(q, s'), (q, 1')\}$ we also use $a_0 a_p$.

Consider $|S'| \geq 2$ and assume the induction hypothesis for subsets S with a smaller core. Since S' contains at least two states different from $0'$, there is a state $p' \in S' \setminus \{1'\}$. Let X' be the previous cyclic shift of $S' \setminus \{p'\}$. Since $p' \notin S' \setminus \{p'\}$, X' does not contain $(p-1)'$, but this is its only difference from the previous cyclic shift of S'. By the inductive assumption, $\{(q, s')\} \cup (\{q\} \times X')$ is reachable. We apply a_p to this subset, which maps X' to its next cyclic shift, and also (q, s') to (q, p'), which yields $\{(q, s'\} \cup (\{q\} \times S')$.

• Now we show reachability of subsets $S = \{(0, s')\} \cup (\{0\} \times S') \cup (\{t\} \times S')$, where $\emptyset \neq S' \subseteq Q'_n$. These are all potentially reachable subsets with selector 0.

First consider the case $0' \notin S'$. For $\{(m-1, s'), (m-1, 1')\}$ we apply $a_0 a_1$, which yields $\{(0, s'), (0, 1'), (t, 1')\}$. Then we continue the induction on $|S'|$ as before when $|S'| \geq 2$, with just $\{t\} \times S'$ added to the subsets.

Now consider the case $0' \in S'$. The case $S' = \{0'\}$ is easily covered by applying a_0 to $\{(0, s'), (0, 1'), (t, 1')\}$. If $S' = \{0', 1'\}$, then from $\{(m-1, s'), (m-1, (n-1)')\}$ we apply a_1 and get $\{(0, s'), (0, 0'), (0, 1'), (t, 0'), (t, 1')\}$ as desired. Let $S' \neq \{0', 1'\}$. We already know that $\{(0, s')\} \cup (\{0, t\} \times X')$ is reachable, where X' is the previous cyclic shift of $S' \setminus \{0'\}$. Since $|S'| \geq 2$ and $S' \neq \{0', 1'\}$, there is a $p' \in S' \setminus \{1'\}$. We apply a_p to $\{(0, s')\} \cup (\{0, t\} \times X')$. We have $X' \setminus \{(p-1)'\}$ mapped to $S' \setminus \{p'\}$ and $(p-1)'$ mapped to $0'$, which gives $(\{0\} \times (S' \cup \{0'\} \setminus \{p'\})$ by transitions (iii), and $(0, p')$ is added by transitions (ii). Thus, after completing by ε-transitions this yields $\{(0, s')\} \cup (\{0, t\} \times S')$.

• Finally, we show that for all subsets $S = \{(q, s')\} \cup (\{q\} \times S') \cup (\{t\} \times T')$, where $q \neq 0$ and $\emptyset \neq T' \subseteq S' \subseteq Q'_n$, either $S \setminus \{(q, 0')\}$ or $S \cup \{(q, 0')\}$ is reachable.

Consider the special case $S' = T' = \{0'\}$. We reach it from $\{(0, s'), (0, 0'), (t, 0')\}$ by applying $a_1^q a_0$. For the rest, assume that $S' \setminus \{0'\}$ is non-empty.

We need an auxiliary argument that from $\{(0, s')\}$ we can reach a subset with selector q, core S', and an empty subcore, using a word from $\{a_1, a_2, \ldots, a_{n-1}\}^*$ (any word without a_0). We prove this by induction on the core size $|S' \setminus \{0'\}|$. For $|S' \setminus \{0'\}| = 1$, at the beginning we use a_1, which yields $\{(1, s'), (1, 1')\}$. Now we can reach $\{(1, s'), (1, 0'), (1, p')\}$ for any $p' \in \{2', \ldots, (n-1)'\}$ by using $a_2 a_3 \ldots a_p$. Then, from $\{(1, s'), (1, 0'), (1, (n-1)')\}$ we reach $\{(2, s'), (2, 0'), (2, 1')\}$, and it remains to repeat the argument to reach every remaining subset of the form $\{(q, s'), (q, 0'), (q, p')\}$ for $q \in Q_m \setminus \{0, 1\}$ and $p' \in Q'_n \setminus \{0'\}$. For $|S' \setminus \{0'\}| \geq 2$ we follow the first part of the reachability argument as before, but we reach either $\{(q, s')\} \cup (\{q\} \times (S' \setminus \{0'\})$ or $\{(q, s')\} \cup (\{q\} \times (S' \cup \{0'\}))$, instead of just the former. Let $w \in \{a_1, a_2, \ldots, a_{n-1}\}^*$ be a word that reaches either $\{(q, s')\} \cup (\{q\} \times (S' \setminus \{0'\})$ or $\{(q, s')\} \cup (\{q\} \times (S' \cup \{0'\}))$.

Suppose that we start from the subset $S_0 = \{(0, s')\} \cup (\{0, t\} \times T'_0)$, where T'_0 is some subset such that $\emptyset \neq T'_0 \subseteq Q'_n$. We already know that for every T'_0, subset S_0 is reachable. After applying $a_1 w$, we reach either

$$S_q = \{(q, s')\} \cup (\{q\} \times (S' \cup T'_q \setminus \{0'\})) \cup (\{t\} \times T'_q),$$

or $S_q \cup \{(q, 0')\}$, where T'_q is obtained by applying some permutation π of Q'_n to T'_0. This is because $\{(0, s')\}$ is mapped by $a_1 w$ to $\{(q, s')\} \cup (\{q\} \times (S' \setminus \{0'\})$ or $\{(q, s')\} \cup (\{q\} \times (S' \cup \{0'\}))$, word $a_1 w$ acts as a permutation on $(\{t\} \times Q'_q)$, and $\{0\} \times T'_0$ is mapped to $(\{q\} \times T'_q)$. Note that $a_1 w$ does not depend on T'_0, so we can choose T'_0 arbitrarily. Let $T'_0 = \pi^{-1}(T')$, so $\pi(T'_0) = T'$. We obtain either

$$S_q = \{(q, s')\} \cup (\{q\} \times ((S' \setminus \{0'\}) \cup T')) \cup (\{t\} \times T'),$$

$$\text{or } S_q = \{(q, s')\} \cup (\{q\} \times ((S' \cup \{0'\}) \cup T')) \cup (\{t\} \times T').$$

Recall that $T' \subseteq S'$ and if $0' \in T$ then also $0' \in S'$; hence $(S' \setminus \{0'\}) \cup T'$ is either S' or $S' \setminus \{0'\}$, and $(S' \cup \{0'\}) \cup T' = S' \cup \{0'\}$. Thus, S_q is either $S \setminus \{(q, 0')\}$ or $S \cup \{(q, 0')\}$.

Distinguishability: Consider two reachable subsets

$$S_1 = \{(q_1, s')\} \cup (\{q_1\} \times S_1') \cup (\{t\} \times T_1'),$$

$$\text{and } S_2 = \{(q_2, s')\} \cup (\{q_2\} \times S_2') \cup (\{t\} \times T_2'),$$

with different selectors, different cores, or different subcores. Thus we have $q_1 \neq q_2$, or $T_1' \neq T_2'$, or $(S_1' \setminus \{(q_1, 0')\}) \neq (S_2' \setminus \{(q_2, 0')\})$. These are precisely all the reachable and potentially distinguishable subsets in view of Lemma 1. Note that the initial subset also has this form, where $q_1 = 0$ and S_1' and T_1' are empty.

If $q_1 \neq q_2$, then without loss of generality let $q_1 < q_2$. We apply $a_1^{m-q_2} a_0 a_{n-1}^2$. For S_1, first $a_1^{m-q_2} a_0$ maps it to a subset $\{(q, s'), (0, s')\}$ or $\{(q, s'), (q, 0'), (t, 0')\}$ (if T_1' is non-empty) for some $q \neq 0$. Then a_{n-1}^2 results in a subset that from the states from $(\{t\} \times Q_n')$ contains at most $(t, 1')$, which is not final. On the other hand, S_2 by $a_1^{m-q_2} a_0$ is mapped to $\{(0, s'), (0, 0'), (t, 0')\}$. Then $a_{n_1}^2$ yields $\{(0, s'), (0, 0'), (t, 1'), (t, (n-1)')\}$, where $(t, (n-1)')$ is final.

So suppose that $q_1 = q_2$. If $q_1 \neq 0$ and $T_1' \neq T_2'$, then we apply a_{n-1}^i for a suitable $i \geq 0$. Since a_{n-1} acts cyclically on all states $(\{t\} \times Q_n')$ and no other states from the subsets are mapped to $(\{t\} \times Q_n')$, we can repeat the cycle so that exactly one of $\eta(\{t\} \times T_1', a_{n-1}^i)$ and $\eta(\{t\} \times T_2', a_{n-1}^i)$ contains the final state $(t, (n-1)')$. If $q_1 = 0$ and $T_1' \neq T_2'$, then also $S_1' \neq S_2'$, so it remains to cover this case.

Suppose that $S_1' \neq S_2'$. If $q_1 = q_2 = 0$, then also $T_1' \neq T_2'$. We apply a_1, which maps S_1 to the subset $\{(1, s')\} \cup (\{1\} \times (\delta_m(S_1', a_1) \cup \{2'\})) \cup (\{t\} \times \delta_n'(T_1', a_1))$, and analogously S_2. Since $T_1' \neq T_2'$ and a_1 acts cyclically on Q_n', we have $\delta_n'(T_1', a_1) \neq \delta_n'(T_2', a_1)$. The case of these subsets has been covered in the previous paragraph.

There remains the case where $T_1' = T_2'$, $S_1' \neq S_2'$, $q_1 = q_2 \neq 0$. We follow the induction on the selector q_1 starting with $q_1 = m - 1$ and decreasing it. We will show for $q_1 = m - 1$ that we can reach subsets with selector 0 that still have different cores. We have already shown in the previous paragraph that the subsets with selector 0 and different cores can be distinguished. For $q_1 < m - 1$ we will show that we can reach subsets with the same property but with selector $q_1 + 1$, which will follow by the inductive assumption. So let p be the largest index such that, without loss of generality, $p' \in S_1'$ and $p' \notin S_2'$. Note that $p \neq 0$, because then the subsets cannot be distinguished. If $p < n - 1$, then we apply a_1, which yields subsets with the desired property. If $p = n - 1$, then we first apply a_2, which yields the subset with $p' = 1'$, and then we can apply a_1 as before. $\square$

5   Conclusions

We have found an upper bound of $2(m-1)3^{n-1} + 2^n$ on the state complexity of overlap assembly, a biologically inspired operation on regular languages, and we have shown that this bound is tight for languages over an alphabet of size n.

For completeness, we state without proof some results about the unary and binary languages. Proofs can be found in [2].

Theorem 4. *Let $m, n \geq 1$, and let L_m and L_n be two unary languages of state complexities m and n, respectively. The state complexity of $L_m \odot L_n$ is at most $m + n$, and this bound is met by $L_m = \{a^{mk+n-1} \mid k \in \mathbb{Z}, mk + n - 1 \geq 0\}$ and $L_n = \{a^{nk+m-1} \mid k \in \mathbb{Z}, nk + m - 1 \geq 0\}$.*

For binary languages we have found an exponential lower bound on the complexity of overlap assembly; the proof is based on ideas similar to those in the proof of Theorem 3.

Theorem 5. *For every $m \geq 2$ and $n \geq 3$, there exist binary DFAs $\mathcal{B}_m$ and $\mathcal{B}'_n$ such that the state complexity of $L(\mathcal{B}_m) \odot L(\mathcal{B}'_n)$ is at least $m(2^{n-1} - 2) + 2$.*

References

1. Brzozowski, J.A.: Towards a theory of complexity of regular languages. J. Autom. Lang. Comb. **23**(1–3), 67–101 (2018). http://arxiv.org/abs/1702.05024
2. Brzozowski, J.A., Kari, L., Li, B., Szykuła, M.: State Complexity of Overlap Assembly (2017). http://arxiv.org/abs/1710.06000
3. Carausu, A., Paun, G.: String intersection and short concatenation. Rev. Roumaine Math. Pures Appl. **26**, 713–726 (1981)
4. Csuhaj-Varjú, E., Petre, I., Vaszil, G.: Self-assembly of strings and languages. Theoret. Comput. Sci. **374**(1–3), 74–81 (2007)
5. Domaratzki, M.: Minimality in template-guided recombination. Inf. Comput. **207**(11), 1209–1220 (2009)
6. Enaganti, S.K., Ibarra, O.H., Kari, L., Kopecki, S.: On the overlap assembly of strings and languages. Nat. Comput. **16**(1), 175–185 (2016)
7. Enaganti, S.K., Ibarra, O.H., Kari, L., Kopecki, S.: Further remarks on DNA overlap assembly. Inform. Comput. **253**, 143–154 (2017)
8. Gao, Y., Moreira, N., Reis, R., Yu, S.: A survey on operational state complexity. J. Autom. Lang. Comb. **21**(4), 251–310 (2016)
9. Golan, J.S.: The Theory of Semirings with Applications in Mathematics and Theoretical Computer Science. Addison-Wesley Longman Ltd., Essex (1992)
10. Holzer, M., Jakobi, S., Kutrib, M.: The chop of languages. Theoret. Comput. Sci. **682**, 122–137 (2017)
11. Hussini, S., Kari, L., Konstantinidis, S.: Coding properties of DNA languages. In: Jonoska, N., Seeman, N.C. (eds.) DNA 2001. LNCS, vol. 2340, pp. 57–69. Springer, Heidelberg (2002). https://doi.org/10.1007/3-540-48017-X_6
12. Ito, M., Lischke, G.: Generalized periodicity and primitivity for words. Math. Logic Q. **53**(1), 91–106 (2007)
13. Kari, L., Kitto, R., Thierrin, G.: Codes, involutions, and DNA encodings. In: Brauer, W., Ehrig, H., Karhumäki, J., Salomaa, A. (eds.) Formal and Natural Computing. LNCS, vol. 2300, pp. 376–393. Springer, Heidelberg (2002). https://doi.org/10.1007/3-540-45711-9_21
14. Maslov, A.N.: Estimates of the number of states of finite automata. Dokl. Akad. Nauk SSSR **194**, 1266–1268 (1970). (in Russian) English translation: Soviet Math. Dokl. **11**, 1373–1375 (1970)
15. Yu, S., Zhuang, Q., Salomaa, K.: The state complexities of some basic operations on regular languages. Theoret. Comput. Sci. **125**, 315–328 (1994)

Online Stochastic Pattern Matching

Marco Cognetta and Yo-Sub Han$^{(\boxtimes)}$

Department of Computer Science, Yonsei University, Seoul, Republic of Korea
{mcognetta,emmous}@yonsei.ac.kr

Abstract. The pattern matching problem is to find all occurrences of a given pattern in an input text. In particular, we consider the case when the pattern is a stochastic regular language where each pattern string has its own probability. Our problem is to find all matching patterns— (start, end) indices in the text—whose probability is larger than a given threshold probability. A pattern matching procedure is frequently used on streaming data in several applications, and often it is very challenging to find the start index of a matching in streaming data. We design an efficient algorithm for the stochastic pattern matching problem over streaming data based on the transformation of the pattern PFA into a weighted automaton and a constant bound on the number of backtracks required to find a start index while reading the streaming input. We also employ heuristics that enable us to reduce the number of backtracks, which improves the practical runtime of our algorithm. We establish the tight theoretical runtime of the proposed algorithm and experimentally demonstrate its practical performance. Finally, we show a possible application of our algorithm to another stochastic pattern matching problem where we search for the maximum probability substring of a text that is a superstring of a specified string.

Keywords: Stochastic pattern matching · Probabilistic automata
Weighted automata · Online matching

1 Introduction

Given a text T and a pattern P, the basic pattern matching problem is to determine whether or not P appears in T [11]. There are several variants for the pattern matching problem; for example, if P is a finite set of strings, we have a keyword pattern matching problem [1]. If P is described by a regular expression, then the problem becomes the regular expression pattern matching problem [14]. There are also several types of problems depending on what we want to report; if we only look for an end index of a matching pattern in T, which is common in grep-like applications, then often the problem is easier compared with the case when we want to find the exact start and end indices of each matching pattern in T.

We consider the case when the pattern set is represented by a probabilistic finite automaton, in which each pattern has a weight and the pattern set

© Springer International Publishing AG, part of Springer Nature 2018
C. Câmpeanu (Ed.): CIAA 2018, LNCS 10977, pp. 121–132, 2018.
https://doi.org/10.1007/978-3-319-94812-6_11

forms a probability distribution. We search for all matching substrings of T that have probability greater than a given threshold and report their (start, end) indices. Additionally, since it is possible for the text to be very large, we consider this problem in a streaming setting in which we do not hold the entire text in memory throughout the computation. We call this problem *Online Stochastic Pattern Matching*.

Online stochastic pattern matching has several practical applications in fields such as natural language processing (NLP) and bioinformatics. Here is a possible example: suppose we have a PFA representing the distribution of RNA subsequences that encode some property we wish to study. In such a distribution, the probability of a subsequence corresponds to how likely it is that the property manifests if that subsequence is present.

Since minor perturbations in the primary structure of an RNA subsequence or the configuration of the neighboring regions of the subsequence often have no effect on its function, the number of subsequences with non-zero probability could be very large. However, we are only interested in subsequences with probability exceeding some minimum threshold for the manifestation of the property. In this setting, given a long RNA sequence to analyze for our property, we want to detect subsequences that are likely to express the property (which are distinguished by their high probability) without having to extract all high probability subsequences from the distribution. Such problems, where PFAs (generally in an equivalent form of a hidden Markov model [6]) are used to model biological settings, is an active area of research [2,18]. As illustrated in this example, the online stochastic pattern matching problem often involves a large input data stream and requires finding high probability substrings without explicitly extracting all of the high probability strings from the distribution ahead of time, which is infeasible due to the complexity of finding the most probable string in a distribution [9]. We describe an algorithm that efficiently, both in theory and in practice, solves such problems. Our algorithm makes use of a weighted automaton construction that can effectively filter out substrings with lower probability than a given threshold probability. We also employ several properties of stochastic languages that enable us to bound the maximum length of substrings needed to be checked independent from the length of T—this is crucial to design an online algorithm for the problem without storing the whole T.

Researchers have studied several problems related to high probability strings in a stochastic language extensively. For the related class of Rabin automata, it is undecidable to determine whether or not there exists a string with probability greater than some given threshold [3]. For general PFAs, it is NP-hard to determine the highest probability string in the distribution described by the PFA [4]. Recently, de la Higuera and Oncina [9,10] gave randomized and deterministic approaches for solving the consensus string problem. Parsing with weighted finite-state transducers is a common method in speech processing and recognition [12]. However, to the best of our knowledge, there is no prior research on detecting high probability strings from a distribution in streaming text.

2   Preliminaries

Let Σ be a finite alphabet and Σ^* be the set of all strings over Σ. The set of all strings of length k over Σ is written Σ^k. Given some string $w = w_1 w_2 \cdots w_n \in \Sigma^*$, we say that the length $|w|$ of w is n. The symbol λ denotes the null string. Given two strings w and x, wx denotes their concatenation. Then, $w\Sigma^*$ and $\Sigma^* w$ are the set of all strings in Σ^* containing w as a prefix and a suffix, respectively.

A semiring is a set $\mathbb{S}$ with two binary operations, $\oplus$ and $\otimes$, and two special elements, 0 and 1, where $(\mathbb{S}, \oplus)$ is a commutative monoid with identity 0 and $(\mathbb{S}, \otimes)$ is a monoid with identity 1. Additionally, $\otimes$ distributes over $\oplus$ and $\forall x \in \mathbb{S}$, $0 \otimes x = x \otimes 0 = 0$. Such a structure is denoted $(\mathbb{S}, \oplus, \otimes, 0, 1)$. We utilize the *probability semiring* or *real semiring* $(\mathbb{R}_{\geq 0}, +, \times, 0, 1)$ and the *Viterbi semiring* $([0,1], \max, \times, 0, 1)$.

2.1   Weighted Automata

Weighted automata are a generalization of finite automata that compute a function $\mathcal{W} : \Sigma^* \to \mathbb{S}$, where $\mathbb{S}$ is the set of elements of some semiring. For a given string $w \in \Sigma^*$, we call the value $\mathcal{W}(w)$ the *weight* of w.

Given a semiring $(\mathbb{S}, \oplus, \otimes, 0, 1)$, a weighted automaton $\mathcal{W}$ is specified by a tuple $(Q, \Sigma, \delta, I, F)$, where Q is a finite set of states, Σ is a finite alphabet, $\delta : Q \times \Sigma \times Q \to \mathbb{S}$ is the transition function, $I : Q \to \mathbb{S}$ is the initial weight function, and $F : Q \to \mathbb{S}$ is the final weight function. An alternative representation of a weighted automaton is in the form of transition matrices where $\mathcal{W} = (Q, \Sigma, \{\mathbb{M}(c)\}_{c \in \Sigma}, \mathbb{I}, \mathbb{F})$. $\{\mathbb{M}(c)\}_{c \in \Sigma}$ is a set of $|Q| \times |Q|$ transition matrices where $\mathbb{M}(c)_{i,j} = \delta(q_i, c, q_j)$. $\mathbb{I}$ and $\mathbb{F}$ are $1 \times |Q|$ and $|Q| \times 1$ vectors corresponding to the initial and final weights; that is, $\mathbb{I}_i = I(q_i)$ and $\mathbb{F}_j = F(q_j)$. For brevity, we denote $\mathbb{M}(\Sigma) = \sum_{c \in \Sigma} \mathbb{M}(c)$.

We now describe how to compute the weight of w in a weighted automaton $\mathcal{W}$. Consider a string $w = w_1 w_2 \cdots w_n$ and its corresponding labeled path $\pi = (q_0, w_1, q_1), (q_1, w_2, q_2), \ldots, (q_{n-1}, w_n, q_n)$. Let the set of all such labeled paths be Φ_w. The weight of a path occurring is given by

$$\mathcal{W}(\pi) = I(q_0) \otimes \left(\bigotimes_{i=1}^{n} \delta(q_{i-1}, w_i, q_i) \right) \otimes F(q_n).$$

Accordingly, the weight of w is $\mathcal{W}(w) = \bigoplus_{\pi \in \Phi_w} \mathcal{W}(\pi)$.

There exists two equivalent dynamic programming approaches—the forward and backward algorithms—for computing the weight of a string in $\mathcal{W}$. We can also use the matrix formulation of $\mathcal{W}$ to compute the weight by replacing regular matrix operations with the operations defined by the semiring and evaluating $\mathcal{W}(w) = \mathbb{I} \prod_{i=1}^{|w|} \mathbb{M}(w_i) \mathbb{F}$.

Using either the dynamic programming approach or the matrix approach, we can compute the weight of a word w in $O(|w||Q|^2)$ time. For an introduction to weighted automata, we direct the reader to Droste et al. [5].

2.2   Probabilistic Finite Automata

A probabilistic finite automaton (PFA) $\mathcal{P} = (Q, \Sigma, \{\mathrm{M}(c)\}_{c \in \Sigma}, \mathbb{I}, \mathbb{F})$ is a weighted automaton over the *probabilistic semiring* with some additional constraints— $\sum_{q \in Q} I(q) = 1$ and $\forall q \in Q,\ F(q) + \sum_{q' \in Q, c \in \Sigma} \delta(q, c, q') = 1$. Furthermore, we assume that all states reachable from an initial state (a state with non-zero initial weight) lie in some non-zero weight path. Then, $\mathcal{P}$ describes a probability distribution over Σ^*; in other words, $\forall w \in \Sigma^*,\ 0 \leq \mathcal{P}(w) \leq 1$ and $\sum_{w \in \Sigma^*} \mathcal{P}(w) = 1$. For PFAs, we use *probability* instead of *weight* to refer to the value $\mathcal{P}(w)$.

We consider only λ-free PFAs, as they are equivalent to regular PFAs in expressive power [5]. A PFA is deterministic (DPFA) if $\mathcal{P}$ has exactly one state with non-zero initial probability, and, for each state and character c, at most one out-transition labeled with c. While DPFAs are strictly weaker than general PFAs in expressive power, we can compute the probability of a string w in a DPFA in only $O(|w|)$ time.

Given a PFA $\mathcal{P}$, we can efficiently compute $\mathcal{P}(w\Sigma^*) = \sum_{x \in \Sigma^*} \mathcal{P}(wx)$ and $\mathcal{P}(\Sigma^* w) = \sum_{x \in \Sigma^*} \mathcal{P}(xw)$ which correspond to the probability of a word appearing as a prefix and as a suffix, respectively [7]. Let $\mathrm{M}(\Sigma^*) = \sum_{i=0}^{\infty} \mathrm{M}(\Sigma)^i = (\mathbb{1} - \mathrm{M}(\Sigma))^{-1}$ where $\mathbb{1}$ is the identity matrix (we use this notation when the dimension is clear). We now have

$$\mathcal{P}(w\Sigma^*) = \mathbb{I}(\prod_{i=1}^{|w|} \mathrm{M}(w_i))\mathrm{M}(\Sigma^*)\mathbb{F} \ \text{ and } \ \mathcal{P}(\Sigma^* w) = \mathbb{I}\mathrm{M}(\Sigma^*)(\prod_{i=1}^{|w|} \mathrm{M}(w_i))\mathbb{F}.$$

One natural question related to PFAs is that of calculating the maximum probability parse of a string w; namely, to compute $\arg \max_{\pi \in \Phi_w} \mathcal{P}(\pi)$. We can solve this by simply coercing the PFA from the probabilistic semiring into the Viterbi semiring and calculating $\mathcal{P}(w)$. For a more detailed survey of PFAs, see Vidal et al. [16,17].

A stochastic language over Σ is the set of strings from Σ^*, each of which has its own probability. That is, given $w \in \Sigma^*$, $0 \leq Pr(w) \leq 1$ is the probability of w and $\sum_{w \in \Sigma^*} Pr(w) = 1$. A regular stochastic language is a stochastic language that can be represented by a PFA—there exists a PFA $\mathcal{P}$ such that $\forall w \in \Sigma^*,\ \mathcal{P}(w) = Pr(w)$. A deterministic regular stochastic language is a stochastic language that can be represented by a DPFA.

We omit all proofs due to space constraints. Omitted proofs can be found in the appendix.

3   Online Stochastic Pattern Matching

The main problem is to identify all locations (start, end) of matching substrings in a large text that have high probability in some given distribution modeled by a PFA.

Online Stochastic Pattern Matching (OSPM): Given a streaming text T, a PFA $\mathcal{P}$, and a threshold probability $0 \leq p \leq 1$, report all pairs (i, j) such that $\mathcal{P}(T_i T_{i+1} \cdots T_j) \geq p$.

3.1   Weighted Automaton Construction

A naive approach would be to simply backtrack at each index of T and find high probability substrings with respect to $\mathcal{P}$. We notice that this method often leads to unnecessary backtracking. Therefore, we transform $\mathcal{P}$ into a weighted automaton that enables us to compute the sum of the probabilities of all suffixes of the current input without backtracking. This helps to skip unnecessary backtracking procedures where we can guarantee no high probability string ends.

Algorithm 1. Weighted Transform

1: **procedure** WEIGHTED_TRANSFORM(PFA $\mathcal{P} = (Q_{\mathcal{P}}, \Sigma, \{\mathbb{M}_{\mathcal{P}}(c)\}_{c \in \Sigma}, \mathbb{I}_{\mathcal{P}}, \mathbb{F}_{\mathcal{P}})$)
2:     $Q_{\mathcal{W}} \leftarrow Q_{\mathcal{P}} \cup \{q'\}$
3:     **for** $c \in \Sigma \cup \{\lambda\}$ **do**
4:         $\mathbb{M}_{\mathcal{W}}(c) \leftarrow |Q_{\mathcal{W}}| \times |Q_{\mathcal{W}}|$-zero matrix
5:         $[\mathbb{M}_{\mathcal{W}}(c)]_{1,1} \leftarrow 1$
6:         **for** $i \in 1 \ldots |Q_{\mathcal{P}}|$ **do**
7:             **for** $j \in 1 \ldots |Q_{\mathcal{P}}|$ **do**
8:                 $[\mathbb{M}_{\mathcal{W}}(c)]_{i+1,j+1} \leftarrow [\mathbb{M}_{\mathcal{P}}(c)]_{i,j}$
9:     $\mathbb{I}_{\mathcal{W}} \leftarrow 1 \times |Q_{\mathcal{W}}|$-zero vector; $\mathbb{F}_{\mathcal{W}} \leftarrow |Q_{\mathcal{W}}| \times 1$-zero vector
10:     $[\mathbb{I}_{\mathcal{W}}]_1 \leftarrow 1$
11:     **for** $i \in 1 \ldots |Q|$ **do**
12:         $[\mathbb{I}_{\mathcal{W}}]_{i+1} \leftarrow 0$; $[\mathbb{F}_{\mathcal{W}}]_{i+1} \leftarrow [\mathbb{F}_{\mathcal{P}}]_i$; $[\mathbb{M}_{\mathcal{W}}(\lambda)]_{1,i+1} \leftarrow [\mathbb{I}_{\mathcal{P}}]_i$
13:     **return** $\mathcal{W} = (Q_{\mathcal{W}}, \Sigma, \{\mathbb{M}_{\mathcal{W}}(c)\}_{c \in \Sigma}, \mathbb{I}_{\mathcal{W}}, \mathbb{F}_{\mathcal{W}})$

Algorithm 1 adds a new state q' that serves as the only initial state, while all other states have initial probability 0. From q' we add λ-transitions to the initial states of $\mathcal{P}$ weighted with their original initial weights and add a weight 1 self-loop for all characters in Σ. Figure 1 shows an example of the construction.

The resulting weighted automaton from Algorithm 1 helps us to compute the sum of the probabilities of all suffixes of the current streaming input. Then, if the sum is smaller than a threshold probability, we can skip the backtracking procedure since there cannot be a high probability string ending at the current index.

Lemma 1. *Given a PFA* $\mathcal{P} = (Q_{\mathcal{P}}, \Sigma, \{\mathbb{M}_{\mathcal{P}}(c)\}_{c \in \Sigma}, \mathbb{I}_{\mathcal{P}}, \mathbb{F}_{\mathcal{P}})$, *the transformed weighted automaton* $\mathcal{W} = (Q_{\mathcal{W}}, \Sigma, \{\mathbb{M}_{\mathcal{W}}(c)\}_{c \in \Sigma}, \mathbb{I}_{\mathcal{W}}, \mathbb{F}_{\mathcal{W}})$, *and a string* $w = w_1 w_2 \cdots w_n$,

$$\mathcal{W}(w) = \mathcal{P}(\lambda) + \sum_{i=1}^{n} \mathcal{P}(w_i w_{i+1} \cdots w_n).$$

Furthermore, we can compute $\mathcal{W}(w)$ *in* $O(|w||Q_{\mathcal{P}}|^2)$ *time.*

Lemma 1 guarantees that if $\mathcal{W}(w) < p$, then no suffix of $w = w_1 w_2 \cdots w_n$ has probability at least p and, thus, none can be valid matching patterns. Note that the converse is not necessarily true. Nevertheless, using Lemma 1, we can skip many backtracking steps at indices of T where no suffix can have probability greater than p.

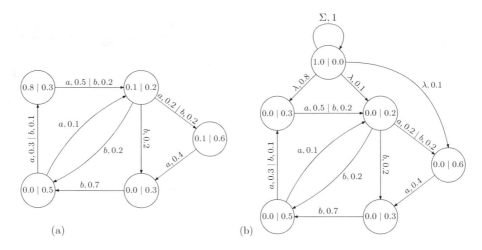

Fig. 1. (a) A PFA and (b) the resulting weighted automaton after Algorithm 1.

3.2   Algorithm Structure

Although we can skip unnecessary backtracking steps when $\mathcal{W}(w) < p$, since $\mathcal{W}(w) \geq p$ does not necessarily imply that there is a suffix of w with sufficiently high probability, we still need to individually check each suffix and report a match only if its probability surpasses the threshold. This gives rise to the algorithm structure shown in Algorithm 2.

Algorithm 2. Online Stochastic Pattern Matching

1: **procedure** OSPM(Text T; PFA $\mathcal{P}$; Probability p)
2:      $\mathcal{W} \leftarrow weighted\_transform(\mathcal{P})$
3:      $\mathbb{V} \leftarrow \mathbb{I}_\mathcal{W}(\mathbb{1} + \mathbb{M}_\mathcal{W}(\lambda))$
4:      $matches \leftarrow \{\}$
5:      **for** $j \in 1 \ldots |T|$ **do**
6:          $\mathbb{V} \leftarrow \mathbb{V}\mathbb{M}_\mathcal{W}(T_j)(\mathbb{1} + \mathbb{M}_\mathcal{W}(\lambda))$
7:          **if** $\mathbb{V}\mathbb{F}_\mathcal{W} \geq p$ **then**
8:              $matches \leftarrow matches \cup backtrack(T, \mathcal{P}, p, j)$
9:      **return** $matches$

In line 2, we transform a pattern PFA into a weighted automaton $\mathcal{W}$. Then using the weighted automaton, we initialize a vector $\mathbb{V}$ that allows us to iteratively compute the weight of a word in line 3. Specifically, by maintaining $\mathbb{V}$, we can quickly evaluate $\mathcal{W}(wa)$ from $\mathcal{W}(w)$ without recomputing the entire word. Then, for each index of T, we backtrack the text only when $\mathbb{V}\mathbb{F}_\mathcal{W} \geq p$, and search for a matching substring whose probability is at least p using the backtrack procedure in lines 5–8. Note that if $\mathbb{V}\mathbb{F}_\mathcal{W} < p$, we know that there is no sufficiently high probability matching substring ending at index j and, thus, skip the backtrack procedure and move to the next streaming input.

Algorithm 3. Naive Backtracking

1: **procedure** BACKTRACK(Text T; PFA $\mathcal{P}$; Probability p; Index j)
2:     $output \leftarrow \{\}$
3:     $\mathbb{X} \leftarrow \mathbb{F}_{\mathcal{P}}$
4:     **for** $i \leftarrow j \ldots 1$ **do**
5:         $\mathbb{X} \leftarrow \mathbb{M}_{\mathcal{P}}(T_i)\mathbb{X}$
6:         **if** $\mathbb{I}_{\mathcal{P}}\mathbb{X} \geq p$ **then**
7:             $output \leftarrow output \cup \{(i,j)\}$
8:     **return** $output$

Algorithm 3 simply checks every suffix ending at a given index j of T. The runtime is $O(|T||Q_{\mathcal{P}}|^2)$ since the algorithm has to backtrack the entire text in the worst-case. Algorithm 2 runs in $O(|T|(|Q_{\mathcal{P}}|^2+|\text{Algorithm 3}|))$ time, and thus has an overall runtime of $O(|T|^2|Q_{\mathcal{P}}|^2)$. Note that, in this case, Algorithm 2 does not fit the definition of an online algorithm since the entire text must be stored in memory. We show that we only need to store a constant number of characters in the length of the text. Note that de la Higuera and Oncina [9,10] established the two bounds relating the probability of a string and its length, and we provide a new bound $c = \max\{i \mid \mathcal{P}(\Sigma^i \Sigma^*) \geq p\}$.

Lemma 2. *Let* $\mathcal{P} = (Q, \Sigma, \{\mathbb{M}(c)\}_{c \in \Sigma}, \mathbb{I}, \mathbb{F})$ *be a PFA,* p *be a threshold probability,* μ *and* σ *be the mean and variance of the string length described by* $\mathcal{P}$, *and* $c = \max\{i \mid \mathcal{P}(\Sigma^i \Sigma^*) \geq p\}$.
At each index of T, *we need only to backtrack at most*

$$\ell = \min\{\mu + \frac{\sigma}{\sqrt{p}}, \ \frac{(|Q|+1)^2}{p}, \ c\}$$

characters, which is independent of T.

The first two bounds are purely theoretical bounds with closed-form representations based on the structure of the PFA and its distribution. The last bound, $c = \max\{i \mid \mathcal{P}(\Sigma^i \Sigma^*) \geq p\}$, must be iteratively searched for, but often provides a much tighter bound, as discussed in Sect. 5. As a pre-processing step, we can choose the minimum of the three as the maximum backtracking length ℓ. Now we are ready to tackle OSPM efficiently using the upper-bound of the backtracking length in Lemma 2 together with Algorithm 2.

Theorem 1. *Given a streaming text* T, *a PFA* $\mathcal{P}$, *and a probability* p, *we can solve the OSPM problem in* $O(\ell|T||Q_{\mathcal{P}}|^2)$ *time with a buffer of size* ℓ.

3.3   OSPM with DPFAs

Despite DPFAs being strictly weaker than PFAs in expressive power, they are still useful in practice [16]. This is mainly because parsing is easier for DPFAs and several difficult problems for general PFAs (most notably, inferring the distribution) can be solved efficiently for DPFAs [8,16]. This motivates us to consider a variant OSPM problem when the distribution is deterministic regular stochastic; in other words, $\mathcal{P}$ is a DPFA. We consider the case of grep-like pattern matching where we only report the end position of matching substrings. We call this problem grep-OSPM. Recall that for PFAs, the Viterbi semiring allows us to compute the most probable parse of a given string. Furthermore, for DPFAs, the probability of the most probable parse of a string w is exactly the probability of w. We combine this result with Algorithm 1 to find the highest probability suffix of a string in a DPFA. We observe that, for grep-OSPM with a DPFA, backtracking is not necessary and obtain a faster algorithm.

Lemma 3. *Given a DPFA $\mathcal{P}$ and its weighted transformation $\mathcal{W}$ over the Viterbi semiring,*

$$\mathcal{W}(w_1 w_2 \cdots w_n) = \max\{\mathcal{P}(\lambda), \mathcal{P}(w_n), \mathcal{P}(w_{n-1}w_n) \ldots, \mathcal{P}(w_1 w_2 \cdots w_n)\}.$$

Moreover, we can iteratively compute $\mathcal{W}(w)$ for each prefix of $w = w_1 w_2 \cdots w_n$ in only $O(|w||Q_\mathcal{P}|)$ time.

Theorem 2. *Given a streaming text T, a DPFA $\mathcal{P}$, and a probability p, we can solve grep-OSPM in $O(|T||Q_\mathcal{P}|)$ time without backtracking.*

4   Heuristic Speedup

The use of the weighted construction in Algorithm 1 is technically a heuristic in the general PFA case because we could simply backtrack at every character with the same asymptotic runtime. We describe another heuristic to further speedup the practical runtime of Algorithm 2 by short-circuiting the backtracking step.

We use the following property of stochastic languages

$$\forall w, x \in \Sigma^*, \ Pr(w) \leq Pr(\Sigma^* w) \text{ and } Pr(\Sigma^* w) \geq Pr(\Sigma^* xw).$$

Lemma 2 shows that the backtracking step only has to consider a constant number of characters when a new character of T arrives in stream. However, it is possible to end the backtracking step early if we can guarantee that no longer suffix can possibly have sufficiently high probability than p. Suppose that, during the backtracking step, we have read a suffix x from the buffer, which is pre-calculated from the upper-bound in Lemma 2. If $\mathcal{P}(\Sigma^* x) \geq p$, there may still be more suffixes (including w) in the buffer with probability at least as large as our threshold p. However, if $\mathcal{P}(\Sigma^* x) < p$ (line 9 of Algorithm 4), then we can immediately terminate the backtracking procedure and move to the next streaming character of T. Thus, Algorithm 4 becomes our new backtracking algorithm. Note that Algorithm 4 performs $O(1)$ matrix-vector multiplications per character and thus runs in $O(\ell|Q_\mathcal{P}|^2)$ time.

Algorithm 4. Backtracking Step

1: **procedure** BACKTRACK(Text T; PFA $\mathcal{P}$; Probability p; Index j)
2:     $matches \leftarrow \{\}$
3:     $\ell \leftarrow$ max backtracking length
4:     $\mathbb{X} \leftarrow \mathbb{F}$
5:     **for** $i \in 0 \ldots \ell$ **do**
6:         $\mathbb{X} \leftarrow \mathbb{M}_{T_{j-i}} \mathbb{X}$
7:         **if** $\mathbb{I}\mathbb{X} \geq p$ **then**
8:             $matches \leftarrow matches \cup \{j - i, j\}$
9:         **if** $\mathbb{I}\mathbb{M}_{\Sigma^*} \mathbb{X} < p$ **then**
10:            **return** $matches$
11:     **return** $matches$

---

5   Experimental Results

Since there is no previous algorithm to address OSPM, we simply analyze the effectiveness of the suggested heuristics, and demonstrate that non-trivial instances of the problem can be solved in reasonable time. We construct two training sets. The first is a set of 20 PFAs with up to 125 states and alphabets of size 3 to 15. This set is generated in a manner similar to the test machines from the PAutomaC PFA learning challenge [15]. We first select up to $\frac{1}{4}$ of all possible state-character-state transitions and assign weights to them before normalization to construct a valid PFA. However, the machines from the PAutomaC competition generally have very short strings with high probability. This causes OSPM to perform well in practice since there will be relatively few high probability strings and the maximum backtracking length is low. We mitigate this by modifying the structure of the PFAs by choosing a random integer n between 5 and 10 and requiring all non-zero probability strings to have length longer than n. So that all prefixes are not equiprobable in expectation, one prefix out of Σ^n is selected and weighted substantially higher than the rest.

For each PFA $\mathcal{P}$, we sample $1,000$ strings from the distribution represented by $\mathcal{P}$ and select the highest probability string as a baseline threshold. For the text, we generate strings of length 10^6 by random sampling. We then run OSPM 20 times using these parameters, halving the threshold probability each time. This gives a spread of thresholds where on one end nearly all indices in the text do not have a sufficiently high probability substring ending at the corresponding indices, whereas at the other nearly all indices do have such substrings. The second training set is drawn from real data. We first build 4, 5, and 6-grams using randomly spliced fruit fly RNA data extracted from RNACentral (http://rnacentral.org/). We use a different fruit fly RNA sequence as our input text. We then construct a 3-gram of characters from Shakespeare's *King Henry VI, Parts I & II* and use *King Henry VI, Part III* as the input text. We run the experiments on an AMD Ryzen 7 1700 (3.0 GHz) 8-Core Processor with 16 GB of RAM.

Table 1. For each PFA, we list the number of states, the alphabet size, the median threshold value, the backtracking bound calculated by $c = \max\{i \mid \mathcal{P}(\Sigma^i \Sigma^*) \geq p\}$, and the average and maximum number of characters backtracked when the backtrack procedure is executed.

PFA	$\|Q\|$	$\|\Sigma\|$	threshold	c	avg	max	time (sec)	PFA	$\|Q\|$	$\|\Sigma\|$	threshold	c	avg	max	time (sec)
1	20	3	1.67E-05	787	6.62	13	5.97	11	54	10	1.22E-06	706	3.23	7	29.75
2	24	5	5.73E-08	2347	9.44	13	5.46	12	69	15	4.15E-05	429	4.02	5	48.42
3	14	10	1.47E-09	1923	6.36	10	3.88	13	109	3	5.44E-06	1890	9.41	14	108.75
4	10	15	3.79E-07	663	4.47	7	2.86	14	107	5	3.93E-08	1655	8.55	13	103.10
5	56	3	7.62E-07	614	9.77	17	35.28	15	104	10	1.46E-05	850	4.10	6	100.39
6	51	5	1.27E-06	1682	4.77	9	25.97	16	103	15	6.14E-06	1376	3.25	5	103.76
7	50	10	3.85E-06	3793	4.07	6	22.53	17	121	3	1.15E-06	1084	9.40	16	130.23
8	53	15	2.74E-06	468	6.20	7	25.69	18	121	5	3.98E-07	1735	10.18	12	119.01
9	74	3	5.75E-07	1528	7.12	14	72.65	19	115	10	7.86E-08	5012	4.31	8	124.29
10	71	5	3.29E-08	3579	3.72	11	88.65	20	115	15	3.57E-10	5196	4.31	8	119.63
RNA 4-gram	341	4	2.06E-04	40	2.10	6	39.19	RNA 5-gram	1145	4	2.20E-04	39	3.26	9	108.10
RNA 6-gram	2096	4	2.08E-04	42	4.45	8	99.87	King Henry	20533	46	1.50E-05	50	2.26	8	489.11

We first consider the bound calculations. Of the three bounds given, our experimental results show $c = \max\{i \mid \Sigma^i \Sigma^* \geq p\}$ performs the best. Furthermore, even in the worst-case, the gap between c and $\mu + \frac{\sigma}{\sqrt{p}}$ or $\frac{(|Q|+1)^2}{p}$ is several orders of magnitude because the latter two depend on the inverse of the threshold value p. This shows that determining c is necessary in practice, since it is impractical to maintain a buffer the size of which is required by the other two bounds. The experiments also show that the suffix probability heuristic allows us to quickly terminate the backtracking procedure when we could guarantee we would not find a string with probability greater than the threshold later in the buffer. Throughout the trials, we recorded the average and maximum number of characters backtracked during each backtracking call. Compared to even the lowest buffer bound, the average number of characters ever backtracked was very low, making the algorithm run very quickly in practice. The worst ratio of the average and maximum backtracking to buffer length is in PFA #5, with ratios $\frac{9.77}{614} \approx 0.016$ and $\frac{17}{614} \approx 0.028$, respectively. In no cases did a backtracking procedure exhaust the entire buffer. Even for very large PFAs, such as 20533-state PFA built from the *King Henry VI* data, our algorithm was able to parse large texts in reasonable time frames. In these cases, the c bound is especially useful as it can be found quickly, while $(\mathbb{1} - \mathbb{M}(\Sigma))^{-1}$ and thus $\mu + \frac{\sigma}{\sqrt{p}}$ takes an impractical amount of time to compute. Table 1 presents our experimental results; we observe that the heuristic in Sect. 4 reduces the number of backtracking characters significantly.

6 Application

Consider again the scenario where we have a PFA representing a distribution of RNA subsequences that are associated with the manifestation of some property. Suppose further that we have a long RNA sequence that exhibits the property, which implies that a non-zero probability subsequence from our distribution is present. Then it is of practical importance to determine what the highest probability subsequence present in the overall RNA sequence is, since that is the subsequence which most likely caused the property to manifest. Here we present a variant of OSPM to solve the aforementioned problem.

Problem 1. **Highest Probability Matching Substring**. Given a streaming text T, a PFA $\mathcal{P}$, and a string $w \in \Sigma^+$, report the highest probability substring of T that is a superstring of w or λ if w never appears in T.

Let $\mathcal{D}$ be the DFA induced by the Knuth-Morris-Pratt next function of w. We construct a new weighted automaton $\mathcal{W} = \mathcal{P} \cap \mathcal{D}$ that has the property $\sum_{w \in \Sigma^*} \mathcal{W}(w) = \sum_{w \in \mathcal{L}(\mathcal{D})} \mathcal{P}(w)$ [13, 16]. We then perform our weighted construction on $\mathcal{W}$ to construct a new automaton $\mathcal{W}'$. Finally, we compute an initial threshold probability that lower bounds the maximum probability of any string containing w. There are several ways to construct such a lower bound, the simplest being to use $\mathcal{P}(w)$. Unfortunately, this can lead to the pathological case where $\mathcal{P}(w) = 0$ and T does not contain any instance of w. A better method is to perform breadth-first search from any starting state to find a non-zero probability path to any final state and use the probability of the corresponding string as our initial threshold. This has the added benefit of allowing us to immediately terminate with λ if no such path exists. We then use Algorithm 2 on T with $\mathcal{W}'$ while adaptively updating the threshold probability and saving only the maximum probability matching substring throughout the computation.

7 Conclusions

We have proposed an algorithm that efficiently solves OSPM and suggested heuristics to speed up its practical runtime. For a variant of OSPM, where only the end index of high probability substrings are reported, we have suggested a faster algorithm without backtracking when a pattern is a deterministic PFA. For the general OSPM problem, we have first introduced a weighted automaton construction that allows us to filter out indices at which no sufficiently high probability substring can end. We have then proposed a new bound on the maximum possible length of a string with probability above a given threshold. This bound is often several orders of magnitude smaller than the previous known bounds. Finally, we have presented a heuristic based on a property of stochastic languages that allows us to terminate the backtracking procedure of our algorithm early when we can guarantee backtracking further would not find a sufficiently high probability string. Experimental results on both artificial and real-life data have showed that our algorithm, combined with the suggested heuristics, solves OSPM quickly in practice.

References

1. Aho, A., Corasick, M.: Efficient string matching: an aid to bibliographic search. Commun. ACM **18**, 333–340 (1975)
2. Birney, E.: Hidden Markov models in biological sequence analysis. IBM J. Res. Dev. **45**, 449–454 (2001)
3. Blondel, V.D., Canterini, V.: Undecidable problems for probabilistic automata of fixed dimension. Theory Comput. Syst. **36**, 231–245 (2003)
4. Casacuberta, F., de la Higuera, C.: Computational complexity of problems on probabilistic grammars and transducers. In: Proceedings of the 5th International Colloquium on Grammatical Inference: Algorithms and Applications, pp. 15–24 (2000)
5. Droste, M., Kuich, W., Volger, H.: Handbook of Weighted Automata. Springer, Heidelberg (2009). https://doi.org/10.1007/978-3-642-01492-5
6. Dupont, P., Denis, F., Esposito, Y.: Links between probabilistic automata and hidden Markov models: probability distributions, learning models and induction algorithms. Pattern Recogn. **38**, 1349–1371 (2005)
7. Fred, A.L.N.: Computation of substring probabilities in stochastic grammars. In: Proceedings of the 5th International Colloquium on Grammatical Inference: Algorithms and Applications, pp. 103–114 (2000)
8. Guttman, O.: Probabilistic automata and distributions over sequences. Ph.D. thesis, The Australian National University (2006)
9. de la Higuera, C., Oncina, J.: Computing the most probable string with a probabilistic finite state machine. In: Proceedings of the 11th International Conference on Finite State Methods and Natural Language Processing, pp. 1–8 (2013)
10. de la Higuera, C., Oncina, J.: The most probable string: an algorithmic study. J. Logic Comput. **24**, 311–330 (2014)
11. Knuth, D.E., Morris Jr., J.H., Pratt, V.R.: Fast pattern matching in strings. SIAM J. Comput. **6**, 323–350 (1977)
12. Mohri, M., Pereira, F., Riley, M.: Speech recognition with weighted finite-state transducers. Comput. Speech Lang. **16**, 69–88 (2002)
13. Nederhof, M., Satta, G.: Computation of infix probabilities for probabilistic context-free grammars. In: Proceedings of the 2011 Conference on Empirical Methods in Natural Language Processing, pp. 1213–1221 (2011)
14. Thompson, K.: Regular expression search algorithm. Commun. ACM **11**, 419–422 (1968)
15. Verwer, S., Eyraud, R., de la Higuera, C.: PAutomaC: a probabilistic automata and hidden Markov models learning competition. Mach. Learn. **96**(1–2), 129–154 (2014)
16. Vidal, E., Thollard, F., de la Higuera, C., Casacuberta, F., Carrasco, R.C.: Probabilistic finite-state machines-part I. IEEE Trans. Pattern Anal. Mach. Intell. **27**, 1013–1025 (2005)
17. Vidal, E., Thollard, F., de la Higuera, C., Casacuberta, F., Carrasco, R.C.: Probabilistic finite-state machines-part II. IEEE Trans. Pattern Anal. Mach. Intell. **27**, 1026–1039 (2005)
18. Yoon, B.J.: Hidden Markov models and their applications in biological sequence analysis. Current Genomics **10**(6), 402–415 (2009)

State Complexity of Reversals
of Deterministic Finite Automata
with Output

Sylvie Davies[(✉)]

Department of Pure Mathematics, University of Waterloo, Waterloo, Canada
sldavies@uwaterloo.ca

Abstract. We investigate the worst-case state complexity of reversals of
deterministic finite automata with output (DFAOs). In these automata,
each state is assigned some output value, rather than simply being
labelled final or non-final. This directly generalizes the well-studied problem of determining the worst-case state complexity of reversals of ordinary deterministic finite automata. If a DFAO has n states and k possible
output values, there is a known upper bound of k^n for the state complexity of reversal. We show this bound can be reached with a ternary input
alphabet. We conjecture it cannot be reached with a binary input alphabet except when $k = 2$, and give a lower bound for the case $3 \leq k < n$.
We prove that the state complexity of reversal depends solely on the
transition monoid of the DFAO and the mapping that assigns output
values to states.

1 Introduction

The problem of determining the worst-case state complexity of the reversal
operation on regular languages has been well-studied. Work on this problem
dates back to the 1960 s; see Jirásková and Šebej [5] for a historical overview.
It is known that if L is recognized by an n-state deterministic finite automaton
(DFA), then the (deterministic) state complexity of the reverse L^R is at most
2^n, and this bound can be reached over a binary alphabet.

We study a generalization of this problem to *deterministic finite automata
with output* (DFAOs). In a DFAO, each state is assigned an output from a
finite *output alphabet* Δ. Rather than recognizing languages, DFAOs compute
functions $f \colon \Sigma^* \to \Delta$, where Σ is the *input alphabet*. The value $f(w)$ is defined to
be the output of the state reached by starting in the initial state and following the
path spelling w. DFAOs directly generalize DFAs; the $|\Delta| = 2$ case is equivalent
to assigning a value of "final" or "non-final" to each state. DFAOs are different
from Moore machines [8], which build up an output word as each state is visited.

DFAOs are used in the study of *automatic sequences* [1]. If we treat the words
$w \in \Sigma^*$ as representations of natural numbers in some base, we can view the
function $f \colon \Sigma^* \to \Delta$ as a function $f \colon \mathbb{N} \to \Delta$, that is, an infinite sequence of

C. Câmpeanu (Ed.): CIAA 2018, LNCS 10977, pp. 133–145, 2018.
https://doi.org/10.1007/978-3-319-94812-6_12

elements of Δ. Sequences for which the corresponding function can be computed by a DFAO are called *automatic*.

The *reverse* of the function $f\colon \Sigma^* \to \Delta$ is the function $f^R\colon \Sigma^* \to \Delta$ defined by $f^R(w) = f(w^R)$. The reversal operation on DFAOs can thus be viewed as changing the direction in which the DFAO reads input: from left-to-right to right-to-left, or vice versa. We are concerned with the maximal blow-up in size (number of states) when the input reading direction of a DFAO is reversed. That is, given a function f computed by an n-state DFAO, what is the worst-case state complexity of f^R? The standard construction for reversal of DFAOs [1, Theorem 4.3.3] gives an upper bound of $|\Delta|^n$, where Δ is the output alphabet. However, it does not seem to be known whether this bound is reachable.

We prove that when the input alphabet has size three or greater, the upper bound $|\Delta|^n$ is indeed reachable. When the input alphabet is binary, the problem becomes much more complicated. We conjecture that if $|\Delta| \geq 3$, the upper bound $|\Delta|^n$ is not reachable over a binary alphabet, despite the fact that it is known to be reachable for $|\Delta| = 2$ (the ordinary DFA case). While we could not prove that the upper bound is unreachable in all cases, we have proved it is unreachable when $|\Delta| = n$ (that is, the cardinality of Δ equals the number of states n) and $|\Delta| \geq 3$, and verified computationally that it is unreachable for $(|\Delta|, n) \in \{(3,4), (3,5), (3,6), (4,5)\}$. We prove a lower bound for the case of a binary input alphabet and $3 \leq |\Delta| < n$.

We also demonstrate that the state complexity of DFAO reversal is completely determined by the transition monoid of the DFAO and the map which assigns outputs to states. In particular, if function f is computed by a minimal n-state DFAO with state set Q, transition monoid M, and output map $\tau\colon Q \to \Delta$, then the state complexity of f^R is exactly $|\tau M|$, where $\tau M = \{\tau \circ m : m \in M\}$ and $\circ$ denotes function composition. Since DFAs are special cases of DFAOs, this gives a new characterization of the state complexity of DFA reversal in terms of the transition monoid and the characteristic function of the final state set.

2   Preliminaries

We assume familiarity with basic concepts and results on regular languages and finite automata. There are many references on this subject, such as [4].

A *deterministic finite automaton with output* (DFAO) is a 6-tuple $\mathcal{D} = (Q, \Sigma, \cdot, q_0, \Delta, \tau)$, where:

- Q is a finite set of *states* and $q_0 \in Q$ is the *initial state*.
- Σ is the *input alphabet* and Δ is the *output alphabet*; both are finite.
- $\cdot\colon Q \times \Sigma \to Q$ is the *transition function*.
- $\tau\colon Q \to \Delta$ is the *output map*.

We use infix notation for the transition function: the image of the pair (q, a) under the transition function is denoted $q \cdot a$. We extend the transition function to words in Σ^* as follows: for $q \in Q$, we define $q \cdot \varepsilon = q$, and for $w = ax$, $a \in \Sigma$, $x \in \Sigma^*$ we inductively define $q \cdot ax = (q \cdot a) \cdot x$. If $p \cdot a = q$ for $p, q \in Q$ and

$a \in \Sigma$, we say there is a *transition* from p to q on a. If $p \cdot w = q$ for $w \in \Sigma^*$, we say there is a *path* from p to q spelling w.

The *function computed by a DFAO* is the function $f \colon \Sigma^* \to \Delta$ defined by $f(w) = \tau(q_0 \cdot w)$. That is, we determine $f(w)$ by starting in the initial state q_0, following the path corresponding to w to reach some state q, then applying the output map τ to get the output value associated with q. A function that can be computed by a DFAO is called a *finite-state function*.

A state $q \in Q$ is *reachable* if there is a path to it from the initial state q_0, i.e., there exists $w \in \Sigma^*$ such that $q_0 \cdot w = q$. The DFAO $\mathcal{D}$ is called *trim* if all states are reachable. Two states $p, q \in Q$ are *distinguishable* if there exists $w \in \Sigma^*$ such that $\tau(p \cdot w) \neq \tau(q \cdot w)$. A DFAO is *minimal* if it has the least possible number of states among all DFAOs computing the same function. The following result is well-known for DFAs, and it can be shown to hold for DFAOs using essentially the same proof.

Proposition 1. *A DFAO is minimal if and only if all states are reachable and every pair of distinct states is distinguishable.*

For further reference on the DFAO model, see [1].

Let Q be a finite set; we usually assume without loss of generality that $Q = \{1, 2, \ldots, n\}$. A *transformation* of Q is a function $t \colon Q \to Q$. The *image* of a transformation $t \colon Q \to Q$ is the set $t(Q) = \{t(q) : q \in Q\}$. The *rank* of a transformation is the size of its image. Transformations of Q (or more generally, functions $f \colon Q \to X$ for some set X) can be specified explicitly using *matrix notation*:

$$t = \begin{pmatrix} 1 & 2 & 3 & \cdots & n \\ t(1) & t(2) & t(3) & \cdots & t(n) \end{pmatrix}.$$

Transformations (or functions $f \colon Q \to X$) can be written concisely using *list notation*; for example, the list $[1, 4, 3, 5, 2, 2, 3]$ denotes $\begin{pmatrix} 1\,2\,3\,4\,5\,6\,7 \\ 1\,4\,3\,5\,2\,2\,3 \end{pmatrix}$.

A bijective transformation is called a *permutation*. Permutations can be written concisely using *disjoint cycle notation*; for example, $(1, 2, 4, 5)(6, 7)$ denotes the permutation $[2, 4, 3, 5, 1, 7, 6]$.

Transformations can be *composed* using the $\circ$ operator; the image of q under $s \circ t$ is $s(t(q))$. A set of transformations of Q that is closed under composition is called a *transformation monoid* on Q. The size of Q is called the *degree* of the transformation monoid. The *full transformation monoid* on Q is the set of all transformations of Q. The *symmetric group* on Q is the set of all permutations of Q. A transformation monoid M is *generated* by a set of transformations T if every transformation in M can be written as a composition of transformations from T. We say a monoid is *k-generated* if it is generated by a set of size k.

Each DFAO $\mathcal{D} = (Q, \Sigma, \cdot, q_0, \Delta, \tau)$ has a transformation monoid associated with it, called the *transition monoid* of the DFAO. It is defined as follows. For each $w \in \Sigma^*$, define the function $\overline{w} \colon Q \to Q$ by $\overline{w}(q) = q \cdot w$. The function $\overline{w}$ is called the *action* of w in $\mathcal{D}$. Composition of actions obeys the following rule:

$$\overline{x} \circ \overline{y} = \overline{yx}, \quad \text{since } \overline{x}(\overline{y}(q)) = q \cdot y \cdot x = q \cdot yx = \overline{yx}.$$

Since the set $\{\overline{w} : w \in \Sigma^*\}$ of all word actions in $\mathcal{D}$ is closed under composition, this set forms a transformation monoid on Q. This is the *transition monoid* of $\mathcal{D}$. The transition monoid is generated by the set $\{\overline{a} : a \in \Sigma\}$ of letter actions.

When working with multiple DFAOs, say $\mathcal{D} = (Q, \Sigma, \cdot, q_0, \Delta, \tau)$ and $\mathcal{D}' = (Q', \Sigma', \cdot', q_0', \Delta', \tau')$, the notation $\overline{w}$ is ambiguous: it is unclear whether this is the action of w in $\mathcal{D}$ or in $\mathcal{D}'$. We adopt the following convention: the notation $\overline{w}$ refers to the action of w in a DFA whose transition function is named "$\cdot$". Thus in this case, $\overline{w}$ would refer to the action of w in $\mathcal{D}$, rather than $\mathcal{D}'$. This convention will be sufficient to keep things unambiguous in this paper.

If $w = a_1 a_2 \cdots a_{n-1} a_n$ is a word over Σ^* with $a_1, \ldots, a_n \in \Sigma$, the *reverse of* w is $w^R = a_n a_{n-1} \cdots a_2 a_1$. Note that $\overline{a_1} \circ \overline{a_2} \circ \cdots \circ \overline{a_{n-1}} \circ \overline{a_n} = \overline{a_n a_{n-1} \cdots a_2 a_1} = \overline{w^R}$. On the other hand, $\overline{a_n} \circ \overline{a_{n-1}} \circ \cdots \circ \overline{a_2} \circ \overline{a_1} = \overline{a_1 a_2 \cdots a_{n-1} a_n} = \overline{w}$. The *reverse* of a finite-state function $f \colon \Sigma^* \to \Delta$ is the function $f^R \colon \Sigma^* \to \Delta$ defined by $f^R(w) = f(w^R)$. Following [1, Theorem 4.3.3], we give a DFAO construction for f^R in terms of a DFAO for f.

Proposition 2. *Let* $\mathcal{D} = (Q, \Sigma, \cdot, q_0, \Delta, \tau)$ *be a DFAO computing the function* f. *There exists a DFAO* $\mathcal{D}^R$ *computing* f^R.

Proof. Let $\mathcal{D}^R = (\Delta^Q, \Sigma, \odot, \tau, \Delta, \Omega)$, where:

- The state set is Δ^Q, the set of all functions from Q to Δ.
- The initial state is $\tau \colon Q \to \Delta$, the output map of $\mathcal{D}$.
- The transition function $\odot$ is defined as follows: $g \odot a = g \circ \overline{a}$, for $g \in \Delta^Q$ and $a \in \Sigma$.
- The output map $\Omega \colon \Delta^Q \to \Delta$ is defined by $\Omega(g) = g(q_0)$.

By definition, the function computed by $\mathcal{D}$ is $f(w) = \tau(q_0 \cdot w)$. The function computed by $\mathcal{D}^R$ is $\Omega(\tau \odot w) = (\tau \odot w)(q_0)$; we must show this equals $f^R(w) = f(w^R)$. If $w = a_1 a_2 \cdots a_n$, then we have

$$\tau \odot w = \tau \odot a_1 \odot a_2 \odot \cdots \odot a_n = \tau \circ \overline{a_1} \circ \overline{a_2} \circ \cdots \circ \overline{a_n} = \tau \circ \overline{w^R}.$$

It follows that

$$(\tau \circ \overline{w^R})(q_0) = \tau(\overline{w^R}(q_0)) = \tau(q_0 \cdot w^R) - f(w^R) - f^R(w)$$

as required.   □

The *state complexity* of a finite-state function is the size of a minimal DFAO computing the function. If a function f is computed by an n-state minimal DFAO (i.e., the function has state complexity n), Proposition 2 shows that the state complexity of f^R is bounded above by $|\Delta|^n$, since the size of the state set Δ^Q of $\mathcal{D}^R$ is $|\Delta|^{|Q|} = |\Delta|^n$.

The following proposition makes it easier to compute the state complexity of f^R. The analogous result for DFAs is known (e.g., see [5, Proposition 3]).

Proposition 3. *If* $\mathcal{D}$ *is trim, then all states of* $\mathcal{D}^R$ *are pairwise distinguishable.*

Proof. Let g and h be distinct states of $\mathcal{D}^R$. There exists $q \in Q$ such that $g(q) \neq h(q)$. Since $\mathcal{D}$ is trim, q is reachable. Choose $w \in \Sigma^*$ such that $q_0 \cdot w^R = q$. Observe that $\Omega(g \odot w) = (g \circ \overline{w^R})(q_0) = g(q_0 \cdot w^R) = g(q)$, and similarly $\Omega(h \odot w) = h(q)$. Since $\Omega(g \odot w) \neq \Omega(h \odot w)$, g and h are distinguishable. □

If we take $\mathcal{D}^R$ and remove all unreachable states from it, we obtain a DFAO for f^R with all states reachable and every pair of distinct states distinguishable. By Proposition 1, this is a minimal DFAO for f^R. Hence given a function f computed by a trim DFAO $\mathcal{D}$, to determine the state complexity of f^R, we can simply count the number of reachable states in $\mathcal{D}^R$.

3   Main Results

We first prove that the state complexity of reversal of DFAOs is completely determined by the transition monoid and the output map.

Proposition 4. *Let $\mathcal{D} = (Q, \Sigma, \cdot, q_0, \Delta, \tau)$ be a trim DFAO computing function f. Let M be the transition monoid of $\mathcal{D}$. The state complexity of f^R is $|\tau M|$, where $\tau M = \{\tau \circ \overline{w} : w \in \Sigma^*\}$.*

Proof. The DFAO $\mathcal{D}^R = (\Delta^Q, \Sigma, \odot, \tau, \Delta, \Omega)$ computes f^R. By Proposition 3, all states of $\mathcal{D}^R$ are distinguishable, so the state complexity of f^R is the number of reachable states in $\mathcal{D}^R$.

Recall from the proof of Proposition 2 that $g \odot w = g \circ \overline{w^R}$ for $g: Q \to \Delta$ and $w \in \Sigma^*$. In particular, since τ is the initial state of $\mathcal{D}^R$, every reachable state of $\mathcal{D}^R$ has the form $\tau \odot w = \tau \circ \overline{w^R}$. Hence the set of reachable states of $\mathcal{D}^R$ is $\{\tau \circ \overline{w^R} : w \in \Sigma^*\}$. But this is the same set as $\tau M = \{\tau \circ \overline{w} : w \in \Sigma^*\}$. It follows that the number of reachable states in $\mathcal{D}^R$ is precisely $|\tau M|$. □

Recall that DFAs are essentially DFAOs with $|\Delta| = 2$, if we view the output map as telling us whether a state is final. Hence we have the following corollary:

Corollary 1. *Let $\mathcal{D} = (Q, \Sigma, \cdot, q_0, F)$ be a trim DFA recognizing language L. Let M be the transition monoid of $\mathcal{D}$. The state complexity of L^R is $|\chi_F M|$, where $\chi_F: Q \to \{0, 1\}$ is the characteristic function of F.*

Throughout the rest of this section, Q and Δ will be finite sets with $|Q| = n$ and $|\Delta| = k$, the monoid M will be a transformation monoid on Q, and $\tau: Q \to \Delta$ will be a surjective function. Note that the surjectivity of τ implies $|\Delta| \leq |Q|$. It is fine to make this assumption, since if $|\Delta| > |Q|$ there are more possible outputs than there are states, and so we can shrink Δ without loss of generality.

Theorem 1. *Let M be the full transformation monoid on Q. Then $|\tau M| = k^n$ for all surjective functions $\tau: Q \to \Delta$.*

Proof. It suffices to show that every function $h\colon Q \to \Delta$ lies in τM, i.e., every such function h can be written as $\tau \circ g$ for some $g\colon Q \to Q$.

For $q \in Q$, we define $g(q)$ as follows. Since τ is surjective, there exists $p_q \in Q$ such that $\tau(p_q) = h(q)$. Define $g(q) = p_q$. Then $(\tau \circ g)(q) = \tau(g(q)) = \tau(p_q) = h(q)$ for all $q \in Q$, so $\tau \circ g = h$ as required. □

Corollary 2. *Let f be a finite-state function computed by a minimal DFAO $\mathcal{D} = (Q, \Sigma, \cdot, q_0, \Delta, \tau)$ with $|\Delta| \leq |Q|$ (i.e., $k \leq n$). The state complexity of f^R is at most $|\Delta|^{|Q|} = k^n$, and this bound can be reached when $|\Sigma| \geq 3$.*

Proof. The upper bound on f^R follows from the construction for $\mathcal{D}^R$. For the lower bound, we use the well-known fact that the full transformation monoid on Q can be generated by three elements: two generators of the symmetric group on Q, and a transformation of rank $|Q| - 1$. If $Q = \{1, \ldots, n\}$, an explicit example of three generators is $f_1 = (1, 2, \ldots, n)$, $f_2 = (1, 2)$ and $f_3 = (1 \to 2)$, where $(1 \to 2)$ is the function that maps 1 to 2 and fixes all other elements. Choose $\{a, b, c\} \subseteq \Sigma$ and let $\mathcal{D}$ be a DFAO such that $\bar{a} = f_1$, $\bar{b} = f_2$ and $\bar{c} = f_3$. Then the transition monoid M of $\mathcal{D}$ is the full transformation monoid. Furthermore, $\mathcal{D}$ is trim (all states can be reached via $\bar{a}$). Hence Proposition 4 applies. If we take the output map τ to be surjective, by Theorem 1 we see that the state complexity of f^R is $|\tau M| = k^n$, as required. □

We now turn to the case where the input alphabet of the DFAO is binary, i.e., $|\Sigma| = 2$. This case is significantly harder than the $|\Sigma| \geq 3$ case. We assume $|\Delta| \geq 3$, since if $|\Delta| = 2$, this case is equivalent to studying reversal of DFAs with binary alphabets, and for DFAs the upper bound of 2^n is reachable [5].

Since the state complexity of DFAO reversal is completely determined by the transition monoid and output map, there are connections between the $|\Sigma| = 2$ case and the problem of finding the largest 2-generated transformation monoids of a particular degree. This problem has been studied by Holzer and König [3] and by Krawetz, Lawrence and Shallit [7].

Following Holzer and König, we define two families of monoids. First and most important are the $U_{\ell,m}$ monoids [3, Definition 5]. The monoid $U_{\ell,m}$ is a transformation monoid on $Q = \{1, \ldots, \ell + m\}$ defined as follows. Let $\alpha\colon Q \to Q$ be the permutation $(1, \ldots, \ell)(\ell + 1, \ldots, \ell + m)$. A function $\gamma\colon Q \to Q$ belongs to $U_{\ell,m}$ if and only if it satisfies one of the following conditions:

1. There exists $i \geq 0$ such that $\gamma = \alpha^i$, that is, $\gamma = \alpha \circ \alpha \circ \cdots \circ \alpha$ (where there are i occurrences of α).
2. $\gamma(\{1, \ldots, \ell\}) \cap \gamma(\{\ell + 1, \ldots, \ell + m\}) \neq \emptyset$, and there exists an element $i \in \{\ell + 1, \ldots, \ell + m\}$ such that i is not in the image of γ.

If $1 < \ell < m$ and $\gcd(\ell, m) = 1$, then $U_{\ell,m}$ can be generated by two elements [3, Theorem 8]. Krawetz [6] gives an explicit generating set: one of the generators is α, and the other is $\beta\colon Q \to Q$, where

$$\beta = \begin{pmatrix} 1 & 2\,3\,4 \cdots \ell + m - 1 & \ell + m \\ \ell + 1 & 2\,3\,4 \cdots \ell + m - 1 & 1 \end{pmatrix}$$

if $k = 2$ or ℓ is even, and otherwise

$$\beta = \begin{pmatrix} 1 & 2\ 3\ 4 \cdots \ell + m - 1\ \ell + m \\ \ell + 1 & 3\ 2\ 4 \cdots \ell + m - 1 \quad 1 \end{pmatrix}.$$

Let $n = \ell + m$. For $n \geq 7$ and n prime, Holzer and König proved that there exist ℓ and m with $1 < \ell < m$ and $\gcd(\ell, m) = 1$ such that $U_{\ell,m}$ is the largest 2-generated transformation monoid [3, Theorem 15]. They conjecture that this also holds when $n \geq 7$ and n is not prime.

When $n \leq 6$, the largest 2-generated transformation monoids belong to a different family: the V_n^d monoids [3, Definition 16]. Let α be the permutation $(1, 2, \ldots, n)$. A function $\gamma \colon Q \to Q$ belongs to V_n^d if and only if it satisfies one of the following conditions:

1. There exists $i \geq 0$ such that $\gamma = \alpha^i$.
2. There exist $i, j \in \{1, \ldots, n\}$ such that $\gamma(i) = \gamma(j)$ and $j \equiv i + d \pmod{n}$.

For $2 \leq n \leq 6$, Holzer and König determined explicit generating sets for the largest 2-generated transformation monoids on $Q = \{1, \ldots, n\}$, which are all V_n^d monoids for some d. One of the generators is always $\alpha_n = (1, 2, \ldots, n)$. For $2 \leq n \leq 6$, the other generator β_n is:

$$\beta_2 = \begin{pmatrix} 1\ 2 \\ 1\ 1 \end{pmatrix}, \quad \beta_3 = \begin{pmatrix} 1\ 2\ 3 \\ 1\ 1\ 3 \end{pmatrix}, \quad \beta_4 = \begin{pmatrix} 1\ 2\ 3\ 4 \\ 1\ 1\ 4\ 3 \end{pmatrix},$$

$$\beta_5 = \begin{pmatrix} 1\ 2\ 3\ 4\ 5 \\ 1\ 1\ 4\ 5\ 3 \end{pmatrix}, \quad \beta_6 = \begin{pmatrix} 1\ 2\ 3\ 4\ 5\ 6 \\ 1\ 4\ 1\ 5\ 6\ 2 \end{pmatrix}.$$

Holzer and König also give a more general construction for 2-element generating sets of V_n^d monoids [3, Theorem 18].

With these definitions done, we return to the problem of computing worst-case state complexity of reversal for binary input alphabets. First we consider the special case $|Q| = |\Delta|$. Here it turns out that the state complexity problem almost completely reduces to the 2-generated monoid problem:

Theorem 2. *Let f be a finite-state function computed by a minimal DFAO $\mathcal{D} = (Q, \Sigma, \cdot, q_0, \Delta, \tau)$ with $|\Sigma| = 2$ and $|Q| = |\Delta| = n$. Let $m_2(n)$ denote the size of the largest 2-generated transformation monoid on $Q = \{1, 2, \ldots, n\}$ that occurs as the transition monoid of some trim DFA. The state complexity of f^R is at most $m_2(n)$, and this bound is reachable.*

Proof. Let $\Sigma = \{a, b\}$. By assumption, we can construct a trim DFAO $\mathcal{D}$ so that $\bar{a}$ and $\bar{b}$ generate a monoid of size $m_2(n)$. and let $\tau \colon Q \to \Delta$ be a bijection. By Proposition 4, the state complexity of f^R is $|\tau M|$. But τ is a bijection, so $|\tau M| = |M| = m_2(n)$. $\qquad\square$

It may be the case that for some values of n, the largest transformation monoid on $\{1, 2, \ldots, n\}$ generated by two elements does *not* occur as the transition monoid of a trim DFA. Thus we do not quite get a complete reduction to the 2-generated monoid problem. Note that the $U_{\ell,m}$ and V_n^d monoids do occur as transition monoids of trim DFAs.

It is well known that if $|Q| \geq 3$, the full transformation monoid on a finite set Q cannot be generated by two elements. Hence $m_2(n)$ never reaches the upper bound of $|\Delta|^{|Q|} = n^n$ except when $|Q| = n = 2$.

Table 1 shows the known values for $m_2(n)$ for $2 \leq n \leq 7$, taken from [3, Table 1]. The value is not known for $n > 7$ except when n is prime, in which case $m_2(n)$ is the size of the largest 2-generated $U_{\ell,m}$ monoid. The values of n^n are also shown for comparison.

Table 1. Values of $m_2(n)$ for $2 \leq n \leq 7$.

n	2	3	4	5	6	7
$m_2(n)$	4	24	176	2110	32262	610871
n^n	4	27	256	3125	46656	823543

We now turn to the case where $|\Delta| < |Q|$. Our main result in this case is a formula for the size of $|\tau U_{\ell,m}|$, which in turn leads to a lower bound on the worst-case state complexity of f^R. The notation $\{\begin{smallmatrix} \ell \\ i \end{smallmatrix}\}$ below means the number of partitions of $\{1, \ldots, \ell\}$ into i parts (a Stirling number of the second kind).

Theorem 3. *Let $|\Delta| = k$ and let $|Q| = \ell + m = n$, with $2 \leq k < n$ and $1 \leq \ell \leq m$. Define*

$$F(k, \ell, m) = \sum_{i=1}^{\ell} \binom{k}{i} i! \left\{ \begin{matrix} \ell \\ i \end{matrix} \right\} (k-i)^m.$$

$$G(k, \ell, m) = \begin{cases} \operatorname{lcm}(\ell, m), & \text{if } k \geq 4; \\ m, & \text{if } k = 3; \\ 1, & \text{if } k = 2. \end{cases}$$

There exists a function $\tau \colon Q \to \Delta$ such that

$$|\tau U_{\ell,m}| = k^n - F(k, \ell, m) + G(k, \ell, m).$$

To prove this theorem, we will need the following technical lemma. For space considerations, we omit the proof of the lemma; the proof can be found in the arXiv version of this paper [2].

Lemma 1. *Let $\Delta = \{1, \ldots, k\}$ and let $Q = \{1, \ldots, n\}$, with $2 \leq k < n$. Fix ℓ and m such that $\ell + m = n$ and $1 \leq \ell \leq m$. Let $\alpha \colon Q \to Q$ be the permutation $\alpha = (1, \ldots, \ell)(\ell+1, \ldots, \ell+m)$. There exists a function $\tau \colon Q \to \Delta$ with the following properties:*

– $\tau\colon Q \to \Delta$ *is surjective.*
– $\tau(\{1,\dots,\ell\}) \cap \tau(\{\ell+1,\dots,\ell+m\}) = \emptyset.$
– *There exist distinct* $p, p' \in \{\ell+1,\dots,\ell+m\}$ *such that* $\tau(p) = \tau(p').$
– *The size of the set* $\{\tau \circ \alpha^i : i \geq 0\}$ *is precisely given by the function* $G(k, \ell, m).$

Proof (Theorem 3). We start with a brief outline of the proof strategy. Without loss of generality, assume $\Delta = \{1,\dots,k\}$ and $Q = \{1,\dots,n = \ell+m\}$. Define $F_{\ell,m} = \{f\colon Q \to \Delta : f(\{1,\dots,\ell\}) \cap f(\{\ell+1,\dots,\ell+m\}) = \emptyset\}.$

– First, we show that $\Delta^Q = \tau U_{\ell,m} \cup F_{\ell,m}$ for certain τ.
– After proving this, the inclusion-exclusion principle gives the formula

$$k^n = |\Delta^Q| = |\tau U_{\ell,m}| + |F_{\ell,m}| - |\tau U_{\ell,m} \cap F_{\ell,m}|.$$

– We show that $|F_{\ell,m}| = F(k, \ell, m)$.
– We show that $|\tau U_{\ell,m} \cap F_{\ell,m}| = G(k, \ell, m)$.
– Rearranging the inclusion-exclusion formula above gives the result.

Let us show that for an appropriate choice of $\tau\colon Q \to \Delta$, we have $\Delta^Q = \tau U_{\ell,m} \cup F_{\ell,m}$. That is, every function from Q to Δ lies in one of $\tau U_{\ell,m}$ or $F_{\ell,m}$.

We select τ with the following properties:

– $\tau\colon Q \to \Delta$ is surjective.
– $\tau(\{1,\dots,\ell\}) \cap \tau(\{\ell+1,\dots,\ell+m\}) = \emptyset$, that is, $\tau \in F_{\ell,m}$.
– There exist distinct $p, p' \in \{\ell+1,\dots,\ell+m\}$ such that $\tau(p) = \tau(p')$.
– The size of the set $\{\tau \circ \alpha^i : i \geq 0\}$ is precisely $G(k, \ell, m)$.

Such a function τ exists by Lemma 1. Note that we need $k < n$ and $\ell \leq m$ to apply Lemma 1; this is the only place we use these hypotheses.

Now, let $g\colon Q \to \Delta$ be arbitrary. We will show that if g is *not* in $F_{\ell,m}$, then it must be in $\tau U_{\ell,m}$, thus proving that $\Delta^Q = \tau U_{\ell,m} \cup F_{\ell,m}$. To show that $g \in \tau U_{\ell,m}$, we define a function $f\colon Q \to Q$ such that $f \in U_{\ell,m}$ and $\tau \circ f = g$.

Since $g \notin F_{\ell,m}$, there exist distinct elements $r \in \{1,\dots,\ell\}$ and $r' \in \{\ell+1,\dots,\ell+m\}$ such that $g(r) = g(r')$. Since τ is surjective, there exists s such that $\tau(s) = g(r)$. Furthermore, we can choose s so that $s \neq p'$. Indeed, if p' is one of the possible choices for s, then by the fact that $\tau(p) = \tau(p')$, we can choose $s = p$ instead. Now, we define $f\colon Q \to Q$ for each $q \in Q$ as follows:

– If $q \in \{r, r'\}$, define $f(q) = s$.
– If $g(q) = \tau(p)$ and $q \notin \{r, r'\}$, define $f(q) = p$.
– Otherwise, choose an element q' such that $\tau(q') = g(q)$ (by surjectivity) and define $f(q) = q'$.

We verify in each case that $\tau \circ f = g$:

– If $q = r$, then $f(r) = s$, so $\tau(f(r)) = \tau(s) = g(r)$.
– If $q = r'$, then $f(q) = s$, and since $g(r) = g(r')$ we have $\tau(f(r')) = \tau(s) = g(r) = g(r')$.

- If $q \notin \{r, r'\}$ and $g(q) = \tau(p)$, then $f(q) = p$, so $\tau(f(q)) = \tau(p) = g(q)$.
- Otherwise, we have $f(q) = q'$ such that $\tau(f(q)) = \tau(q') = g(q)$.

Now, we show that $f \in U_{\ell,m}$. First, note that there exist elements $r \in \{1, \ldots, \ell\}$ and $r' \in \{\ell+1, \ldots, \ell+m\}$ such that $f(r) = f(r')$. Next, observe that the element $p' \in \{\ell+1, \ldots, \ell+m\}$ is not in the image of f. To see this, note that if we have $f(q) = p'$, then we have $\tau(f(q)) = \tau(p') = \tau(p)$. But $\tau(f(q)) = g(q)$, so this implies $g(q) = \tau(p)$. In the case where $g(q) = \tau(p)$, we defined $f(q) = p \neq p'$, so this is a contradiction. It follows that f meets the conditions to belong to $U_{\ell,m}$.

This proves that if $g \colon Q \to \Delta$ is not in $F_{\ell,m}$, then $g \in \tau U_{\ell,m}$ and thus $\Delta^Q = \tau U_{\ell,m} \cup F_{\ell,m}$. Next, we show that $|F_{\ell,m}| = F(k, \ell, m)$.

Write $f \in F_{\ell,m}$ in list notation as $[a_1, a_2, \ldots, a_\ell, b_1, b_2, \ldots, b_m]$, where $f(i) = a_i$ and $f(\ell + i) = b_i$. For this function to lie in $F_{\ell,m}$, we must have the property that $\{a_1, a_2, \ldots, a_\ell\} \cap \{b_1, b_2, \ldots, b_m\} = \emptyset$. Note that since $F_{\ell,m}$ is a set of functions from Q to Δ, we have $\{a_1, \ldots, a_\ell\}, \{b_1, \ldots, b_m\} \subseteq \Delta$. We count the number of distinct "function lists" in $F_{\ell,m}$ as follows:

- Fix a set $S \subseteq \Delta$ and assume $\{a_1, \ldots, a_\ell\} = S$. Let $|S| = i$.
- In the first segment $[a_1, \ldots, a_\ell]$ of the list, each a_i can be an arbitrary element of S. However, since $\{a_1, \ldots, a_\ell\} = S$, each element of S must appear at least once in the list. Thus the first segment $[a_1, \ldots, a_\ell]$ of the list represents a *surjective* function from $\{1, \ldots, \ell\}$ onto S. Since $|S| = i$, the number of such surjective functions is $i! \{ {\ell \atop i} \}$. (It is known in general that the number of surjective functions from $\{1, \ldots, m\}$ to $\{1, \ldots, n\}$ is $n! \{ {m \atop n} \}$.)
- In the second segment $[b_1, \ldots, b_m]$ of the list, each b_i must be an element of $\Delta \setminus S$, since we want $\{a_1, \ldots, a_\ell\} \cap \{b_1, \ldots, b_m\} = \emptyset$. Since $|S| = i$ and $|\Delta| = k$, there are $k - i$ elements to pick from in $\Delta \setminus S$, and we need to choose m of them. Thus there are $(k - i)^m$ choices for the second segment of the list. In total, for a fixed set S of size i, there are $i! \{ {\ell \atop i} \} (k - i)^m$ distinct lists with $\{a_1, \ldots, a_k\} = S$.
- Now, we take the sum over all possible choices for the set S. Since $S = \{a_1, \ldots, a_\ell\}$ and S is non-empty, we have $1 \leq |S| \leq \ell$. For each set size i, there are $\binom{k}{i}$ ways to choose $S \subseteq \Delta$ with $|S| = i$. Thus the total number of functions in $F_{\ell,m}$ is

$$\sum_{i=1}^{\ell} \binom{k}{i} i! \left\{ {\ell \atop i} \right\} (k - i)^m = F(k, \ell, m).$$

Next, we show that $|\tau U_{\ell,m} \cap F_{\ell,m}| = G(k, \ell, m)$. We claim that

$$\tau U_{\ell,m} \cap F_{\ell,m} = \begin{cases} \emptyset, & \text{if } \tau \notin F_{\ell,m}; \\ \{\tau \circ \alpha^i : i \geq 0\}, & \text{if } \tau \in F_{\ell,m}. \end{cases}$$

Then the size equality with $G(k, \ell, m)$ follows from the properties of τ.

To see the claim, suppose that $\tau \circ g \in F_{\ell,m}$ for some $g \in U_{\ell,m}$. Since $g \in U_{\ell,m}$, either $g = \alpha^i$ for some i, or there exists $p \in \{1, \ldots, \ell\}$ and $q \in \{\ell+1, \ldots, \ell+m\}$

such that $g(p) = g(q)$. In the latter case, $\tau(g(p)) = \tau(g(q))$, which contradicts the assumption that $\tau \circ g$ is in $F_{\ell,m}$. Hence $g = \alpha^i$ for some $i \geq 0$, and so $\tau \circ g = \tau \circ \alpha^i$. Now, note that $\tau(\alpha^i(\{1, \ldots, \ell\})) = \tau(\{1, \ldots, \ell\})$, and $\tau(\alpha^i(\{\ell+1, \ldots, \ell+m\})) = \tau(\{\ell+1, \ldots, \ell+m\})$. Thus $\tau \circ \alpha^i$ is in $F_{\ell,m}$ if and only if τ is in $F_{\ell,m}$, and the claim follows.

Finally, we can conclude the proof. Recall that $|\Delta| = k$ and $|Q| = n$, and thus $|\Delta^Q| = |\Delta|^{|Q|} = k^n$. Thus by the inclusion-exclusion principle, we have

$$k^n = |\Delta^Q| = |\tau U_{\ell,m}| + |F_{\ell,m}| - |\tau U_{\ell,m} \cap F_{\ell,m}|.$$

Rearranging this, we get:

$$|\tau U_{\ell,m}| = k^n - |F_{\ell,m}| + |\tau U_{\ell,m} \cap F_{\ell,m}|.$$

We proved that $|F_{\ell,m}| = F(k, \ell, m)$ and $|\tau U_{\ell,m} \cap F_{\ell,m}| = G(k, \ell, m)$. It follows that $|\tau U_{\ell,m}| = k^n - F(k, \ell, m) + G(k, \ell, m)$, as required.   □

This theorem gives the following lower bound on the worst-case state complexity of DFAO reversal when $|\Sigma| = 2$.

Corollary 3. *Let $|Q| = n \geq 2$ and $|\Delta| = k \geq 2$. There exists a trim DFAO $\mathcal{D} = (Q, \Sigma, \cdot, q_0, \Delta, \tau)$ computing function f, with $|\Sigma| = 2$ and $k < n$, such that the state complexity of f^R is*

$$\max\{k^n - F(k, \ell, m) + G(k, \ell, m) : 1 < \ell < m, \ell + m = n, \gcd(\ell, m) = 1\}.$$

Proof. Pick ℓ and m such that $1 < \ell < m$, $\ell + m = n$ and $\gcd(\ell, m) = 1$. Then $U_{\ell,m}$ can be generated by two elements. Hence we can construct a DFAO $\mathcal{D}$ over a binary alphabet with state set $Q = \{1, \ldots, n\}$ and transition monoid $U_{\ell,m}$. This DFAO will be trim: all states in $\{1, \ldots, \ell\}$ are reachable by $\alpha = (1, \ldots, \ell)(\ell+1, \ldots, \ell+m)$, and $U_{\ell,m}$ contains elements which map 1 to $\ell+1$, so the rest of the states are reachable. By Theorem 3, there exists $\tau \colon Q \to \Delta$ such that

$$|\tau U_{\ell,m}| = k^n - F(k, \ell, m) + G(k, \ell, m).$$

Take τ as the output map of $\mathcal{D}$. Then by Proposition 4, the state complexity of f^R is $|\tau U_{\ell,m}|$. Taking the maximum over all values of ℓ and m that satisfy the desired properties gives the result.   □

Table 2 gives the values of this lower bound for various values of $|\Delta| = k$ and $|Q| = n$ with $k < n$. For $n \in \{1, 2, 3, 4, 6\}$ there are no pairs (ℓ, m) such that $1 < \ell < m$, $\ell + m = n$ and $\gcd(\ell, m) = 1$, so those values of n are ignored.

Note that for $|\Delta| = 2$, this lower bound is off by one from the upper bound of 2^n. The known examples where 2^n is achieved do not use $U_{\ell,m}$ monoids. We conjecture that for $|\Delta| \geq 3$, the upper bound $|\Delta|^n = k^n$ is not reachable. Jason Bell has recently claimed a proof of this conjecture (private communication).

We close this section by mentioning the results of some computational experiments. The goal of these experiments was to find, for small values of $|Q| = n$

Table 2. Values for the lower bound of Corollary 3.

$k \backslash n$	5	6	7	8	9
2	31	-	127	255	511
3	216	-	2125	6452	19550
4	826	-	15472	63403	258360
5	-	-	71037	368020	1902365
6	-	-	243438	1539561	9657446

and $|\Delta| = k$, the maximal size of $|\tau M|$, where M is a monoid generated by two functions $\alpha \colon Q \to Q$ and $\beta \colon Q \to Q$, and $\tau \colon Q \to \Delta$ is a surjective function. The results of our experiments are shown in Table 3. The values in **bold** are true maximal values for $|\tau M|$ (and thus for the state complexity of binary DFAO reversal), which have been confirmed by brute force search. The other, non-bold values in the table are simply the largest we found through random search.

Table 3. Largest known values for $|\tau M|$, where M is a 2-generated transformation monoid on $\{1, \ldots, n\}$ and $\tau \colon \{1, \ldots, n\} \to \{1, \ldots, k\}$ is surjective. **Bold** values have been confirmed to be maximal by brute force search.

$k \backslash n$	3	4	5	6	7	8
3	**24**	**67**	**218**	**699**	2125	6452
4	-	**176**	**826**	3526	15472	63403

Note that for $n \geq 7$, the conjectured maximal values in Table 3 match the values in Table 2 for lower bound of Corollary 3. For this reason, we suspect the bound of Corollary 3 may in fact be optimal for $n \geq 7$. However, the evidence at this point is limited.

4   Conclusions

For DFAs, the worst-case state complexity of the reversal operation is 2^n for languages of state complexity n. When we generalize to DFAOs, the worst-case state complexity is bounded above by k^n, where k is the number of outputs of the DFAO. We proved that this upper bound can be attained by DFAOs over a ternary input alphabet. For binary input alphabets, we demonstrated there are connections with the problem of finding the largest 2-generated transformation monoid, and gave a lower bound on the worst-case state complexity for the $k < n$ case. Computational experiments suggest that the upper bound k^n is not reachable using binary input alphabets if $k \geq 3$.

Acknowledgements. I thank Jason Bell, Janusz Brzozowski, Jeffrey Shallit, and the anonymous referees for proofreading and helpful comments. This work was supported by the Natural Sciences and Engineering Research Council of Canada under grant No. OGP0000871.

References

1. Allouche, J.P., Shallit, J.: Automatic Sequences: Theory, Applications, Generalizations. Cambridge University Press, Cambridge (2003)
2. Davies, S.: State complexity of reversals of deterministic finite automata with output. CoRR abs/1705.07150 (2017). http://arxiv.org/abs/1705.07150
3. Holzer, M., König, B.: On deterministic finite automata and syntactic monoid size. Theoret. Comput. Sci. **327**(3), 319–347 (2004)
4. Hopcroft, J.E., Ullman, J.D.: Introduction to Automata Theory Languages and Computation, 1st edn. Addison-Wesley Longman Publishing Co., Inc., Boston (1979)
5. Jirásková, G., Šebej, J.: Reversal of binary regular languages. Theoret. Comput. Sci. **449**, 85–92 (2012)
6. Krawetz, B.: Monoids and the state complexity of root(L). Master's thesis (2003). https://cs.uwaterloo.ca/~shallit/krawetz.pdf
7. Krawetz, B., Lawrence, J., Shallit, J.: State complexity and the monoid of transformations of a finite set. Int. J. Found. Comput. Sci. **16**(03), 547–563 (2005)
8. Moore, E.F.: Gedanken experiments on sequential machines. In: Automata Studies, pp. 129–153. Princeton University Press (1956)

Algorithms and Training for Weighted Multiset Automata and Regular Expressions

Justin DeBenedetto[(✉)] and David Chiang

Department of Computer Science and Engineering,
University of Notre Dame, Notre Dame, IN 46556, USA
{jdebened,dchiang}@nd.edu

Abstract. Multiset automata are a class of automata for which the symbols can be read in any order and obtain the same result. We investigate weighted multiset automata and show how to construct them from weighted regular expressions. We present training methods to learn the weights for weighted regular expressions and for general multiset automata from data. Finally, we examine situations in which inside weights can be computed more efficiently.

Keywords: Multiset automata · Multiset regular expressions
Weighted automata · Weighted regular expressions

1 Introduction

Automata have been widely studied and utilized for pattern and string matching problems. A string automaton reads the symbols of an input string one at a time, after which it accepts or rejects the string. But in certain instances, the order in which the symbols appear is irrelevant.

For example, in a set of graphs, the edges incident to a node are unordered and therefore their labels form a commutative language. Or, in natural language processing, applications might arise in situations where a sentence is generated by a context-free grammar subject to (hard or soft) order-independent constraints. For example, in summarization, there might be an unordered set of facts that must be included. Or, there might be a constraint that among the references to a particular entity, exactly one is a full NP.

To handle these scenarios, we are interested in weighted automata and weighted regular expressions for multisets. This paper makes three main contributions:

- We define a new translation from weighted multiset regular expressions to weighted multiset automata, more direct than that of Chiang et al. [3] and more compact (but less general) than that of Droste and Gastin [4].
- We discuss how to train weighted multiset automata and regular expressions from data.

© Springer International Publishing AG, part of Springer Nature 2018
C. Câmpeanu (Ed.): CIAA 2018, LNCS 10977, pp. 146–158, 2018.
https://doi.org/10.1007/978-3-319-94812-6_13

– We give a new composable representation of partial runs of weighted multiset automata that is more efficient than that of Chiang et al. [3].

2   Definitions

We begin by defining weighted multiset automata (Sect. 2.2) and the related definitions from previous papers for weighted multiset regular expressions (Sect. 2.3).

2.1   Preliminaries

For any natural number n, let $[n] = \{1, \ldots, n\}$.

A *multiset* over a finite alphabet Σ is a mapping from Σ to $\mathbb{N}_0$. For consistency with standard notation for strings, we write a (where $a \in \Sigma$) instead of $\{a\}$, uv for the multiset union of multisets u and v, and ϵ for the empty multiset.

The *Kronecker product* of a $m \times n$ matrix A and a $p \times q$ matrix B is the $mp \times nq$ matrix

$$A \otimes B = \begin{bmatrix} A_{11}B & \cdots & A_{1m}B \\ \vdots & \ddots & \vdots \\ A_{n1}B & \cdots & A_{mn}B \end{bmatrix}.$$

If w is a string over Σ, we write $\mathrm{alph}(w)$ for the subset of symbols actually used in w; similarly for $\mathrm{alph}(L)$ where L is a language. If $|\mathrm{alph}(L)| = 1$, we say that L is *unary*.

2.2   Weighted Multiset Automata

We formulate weighted automata in terms of matrices as follows. Let $\mathbb{K}$ be a commutative semiring.

Definition 1. *A $\mathbb{K}$-weighted finite automaton (WFA) over Σ is a tuple $M = (Q, \Sigma, \lambda, \mu, \rho)$, where $Q = [d]$ is a finite set of states, Σ is a finite alphabet, $\lambda \in \mathbb{K}^{1 \times d}$ is a row vector of initial weights, $\mu : \Sigma \to \mathbb{K}^{d \times d}$ assigns a transition matrix to every symbol, and $\rho \in \mathbb{K}^{d \times 1}$ is a column vector of final weights.*

For brevity, we extend μ to strings: If $w \in \Sigma^*$, then $\mu(w) = \mu(w_1) \cdots \mu(w_n)$. Then, the weight of all paths accepting w is $M(w) = \lambda \, \mu(w) \, \rho$. Note that in this paper we do not consider ϵ-transitions. Note also that one unusual feature of our definition is that it allows a WFA to have more than one initial state.

Definition 2. *A $\mathbb{K}$-weighted multiset finite automaton is one whose transition matrices commute pairwise. That is, for all $a, b \in \Sigma$, we have $\mu(a)\mu(b) = \mu(b)\mu(a)$.*

2.3   Weighted Multiset Regular Expressions

This definition follows that of Chiang et al. [3], which in turn is a special case of that of Droste and Gastin [4].

Definition 3. *A* $\mathbb{K}$-weighted multiset regular expression *over* Σ *is an expression belonging to the smallest set* $\mathcal{R}(\Sigma)$ *satisfying:*

- *If* $a \in \Sigma$, *then* $a \in \mathcal{R}(\Sigma)$.
- $\epsilon \in \mathcal{R}(\Sigma)$.
- $\emptyset \in \mathcal{R}(\Sigma)$.
- *If* $\alpha, \beta \in \mathcal{R}(\Sigma)$, *then* $\alpha \cup \beta \in \mathcal{R}(\Sigma)$.
- *If* $\alpha, \beta \in \mathcal{R}(\Sigma)$, *then* $\alpha\beta \in \mathcal{R}(\Sigma)$.
- *If* $\alpha \in \mathcal{R}(\Sigma)$, *then* $\alpha^* \in \mathcal{R}(\Sigma)$.
- *If* $\alpha \in \mathcal{R}(\Sigma)$ *and* $k \in \mathbb{K}$, *then* $k\alpha \in \mathcal{R}(\Sigma)$.

We define the language described by a regular expression, $\mathcal{L}(\alpha)$, by analogy with string regular expressions. Note that ϵ matches the empty multiset, while $\emptyset$ does not match any multisets. Interspersing weights in regular expressions allows regular expressions to describe weighted languages.

Definition 4. *A multiset* mc-regular expression *is one where in every subexpression* α^*, α *is:*

- *proper:* $\epsilon \notin \mathcal{L}(\alpha)$, *and*
- *monoalphabetic and connected:* $\mathcal{L}(\alpha)$ *is unary.*

As an example of why these restrictions are needed, consider the regular expression $(ab)^*$. Since the symbols commute, this is equivalent to $\{a^n b^n\}$, which multiset automata would not be able to recognize. From now on, we assume that all multiset regular expressions are mc-regular and do not write "mc-."

3   Matching Regular Expressions

In this section, we consider the problem of computing the weight that a multiset regular expression assigns to a multiset. The bad news is that this problem is NP-complete (Sect. 3.1). However, we can convert a multiset regular expression to a multiset automaton (Sect. 3.2) and run the automaton.

3.1   NP-Completeness

Theorem 1. *The membership problem for multiset regular expressions is NP-complete.*

Proof. Define a transformation T from Boolean formulas in CNF over a set of variables X to multiset regular expressions over the alphabet $X \cup \{\bar{x} \mid x \in X\}$:

$$T(\phi_1 \vee \phi_2) = T(\phi_1) \cup T(\phi_2)$$
$$T(\phi_1 \wedge \phi_2) = T(\phi_1) T(\phi_2)$$
$$T(x) = x$$
$$T(\neg x) = \bar{x}$$

Given a formula ϕ in 3CNF, construct the multiset regular expression $\alpha = T(\phi)$. Let n be the number of clauses in ϕ. Then form the expression

$$\beta = \prod_x \left(x^n (\bar{x} \cup \epsilon)^n \cup (x \cup \epsilon)^n \bar{x}^n \right)$$

Both α and β clearly have length linear in n. We claim that ϕ is satisfiable if and only if $L(\alpha\beta)$ contains $w = \prod_x x^n \bar{x}^n$.

($\Rightarrow$) If ϕ is satisfiable, form a string $u = u_1 \cdots u_n$ as follows. For $i = 1, \ldots n$, the ith clause of ϕ has at least one literal made true by the satisfying assignment. If it's x, then $u_i = x$; if it's $\neg x$, then $u_i = \bar{x}$. Clearly, $u \in L(\alpha)$. Next, form a string $v = \prod_x v_x$, where the v_x are defined as follows. For each x, if x is true under the assignment, then there are $k \geq 0$ occurrences of x in u and zero occurrences of $\bar{x}$ in u. Let $v_x = x^{n-k} \bar{x}^n$. Likewise, if x is false under the assignment, then there are $k \geq 0$ occurrences of $\bar{x}$ and zero occurrences of x, so let $v_x = x^k \bar{x}^{n-k}$. Clearly, $uv = w$ and $v \in L(\beta)$.

($\Leftarrow$) If $w \in L(\alpha\beta)$, then there exist strings $uv = w$ such that $u \in L(\alpha)$ and $v \in L(\beta)$. For each x, it must be the case that v contains either x^n or $\bar{x}^n$, so that u must either not contain x or not contain $\bar{x}$. In the former case, let x be false; in the latter case, let x be true. The result is a satisfying assignment for ϕ. $\qquad\square$

3.2   Conversion to Multiset Automata

Given a regular expression α, we can construct a finite multiset automaton corresponding to that regular expression. In addition to λ, $\mu(a)$, and ρ, we compute Boolean matrices $\kappa(a)$ with the same dimensions as $\mu(a)$. The interpretation of these matrices is that whenever the automaton is in state q, then $[\kappa(a)]_{qq} = 1$ iff the automaton has not read an a yet.

If $\alpha = a$, then for all $b \neq a$:

$$\lambda = \begin{bmatrix} 1 & 0 \end{bmatrix} \qquad \mu(a) = \begin{bmatrix} 0 & 1 \\ 0 & 0 \end{bmatrix} \qquad \kappa(a) = \begin{bmatrix} 1 & 0 \\ 0 & 0 \end{bmatrix} \qquad \rho = \begin{bmatrix} 0 \\ 1 \end{bmatrix}$$

$$\mu(b) = \begin{bmatrix} 0 & 0 \\ 0 & 0 \end{bmatrix} \qquad \kappa(b) = \begin{bmatrix} 1 & 0 \\ 0 & 1 \end{bmatrix}.$$

If $\alpha = k\alpha_1$ (where $k \in \mathbb{K}$), then for all $a \in \Sigma$:

$$\mu(a) = \mu_1(a) \qquad \lambda = \lambda_1 \qquad \rho = k\rho_1 \qquad \kappa(a) = \kappa(a).$$

If $\alpha = \alpha_1 \cup \alpha_2$, then for all $a \in \Sigma$:

$$\mu(a) = \begin{bmatrix} \mu_1(a) & 0 \\ 0 & \mu_2(a) \end{bmatrix} \quad \lambda = \begin{bmatrix} \lambda_1 & \lambda_2 \end{bmatrix} \quad \rho = \begin{bmatrix} \rho_1 \\ \rho_2 \end{bmatrix} \quad \kappa(a) = \begin{bmatrix} \kappa_1(a) & 0 \\ 0 & \kappa_2(a) \end{bmatrix}$$

If $\alpha = \alpha_1\alpha_2$, then for all $a \in \Sigma$:

$$\mu(a) = \mu_1(a) \otimes \kappa_2(a) + I \otimes \mu_2(a) \qquad\qquad \lambda = \lambda_1 \otimes \lambda_2$$
$$\kappa(a) = \kappa_1(a) \otimes \kappa_2(a) \qquad\qquad\qquad\qquad\quad \rho = \rho_1 \otimes \rho_2.$$

If $\alpha = \alpha_1^*$ and α_1 is unary, then for all $a \in \Sigma$:

$$\mu(a) = \mu_1(a) + \rho\lambda\mu_1(a) \qquad \lambda = \lambda_1 \qquad \rho = \rho_1 + \lambda_1^\top \qquad \kappa(a) = \kappa_1(a).$$

This construction can be explained intuitively as follows. The case $\alpha = a$ is standard. The union operation is standard except that the use of two initial states makes for a simpler formulation. The shuffle product is similar to a conventional shuffle product except for the use of κ_2. It builds an automaton whose states are pairs of states of the automata for α_1 and α_2. The first term in the definition of $\mu(a)$ feeds a to the first automaton and the second term to the second; but it can be fed to the first only if the second has not already read an a, as ensured by $\kappa_2(a)$. Finally, Kleene star adds a transition from final states to "second" states (states that are reachable from the initial state by a single a-transition), while also changing all initial states into final states.

Let $A(\alpha)$ denote the multiset automaton constructed from α. We can bound the number of states of $A(\alpha)$ by $2^{|\alpha|}$ by induction on the structure of α. For $\alpha = \epsilon$, $|A(\alpha)| = 1 \leq 2^{|\alpha|}$. For $\alpha = a$, $|A(\alpha)| = 2 \leq 2^{|\alpha|}$. For $\alpha = \alpha_1 \cup \alpha_2$, $|A(\alpha)| = |A(\alpha_1)| + |A(\alpha_2)| \leq 2^{|\alpha|}$. For $\alpha = \alpha_1\alpha_2$, $|A(\alpha)| = |A(\alpha_1)||A(\alpha_2)| \leq 2^{|\alpha|}$. For $\alpha = \alpha_1^*$, $|A(\alpha)| = |A(\alpha_1)| \leq 2^{|\alpha|}$.

3.3   Related Work

Droste and Gastin [4] show how to perform regular operations for the more general case of trace automata (automata on monoids). Our use of κ resembles their forward alphabet. Our construction does not utilize anything akin to their backward alphabet, so that we allow outgoing edges from final states and we allow initial states to be final states. Their construction, when converting α_1^*, creates $m = |\text{alph}(\alpha_1)|$ simultaneous copies of $A(\alpha_1)$, that is, it creates an automaton with $|A(\alpha_1)|^m$ states. Since our Kleene star is restricted to the unary case, we can use the standard, much simpler, Kleene star construction [2].

Our construction is a modification of a construction from previous work [3]. Previously, the shuffle operation required $\text{alph}(\alpha_1)$ and $\text{alph}(\alpha_2)$ to be disjoint; to ensure this required some rearranging of the regular expression before converting to an automaton. Our construction, while sharing the same upper bound on the number of states, operates directly on the regular expression without any preprocessing.

4   Learning Weights

Given a collection of multisets, the weights of the transition matrices and the initial and final weights can be learned automatically from data. Given a multiset w, we let $\mu(w) = \prod_i \mu(w_i)$. The probability of w over all possible multisets is

$$P(w) = \frac{1}{Z}\lambda\mu(w)\rho$$
$$Z = \sum_{\text{multisets } w'} \lambda\mu(w')\rho.$$

We must restrict w' to multisets up to a given length bound, which can be set based on the size of the largest multiset which is reasonable to occur in the particular setting of use. Without this restriction, the infinite sum for Z will diverge in many cases. For example, if $\alpha = a^*$, then $\mu(a)^n = \mu(a)$ and thus $\lambda\mu(a)\rho = \lambda\mu(a)^n\rho$. Since this value is non-zero, the sum diverges.

The goal is to minimize the negative log-likelihood given by

$$L = -\sum_{w \in \text{data}} \log P(w).$$

To this end, we envision and describe two unique scenarios for how the multiset automata are formed.

4.1   Regular Expressions

In certain circumstances, we may start with a set of rules as weighted regular expressions and wish to learn the weights from data. Conversion from weighted regular expressions to multiset automata can be done automatically, see Sect. 3.2. Now the multiset automata that result already have commuting transition matrices. The weights from the weighted regular expression are the parameters to be learned. These parameters can be learned through stochastic gradient descent with the gradient computed through automatic differentiation, and the transition matrices will retain their commutativity by design.

4.2   Finite Automata

We can learn the weighted automaton entirely from data by starting with a fully connected automaton on n nodes. All initial, transition, and final weights are initialized randomly. Learning proceeds by gradient descent on the log-likelihood with a penalty to encourage the transition matrices to commute. Thus our modified log-likelihood is

$$L' = L + \alpha \sum_{a,b} (\mu(a)\mu(b) - \mu(b)\mu(a))$$

Over time we increase the penalty by increasing α. This method has the benefit of allowing us to learn the entire structure of the automaton directly from data without having to form rules as regular expressions. Additionally, since we set n at the start, the number of states can be kept small and computationally feasible. The main drawback of this method is that the transition matrices, while penalized for not commuting, may not exactly satisfy the commuting condition.

5   Computing Inside Weights

We can compute the total weight of a multiset incrementally by starting with λ and multiplying by $\mu(a)$ for each a in the multiset. But in some situations, we might need to compose the weights of two partial runs. That is, having computed $\mu(u)$ and $\mu(v)$, we want to compute $\mu(uv)$ in the most efficient way. Sometimes we also want to be able to compute $\mu(u) + \mu(v)$ in the most efficient way.

For example, if we divide w into parts u and v to compute $\mu(u)$ and $\mu(v)$ in parallel [9], afterwards we need to compose them to form $\mu(w)$. Or, we could intersect a context-free grammar with a multiset automaton, and parsing with the CKY algorithm would involve multiplying and adding these weight matrices. The recognition algorithm for extended DAG automata [3] uses multiset automata in this way as well.

Let M be a multiset automaton and $\mu(a)$ its transition matrices. Let us call $\mu(w)$ the matrix of *inside weights* of w. If stored in the obvious way, it takes $\mathcal{O}(d^2)$ space. If $w = uv$ and we know $\mu(u)$ and $\mu(v)$, we can compute $\mu(w)$ by matrix multiplication in $\mathcal{O}(d^3)$ time. Can we do better?

The set of all matrices $\mu(w)$ spans a module which we call Ins(M). We show in this section that, under the right conditions, if M has d states, then Ins(M) has a generating set of size d, so that we can represent $\mu(w)$ as a vector of d coefficients. We begin with the special case of unary languages (Sect. 5.1), then after a brief digression to more general languages (Sect. 5.2), we consider multiset regular expressions converted to multiset automata (Sect. 5.3).

5.1   Unary Languages

Suppose that the automaton is unary, that is, over the alphabet $\Sigma = \{a\}$. Throughout this section, we write μ for $\mu(a)$ for brevity.

Ring-Weighted. The inside weights of a string $w = a^n$ are simply the matrix μ^n, and the inside weights of a set of strings is a polynomial in μ. We can take this polynomial to be our representation of inside weights, if we can limit the degree of the polynomial.

The Cayley-Hamilton theorem (CHT) says that any matrix μ over a commutative ring satisfies its own *characteristic equation*, $\det(\lambda I - \mu) = 0$, by substituting μ for λ. The left-hand side of this equation is the *characteristic polynomial*; its highest-degree term is λ^d. So if we substitute μ into the characteristic equation and solve for μ^d, we have a way of rewriting any polynomial in μ of degree d or more into a polynomial of degree less than d.

So representing the inside weights as a polynomial in μ takes only $O(d)$ space, and addition takes $O(d)$ time. Naive multiplication of polynomials takes $O(d^2)$ time; fast Fourier transform can be used to speed this up to $O(d \log d)$ time, although d would have to be quite large to make this practical.

Semiring-Weighted. Some very commonly used weights do not form rings: for example, the Boolean semiring, used for unweighted automata, and the Viterbi semiring, used to find the highest-weight path for a string.

There is a version of CHT for semirings due to Rutherford [10]. In a ring, the characteristic equation can be expressed using the sums of determinants of principal minors of order r. Denote the sum of positive terms (even permutations) as p_r and sum of negative terms (odd permutations) as $-q_r$. Then Rutherford expresses the characteristic equation applicable for both rings and semirings as

$$\lambda^n + q_1\lambda^{n-1} + p_2\lambda^{n-2} + q_3\lambda^{n-3} + \ldots = p_1\lambda^{n-1} + q_2\lambda^{n-2} + p_3\lambda^{n-3} + \ldots$$

For any $K \subseteq \mathbb{N}$, let S_K be the set of all permutations of K, and let $\text{sgn}(\sigma)$ be $+1$ for an even permutation and -1 for an odd permutation. The characteristic polynomial is

$$\sum_{K \subseteq [d]} \sum_{\substack{\pi \in S_K \\ \text{sgn}(\pi) \neq (-1)^{|K|}}} \left(\prod_{i \in K} \mu_{i,\pi(i)} \right) \lambda^{d-|K|} = \sum_{K \subseteq [d]} \sum_{\substack{\pi \in S_K \\ \text{sgn}(\pi) = (-1)^{|K|}}} \left(\prod_{i \in K} \mu_{i,\pi(i)} \right) \lambda^{d-|K|}.$$

$$(1)$$

If we can ensure that the characteristic equation has just λ^d on the left-hand side, then we have a compact representation for inside weights. The following result characterizes the graphs for which this is true.

Theorem 2. *Given a semiring-weighted directed graph G, the characteristic equation of G's adjacency matrix, given by the semiring version of CHT, has only λ^d on its left-hand side if and only if G does not have two node-disjoint cycles.*

Proof. Let K be a node-induced subgraph of the directed graph G. A *linear subgraph* of K is a subgraph of K that contains all nodes in K and each node has indegree and outdegree 1 within the subgraph, that is, a collection of directed cycles such that each node in K occurs in exactly one cycle. Every permutation π of K corresponds to the linear subgraph of K containing edges $(i, \pi(i))$ for each $i \in K$ [6].

Note that $\text{sgn}(\pi) = +1$ iff the corresponding linear subgraph has an even number of even-length cycles. Moreover, note that $\text{sgn}(\pi) = (-1)^{|K|}$ appearing in (1) holds iff the corresponding linear subgraph has an even number of cycles (of any length). So if the transition graph does not have two node-disjoint cycles, the only nonzero term in (1) with $\text{sgn}(\pi) = (-1)^{|K|}$ is that for which $K = \emptyset$, that is, λ^d. To prove the other direction, suppose that the graph does have two node-disjoint cycles; then the linear subgraph containing just these two cycles corresponds to a π that makes $\text{sgn}(\pi) = (-1)^{|K|}$. $\square$

The coefficients in (1) look difficult to compute; however, the product inside the parentheses is zero unless the permutation π corresponds to a cycle in the transition graph of the automaton. Given that we are interested in computing this product on linear subgraphs, we are only concerned with simple cycles. Using an algorithm by Johnson [8], all simple cycles in a directed graph can be found in $\mathcal{O}((n+e)(c+1))$ with n = number of nodes, e = number of edges, and c = number of simple cycles.

Theorem 3. *A digraph D with no two disjoint dicycles has at most $2^{|V|-1}$ simple dicycles.*

Proof. First, a theorem from Thomassen [11] limits the number of cases we must consider. In the first case, one vertex, v_s, is contained in every cycle. If we consider $G \setminus \{v_s\}$, this is a directed acyclic graph (DAG) and thus there is a partial order determined by reachability. This partial order determines the order that vertices appear in any cycle in G, which limits the number of simple cycles to the number of choices for picking vertices to join v_s in each cycle. This is a binary choice on $|V| - 1$ vertices, thus $2^{|V|-1}$ possible cycles (see Fig. 1).

In the second case, the graph contains a subgraph with 3 vertices with no self loops, but all 6 other possible edges between them. If we let S be the set of these three vertices, then $G \setminus S$ has a partial order on it just as in the first case. Additionally, for each $s \in S$, there exists a partial order on $G \setminus (S \setminus \{s\})$, and these uniquely determine the order of vertices in any cycle in G. While the bound could be lowered, this is bounded above by $2^{|V|-1}$.

All other cases can be combined with the second case by observing that they all start with the same graph as the second case, then modified by subdivision (breaking an edge in two by inserting a vertex in the middle) or splitting (breaking a vertex in two, one with all in edges, one with all out edges, then adding one edge from the in vertex to the out vertex). These cases do not violate the arguments of the second case, nor add any additional cycles. Intuitively, these are graphs from case two with some edge(s) deleted.   □

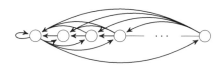

Fig. 1. A directed graph achieving the $2^{|V|-1}$ simple cycle bound.

5.2   Digression: Binary Languages and Beyond

If Σ has two symbols and the transition matrices are commuting matrices over a field, then inside weights can still be represented in d dimensions [5]. We give only a brief sketch here of the simpler, algebraically closed case [1].

Given a matrix M with entries in an algebraically closed field, there exists a matrix S such that $S^{-1}MS$ is in *Jordan form*. A matrix in Jordan form has the following block structure. Each A_i is a square matrix and λ_i is an eigenvalue.

$$S^{-1}MS = \begin{bmatrix} A_1 & & 0 \\ & \ddots & \\ 0 & & A_p \end{bmatrix} \qquad A_i = \begin{bmatrix} \lambda_i & 1 & & 0 \\ & \lambda_i & \ddots & \\ & & \ddots & 1 \\ 0 & & & \lambda_i \end{bmatrix}$$

Let the number of rows in A_i be k_i. Here let $M = \mu(a)$ be one of the commuting transition matrices. Then the following matrices span the algebra generated by the commuting transition matrices $\mu(a)$ and $\mu(b)$:

$$1, \mu(a), \ldots, \mu(a)^{k_1-1},$$
$$\mu(b), \mu(a)\mu(b), \ldots, \mu(a)^{k_2-1}\mu(b),$$
$$\vdots$$
$$\mu(b)^{p-1}, \mu(a)\mu(b)^{p-1}, \ldots, \mu(a)^{k_p-1}\mu(b)^{p-1}.$$

The number of matrices in this span is equal to the dimension of $\mu(a)$ and $\mu(b)$, which in our case is d. Further, a basis for the algebra is contained within this span. Therefore the inside weights can be represented in d dimensions.

On the other hand, if the weights come from a ring, the above fact does not hold in general [7]. Going beyond binary languages, if Σ has four or more symbols, then inside weights might need as many as $\lfloor d^2/4 \rfloor + 1$ dimensions, which is not much of an improvement [5]. The case of three symbols remains open [7] (Fig. 2).

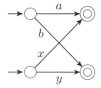

Fig. 2. Example commutative automaton whose inside weights require storing more than d values.

5.3   Regular Expressions

Based on the above results, we might not be optimistic about efficiently representing inside weights for languages other than unary languages. But in this subsection, we show that for multiset automata converted from multiset regular expressions, we can still represent inside weights using only d coefficients. We show this inductively on the structure of the regular expression.

First, we need some properties of the matrices $\kappa(a)$.

Lemma 1. *If $\mu(a)$ and $\kappa(a)$ are constructed from a multiset regular expression, then*

1. $\kappa(a)\kappa(a) = \kappa(a)$.
2. $\kappa(a)\kappa(b) = \kappa(b)\kappa(a)$.
3. $\mu(a)\kappa(a) = 0$.
4. $\mu(a)\kappa(b) = \kappa(b)\mu(a)$ *if $a \neq b$.*

To show that $\mathrm{Ins}(M)$ can be expressed in d dimensions, we will need to prove an additional property about the structure of $\mathrm{Ins}(M)$. Note that if $\mathrm{Ins}(M)$ is not a free-module, then $\dim \mathrm{Ins}(M)$ is the size of the generating set we construct.

Theorem 4. *If M is a ring-weighted multiset automaton with d states converted from a regular expression, then*

1. $\dim \mathrm{Ins}(M) = d$.
2. $\mathrm{Ins}(M)$ *can be decomposed into a direct sum*

$$\mathrm{Ins}(M) \cong \bigoplus_{\Delta \subseteq \Sigma} \mathrm{Ins}_\Delta(M)$$

where $\mu(w) \in \mathrm{Ins}_\Delta(M)$ iff $\mathrm{alph}(w) = \Delta$.

Proof. By induction on the structure of the regular expression α.

If α is unary: the Cayley-Hamilton theorem gives a generating set $\{I, \mu(a), \ldots, \mu(a)^{d-1}\}$, which has size d. Moreover, let $\mathrm{Ins}_\emptyset(M)$ be the span of $\{I\}$ and $\mathrm{Ins}_{\{a\}}(M)$ be the span of the $\mu(a)^i$ ($i > 0$). The automaton M, by construction, has a state (the initial state) with no incoming transitions. That is, its transition matrix has a zero column, which means that its characteristic polynomial has no I term. Therefore, if $w \neq \epsilon$, $\mu(w) \in \mathrm{Ins}_{\{a\}}(M)$.

If $\alpha = k\alpha_1$, then $\mathrm{Ins}(M) = \mathrm{Ins}(M_1)$, so both properties hold of $\mathrm{Ins}(M)$ if they hold of $\mathrm{Ins}(M_1)$.

If $\alpha = \alpha_1 \cup \alpha_2$, the inside weights of $M_1 \cup M_2$ for w are

$$\mu(w) = \prod_{a \in w} \mu(a) = \prod_a \begin{bmatrix} \mu_1(a) & 0 \\ 0 & \mu_2(a) \end{bmatrix} = \begin{bmatrix} \prod_a \mu_1(a) & 0 \\ 0 & \prod_a \mu_2(a) \end{bmatrix} = \begin{bmatrix} \mu_1(w) & 0 \\ 0 & \mu_2(w) \end{bmatrix}.$$

Thus, $\mathrm{Ins}(M) \cong \mathrm{Ins}(M_1) \oplus \mathrm{Ins}(M_2)$, and $\dim \mathrm{Ins}(M) = \dim \mathrm{Ins}(M_1) + \dim \mathrm{Ins}(M_2)$. Moreover, $\mathrm{Ins}_\Delta(M) \cong \mathrm{Ins}_\Delta(M_1) \oplus \mathrm{Ins}_\Delta(M_2)$.

If $\alpha = \alpha_1\alpha_2$, the inside weights of $M_1 \sqcup M_2$ for w are

$$\mu(w) = \prod_{a \in w} \mu(a) = \prod_{a \in w} (\mu_1(a) \otimes \kappa_2(a) + I \otimes \mu_2(a))$$

$$= \sum_{uv=w} \left(\prod_{a \in u} \mu_1(a) \otimes \prod_{a \in u} \kappa_2(a) \prod_{a \in v} \mu_2(a) \right)$$

$$= \sum_{uv=w} \mu_1(u) \otimes \kappa_2(u)\mu_2(v)$$

where we have used Lemma 1 and properties of the Kronecker product. Let $\{e_i\}$ and $\{f_i\}$ be a generating set for $\mathrm{Ins}(M_1)$ and $\mathrm{Ins}(M_2)$, respectively. Then the above can be written as a linear combination of terms of the form $e_i \otimes \kappa_2(u)f_j$. We take these as a generating set for $\mathrm{Ins}(M)$. Although it may seem that there are too many generators, note that if both $\mu_1(u)$ and $\mu_1(u')$ depend on e_i, they belong to the same submodule and therefore use the same symbols, so $\kappa_2(u) = \kappa_2(u')$ (Lemma 1.1). Therefore, the $e_i \otimes \kappa_2(u)f_j$ form a generating set of size $\dim \mathrm{Ins}(M_1) \cdot \dim \mathrm{Ins}(M_2)$.

Moreover, let $\mathrm{Ins}_\Delta(M)$ be the submodule spanned by all the $\mu_1(u) \otimes \kappa_2(u)\mu_2(v)$ such that $\mathrm{alph}(uv) = \Delta$. $\qquad\square$

6 Conclusion

We have examined weighted multiset automata, showing how to construct them from weighted regular expressions, how to learn weights automatically from data, and how, in certain cases, inside weights can be computed more efficiently in terms of both time and space complexity. We leave implementation and application of these methods for future work.

Acknowledgements. We would like to thank the anonymous reviewers for their very detailed and helpful comments.

This research is based upon work supported by the Office of the Director of National Intelligence (ODNI), Intelligence Advanced Research Projects Activity (IARPA), via AFRL Contract #FA8650-17-C-9116. The views and conclusions contained herein are those of the authors and should not be interpreted as necessarily representing the official policies or endorsements, either expressed or implied, of the ODNI, IARPA, or the U.S. Government. The U.S. Government is authorized to reproduce and distribute reprints for Governmental purposes notwithstanding any copyright annotation thereon.

References

1. Barría, J., Halmos, P.R.: Vector bases for two commuting matrices. Linear and Multilinear Algebra **27**, 147–157 (1990)
2. Berry, G., Sethi, R.: From regular expressions to deterministic automata. Theor. Comput. Sci. **48**, 117–126 (1986)
3. Chiang, D., Drewes, F., Lopez, A., Satta, G.: Weighted DAG automata for semantic graphs. Comput. Linguist. **44**, 119–186 (2018)
4. Droste, M., Gastin, P.: The Kleene-Schützenberger theorem for formal power series in partially commuting variables. Inf. Comput. **153**, 47–80 (1999)
5. Gerstenhaber, M.: On dominance and varieties of commuting matrices. Ann. Math. **73**(2), 324–348 (1961)
6. Harary, F.: The determinant of the adjacency matrix of a graph. SIAM Rev. **4**(3), 202–210 (1962)
7. Holbrook, J., O'Meara, K.C.: Some thoughts on Gerstenhaber's theorem. Linear Algebra Appl. **466**, 267–295 (2015)
8. Johnson, D.B.: Finding all the elementary circuits of a directed graph. SIAM J. Comput. **4**(1), 77–84 (1975)

9. Ladner, R.E., Fischer, M.J.: Parallel prefix computation. J. ACM (JACM) **27**(4), 831–838 (1980)
10. Rutherford, D.E.: The Cayley-Hamilton theorem for semi-rings. Proc. Roy. Soc. Edinb. **66**(4), 211–215 (1964)
11. Thomassen, C.: On digraphs with no two disjoint directed cycles. Combinatorica **7**(1), 145–150 (1987)

Solving Parity Games:
Explicit vs Symbolic

Antonio Di Stasio[1(✉)], Aniello Murano[1], and Moshe Y. Vardi[2]

[1] Università di Napoli "Federico II", Naples, Italy
distasio.antonio@gmail.com
[2] Rice University, Houston, USA

Abstract. In this paper we provide a broad investigation of the symbolic approach for solving Parity Games. Specifically, we implement in a fresh tool, called SymPGSolver, four symbolic algorithms to solve Parity Games and compare their performances to the corresponding explicit versions for different classes of games. By means of benchmarks, we show that for random games, even for constrained random games, explicit algorithms actually perform better than symbolic algorithms. The situation changes, however, for structured games, where symbolic algorithms seem to have the advantage. This suggests that when evaluating algorithms for parity-game solving, it would be useful to have real benchmarks and not only random benchmarks, as the common practice has been.

1 Introduction

Parity games (PGs) [12,24] are abstract games with a key role in automata theory and formal verification [7,9,18,19,23]. PGs are two-player turn-based games played on directed graphs whose nodes are labeled with priorities. Players take turns moving a token along the graph's edges, starting from an initial node. A play induces an infinite path and Player 0 wins the play if the smallest priority visited infinitely often is even. Solving a PG amounts checking whether Player 0 can force such a winning play. Several algorithms to solve PGs have been proposed aiming to tighten the asymptotic complexity of the problem, as well as to work well in practice. Well known are *Recursive* (RE) [24], small-progress measures (SPM) [14], and APT [10,18], the latter originated to deal with the emptiness of parity automata. Notably, all these algorithms are *explicit*, that is, they are formulated in terms of the underlying game graphs. Due to the exponential growth of finite-state systems, and, consequently, of the corresponding game graphs, the state-explosion problem limits the scalability of these algorithms in practice.

Symbolic algorithms are an efficient way to deal with extremely large graphs. They avoid explicit access to graphs by using a set of predefined operations that manipulate Binary Decision Diagrams (BDDs) [3] representing these graphs.

Work supported by NSF grants CCF-1319459 and IIS-1527668, NSF Expeditions in Computing project "ExCAPE: Expeditions in Computer Augmented Program Engineering" and GNCS 2018: Logica, Automi e Giochi per Sistemi Auto-adattivi.

C. Câmpeanu (Ed.): CIAA 2018, LNCS 10977, pp. 159–172, 2018.
https://doi.org/10.1007/978-3-319-94812-6_14

This enables handling large graphs succinctly, and, in general, it makes symbolic algorithms scale better than explicit ones. For example, in hardware model checking symbolic algorithms enable going from millions of states to 10^{20} states and more [4,20]. In contrast, in the context of PG solvers, symbolic algorithms have been only marginally explored. In this direction we just mention a symbolic implementation of RE [2,16], which, however, has been done for different purposes and no benchmark comparison with the explicit version has been carried out. Other works close to this topic and worth mentioning are [5,8], where a symbolic version of SPM has been theoretically studied but not implemented.

In this work we provide the first broad investigation of the symbolic approach for solving PGs. We implement four symbolic algorithms and compare their performances to the corresponding explicit versions for different classes of PGs. Specifically, we implement in a new tool, called SymPGSolver, the symbolic versions of RE, APT, and two variants of SPM. The tool also allows to generate random games, as well as compare the performance of different symbolic algorithms.

The main result we obtain from our comparisons is that for random games, and even for constrained random games (see Sect. 4), explicit algorithms actually perform better than symbolic ones, most likely because BDDs do not offer any compression for random sets. The situation changes, however, for structured games, where symbolic algorithms sometimes outperform explicit algorithms. This is similar to what has been observed in the context of model checking [11]. We take this as an important development because it suggests a methodological weakness in this field of investigation, due to the excessive reliance on random benchmarks. We believe that, in evaluating algorithms for PG solving, it would be useful to have real benchmarks and not only random benchmarks, as the common practice has been. This would lead to a deeper understanding of the relative merits of PG solving algorithms, both explicit and symbolic.

2   Explicit and Symbolic Parity Games

Explicit Parity Games. A *Parity Game* (PG, for short) is a tuple $\mathcal{G} \triangleq \langle P_0, P_1, Mv, p \rangle$, where P_0 and P_1 are two finite disjoint sets of nodes for Player 0 and Player 1, respectively, with $P = P_0 \cup P_1$, $Mv \subseteq P \times P$ is the binary relation of moves, and $p : P \rightarrow \mathbb{N}$ is the priority function. By $Mv(q) \triangleq \{q' \in P : (q, q') \in Mv\}$ we denote the set of nodes to which the token can be moved, starting from q.

A *play* over $\mathcal{G}$ is an infinite sequence $\pi = q_1 q_2 \ldots \in P^\omega$ of nodes that agree with Mv, i.e., $(q_i, q_{i+1}) \in Mv$, for each $i \in \mathbb{N}$. By $p(\pi) = p(q_1)p(q_2) \ldots \in \mathbb{N}^\omega$ we denote the priority sequence associated to π, and by $\mathsf{Inf}(\pi)$ and $\mathsf{Inf}(p(\pi))$, the sets of nodes and priorities that occur infinitely often in π and $p(\pi)$, respectively. A play π is *winning* for Player 0 if $\min(\mathsf{Inf}(p(\pi)))$ is even. Player 0 (Player 1) strategy is a function $\mathsf{str}_0 : P^* P_0 \rightarrow P$ ($\mathsf{str}_1 : P^* P_1 \rightarrow P$) that agrees with Mv. Given a node q, $\mathsf{play}(q, \mathsf{str}_0, \mathsf{str}_1)$ is the unique play starting in q that agrees with both str_0 and str_1. Player 0 *wins* the game $\mathcal{G}$ from q if a strategy str_0

exists such that, for all strategies str_1 it holds that $\mathsf{play}(q, \mathsf{str}_0, \mathsf{str}_1)$ is winning for Player 0. Then q is declared *winning* for Player 0. By $\mathrm{Win}_0(\mathcal{G})$ we denote the set of winning nodes in $\mathcal{G}$ for Player 0. Parity games enjoy determinacy, *i.e.*, for every node q, either $q \in \mathrm{Win}_0(\mathcal{G})$ or $q \in \mathrm{Win}_1(\mathcal{G})$ [12]. Also, if Player 0 has a winning strategy from a node q, then she has a memoryless one from q [24]. A strategy str_0 is *memoryless* if, for all prefixes of plays ρ_1, ρ_2, it holds that $\mathsf{str}_0(\rho_1) = \mathsf{str}_0(\rho_2)$ iff last nodes of ρ_1 and ρ_2 coincide. Then, one can use str_0 defined as $\mathsf{str}_0 : \mathrm{P}_0 \to \mathrm{P}$.

Symbolic Parity Games. We start with some notation. In the sequel we use symbols x_i for propositions (variables), l_i for literals, *i.e.*, positive or negative variables, f for a generic Boolean formula, $\|f\|$ for the set of interpretations that makes the formula f true, and $\lambda(f) \subseteq V$ for the set of variables in f.

Definition 1. *Given a PG $\mathcal{G} \triangleq \langle \mathrm{P}_0, \mathrm{P}_1, Mv, \mathsf{p} \rangle$, the corresponding symbolic PG (SPG, for short) is the tuple $\mathcal{F} = (\mathcal{X}, \mathcal{X}_M, f_{\mathrm{P}_0}, f_{\mathrm{P}_1}, f_{Mv}, \eta_{\mathsf{p}})$ defined as follows:*

- *$\mathcal{X} = \{x_1, \dots, x_n\}$, with $n = \lceil log_2(|\mathrm{P}|) \rceil$, is the set of propositions used to encode nodes in $\mathcal{G}$, i.e., to each $v \in \mathrm{P}$ we associate a Boolean formula $f_v = l_{v,1} \wedge \dots \wedge l_{v,n}$ where $l_{v,i}$ is either x_i or $\overline{x_i}$. We also associate to v the interpretation $\mathcal{X}_v \in 2^{\mathcal{X}}$, i.e., the subset of variables appearing positively in f_v.*
- *$\mathcal{X}_M = \{x'_1, \dots, x'_n\}$, with $n = \lceil log_2(|\mathrm{P}|) \rceil$, is the set of propositions used to encode the successor nodes such that $\mathcal{X} \cap \mathcal{X}_M = \emptyset$. We extend to $\mathcal{X}_M$ the definitions of f_v and X_v as used in the previous item.*
- *f_{P_i}, for $i \in \{0, 1\}$, is a Boolean formula such that $\|f_{\mathrm{P}_i}\| = \mathrm{P}_i$.*
- *f_{Mv} is a Boolean formula over the propositions $\mathcal{X} \cup \mathcal{X}_M$ such that $\|f_{Mv}\| = Mv$.*
- *η_{p} is the symbolic representation of the priority function p; formally, it is a function $\eta_{\mathsf{p}} : 2^{\mathcal{X}} \to \mathbb{N}$ associating to each interpretation X_v a natural number.*

Example. Consider the PG depicted in Fig. 1. It has $\mathrm{P}_0 = \{q_0, q_2\}$ (circles) and $\mathrm{P}_1 = \{q_1\}$ (squares); Mv is given by arrows; and $\mathsf{p}(q_i) = i$, for $1 \leq i \leq 3$.

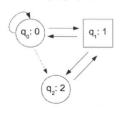

Fig. 1. A parity game

The correlating SPG $\mathcal{F} = (\mathcal{X}, \mathcal{X}_M, f_{\mathrm{P}_0}, f_{\mathrm{P}_1}, f_{Mv}, \eta_{\mathsf{p}})$ is as follows: $\mathcal{X} = \{x_1, x_2\}$ and $\mathcal{X}_M = \{y_1, y_2\}$ are the set of propositions; $f_{\mathrm{P}_0} = (\overline{x_1} \wedge \overline{x_2}) \vee (x_1 \wedge \overline{x_2})$ and $f_{\mathrm{P}_1} = (\overline{x_1} \wedge x_2)$ are Boolean formulas representing P_0 and P_1, respectively; $f_{Mv} = (\overline{x_1} \wedge \overline{y_1} \wedge \overline{x_2} \wedge \overline{y_2}) \vee (\overline{x_1} \wedge \overline{y_1} \wedge \overline{x_2} \wedge y_2) \vee (\overline{x_1} \wedge \overline{y_1} \wedge x_2 \wedge \overline{y_2}) \vee (\overline{x_1} \wedge y_1 \wedge \overline{x_2} \wedge \overline{y_2}) \vee (\overline{x_1} \wedge y_1 \wedge x_2 \wedge \overline{y_2}) \vee (x_1 \wedge \overline{y_1} \wedge \overline{x_2} \wedge y_2)$ is the Boolean formula for Mv; finally, the function η_{p}, given by $\eta_{\mathsf{p}}(0, i) - i$, for $1 \leq i \leq 3$, represents the priority function p.

To solve an SPG we compute the Boolean formulas f_{Win_0} over $\mathcal{X}$ that is satisfied by those interpretations that correspond to winning nodes for Player 0.

For technical reasons, we also need the definition of symbolic sub-games.

Definition 2. *Let* $\mathcal{G} \triangleq \langle P_0, P_1, Mv, p \rangle$ *be a PG and* $U \subseteq P$. *By* $\mathcal{G} \setminus U = (P_0 \setminus U, P_1 \setminus U, Mv \setminus (U \times P \cup P \times U), p_{|P \setminus U})$ *we denote the PG restricted to nodes* $P \setminus U$.

Let f_U *be a Boolean formula such that* $\|f_U\| = U$ *and* $\mathcal{F} = (\mathcal{X}, \mathcal{X}_M, f_{P_0}, f_{P_1}, f_{Mv}, \eta_p)$ *be the corresponding SPG of the PG* $\mathcal{G}$. *By* $\mathcal{F}_{P \setminus U} = (\mathcal{X}, \mathcal{X}_M, f'_{P_0}, f'_{P_1}, f'_{Mv}, \eta'_p)$ *we denote the SPG of* $\mathcal{G} \setminus U$, *where:*

- $f'_{P_i} = f_{P_i} \wedge \neg f_U$, *for* $i \in \{0, 1\}$, *is the Boolean formula for nodes* $v \in P_i \setminus U$;
- $f'_{Mv} = f_{Mv} \wedge \neg(f_U \vee f'_U)$, *where* $\|f'_U\| = U$ *and* $\lambda(f'_U) = \mathcal{X}_M$, *is the Boolean formula representing moves restricted to* $Mv \setminus (U \times P \cup P \times U)$;
- $\eta'_p = 2^{\mathcal{X}} \to \mathbb{N}$ *is the symbolic representation of* $p_{|P \setminus U}$ *that associates to the interpretations* X_v *satisfying the Boolean formula* $f_P \wedge \neg f_U$ *a natural number.*

3   Solving Parity Games: Explicit vs Symbolic Algorithms

3.1   Explicit Algorithms

Small Progress Measures Algorithm (SPM) [13]. The core idea of SPM is a *ranking function* that assigns to each node a vector of counters (namely a *progress measure*) collecting the number n of times Player 1 can force a play to visit an odd priority until a lower priority is seen. If this value is sufficiently large, then the node is declared winning for Player 1. SPM computes the *progress measure* by updating the values of a node according to those associated to its successors, *i.e.*, by computing a least fixed-point for all nodes with respect to the ranking function.

We fix some notation. Let $\mathcal{G}$ be a PG with maximal priority c and $d \in \mathbb{N}^c$ be a c-tuple of non-negative integers. By $<$ we denote the usual lexicographic ordering over $\mathbb{N}^c$. For each odd number i, by n_i we denote the number of nodes in $\mathcal{G}$ with priority i. For i even, we set $n_i = 0$. The progress measure domain is defined as $M_G^\top = M_G \cup \{\top\}$ with $M_G = (M_0 \times \ldots \times M_{c-1})$ and $M_i = [n_i]$. The element $\top$ is the biggest value such that $m < \top$ for all $m \in M_G$. For $d = (d_0, \ldots, d_{c-1})$ and $l < c$, we set $\langle d \rangle_l = (d_0, \ldots, d_l, 0, \ldots, 0)$, i.e., all $d_{i>l}$ in d are set to 0. By $\mathrm{inc}(d)$ we denote the smallest tuple $d' \in M_G^\top$ such that $d < d'$. This notion easily extends to tuples in $\mathbb{N}^l$ by defining $\mathrm{inc}_l(d)$ with $l > 0$ to be the smallest tuple $d' \in M_G^\top$ such that $d <_l d'$ iff $\langle d \rangle_l < \langle d' \rangle_l$. In particular, for $d = \top$ we have $\mathrm{inc}_l(d) = d$. Otherwise, $\mathrm{inc}_l(d) = \langle d \rangle_l$ if l is even and $\min\{y \in M_G^\top | y >_l d\}$ if l is odd. To conclude we introduce a *ranking function* $\varrho : P \to M_G^\top$ that associates to each node either a c-tuple in M_G or the value $\top$, and a function *Lift* that defines the increment of a node v based on its priority and the values of its neighbors. The formal definition of *Lift* follows.

$$
\mathrm{Lift}(\varrho, v)(u) = \begin{cases} \mathrm{inc}_{p(v)}(\min\{\varrho(w) | (v, w) \in Mv\}), & \text{if } v \in P_0 \\ \mathrm{inc}_{p(v)}(\max\{\varrho(w) | (v, w) \in Mv\}), & \text{if } v \in P_1 \\ \varrho(u), & \text{otherwise} \end{cases}
$$

Lift is monotone and the progress measures over v is the least fixed point of $Lift(\cdot, v)$. The solution algorithm starts by setting 0 to every node. Then, it applies the lift as long as $\text{Lift}(\varrho, v)(u) > \varrho(v)$ for some node v. Next lemma relates the solution of a PG $\mathcal{G}$ with the least fixed point calculation of Lift.

Lemma 1 ([13]). *If ϱ is a progress measures function then the set of nodes v with $\varrho(v) < \top$ is the set of winning nodes for Player 0.*

The APT Algorithm (APT) [10]. APT was first introduced by Kupferman and Vardi in [18] to solve parity games via emptiness checking of parity automata. It makes use of two special sets of nodes, V and A, called *Visiting* and *Avoiding*, respectively. Intuitively, a node is visiting for a player at the stage in which it is clear that, by reaching that node, he can surely induce a winning play. The reasoning is symmetric for the avoiding set. The algorithm, in turns, tries to partition all nodes of the game into these two sets. Some formal details follow.

Given a PG $\mathcal{G}$, an *Extended Parity Game*, (EPG, for short) is a tuple $\langle P_0, P_1, V, A, Mv, p \rangle$ where P_0, P_1, $P = P_0 \cup P_1$, Mv, and p are as in PG. Moreover, the sets $V, A \subseteq P$ are two disjoint sets of *Visiting* and *Avoiding* nodes, respectively. For EPGs we make use of the same notion of play as given for PG. A play π in $P \cdot (P \setminus (V \cup A))^* \cdot V \cdot P^\omega$ is winning for Player 0, while a play π in $P \cdot (P \setminus (V \cup A))^* \cdot A \cdot P^\omega$ is winning for Player 1. A play π that never hits either V or A is declared winning for Player 0 iff it satisfies the parity condition, *i.e.*, $\min(\mathsf{Inf}(p(\pi)))$ is even, otherwise it is winning for Player 1.

To solve an EPG, APT makes use of two functions: $\mathsf{force}_i(X)$ and $\mathsf{Win}_i(\alpha, V, A)$. For $X \subseteq P$, $\mathsf{force}_i(X) = \{q \in P_i : X \cap Mv(q) \neq \emptyset\} \cup \{q \in P_{1-i} : X \subseteq Mv(q)\}$ is the set of nodes from which Player i can force, in one step, a move to X. The function $\mathsf{Win}_i(\alpha, V, A)$ denotes the nodes from which Player i has a strategy that avoids A, and either forces a visit to V or satisfies the parity condition α. Note that in APT α is given as a finite sequence $\alpha = F_0 \cdot \ldots \cdot F_k$ of sets, where $F_j = p^{-1}(j)$, i.e., the set of nodes with priority j. Formally, $\mathsf{Win}_i(\alpha, V, A)$ is defined as follows. If $\alpha = \varepsilon$, then $\mathsf{Win}_i(\alpha, V, A) = \mathsf{force}_i(V)$. Otherwise, if $\alpha = F \cdot \alpha'$, for some set F, then $\mathsf{Win}_i(\alpha, V, A) = P \setminus \mu Y(\mathsf{Win}_{1-i}(\alpha', A \cup (F \setminus Y), V \cup (F \cap Y)))$, where μ is the least fixed-point operator.

Recursive Zielonka Algorithm (RE) [24]. Introduced by Zielonka, RE makes use of a divide and conquer technique. The core subroutine of RE is the *attractor*. Intuitively, given a set of nodes U the attractor of U for a Player i represents those nodes that i can force the play toward. At each step, the algorithm removes all nodes with the highest priority p, together with all nodes Player $i = p \bmod 2$ can attract to them, and recursively computes the winning sets (W_0, W_1) for Player 0 and Player 1, respectively, on the remaining subgame. If Player i wins the subgame, then he also wins the whole starting game. Otherwise if Player i does not win the subgame, *i.e.*, W_{1-i} is non empty, the algorithm computes the attractor for Player $1 - i$ of W_{1-i} and recursively solves the subgame.

3.2   Symbolic Algorithms

We now describe symbolic versions of the explicit algorithms listed in Sect. 3.1.

SPG Implementation. An SPG can be implemented using Binary Decision Diagrams (BDDs) and Algebraic Decision Diagrams (ADDs) [1] to represent and manipulate the associated Boolean functions introduced along with its definition. ADDs were introduced to extend BDDs by allowing values from any arbitrary finite domain to be associated with the terminal nodes of the diagram, *i.e.*, an ADD can be seen as a BDD whose leaves may take on values belonging to a set of constants different from 0 and 1. Given an SPG $\mathcal{F} = (\mathcal{X}_1, \mathcal{X}_2, f_{P_0}, f_{P_1}, f_{Mv}, \eta_p)$ with maximal priority c, we use BDDs to represent the Boolean formulas f_{P_0}, f_{P_1} and f_{Mv}, and an ADD for the function η_p. Moreover, we decompose the function η_p into a sequence of BDDs $\mathcal{B} = \langle B_0, \ldots, B_{c-1} \rangle$ where each B_i encodes the nodes with priority i, to easily manage the selection of a set of nodes with a specific priority. In the sequel, by BDD (*resp.*, ADD) f, we denote the BDD (*resp.*, ADD) representing the function f.

Symbolic SPM (SSP) [5]. This is the first symbolic implementation of SPM we are aware of, and which we describe with some minor corrections compared to the one in [5]. Lift is encoded by using ADDs and the algorithm computes the progress measure as the least fixed point f_G of Lift(f, v) on a ranking function here given by the function $f : P \to D$, with $D = M_G \cup \{\infty, -\infty\}$. The algorithm takes as input an SPG $\mathcal{F}$ and returns an ADD representing the least fixed point f_G such that the set of winning nodes for Player 0 is $\{v | f_G(v) < \infty\}$, and the set of winning nodes for Player 1 is $\{v | f_G(v) = \infty\}$. See Algorithm 1.

Algorithm 1. Symbolic Small Progress Measures

```
1: procedure PARITY (ℱ)
2:     f =→ (f_P, −∞);
3:     repeat
4:         f_old = f; f = false;
5:         for  j = 0 to c − 1 do
6:             f = f OR MAXeo(f_old, j) OR MINeo(f_old, j);
7:     until f = f_old
```

The algorithm calls the procedure MAXeo (*resp.*, MINeo), which given an ADD $f : P \to D$, the BDD f_{Mv}, and $1 \le j \le k$, returns an ADD that assigns to every node $v \in P_1$ (*resp.*, $v \in P_0$,), with $p(v) = j$, the value $inc_j(\max\{f(v')|(v, v') \in Mv\})$ (*resp.*, $inc_j(\min\{f(v')|(v, v') \in Mv\})$).

MINeo (*resp.*, MAXeo) aims at constructing an ADD that represents the ranking function $f_{\min}(v) = \min\{f(v')|(v, v') \in Mv\}$ (*resp.*, $f_{\max}(v) = \max\{f(v')|(v, v') \in Mv\}$). To do this, given an ADD $f : P \to D$ and the BDD f_{Mv}, it is generated an ADD $f_{suc} : (P \times P) \to D$ such that $f_{suc}(v, v') = d$ if $(v, v') \in Mv$ and $f(v') = d$. Then, the ADD f_{suc} is given in input to the procedure MIN, described in Algorithm 2, that constructs the ADD for f_{min}. The procedure MAX is defined similarly. Let n be an ADD node, we refer to the left and right successors of n as $n.l$ and $n.r$, respectively, and refer to the variable that n represents as $n.v$.

Algorithm 2. Procedure MIN

1: **procedure** MIN(ADD n)
2:     **if** n is a terminal node **then**
3:         return n
4:     **if** $n.v$ is in $\mathcal{X}$ **then**
5:         return $(n.v$ AND MIN$(n.r))$ OR (NOT $n.v$ AND MIN$(n.l))$
6:     **if** $n.v$ is in $\mathcal{X}'$ **then**
7:         return MERGE(MIN$(n.r)$, MIN$(n.l)$)

The procedure MIN calls the procedure MERGE, reported in Algorithm 3, that gets in input the pointer to the roots n_1 and n_2 of two ADDs representing the functions f_1 and f_2, both from some set $U \subseteq P$ to D, and merges them to an ADD in which every $u \in U$ is mapped into $\min(f_1(u), f_2(u))$.

Algorithm 3. Procedure MERGE

1: **procedure** MERGE(ADD n_1, ADD n_2)
2:     **if** n_1 and n_2 are a terminal nodes **then**
3:         return $\min(n1, n2)$
4:     **if** $o(n_1.v) < o(n_2.v)$ **then**
5:         return $(n_1.v$ AND MERGE$(n_1.r, n_2))$ OR (NOT $n_1.v$ AND MERGE$(n_1.l, n_2))$
6:     **if** $o(n_1.v) > o(n_2.v)$ **then**
7:         return $(n_2.v$ AND MERGE$(n_2.r, n_1))$ OR (NOT $n_2.v$ AND MERGE$(n_2.l, n_1))$
8:     return $(n_1.v$ AND MERGE$(n_1.r, n_2.r))$ OR (NOT $n_1.v$ AND MERGE$(n_1.l, n_2.l))$

Set-Based Symbolic SPM (SSP2) [8]. This is a symbolic implementation of SPM that has been introduced very recently. It allows to use only basic set operations like $\cup, \cap, \backslash, \subseteq$, and one-step predecessor operations for its description. Unlike the implementation described previously, the ranking function is implicitly encoded by using sets of nodes. This allows representing the *Lift* operator just by BDDs.

To encode the ranking function the algorithm defines for each rank $r \in M_G^\top$ the set S_r containing the nodes with rank r or higher. Formally, given the ranking function $\varrho : P \to M_G^\top$, the corresponding sets are defined as $S_r = \{v | \varrho(v) \geq r\}$. Conversely, given the family of sets $\{S_r\}_r$, the corresponding ranking function, say $\varrho_{\{S_r\}_r}$, is given by $\varrho_{\{S_r\}_r}(v) = \max\{r \in M_G^\top | v \in S_r\}$. This formulation encodes the ranking function with sets but uses exponential in c many sets.

Space is reduced to a linear number of sets by encoding the value of each coordinate of the rank r, separately. In detail, for each odd priority i, the algorithm defines the sets $C_0^i, \ldots, C_{n_i}^i$. Each set C_x^i with $x \in \{0, \ldots, n_i\}$ contains the nodes that have x as i-th coordinate of their rank. Therefore, the algorithm has to construct the set S_r whenever it needs it.

Let $Cpre_i(X) = \{q \in P_i : X \cap Mv(q) \neq \emptyset\} \cup \{q \in P_{1-i} : X \subseteq Mv(q)\}$ the one-step controllable predecessor operator. The algorithm starts initializing the sets S_r for $r > 0$ to empty, and S_0 with the set of all nodes P. The rank r initially is set to the second lowest rank $\mathrm{inc}((0,\dots,0))$. Then, at each iteration the set S_r is updated for the current value of r by using the *Lift* encoded by the $Cpre_i$ operator. After the update of S_r, it is checked if $S'_r \supseteq S_r$ for all $r' < r$, *i.e.*, if the property of the *anti-monotonicity* is preserved. Anti-monotonicity together with the definition of the sets S'_r allows to decide whether the rank of a node v can be increased to r by only considering one set $S'_{r'}$. If the anti-monotonicity is preserved, then for $r < \top$ the value of r is increased to the next highest rank and for $r = \top$ the algorithm terminates. Otherwise the nodes newly added to S_r are also added to all sets with $r' < r$ that do not already contain them; the variable r is then updated to the lowest r' for which a new node is added to S'_r in this iteration. Due to lack of space, we omit the algorithm (see [8] for more details).

Symbolic Versions of RE (SRE) and APT (SAPT). RE and APT can be easily rephrased symbolically by using BDDs to represent the operations they make use of set basic operations like union, intersection, complement, and inclusion; the controllable predecessor operators used to implement the function force$_i$ in APT, and the attractor in RE; the symbolic construction of a subgame used in RE and implemented following the definition of symbolic subgame reported previously.

4   Experimental Evaluations: Methodology and Results

We now analyze the performance of the introduced symbolic approach to solve PGs and compare with the explicit one. We have implemented the symbolic algorithms described in Sect. 3.2 in a fresh tool, called SymPGSolver (Symbolic Parity Games Solver). SymPGSolver[1] is implemented in C++ and uses the CUDD[2] package as the underlying BDD and ADD library. The platform provides a collection of tools to randomly generate and solve SPGs, as well as compare the performance of different symbolic algorithms.

We have also compared them with *Oink*, a platform recently developed in C++ by van Dijk [22], which collects the large majority of explicit PGs algorithms introduced in the literature [6,14,15,24].

4.1   Experimental Results

In this section we report on some experimental results on evaluating the performance for the explicit algorithms RE, APT, and SPM, as well as their corresponding

---

[1] The tool is available for download from https://github.com/antoniodistasio/sympgsolver.

[2] http://vlsi.colorado.edu/~fabio/CUDD/.

symbolic versions SRE, SAPT, SSP and SSP2. All tests have been run on an Intel Core i7 @2.40 GHz, with 16 GB of RAM running macOS 10.12. We have used different classes of parity games: random games with linear structures, ladder games, clique games as well as games corresponding to practical model checking problems. Random games are generated by SymPGSolver, while for ladder and clique games we use *Oink*. We have taken 100 different instances for each class of games and used the average time execution. In all tests, we use $abort_T$ to denote an aborted execution due to time-out (greater than 200 s). On the class of ladder games and in model checking problems the benchmarks have been executed using the variable ordering given by the heuristic WINDOW2 module available in the CUDD package.

Random Games with Linear Structure. Tabakov and Vardi showed that in the context of automata-theoretic problems, explicit algorithms generally dominate symbolic algorithms, as BDDs do not offer any compression for random sets [21]. We found that the same holds for parity-game solving (we omit details due to lack of space). In [21] it was observed that, in case of random games with linear structures, the symbolic algorithms are the best performing ones. Hence, we have investigated the same class here as well, but with a different outcome.

A random game with *linear structure* is built by restricting the transition relation as follows: a node v_i can make a transition to node v_j, where $0 \leq i, j \leq |P| - 1$, if and only if $|i - j| \leq d$, where d is named as the *distance* parameter.

Table 1. Runtime executions of the symbolic algorithms

n	2 Pr				3 Pr				5 Pr			
	SRE	SAPT	SSP	SSP2	SRE	SAPT	SSP	SSP2	SRE	SAPT	SSP	SSP2
1,000	0.04	0.03	29.89	0,95	0.05	0.10	18.9	1,44	0.05	0.45	15.75	$abort_T$
2,000	0.14	0.12	128.06	2,87	0.13	0.18	79.22	26,24	0.12	1.34	69.6	$abort_T$
3,000	0.25	0.23	$abort_T$	10,15	0.21	0.41	193.06	75,49	0.21	2.03	135.04	$abort_T$
4,000	0.33	0.30	$abort_T$	32,42	0.28	0.60	$abort_T$	146,58	0.3	3.01	$abort_T$	$abort_T$
7,000	0.79	0.73	$abort_T$	$abort_T$	0.65	1.44	$abort_T$	$abort_T$	0.59	7.20	$abort_T$	$abort_T$
10,000	1.16	1.12	$abort_T$	$abort_T$	0.93	2.19	$abort_T$	$abort_T$	1.08	11.72	$abort_T$	$abort_T$
20,000	2.78	3.10	$abort_T$	$abort_T$	2.33	6.34	$abort_T$	$abort_T$	3.69	43.87	$abort_T$	$abort_T$
100,000	19.21	24.4	$abort_T$	$abort_T$	24.38	65.11	$abort_T$	$abort_T$	24.89	$abort_T$	$abort_T$	$abort_T$

Table 1 collects the running time of the symbolic algorithms on random games with linear structures having priorities 2, 3, and 5, and distance $d = 25$. The results show that SAPT performs better than the others in solving games with $n \leq 10,000$ nodes and 2 priorities, while SRE is the best performing in all other cases. Also, they show that SSP and SSP2 have the worst performances in all instances, with SSP overcoming SSP2 of more than 200 s on games with 3,000 nodes. In Table 2 we collect the execution time of the explicit algorithms on the same set of games. The results highlight that the explicit algorithms are faster than the symbolic ones in all instances.

Table 2. Runtime executions of the explicit algorithms

n	2 Pr			3 Pr			5 Pr		
	RE	APT	SPM	RE	APT	SPM	RE	APT	SPM
1,000	0.0008	0.0006	0.0043	0.0008	0.0007	0.0049	0.0008	0.0008	0.0053
2,000	0.0015	0.0012	0.0084	0.0017	0.0016	0.0096	0.0019	0.0029	0.011
3,000	0.0023	0.0017	0.012	0.0025	0.0022	0.014	0.0029	0.0073	0.020
4,000	0.0031	0.0022	0.016	0.0033	0.0028	0.019	0.0035	0.0066	0.027
7,000	0.0051	0.0039	0.025	0.0053	0.0048	0.032	0.0056	0.012	0.039
10,000	0.0065	0.0057	0.035	0.0067	0.0076	0.046	0.0069	0.018	0.051
20,000	0.013	0.011	0.078	0.014	0.021	8.32	0.17	0.019	107.2
100,000	0.094	0.081	0.44	0.099	0.10	1.47	0.10	0.59	80.37

Ladder Games. In a ladder game, every node in P_i has priority i. In addition, each node $v \in P$ has two successors: one in P_0 and one in P_1, which form a node pair. Every pair is connected to the next pair forming a ladder of pairs. Finally, the last pair is connected to the top. The parameter m specifies the number of node pairs. Formally, a ladder game of index m is $\mathcal{G} = (P_0, P_1, Mv, \mathsf{p})$ where $P_0 = \{0, 2, \ldots, 2m - 2\}, P_1 = \{1, 3, \ldots, 2m - 1\}, Mv = \{(v, w) | w \equiv_{2m} v + i$ for $i \in \{1, 2\}\}$, and $\mathsf{p}(v) = v \bmod 2$. Tables 3 and 4 report the benchmarks.

Benchmarks indicate that SRE and SAPT outperform their explicit versions, showing an excellent runtime execution even on fairly large instances. Indeed, while RE needs 6.31 s for games with index $m = 10M$, SRE takes just 0.00015 s. Tests also show that SSP and SSP2 have yet the worst performance (Table 3).

Clique Games. Clique games are fully connected games without self-loops, where P_0 (*resp.*, P_1) contains the nodes with an even index (*resp.*, *odd*) and

Table 3. Runtime executions of the symbolic algorithms on ladder games.

m	SRE	SAPT	SSP	SSP2
1,000	0	0.00013	24.86	0.47
10,000	0.00009	0.00016	abort$_T$	41.22
100,000	0.0001	0.00018	abort$_T$	abort$_T$
1,000,000	0.00012	0.00022	abort$_T$	abort$_T$
10,000,000	0.00015	0.00025	abort$_T$	abort$_T$

Table 4. Runtime executions of the explicit algorithms on ladder games.

m	RE	APT	SPM
1,000	0.0007	0.0006	0.002
10,000	0.006	0.005	0.0017
100,000	0.057	0.054	0.18
1,000,000	0.59	0.56	1.84
10,000,000	6.31	5.02	20.83

each node $v \in P$ has as priority the index of v. An important feature of the clique games is the high number of cycles, which may pose difficulties for certain algorithms. Formally, a clique game of index n is $\mathcal{G} = (P_0, P_1, Mv, p)$ where $P_0 = \{0, 2, \ldots, n-2\}, P_1 = \{1, 3, \ldots, n-1\}, Mv = \{(v, w) | v \neq w\}$, and $p(v) = v$. Benchmarks on clique games are reported in Tables 5 and 6.

Table 5. Runtime executions of the symbolic algorithms on clique games

n	SRE	SAPT	SSP	SSP2
2,000	0.007	0.003	5.53	abort$_T$
4,000	0.018	0.008	19.27	abort$_T$
6,000	0.025	0.012	39.72	abort$_T$
8,000	0.037	0.017	76.23	abort$_T$

Table 6. Runtime executions of the explicit algorithms on clique games

n	RE	APT	SPM
2,000	0.021	0.0105	0.0104
4,000	0.082	0.055	0.055
6,000	0.19	0.21	0.22
8,000	0.35	0.59	0.63

Benchmarks show that SAPT is the best one among the symbolic algorithms in all instances, SAPT and SRE outperform the explicit ones (as in ladder games), and the symbolic versions of SPM do not show good results even on small games.

Finally, we evaluate the symbolic and explicit approaches on some practical model checking problems as in [17]. Specifically, we use models coming from: the Sliding Window Protocol (SWP) with window size (WS) of 2 and 4 (WS represents the boundary of the total number of packets to be acknowledged by the receiver), the Onebit Protocol (OP), and the Lifting Truck (Lift). The properties we check on these models concern: absence of deadlock (ND), a message of a certain type (d1) is received infinitely often (IORD1), if there are infinitely many read steps then there are infinitely many write steps (IORW), liveness, and safety. Note that, in all benchmarks, data size (DS) denotes the number of messages.

Table 7. SWP (Sliding Window Protocol)

n	Pr	Property	SRE	SAPT	SSP	SSP2	RE	APT	SPM	WS	DS
14,065	3	ND	0.00009	0.00006	3.30	0.0001	0.004	0.004	0.029	2	2
17,810	3	IORD1	0.0003	0.0005	abort$_T$	85.4	0.006	0.006	0.037	2	2
34,673	3	IORW	0.0006	0.0008	164.73	56.44	0.015	0.014	0.053	2	2
2,589,056	3	ND	0.0002	abort$_T$	abort$_T$	0.29	1.02	0.93	9.09	4	2
3,487,731	3	IORD1	abort$_T$	abort$_T$	abort$_T$	abort$_T$	1.81	1.4	17.45	4	2
6,823,296	3	IORW	0.3	abort$_T$	abort$_T$	abort$_T$	3.87	3.13	22.26	4	2

As we can see, by comparing Tables 7, 8, and 9, the experiments indicate more nuanced relationship between the symbolic and explicit approaches. Indeed, they show a different behavior depending on the protocol and the property we are

Table 8. OP (Onebit Protocol)

n	Pr	Property	SRE	SAPT	SSP	SSP2	RE	APT	SPM	DS
81,920	3	ND	0.00002	31.69	1.37	0.0016	0.031	0.034	0.22	2
88,833	3	IORD1	0.0027	0.003	abort$_T$	abort$_T$	0.036	0.0038	0.27	2
170,752	3	IORW	14.37	98.4	abort$_T$	abort$_T$	0.07	0.07	0.47	2
289,297	3	ND	0.0001	154.89	12.3	0.0058	0.13	0.12	1.34	4
308,737	3	IORD1	0.0088	0.009	abort$_T$	abort$_T$	0.14	0.13	1.37	4
607,753	3	IORW	43.7	abort$_T$	abort$_T$	abort$_T$	0.29	0.27	2.06	4

Table 9. Lift (Lifting Truck)

n	Pr	Property	SRE	SAPT	SSP	SSP2	RE	APT	SPM	DS
328	1	ND	0.00002	0.002	0.005	0.00002	0.0001	0.0001	0.0004	2
308	1	Safety	0.00002	0.003	0.028	0.00002	0.0001	0.0001	0.0004	2
655	3	Liveness	0.00008	0.0001	5.52	0.09	0.0003	0.0002	0.001	2
51.220	1	Safety	0.0001	1.48	32.14	0.00002	0.01	0.01	0.09	4
53.638	1	ND	0.0001	0.2	4.67	0.0001	0.017	0.015	0.07	4
107,275	3	Liveness	0.005	0.001	abort$_T$	abort$_T$	0.03	0.03	0.18	4

checking. Overall, we note that SRE outperforms the other symbolic algorithms in all protocols, although the advantage over RE is discontinued. Specifically, SRE is the best performing in checking absence of deadlock in all three protocols, but for IORD1 in the SWP protocol with $WS = 2$, or for IORW in the OP protocol, RE exhibits a significant advantage. Differently, SAPT and SSP2 show better performances on a smaller number of properties. Moreover, the results highlights that SSP exhibits the worst performances in all protocols and properties.

5   Concluding Remarks

In this paper we have compared for the first time the performances of different symbolic and explicit versions of classic algorithms to solve parity games. To this aim we have implemented in a fresh tool, which we have called SymPGSolver, the symbolic versions of Recursive [24], APT [10,18], and the small-progress-measures algorithms presented in [5,8].

Our analysis started from constrained random games [21]. The results show that on these games the explicit approach is better than the symbolic one, exhibiting a different behavior than the one showed in [21]. To gain a fuller understanding of the performances of the symbolic and the explicit algorithms, we have further tested the two approaches on structured games. Precisely, we have considered ladder games, clique games, as well as game models coming from practical model-checking problems. We have showed several cases in which the symbolic algorithms have the advantage over the explicit ones.

Our empirical study let us to conclude that on comparing explicit and symbolic algorithms for solving parity games, it would be useful to have real scenarios and not only random games, as the common practice has been.

References

1. Iris Bahar, R., Frohm, E.A., Gaona, C.M., Hachtel, G.D., Macii, E., Pardo, A., Somenzi, F.: Algebraic decision diagrams and their applications. Formal Methods Syst. Des. **10**, 171–206 (1997)
2. Bakera, M., Edelkamp, S., Kissmann, P., Renner, C.D.: Solving μ-calculus parity games by symbolic planning. In: Peled, D.A., Wooldridge, M.J. (eds.) MoChArt 2008. LNCS (LNAI), vol. 5348, pp. 15–33. Springer, Heidelberg (2009). https://doi.org/10.1007/978-3-642-00431-5_2
3. Bryant, R.E.: Graph-based algorithms for boolean function manipulation. IEEE Trans. Comput. **35**, 677–691 (1986)
4. Burch, J.R., Clarke, E.M., McMillan, K.L., Dill, D.L., Hwang, L.J.: Symbolic model checking: 10^{20} states and beyond. In: LICS 1990, pp. 428–439 (1990)
5. Bustan, D., Kupferman, O., Vardi, M.Y.: A measured collapse of the modal μ-calculus alternation hierarchy. In: Diekert, V., Habib, M. (eds.) STACS 2004. LNCS, vol. 2996, pp. 522–533. Springer, Heidelberg (2004). https://doi.org/10.1007/978-3-540-24749-4_46
6. Calude, C.S., Jain, S., Khoussainov, B., Li, W., Stephan, F.: Deciding parity games in quasipolynomial time. In: STOC 2017, pp. 252–263 (2017)
7. Cermák, P., Lomuscio, A., Murano, A.: Verifying and synthesising multi-agent systems against one-goal strategy logic specifications. In: AAAI 2015, pp. 2038–2044 (2015)
8. Chatterjee, K., Dvorák, W., Henzinger, M., Loitzenbauer, V.: Improved set-based symbolic algorithms for parity games. In: CSL 2017, pp. 18:1–18:21 (2017)
9. Clarke, E.M., Emerson, E.A.: Design and synthesis of synchronization skeletons using branching time temporal logic. In: Kozen, D. (ed.) LP 1981. LNCS, vol. 131, pp. 52–71. Springer, Heidelberg (1982). https://doi.org/10.1007/BFb0025774
10. Di Stasio, A., Murano, A., Perelli, G., Vardi, M.Y.: Solving parity games using an automata-based algorithm. In: Han, Y.-S., Salomaa, K. (eds.) CIAA 2016. LNCS, vol. 9705, pp. 64–76. Springer, Cham (2016). https://doi.org/10.1007/978-3-319-40946-7_6
11. Eisner, C., Peled, D.: Comparing symbolic and explicit model checking of a software system. In: Bošnački, D., Leue, S. (eds.) SPIN 2002. LNCS, vol. 2318, pp. 230–239. Springer, Heidelberg (2002). https://doi.org/10.1007/3-540-46017-9_18
12. Emerson, E.A., Jutla, C.: Tree automata, μ-calculus and determinacy. In: FOCS 1991, pp. 368–377 (1991)
13. Jurdzinski, M.: Deciding the winner in parity games is in UP ∩ co-Up. Inf. Process. Lett. **68**(3), 119–124 (1998)
14. Jurdziński, M.: Small progress measures for solving parity games. In: Reichel, H., Tison, S. (eds.) STACS 2000. LNCS, vol. 1770, pp. 290–301. Springer, Heidelberg (2000). https://doi.org/10.1007/3-540-46541-3_24
15. Jurdzinski, M., Lazic, R.: Succinct progress measures for solving parity games. In: LICS 2017, pp. 1–9 (2017)
16. Kant, G., van de Pol, J.: Generating and solving symbolic parity games. In: GRAPHITE 2014, pp. 2–14 (2014)

17. Keiren, J.J.A.: Benchmarks for parity games. In: Dastani, M., Sirjani, M. (eds.) FSEN 2015. LNCS, vol. 9392, pp. 127–142. Springer, Cham (2015). https://doi.org/10.1007/978-3-319-24644-4_9
18. Kupferman, O., Vardi, M.Y.: Weak alternating automata and tree automata emptiness. In: STOC 1998, pp. 224–233 (1998)
19. Kupferman, O., Vardi, M.Y., Wolper, P.: An automata theoretic approach to branching-time model checking. J. ACM **47**(2), 312–360 (2000)
20. McMillan, K.L.: Symbolic Model Checking. Kluwer Academic Publishers, Norwell (1993)
21. Tabakov, D.: Evaluation of explicit and symbolic automata-theoretic algorithm. Master's thesis, Rice University (2005)
22. van Dijk, T.: Oink: an implementation and evaluation of modern parity game solvers. In: Beyer, D., Huisman, M. (eds.) TACAS 2018. LNCS, vol. 10805, pp. 291–308. Springer, Cham (2018). https://doi.org/10.1007/978-3-319-89960-2_16
23. Wilke, T.: Alternating tree automata, parity games, and modal μ-calculus. Bull. Belg. Math. Soc. Simon Stevin **8**(2), 359 (2001)
24. Zielonka, W.: Infinite games on finitely coloured graphs with applications to automata on infinite trees. Theor. Comput. Sci. **200**(1–2), 135–183 (1998)

Generalised Twinning Property

Stefan Gerdjikov[1,2]([✉])

[1] Faculty of Mathematics and Informatics,
Sofia University, 5, James Bourchier Blvd., 1164 Sofia, Bulgaria
stefangerdzhikov@fmi.uni-sofia.bg
[2] Institute of Information and Communication Technologies,
Bulgarian Academy of Sciences, 25A, Acad. G. Bonchev Str., 1113 Sofia, Bulgaria

Abstract. In this paper we consider the problem of sequentialisation of rational functions $f : \Sigma^* \to \mathcal{M}$. We introduce a class of monoids that includes infinitary groups, free monoids, tropical monoids and is closed under Cartesian Product. For this class of monoids we provide a sequentialisation construction for transducers and appropriately generalise the notion of Twinning Property. We provide a construction to test the Twinning Property for transducers over the considered class of monoids and prove that it is a necessary and sufficient condition for the sequentialisation construction to terminate.

Keywords: Sequential functions · Transducers · Sequentialisation
Monoid

1 Introduction

Finite State Transducers (FST) provide a natural effective way to represent a large class of relations, called *rational relations*, applied in Natural Language Processing [12,14–17]. In their essence the FST's are formal devices that generalise the classical Finite State Automata (FSA).

Aiming at linear on-line algorithms for processing words, one prefers the Deterministic FSA to the general FSA. In the case of FSA it is well known that both formalisms are equivalent in their expressive power, [11]. However, for the FST's and the deterministic, called *sequential*, FST's this is not the case, [2,13, 15]. The constraint for an FST to deterministically process an input word clearly implies that it represents a graph of a function $f : \Sigma^* \to \mathcal{M}$. But it is by far not sufficient that an FST to be *functional* to be turned into a sequential FST. Functions recognised by some sequential FST are called *sequential functions*.

The problem we are looking at in this paper is to recognise if a given transducer $\mathcal{T}$ represents a sequential function and if so to construct a sequential transducer equivalent to $\mathcal{T}$.

In the case where $\mathcal{M}$ is a free monoid this problem has been solved by Choffrut [2]. The case where $\mathcal{M}$ is the tropical monoid was solved by Mohri [14, 15]. For a survey see also [13]. In [9] a class of monoids, sequentiable structures,

© Springer International Publishing AG, part of Springer Nature 2018
C. Câmpeanu (Ed.): CIAA 2018, LNCS 10977, pp. 173–185, 2018.
https://doi.org/10.1007/978-3-319-94812-6_15

has been introduced and the results from [2,13–15] have been generalised. The case where $\mathcal{M}$ is an infinitary group was solved in [3]. In this paper we consider a class of monoids that contains the free monoids, the tropical monoids, the sequentiable structures, and infinitary groups and additionally is closed under Cartesian Product. In its essence the class of monoids that we consider is a subclass of mge monoids [10] and the monoids considered in [7] obtained by adding three more axioms. We formally introduce it in Sect. 3.

Typically, the problem for sequentialisation of an FST starts with a functionality test. This problem can be efficiently solved for free monoids, [1], and groups, [5]. These techniques were generalised to arbitrary mge monoids in [10]. The second step is usually to characterise the sequential functions as rational functions of *bounded variation*, [2,3,9,13,15]. The third step is to introduce an appropriate notion of *Twinning Property*, [2,3,13,18].

We generalise the notion of Twinning Property in Sect. 4.2, but we do not have an appropriate notion for bounded variation. Thus, we cannot follow the common way, [2,3,9,13,15,18], of proving the characterisation theorem in order (i) sequential; (ii) bounded variation; (iii) Twinning Property; (iv) termination of a power set construction. The proof in Sect. 4.3 skips (ii) and also requires a modification of the power set construction. The latter is presented in Sect. 4.1.

2   Preliminaries

The reader familiar with the main notions on monoids and automata[1], [4,18], may prefer to skip this section.

A *monoid* $\mathcal{M} = \langle M, \circ, e \rangle$ is a semigroup $\langle M, \circ \rangle$ with a unit element e. A special case of monoids are the free monoids Σ^* generated by a finite set Σ. The support of Σ^* is the set of all finite sequence over Σ, called *words*, the multiplication is the *concatenation* of words, and the unit element is *the empty word*, ε. For monoids $\mathcal{M}_i = \langle M_i, \circ_i, e_i \rangle$ for $i = 1, 2$, the Cartesian Product $\mathcal{M} = \mathcal{M}_1 \times \mathcal{M}_2$ is defined as $\mathcal{M} = \langle M_1 \times M_2, \circ, \langle e_1, e_2 \rangle \rangle$ where:

$$\langle a_1, a_2 \rangle \circ \langle b_1, b_2 \rangle = \langle a_1 \circ_1 b_1, a_2 \circ_2 b_2 \rangle.$$

It is straightforward to see that $\mathcal{M}$ is also a monoid, [4]. For an element $a \in M$ and set $S \subseteq M$, we use aS and Sa as abbreviations for:

$$aS = \{as \mid s \in S\} \text{ and } Sa = \{sa \mid s \in S\}.$$

A *finite automaton* over a monoid $\mathcal{M}$ is a tuple $\mathcal{A} = \langle \mathcal{M}, Q, s, F, \Delta, \iota, \Psi \rangle$ where Q is a finite set of *states*, $s \in Q$ is the *initial state*, $F \subseteq Q$ is the set of *final states*, $\Delta \subseteq Q \times M \times Q$ is a finite relation of *transitions*, $\iota \in M$, and $\Psi : F \to M$ is the *terminal function*.

A *non-trivial path* in an automaton $\mathcal{A}$ is a non-empty sequence of transitions $\pi = \langle p_0, m_1, p_1 \rangle \ldots \langle p_{n-1}, m_n, p_n \rangle$. For each state $p \in Q$ we also have the *trivial*

---

[1] We consider one-letter transducers with unique initial state. It emits an initial output. Final states emit final outputs.

path $\pi = (p)$. A *path* is either a trivial or a non-trivial path. Each path π has a *source state*, $\sigma(\pi)$, a *terminal state*, $\tau(\pi)$, *label*, $\ell(\pi)$, and *length*, $|\pi|$. For a non-trivial path $\pi = \langle p_0, m_1, p_1 \rangle \dots \langle p_{n-1}, m_n, p_n \rangle$ they are defined as: $\sigma(\pi) = p_0$, $\tau(\pi) = p_n$, $\ell(\pi) = \prod_{i=1}^{n} m_i$, and $|\pi| = n$. For a trivial path $\pi = (p)$, $\sigma(\pi) = \tau(\pi) = p$, $\ell(\pi) = e$, $|\pi| = 0$.

A path π is called *successful* if $\sigma(\pi) = s$ and $\tau(\pi) \in F$. In these notions, the *language* of a finite automaton $\mathcal{A} = \langle \mathcal{M}, Q, s, F, \Delta, \iota, \Psi \rangle$ is:

$$\mathcal{L}(\mathcal{A}) = \{\iota \circ \ell(\pi) \circ \Psi(\tau(\pi)) \mid \pi \text{ is a successful path in } \mathcal{A}\}.$$

We also denote $\Delta^* = \{\langle \sigma(\pi), \ell(\pi), \tau(\pi) \rangle \mid \pi \text{ is a path in } \mathcal{A}\}$. A state p is called *accessible* if there exists a path π with $\sigma(\pi) = s$ and $\tau(\pi) = p$. A state p is called *co-accessible* if there exists a path π with $\sigma(\pi) = p$ and $\tau(\pi) \in F$. We say that an automaton is *trimmed* if all its states are both accessible and co-accessible. For a state $p \in Q$ we denote with $\mathcal{A}_p = \langle \mathcal{M}, Q, p, F, \Delta, e, \Psi \rangle$ and we set $\mathcal{L}(p) = \mathcal{L}(\mathcal{A}_p)$.

$Rng(f)$ stays for the range of a function, f. Given a finite set Σ and a monoid $\mathcal{M}$, a *finite state transducer* is an automaton $\mathcal{T} = \langle \Sigma^* \times \mathcal{M}, Q, s, F, \Delta, \iota, \Psi \rangle$. If:

$$\Delta \subseteq Q \times ((\Sigma \cup \{\varepsilon\}) \times M) \times Q, \ \iota \in \{\varepsilon\} \times M \text{ and } Rng(\Psi) \subseteq \{\varepsilon\} \times M,$$

then $\mathcal{T}$ is called *one-letter transducer*. Clearly, an FST over some monoid, $\mathcal{M}$, is equivalent to a one-letter transducer, [4]. We denote one-letter transducers like $\mathcal{T} - \langle \Sigma \times \mathcal{M}, Q, s, F, \Delta, \iota, \Psi \rangle$ and we tacitly identify $\iota = \langle \varepsilon, \iota_2 \rangle$ with ι_2 and, similarly, with $\Psi(f) = \langle \varepsilon, \Psi_2(f) \rangle$ we intend $\Psi(f) = \Psi_2(f) \in M$. By definition, a one-letter transducer recognises a relation $\mathcal{L}(\mathcal{T}) \subseteq \Sigma^* \times \mathcal{M}$. We say that $\mathcal{T}$ is *functional* if $\mathcal{L}(\mathcal{T})$ is a graph of a function $\mathcal{O}_{\mathcal{T}} : \Sigma^* \to M$. If $\mathcal{T}_p$ is functional, we use $\mathcal{O}_{\mathcal{T}}^{(p)}$ to denote the function corresponding to $\mathcal{T}_p$.

A special class of functional one-letter transducers are the *sequential transducers*. Formally, these are one-letter transducers, $\mathcal{T} = \langle \Sigma \times \mathcal{M}, Q, s, F, \Delta, \iota, \Psi \rangle$ such that there exist functions $\delta : Q \times \Sigma \to Q$ and $\lambda : Q \times \Sigma \to M$ with $Dom(\delta) = Dom(\lambda)$ satisfying: $\Delta = \{\langle p, \langle a, \lambda(p, a) \rangle, \delta(p, a) \rangle \mid \langle p, a \rangle \in Dom(\delta)\}$. To stress these particularities of the sequential transducers, we denote them as $\mathcal{T} = \langle \Sigma \times \mathcal{M}, Q, s, F, \delta, \lambda, \iota, \Psi \rangle$. As usual, $\delta^* : Q \times \Sigma^* \to Q$ and $\lambda^* : Q \times \Sigma^* \to M$ denote the natural extensions of δ and λ with $Dom(\lambda^*) = Dom(\delta^*)$ s.t.:

$$\Delta^* = \{\langle p, \langle w, \lambda^*(p, w) \rangle, \delta^*(p, w) \rangle \mid \langle p, w \rangle \in Dom(\delta^*)\}.$$

With these notions we can express the function $\mathcal{O}_{\mathcal{T}} : \Sigma^* \to M$ as:

$$\mathcal{O}_{\mathcal{T}}(w) = \iota \circ \lambda^*(s, w) \circ \Psi(f), \text{ where } f = \delta^*(s, w).$$

3 Classes of Monoids

In this section we define the class of monoids that we shall be interested in. It represents a subclass of the monoids considered in [7]. Similarly to the monoids considered in [7], it contains the free monoids, the tropical monoid, and sequentiable structures, [8,9], and it is closed under Cartesian Product. It also contains the infinitary groups, [3].

In the first paragraph, below, we revisit the basic notions from [7] and summarise the results obtained there. In the second paragraph, we introduce the new concepts that are important for the outline in next section.

3.1   MGE Monoids with LSL- and GCLF-axioms

First, we generalise the notions of a prefix and longest common prefix to monoids:

Definition 1. *For a monoid $\mathcal{M}$ and elements $a, b \in M$ we say that $a \leq_M b$ if there is an element $c \in M$ with $a \circ c = b$. We use $a \sim_M b$ as an abbreviation for the induced equivalence relation, $a \leq_M b \,\&\, b \leq_M a$. For a set $S \subseteq \mathcal{M}$, we define the sets $low(S)$ and $up(S)$ of lower and upper bounds for S, resp. as follows:*

$$low(S) = \{a \in M \mid \forall s \in S(a \leq_M s)\} \quad up(S) = \{b \in M \mid \forall s \in S(s \leq_M b)\}.$$

We define the sets of infimums and supremums for S as:

$$\inf S = low(S) \cap up(low(S)) \text{ and } \sup S = up(S) \cap low(up(S)).$$

Definition 2. *Let $\mathcal{T} = \langle \Sigma \times \mathcal{M}, Q, s, F, \Delta, \iota, \Psi \rangle$ be a one-letter transducer. We say that $\mathcal{T}$ is onward if for every accessible $p \in Q$ it holds $e \in \inf \mathrm{Rng}(\mathcal{L}(p))$.*

Definition 3. *An mge monoid is a monoid $\mathcal{M}$ with the following properties:*

1. *(LC, left cancellation) for all $a, b \in M$ there is at most one element $c = \frac{b}{a}$ with $a \circ c = b$.*
2. *(RC, right cancellation) for all $a, b \in M$ there is at most one element $c = b - a$ with $c \circ a = b$.*
3. *(RMGE, right most general equaliser) for all $a, b \in M$ s.t. $up(\{a, b\}) \neq \emptyset$, there is an element $a \vee b \in \sup\{a, b\}$.*

An mge monoid $\mathcal{M}$ is called effective, if $\mathcal{M}$ is effective and the functions $\frac{a}{b}$, $a - b$, and $a \vee b$ are computable and their domains are recursive.

Theorem 1 ([10]). *Let $\mathcal{M}$ be an effective mge monoid. Then it is decidable given a one-letter $\Sigma - \mathcal{M}$-transducer $\mathcal{T}$ whether $\mathcal{T}$ is functional.*

Definition 4. *We say that a monoid $\mathcal{M}$ satisfies the left semi-lattice and greatest common left factor axioms, respectively, if:*

1. *the LSL-axiom[2] iff for all $a, b \in M$ there is an element $a \sqcap b \in \inf\{a, b\}$.*
2. *the GCLF-axiom[3] iff for all $a, b, c \in M$, $b \leq_M c$ and $b \leq_M ac$ imply $b \leq_M ab$.*

Theorem 2 ([7]). *Let $\mathcal{M}$ be an (effective) mge monoid with LSL- and GCLF-axioms. Then there is an (effective) construction that for every one-letter $\Sigma - \mathcal{M}$-transducer produces an equivalent onward transducer with the same states and input[4] transitions.*

Remark 1 ([7]). Groups, free monoids, and tropical monoids are all mge monoids with LSL- and GCLF-axioms. Furthermore the mge monoids and mge monoids with LSL- and GCLF-axioms are closed under Cartesian Product.

---

[2] LSL stays for *lower semi-lattice*.
[3] GCLF stays for *greatest common left factor*.
[4] That is, the only difference in the transitions is their $\mathcal{M}$-coordinate.

3.2   Sequentialisation Axioms

In this section we define some new notions that will be used in the constructions and proofs to come in the subsequent paragraphs.

Definition 5. *Let $\mathcal{M}$ be a monoid. For a natural number $n \in \mathbb{N}$ we define the relation $\equiv_M^{(n)} \subseteq M^n \times M^n$ as:*

$$\mathbf{a} \equiv_M^{(n)} \mathbf{b} \iff \exists u \in M(\forall i \leq n(u\mathbf{a}_i = \mathbf{b}_i) \text{ and } u \text{ is invertible}).$$

Lemma 1. *For each $n \in \mathbb{N}$, the relation $\equiv_M^{(n)}$ is an equivalence relation.*

The following definition is the symmetric variant[5] of the RMGE-axiom. In terms of free monoids, it requires that if two words are suffixes of the same word, then there is a shortest word with this property.

Definition 6. *A monoid $\mathcal{M}$ satisfies the Left Most General Equaliser Axiom (LMGE-axiom) if:*

$$\forall a, b \in M(Ma \cap Mb \neq \emptyset \Rightarrow \exists c \in \mathcal{M}(Ma \cap Mb = Mc)).$$

Definition 7. *A monoid $\mathcal{M}$ is an (effective) 2mge-monoid if it is an (effective) mge monoid and satisfies the LMGE-axiom.*

Definition 8. *Let $\mathcal{M}$ be a monoid. A left equaliser for $\mathbf{u} \in M^n$ is an n-tuple $\mathbf{a} \in M^n$ such that $a_i u_i = a_j u_j$ for all $i, j \leq n$. An element $\mathbf{u} \in M^n$ is called left equalisable if it admits a left equaliser. We say that $\mathbf{a}$ is a left mge for $\mathbf{u}$ if both:*

1. $\mathbf{a}$ is a left equaliser for $\mathbf{u}$,
2. for every left equaliser, $\mathbf{b}$, for $\mathbf{u}$ there is $c \in \mathcal{M}$ such that: $\mathbf{b}_j = c\mathbf{a}_j$ for $j \leq n$.

Lemma 2. *If $\mathcal{M}$ is a 2mge-monoid, and $\mathbf{u} \in \mathcal{M}^n$ is left equalisable, then $\mathbf{u}$ admits a unique up to equivalence w.r.t. $\equiv_M^{(n)}$ left mge $\mathbf{a} \in \mathcal{M}^n$.*

Definition 9. *A monoid $\mathcal{M}$ satisfies the Conjugate Closeness Axiom (CC) if:*

$$\forall u, r \in M(\exists k \geq 1(ru^k \in Mr)) \Rightarrow ru \in Mr.$$

Next definition captures the property that is characteristic for infinitary groups.

Definition 10. *A monoid $\mathcal{M}$ satisfies the Prime Root Axiom (PR) if:*

$$\forall u, v \in M(\exists k > 1(u^k = v^k)) \Rightarrow u = v.$$

Lemma 3. *LMGE, CC, and PR-axioms hold for free and tropical monoids[6].*

---

[5] Note that $up(\{a, b\}) = aM \cap bM$.
[6] The result extends to sequentiable structures, for the definition see [9].

Lemma 4. *If $\mathcal{G}$ is a group then it satisfies the LMGE- and the CC-axiom. Furthermore, $\mathcal{G}$ is an infinitary group if and only if $\mathcal{G}$ satisfies the PR-axiom.*

Lemma 5. *Let $\mathcal{M}_1$ and $\mathcal{M}_2$ be monoids. If $A \in \{LMGE, CC, PR\}$ and $\mathcal{M}_i$ satisfies A for $i = 1, 2$, then so does $\mathcal{M} = \mathcal{M}_1 \times \mathcal{M}_2$.*

Lemma 6. *Let $\mathcal{M}$ be an mge-monoid satisfying the CC-axiom and the PR-axiom. If $r_1, r_2, u_1, u_2, t \in M$ and $k \geq 1$ are such that: $r_i u_i^k = t r_i$ for $i \in \{1, 2\}$, then there is $s \in M$ with $r_i u_i = s r_i$ for $i \in \{1, 2\}$.*

4   Sequentialisation

In this section we will be interested in the Sequentialisation Problem:

```
Given:M effective 2mge-monoid with LSL and GCLF
      T = ⟨Σ × M, Q, i, F, Δ, ι, Ψ⟩ transducer
Output:TD, sequential transducer with O_TD = O_T, if such exists.
      No, alternatively.
```

In view of Theorems 1 and 2 this problem is equivalent to the following Restricted Sequentialisation Problem:

```
Given:M effective 2mge-monoid with LSL and GCLF
      T = ⟨Σ × M, Q, i, F, Δ, ι, Ψ⟩ trimmed, functional, onward
Output:TD, sequential transducer with O_TD = O_T, if such exists.
      No, alternatively.
```

4.1   Sequentialisation Construction

We start by providing a natural semi-decision construction for the Restricted Sequentialisation Problem. It specialises the classical power-set construction of Choffrut, [2]. Under additional assumptions for the monoid $\mathcal{M}$, namely the PR- and CC-axioms, we are going to give necessary and sufficient condition for this procedure to halt.

First, note that since $\mathcal{T}$ is functional and trimmed whereas $\mathcal{M}$ satisfies LC- and RC-axioms, every cycle $\langle p, \langle \varepsilon, m \rangle, p \rangle \in \Delta^*$ satisfies $m = e$. The sequentialisation of $\mathcal{T}$ proceeds stepwise and constructs a sequence of sequential transducers: $\mathcal{T}_k = \langle \Sigma, \mathcal{M}, Q_k, s, F_k, \delta_k, \lambda_k, \iota, \Psi_k \rangle$. The states, Q_k, are sets of pairs, $Q_k \subseteq 2^{Q \times M}$. The initial state is defined as $s = \{\langle p, m \rangle \mid \langle i, \langle \varepsilon, m \rangle, p \rangle \in \Delta^*\}$.

The main difference of our construction from the classical constructions [2, 13, 16, 18] lies in the special cares in Step 2.(c), below. Intuitively, they aim at preventing the unnecessary creation of equivalent states w.r.t. $\equiv_\mathcal{M}$.

1. At step $k = 0$, set $Q_0 = \{s\}$, $Q_{-1} = \emptyset$, and $\mathcal{T}_0 = \langle \Sigma, \mathcal{M}, \{s\}, s, \emptyset, \emptyset, \emptyset, \iota, \emptyset \rangle$.
2. If $Q_k = Q_{k-1}$, then $\mathcal{T}_D = \mathcal{T}_k$ and stop. Otherwise, set $\delta_{k+1} = \delta_k$, $\lambda_{k+1} = \lambda_k$:
   (a) $F_{k+1} = F_k \cup \{P \in Q_k \setminus Q_{k-1} \mid \exists \langle p, v \rangle \in P(p \in F)\}$.

(b) $\Psi_{k+1}(P) = v \circ \Psi(f)$ s.t. there is $\langle f, v \rangle \in P$ with $f \in F$.
(c) for each $P \in Q_k \setminus Q_{k-1}$ and each character $a \in \Sigma$:
   i. compute the monoid element and the set of pairs:

$$\ell(P, a) = \prod \{v \circ m \mid \langle p, v \rangle \in P \text{ and } \exists q \in Q(\langle p, \langle a, m \rangle, q \rangle \in \Delta^*)\}$$

$$\partial(P, a) = \left\{ \left\langle q, \frac{v \circ m}{\ell(P, a)} \right\rangle \mid \langle p, v \rangle \in P \text{ and } (\langle p, \langle a, m \rangle, q \rangle \in \Delta^*) \right\}$$

      Denote $\partial(P, a) = \{\langle q_k, u_k \rangle\}_{k=1}^K$.
   ii. check if there is already a state $P' \in Q_k \cup Rng(\delta_{k+1})$ satisfying:
      A. $P' = \{\langle q_k, u'_k \rangle\}_{k=1}^K$ for some $u'_k \in \mathcal{M}$,
      B. $\langle u_1, u_2, \ldots, u_K \rangle \equiv_M^{(K)} \langle u'_1, u'_2, \ldots, u'_K \rangle$.
      If such a state P' exists, set $u = u'_1 - u_1$ if $K \geq 1$ and $u = e$ otherwise.
   iii. Update:

$$\langle \delta_{k+1}(P, a), \lambda_{k+1}(P, a) \rangle = \begin{cases} \langle P', \ell(P, a) \circ u \rangle & \text{if } u \text{ is defined} \\ \langle \partial(P, a), \ell(P, a) \rangle & \text{otherwise.} \end{cases}$$

(d) $Q_{k+1} = Q_k \cup Rng(\delta_{k+1})$ and increase k to $k + 1$. Goto 2.

Lemma 7. *Let $\mathcal{T}$ be an onward functional transducer with unique initial state. Let $k \in \mathbb{N}$ and $\alpha \in \Sigma^*$ be such that $P = \delta_k^*(s, \alpha)$ is defined. Then $\lambda_k^*(s, \alpha) = u$ is defined and:*

1. if $P \neq \emptyset$, then $\prod \{v \mid \exists p \in Q(\langle p, v \rangle \in P)\} \sim_M e$.
2. for each $p \in Q$ and $v \in \mathcal{M}$ it holds: $\langle p, v \rangle \in P \iff \langle i, \langle \alpha, uv \rangle, p \rangle \in \Delta^*$.

Proof. The proof follows by a straightforward induction on the length of α. $\square$

As a corollary we get:

Corollary 1. *If $Q_{k-1} = Q_k$, then $\mathcal{T}_k$ is a sequential transducer and $\mathcal{O}_{\mathcal{T}_k} = \mathcal{O}_{\mathcal{T}}$.*

4.2 Squared Automaton and Twinning Property

Let $\mathcal{T} = \langle \Sigma \times \mathcal{M}, Q, i, F, \Delta \rangle$ be an onward trimmed functional transducer over a regular 2mge-monoid. We denote with $\mathcal{A}^2$ the squared automaton for $\mathcal{T}$:

$$\mathcal{A}^2 = \langle \Sigma \times \mathcal{M}^2, Q^2, \langle i, i \rangle, F^2, \Delta_2, e, \mathbf{e} \rangle, \text{ where}$$
$$\Delta_2 = \{\langle \langle p_1, p_2 \rangle, \langle a, \langle m_1, m_2 \rangle \rangle, \langle p'_1, p'_2 \rangle \rangle \mid a \in \Sigma, \langle p_j, \langle a, m_j \rangle, p'_j \rangle \in \Delta \text{ for } j \leq 2\}$$
$$\cup \{\langle \langle p_1, p_2 \rangle, \langle \varepsilon, \langle m_1, e \rangle \rangle, \langle p'_1, p_2 \rangle \rangle \mid \langle p_1, \langle \varepsilon, m_1 \rangle, p'_1 \rangle \in \Delta\}$$
$$\cup \{\langle \langle p_1, p_2 \rangle, \langle \varepsilon, \langle e, m_2 \rangle \rangle, \langle p_1, p'_2 \rangle \rangle \mid \langle p_2, \langle \varepsilon, m_2 \rangle, p'_2 \rangle \in \Delta\}$$

The squared automaton $\mathcal{A}^2$ has the following structural property:

Lemma 8. *Let $\mathbf{q}, \mathbf{q}' \in Q^2$ be arbitrary. Then for a word $\alpha \in \Sigma^*$ and $\mathbf{m} \in \mathcal{M}^2$ the following are equivalent:*

1. $\langle \mathbf{q}, \langle \alpha, \mathbf{m} \rangle, \mathbf{q}' \rangle \in \Delta_2^*$,
2. *for each* $i \leq 2$, $\langle \mathbf{q}_i, \langle \alpha, \mathbf{m}_i \rangle, \mathbf{q}_i' \rangle \in \Delta^*$,

Proof. The implication $\mathbf{1} \Rightarrow \mathbf{2}$ follows by induction on the length of the generalised transition, $\langle \mathbf{q}, \langle \alpha, \mathbf{m} \rangle, \mathbf{q}' \rangle$. In turn, the implication $\mathbf{2} \Rightarrow \mathbf{1}$ follows by induction on the sum of the lengths of the generalised transitions, $\langle \mathbf{q}_i, \langle \alpha, \mathbf{m}_i \rangle, \mathbf{q}_i' \rangle$ □

Next, we introduce the *advance action*. It generalises the *delay of runs*, [1,3], by factorising w.r.t. the equivalence relation $\equiv_M^{(2)}$. Let $t = \langle \mathbf{q}, a, \mathbf{m}, \mathbf{q}' \rangle \in \Delta_2$ be a transition. We introduce $adv_t : \mathcal{M}^2 \to \mathcal{M}^2$ as:

$$adv_t(v) = \left\langle \frac{(\mathbf{v}_1 \circ \mathbf{m}_1)}{m}, \frac{(\mathbf{v}_2 \circ \mathbf{m}_2)}{m} \right\rangle, \text{ where } m = (\mathbf{v}_1 \circ \mathbf{m}_1) \sqcap (\mathbf{v}_2 \circ \mathbf{m}_2).$$

For a path $\pi = t_1 t_2 \ldots t_n$ in $\mathcal{A}^2$, we denote with $adv^{(\pi)} : \mathcal{M}^2 \to \mathcal{M}^2$ the function:

$$adv^{(\pi)} = adv_{t_1} \circ adv_{t_2} \circ \cdots \circ adv_{t_n}.$$

Next we list some useful properties of the advance action.

Lemma 9. *Let* $v \leq_M \mathbf{v}_1$ *and* $v \leq_M \mathbf{v}_2$, *then* $adv_t(\langle \mathbf{v}_1, \mathbf{v}_2 \rangle) \equiv_M^{(2)} adv_t(\langle \frac{\mathbf{v}_1}{v}, \frac{\mathbf{v}_2}{v} \rangle)$.

Corollary 2. *Let* $\mathbf{v}' \equiv_M^{(2)} \mathbf{v}''$ *and* $t \in \Delta_2$, *then* $adv_t(\mathbf{v}') \equiv_M^{(2)} adv_t(\mathbf{v}'')$.

Proof. Since $\mathbf{v}' \equiv_M^{(2)} \mathbf{v}''$ there is an invertible element c with $\frac{\mathbf{v}_j'}{c} = \mathbf{v}_j''$ for $j = 1, 2$. Now the result follows by the previous lemma. □

Corollary 3. *Let* π_1 *and* π_2 *be paths in* $\mathcal{A}^2$ *that start at* $\langle i, i \rangle$ *and terminate in the same state* $\mathbf{q}$ *be such that:* $adv^{(\pi_1)}(e, e) \equiv_M^{(2)} adv^{(\pi_2)}(e, e)$. *Then for any path* π *in* $\mathcal{A}^2$ *that starts at* $\mathbf{q}$ *it holds that:* $adv^{(\pi_1 \pi)}(e, e) \equiv_M^{(2)} adv^{(\pi_2 \pi)}(e, e)$.

Proof. The proof follows by Corollary 2 and straightforward induction on the length of the path π. □

Lemma 10. *Let* π *be a path in* $\mathcal{A}^2$ *from* $\mathbf{i} = \langle i, i \rangle$ *to some state* $\mathbf{q} \in Q^2$. *Let* $\ell(\pi) = \langle \alpha, \mathbf{m} \rangle$ *be the label of* π, *and* $m = \mathbf{m}_1 \sqcap \mathbf{m}_2$, *then:*

$$adv^{(\pi)}(\langle e, e \rangle) \equiv_M^{(2)} \left\langle \frac{\mathbf{m}_1}{m}, \frac{\mathbf{m}_2}{m} \right\rangle.$$

Definition 11. *Let* $\mathcal{A}^2$ *be a squared automaton for a trimmed onward transducer with unique initial state. We say that* $\mathcal{A}^2$ *satisfies the Twinning Property iff for any two paths* π_1 *and* π_2 *in* $\mathcal{A}^2$ *such that* $\sigma(\pi_1) = \langle i, i \rangle$ *and* $\tau(\pi_1) = \sigma(\pi_2) = \tau(\pi_2)$, *i.e.* π_2 *is a cycle starting at* $\tau(\pi_1)$, *it holds:*

$$adv^{(\pi_1)}(e, e) \equiv_M^{(2)} adv^{(\pi_1 \pi_2)}(e, e).$$

We conclude this section by showing that the Twinning Property is decidable:

Lemma 11. *Given a squared automaton $\mathcal{A}^2$ over an effective 2mge-monoid, $\mathcal{M}$, with LSL- and GCLF-axioms we can effectively test whether $\mathcal{A}^2$ obeys the Twinning Property.*

Proof. (Idea) Let $n = |Q_2|$. We denote with Π_{2n} and $\mathcal{C}$ the sets:

$$\Pi_{2n} = \{\pi \text{ path in } \mathcal{A}^2 \,|\, \sigma(\pi) = \langle i, i\rangle, \, |\pi| < 2n\} \text{ and } \mathcal{C} = \{\pi \text{ simple cycle in } \mathcal{A}^2\}.$$

We say that $\mathcal{A}^2$ satisfies the *restricted* Twinning Property if and only if for every $\pi_1 \in \Pi_{2n}$ and any $\pi_2 \in \mathcal{C}$ such that $\tau(\pi_1) = \sigma(\pi_2)$:

$$adv^{(\pi_1)}(e, e) \equiv_M^{(2)} adv^{(\pi_1\pi_2)}(e, e).$$

Clearly, under the assumptions of the lemma, the restricted Twinning Property is decidable. It is also clear that the Twinning Property implies the restricted Twinning Property. The reverse is also true. This follows by induction, the Pigeonhole Principle, and Corollary 3.   □

4.3   Twinning Property ⇔ Sequentialisation Algorithm Halts

The main result in this section is the following:

Theorem 3. *Assume that $\mathcal{M}$ is a 2mge-monoid satisfying the PR- and CC-axioms. Let $\mathcal{T} = \langle \Sigma \times \mathcal{M}, Q, i, F, \Delta, \iota, \Psi\rangle$ be an onward, trimmed, functional transducer and let $f = \mathcal{O}_{\mathcal{T}}$. Then the following are equivalent:*

1. *the sequentialisation procedure on $\mathcal{T}$ terminates.*
2. *f is sequential.*
3. *$\mathcal{A}^2$ satisfies the Twinning Property.*

Before we step to the formal proof of Theorem 3, we note the important consequence of this theorem:

Theorem 4. *Let $\mathcal{M}$ be an effective 2mge-monoid with PR-, CC-, LSL-, and GCLF-axioms. Then it is decidable given a transducer $\mathcal{T}$ over $\Sigma^* \times \mathcal{M}$ whether $\mathcal{T}$ represents a sequential function.*

Proof. Immediate from Theorem 1, Theorem 2, Lemma 11, and Theorem 3.   □

The rest of this section is devoted to the proof of Theorem 3. The implication **1 ⇒ 2** is obvious and follows immediately from Corollary 1. The implication **3 ⇒ 1** is standard as it appropriately generalises the main ideas from [2,3,9, 13,15,18]. Yet, the implication **2 ⇒ 3** is more involved since it has to surmount the lack of *Bounded Variation Property* that is usually the bridge between the sequential functions and the Twinning Property. This is also the only place in the proof where we need the PR- and the CC-axioms and more precisely their consequence Lemma 6. With these remarks we delve into the proof of Theorem 3:

Proof (of Theorem 3). **1 $\Rightarrow$ 2**. Follows by Corollary 1.

2 $\Rightarrow$ 3 Let the paths π_1, π_2, with $\mathbf{q} = \tau(\pi_1) = \sigma(\pi_2) = \tau(\pi_2)$ satisfy the premise of the Twinning Property. Let $\ell(\pi_1) = \langle \alpha, \mathbf{m} \rangle$ and $\ell(\pi_2) = \langle \beta, \mathbf{n} \rangle$. First consider the case where $\beta = \varepsilon$. Since, $\mathcal{T}$ is trimmed and functional over an mge monoid (LC- and RC-axiom), we conclude that $\mathbf{m} = \mathbf{e}$. Therefore $\ell(\pi_1) = \ell(\pi_1 \pi_2)$. Thus by Lemma 10 we deduce that:

$$adv^{(\pi_1)}(e, e) \equiv_M^{(2)} adv^{(\pi_1 \pi_2)}(e, e).$$

In the sequel we assume that $\beta \neq \varepsilon$. Let $\Gamma \subseteq \Sigma^*$ be the language[7] $\Gamma = \{\alpha\} \circ \bigcup_{j=1}^2 Dom(\mathcal{O}_{\mathcal{T}}^{(\mathbf{q}_j)})$. We set $g = f \restriction \Gamma$, i.e. the restriction of f to Γ. Since there is a sequential transducer for f and Γ is regular, it follows that there is also a sequential transducer for g. Let

$$m^{(k)} = (\mathbf{m}_1 \circ \mathbf{n}_1^k) \sqcap (\mathbf{m}_2 \circ \mathbf{n}_2^k) \text{ and } \mathbf{r}^{(k)} = \left\langle \frac{\mathbf{m}_1 \circ \mathbf{n}_1^k}{m^{(k)}}, \frac{\mathbf{m}_2 \circ \mathbf{n}_2^k}{m^{(k)}} \right\rangle.$$

Note that by Lemma 10 we have that $\mathbf{r}^{(k)} \equiv_M^{(2)} adv^{(\pi_1 \pi_2^k)}(e, e)$. To complete the proof we need the following:

Lemma 12. *If $\mathcal{T}$ is trimmed and onward, and $g = f \restriction \Gamma$ is sequential, then there is some $l \in \mathbb{N}$ with $\mathbf{r}^{(l)} \equiv_M \mathbf{r}^{(l+1)}$.*

Proof (Idea). First, using the sequential transducer for g we find two integers $k > l$ such that $\alpha\beta^k$ and $\alpha\beta^l$ lead to the same state in this transducer. Then, we establish the existence of $u' \sim_M m^{(l)}$ and $v' \sim_M m^{(k)}$ and a function $\widehat{g}' : \Sigma^* \to M$ such that for any $\gamma \in Dom(\mathcal{O}_{\mathcal{T}}^{(\mathbf{q}_1)}) \cup Dom(\mathcal{O}_{\mathcal{T}}^{(\mathbf{q}_2)})$ it holds:

$$g(\alpha\beta^l \gamma) = u' \circ \widehat{g}'(\gamma) \text{ and } g(\alpha\beta^k \gamma) = v' \circ \widehat{g}'(\gamma). \tag{1}$$

The mere existence of u, v, and $\widehat{g}$ satisfying Eq. 1 can be easily derived from the sequential transducer for g. The onward property of the original transducer $\mathcal{T}$, allows us to conclude that $u \leq_M m^{(l)}$ and $v \leq_M m^{(k)}$. Using the RMGE-axiom it is then easy to construct $u' \sim_M m^{(l)}$, $v' \sim_M m^{(k)}$, and $\widehat{g}'$ satisfying Eqs. 1.

Next, the function $\widehat{g}'$ allows us to transfer information from the reduct, $\mathbf{r}^{(l)}$, to the reduct, $\mathbf{r}^{(k)}$, and obtain that $\mathbf{r}^{(l)} \equiv_M^{(2)} \mathbf{r}^{(k)}$. Finally, using that $\mathbf{m}_j \circ \mathbf{n}_j^k = m^{(k)} \mathbf{r}_j^{(k)}$ and $\mathbf{m}_j \circ \mathbf{n}_j^k = m^{(l)} \mathbf{r}_j^{(l)} \mathbf{n}_j^{k-l}$ and $\mathbf{r}^{(l)} \equiv_M \mathbf{r}^{(k)}$ we can see that $tr_j^{(l)} = \mathbf{r}_j^{(l)} \mathbf{n}_j^{k-l}$ where t does not depend on $j = 1, 2$. Now, the result follows by Lemma 6. □

Back to the Proof of 2 $\Rightarrow$ 3. Let l be such $\mathbf{r}^{(l)} \equiv_M^{(2)} \mathbf{r}^{(l+1)}$. Then by $\mathbf{r}^{(0)} \equiv_M^{(2)} adv^{(\pi_1)}(\langle e, e \rangle)$ and $\mathbf{r}^{(1)} \equiv_M^{(2)} adv^{(\pi_1 \pi_2)}(\langle e, e \rangle)$ Lemma 10 implies:

$$\mathbf{r}^{(l)} \equiv_M^{(2)} adv^{(\pi_2^l)}(\mathbf{r}^{(0)}) \text{ and } \mathbf{r}^{(l)} \equiv_M^{(2)} \mathbf{r}^{(l+1)} \equiv_M^{(2)} adv^{(\pi_2^l)}(\mathbf{r}^{(1)}).$$

---

[7] Note that $\mathcal{T}$ is functional and $\mathcal{M}$ satisfies the LC-axiom. Therefore $\mathcal{T}_q$ is functional for any accessible state q, hence $\mathcal{O}_{\mathcal{T}}^{(\mathbf{q}_j)}$ are well-defined.

This means that $y\mathbf{r}_j^{(l)} = \mathbf{r}_j^{(0)}\mathbf{n}_j^l$ and $w\mathbf{r}_j^{(l)} = \mathbf{r}_j^{(1)}\mathbf{n}_j^l$ for appropriate $y, w \in \mathcal{M}$ that are independent of $j = 1, 2$. This shows that for $j = 1, 2$ the pairs $\left\langle \mathbf{r}_j^{(l)}, \mathbf{n}_j^{(l)} \right\rangle$ are left equalisable. We conclude that both $\left\langle y, \mathbf{r}_j^{(0)} \right\rangle$ and $\left\langle w, \mathbf{r}_j^{(1)} \right\rangle$ are equalisers for this pair. Let $\langle a_j, b_j \rangle$ be a left mge for the pair $\left\langle \mathbf{r}_j^{(l)}, \mathbf{n}_j^{(l)} \right\rangle$. Therefore there are $c_j, d_j \in \mathcal{M}$ with:

$$y = c_j a_j \text{ and } w = d_j a_j, \quad \mathbf{r}_j^{(0)} = c_j b_j \text{ and } \mathbf{r}_j^{(1)} = d_j b_j$$

Considering the first pair of equalities, we have that $\langle a_1, a_2 \rangle$ is left equalisable and $\langle c_1, c_2 \rangle$ and $\langle d_1, d_2 \rangle$ are left equalisers for this pair. Hence, if $\langle a_1', a_2' \rangle$ is the left mge for $\langle a_1, a_2 \rangle$, then there are c, d with $c_j = ca_j'$ and $d_j = da_j'$. This shows that $d \leq_M \mathbf{r}_j^{(1)}$ for $j = 1, 2$ and similarly, $c \leq_M \mathbf{r}_j^{(0)}$. Since $\mathbf{r}_1^{(0)} \sqcap \mathbf{r}_2^{(0)} \sim_M e$ and $\mathbf{r}_1^{(1)} \sqcap \mathbf{r}_2^{(1)} \sim_M e$ we conclude that c and d are invertible. Therefore $w \equiv_M y$. Let $uw = y$ where u is invertible. Therefore:

$$u\mathbf{r}_j^{(0)}\mathbf{n}_j^l = uy\mathbf{r}_j^{(l)} = uy\mathbf{r}_j^{(l)} = w\mathbf{r}_j^{(l)} = \mathbf{r}_j^{(1)}\mathbf{n}_j^l$$

and by the RC-axiom, we derive that $\mathbf{r}_j^{(0)} = u\mathbf{r}_j^{(1)}$ for $j = 1, 2$ with $u \sim_M e$. Therefore $\mathbf{r}^{(0)} =_M^{(2)} \mathbf{r}^{(1)}$, i.e. $adv^{(\pi_1)}(e, e) \equiv_{\mathcal{M}}^{(2)} adv^{(\pi_1 \pi_2)}(e, e)$, as required.

$3 \Rightarrow 1$. By Corollary 1, it suffices to show that if $\mathcal{A}^2$ obeys the Twinning Property, then $Q_{k+1} = Q_k$ for some k. We set out to show that there are only finitely many tuples in $2^{Q \times M}$ that can be generated by the algorithm. Let:

$$Adv(q_1, q_2) = \{[adv^{(\pi)}(\langle e, e \rangle)]_{\equiv_{\mathcal{M}}^{(2)}} \mid \pi \text{ is a path from } \langle i, i \rangle \text{ to } \langle q_1, q_2 \rangle \text{ in } \mathcal{A}^2 \}$$

for $q_1, q_2 \in Q$. The Twinning Property implies that $Adv(q_1, q_2)$ is generated entirely by cycle-free paths, thus it is finite.

Next, consider a state $P = \{\langle p_j, v_j \rangle\}_{j=1}^J \in Q_{k-1}$ for some k. Let α be a word such that: $\delta_k^*(s, \alpha) = P$ and $\lambda_k^*(s, \alpha) = u$. By Lemma 7 for each j we have: $\langle i, \langle \alpha, uv_j \rangle, p_j \rangle \in \Delta^*$. Therefore in the squared automaton $\mathcal{A}^2$ there are paths:

$$\langle \langle i, i \rangle, \langle \alpha, \langle uv_{j_1}, uv_{j_2} \rangle \rangle, \langle p_{j_1}, p_{j_2} \rangle \rangle \in \Delta_2^*$$

for all $j_1, j_2 \leq J$. Hence there is an element $\mathbf{r}(j_1, j_2) = \langle \mathbf{r}_1(j_1, j_2), \mathbf{r}_2(j_1, j_2) \rangle$ such that $[\mathbf{r}(j_1, j_2)] \in Adv(p_{j_1}, p_{j_2})$ and:

$$uv_{j_i} = t(j_1, j_2)\mathbf{r}_i(j_1, j_2) \text{ for } i = 1, 2 \text{ where } t(j_1, j_2) = uv_{j_1} \sqcap uv_{j_2}.$$

Consider the sequence $\langle \mathbf{r}_1(1, j) \rangle_{j=1}^J$. It is left equalisable for $uv_1 = t(1, j)\mathbf{r}_1(1, j)$. Thus, by Lemma 2, it has a left mge $\langle a_1, a_2, \dots, a_J \rangle$. In particular, there exists a t' s.t. $t(1, j) = t' \circ a_j$ for all $j \leq J$. Since $t' \sim_M \bigsqcap_j t(1, j) \sim_M \bigsqcap_j uv_j$ and, by construction, $\bigsqcap v_j \sim_M e$, we get that $t' \sim_M u$. Finally, the equalities $u \circ v_j = t(1, j)\mathbf{r}_2(1, j) = t'a_j\mathbf{r}_2(1, j)$, show that $v_j = \frac{t'}{u}a_j\mathbf{r}_2(1, j)$. Since $\frac{t'}{u}$ is invertible, $\langle v_j \rangle_{j=1}^J \equiv_M^{(J)} \langle a_j \mathbf{r}_2(1, j) \rangle_{j=1}^J$ is determined by $\{\mathbf{r}(1, j)\}_{j=1}^J$ up to equivalence w.r.t. $\equiv_M^{(J)}$. This is exactly what Step 2.(c) in our algorithm guards. This proves the existence of an injection between the states in $\bigcup_{k=0}^{\infty} Q_k$ and the subsets of $Q \times \left(\bigcup_{p,q \in Q} Adv(p,q) \right)$, which is finite. Since $Q_k \subseteq Q_{k+1}$ for all k, this implies that the algorithm halts. $\qquad\square$

5   Conclusion

In this paper we described a general class of monoids and characterised the sequential functions w.r.t. this class in terms of and appropriately generalised Twinning Property. We consider that the axiomatisation approach should make it easier to strengthen these results or alternatively to recognise that some of these axioms are necessary.

Most of the axioms seem natural from algebraic point of view. Yet, the GCLF- and PR-axioms are odd. From [7] we know that there are mge monoids with LSL-axiom that violate the GCLF-axiom and that admit regular languages with inf $L = \emptyset$. Yet, the GCLF-axiom is the only axiom from the mge and LSL-axioms not satisfied by the gcd monoids, [19]. Actually, both GCLF- and PR-axioms have the intrinsic property we need to surmount the cycles in the transducers and effectively reduce the infinite nature of the problem to a finite one. Can we relax them?

Notably, we have a characterisation of the sequential functions in terms of congruence relations, both for gcd monoids [19] and mge monoids with GCLF-axiom and additional (but rather tight) second order axiom, [6]. This challenges the necessity of all: LMGE-, PR-, and CC-axioms. Are there monoids that admit characterisation of sequential functions in terms of congruence relations but do not admit sequentialisation algorithm?

References

1. Béal, M.P., Carton, O., Prieur, C., Sakarovitch, J.: Squaring transducers: an efficient procedure for deciding functionality and sequentiality. TCS **292**(1), 45–63 (2003)
2. Choffrut, C.: Une caractérisation des fonctions séquentielles et des fonctions sous-séquentielles en tant que relations rationelles. TCS **5**, 325–338 (1977)
3. Daviaud, L., Reynier, P.A., Talbot, J.M.: A generalised twinning property for minimisation of cost register automata. In: Symposium on Logic in Computer Science, pp. 857–866 (2016)
4. Eilenberg, S.: Automata, Languages and Machines. Academic Press, New York and London (1974)
5. Filiot, E., Gentilini, R., Raskin, J.-F.: Quantitative languages defined by functional automata. In: Koutny, M., Ulidowski, I. (eds.) CONCUR 2012. LNCS, vol. 7454, pp. 132–146. Springer, Heidelberg (2012). https://doi.org/10.1007/978-3-642-32940-1_11
6. Gerdjikov, S.: Characterisation of (sub)sequential rational functions over a general class monoids. CoRR abs/1801.10063 (2018)

7. Gerdjikov, S.: A general class of monoids supporting canonisation and minimisation of (Sub)sequential transducers. In: Klein, S.T., Martín-Vide, C., Shapira, D. (eds.) LATA 2018. LNCS, vol. 10792, pp. 143–155. Springer, Cham (2018). https://doi.org/10.1007/978-3-319-77313-1_11

8. Gerdjikov, S., Mihov, S.: Myhill-Nerode Relation for Sequentiable Structures. ArXiv e-prints, June 2017. https://arxiv.org/abs/1706.02910

9. Gerdjikov, S., Mihov, S.: Over which monoids is the transducer determinization procedure applicable? In: Drewes, F., Martín-Vide, C., Truthe, B. (eds.) LATA 2017. LNCS, vol. 10168, pp. 380–392. Springer, Cham (2017). https://doi.org/10.1007/978-3-319-53733-7_28

10. Gerdjikov, S., Mihov, S., Schulz, K.U.: Space-efficient bimachine construction based on the equalizer accumulation principle. CoRR abs/1803.04312 (2018)

11. Hopcroft, J.E., Motwani, R., Ullman, J.D.: Introduction to Automata Theory, Languages, and Computation, 2nd edn. Addison-Wesley, Reading (2001)

12. Kempe, A.: Part of speech tagging with two sequential transducers. CoRR cs.CL/0110027 (2001). http://arxiv.org/abs/cs.CL/0110027

13. Lombardy, S., Sakarovitch, J.: Sequential? TCS **356**(1–2), 224–244 (2006)

14. Mohri, M.: On some applications of finite-state automata theory to natural language processing. J. Nat. Lang. Eng. **2**, 1–20 (1996)

15. Mohri, M.: Finite-state transducers in language and speech processing. Comput. Linguist. **23**(2), 269–311 (1997)

16. Mohri, M.: Minimization algorithms for sequential transducers. TCS **234**, 177–201 (2000)

17. Roche, E., Schabes, Y.: Introduction. In: Roche, E., Schabes, Y. (eds.) Finite-State Language Processing, pp. 1–66. MIT Press (1997)

18. Sakarovitch, J.: Elements of Automata Theory. Cambridge University Press, Cambridge (2009)

19. Souza, R.N.P.d.: Properties of some classes of rational relations (short version in English). Master's thesis, University of Sao Paulo (2004)

Non-self-embedding Grammars, Constant-Height Pushdown Automata, and Limited Automata

Bruno Guillon, Giovanni Pighizzini, and Luca Prigioniero$^{(\boxtimes)}$

Dipartimento di Informatica, Università degli Studi di Milano, Milan, Italy
{guillonb,pighizzini,prigioniero}@di.unimi.it

Abstract. Non-self-embedding grammars are a restriction of context-free grammars which does not allow to describe recursive structures and, hence, which characterizes only the class of regular languages. A double exponential gap in size from non-self-embedding grammars to deterministic finite automata is known. The same size gap is also known from constant-height pushdown automata and 1-limited automata to deterministic finite automata. Constant-height pushdown automata and 1-limited automata are compared with non-self-embedding grammars. It is proved that non-self-embedding grammars and constant-height pushdown automata are polynomially related in size. Furthermore, a polynomial size simulation by 1-limited automata is presented. However, the converse transformation is proved to cost exponential.

1 Introduction

It is well known that the extra capability of context-free grammars with respect to regular ones is that of describing recursive structures as, for instance, nested parentheses, arithmetic expressions, typical programming language constructs. In terms of recognizing devices, this capability is implemented through the pushdown store, which is used to extend finite automata in order to make the resulting model, namely pushdown automata, equivalent to context-free grammars.

To emphasize this capability, in one of his pioneering papers, Chomsky investigated the *self-embedding* property [4]: a context-free grammar is self-embedding if it contains a variable A which, in some sentential form, is able to reproduce itself surrounded by two nonempty strings α and β, in symbols $A \stackrel{*}{\Rightarrow} \alpha A \beta$. Roughly speaking, this means that the variable A is "truly" recursive. He proved that, among all context-free grammars, only self-embedding ones can generate nonregular languages. Hence, *non-self-embedding grammars* are no more powerful than finite automata.

The relationships between the description sizes of non-self-embedding grammars and finite automata have been investigated in [1,15]. In the worst case, the size of a deterministic automaton equivalent to a given non-self-embedding grammar is doubly exponential in the size of the grammar. The gap reduces to a simple exponential in the case of nondeterministic automata.

© Springer International Publishing AG, part of Springer Nature 2018
C. Câmpeanu (Ed.): CIAA 2018, LNCS 10977, pp. 186–197, 2018.
https://doi.org/10.1007/978-3-319-94812-6_16

Other formal models characterizing the class of regular languages and exhibiting gaps of the same order with respect to deterministic and nondeterministic automata have been investigated in the literature. Two of them are *constant-height pushdown automata* and 1-*limited automata*. The aim of this paper is to study the size relationships between non-self-embedding grammars, constant-height pushdown automata, and 1-limited automata, three models that restrict context-free acceptors to the level of regular recognizers.

Constant-height pushdown automata are standard nondeterministic pushdown automata where the amount of available pushdown store is fixed. Hence, the number of their possible configurations is finite. This implies that they are no more powerful than finite automata. The exponential and double exponential gaps from constant-height pushdown automata to nondeterministic and deterministic automata have been proved in [5]. Furthermore, in [2] the authors showed the interesting result that also the gap from nondeterministic to deterministic constant-height pushdown automata is double exponential. We can observe that both non-self-embedding grammars and constant-height pushdown automata are restrictions of the corresponding general models, where true recursions are not possible. In the first part of the paper we compare these two models by proving that they are polynomially related in size.

In the second part, we turn our attention to the size relationships between 1-limited automata and non-self-embedding grammars. For each integer $d > 0$, a d-*limited automaton* is a one-tape nondeterminstic Turing machine which is allowed to rewrite the content of each tape cell only in the first d visits. These models have been introduced by Hibbard in 1967, who proved that for each $d \geq 2$ they characterize context-free languages [6]. This yields a hierarchy of acceptors, merely obtained by restricting one-tape Turing machines, corresponding to Chomsky's classification. Furthermore, as shown in [16, Theorem 12.1], 1-limited automata are equivalent to finite automata. This equivalence has been investigated from the descriptional complexity point of view in [13], by proving exponential and double exponential gaps from 1-limited automata to nondeterministic and deterministic finite automata, respectively. Our main result is a construction transforming each non-self-embedding grammar into a 1-limited automaton of polynomial size. For the converse transformation, we show that an exponential size is necessary. Indeed, we prove a stronger result by exhibiting, for each $n > 0$, a language L_n accepted by a two-way deterministic finite automaton with $O(n)$ states, which requires exponentially many states to be accepted even by an unrestricted pushdown automaton. From the cost of the conversion of 1-limited automata into nondeterministic automata, it turns out that for the conversion of 1-limited automata into non-self-embedding grammars an exponential size is also sufficient. Figure 1 summarizes the main results discussed in the paper.

For brevity reasons some proofs are omitted in this version of the paper.

2   Preliminaries

Given a set S, we denote by $\#S$ its cardinality, and by 2^S the family of all its subsets. We assume the reader familiar with notions from formal languages and

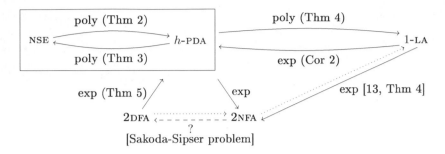

Fig. 1. Some bounds discussed in the paper. Dotted arrows denote trivial relationships, while the dashed arrow indicates the famous Sakoda and Sipser's question. The exponential cost of the simulation of h-PDAS by 2NFAs is discussed at the end of Sect. 4.2.

automata theory, in particular with the fundamental variants of finite automata (1DFAs, 1NFAs, 2DFAs, 2NFAs, for short, where 1 and 2 mean *one-way* and *two-way*, respectively, and D and N mean *deterministic* and *nondeterministic*, respectively). For further details see, *e.g.*, [7]. The empty word is denoted by ε. Given a word $u \in \Sigma^*$, we denote by $|u|$ its length. The set of all nonempty words over Σ is denoted by Σ^+. For two-way devices operating on a tape, we use the special symbols $\rhd$ and $\lhd$ not belonging to the input alphabet, respectively called the *left* and the *right endmarkers*, that surround the input word.

Given a *context-free grammar* (CFG, for short) $G = \langle V, \Sigma, P, S \rangle$, we denote by $L(G)$ the language generated by it. The relations $\Rightarrow$ and $\overset{*}{\Rightarrow}$ are defined in the usual way. The *production graph* of G is a directed graph which has V as vertex set and contains an edge from A to B if and only if there is a production $A \to \alpha B \beta$ in P, for $A, B \in V$ and some $\alpha, \beta \in (V \cup \Sigma)^*$. The strongly connected components of the production graph induce a partial order on variables, namely, a variable A is *smaller than* B if there exist a path from A to B and no path from B to A.

Definition 1. *Let* $G = \langle V, \Sigma, P, S \rangle$ *be a context-free grammar. A variable* $A \in V$ *is said to be* self-embedded *when there are two strings* $\alpha, \beta \in (V \cup \Sigma)^+$ *such that* $A \overset{*}{\Rightarrow} \alpha A \beta$. *The grammar* G *is* self-embedding *if it contains at least one self-embedded variable, otherwise* G *is* non-self-embedding *(*NSE*, for short).*

Chomsky proved that NSE grammars generate only regular languages, *i.e.*, they are no more powerful than finite automata [3,4]. As shown in [1], given a grammar G it is possible to decide in polynomial time whether or not it is NSE.

A *pushdown automaton* (PDA) is usually obtained from a nondeterministic finite automaton by adding a pushdown store, containing symbols from a *pushdown alphabet* Γ. Following [2,5], we consider PDAs in the following form, where the transitions manipulating the pushdown store are clearly distinguished from those reading the input tape. Furthermore, we consider a restriction of the model in which the capacity of the pushdown store is bounded by some constant $h \in \mathbb{N}$.

Definition 2. *For* $h \in \mathbb{N}$, *a* pushdown automaton of height h (h-PDA) *is a tuple* $\mathcal{A} = \langle Q, \Sigma, \Gamma, \delta, q_0, F \rangle$ *where* Q *is the set of states,* $q_0 \in Q$ *is the initial state,* $F \subseteq Q$ *is the set of final states,* Σ *is the input alphabet,* Γ *is the pushdown alphabet, and* $\delta \subseteq Q \times (\{\varepsilon\} \cup \Sigma \cup \{-, +\}\Gamma) \times Q$ *is the transition relation with the following meaning:*

- $(p, \varepsilon, q) \in \delta$: $\mathcal{A}$ *can reach the state* q *from the state* p *without using the input tape nor the pushdown store (these transitions are also called* ε-*moves);*
- $(p, a, q) \in \delta$: $\mathcal{A}$ *can reach the state* q *from the state* p *by reading the symbol* a *from the input but without using the pushdown store;*
- $(p, -X, q) \in \delta$: *if the symbol on the top of the pushdown store is* X, $\mathcal{A}$ *can reach the state* q *from the state* p *by popping off* X, *not using the input tape;*
- $(p, +X, q) \in \delta$: *if the number of symbols contained in the pushdown store is less than* h, $\mathcal{A}$ *can reach the state* q *from the state* p *by pushing* X *on the pushdown store, without using the input tape.*

The model *accepts* an input word $w \in \Sigma^*$ if, starting from the initial state q_0 with an empty pushdown store, it can eventually reach an accepting state $q_f \in F$, after having read all the input symbols.

Without the restriction on the pushdown height, the model is equivalent to classical pushdown automata, while preserving comparable size (namely, translations both ways have at most polynomial costs, see [2]). By contrast, 0-PDAS are exactly 1NFAs, since they can never push symbols.

One-limited automata (1-LAS, for short) extend two-way finite automata by providing the ability to overwrite each tape cell at its first visit by the head. This extension does not increase the expressiveness of the model. However, they can be significantly smaller than equivalent finite automata. For instance, the size gaps from 1-LAS to 1NFAs and 1DFAs are exponential and double exponential, respectively [13], while 2NFAS size with respect to deterministic 1-LAS even in the unary case, as shown in [9] and improved in [14].

Definition 3. *A* 1-limited automaton *is a tuple* $\mathcal{A} = \langle Q, \Sigma, \Gamma, \delta, q_0, F \rangle$, *where* Q, Σ, q_0, F *are defined as for* 2NFAs, Γ *is a finite* working alphabet *such that* $\Sigma \subseteq \Gamma$, *and* $\delta : Q \times \Gamma_{\triangleright\triangleleft} \to 2^{Q \times \Gamma_{\triangleright\triangleleft} \times \{-1, +1\}}$ *is the transition function, where* $\Gamma_{\triangleright\triangleleft} = \Gamma \cup \{\triangleright, \triangleleft\}$ *with* $\triangleright, \triangleleft \notin \Gamma$.

In one move, according to δ and to the current state, $\mathcal{A}$ reads a symbol from the tape, changes its state, replaces the symbol just read by a new symbol, and moves its head to one position backward or forward. However, replacing symbols is subject to some restrictions, which, essentially, allow to modify the content of a cell during the first visit only. Formally, symbols from Σ shall be replaced by symbols from $\Gamma \setminus \Sigma$, while symbols from $\Gamma_{\triangleright\triangleleft} \setminus \Sigma$ are never overwritten. In particular, at any time, both special symbols $\triangleright$ and $\triangleleft$ occur exactly once on the tape at the respective left and right boundaries. *Acceptance* for 1-LAS can be defined in several ways, for instance we can say that a 1-LA $\mathcal{A}$ accepts an input word if, starting from the left endmarker in the initial state, a computation eventually reaches the right endmarker in an accepting state. The language accepted by $\mathcal{A}$ is denoted by $L(\mathcal{A})$.

For each model under consideration, we evaluate its size as the total number of symbols used to define it. Hence, as a measure for the *size of a grammar* $\langle V, \Sigma, P, S \rangle$, we consider the total number of symbols used to specify it, defined as $\sum_{(A \to \alpha) \in P} (2 + |\alpha|)$, *cf.* [8]. Since we consider simulations between models, we can suppose that the input alphabet is fixed. Fixed a constant $h \geq 0$, the *size of an h*-PDA $\langle Q, \Sigma, \Gamma, \delta, q_0, F \rangle$ is given by a polynomial in $\#Q$ and $\#\Gamma$. The *size of an n-state* NFA (resp., DFA) is quadratic (resp., linear) in n. Finally, the *size of a* 1-LA $\langle Q, \Sigma, \Gamma, \delta, q_0, F \rangle$ is given by a polynomial in $\#Q$ and $\#\Gamma$.

3   NSE Grammars Versus *h*-PDAs

We prove here that NSE grammars and h-PDAs are polynomially related in size.

3.1   From NSE Grammars to *h*-PDAs

In [1], the authors showed that NSE grammars admit a particular form based on a decomposition into finitely many simpler grammars, that will be now recalled.

First of all, we remind the reader that a grammar is said *right-linear* (resp., *left-linear*), if each production is either of the form $A \to wB$ (resp., $A \to Bw$), or of the form $A \to w$, for some $A, B \in V$ and $w \in \Sigma^*$. It is well known that right- or left-linear grammars generate exactly the class of regular languages.

Given two CFGs $G_1 = \langle V_1, \Sigma_1, P_1, S_1 \rangle$ and $G_2 = \langle V_2, \Sigma_2, P_2, S_2 \rangle$ with $V_1 \cap V_2 = \emptyset$, the $\oplus$-composition of G_1 and G_2 is the grammar $G_1 \oplus G_2 = \langle V, \Sigma, P, S \rangle$, where $V = V_1 \cup V_2$, $\Sigma = (\Sigma_1 \setminus V_2) \cup \Sigma_2$, $P = P_1 \cup P_2$, and $S = S_1$. Intuitively, the grammar $G_1 \oplus G_2$ generates all the strings which can be obtained by replacing in any string $w \in L(G_1)$ each symbol $A \in \Sigma_1 \cap V_2$ with some string derived in G_2 from the variable A (notice that the definition of $G_1 \oplus G_2$ does not depend on the start symbol S_2 of G_2). The $\oplus$-composition is associative and preserves the property of being non-self-embedding [1]. The decomposition presented in the following result was obtained in [1], while its size is discussed in [15].

Theorem 1. *For each* NSE *grammar G there exist g grammars $G_1, G_2, \ldots, G_g$ such that $G = G_1 \oplus G_2 \oplus \cdots \oplus G_g$, where each G_i is either left- or right-linear. Furthermore the sum of sizes of G_i's is linear in the size of G.*

Studying the relationships between NSE grammars and PDAs, in [1] the authors claimed that from any NSE grammar in *canonical normal form* (namely with productions $A \to a\gamma$ or $A \to \gamma$, $A \in V$, $a \in \Sigma$ and $\gamma \in V^*$), by applying a standard transformation, it is possible to obtain an equivalent constant-height PDA. Unfortunately, the argument fails when the grammar contains left-recursive derivations, *i.e.*, derivations of the form $A \overset{*}{\Rightarrow} A\gamma$, with $\gamma \neq \varepsilon$. For them, the resulting PDA has computations with arbitrarily high pushdown stores. This problem can be fixed by replacing each left-linear grammar corresponding to a strongly connected component of the production graph of the given NSE grammar by a set of right-linear grammars.

Theorem 2. *Each* NSE *grammar* $G = \langle V, \Sigma, P, S \rangle$ *can be converted into an* h-PDA $\mathcal{A}$ *with both* h *and the size of* $\mathcal{A}$ *polynomial in the size of* G.

Proof (sketch). With a polynomial increase of the size, $G = G_1 \oplus G_2 \oplus \cdots \oplus G_g$, where each G_i is right-linear. As in the construction in [1], we can prove that if a variable $A \in V_i$ derives a string $x\alpha$ by a leftmost derivation, where x is the longest prefix of $x\alpha$ consisting only of terminal symbols, then $|\alpha| \leq K(g-i)+1$, where K is the maximum length of production right-hand sides.

From the grammar G, by a standard construction, we obtain a PDA M which simulates any leftmost derivation of G by replacing each variable A occurring on the top of the pushdown by the right-hand side of a production $A \to \alpha$, and by popping off the pushdown any terminal symbol occurring on the top and matching the next input symbol (for details see, *e.g.*, [7]). After consuming an input prefix y, the pushdown store of M can contain any string $z\alpha$ such that $S \overset{\star}{\Longrightarrow} yz\alpha$ by a leftmost derivation, yz is the longest prefix of $yz\alpha$ consisting only of terminal symbols, and z is a suitable factor of the string which was most recently pushed on the pushdown. Since $|z| \leq K$ and according to the first part of the proof $|\alpha| \leq K(g-1)+1$, we conclude that the pushdown height is bounded by $Kg + 1$. Hence, M is a constant-height PDA. $\qquad\square$

3.2   From h-PDAs to NSE Grammars

We first show that, modulo acceptance of the empty word, with only a polynomial increase in the size we can transform any h-PDA in a special form.

Lemma 1. *For each* h-PDA $\mathcal{A} = \langle Q, \Sigma, \Gamma, \delta, q_0, F \rangle$ *there exists an* h-PDA $\mathcal{A}' = \langle Q', \Sigma, \Gamma', \delta', q_-, \{q_+\} \rangle$ *and a mapping* $\tilde{h} : \Gamma' \to \{1, \ldots\}$ *such that:*

- $L(\mathcal{A}') = L(\mathcal{A}) \setminus \{\varepsilon\}$;
- $\mathcal{A}'$ *has polynomial size with respect to* $\mathcal{A}$;
- $\mathcal{A}'$ *accepts with empty pushdown;*
- *each symbol* $X \in \Gamma'$ *can appear on the pushdown only at height* $\tilde{h}(X)$;
- *every nonempty computation path of* $\mathcal{A}'$ *starting and ending with the same symbol* X *on the top of the pushdown, and never popping off* X *in the meantime, consumes some input letters.*

From an h-PDA $\mathcal{A} = \langle Q, \Sigma, \Gamma, \delta, q_-, \{q_+\} \rangle$ in the form of Lemma 1, we define a grammar $G = \langle V, \Sigma, P, S \rangle$, where V consists of an initial symbol S and of triples of the form $[qAp]$ and $\langle qAp \rangle$, for $q, p \in Q$, $A \in \Gamma \cup \{\perp\}$, with the new symbol $\perp \notin \Gamma$ denoting the "missed top" in the empty pushdown store. The set P consists of the following productions:

(i) $\langle pAq \rangle \to a$, for $(p, a, q) \in \delta$
(ii) $\langle pAq \rangle \to [p'Xq']$, for $(p, +X, p'), (q', -X, q) \in \delta$, *i.e.*, push and pop of a same symbol X
(iii) $[pAq] \to \langle pAr \rangle [rAq]$, for $p, q, r \in Q$, $A \in \Gamma$

(iv) $[pAq] \rightarrow \langle pAq \rangle$, for $p, q \in Q$, $A \in \Gamma$

(v) $S \rightarrow [q_- \perp q_+]$.

The above definition is derived from the classical construction of CFGs from PDAs, introducing two types of triples in order to obtain an NSE grammar. We can prove that the grammar G generates $L(\mathcal{A})$ and has size polynomial in $\#Q$ and $\#\Gamma$, so obtaining:

Theorem 3. *For each h-PDA there exists an equivalent NSE grammar of polynomial size.*

By applying the conversion in Theorem 2, the above construction, and a further standard transformation, we obtain that each NSE grammar can be transformed into a particular form, by paying a polynomial size increase.

Corollary 1. *Each NSE grammar is equivalent (modulo the empty word) to a grammar in Chomsky normal form of polynomial size in which, for each production $X \rightarrow YZ$, Y is greater than X according to the order induced by the production graph.*

4   NSE Grammars versus 1-LAS

In this section, we compare the sizes of NSE grammars and of h-PDAS with the size of equivalent 1-limited automata. We prove that for each NSE grammar there exists an equivalent 1-LA of polynomial size. As a consequence, the simulation of constant-height PDAs by 1-LAS is polynomial in size.

Concerning the converse transformation, we prove that 1-LAS can be more succinct than NSE grammars and constant-height PDAs. Actually, we prove a stronger result showing the existence of a family $(L_n)_{n>0}$ of languages such that each L_n is accepted by a 2DFA with $O(n)$ states, while each Chomsky normal form grammar or PDA accepting L_n would require an exponential size in n.

4.1   From NSE Grammars to 1-LAS

We start from an NSE grammar $G = \langle V, \Sigma, P, S \rangle$ in the form given by Corollary 1. Thus, there exists a constant $c \leq \#V$, such that every derivation tree of G has the following properties:

– Each internal node is either *saturated* (*i.e.*, it has exactly two children) and its children are labeled by some variables, or it has a unique child which is labeled by a terminal symbol.

– Along every path, the number of *left turns* (*i.e.*, the number of nodes which are left child of some node) is bounded by c.

These properties allow us to compress the representation of a derivation tree generating a word w of length m into a word u of length m over the alphabet $\Gamma = \Sigma \times V \times \{0, \dots, c\}$. The compression is non-injective, thus u may encode different derivation trees. However, each of these trees should generate the same word w, which is the projection of u over Σ. We now describe the compression, which is illustrated in Fig. 2. Given a derivation tree T of G, we inductively index its internal nodes according to the following rules:

- the root of T, labeled by the start symbol S, has index 0;
- the left child of a node with index i, has index $i + 1$;
- the right child of a node with index i, has index i.

In other words, the index of an internal node indicates the number of left turns along the path from the root to it. By assumption this number is bounded by c.

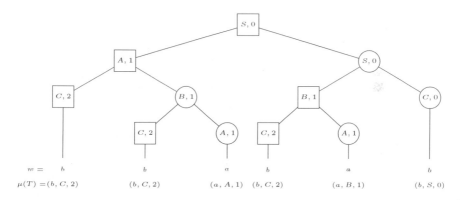

Fig. 2. An example of derivation tree

For a leaf ℓ of the tree labeled by a symbol $a \in \Sigma$, we define $\sigma_\ell = (a, X, i) \in \Gamma$ where (X, i) is the indexed label of the deepest ancestor of ℓ which is not a right child of any node (such nodes have square shape in Fig. 2). The *compression* of the derivation tree T is defined as the word $\mu(T) = \sigma_{\ell_1} \cdots \sigma_{\ell_m}$ where $\ell_1, \ldots, \ell_m$ are the leaves of T taken from left to right.

We now show how to check that a word $u \in \Gamma^+$ is the compression of some derivation tree. To this end, we highlight the recursive structure of compressions. We first define the three natural projections over Γ: for a symbol $\sigma = (a, X, i) \in \Gamma$, we set $\texttt{letter}(\sigma) = a$, $\texttt{var}(\sigma) = X$ and $\texttt{index}(\sigma) = i$. We fix the convention $\texttt{index}(\triangleright) = \texttt{index}(\triangleleft) = -1$. For $i = 0, \ldots, c$, we define $\Gamma_{>i} = \{\sigma \in \Gamma \mid \texttt{index}(\sigma) > i\}$, the restriction of Γ to symbols of index greater than i.

A word $u \in \Gamma^+$ is a *valid compression of level* i, $0 \le i \le c$, if, on the one hand, $u = w \cdot (a, X, i)$ for some $w \in \Gamma_{>i}^*$, $a \in \Sigma$ and $X \in V$, and, on the other hand, one of the following two cases holds:

1. $w = \varepsilon$ and $X \to a$ belongs to P;
2. there exist $Y, Z \in V$, $b \in \Sigma$, and $v, w' \in \Gamma^*$ such that:
   (a) $X \to YZ$ belongs to P;
   (b) $w = v(b, Y, i + 1)w'$

(c) $v(b, Y, i+1)$ is a valid compression of level $i + 1$;

(d) $w'(a, Z, i)$ is a valid compression of level i.

In particular, valid compressions of level c are exactly the single-letter words (a, X, c) such that $X \to a \in P$. Observe that Item 2c implies $v \in \Gamma^*_{>i+1}$ and therefore, Y and b are read from the leftmost symbol of index $i + 1$ of u. Hence, in order to reconstruct the tree, only the variables "Z's" should be guessed (these variables correspond indeed to nodes that are right child of some node, drawn with circle shape on Fig. 2, which are therefore not represented in the compression of the tree). By construction, we have:

Lemma 2. *A word $u \in \Gamma^+$ is a valid compression of level 0 if and only if $u = \mu(T)$ for some derivation tree T of G. Furthermore, T generates a word $w \in \Sigma^+$ which equals the projection of u over Σ^*.*

Proof (sketch). The result can be proved in a more general statement concerning any level i. Observe that Items 1 and 2a check that the tree recovered from a word u is consistent with the productions of G, and that Items 2c and 2d are obtained by induction on the left and right subtrees, respectively. Conversely, a correct derivation tree can be recovered from its (valid) compression. □

In every compression $\mu(T)$ of some derivation tree T, and for every level index i, a valid compression of level i is a factor delimited to the left, by a symbol of index less than or equal to i (not included in the factor), and to the right, by the symbol of index i corresponding to its root node (included in the factor). This allows a reading head to locally detect the boundaries of such a factor of an input. This also implies, that the index of a symbol preceding a symbol of index i, is always less than or equal to $i + 1$. For instance, the compression illustrated in Fig. 2 admits two valid compressions of level 1, namely the factors $(b, C, 2)(b, C, 2)(a, A, 1)$ and $(b, C, 2)(a, B, 1)$ which correspond to the subtree rooted in the square-shape nodes $(A, 1)$ and $(B, 1)$, respectively.

We now describe how a 2NFA $\mathcal{A}$ can check that a word $u \in \Gamma^+$ is a valid compression. First of all, the device checks that u belongs to $\Gamma^*_{>0}(a, S, 0)$ for some letter $a \in \Sigma$. Then, it iteratively verifies that every maximal factor of the form $\Gamma^*_{>i}(a, X, i)$ is a valid compression of level i. In order to do this, once the verification has been performed for the level $i + 1$, it just needs to check that the letter before (a, X, i) is of index at most $i + 1$, and that there is some consistency between letters of index $i + 1$ and (a, X, i) of such maximal word, as follows: sweeping these letters $(a_1, Y_1, i + 1), \ldots, (a_k, Y_k, i + 1)$ from left to right and setting $Z_0 = X$, the 2NFA sequentially guesses letters $Z_1, \ldots, Z_k$ such that $Z_{i-1} \to Y_i Z_i \in P$ for $i = 1, \ldots, k$, and $Z_k \to a \in P$. In other words, the device implements the above-given inductive definition of valid compressions, with the difference that it tests each subtree of level from c downto 0 instead of performing recursive calls. This allows to store only one guessed variable Z at each time.

The 2NFA $\mathcal{A}$ implements a collection of nondeterministic subroutines, the top-level of which is the procedure `CheckTree`. In each subroutine, σ denotes

---

Procedure `CheckTree`

/* start with the head on the left endmarker */

1 `CheckZeroes`
2 **for** $i \leftarrow c$ **downto** 0 **do**
3   move the head to the right until reaching the next symbol with index i
4   **while** $\text{index}(\sigma) = i$ **do**
5   `CheckSubtree`(i)
6   move the head to the right until reaching the next symbol with index i
7   move the head to the left until reaching the left endmarker
8 ACCEPT

Procedure `CheckSubtree`(i)

/* start with the head scanning a symbol of index i */

9    $C \leftarrow \text{var}(\sigma)$
10 **repeat** move the head to the left **until** $\text{index}(\sigma) \leq i$
11 `SelectNext`$(i + 1)$
12 **while** $\text{index}(\sigma) \neq i$ **do**
13   guess Z
14   **if** $C \rightarrow YZ \notin P$, *where* $Y = \text{var}(\sigma)$ **then** REJECT
15      $C \leftarrow Z$
16   `SelectNext`$(i + 1)$
17 **if** $C \rightarrow a \notin P$, *where* $a = \text{letter}(\sigma)$ **then** REJECT

---

the symbol currently scanned by the head, which is automatically updated at each head move. Moreover, the special instruction REJECT causes the whole computation to halt and reject.

As initial phase, a subroutine `CheckZeroes` checks that the input word belongs to $\Gamma_{>0}^* \cdot (a, S, 0)$ for some letter $a \in \Sigma$. Then, $\mathcal{A}$ checks the validity of each compression of each level from c downto 0 (Lines 2 to 7). This verification uses the procedure `CheckSubtree` (Line 5).

This latter subroutine is the direct implementation of the inductive definition of valid compressions, where the recursive call to incremented level (Item 2c) is omitted (the validity of these sub-compressions have already been checked by previous call to `CheckSubtree`). It uses the subroutine `SelectNext` to locate the leftmost symbol of index $i + 1$ in the factor under consideration, if any, or to check if the factor has length 1, otherwise, thus checking Item 2b (or, partially, Item 1). Items 1 and 2a correspond to Lines 17 and 14, respectively, where C contains the variable Z (Line 15) which is initially set to X, the variable label of the root of the subtree (Line 9), thus allowing to verify Item 2d (Lines 12 to 16).

To summarize, we obtained the following result.

Lemma 3. *The language of valid compressions of derivation trees of G is recognized by a* 2NFA *which uses $O(\#V^2)$ states.*

Procedure `SelectNext(`j`)`

18	move the head to the right
19	**if** `index(`σ`)` $\neq j - 1$ **then**
20	$\quad$ **while** `index(`σ`)` $> j$ **do** move the head to the right
21	$\quad$ **if** `index(`σ`)` $\neq j$ **then** REJECT

We are now ready to state our main result.

Theorem 4. *For every* NSE *grammar* G, *there exist a 1-state letter-to-letter nondeterministic transducer* $\mathcal{T}$ *and a* 2NFA $\mathcal{A}$ *of polynomial size, such that a word* w *is generated by* G *if and only if* $\mathcal{A}$ *accepts an image* u *of* w *by* $\mathcal{T}$. *As a consequence,* G *can be transformed into a* 1-LA *of polynomial size.*

Proof. From an NSE grammar G, we obtain an NSE grammar G' over Σ of polynomial size in the form given by Corollary 1, such that $L(G') = L(G) \setminus \{\varepsilon\}$. The transducer $\mathcal{T}$ replaces each letter $a \in \Sigma$ by a symbol (a, X, i) for some variable X of G' and some index $i \leq \#V$. Finally, we build $\mathcal{A}$, using Lemma 3, which recognizes an output of $\mathcal{T}$, if and only if its pre-image was generated by G', by Lemma 2. In case $\varepsilon \in L(G)$, we modify $\mathcal{A}$ in order to accept ε. $\quad\square$

4.2   From 2DFAs to PDAs: An Exponential Gap

In this section, we exhibit an infinite family $(L_n)_{n \geq 0}$ of languages over the alphabet $\{0, 1\}$, such that each L_n is recognized by a 1-LA with size polynomial in n, but requires an exponential size in order to be recognized by any h-PDA. We can actually prove a stronger result, since each L_n is recognized by a 2DFA (and even by a *rotating* deterministic automaton, in which all passes over the input are from left to right) of linear size, while any grammar in Chomsky normal form generating L_n requires an exponential number of variables. As a consequence, every PDA recognizing L_n requires an exponential size. The proof of this lower bound is obtained by using the *interchange lemma for context-free languages* [11].

Theorem 5. *For each* $n > 0$, *let* L_n *be the language of the powers of any string of length* n *over* $\{0, 1\}$, *i.e.,* $L_n = \{u^k \mid u \in \{0, 1\}^n,\ k \geq 0\}$. *Then:*

- L_n *is accepted by a* 2DFA *of size* $O(n)$;
- *each context-free grammar in Chomsky normal form needs exponentially many variables in* n *to generate* L_n;
- *the size of any* PDA *accepting* L_n *is at least exponential in* n.

Corollary 2. *The size cost of the conversion of* 1-LA*s into* NSE *grammars and* h-PDA*s is exponential.*

Proof. The lower bound derives from Theorem 5. For the upper bound, in [13] it was proved that each 1-LA can be transformed into a 1NFA of exponential size from which, by a standard construction, we can obtain a regular (and, so, NSE) grammar, without increasing the size asymptotically. $\quad\square$

In [2], the question of the cost of the conversion of deterministic h-PDAs into 1NFAs was raised. To this regard, we observe that the language $(a^{2^n})^*$ is accepted by a deterministic h-PDA of size polynomial in n for large enough h (see, *e.g.*, [12]) but, by a standard pumping argument, it requires at least 2^n states to be accepted by 1NFAs. Actually, as a consequence of state lower bound presented in [10], 2^n states are also necessary to accept it on each 2NFA. Considering Theorem 5, we can conclude that both simulations from two-way automata to h-PDAs and from h-PDAs to two-way automata cost at least exponential.

References

1. Anselmo, M., Giammarresi, D., Varricchio, S.: Finite automata and non-self-embedding grammars. In: Champarnaud, J.-M., Maurel, D. (eds.) CIAA 2002. LNCS, vol. 2608, pp. 47–56. Springer, Heidelberg (2003). https://doi.org/10.1007/3-540-44977-9_4
2. Bednárová, Z., Geffert, V., Mereghetti, C., Palano, B.: Removing nondeterminism in constant height pushdown automata. Inf. Comput. **237**, 257–267 (2014)
3. Chomsky, N.: On certain formal properties of grammars. Inf. Control **2**(2), 137–167 (1959)
4. Chomsky, N.: A note on phrase structure grammars. Inf. Control **2**(4), 393–395 (1959)
5. Geffert, V., Mereghetti, C., Palano, B.: More concise representation of regular languages by automata and regular expressions. Inf. Comput. **208**(4), 385–394 (2010)
6. Hibbard, T.N.: A generalization of context-free determinism. Inf. Control **11**(1/2), 196–238 (1967)
7. Hopcroft, J.E., Motwani, R., Ullman, J.D.: Introduction to Automata Theory, Languages, and Computation, 2nd edn. Addison-Wesley-Longman, Reading (2001)
8. Kelemenová, A.: Complexity of normal form grammars. Theor. Comput. Sci. **28**, 299–314 (1984)
9. Kutrib, M., Wendlandt, M.: On simulation cost of unary limited automata. In: Shallit, J., Okhotin, A. (eds.) DCFS 2015. LNCS, vol. 9118, pp. 153–164. Springer, Cham (2015). https://doi.org/10.1007/978-3-319-19225-3_13
10. Mereghetti, C., Pighizzini, G.: Two-way automata simulations and unary languages. J. Automata Lang. Comb. **5**(3), 287–300 (2000)
11. Ogden, W.F., Ross, R.J., Winklmann, K.: An "interchange lemma" for context-free languages. SIAM J. Comput. **14**(2), 410–415 (1985)
12. Pighizzini, G.: Deterministic pushdown automata and unary languages. Int. J. Found. Comput. Sci. **20**(4), 629–645 (2009)
13. Pighizzini, G., Pisoni, A.: Limited automata and regular languages. Int. J. Found. Comput. Sci. **25**(7), 897–916 (2014)
14. Pighizzini, G., Prigioniero, L.: Limited automata and unary languages. In: Charlier, É., Leroy, J., Rigo, M. (eds.) DLT 2017. LNCS, vol. 10396, pp. 308–319. Springer, Cham (2017). https://doi.org/10.1007/978-3-319-62809-7_23
15. Pighizzini, G., Prigioniero, L.: Non-self-embedding grammars and descriptional complexity. NCMA **2017**, 197–209 (2017)
16. Wagner, K.W., Wechsung, G.: Computational Complexity. D. Reidel Publishing Company, Dordrecht (1986)

The Ranges of Accepting State Complexities of Languages Resulting From Some Operations

Michal Hospodár[1] and Markus Holzer[2]([⊠])

[1] Mathematical Institute, Slovak Academy of Sciences,
Grešákova 6, 040 01 Košice, Slovakia
hosmich@gmail.com
[2] Institut für Informatik, Universität Giessen,
Arndtstr. 2, 35392 Giessen, Germany
holzer@informatik.uni-giessen.de

Abstract. We examine the accepting state complexity, i.e., the minimal number of *accepting states* of deterministic finite automata (DFAs) for languages resulting from unary and binary operations on languages with accepting state complexity given as a parameter. This is continuation of the work of [J. Dassow: On the number of accepting states of finite automata, *J. Autom., Lang. Comb.*, 21, 2016]. We solve most of the open problems mentioned thereof. In particular, we consider the operations of intersection, symmetric difference, right and left quotients, reversal, and permutation (on finite languages), where we obtain precise ranges of the accepting state complexities.

1 Introduction

The descriptive complexity of regular languages, to be more precise the state complexity of deterministic and nondeterministic finite automata and regularity preserving operations thereof, is well understood. While the deterministic state complexity of a regular language can be read of from the minimal deterministic finite automaton (DFA) for the language in question, it is well-known that this is not the case for the nondeterministic state complexity. Moreover, it is folklore, that the deterministic and nondeterministic state complexity forms a strict infinite hierarchy w.r.t. the number of states. Yet another well known result is that for DFAs the number of accepting states is a host for an infinite strict hierarchy, while for nondeterministic finite automata (NFAs) two accepting states suffice, and if λ-transitions (spontaneous transitions) are allowed for NFAs even a single accepting state is enough to accept every regular language. But what else

M. Hospodár—Research supported by VEGA grant 2/0084/15 and grant APVV-15-0091. This work was conducted during a research visit at the Institut für Informatik, Universität Giessen, Germany, funded by the DAAD short-term grant ID 57314022.

C. Câmpeanu (Ed.): CIAA 2018, LNCS 10977, pp. 198–210, 2018.
https://doi.org/10.1007/978-3-319-94812-6_17

can be said about the number of accepting states for finite automata, in particular, when regularity preserving operations such as, e.g., Boolean operations, concatenation, Kleene star, etc., are applied to the finite state devices?

A partial answer to these questions was recently given in [3]. There the accepting state complexity of DFAs and NFAs was introduced and investigated in detail. To be more precise, the *(deterministic) accepting state complexity* of a regular language L is defined as the minimal number of accepting states needed for a DFA to accept L. Analogously one defines the *nondeterministic accepting state complexity* of a regular language. Similarly as for ordinary deterministic state complexity the deterministic *accepting state complexity* of a regular language can be determined from the minimal DFA for the language under consideration. On the other hand, the nondeterministic accepting state complexity is trivial as already mentioned above. The major contribution of [3] is the investigation of the deterministic accepting state complexity or for short the accepting state complexity w.r.t. the operations of complementation, union, concatenation, set difference, and Kleene star, which are summarized on the left in Table 1— a number within the range is *magic* if it cannot be produced by the operation from any K and L with the appropriate complexities. Hence, the quest to understand the accepting state complexity of operations can be seen as a variant of the magic number problem—see, e.g., [5,8,10], but now for the descriptional complexity measure accepting states instead of ordinary states.

Table 1. Results obtained in [3] (left) and the results of this paper (right). It is assumed that K and L have accepting state complexity m and n, respectively, for $m, n \geq 1$. Then the range indicates the obtainable accepting state complexities of the operation under consideration and the status of the magic number problem refers to whether there are magic numbers in the given range or not.

Op.	Range	Magic num.	$|\Sigma|$	Op.	Range	Magic num.	$|\Sigma|$
$\Sigma^* \setminus L$	$\mathbb{N} \cup \{0 \mid n = 1\}$	no	1	$K \cap L$	$[0, mn]$	no	2
$K \cup L$	$\mathbb{N}$	no	1	$K \oplus L$	$\{0\} \cup \mathbb{N}$	no	1
KL	$\mathbb{N}$	no	1	KL^{-1}	$\{0\} \cup \mathbb{N}$	no	1
$K \setminus L$	$\{0\} \cup \mathbb{N}$	no	1	$L^{-1}K$	$\{0\} \cup \mathbb{N}$	no	1
L^*	$\mathbb{N}$	no	1	L^R	$\mathbb{N}$	no	2
$K \cap L$	$[0, mn]$	?		$\mathrm{per}(L)$	$\mathbb{N} \setminus \{1 \mid n \geq 2\}$	no	2

This is the starting point of our investigation. We study the accepting state complexity of the operations intersection, symmetric difference, right and left quotients, reversal, and permutation. The latter operation is only considered on finite languages, since regular languages are not closed under permutation. The obtained results are summarized on the right of Table 1. We solve most open problems from [3]. It is worth mentioning that intersection has an accepting state complexity bounded from above and no magic numbers within this interval.

2   Preliminaries

We recall some definitions on finite automata as contained in [6]. Let Σ^* denote the set of all words over the finite alphabet Σ. The *empty word* is denoted by λ. Further, we denote the set $\{i, i+1, \ldots, j\}$ by $[i, j]$, if i and j are integers.

A *nondeterministic finite automaton* (NNFA) is a 5-tuple $A = (Q, \Sigma, \delta, I, F)$, where Q is a finite set of states, Σ is a finite nonempty alphabet, $\delta \colon Q \times \Sigma \to 2^Q$ is the transition function which is naturally extended to the domain $2^Q \times \Sigma^*$, $I \subseteq Q$ is the set of initial states, and $F \subseteq Q$ is the set of accepting (or final) states. We say that (p, a, q) is a *transition* in A if $q \in \delta(p, a)$. If (p, a, q) is a transition in A, then we say that the state q has an *ingoing transition*, and the state p has an *outgoing transition*. We sometimes write $p \xrightarrow{w} q$, if $q \in \delta(p, w)$. The *language accepted by* A is the set $L(A) = \{ w \in \Sigma^* \mid \delta(I, w) \cap F \neq \emptyset \}$. If $|I| \geq 2$, we say that A is a *nondeterministic finite automaton with nondeterministic choice of initial state* (so we use the abbreviation NNFA, cf. [15]). Otherwise, if $|I| = 1$, we say that A is a *nondeterministic finite automaton* (NFA). In this case we simple $A = (Q, \Sigma, \delta, s, F)$ instead of $A = (Q, \Sigma, \delta, \{s\}, F)$. Moreover, an NFA A is a (partial) *deterministic finite automaton* (DFA), if $|\delta(q, a)| \leq 1$, for each q in Q and each a in Σ, and it is a *complete* DFA, if $|\delta(q, a)| = 1$, for each q in Q and each a in Σ.

Every NNFA $A = (Q, \Sigma, \delta, I, F)$ can be converted to an equivalent complete DFA $\mathcal{D}(A) = (2^Q, \Sigma, \delta, I, \{ S \in 2^Q \mid S \cap F \neq \emptyset \})$, where $\delta(S, a) = \bigcup_{q \in S} \delta(q, a)$, for $S \in 2^Q$ and $a \in \Sigma$. We call the DFA $\mathcal{D}(A)$ the *subset automaton* of A.

The *state complexity of a regular language* L, referred to as $\mathrm{sc}(L)$, is the smallest number of states in any complete DFA accepting L. The *state complexity of a regular operation* is the number of states that are sufficient and necessary in the worst case for a DFA to accept the language resulting from the operation, considered as a function of the number of states of DFAs for the given operands. Similarly we define the *accepting state complexity* of a language L by

$$\mathrm{asc}(L) = \min\{ \, n \mid L \text{ is accepted by a DFA with } n \text{ accepting states} \, \}.$$

An automaton is *minimal* (a-minimal, respectively) if it admits no smaller equivalent automaton w.r.t. the number of states (accepting states, respectively). For DFAs both properties can be easily verified. Minimality can be shown if all states are reachable from the initial state and all states are pairwise inequivalent. For a-minimality the following result shown in [3, Theorem 1] applies.

Theorem 1. *Let L be a language accepted by a minimal DFA A. Then the number of accepting states of A is equal to $\mathrm{asc}(L)$.*

Note that a-minimality can be shown if all states are reachable from the initial state and all *accepting* states are pairwise inequivalent. In fact, we do not need to prove distinguishability of all (including rejecting) states.

In order to characterize the behaviour of complexities under operations we introduce the following notation: for $c \in \{sc, asc\}$, a k-ary regularity preserving operation $\circ$ on languages, and natural numbers $n_1, n_2, \ldots, n_k$, we define

$$g_\circ^c(n_1, n_2, \ldots, n_k)$$

as the set of all integers α such that there are k regular languages $L_1, L_2, \ldots, L_k$ with $c(L_i) = n_i$, for $1 \leq i \leq k$, and $c(\circ(L_1, L_2, \ldots, L_k)) = \alpha$. In case we only consider unary (finite, respectively) languages $L_1, L_2, \ldots, L_k$ we write $g_\circ^{c,u}$ ($g_\circ^{c,f}$, respectively) instead. Let $I_\circ^c$ be the smallest integer interval containing all elements from the set $g_\circ^c(n_1, n_2, \ldots, n_k)$. Then any element from $I_\circ^c \setminus g_\circ^c(n_1, n_2, \ldots, n_k)$ is said to be a *magic number* for the operation $\circ$ with respect to the complexities $n_1, n_2, \ldots, n_k$. This notion was introduced in [8,9].

The *nondeterministic accepting state complexity* of a language L, denoted by $\mathrm{nasc}(L)$, refers to the minimal number of accepting states in any NFA for L. It was shown in [3] that for every nonempty regular language L we have $\mathrm{nasc}(L) = 1$, if $\lambda \notin L$, but $\mathrm{nasc}(L) \leq 2$, if $\lambda \in L$. Thus, the nondeterministic accepting state complexity is not too interesting. Nevertheless, it was left open to give a sufficient and necessary condition for a language L such that $\mathrm{nasc}(L) = 1$ and $\lambda \in L$. This problem was solved in [11].

Lemma 2. *A language L satisfies $\lambda \in L$ and $\mathrm{nasc}(L) = 1$ if and only if $L = L^*$.*

Proof. If $\lambda \in L$ and $\mathrm{nasc}(L) = 1$, then there is an NFA for L in which the single accepting state is the initial state. Therefore $L = L^*$.

Conversely, let $A = (Q, \Sigma, \delta, s, F)$ be an NFA accepting the set L. If $L = L^*$, then $\lambda \in L$, so the initial state s of A is accepting. For every accepting state q_f in $F \setminus \{s\}$ and every transition (q, a, q_f) we add the transition (q, a, s) to A and make the state q_f rejecting. Since $L = L^*$, the resulting automaton, which has exactly one accepting state, accepts L. It follows that $\mathrm{nasc}(L) = 1$.   □

3   Results

We investigate the accepting state complexity of various regularity preserving language operations such as, e.g., intersection, symmetric difference, right and left quotients, reversal, and permutation on finite languages. We start with the accepting state complexity of intersection solving an open problem stated in [3].

3.1   Intersection

For two DFAs $A = (Q_A, \Sigma, \delta_A, s_A, F_A)$ and $B = (Q_B, \Sigma, \delta_B, s_B, F_B)$ we apply the standard cross-product construction in order to construct an automaton for the intersection of $L(A)$ and $L(B)$. Thus, define $C = (Q_C, \Sigma, \delta_C, s_C, F_C)$ with $Q_C = Q_A \times Q_B$, $s_C = (q_A, q_B)$, and $F_C = F_A \times F_B$. The transition function is set to $\delta_C((p, q), a) = (\delta_A(p, a), \delta_B(q, a))$. Thus, we have $L(C) = L(A) \cap L(B)$. If A is an m-state and B an n-state DFA then the above construction results in an

mn-state DFA C. In [16] it was shown that this upper bound is necessary in the worst case, that is, it can be reached by two appropriately chosen minimal DFAs with m and n states, respectively. Moreover, in [7] it was shown that there are no magic numbers for intersection on a binary alphabet. This is a direct consequence of the theorem that there are no magic numbers for union, De Morgan's law, and the fact the complementation preserves the state complexity. Thus, for every α with $1 \leq \alpha \leq mn$ there are minimal m-state and n-state DFAs such that the intersection of the languages described by these automata requires a minimal DFA with exactly α states.

Now let us turn our attention to the accepting state complexity of intersection. The next theorem solves an open problem stated in [3].

Theorem 3. *We have* $g_\cap^{\mathrm{asc}}(m,n) = g_\cap^{\mathrm{asc}}(n,m) = [0, mn]$.

Proof. Since intersection is commutative we have $g_\cap^{\mathrm{asc}}(m,n) = g_\cap^{\mathrm{asc}}(n,m)$. Now let $0 \leq \alpha \leq mn$. We are going to describe minimal DFAs A and B with m and n accepting states, respectively, such that $\mathrm{asc}(L(A) \cap L(B)) = \alpha$. Notice that α can be expressed as $\alpha = kn + \ell$, for some integers k and ℓ with $0 \leq k \leq m$ and $0 \leq \ell \leq n-1$.

Define the DFA $A = ([1, m+1], \{a, b\}, \delta_A, m+1, [1, m])$, where

$$\delta_A(i, a) = i - 1, \text{ if } 2 \leq i \leq m+1; \qquad \delta_A(i, b) = \begin{cases} i, & \text{if } 1 \leq i \leq m; \\ k+1, & \text{if } i = m+1. \end{cases}$$

Next, define the DFA $B = ([0, n+1], \{a, b\}, \delta_B, n+1, [1, n])$, where

$$\delta_B(j, a) = n, \text{ if } j = 0; \qquad \delta_B(j, b) = \begin{cases} j - 1, & \text{if } 1 \leq j \leq n; \\ \ell, & \text{if } j = n+1. \end{cases}$$

The DFAs A and B are depicted in Fig. 1. It is easy to see that both DFAs are minimal.

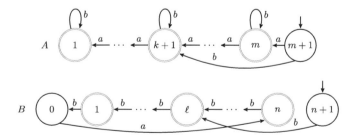

Fig. 1. Let α satisfy $0 \leq \alpha \leq mn$. The witness DFAs A (top) and B (bottom) for intersection with $\alpha = kn + \ell$, for $0 \leq k \leq m$ and $0 \leq \ell \leq n$.

We construct the automaton C of A and B according to the previously given construction. The product automaton C has the following transitions:

1. $\to (m+1, n+1) \xrightarrow{b} (k+1, \ell) \xrightarrow{b} (k+1, \ell-1) \xrightarrow{b} \dots \xrightarrow{b} (k+1, 1) \xrightarrow{b} (k+1, 0)$,

2. $(k+1, 0) \xrightarrow{a} (k, n) \xrightarrow{b} (k, n-1) \xrightarrow{b} \dots \xrightarrow{b} (k, 1) \xrightarrow{b} (k, 0)$,

3. $(k, 0) \xrightarrow{a} (k-1, n) \xrightarrow{b} (k-1, n-1) \xrightarrow{b} \dots \xrightarrow{b} (k-1, 1) \xrightarrow{b} (k-1, 0)$, etc., and

4. $(2, 0) \xrightarrow{a} (1, n) \xrightarrow{b} (1, n-1) \xrightarrow{b} \dots \xrightarrow{b} (1, 1) \xrightarrow{b} (1, 0)$.

No other transitions are present in C. It follows that $L(C)$ is a finite language with the longest word $b^{\ell+1}(ab^n)^{k-1}ab^{n-1}$. Hence every NFA for the language $L(C)$ has at least $k(n+1) + \ell + 1$ states. Thus C with the state $(1, 0)$ removed is a minimal NFA for $L(C) = L(A) \cap L(B)$. Next, since C is a DFA it is a minimal DFA. So every state pair is distinguishable. Note that the states (i, j), for $1 \leq i \leq k$ and $1 \leq j \leq n$, and $(k+1, j)$, for $1 \leq j \leq \ell$, are reachable and accepting in C. It follows that we have $kn + \ell$ reachable and pairwise distinguishable accepting states. Thus $\mathrm{asc}(L(A) \cap L(B)) = kn + \ell = \alpha$, and the theorem follows.   □

3.2   Symmetric Difference

The symmetric difference ($\oplus$) of two languages accepted by finite automata can also be obtained by a product construction, similar as in the case of intersection. The only difference to the construction used for intersection is the definition of the set of accepting states, which in case of symmetric difference is set to $F_C = F_A \times (Q_B \setminus F_B) \cup (Q_A \setminus F_A) \times F_B$, where the notation is that for intersection used in Subsect. 3.1. Thus, for the ordinary state complexity the upper bound is mn, which was shown to be tight in [17]. To our knowledge the magic number problem for state complexity of the symmetric difference operation was not investigated so far. For the accepting state complexity we find the following situation, where we utilize the fact that for unary finite and unary co-finite languages it is very easy to determine the number of accepting states, from a description of the language in question. For instance, the unary language $L = \{ a^i \mid 2 \leq i \leq 5\} \cup \{ a^j \mid j \geq 7 \}$ is accepted by a minimal DFA with $(5-2)+1+1 = 5$ accepting states. For the structure of (minimal) unary DFAs in general we refer to [2].

Lemma 4. *Let $m, n \geq 1$ and $m \leq n$. Then for every α with $\alpha \geq 1$ there are minimal unary DFAs A and B with m and n accepting states, respectively, such that the minimal DFA for $L(A) \oplus L(B)$ has α accepting states.*

Proof. Define the unary languages $K = \{ a^i \mid 0 \leq i \leq m-2 \text{ or } i \geq m \}$ and $L = \{ a^i \mid 0 \leq i \leq m-2 \text{ or } m \leq i \leq n-1 \text{ or } i \geq n+\alpha \}$. Let A and B be minimal DFAs for K and L, respectively. Then A and B have m and n accepting states, respectively. Moreover, $L(A) \oplus L(B) = \{ a^i \mid n \leq i \leq n+\alpha-1 \}$, which is accepted by a minimal DFA with α accepting states.   □

Now we are ready to describe the behaviour of the accepting state complexity measure w.r.t. the symmetric difference operation.

Theorem 5. *We have*

$$
g_{\oplus}^{\mathrm{asc},u}(m,n) = g_{\oplus}^{\mathrm{asc}}(m,n) = g_{\oplus}^{\mathrm{asc}}(n,m) = \begin{cases} \{n\} & \text{if } m = 0; \\ \{m\} & \text{if } n = 0; \\ \{0\} \cup \mathbb{N} & \text{if } m,n \geq 1 \text{ and } m = n; \\ \mathbb{N} & \text{otherwise.} \end{cases}
$$

Proof. The symmetric difference of two languages is commutative. Therefore $g_{\oplus}^{\mathrm{asc}}(m,n) = g_{\oplus}^{\mathrm{asc}}(n,m)$. The only language with accepting state complexity 0 is the empty language $\emptyset$. For nonempty languages Lemma 4 applies. Since we have $\emptyset \oplus L = L$, $K \oplus \emptyset = K$, and $K \oplus L = \emptyset$ if and only if $K = L$, the first three cases of $g_{\oplus}^{\mathrm{asc}}$ are covered. Thus, all natural numbers can be obtained as the number of accepting states of a DFA accepting the symmetric difference of DFAs A and B with m and n accepting states, respectively; notice that $m \neq n$ implies $K \neq L$. Additionally, in case $m = n$ one can also obtain the value 0, since in this case we can force both languages K and L to be the same, which gives $K \oplus L = \emptyset$. Finally, $g_{\oplus}^{\mathrm{asc}}(m,n) = g_{\oplus}^{\mathrm{asc},u}(m,n)$ since all our witnesses are unary languages. $\square$

3.3   Right and Left Quotients

The *right quotient* of a language K by a language L is defined as follows:

$$KL^{-1} = \{\, w \mid \text{there is a } x \in L \text{ such that } wx \in K \,\}.$$

The DFA accepting KL^{-1} is the same as the DFA accepting K except that the set of accepting states is different. To be more precise, let $A = (Q, \Sigma, \delta, s, F)$ be the DFA accepting K, then $B = (Q, \Sigma, \delta, s, \{\, q \mid \exists x \in L : \delta(q,x) \in F \,\})$ accepts the language KL^{-1}. Thus, for an m-state DFA the upper bound for the state complexity of the right quotient w.r.t. any language is m, which is known to be tight [17]. Similarly one defines the *left quotient* of K by L as

$$L^{-1}K = \{\, w \mid \text{there is a } x \in L \text{ such that } xw \in K \,\}.$$

It was proven that for an m-state DFA language K, the state complexity of the left quotient of K by any language L is at most $2^m - 1$. Again, this bound is tight [17]. Note, when considering unary languages K and L, the right and left quotient coincide, i.e., $KL^{-1} = L^{-1}K$. Thus, in this case, the state complexity is bounded by the state complexity of K. To our knowledge the magic number problem for state complexity of the quotient operations was not investigated so far. Next we consider the magic number problem for accepting state complexity of the quotient operations.

Lemma 6. *Let $m,n \geq 1$. Then for every α with $\alpha \geq 0$ there are minimal unary DFAs A and B with m and n accepting states, respectively, such that the minimal DFA for $L(A)L(B)^{-1}$ has α accepting states.*

Proof. We consider two cases:

1. Let $\alpha < n$. Define the languages $K = \{\, a^i \mid 0 \le i \le m - 2 \text{ or } i = m + \alpha \,\}$ and $L = \{\, a^i \mid m + 1 \le i \le m + n \,\}$. The language K (L, respectively) is accepted by a minimal DFA with m (n, respectively) accepting states. Next $KL^{-1} = \{\, a^i \mid 0 \le i \le \alpha - 1 \,\}$, whose minimal DFA has α accepting states. Observe, that this case also covers $\alpha = 0$, where KL^{-1} becomes empty.
2. Now let $\alpha \ge n$. Let K be the same language as above and define the set $L = \{\, a^i \mid m \le i \le m + n - 2 \text{ or } i \ge m + n \,\}$. The language K (L, respectively) is accepted by a minimal DFA with m (n, respectively) accepting states. Next $KL^{-1} = \{\, a^i \mid 0 \le i \le \alpha - n \text{ or } \alpha - n + 2 \le i \le \alpha \,\}$, whose minimal DFA has α accepting states.   □

In the next theorem we use an alternative notation for the quotients, namely $K/L := KL^{-1}$ for the right quotient and $L\backslash K := L^{-1}K$ for the left quotient.

Theorem 7. *We have $g_{/}^{\mathrm{asc},u}(m,n) = g_{/}^{\mathrm{asc}}(m,n)$ and*

$$g_{/}^{\mathrm{asc}}(m,n) = \begin{cases} \{0\} & \text{if } m = 0 \text{ or } n = 0; \\ \{0\} \cup \mathbb{N} & \text{otherwise.} \end{cases}$$

Next, we have $g_{\backslash}^{\mathrm{asc}}(m,n) = g_{/}^{\mathrm{asc}}(m,n)$ and $g_{\backslash}^{\mathrm{asc},u}(m,n) = g_{/}^{\mathrm{asc},u}(m,n)$.   □

3.4   Reversal

As usual, the *reverse of a word* over Σ is defined by $\lambda^R = \lambda$ and $(va)^R = av^R$, for every a in Σ and v in Σ^*. The *reverse of a language* L is defined as $L^R = \{\, w^R \mid w \in L \,\}$. In order to obtain an NNFA accepting the reverse of a language L accepted by a DFA $A = (Q, \Sigma, \delta, s, F)$ one reverses all transitions and swaps the role of initial and accepting states. This results in an NNFA that accepts the language L^R. More formally, this automaton can be described as $A^R = (Q, \Sigma, \delta^R, F, \{s\})$, where $\delta^R(p, a) = \{q \in Q \mid \delta(q, a) = p\}$. Finally, we obtain the DFA $\mathcal{D}(A^R)$ for the language L^R, which provides the upper bound 2^n on the state complexity of the reversal operation on complete DFAs. In [13] it was shown that this bound is tight for languages over an alphabet of at least two letters. This alphabet size is optimal since the reverse of every unary language is the same language, hence n is a tight upper bound for the ordinary state complexity of the reversal operation. Moreover, every value from $\log n$ to 2^n can be obtained as the state complexity of L^R if the state complexity of L is n [14].

Before we consider the accepting state complexity of the reversal operation we take a closer look on the automaton $\mathcal{D}(A^R)$. Observe, that the state s is the single accepting state of the NNFA A^R. Therefore the accepting subsets of the corresponding subset automaton $\mathcal{D}(A^R)$ are those containing the state s. Moreover, if A is a DFA without unreachable states, then the subset automaton $\mathcal{D}(A^R)$ does not have equivalent states [12, Proposition 3]. Now we are ready to consider accepting state complexity of reversal in general.

Lemma 8. *Let $n \ge 1$. Then for every α with $\alpha \ge 1$ there exists a minimal binary DFA A with n accepting states such that the minimal DFA for $L(A^R)$ has α accepting states.*

Proof. Let $A = ([1, \alpha + n], \{a, b\}, \delta, 1, F)$, where $F = [\alpha + 1, \alpha + n]$, and

$$\delta(i, a) = \begin{cases} i & \text{if } i = 1 \text{ or } i = \alpha + 1; \\ i - 1 & \text{otherwise,} \end{cases} \qquad \delta(i, b) = \begin{cases} \alpha + n & \text{if } i = 1; \\ \alpha & \text{if } i = \alpha + 1. \end{cases}$$

The DFA A is shown in Fig. 2. Two rejecting states are distinguished by a word in a^*b and two accepting states by a word in $a^*ba^{\alpha-1}b$. Hence A is minimal.

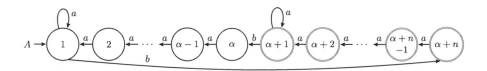

Fig. 2. The witness DFA A for the reversal operation with $n, \alpha \geq 1$.

We construct the NNFA $A^R = ([1, \alpha + n], \{a, b\}, \delta^R, F, \{1\})$ from the DFA A by reversing all the transitions, and by swapping the roles of the initial and accepting states. The subset automaton $\mathcal{D}(A^R)$ has the initial state F and the following transitions:

1. $\rightarrow F \xrightarrow{a} F \xrightarrow{b} \{1\} \xrightarrow{a} [1, 2] \xrightarrow{a} [1, 3] \xrightarrow{a} \cdots \xrightarrow{a} [1, \alpha] \xrightarrow{a} [1, \alpha] \xrightarrow{b} \{\alpha + 1\}$ and
2. $\{\alpha + 1\} \xrightarrow{a} [\alpha + 1, \alpha + 2] \xrightarrow{a} [\alpha + 1, \alpha + 3] \xrightarrow{a} \cdots \xrightarrow{a} [\alpha + 1, \alpha + n - 1] \xrightarrow{a} F$.

Since every other transition from these reachable states goes to the empty set, no more states are reachable. Since only the subsets containing 1 are accepting, there are α reachable accepting subsets. By [12, Proposition 3], the subset automaton $\mathcal{D}(A^R)$ does not have equivalent states, and the theorem follows. □

Taking into account that the only language with accepting state complexity 0 is the empty language $\emptyset$, and for nonempty languages Lemma 8 applies, we obtain the next result. Moreover, since the reverse of a unary language is the same language, we immediately get the result on the accepting state complexity of reversal for unary regular languages, too.

Theorem 9. *We have*

$$g_R^{\mathrm{asc}}(n) = \begin{cases} \{0\} & \text{if } n = 0; \\ \mathbb{N} & \text{otherwise.} \end{cases}$$

For unary regular languages, we have $g_R^{\mathrm{asc},u}(n) = \{n\}$, *if* $n \geq 0$. □

3.5 Permutation on Finite Languages

The *permutation* of a language L is defined as $\mathrm{per}(L) = \bigcup_{w \in L} \mathrm{per}(w)$, where $\mathrm{per}(w) = \{u \in \Sigma^* \mid \psi(u) = \psi(w)\}$ with $\psi(v) = (|v|_{a_1}, |v|_{a_2}, \ldots, |v|_{a_k})$, the

Parikh vector of a word v over the alphabet $\Sigma = \{a_1, a_2, \ldots, a_k\}$. Here $|v|_a$ refers to the number of occurrences of the letter a in v. It is known that the permutation operation is not regular on infinite languages. For example, $\mathrm{per}(\{ab\}^*) = \{w \in \{a, b\}^* \mid |w|_a = |w|_b\}$ is *not* regular. On the other hand, permutation of a finite language is always finite, and every finite language is regular. So permutation is a regular operation on finite languages. Moreover, note that every unary language is a permutation of itself, thus one may consider the ordinary state as well as the accepting state complexity of permutation on *binary* finite languages. Ordinary deterministic state complexity was considered in [1], where an upper bound of $\frac{n^2-n+2}{2}$ states for the permutation of a finite binary language with state complexity n was shown. This was slightly improved for permutations of chain DFAs where a matching upper and lower bound was obtained. To our knowledge the magic number problem for state complexity of permutation on (binary) finite languages was not considered so far. For the accepting state complexity we can prove the following three lemmata:

Lemma 10. *Let $n \geq 1$. Then for every α with $\alpha \geq n$ there exists a minimal binary DFA A with n accepting states such that the minimal DFA for $\mathrm{per}(L(A))$ has α accepting states.*

Proof. Define the finite language $L = \{b^i a b^j \mid 0 \leq i \leq \alpha - n$ and $0 \leq j \leq n-1\}$. Since $L = \bigcup_{0 \leq j \leq n-1}[ab^j]$, where $[ab^j]$ is the Myhill-Nerode equivalence class with $[ab^j] = \{b^i a b^j \mid 0 \leq i \leq \alpha - n\}$, it is accepted by a minimal DFA with n accepting states. Observe, that every word w in L satisfies $|w|_a = 1$ and $0 \leq |w|_b \leq \alpha - 1$. Thus, $\mathrm{per}(L) = \{w \in \{a, b\}^* \mid |w|_a = 1$ and $0 \leq |w|_b \leq \alpha - 1\}$. Hence, $\mathrm{per}(L) = \bigcup_{0 \leq i \leq \alpha - 1}[ab^i]$, where $[ab^i]$ is now the Myhill-Nerode equivalence class $[ab^i] = \{w \in \{a, b\}^* \mid |w|_a = 1$ and $|w|_b = i\}$. Therefore, we deduce that $\mathrm{per}(L)$ has accepting state complexity α. $\square$

The next lemma follows from [4, Lemma 1].

Lemma 11. *Let $n \geq 2$. Let L be a finite language accepted by a minimal DFA with n accepting states. Then the minimal DFA for $\mathrm{per}(L)$ has at least 2 accepting states.* $\square$

The magic status of numbers from 2 to n is considered next.

Lemma 12. *Let $n \geq 2$. Then for every α with $2 \leq \alpha \leq n$ there exists a minimal binary DFA A with n accepting states such that the minimal DFA for $\mathrm{per}(L(A))$ has α accepting states.*

Proof. We prove a slightly stronger statement, namely: let $m \geq 1$. Then for every α with $\alpha \geq 2$ there is a minimal binary DFA A with $2^m + (\alpha - 1)$ accepting states such that the minimal DFA for $\mathrm{per}(L(A))$ has α accepting states. The idea for the construction is as follows: for a word $w \in \{a, b\}^m$ let x_w refer to the length m word $b^{m-|w|_a}a^{m-|w|_b}$. Then define the finite language

$$L = \{wx_w \in \{a, b\}^* \mid |w| = m\}$$
$$\cup \{wx_w w^R y \in \{a, b\}^* \mid |w| = m \text{ and } 0 \leq |y| \leq \alpha - 2\}.$$

By construction every word of the form wx_w, for $w \in \{a,b\}^m$, has the Parikh vector (m,m). Moreover, the Parikh vector of every word of the form $wx_w w^R$, for $w \in \{a,b\}^m$, lies in the set $\{\,(m+i, 2m-i) \mid 0 \le i \le m\,\}$. By considering the Myhill-Nerode equivalence classes for the words in L one deduces that the accepting state complexity of L is $2^m + (\alpha - 1)$.

The automaton B accepting $\mathrm{per}(L)$ is constructed according to [1, Lemma 3.1]. Thus, the DFA B has a grid like structure (with a truncated lower right) where the b-transitions connect neighboring columns and the a-transitions neighboring rows and every state can be identified with a Parikh vector. A schematic drawing is given on the left of Fig. 3. The states in B that correspond to a Parikh vector of a word in L are marked accepting. Since every word wx_w, for $w \in \{a,b\}^m$, has the Parikh vector (m,m), the corresponding state is marked accepting—see the accepting state in the middle of the schematic drawing on the left of Fig. 3. The words of the form $wx_w w^R$, for $w \in \{a,b\}^m$, which Parikh vector lies in the set $\{\,(m+i, 2m-i) \mid 0 \le i \le m\,\}$ induce the topmost anti-diagonal of accepting states. This anti-diagonal is followed by $\alpha - 2$ further anti-diagonals of accepting states, since every word $wx_w w^R$ can be extended by any word of length at most $\alpha - 2$. Again, see the left of Fig. 3. A close inspection reveals that this automaton is not minimal, because all states in a fixed anti-diagonal are equivalent. A schematic drawing of the minimal DFA accepting the permutation of the finite language L is shown on the right of Fig. 3. The tedious details of the construction are left to the reader.

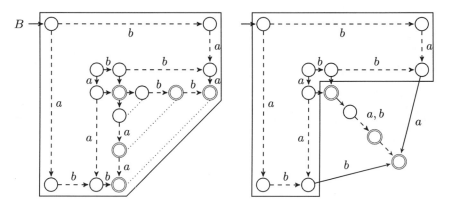

Fig. 3. A schematic drawing of the grid like DFA B (left) accepting $\mathrm{per}(L(A))$ and its minimal DFA (right) obtained from B by identifying accepting states that are connect by dotted lines.

In order to decrease the accepting state complexity of L one removes all words with prefix wx_w, for some words $w \in \{a,b\}^m$. Let L' refer to the resulting language. In order to keep the construction working as described above, one must ensure that all accepting states in the topmost anti-diagonal can be reached. This requirement is fulfilled if the Parikh vectors of all words $wx_w w^R$ with $wx_w \in L'$

form the set $\{\,(m+i, 2m-i) \mid 0 \leq i \leq m\,\}$, which can always be achieved. Thus, at least $m+1$ words of the form wx_w, for $w \in \{a,b\}^*$, must belong to L'. Finally, this allows us to set the accepting state complexity of L' to n by choosing the parameter m appropriately, which proves the original statement. $\square$

Taking into account Lemmata 10, 11, and 12, we get the following result.

Theorem 13. *We have*

$$g_{\mathrm{per}}^{\mathrm{asc}}(n) = g_{\mathrm{per}}^{\mathrm{asc},f}(n) = \begin{cases} \{0\} & \text{if } n = 0; \\ \mathbb{N} & \text{if } n = 1; \\ \mathbb{N} \setminus \{1\} & \text{if } n \geq 2. \end{cases}$$

For unary regular languages, we have $g_{\mathrm{per}}^{\mathrm{asc},u}(n) = \{n\}$ *if* $n \geq 0$. $\square$

References

1. Cho, D.-J., Goč, D., Han, Y.-S., Ko, S.-K., Palioudakis, A., Salomaa, K.: State complexity of permutation on finite languages over a binary alphabet. Theoret. Comput. Sci. **682**, 67–78 (2017)
2. Chrobak, M.: Finite automata and unary languages. Theoret. Comput. Sci. **47**, 149–158 (1986)
3. Dassow, J.: On the number of accepting states of finite automata. J. Autom. Lang. Comb. **21**(1–2), 55–67 (2016)
4. Dassow, J.: Descriptional complexity and operations – two non-classical cases. In: Pighizzini, G., Câmpeanu, C. (eds.) DCFS 2017. LNCS, vol. 10316, pp. 33–44. Springer, Cham (2017). https://doi.org/10.1007/978-3-319-60252-3_3
5. Geffert, V.: Magic numbers in the state hierarchy of finite automata. Inf. Comput. **205**(11), 1652–1670 (2007)
6. Harrison, M.A.: Introduction to Formal Language Theory. Addison-Wesley, Boston (1978)
7. Hricko, M., Jirásková, G., Szabari, A.: Union and intersection of regular languages and descriptional complexity. In: DCFS 2005, pp. 170–181 (2005)
8. Iwama, K., Kambayashi, Y., Takaki, K.: Tight bounds on the number of states of DFAs that are equivalent to n-state NFAs. Theoret. Comput. Sci. **237**(1–2), 485–494 (2000)
9. Iwama, K., Matsuura, A., Paterson, M.: A family of NFAs which need $2^n - \alpha$ deterministic states. Theoret. Comput. Sci. **301**(1–3), 451–462 (2003)
10. Jirásková, G.: Magic numbers and ternary alphabet. Internat. J. Found. Comput. Sci. **22**(2), 331–344 (2011)
11. Jirásková, G.: Personal communication (2017)
12. Jirásková, G., Šebej, J.: Reversal of binary regular languages. Theoret. Comput. Sci. **449**, 85–92 (2012)
13. Leiss, E.: Succinct representation of regular languages by Boolean automata. Theoret. Comput. Sci. **13**, 323–330 (1981)
14. Šebej, J.: Reversal on regular languages and descriptional complexity. In: Jurgensen, H., Reis, R. (eds.) DCFS 2013. LNCS, vol. 8031, pp. 265–276. Springer, Heidelberg (2013). https://doi.org/10.1007/978-3-642-39310-5_25

15. Yu, S.: Regular languages. In: Rozenberg, G., Salomaa, A. (eds.) Handbook of Formal Languages, vol. 1, pp. 41–110. Springer, Heidelberg (1997). https://doi.org/10.1007/978-3-642-59136-5
16. Yu, S., Zhuang, Q.: On the state complexity of intersection of regular languages. SIGACT News **22**(3), 52–54 (1991)
17. Yu, S., Zhuang, Q., Salomaa, K.: The state complexity of some basic operations on regular languages. Theoret. Comput. Sci. **125**, 315–328 (1994)

Semilinearity of Families of Languages

Oscar H. Ibarra[1]([✉]) and Ian McQuillan[2]

[1] Department of Computer Science, University of California,
Santa Barbara, CA 93106, USA
ibarra@cs.ucsb.edu
[2] Department of Computer Science, University of Saskatchewan,
Saskatoon S7N 5A9, Canada
mcquillan@cs.usask.ca

Abstract. Techniques are developed for creating new and general language families of only semilinear languages, and for showing families only contain semilinear languages. It is shown that for language families $\mathcal{L}$ that are semilinear full trios, the smallest full AFL containing the languages obtained by intersecting languages in $\mathcal{L}$ with languages in NCM (where NCM is the family of languages accepted by NFAs augmented with reversal-bounded counters), is also semilinear. If these closure properties are effective, this also immediately implies decidability of membership, emptiness, and infiniteness for these general families. From the general techniques, new grammar systems are given that are extensions of well-known families of semilinear full trios, whereby it is implied that these extensions must only describe semilinear languages. This also implies positive decidability properties for the new systems. Some characterizations of the new families are also given.

1 Introduction

One-way nondeterministic reversal-bounded multicounter machines (NCM) operate like NFAs with λ transitions, where there are some number of stores that each can contain some non-negative integer. The transition function can detect whether each counter is zero or non-zero, and optionally increment or decrement each counter; however, there is a bound on the number of changes each counter can make between non-decreasing and non-increasing. These machines have been extensively studied in the literature, for example in [15], where it was shown that NCMs only accept semilinear languages (defined in Sect. 2). As the semilinear property is effective for NCM (in that, the proof consists of an algorithm for constructing a finite representation of the semilinear sets), this implies that NCMs have decidable membership, emptiness, and infiniteness properties, as emptiness and infiniteness can be decided easily on semilinear sets (and membership follows from emptiness by effective closure under intersection with regular languages).

The research of O. H. Ibarra was supported, in part, by NSF Grant CCF-1117708.
The research of I. McQuillan was supported, in part, by the Natural Sciences and Engineering Research Council of Canada.

© Springer International Publishing AG, part of Springer Nature 2018
C. Câmpeanu (Ed.): CIAA 2018, LNCS 10977, pp. 211–222, 2018.
https://doi.org/10.1007/978-3-319-94812-6_18

NCM machines have been applied extensively in the literature, for example, to model checking and verification [16,17,21,22], often using the positive decidability properties of the family.

More general machine models have been studied with an unrestricted pushdown store augmented by some number of reversal-bounded counters (NPCM, [15]). Despite the unrestricted pushdown, the languages accepted are all semilinear, implying they have the same decidable properties. This family too has been applied to several verification problems [4,18], including model checking recursive programs with numeric data types [10], synchronization- and reversal-bounded analysis of multithreaded programs [8], for showing decidable properties of models of integer-manipulating programs with recursive parallelism [9], and for decidability of problems on commutativity [19]. In these papers, the positive decidability properties—the result of the semilinearity—plus the use of the main store (the pushdown), plus the counters, played a key role. Hence, (effective) semilinearity is a crucial property for families of languages.

The ability to augment a machine model with reversal-bounded counters and to only accept semilinear languages is not unique to pushdown automata; in [11], it was found that many classes of machines $\mathcal{M}$ accepting semilinear languages could be augmented with reversal-bounded counters, and the resulting family $\mathcal{M}_c$ would also only accept semilinear languages. This includes models such as Turing machines with a one-way read-only input tape and a finite-crossing[1] work-tape. However, a precise formulation of which classes of machines this pertains to was not given.

Here, a precise formulation of families of languages that can be "augmented" with counters will be examined in terms of closure properties rather than machine models. This allows for application to families described by machine models, or grammatical models. It is shown that for any full trio (a family closed under homomorphism, inverse homomorphism, and intersection with regular languages) of semilinear languages $\mathcal{L}_0$, then the smallest full AFL $\mathcal{L}$ (a full trio also closed under union, concatenation, and Kleene-*) containing all languages obtained from intersecting a language in $\mathcal{L}_0$ with a language in NCM, must only contain semilinear languages. Furthermore, if the closure properties and semilinearity are effective in $\mathcal{L}_0$, this implies a decidable membership, emptiness, and infiniteness problem in $\mathcal{L}$. Hence, this provides a new method for creating general families of languages with positive decidability properties.

Several specific models are created by adding counters. For example, indexed grammars are a well-studied general grammatical model like context-free grammars except where nonterminals keep stacks of "indices". Although this system can generate non-semilinear languages, linear indexed grammars (indexed grammars with at most one nonterminal in the right hand side of every production) generate only semilinear languages [5]. Here, we define *linear indexed grammars with counters*, akin to linear indexed grammars, where every sentential form contains the usual sentential form, plus k counter values; each production operates as

---

[1] A worktape is finite-crossing if there is a bound on the number of times the boundary of all neighboring cells on the worktape are crossed.

usual and can also optionally increase each counter by some amount; and a terminal word can be generated only if it can be produced with all counter values equal. It is shown that the family of languages generated must be semilinear since it is contained in the smallest full AFL containing the intersection of linear indexed languages and NCM languages. A characterization is also shown: linear indexed grammars with counters generate exactly those languages obtained by intersecting a linear indexed language with an NCM and then applying a homomorphism. Furthermore, it is shown that right linear indexed grammars (where terminals only appear to the left of nonterminals in productions) with counters coincide exactly with the machine model NPCM. Therefore, linear indexed grammars with counters are a natural generalization of NPCM containing only semilinear languages. This model is generalized once again as follows: an indexed grammar is uncontrolled finite-index if, there is a value k such that, for every derivation in the grammar, there are at most k occurrences of nonterminals in every sentential form. It is known that every uncontrolled finite-index indexed grammar generates only semilinear languages [3,25]. It is shown here that uncontrolled finite-index indexed grammars with counters generate only semilinear languages, which is also a natural generalization of both linear indexed grammars with counters and NPCM. This immediately shows decidability of membership, emptiness, and infiniteness for this family.

Lastly, the closure property theoretic method of adding counters is found to often be more helpful than the machine model method of [11] in terms of determining whether the resulting family is semilinear, as here a machine model $\mathcal{M}$ is constructed such that the language family accepted by $\mathcal{M}$ is a semilinear full trio, but adding counters to the model to create $\mathcal{M}_c$ accepts non-semilinear languages. This implies from our earlier results, that $\mathcal{M}_c$ can accept languages that cannot be obtained by intersecting a language accepted by a machine in $\mathcal{M}$ with a NCM and then applying any of the full AFL properties.

This paper therefore contains useful new techniques for creating new language families, and for showing existing language families only contain semilinear languages, which can then be used to immediately obtain decidable emptiness, membership, and infiniteness problems. Such families can perhaps also be applied to various areas, such as to verification, similarly to the use of NPCM.

All proofs are omitted due to space constraints.

2   Preliminaries

In this section, preliminary background and notation is given.

Let $\mathbb{N}_0$ be the set of non-negative integers, and let $\mathbb{N}_0^k$ be the set of all k-tuples of non-negative integers. A set $Q \subseteq \mathbb{N}_0^k$ is *linear* if there exists vectors $\boldsymbol{v_0}, \boldsymbol{v_1}, \ldots, \boldsymbol{v_l} \in \mathbb{N}_0^k$ such that $Q = \{\boldsymbol{v_0} + i_1 \boldsymbol{v_1} + \cdots + i_l \boldsymbol{v_l} \mid i_1, \ldots, i_l \in \mathbb{N}_0\}$. Here, $\boldsymbol{v_0}$ is called the *constant*, and $\boldsymbol{v_1}, \ldots, \boldsymbol{v_l}$ are called the *periods*. A set Q is called semilinear if it is a finite union of linear sets.

Introductory knowledge of formal language and automata theory is assumed such as nondeterministic finite automata (NFAs), pushdown automata (NPDAs),

214 O. H. Ibarra and I. McQuillan

Turing machines, and closure properties. [14]. An *alphabet* Σ is a finite set of symbols, a *word* w over Σ is a finite sequence of symbols from Σ, and Σ^* is the set of all words over Σ which includes the empty word λ. A *language* L over Σ is any $L \subseteq \Sigma^*$. The *complement* of a language $L \subseteq \Sigma^*$, denoted by $\overline{L}$, is $\Sigma^* - L$.

Given a word $w \in \Sigma^*$, the length of w is denoted by $|w|$. For $a \in \Sigma$, the number of a's in w is denoted by $|w|_a$. Given a word w over an alphabet $\Sigma = \{a_1, \ldots, a_k\}$, the Parikh map of w, $\psi(w) = (|w|_{a_1}, \ldots, |w|_{a_k})$, and the Parikh map of a language L is $\{\psi(w) \mid w \in L\}$. The commutative closure of a language L is the language $\mathrm{comm}(L) = \{w \in \Sigma^* \mid \psi(w) = \psi(v), v \in L\}$. Two languages are *letter-equivalent* if $\psi(L_1) = \psi(L_2)$.

A language L is *semilinear* if $\psi(L)$ is a semilinear set. Equivalently, a language is semilinear if and only if it is letter-equivalent to some regular language [12]. A family of languages is semilinear if all languages in it are semilinear, and it is said that it is effectively semilinear if there is an algorithm to construct the constant and periods for each linear set from a representation of each language in the family. For example, it is well-known that all context-free languages are effectively semilinear [23].

Notation from AFL (abstract families of languages) theory is used from [6]. A *full trio* is any family of languages closed under homomorphism, inverse homomorphism, and intersection with regular languages. Furthermore, a *full AFL* is a full trio closed under union, concatenation, and Kleene-*. Given a language family $\mathcal{L}$, the smallest family containing $\mathcal{L}$ that is closed under arbitrary homomorphism is denoted by $\hat{\mathcal{H}}(\mathcal{L})$, the smallest full trio containing $\mathcal{L}$ is denoted by $\hat{\mathcal{M}}(\mathcal{L})$, and the smallest full AFL containing $\mathcal{L}$ is denoted by $\hat{\mathcal{F}}(\mathcal{L})$. Given families $\mathcal{L}_1$ and $\mathcal{L}_2$, let $\mathcal{L}_1 \wedge \mathcal{L}_2 = \{L_1 \cap L_2 \mid L_1 \in \mathcal{L}_1, L_2 \in \mathcal{L}_2\}$.

We will only define NCM and NPCM informally here, and refer to [15] for a formal definition. A one-way nondeterministic counter machine can be defined equivalently to a one-way nondeterministic pushdown automaton [14] with only a bottom-of-pushdown marker plus one other symbol. Hence, the machine can add to the counter (by pushing), subtract from the counter (by popping), and can detect emptiness and non-emptiness of the pushdown. A k-counter machine has k independent counters. A k-counter machine M is l-reversal-bounded, if M makes at most l changes between non-decreasing and non-increasing of each counter in every accepting computation. Let NCM be the class of one-way nondeterministic l-reversal-bounded k-counter machines, for some k, l (DCM for deterministic machines). Let NPCM be the class of machines with one unrestricted pushdown plus some number of reversal-bounded counters. By a slight abuse of notation, we also use these names for the family of languages they accept.

3 Full AFLs Containing Counter Languages

This section will start by showing that for every semilinear full trio $\mathcal{L}$, the smallest full AFL containing $\mathcal{L} \wedge$ NCM is a semilinear full AFL. First, the following intermediate result is required.

Lemma 1. *If $\mathcal{L}$ is a semilinear full trio, then $\hat{\mathcal{M}}(\mathcal{L} \wedge \mathsf{NCM}) = \hat{\mathcal{H}}(\mathcal{L} \wedge \mathsf{NCM})$ is a semilinear full trio.*

The next result is relatively straightforward from results in [6,7], however we have not seen it explicitly stated as we have done. From Corollary 2, Sect. 3.4 of [6], for any full trio $\mathcal{L}$, the smallest full AFL containing $\mathcal{L}$ is the substitution of the regular languages into $\mathcal{L}$. And from [7], the substitution closure of one semilinear family into another is semilinear. Therefore, we obtain:

Lemma 2. *If $\mathcal{L}$ is a semilinear full trio, then the smallest full AFL containing $\mathcal{L}$ is semilinear.*

From these, it is immediate that for semilinear full trios $\mathcal{L}$, the smallest full AFL containing intersections of languages in $\mathcal{L}$ with NCM is semilinear.

Theorem 3. *If $\mathcal{L}$ is a semilinear full trio $\mathcal{L}$, then $\hat{\mathcal{F}}(\mathcal{L} \wedge \mathsf{NCM})$ is semilinear.*

It is worth noting that this procedure can be iterated, as therefore $\hat{\mathcal{F}}(\hat{\mathcal{F}}(\mathcal{L} \wedge \mathsf{NCM}) \wedge \mathsf{NCM})$ must also be a semilinear full AFL, etc. for additional levels, but it is not clear whether this can increase the capacity or not.

Many acceptors and grammar systems are known to be semilinear full trios, such as finite-index ETOL systems [24], indexed grammars with a bound on the number of variables appearing in every sentential form (called uncontrolled finite-index) [3], multi-push-down machines (which have k pushdowns that can simultaneously be written to, but they can only pop from the first non-empty pushdown) [2], a Turing machine variant with one finite-crossing worktape [11], and pushdown machines that can flip their pushdown up to k times [13].

Corollary 4. *Let $\mathcal{L}$ be any of the following families:*

- *languages generated by context-free grammars,*
- *languages generated by finite-index ETOL,*
- *languages generated by uncontrolled finite-index indexed languages,*
- *languages accepted by one-way multi-push-down machine languages,*
- *languages accepted by one-way read-only input nondeterministic Turing machines with a two-way finite-crossing read/write worktape,*
- *languages accepted by one-way k-flip pushdown automata.*

Then the smallest full AFL containing $\mathcal{L} \wedge \mathsf{NCM}$ is a semilinear full AFL.

A simplified analogue to this result is known for certain types of machines [11], although the new result here is defined entirely using closure properties rather than machines. Furthermore, the results in [11] do not allow Kleene-* type closure as part of the full AFL properties. For the machine models $\mathcal{M}$ above, it is an easy exercise to show that augmenting them with reversal-bounded counters to produce $\mathcal{M}_c$, the languages accepted by $\mathcal{M}_c$ are a subset of the smallest full AFL containing intersections of languages in $\mathcal{M}$ with NCM. Hence, these models augmented by counters only accept semilinear languages. Similarly, this type of technique also works for grammar systems, as seen in Sect. 5.

In addition, in [7], it was shown that if $\mathcal{L}$ is a semilinear family, then the smallest AFL containing the commutative closure of $\mathcal{L}$ is a semilinear AFL. It is known that the commutative closure of every semilinear language is in NCM [19], and we know now that if we have a semilinear full trio $\mathcal{L}$, then the smallest full AFL containing $\mathcal{L}$ is also semilinear. So, we obtain an alternate proof that is an immediate corollary since we know that the smallest full AFL containing NCM is a semilinear full AFL.

For any semilinear full trio $\mathcal{L}$ where the semilinearity and the intersection with regular language properties are effective, the membership and emptiness problems in $\mathcal{L}$ are decidable. Indeed, to decide emptiness, it suffices to check if the semilinear set is empty. And to decide if a word w is in L, one constructs the language $L \cap \{w\}$, then emptiness is decided.

Corollary 5. *For any semilinear full trio $\mathcal{L}$ where the semilinearity and intersection with regular language properties are effective, then the membership, emptiness, and infiniteness problems are decidable for languages in $\hat{\mathcal{F}}(\mathcal{L} \wedge \mathsf{NCM})$. In these cases, $\hat{\mathcal{F}}(\mathcal{L} \wedge \mathsf{NCM})$ are a strict subset of the recursive languages.*

As membership is decidable, the family must only contain recursive languages, and the inclusion must be strict as the recursive languages are not closed under homomorphism.

The next property on commutative closure also follows.

Proposition 6. *Let $\mathcal{L}$ be a semilinear full trio, where these properties are effective. Then, the problem, for $L_1, L_2 \in \hat{\mathcal{F}}(\mathcal{L} \wedge \mathsf{NCM})$ is $L_1 \subseteq \mathrm{comm}(L_2)$, is decidable. Furthermore, the problem, is $L_1 \cap \mathrm{comm}(L_2) = \emptyset$ is decidable.*

Next, we provide an interesting decomposition theorem of semilinear languages into linear parts. Consider any semilinear language L, where its Parikh image is a finite union of linear sets $A_1, \ldots, A_k$, and the constant and periods for each linear set can be constructed. Then we can effectively create languages in perhaps another semilinear full trio separately accepting those words in $L_i = \{w \in L \mid \psi(w) \in A_i\}$, for each $1 \leq i \leq k$.

Corollary 7. *Let $\mathcal{L}$ be a semilinear full trio, where semilinearity is effective. Then, given $L \in \mathcal{L}$, we can determine that the Parikh map of L is $A = A_1 \cup \cdots \cup A_k$, $A_1, \ldots, A_k$ are linear sets, and we can effectively construct languages $L_1, \ldots, L_k$ in the semilinear full trio $\hat{\mathcal{M}}(\mathcal{L} \wedge \mathsf{NCM})$ such that $L_i = \{w \in L \mid \psi(w) \in A_i\}$.*

Proof. Since semilinearity is effective, we can construct a representation of linear sets $A_1, \ldots, A_k$. An NCM M_i can be created to accept $\psi^{-1}(A_i)$, for each i, $1 \leq i \leq k$. Then, $L_i = L \cap L(M_i) \in \hat{\mathcal{M}}(\mathcal{L} \wedge \mathsf{NCM})$, for each i, $1 \leq i \leq k$.   □

4   Application to General Multi-store Machine Models

In [6], a generalized type of multitape automata was studied, called multitape abstract families of automata (multitape AFAs). We will not define the notation used there, but in Theorem 4.6.1 (and Exercise 4.6.3), it is shown that if we have two types of automata $\mathcal{M}_1$ and $\mathcal{M}_2$ (defined using the AFA formalism), accepting language families $\mathcal{L}_1$ and $\mathcal{L}_2$ respectively, then the languages accepted by automata combining together the stores of $\mathcal{M}_1$ and $\mathcal{M}_2$, accepts exactly the family $\hat{\mathcal{H}}(\mathcal{L}_1 \wedge \mathcal{L}_2)$. This is shown for machines accepting full AFLs in Theorem 4.6.1 of [6], and for union-closed full trios mentioned in Exercise 4.6.3. We will show that this is tightly coupled with this precise definition of AFAs, as we will define a simple type of multitape automata where this is not the case, but each type still satisfies the same closure properties. This result uses the characterization of Theorem 3.

A checking stack automaton (NCSA) M is a one-way NFA with a store tape, called a stack. At each move, M pushes a string (possibly λ) on the stack, but M cannot pop. And, M can enter and read from the inside of the stack in two-way read-only fashion. But once the machine enters the stack, it can no longer change the contents. The checking stack automaton is said to be *restricted* (or *no-read* using the terminology of [20]), if it does not read from the inside of the stack until the end of the input. We denote by RNCSA the family of machines, as well as the family of languages described by the machines above, with RDCSA being the deterministic version. Let RNCSA_c (RDCSA_c) be the family of machines and languages in RNCSA (RDCSA) augmented with reversal-bounded counters. A preliminary investigation of RNCSA_c and RDCSA_c was done in [20].

Here, we will show the following:

1. RNCSA is a full trio of semilinear languages,
2. $\hat{\mathcal{F}}(\text{RNCSA} \wedge \text{NCM})$ is a semilinear full AFL,
3. every language in RNCSA $\wedge$ NCM is accepted by some machine in RNCSA_c,
4. there are non-semilinear languages accepted by machines in RNCSA_c.

Therefore, RNCSA_c contains some languages not in the smallest full AFL containing RNCSA $\wedge$ NCM, and the multitape automata and results from [6,11] do not apply to this type of automata.

Proposition 8. *RNCSA accepts exactly the regular languages, which is a full trio of semilinear languages.*

From Theorem 3, the following is true:

Corollary 9. $\hat{\mathcal{F}}(RNCSA \wedge NCM)$ *is a semilinear full AFL.*

Since RNCSA accepts the regular languages, and NCM is closed under intersection with regular languages, the following is true:

Proposition 10. $RNCSA \wedge \text{NCM} = \text{NCM} \subseteq RNCSA_c$.

Proposition 11. *The non-semilinear* $L = \{a^i b^j \mid i,j \geq 1, j$ *is divisible by* $i\}$ *can be accepted by an* $RDCSA_c$ M *with one counter that makes only one reversal.*

It is concluded that RNCSA_c contains some languages not in RNCSA$\wedge$NCM $=$ NCM, since NCM is semilinear [15]. Moreover, $\hat{\mathcal{F}}(\text{RNCSA} \wedge \text{NCM})$ is semilinear as well, so it does not contain all languages of RNCSA_c. Then it is clear that combining together the stores of RNCSA and NCM accepts significantly more than $\hat{\mathcal{H}}(\mathsf{RNCSA} \wedge \mathsf{NCM})$ as is the case for multitape AFA [6]. The reason for the discrepancy between this result and Ginsburg's result is that the definition of multitape AFA allows for reading the input while performing instructions (like operating in two-way read-only mode in the stack). In contrast, RNCSA does not allow this behavior. And if this behavior is added into the definition, the full capability of checking stack automata is achieved which accepts non-semilinear languages, and not regular languages.

A similar analysis can be done using the method developed in [11] for augmenting the machine models with counters. Let $\mathcal{M}$ be a family of one-way acceptors with some type of store structure X. For example, if the storage X is a pushdown stack, then $\mathcal{M}$ is the family of nondeterministic pushdown automata (NPDAs). Let the machines in $\mathcal{M}$ be augmented with reversal-bounded counters, and call the resulting family $\mathcal{M}_c$. In [11], the following was shown for many families $\mathcal{M}$:

(*) If $\mathcal{M}$ is a semilinear family (i.e., the languages accepted by the machines in $\mathcal{M}$ have semilinear Parikh map), then $\mathcal{M}_c$ is also a semilinear family.

It was not clear in [11] whether the result above is true for all types of one-way acceptors, in general. However, the family RNCSA is semilinear (Proposition 8), but RDCSA_c is not semilinear (Proposition 11).

5   Applications to Indexed Grammars with Counters

In this section, we describe some new types of grammars obtained from existing grammars generating a semilinear language family $\mathcal{L}$, by adding counters. The languages generated by these new grammars are then shown to be contained in $\mathcal{F}(\mathcal{L} \wedge \mathsf{NCM})$, and by an application of Theorem 3, are all semilinear with positive decidability properties.

We need the definition of an indexed grammar introduced in [1] by following the notation of [14], Sect. 14.3.

Definition 12. *An indexed grammar is a 5-tuple* $G = (V, \Sigma, I, P, S)$, *where* V, Σ, I *are finite pairwise disjoint sets: the set of nonterminals, terminals, and indices, respectively,* S *is the start nonterminal, and* P *is a finite set of productions, each of the form either*

$$(1) \; A \to \nu, \quad (2) \; A \to Bf, \quad or \quad (3) \; Af \to \nu,$$

where $A, B \in V$, $f \in I$ *and* $\nu \in (V \cup \Sigma)^*$.

Let ν be an arbitrary sentential form of G, which is of the form

$$\nu = u_1 A_1 \alpha_1 u_2 A_2 \alpha_2 \cdots u_k A_k \alpha_k u_{k+1},$$

where $A_i \in V, \alpha_i \in I^*, u_i \in \Sigma^*, 1 \leq i \leq k, u_{k+1} \in \Sigma^*$. For a sentential form $\nu' \in (VI^* \cup \Sigma)^*$, we write $\nu \Rightarrow_G \nu'$ if one of the following three conditions holds:

1. There exists a production in P of the form (1) $A \rightarrow w_1 C_1 \cdots w_\ell C_\ell w_{\ell+1}$, $C_j \in V, w_j \in \Sigma^*$, and there exists i with $1 \le i \le k$, $A_i = A$ and

$$\nu' = u_1 A_1 \alpha_1 \cdots u_i(w_1 C_1 \alpha_i \cdots w_\ell C_\ell \alpha_i w_{\ell+1}) u_{i+1} A_{i+1} \alpha_{i+1} \cdots u_k A_k \alpha_k u_{k+1}.$$

2. There exists a production in P of the form (2) $A \rightarrow Bf$ and there exists i, $1 \le i \le k$, $A_i = A$ and $\nu' = u_1 A_1 \alpha_1 \cdots u_i(Bf\alpha_i)u_{i+1}A_{i+1}\alpha_{i+1} \cdots u_k A_k \alpha_k u_{k+1}$.

3. There exists a production in P of the form (3) $Af \rightarrow w_1 C_1 \cdots w_\ell C_\ell w_{\ell+1}$, $C_j \in V, w_j \in \Sigma^*$, and an i, $1 \le i \le k$, $A_i = A$, $\alpha_i = f\alpha_i'$, $\alpha_i' \in I^*$, with $\nu' = u_1 A_1 \alpha_1 \cdots u_i(w_1 C_1 \alpha_i' \cdots w_\ell C_\ell \alpha_i' w_{\ell+1}) u_{i+1} A_{i+1} \alpha_{i+1} \cdots u_k A_k \alpha_k u_{k+1}$.

Then, $\Rightarrow_G^*$ denotes the reflexive and transitive closure of $\Rightarrow_G$. The language $L(G)$ generated by G is the set $L(G) = \{u \in \Sigma^* \mid S \Rightarrow_G^* u\}$.

This type of grammar can be generalized to include counters as follows:

Definition 13. *An* indexed grammar with k counters *is defined as in indexed grammars, except where rules (1), (2), (3) above are modified so that a rule $\alpha \rightarrow \beta$ now becomes:*

$$\alpha \rightarrow (\beta, c_1, \ldots, c_k), \tag{1}$$

where $c_i \ge 0$, $1 \le i \le k$. Sentential forms are of the form $(\nu, n_1, \ldots, n_k)$, and $\Rightarrow_G$ operates as do indexed grammars on ν, and for a production in Eq. 1, adds c_i to n_i, for $1 \le i \le k$. The language generated by G with terminal alphabet Σ and start nonterminal S is, $L(G) = \{w \mid w \in \Sigma^*, (S, 0, \ldots, 0) \Rightarrow_C^* (w, n_1, \ldots, n_k), n_1 = \cdots = n_k\}$.

Given an indexed grammar with counters, the underlying grammar *is the indexed grammar obtained by removing the counter components from productions.*

Although indexed grammars generate non-semilinear languages, restrictions will be studied that only generate semilinear languages.

An indexed grammar G is *linear* [5] if the right side of every production of G has at most one variable. Furthermore, G is *right linear* if it is linear, and terminals can only appear to the left of a nonterminal in productions. Let L-IND be the family of languages generated by linear indexed grammars, and let RL-IND be the family of languages generated by right linear indexed grammars.

Similarly, indexed grammars with counters can be restricted to be linear. An indexed grammar with k-counters is said to be *linear indexed* (resp. *right linear*) with k counters, if the underlying grammar is linear (resp. right linear). Let L-IND$_c$ (resp. RL-IND$_c$) be the family of languages generated by linear (resp. right linear) indexed grammars with counters.

Example 14. Consider the language $L = \{v\$w \mid v, w \in \{a, b, c\}^*, |v|_a = |v|_b = |v|_c, |w|_a = |w|_b = |w|_c\}$ which can be generated by a linear indexed grammar with counters $G = (V, \Sigma, I, P, S)$ where P contains

$S \rightarrow (S, 1, 1, 1, 0, 0, 0) \mid (S, 0, 0, 0, 1, 1, 1) \mid (T, 0, 0, 0, 0, 0, 0)$

$T \rightarrow (aT, 1, 0, 0, 0, 0, 0) \mid (bT, 0, 1, 0, 0, 0, 0) \mid (cT, 0, 0, 1, 0, 0, 0) \mid (\$R, 0, 0, 0, 0, 0, 0)$

$R \rightarrow (aR, 0, 0, 0, 1, 0, 0) \mid (bR, 0, 0, 0, 0, 1, 0) \mid (cR, 0, 0, 0, 0, 0, 1) \mid (\lambda, 0, 0, 0, 0, 0, 0)$.

This language cannot be generated by a linear indexed grammar [3].

The following is a characterization of languages generated by these grammars.

Proposition 15. *$L \in$ L-IND$_c$ if and only if there is a homomorphism h, $L_1 \in$ L-IND, and $L_2 \in$ NCM such that $L = h(L_1 \cap L_2)$.*

Implied from the above result and Theorem 3 and since L-IND is an effectively semilinear trio [5] is that L-IND$_c$ $\subseteq \hat{\mathcal{F}}($L-IND $\wedge$ NCM$)$, and therefore L-IND$_c$ is effectively semilinear.

Corollary 16. *The languages generated by linear indexed grammar with counters are effectively semilinear, with decidable emptiness, membership, and infiniteness problems.*

Next, a machine model characterization of right linear indexed grammars with counters will be provided. Recall that an NPCM is a pushdown automaton augmented by reversal-bounded counters. The proof uses the fact that every context-free language can be generated by a right-linear indexed grammar [5].

Theorem 17. *RL-IND$_c$ = NPCM.*

We conjecture that the family of languages generated by right-linear indexed grammars with counters (the family of NPCM languages) is properly contained in the family of languages generated by linear indexed grammars with counters. Candidate witness languages are $L = \{w\$w \mid w \in \{a,b,c\}^*, |w|_a + |w|_b = |w|_c\}$ and $L' = \{w\$w \mid w \in \{a,b\}^*\}$. It is known that L' is generated by a linear indexed grammar [5], and hence L can be generated by such a grammar with two counters. But, both L' and L seem unlikely to be accepted by any NPCM. Therefore, indexed grammars with counters form quite a general semilinear family as it seems likely to be more general than NPCM.

Next, another subfamily of indexed languages is studied that are even more expressive than linear indexed grammars but only generate semilinear languages.

An indexed grammar $G = (V, \Sigma, I, P, S)$ is said to be *uncontrolled* index-r if, every sentential form in every successful derivation has at most r nonterminals. G is uncontrolled finite-index if G is uncontrolled index-r, for some r. Let U-IND be the languages generated by uncontrolled finite-index indexed grammars.

Uncontrolled finite-index indexed grammars have also been studied under the name of breadth-bounded indexed grammars in [3,25], where it was shown that the languages generated by these grammars are a semilinear full trio.

This concept can then be carried over to indexed grammars with counters.

Definition 18. *An indexed grammar with k-counters is uncontrolled index-r (resp. uncontrolled finite-index) if the underlying grammar is uncontrolled index-r (resp. uncontrolled finite-index). Let U-IND$_c$ be the languages generated by uncontrolled finite-index indexed grammar with k-counters, for some k.*

One can easily verify that Proposition 15 also applies to uncontrolled finite-index indexed grammars with counters. Hence, we have:

Proposition 19. $L \in$ *U-IND$_c$ if and only if there is a homomorphism h, $L_1 \in$ U-IND, $L_2 \in$* NCM *such that $L = h(L_1 \cap L_2)$.*

Implied from the above Proposition and Theorem 3 also is that these new languages are all semilinear.

Corollary 20. *U-IND$_c$ is effectively semilinear, with decidable emptiness, membership, and infiniteness problems.*

Hence, RL-IND$_c \subseteq$ L-IND$_c \subseteq$ U-IND$_c$. We conjecture that both containments are strict; the first was discussed previously, and the second is likely true since L-IND $\subsetneq$ U-IND [3]. Hence, U-IND$_c$ forms quite a general semilinear family, containing NPCM with positive decidability properties.

References

1. Aho, A.V.: Indexed grammars–an extension of context-free grammars. J. ACM **15**(4), 647–671 (1968)
2. Breveglieri, L., Cherubini, A., Citrini, C., Reghizzi, S.: Multi-push-down languages and grammars. Int. J. Found. Comput. Sci. **7**(3), 253–291 (1996)
3. D'Alessandro, F., Ibarra, O.H., McQuillan, I.: On finite-index indexed grammars and their restrictions. In: Drewes, F., Martín-Vide, C., Truthe, B. (eds.) LATA 2017. LNCS, vol. 10168, pp. 287–298. Springer, Cham (2017). https://doi.org/10.1007/978-3-319-53733-7_21
4. Dang, Z., Ibarra, O.H., Bultan, T., Kemmerer, R.A., Su, J.: Binary reachability analysis of discrete pushdown timed automata. In: Emerson, E.A., Sistla, A.P. (eds.) CAV 2000. LNCS, vol. 1855, pp. 69–84. Springer, Heidelberg (2000). https://doi.org/10.1007/10722167_9
5. Duske, J., Parchmann, R.: Linear indexed languages. Theoret. Comput. Sci. **32**(1–2), 47–60 (1984)
6. Ginsburg, S.: Algebraic and Automata-Theoretic Properties of Formal Languages. North-Holland Publishing Company, Amsterdam (1975)
7. Ginsburg, S., Spanier, E.H.: AFL with the semilinear property. J. Comput. Syst. Sci. **5**(4), 365–396 (1971)
8. Hague, M., Lin, A.W.: Synchronisation- and reversal-bounded analysis of multi-threaded programs with counters. In: Madhusudan, P., Seshia, S.A. (eds.) CAV 2012. LNCS, vol. 7358, pp. 260–276. Springer, Heidelberg (2012). https://doi.org/10.1007/978-3-642-31424-7_22
9. Hague, M., Lin, A.W.: Decidable models of integer-manipulating programs with recursive parallelism. In: Larsen, K.G., Potapov, I., Srba, J. (eds.) RP 2016. LNCS, vol. 9899, pp. 148–162. Springer, Cham (2016). https://doi.org/10.1007/978-3-319-45994-3_11
10. Hague, M., Lin, A.W.: Model checking recursive programs with numeric data types. In: Gopalakrishnan, G., Qadeer, S. (eds.) CAV 2011. LNCS, vol. 6806, pp. 743–759. Springer, Heidelberg (2011). https://doi.org/10.1007/978-3-642-22110-1_60
11. Harju, T., Ibarra, O.H., Karhumäki, J., Salomaa, A.: Some decision problems concerning semilinearity and commutation. J. Comput. Syst. Sci. **65**(2), 278–294 (2002)
12. Harrison, M.: Introduction to Formal Language Theory. Addison-Wesley Series in Computer Science. Addison-Wesley Pub. Co., Boston (1978)

13. Holzer, M., Kutrib, M.: Flip-pushdown automata: nondeterminism is better than determinism. In: Ésik, Z., Fülöp, Z. (eds.) DLT 2003. LNCS, vol. 2710, pp. 361–372. Springer, Heidelberg (2003). https://doi.org/10.1007/3-540-45007-6_29
14. Hopcroft, J.E., Ullman, J.D.: Introduction to Automata Theory, Languages, and Computation. Addison-Wesley, Reading (1979)
15. Ibarra, O.H.: Reversal-bounded multicounter machines and their decision problems. J. ACM **25**(1), 116–133 (1978)
16. Ibarra, O.H., Bultan, T., Su, J.: Reachability analysis for some models of infinite-state transition systems. In: Palamidessi, C. (ed.) CONCUR 2000. LNCS, vol. 1877, pp. 183–198. Springer, Heidelberg (2000). https://doi.org/10.1007/3-540-44618-4_15
17. Ibarra, O.H., Bultan, T., Su, J.: On reachability and safety in infinite-state systems. Int. J. Found. Comput. Sci. **12**(6), 821–836 (2001)
18. Ibarra, O.H., Dang, Z.: Eliminating the storage tape in reachability constructions. Theoret. Comput. Sci. **299**(1–3), 687–706 (2003)
19. Ibarra, O.H., McQuillan, I.: The effect of end-markers on counter machines and commutativity. Theoret. Comput. Sci. **627**, 71–81 (2016)
20. Ibarra, O.H., McQuillan, I.: Variations of checking stack automata: obtaining unexpected decidability properties. In: Charlier, É., Leroy, J., Rigo, M. (eds.) DLT 2017. LNCS, vol. 10396, pp. 235–246. Springer, Cham (2017). https://doi.org/10.1007/978-3-319-62809-7_17
21. Ibarra, O.H., Su, J., Dang, Z., Bultan, T., Kemmerer, R.: Counter machines and verification problems. Theoret. Comput. Sci. **289**(1), 165–189 (2002)
22. Ibarra, O.H., Su, J., Dang, Z., Bultan, T., Kemmerer, R.: Counter machines: decidable properties and applications to verification problems. In: Nielsen, M., Rovan, B. (eds.) MFCS 2000. LNCS, vol. 1893, pp. 426–435. Springer, Heidelberg (2000). https://doi.org/10.1007/3-540-44612-5_38
23. Parikh, R.: On context-free languages. J. ACM **13**(4), 570–581 (1966)
24. Rozenberg, G., Vermeir, D.: On ET0L systems of finite index. Inf. Control **38**, 103–133 (1978)
25. Zetzsche, G.: An approach to computing downward closures. In: Halldórsson, M.M., Iwama, K., Kobayashi, N., Speckmann, B. (eds.) ICALP 2015. LNCS, vol. 9135, pp. 440–451. Springer, Heidelberg (2015). https://doi.org/10.1007/978-3-662-47666-6_35

The Exact Complexity
of Star-Complement-Star

Jozef Jirásek[1] and Galina Jirásková[2(✉)]

[1] Institute of Computer Science, Faculty of Science,
P. J. Šafárik University, Jesenná 5, 040 01 Košice, Slovakia
jozef.jirasek@upjs.sk
[2] Mathematical Institute, Slovak Academy of Sciences,
Grešákova 6, 040 01 Košice, Slovakia
jiraskov@saske.sk

Abstract. We show that the state complexity of the star-complement-star operation is given by $\frac{3}{2}f(n-1) + 2f(n-2) + 2n - 5$, where $f(2) = 2$ and $f(n) = \sum_{i=1}^{n-2} \binom{n}{i} f(n-i) + 2$. The function $f(n)$ counts the number of distinct resistances possible for n arbitrary resistors each connected in series or parallel with previous ones, or the number of labeled threshold graphs on n vertices, and $f(n) \sim n!(1 - \ln 2)/(\ln 2)^{n+1} = 2^{n \log n - 0.91n + o(n)}$. Our witness language is defined over a quaternary alphabet, and we strongly conjecture that the size of the alphabet cannot be decreased.

1 Introduction

The Kuratowski 14-theorem states that applying the operations of closure and complementation to a set in a topological space in any order and any number of times results in at most 14 distinct sets. The Kuratowski algebras in the settings of formal languages have been investigated by Brzozowski et al. [3]. They showed that at most 14 distinct languages may be produced by applying the star and complementation operations to a given language. Moreover, every such language can be expressed, up to inclusion of the empty string, as one of the following 5 languages and their complements: L, L^+, L^{c+}, L^{+c+}, and L^{+c+c}; here L^c denotes the complement and L^+ denotes the positive closure of L, and we use an exponent notation as follows: $L^{+c} = (L^+)^c$, $L^{+c+} = ((L^+)^c)^+$, etc.

While a language and its complement have the same complexity, and the complexity of L^+ is known to be $\frac{3}{4}2^n - 1$ since 70's [6], the only language in this chain which could possibly have a double-exponential state complexity was L^{+c+}. Surprisingly, as shown in [4], its state complexity is in $2^{\Theta(n \log n)}$, and lower bound

J. Jirásek—Research supported by VEGA grant 1/0056/18 and grant APVV-15-0091.
G. Jirásková—Research supported by VEGA grant 2/0084/15 and grant APVV-15-0091.

© Springer International Publishing AG, part of Springer Nature 2018
C. Câmpeanu (Ed.): CIAA 2018, LNCS 10977, pp. 223–235, 2018.
https://doi.org/10.1007/978-3-319-94812-6_19

example has been defined over a seven-letter alphabet. Nevertheless, since Θ is in the exponent, the gap between lower and upper bound remained large.

In this paper, we continue this research by a careful inspection of reachable and unreachable states in the resulting automaton, and we get the exact state complexity of the star-complement-star operation.

This complexity is given by $\frac{3}{2}f(n-1) + 2f(n-2) + 2n - 5$, where the function $f(n)$ counts, for example, the number of distinct resistances possible for n arbitrary resistors each connected in series or parallel with previous ones [1,12], or the number of labeled threshold graphs on n vertices [2], and $f(n) \sim n!(1 - \ln 2)/(\ln 2)^{n+1}$. Our witness language is defined over a quaternary alphabet, and we strongly conjecture that the size of alphabet is optimal.

2   Preliminaries

Let Σ be a finite non-empty alphabet of symbols. Then Σ^* denotes the set of strings over Σ including the empty string ε. A language is any subset of Σ^*. For a language L over Σ, the complement of L is the language $L^c = \Sigma^* \setminus L$. The (Kleene) star of a language L is the language $L^* = \bigcup_{i \geq 0} L^i$ where $L^0 = \{\varepsilon\}$ and $L^i = LL^{i-1}$. The positive closure of L is the language $L^+ = \bigcup_{i \geq 1} L^i$.

A *nondeterministic finite automaton* (NFA) is a quintuple $A = (Q, \Sigma, \cdot, I, F)$, where Q is a finite non-empty set of states, Σ is a finite non-empty input alphabet, the function $\cdot$ is the transition function that maps $Q \times \Sigma$ to 2^Q, $I \subseteq Q$ is the set of initial states, and $F \subseteq Q$ is the set of final (or accepting) states [9]. We say that (p, a, q) is a transition in the NFA A if $q \in p \cdot a$. The transition function is extended to the domain $2^Q \times \Sigma^*$ in the natural way. The language accepted by the NFA A is the set of strings $L(A) = \{w \in \Sigma^* \mid I \cdot w \cap F \neq \emptyset\}$.

An NFA A is a (complete) *deterministic finite automaton* (DFA) if $|I| = 1$ and for each state p and each input symbol a, the set $p \cdot a$ has exactly one element. In such a case, we write $p \cdot a = q$ instead of $p \cdot a = \{q\}$. We also use $p \xrightarrow{a} q$ to denote that $p \cdot a = q$. A DFA $A = (Q, \Sigma, \cdot, s, F)$ is minimal if all its states are reachable from the initial state, and every two distinct states are distinguishable.

The state complexity of a regular language L, $\mathrm{sc}(L)$, is the number of states of the minimal DFA recognizing the language L. The state complexity of the star-complement-star operation is the function from $\mathbb{N}$ to $\mathbb{N}$ defined as $n \mapsto \max\{\mathrm{sc}(L^{*c*}) \mid \mathrm{sc}(L) \leq n\}$.

The transitions on symbol a in a DFA A perform a transformation $a \colon Q \to Q$ defined by $qa = q \cdot a$. For a subset S of Q, we denote $Sa = \{qa \mid q \in S\}$ and $aS = \{q \in Q \mid qa \in S\}$. We say that a acts as a permutation on $S \subseteq Q$ if $Sa = S$; in such a case, for each $q \in S$ the set $aq = \{p \in Q \mid pa = q\}$ is nonempty.

A *cyclic permutation* of a set $\{q_1, q_2, \ldots, q_k\} \subseteq Q$ is a permutation a such that $q_i a = q_{i+1}$ if $1 \leq i \leq k-1$, $q_k a = q_1$, and $qa = q$ if $q \in Q \setminus \{q_1, q_2, \ldots, q_k\}$. We denote such a permutation as $a \colon (q_1, q_2, \ldots, q_k)$. For two states p and q, we use $(p \to q)$ to denote the transformation that maps p to q and fixes every state different from p. Each input string u also performs a transformation on Q given by the composition of its input symbols, that is, if $w = av$ with $a \in \Sigma$

and $v \in \Sigma^*$, then $w\colon Q \to Q$ is given by $qw = qav = (q \cdot a) \cdot v$. For $S \subseteq Q$ and $w \in \Sigma^*$, we denote $Sw = \{qw \mid q \in S\}$ and $wS = \{q \in Q \mid qw \in S\}$.

Every NFA $A = (Q, \Sigma, \cdot, I, F)$ can be converted to an equivalent deterministic automaton $\mathcal{D}(A) = (2^Q, \Sigma, \cdot, I, \{S \in 2^Q \mid S \cap F \neq \emptyset\})$ [8]. The DFA $\mathcal{D}(A)$ is called the *subset automaton* of the NFA A.

In what follows we use $[i, j]$ to denote the set of integers $\{\ell \mid i \leq \ell \leq j\}$ and we set $Q_n = [0, n-1]$.

3   Constructions of Automata for Plus-Complement-Plus

Let a language L be accepted by a DFA $A = (Q_n, \Sigma, \cdot, 0, F)$. Let $F^c = Q_n \setminus F$. Let us construct the following automata.

- NFA A^+ for L^+ is constructed from the DFA A by adding the transition $(q, a, 0)$ whenever $q \cdot a \in F$. The set of final states of A^+ is F.
- DFA B for L^+ is the subset automaton $\mathcal{D}(A^+)$ restricted to reachable states. Thus, states of B are subsets of Q_n, its initial state is $\{0\}$, and its state S is final if $S \cap F \neq \emptyset$. Moreover, if a state of B contains a final state of A, then it also contains the state 0 since A^+ always has the transition $(q, a, 0)$ if $q \cdot a \in F$.
- DFA C for L^{+c} is constructed from the DFA B by interchanging the final and non-final states. Thus, states of C are subsets of Q_n, its initial state is $\{0\}$, and its state S is final if $S \subseteq F^c$, and it is non-final if $S \not\subseteq F^c$ in which case it also must contain the initial state 0 of A.
- NFA C^+ for L^{+c+} is constructed from the DFA C by adding the transition $(S, a, \{0\})$ whenever $S \cdot a$ is final, that is, whenever $S \cdot a \subseteq F^c$.

Then, the subset automaton $\mathcal{D}(C^+)$ is a DFA for $(L(A))^{+c+}$, and we are interested in the number of its reachable and distinguishable states. A DFA for L^{*c*} may require one more state to accept the empty string.
It follows from the constructions above that in the subset automaton $\mathcal{D}(C^+)$:

- each state $\mathcal{T} = \{T_1, T_2, \ldots, T_k\}$ with $T_i \subseteq Q_n$ is a set of subsets of Q_n;
- if some $T_i \subseteq F^c$, then $\{0\} \in \mathcal{T}$;
- otherwise, for each i, we have $T_i \not\subseteq F^c$ and $0 \in T_i$;
- the transitions are given by

$$\mathcal{T} \xrightarrow{a} \bigcup_{\substack{T \in \mathcal{T} \\ T \cdot a \subseteq F^c}} \{T \cdot a, \{0\}\} \cup \bigcup_{\substack{T \in \mathcal{T} \\ T \cdot a \not\subseteq F^c}} \{T \cdot a \cup \{0\}\}.$$

It is known that each state of $\mathcal{D}(C^+)$ is equivalent to an antichain of subsets of Q_n [4, Lemma 1]; recall that a set of subsets of Q_n is an antichain if every two distinct elements in it are incomparable with respect to the set inclusion. This means that each final state of $\mathcal{D}(C^+)$ is equivalent to an antichain $\mathcal{T} = \{\{0\}, T_2, \ldots, T_k\}$ with $k \geq 2$ and all $T_i \subseteq F^c$ $(2 \leq i \leq k)$, while each its non-final state is equivalent to an antichain $\mathcal{T} = \{T_1, T_2, \ldots, T_k\}$ with $k \geq 1$, $T_i \not\subseteq F^c$

and $0 \in T_i$ $(1 \le i \le k)$. Thus, the upper bound on the number of reachable and pairwise distinguishable states of $\mathcal{D}(C^+)$ is given by the number of antichains of subsets of an n-element set, known as the Dedekind number; see, for example, [5]. This number still grows double-exponentially. The next two propositions show that all these antichains can be distinguished using a growing alphabet.

Proposition 1. *Every two distinct antichains differ in a set S such that S is in one of them, and no subset of S is in the other one.*

Proof. Let $\mathcal{S}$ and $\mathcal{T}$ be two distinct antichains. Then without loss of generality, there is a set S with $S \in \mathcal{S} \setminus \mathcal{T}$. If no subset of S is in $\mathcal{T}$, then S is the desired set. Otherwise, $\mathcal{T}$ contains some subset T of S. Since $\mathcal{S}$ is an antichain, it cannot contain T and it cannot contain any of its subsets. Then T is the desired set. □

Proposition 2. *There exists an n-state DFA A defined over an alphabet of size 2^n such that all the antichains are pairwise distinguishable in the subset automaton $\mathcal{D}(C^+)$.*

Proof. Define an n-state DFA $A = (Q_n, \{b_S \mid S \subseteq Q_n\}, \cdot, 0, \{0,1\})$ where for each $q \in Q_n$ and $S \subseteq Q_n$, we have $q \cdot b_S = 2$ if $q \in S$, and $q \cdot b_S = 0$ otherwise. Let $\mathcal{S}$ and $\mathcal{T}$ be two distinct antichains. By Proposition 1, we may assume that there is a set S in $\mathcal{S} \setminus \mathcal{T}$ such that no subset of S is in $\mathcal{T}$. Then by b_S, the antichain $\mathcal{S}$ is sent to a final antichain containing $\{2\}$, while $\mathcal{T}$ is sent to a non-final antichain since each of its components is sent to a set containing the state 0. □

Hence, all the antichains can be distinguished, and the question about how many of them are reachable was partially answered in [4]. It has been shown that each reachable state of $\mathcal{D}(C^+)$ is equivalent to some antichain $\mathcal{T} = \{T_1, T_2, \ldots, T_k\}$ which satisfies (1) $1 \le k \le n$; (2) $T_i = \{q_i\} \cup S_i$ where $S_1 \subseteq S_2 \subseteq \cdots \subseteq S_k$ and $q_1, q_2, \ldots, q_k$ are pairwise distinct states in $Q_n \setminus S_k$ [4, Lemma 2].

This reduced the number of reachable antichains from a double-exponential to at most $\sum_{k=1}^{n} \binom{n}{k} k! (k+1)^{n-k} \in 2^{O(n \log n)}$. Moreover, a language over a seven-letter alphabet was described in [4, Proof of Corollary 2] such that every DFA for its star-complement-star has at least $\lceil \frac{n}{2} \rceil^{n-\lceil \frac{n}{2} \rceil} \in 2^{\Omega(n \log n)}$ states. Thus the state complexity of the star-complement-star operation is in $2^{\Theta(n \log n)}$. However, since Θ is in an exponent, the gap between the lower and upper bound is large.

In what follows we aim to get the exact state complexity of this combined operation. We call an antichain valid if it satisfies the above mentioned two conditions, and we count the number of valid antichains in the next section.

4   The Number of Valid Antichains

The aim of this section is to count all the valid antichains. After giving their explicit definition, we first get the number of the valid antichains such that each element occurs in their union. Then we use this number to count all valid antichains. Recall that we denote by $[i, j]$ the set of integers $\{\ell \mid i \le \ell \le j\}$.

Definition 3. *An antichain* $\mathcal{T} = \{T_1, T_2, \ldots, T_k\}$ *of subsets of* $[1, n]$ *is* valid *if*

(1) $1 \leq k \leq n$;
(2) for each i, we have $T_i = \{q_i\} \cup S_i$ where
  - $S_1 \subseteq S_2 \subseteq \cdots \subseteq S_k$,
  - $q_1, q_2, \ldots, q_k$ *are pairwise distinct states in* $[1, n] \setminus S_k$.

For an antichain $\mathcal{T} = \{T_1, T_2, \ldots, T_k\}$, let $\cup \mathcal{T} = \bigcup_{i=1}^{k} T_i$ and $\cap \mathcal{T} = \bigcap_{i=1}^{k} T_i$.

Lemma 4. *Let $n \geq 2$ and $f(n)$ denote the number of valid antichains $\mathcal{T}$ of subsets of $[1, n]$ such that $\cup \mathcal{T} = [1, n]$. Then*

$$f(2) = 2 \text{ and } f(n) = \sum_{i=1}^{n-2} \binom{n}{i} f(n - i) + 2 \text{ if } n \geq 3. \qquad (1)$$

Proof. Denote by $f_1(n)$ the number of valid antichains such that $\cup \mathcal{T} = [1, n]$ and $\{i\} \in \mathcal{T}$ for some i. Next, denote by $f_2(n)$ the number of valid antichains with $\cup \mathcal{T} = [1, n]$ and $i \in \cap \mathcal{T}$ for some i; notice that if $\mathcal{T}$ does not contain any singleton set, than $\cap \mathcal{T} \neq \emptyset$. A valid antichain with $\cup \mathcal{T} = [1, n]$ and containing a singleton set may contain either exactly one singleton set, or exactly two singleton sets, etc. Therefore,

$$f_1(n) = \sum_{i=1}^{n-2} \binom{n}{i} f_2(n - i) + 1; \qquad (2)$$

notice that we cannot have exactly $n - 1$ one-element sets in an antichain. Similarly, if a valid antichain with $\cup \mathcal{T} = [1, n]$ does not contain any singleton set, then $\cap \mathcal{T}$ may have exactly one element, or exactly two elements, etc. Therefore,

$$f_2(n) = \sum_{i=1}^{n-2} \binom{n}{i} f_1(n - i) + 1; \qquad (3)$$

First, let us prove that $f_1(n) = f_2(n)$. The proof is by induction on n. The basis, $n = 2$, holds true since $f_1(2) = 1$ because of the unique antichain $\{\{1\}, \{2\}\}$, and $f_2(2) = 1$ because of $\{\{1, 2\}\}$. Assume that $n \geq 3$ and that $f_1(i) = f_2(i)$ if $2 \leq i \leq n - 1$. Then $f_1(n) = f_2(n)$ follows from (2) and (3).

Next, consider all valid antichains $\mathcal{T}$ of subsets of $[1, n]$ with $\cup \mathcal{T} = [1, n]$, and denote the number of such antichains by $f(n)$. Notice that every such valid antichain either contains a singleton set or the intersection $\cap \mathcal{T}$ is non-empty. Therefore, $f(n) = f_1(n) + f_2(n)$, and we get

$$f(n) = \sum_{i=1}^{n-2} \binom{n}{i} (f_1(n - i) + f_2(n - i)) + 2 = \sum_{i=1}^{n-2} \binom{n}{i} f(n - i) + 2,$$

which concludes the proof. $\qquad \square$

Remark 5. The function $f(n)$ defines Sloane's sequence A005840 [10,11], and it counts the number of distinct resistances possible for n arbitrary resistors each connected in series or parallel with previous ones [1,12]. It also counts the number of labeled threshold graphs on n vertices [2]. The table of $f(n)$ for $n \leq 100$ can be found in [7]. These numbers are the coefficients of the generating function $(1 - x)e^x/(2 - e^x)$ [2], and

$$f(n) \sim n!(1 - \ln 2)/(\ln 2)^{n+1} \in 2^{n \log n - n(\log \ln 2 + \log e) + o(n)} \doteq 2^{n \log n - 0.9139n + o(n)}.$$

Theorem 6. *Let $V(n)$ be the number of valid antichains of subsets of $[1, n]$. Then $V(n) = 2f(n) + n - 2$, where $f(n)$ is the function defined by (1).*

Proof. In $\cup \mathfrak{T}$, nothing may be missing, or exactly one element may be missing, or exactly two elements may be missing, etc. Therefore,

$$V(n) = f(n) + \sum_{i=1}^{n-2} \binom{n}{i} f(n - i) + n,$$

where n is the number of antichains $\{\{i\}\}$ in which $n - 1$ elements are missing in $\cup \mathfrak{T}$. Hence $V(n) = 2f(n) + n - 2$, and the theorem follows.   □

5   Upper Bound

Our first aim is to show that some valid antichains are always unreachable. Recall that for an antichain $\mathfrak{T} = \{T_1, T_2, \ldots, T_k\}$, $\cup \mathfrak{T} = \bigcup_{i=1}^k T_i$ and $\cap \mathfrak{T} = \bigcap_{i=1}^k T_i$.

Lemma 7 (Unreachable Antichains). *Let $n \geq 4$ and $A = (Q_n, \Sigma, \cdot, 0, F)$ be a DFA with $|F| \geq 1$. Let $\mathfrak{T}$ be a valid antichain as defined in Definition 3. If*

$$\{0, j\} \in \mathfrak{T} \text{ for some } j \text{ in } Q_n \setminus \{0\}, \text{ and } \cup \mathfrak{T} = Q_n, \tag{4}$$

then $\mathfrak{T}$ is unreachable in the subset automaton $\mathcal{D}(C^+)$.

Proof. Let $\mathfrak{T} = (T_1, T_2, \ldots, T_k)$ be a valid antichain satisfying (4). Then $k \geq 2$. Assume that $\mathfrak{T}$ can be reached from a reachable antichain $\mathcal{S}$ by reading a symbol a in Σ. Our aim is to show that $\mathcal{S}$ satisfies (4) as well. Then, the lemma follows.

Denote by $\mathrm{Im}(a) = \{qa \mid q \in Q_n\}$. Since each state is in $\cup \mathfrak{T}$, each state, with a possible exception of the state 0, must be in $\mathrm{Im}(a)$. Thus $0 \in \mathrm{Im}(a)$ implies that a performs a permutation on Q_n, and in such a case, we must have $\{a1, a2, \ldots, a(n-1)\} \subseteq \cup \mathcal{S}$. If $0 \notin \mathrm{Im}(a)$, then there is exactly one state r in $Q_n \setminus \{0\}$ such that $r = pa = qa$ and $p \neq q$. Consider three cases:

(a) $\{0, j\}$ is reached from a state S in $\mathcal{S}$ with $|S| \geq 3$. Let p, q, r be three distinct states in S. Since we can have neither $pa = qa = ra$ nor $pa = qa = 0$, we must have $pa = 0$ and $qa = ra = j$. This is a contradiction since $0 \in \mathrm{Im}(a)$ implies that a is a permutation.

(b) $\{0,j\}$ is reached from a state in a final antichain $\mathcal{S}$. Then we have $\cup\mathcal{S} \subseteq (Q_n \setminus F) \cup \{0\}$, so $|\cup\mathcal{S}| \leq n-1$. If $|F| \geq 2$, then $|\cup\mathcal{S}| \leq n-2$, and therefore

$$|\cup\mathcal{T}| \leq |(\cup\mathcal{S})a| \leq n-1,$$

a contradiction. If $|F| = 1$, then we must have $0a \in F$ to get a set $\{0, 0a\}$ in $\mathcal{T}$ from the set $\{0\}$ in $\mathcal{S}$. However, then the unique final state $0a$ cannot be in any other component of the antichain $\mathcal{T}$. Since $k \geq 2$, we must have $0 \in \mathrm{Im}(a)$ and $a0 \in \cup\mathcal{S}$. However, then a is a permutation and $\{a1, a2, \ldots, a(n-1)\} \subseteq \cup\mathcal{S}$. This is a contradiction since we have $|\cup\mathcal{S}| \leq n-1$. Notice that this case covers the reachability of $\{0, j\}$ from one-element sets, or from two-element sets $\{p, q\}$ with $p \neq 0$ and $q \neq 0$.

(c) $\{0, j\}$ is reached from a two-element state $\{0, q\}$ in $\mathcal{S}$ where $q \neq 0$. Then $\mathcal{S}$ is a non-final antichain of size at least 2, and therefore the state 0 is in each of its components. If $0a = j$, then we would have j in each component of $\mathcal{T}$, so $\mathcal{T}$ would not be an antichain, a contradiction. Therefore $0a = 0$ and $qa = j$. This means that $0 \in \mathrm{Im}(a)$, so a is a permutation, and $\{a1, a2, \ldots, a(n-1)\} \subseteq \cup\mathcal{S}$. Since $a0 = 0$ and $0 \in \cup\mathcal{S}$, we get $\cup\mathcal{S} = Q_n$, so $\mathcal{S}$ satisfies (4). $\square$

Our next result provides an upper bound on the state complexity of star-complement-star. We discuss all possible choices of the final states in a given DFA, and show that the number of reachable valid antichains in the subset automaton for plus-complement-plus is maximal if the initial state of the given DFA is final, and if there is exactly one non-initial final state.

Theorem 8 (Star-Complement-Star: Upper Bound). *Let $n \geq 4$ and $A = (Q_n, \Sigma, \cdot, 0, F)$ be an n-state DFA. Then the language $L(A)^{*c*}$ is accepted by a DFA of at most $\frac{3}{2}f(n-1) + 2f(n-2) + 2n - 5$ states, where $f(n)$ is the function defined by (1).*

Proof. Recall that we denoted the number of valid antichains of subsets of $[1, n]$ by $V(n)$, and $V(n) = 2f(n) + n - 2$ by Theorem 6. We now discuss possible choices of the set of final states F of the DFA A. If $F = \emptyset$ then $L(A) = \emptyset$ and $L(A)^{*c*} = \Sigma^*$. If $F = \{0\}$, then $L(A) = L(A)^*$, so $L(A)^{*c} = L(A)^c$. Thus the state complexity of $L(A)^{*c}$ is n, and therefore the state complexity of $(L(A))^{*c*}$ is at most $\frac{3}{4}2^n$ [6,13], which is less than $\frac{3}{2}f(n-1) + 2f(n-2) + 2n - 5$ if $n \geq 4$.

Let $|F \cap [1, n-1]| = k$ where $k \geq 1$. By Lemma 7, the antichains containing $\{0, j\}$ for some j and with $\cup\mathcal{T} = Q_n$ are always unreachable in $\mathcal{D}(C^+)$, and there are $f_1(n-1) = f(n-1)/2$ of them. Next, only the following valid antichains may be reachable in $\mathcal{D}(C^+)$:

(i) the initial antichain $\{\{0\}\}$;
(ii) the final antichains $\{\{0\}, T_2, T_3, \ldots, T_k\}$ with $k \geq 2$ and $T_i \subseteq [1, n-1] \setminus F$;
(iii) the non-final antichains $\{T_1, T_2, \ldots, T_k\}$ with $k \geq 1$ and $T_i \cap F \neq \emptyset$, except for those containing $\{0, j\}$ for some j and with $\cup\mathcal{T} = Q_n$.

Notice that in case (ii), the antichain $\{T_2, T_3, \ldots, T_k\}$ is a valid antichain of subsets of $[1, n-1] \setminus F$, and that there are $V(n-1-k)$ such valid antichains.

Now consider antichains in case (iii). Since each T_i contains a final state of A, it also must contain the state 0, because in the construction of A^+ we added the transition $(p, a, 0)$ whenever $p \cdot a \in F$ in A.

If $0 \in F$, then each subset containing 0, is final in B, so non-final in C^+, so every antichain of the form $\{\{0\} \cup T_1, \{0\} \cup T_2, \ldots, \{0\} \cup T_k\}$ with $k \geq 1$ and $T_i \subseteq [1, n-1]$ $(1 \leq i \leq k)$ may possibly be reachable, except for those containing $\{0, j\}$ for some j and with $\cup \mathcal{T} = Q_n$. The number of such valid antichains is $V(n-1) - f(n-1)/2$.

However, if $0 \notin F$ and there is a state $q \in [1, n-1] \setminus F$, then the state $\{0, f\}$ is final in C^+, and therefore, in $\mathcal{D}(C^+)$ it only may be reached together with the initial state $\{0\}$ since in the construction of C^+, we added the transition $(S, a, \{0\})$ whenever $S \cdot a \subseteq F^c$. Thus the antichain $\{\{0, f\}\}$ considered in case (iii) is unreachable in this case. So the only way how to reach $V(n-1) - f(n-1)/2$ antichains in (iii) with $0 \notin F$ is to have $F = [1, n-1]$. However, in such a case, we do not have any final antichain.

Hence to get $V(n-1) - f(n-1)/2$ antichains in (iii) and at least one final antichain, we must have $0 \in F$. Finally, to get the maximal number of final antichains, we must have $k = 1$.

It follows that the number of reachable antichains in $\mathcal{D}(C^+)$ is maximal if $0 \in F$ and $|F \cap [1, n-1]| = 1$. In such a case, this number is equal to $1 + V(n-2) + V(n-1) - f(n-1)/2 = (3/2)f(n-1) + 2f(n-2) + 2n - 6$. Finally, to get a DFA for L^{*c*}, a new initial and final state may be required to accept the empty string. Our proof is complete. □

6   Matching Lower Bound

Our next aim is to define a quaternary language such that the state complexity of its star-complement-star meets our upper bound given in Theorem 8. Recall that $[i, j] = \{\ell \mid i \leq \ell \leq j\}$ and $Q_n = [0, n-1]$.

Definition 9 (Quaternary Witness Language). *Let $n \geq 4$. Define an n-state DFA $A = (Q_n, \{a, b, c, d\}, \cdot, 0, \{0, 1\})$, where $a\colon (0, 1, 2)$, $b\colon (1, 2, \ldots, n-1)$, $c\colon (2, 3, \ldots, n-1)$, and $d\colon (0 \to 2)$. The DFA A is shown in Fig. 1.*

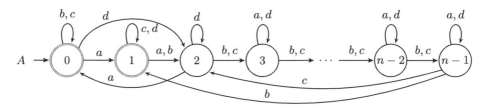

Fig. 1. A quaternary witness for star-complement-star meeting the upper bound $\frac{3}{2}f(n-1) + 2f(n-2) + 2n - 5$, where $f(n) = \sum_{i=1}^{n-2} \binom{n}{i} f(n-i) + 2$ and $f(2) = 2$.

Lemma 10. *Let $n \geq 4$ and A be an n-state DFA described in Definition 9. Let C^+ be the NFA for $L(A)^{+c+}$ described in Sect. 3. Let $\mathcal{T} = \{T_1, T_2, \ldots, T_k\}$ be an antichain of subsets of Q_n such that*

(i) $1 \leq k \leq n$;
(ii) $T_i = \{q_i\} \cup S_i$ $(1 \leq i \leq k)$, where $S_1 \subseteq S_2 \subseteq \cdots \subseteq S_k$ and $q_1, q_2, \ldots, q_k$ are pairwise distinct states in $Q_n \setminus S_k$;
(iii) either $T_1 = \{0\}$ and $T_i \subseteq [2, n-1]$ if $2 \leq i \leq k$, or $0 \in T_i$ for each i;
(iv) if $\{0, j\} \in \mathcal{T}$ for some $j \geq 1$, then there is q in $[1, n-1]$ such that $q \notin \cup \mathcal{T}$.

Then $\mathcal{T}$ is reachable in the subset automaton $\mathcal{D}(C^+)$. All these antichains are pairwise distinguishable, and there are $\frac{3}{2}f(n-1) + 2f(n-2) + 2n - 6$ of them.

Proof. To simplify the notation let us set $m := n - 1$. The proof is by induction on the size of an antichain $\mathcal{T} = \{T_1, T_2, \ldots, T_k\}$. Let $k = 1$, so $\mathcal{T} = \{T\}$. Then T must be a non-final state of the NFA C^+. This means that $0 \in T$. Let us show by induction on $|T|$ that the state $\{T\}$ is reachable in the subset automaton $\mathcal{D}(C^+)$. The set $\{\{0\}\}$ is the initial state of $\mathcal{D}(C^+)$. Let $T \subseteq Q_n$ and $0 \in T$. Let $j = \min(T \setminus \{0\})$. Then $T \setminus \{0, j\} \subseteq [j+1, m]$, $b^{j-1}(T \setminus \{0, j\}) \subseteq [2, m]$, and

$$\{\{0\} \cup ab^{j-1}(T \setminus \{0, j\})\} \xrightarrow{a} \{\{0, 1\} \cup b^{j-1}(T \setminus \{0, j\})\} \xrightarrow{b^{j-1}}$$
$$\{\{0, j\} \cup (T \setminus \{0, j\})\} = \{T\},$$

where the starting set is reachable by the induction assumption; notice that $(0, a, 0)$ and $(0, b, 0)$ are transitions in the NFA A^+, so while reading any string over $\{a, b\}$, the NFA C^+ is always in a state containing 0, that is, in a rejecting state, therefore the initial state $\{0\}$ of C^+ cannot be added while reading such a string.

Now let $2 \leq k \leq n$ and assume that each antichain satisfying (i)–(iv) of size $k - 1$ is reachable. Let $\mathcal{T} = \{T_1, T_2, \ldots, T_k\}$ be an antichain odd size k satisfying (i)–(iv).

To simplify the exposition, let us use $q + S$ to denote the set $\{q\} \cup S$, where $q \in Q_n$ and $S \subseteq Q_n$. Then by (ii), $T_i = q_i + S_i$ where $S_1 \subseteq S_2 \subseteq \cdots \subseteq S_k$, and $q_1, q_2, \ldots, q_k$ are pairwise distinct states in $Q_n \setminus S_k$. Consider several cases:

(1) Let $T_1 = \{0\}$. Then $T_i \subseteq [2, m]$ if $2 \leq i \leq k$, so $1 \notin \cup \mathcal{T}$.
   (a) First, let $T_2 = \{j\}$ for some j in $[2, m]$. Let u be a string in c^* such that $uj = 2$. Let $\mathcal{T}' = \{\{0\}, uT_3, \ldots, uT_k\}$. Then $\mathcal{T}'$ is an antichain of size $k - 1$ which satisfies (i)–(iv). Therefore, $\mathcal{T}'$ is reachable by the induction assumption. Since

$$\mathcal{T}' = \{\{0\}, uT_3, \ldots, uT_k\} \xrightarrow{d} \{\{0\}, \{2 = uj\}, uT_3, \ldots, uT_k\} \xrightarrow{u}$$
$$\{\{0\}, \{j\}, T_3, \ldots, T_k\} = \mathcal{T},$$

   the antichain $\mathcal{T}$ is reachable.

232   J. Jirásek and G. Jirásková

(b) Now let $|T_2| \geq 2$, so there is a state $j \in [2, m]$ such that $j \in \cap \mathcal{T}$. Let u be a string in c^* such that $uj = 2$, and therefore $2 \in \cap u\mathcal{T}$. Let $\mathcal{T}' = \{0 + uT_2, 0 + uT_3, \ldots, 0 + uT_k\}$. Then $1 \notin \cup \mathcal{T}'$, so $\mathcal{T}'$ is an antichain of size $k - 1$ satisfying (i)–(iv), and therefore it is reachable by the induction assumption. Since

$$\mathcal{T}' = \{0 + uT_2, 0 + uT_3, \ldots, 0 + uT_k\} \xrightarrow{d} \{\{0\}, uT_2, uT_3, \ldots, uT_k\} \xrightarrow{u} \{\{0\}, T_2, T_3, \ldots, T_k\} = \mathcal{T},$$

the antichain $\mathcal{T}$ is reachable.

(2) Let $T_1 = \{0, 1\}$. Then $0 \in T_i$ and $1 \notin T_i$ if $2 \leq i \leq k$. By (iv), there is a state q in $[2, m]$ such that $q \notin \cup \mathcal{T}$. Let u be the string in c^* such that $uq = 2$. Let $T_i' = T_i \setminus \{0\}$. Then

$$\{\{0\}, uq + uT_2', \ldots, uq + uT_k'\} \xrightarrow{a} \{\{0, 1\}, 0 + uT_2', \ldots, 0 + uT_k'\} \xrightarrow{u} \{\{0, 1\}, T_2, \ldots, T_k\} = \mathcal{T},$$

where the starting antichain satisfies (i)–(iv) and it is considered in case (1).

(3) Let $T_1 = \{0, j\}$ and $j \geq 2$. Then $0 \in T_i$ and $j \notin T_i$ if $2 \leq i \leq k$. By (iv), there is a state q in $[1, m]$ and $q \neq j$ such that $q \notin \cup \mathcal{T}$. Let u be a string in b^* such that $uj = 1$. Then $uq \neq 1$ and $uq \notin \cup u\mathcal{T}$. Next,

$$\{\{0, 1\}, uT_2, \ldots, uT_k\} \xrightarrow{u} \{\{0, j\}, T_2, \ldots, T_k\},$$

where the starting antichain satisfies (i)–(iv), and it is considered in case (2).

(4) Let $|T_1| \geq 3$. We prove this case by induction on $|T_1|$. First, let $|T_1| = 3$. Then $0 \in \cap \mathcal{T}$ and there is a state $q \in T_1 \setminus \{0\}$ such that $q \in \cap \mathcal{T}$. Let u be a string in b^* such that $uq = 1$ and let $T_i' = T_i \setminus \{0, q\}$. Then $uT_i' \subseteq [2, m]$. Therefore,

$$\{0 + auT_1', 0 + auT_2', \ldots, 0 + auT_k'\} \xrightarrow{a}$$
$$\{\{0, 1\} \cup uT_1', \{0, 1\} \cup uT_2', \ldots, \{0, 1\} \cup uT_k'\} \xrightarrow{u} \mathcal{T}$$

since $0u = 0$ and $1u = uqu = q$. The starting antichain is considered in cases (2)–(3). The induction step is exactly the same, except that the starting set is reachable by induction on $|T_1|$.

To prove distinguishability, let $\mathcal{S}$ and $\mathcal{T}$ be two distinct antichains. By Proposition 1, we may assume that there is a set $S \in \mathcal{S} \setminus \mathcal{T}$ such that no subset of S is in $\mathcal{T}$. Notice that the set S must be different from $[0, m]$ because otherwise it is not true that no subset of $[0, m]$ is in $\mathcal{T}$. We also must have $S \neq [1, m]$ since $1 \in S$ implies $0 \in S$. Then S may be send to S' with $1 \notin S'$ using a string u in b^*; while still no subset of S' is in $\mathcal{T}u$. Thus, we may assume that $1 \notin S$.

First, let $\mathcal{S}$ and $\mathcal{T}$ be two final antichains. Then $S \subseteq [2, m]$. Let $i \in [2, m] \setminus S$. Then the string $u_i = c^{n-1-i} b c^{i-2}$ sends each state of S to itself, and the state i

to the state 1 in the DFA A. It follows that for each subset S of $[2, m]$, there is a string $u_S \in \{b, c\}^*$ (equal to the concatenation of strings u_i for $i \notin S$) by which S is sent to itself, while each set containing a state in $[2, m] \setminus S$ is sent to a set containing $\{0, 1\}$ in the NFA C^+; recall that $0 \cdot c = 0 \cdot b = 0$ and $1 \cdot c = 1$. It follows that the antichain $\mathcal{S}$ is send to a final antichain containing the state S by u_S. On the other hand, the antichain $\mathcal{T}$ is send to a non-final antichain equivalent to $\{\{0\}\}$ since $\{\{0\}\}$ remains in itself upon reading $u_S \in \{b, c\}^*$, while any other set in $\mathcal{T}$ is sent to a superset of $\{0, 1\}$ since it is not a subset of S.

If $\mathcal{S}$ and $\mathcal{T}$ are non-final, let $S' = S \setminus \{0\}$. Then $\mathcal{S}$ is sent to an antichain containing the set S by $u_{S'}$, while each set in $\mathcal{T}$ is sent to a superset of $\{0, 1\}$. Now we use the symbol d. Then $\mathcal{S}u_{S'}d$ is a final antichain containing the set $S' \cup \{2\}$, while $\mathcal{T}u_{S'}d$ is a non-final antichain of supersets of $\{0, 1\}$. □

Theorem 11 (Star-Complement-Star: Lower Bound; $|\Sigma| = 4$). *Let $n \geq 4$ and A be an n-state DFA from Definition 9. Then every DFA for the language $L(A)^{*c*}$ has at least $\frac{3}{2}f(n-1) + 2f(n-2) + 2n - 5$ states where $f(n)$ is the function defined in (1).*

Proof. First, notice that we have $L(A)^{*c*} = L(A)^{+c+} \cup \{\varepsilon\}$. To get an NFA C^* for $L(A)^{*c*}$, we add a new initial and final state q_0 to the NFA C^+ for $L(A)^{+c+}$. Thus C^* has two initial states, namely, q_0 and $\{0\}$, so the initial state of $\mathcal{D}(C^*)$ is $\{q_0, \{0\}\}$, and it is final. It is also the unique state of $\mathcal{D}(C^*)$ which contains the state q_0. By reading c it is sent to the initial state $\{\{0\}\}$ of the subset automaton $\mathcal{D}(C^+)$, which has $\frac{3}{2}f(n-1) + 2f(n-2) + 2n - 6$ reachable and pairwise distinguishable antichains by Lemma 10.

Let us show that the final state $\{q_0, \{0\}\}$ is distinguishable from any final antichain. To this aim, let $\mathcal{T} = \{\{0\}, T_2, \ldots, T_k\}$ be a final antichain where $k \geq 2$ and each T_i is a non-empty subset of $[2, n-1]$. Then, by c, the antichain $\mathcal{T}$ is sent to a final antichain, while $\{q_0, \{0\}\}$ is sent to the non-final antichain $\{\{0\}\}$. □

The next theorem summarizes our results.

Theorem 12 (State Complexity of Star-Complement-Star). *Let $n \geq 4$ and L be a language accepted by an n-state DFA. Then the language L^{*c*} is accepted by a DFA with $\frac{3}{2}f(n-1) + 2f(n-2) + 2n - 5$ states, where $f(2) = 2$ and $f(n) = \sum_{i=1}^{n-2}\binom{n}{i}f(n-i) + 2$, and $f(n) \sim n!(1 - \ln 2)/(\ln 2)^{n+1} \doteq 2^{n\log n - 0.91n + o(n)}$. This upper bound is tight, and it is met by the quaternary language recognized by the DFA $A = (\{0, 1, \ldots, n - 1\}, \{a, b, c, d\}, \cdot, 0, \{0, 1\})$ where $a\colon (0, 1, 2)$, $b\colon (1, 2, \ldots, n-1)$, $c\colon (2, 3, \ldots, n-1)$, $d\colon (0 \to 2)$.* □

7   Conclusions

We proved that the exact state complexity of the star-complement-star operation is given by $\frac{3}{2}f(n-1) + 2f(n-2) + 2n - 5$ where $f(n)$ is the function that counts, for example, the number of distinct resistances possible for n arbitrary resistors, each connected in series or parallel with previous ones, or the number of labeled threshold graphs on n vertices. It defines Sloane's sequence A005840. These numbers are the coefficients of the generating function $(1-x)e^x/(2-e^x)$, and $f(n) \sim n!(1 - \ln 2)/(\ln 2)^{n+1}$.

Our witness language is defined over a quaternary alphabet, we are most likely able to show that at least three symbols are necessary. Our computations, summarized in Table 1, show that the upper bound cannot be met by any ternary language if $n \geq 5$, but to prove this seems to be a challenging problem. A lower bound in the binary case is of interest too. On the other hand, the unary case is easy since L^{*c*} equals $\{\varepsilon\}$ if $a \in L$, and it equals a^* otherwise.

Table 1. Computations—the state complexity of plus-complement-plus: the binary and ternary case; lower bound from [4] with a witness over a seven-letter alphabet; the exact complexity with a quaternary lower bound example; the upper bound from [4].

n	$\lvert\Sigma\rvert=2$	$\lvert\Sigma\rvert=3$	$\lceil\frac{n}{2}\rceil^{n-\lceil\frac{n}{2}\rceil}$	State complexity of $L \mapsto L^{+c+}$ with a quaternary witness	$\sum_{k=1}^{n}\binom{n}{k}k!(k+1)^{n-k}$
4	11	18	4	18	260
5	29	77	9	89	2 300
6	134	468	27	596	24 342
7	826		64	4 983	300 454
8			256	49 294	4 238 152
9			625	560 533	67 255 272
10			3 125	7 194 216	1 185 860 330

Acknowledgement. We would like to thank Jeffrey Shallit for proposing such an interesting problem. The work on finding its solution was really funny for both of us, and it helped us to almost forget that our children eventually left our place.

References

1. Amengual, A.: The intriguing properties of the equivalent resistances of n equal resistors combined in series and in parallel. Am. J. Phys. **68**(2), 175–179 (2000). https://doi.org/10.1119/1.19396
2. Beissinger, J.S., Peled, U.N.: Enumeration of labelled threshold graphs and a theorem of Frobenius involving Eulerian polynomials. Graph. Comb. **3**(1), 213–219 (1987). https://doi.org/10.1007/BF01788543
3. Brzozowski, J.A., Grant, E., Shallit, J.: Closures in formal languages and Kuratowski's theorem. Int. J. Found. Comput. Sci. **22**(2), 301–321 (2011). https://doi.org/10.1142/S0129054111008052

4. Jirásková, G., Shallit, J.: The state complexity of star-complement-star. In: Yen, H.-C., Ibarra, O.H. (eds.) DLT 2012. LNCS, vol. 7410, pp. 380–391. Springer, Heidelberg (2012). https://doi.org/10.1007/978-3-642-31653-1_34

5. Kleitman, D., Markowsky, G.: On Dedekind's problem: the number of isotone boolean functions. II. Trans. Amer. Math. Soc. **213**, 373–390 (1975)

6. Maslov, A.N.: Estimates of the number of states of finite automata. Sov. Math. Dokl. **11**(5), 1373–1375 (1970)

7. Noe, T.D.: Table of $f(n)$ for $n = 0..100$ (2018). https://oeis.org/A005840/b005840.txt

8. Rabin, M.O., Scott, D.S.: Finite automata and their decision problems. IBM J. Res. Dev. **3**(2), 114–125 (1959). https://doi.org/10.1147/rd.32.0114

9. Sipser, M.: Introduction to the Theory of Computation. Cengage Learning, Florence (2012). https://doi.org/10.1016/S0304-3975(81)80005-9

10. Sloane, N.J.A.: Online encyclopedia of integer sequences (2018). http://oeis.org

11. Sloane, N.J.A., Plouffe, S.: The Encyclopedia of Integer Sequences. Academic Press, San Diego (1995)

12. Weisstein, E.W.: "Resistor network." from mathworld-a wolfram web resource (2018). http://mathworld.wolfram.com/ResistorNetwork.html

13. Yu, S., Zhuang, Q., Salomaa, K.: The state complexities of some basic operations on regular languages. Theor. Comput. Sci. **125**(2), 315–328 (1994). https://doi.org/10.1016/0304-3975(92)00011-F

Parametrizing String Assembling Systems

Martin Kutrib[(⊠)] and Matthias Wendlandt

Institut für Informatik, Universität Giessen, Arndtstr. 2, 35392 Giessen, Germany
{kutrib,matthias.wendlandt}@informatik.uni-giessen.de

Abstract. String assembling systems are biologically inspired mechanisms that generate strings from copies out of finite sets of assembly units. The underlying mechanism is based on piecewise assembly of a double-stranded sequence of symbols, where the upper and lower strand have to match. The generation is additionally controlled by the requirement that the first symbol of a unit has to be the same as the last symbol of the strand generated so far, as well as by the distinction of assembly units that may appear at the beginning, during, and at the end of the assembling process. We investigate the power of these model-inherent control mechanisms by considering variants where one or more of these mechanisms are relaxed. Additionally, we study the case where the length of the substrings in the assembly units is bounded. The generative capacities and the relative power of the variants are our main interest.

1 Introduction

In 1965 Gordon E. Moore predicted that the number of components per integrated circuit will double every year [7]. Up to now this forecast that is also known as *Moore's Law* became more or less reality. Nevertheless, there are many real world problems requiring such a huge computational complexity that they cannot be solved for an appropriate size of the instance in this day and age, and also will not be solvable under the assumption of Moore's Law in a thousand years unless new computing techniques are developed. This motivated the advent of investigations of devices and operations that are inspired by the study of biological processes, and the growing interest in nature-based problems modeled in formal systems. Among the realms of string generating mechanisms examples are Lindenmayer systems [11], splicing systems and sticker systems [10]. The latter two types of devices model operations on DNA molecules and are therefore based upon double stranded strings as raw material of the string generation process, where corresponding symbols are uniquely related. Sticker systems were introduced in [3] in their basic one-way variant. Basically, they consist of dominoes that can be seen as double stranded molecules. The dominoes are sticked together in a derivation process until a complete double strand is derived. Different variants especially of two-way systems have been investigated in [2,9,10]. A main feature of sticker systems is that the upper and lower fragment of the dominoes are glued together. So, when a domino is added to a double strand

© Springer International Publishing AG, part of Springer Nature 2018
C. Câmpeanu (Ed.): CIAA 2018, LNCS 10977, pp. 236–247, 2018.
https://doi.org/10.1007/978-3-319-94812-6_20

the length difference of upper and the lower strand derived is the same as the length difference between the upper and the lower fragment of the domino. This implies that many variants of sticker systems are at most as powerful as linear context-free grammars [10]. String assembling systems, introduced in [4], are another string generating mechanism based on double strands. The idea of string assembling systems [1, 4, 5] is basically motivated by the mechanisms of the Post's Correspondence Problem. In particular, the basic assembly units are pairs of substrings that have to be connected to the upper and lower string generated so far synchronously. In comparison to sticker systems, the substrings are not connected. This property enables the possibility to increase the length difference between the two strands arbitrarily and, moreover, to compare positions that are an arbitrarily far from each other in a given input word. Thus, it is possible to generate non-context-free languages. Apart from the double strand, essentially, derivations in string assembling systems are controlled by the requirement that the first symbol of a string to be assembled has to match the last symbol of the strand generated so far, as well as by the distinction of assembly units that may appear at the beginning, during, and at the end of the assembling process. Moreover, the lengths of the strings in the assembly units are not limited.

Here we investigate the power of these model-inherent control mechanisms by considering variants where one or more of these mechanisms are relaxed. Additionally, we study the case where the length of the substrings in the assembly units is bounded. It turns out that the generative capacities and the relative power gained in the different control mechanisms may yield strictly more powerful systems and incomparable capacities. Special attention is paid to unary languages and non-context-free languages. The relative power of the systems is summarized in Fig. 1. The last section studies the impact of the lengths of the assembling fragments. It is shown that increasing the lengths gives strictly more capacity, that is, an infinite and tight hierarchy follows.

2   Preliminaries and Definitions

We write Σ^* for the set of all words (strings) over the finite alphabet Σ. The empty word is denoted by λ, and $\Sigma^+ = \Sigma^* \setminus \{\lambda\}$. The reversal of a word w is denoted by w^R and for the length of w we write $|w|$. Generally, for a singleton set $\{a\}$ we also simply write a. We use $\subseteq$ for inclusions and $\subset$ for strict inclusions. In order to avoid technical overloading in writing, two languages L and L' are considered to be equal, if they differ at most by the empty word, that is, $L \setminus \{\lambda\} = L' \setminus \{\lambda\}$.

A string assembling system generates a double-stranded string by assembling units. Each unit consists of two substrings, the first one is connected to the upper and the second one to the lower strand. The corresponding symbols of the upper and lower strand have to be equal. In the general form as studied in [4], the first symbols of the substrings have to match the last symbols of the current strands. In this case the matching symbols are glued together on at the top of the other. The generation has to begin with a unit from the set of initial units. Then it may continue with units from a different set. When a unit from a third set of ending units is applied the process necessarily stops. The generation is said to be successful if and only if both strands are identical when the process stops. More precisely:

A *string assembling system* (SAS) is a quadruple $\langle \Sigma, A, T, E \rangle$, where Σ is the finite, nonempty set of *symbols* or *letters*, $A \subset \Sigma^+ \times \Sigma^+$ is the finite set of *axioms* of the forms (uv, u) or (u, uv), where $u \in \Sigma^+$ and $v \in \Sigma^*$, $T \subset \Sigma^+ \times \Sigma^+$ is the finite set of *assembly units*, and $E \subset \Sigma^+ \times \Sigma^+$ is the finite set of *ending assembly units* of the forms (vu, u) or (u, vu), where $u \in \Sigma^+$ and $v \in \Sigma^*$,

The *derivation relation* $\Rightarrow$ is defined on specific subsets of $\Sigma^+ \times \Sigma^+$ by

1. $(uv, u) \Rightarrow (uvx, uy)$ if
   (i) $uv = ta$, $u = sb$, and $(ax, by) \in T \cup E$, for $a, b \in \Sigma$, $x, y, s, t \in \Sigma^*$, and
   (ii) $vx = yz$ or $vxz = y$, for $z \in \Sigma^*$.
2. $(u, uv) \Rightarrow (uy, uvx)$ if
   (i) $uv = ta$, $u = sb$, and $(by, ax) \in T \cup E$, for $a, b \in \Sigma$, $x, y, s, t \in \Sigma^*$, and
   (ii) $vx = yz$ or $vxz = y$, for $z \in \Sigma^*$.

A derivation is said to be *successful* if it initially starts with an axiom from A, continues with assembling units from T, and ends with assembling an ending unit from E. The process necessarily stops when an ending assembly unit is added. The sets A, T, and E are not necessarily disjoint.

The *language $L(S)$ generated* by S is defined to be the set

$$L(S) = \{ w \in \Sigma^+ \mid (p, q) \Rightarrow^* (w, w) \text{ is a successful derivation} \},$$

where $\Rightarrow^*$ refers to the reflexive, transitive closure of the derivation relation $\Rightarrow$.

In order to illustrate the definitions we continue with meaningful examples.

Example 1 ([4]). The non-context-free language $\{ a^n b^n c^n \mid n \geq 1 \}$ is generated by the SAS $S = \langle \{a, b, c\}, A, T, E \rangle$, where the units are defined as follows.

1. $(a, a) \in A$ 4. $(bb, aa) \in T$ 7. $(c, bc) \in T$
2. $(aa, a) \in T$ 5. $(bc, ab) \in T$ 8. $(c, cc) \in T$
3. $(ab, a) \in T$ 6. $(cc, bb) \in T$ 9. $(c, c) \in E$

The units (2) and (3) are used to generate the prefixes $a^n b$. Initially, only the unit (aa, a) is applicable repeatedly. Then only (ab, a) can be used to generate the upper string $a^n b$ and the lower string a. After that the unit (bb, aa) has to be used exactly as many times as the unit (aa, a) has been applied before. Then an application of unit (bc, ab) is the sole possibility. This generates the upper string $a^n b^n c$ and the lower string $a^n b$. For the last part the units (6) and (7) are used. Similarly as before, repeated applications of (cc, bb) yield to the upper string $a^n b^n c^n$ and the lower string $a^n b^n$. So, it remains to complement the c's in the lower string. This is done by the units (c, bc), which can be applied only once, and (c, cc) which can be applied arbitrarily often. However, the derivation is successful only if the number of c's in the upper and lower string match when the unit from E is applied.   ∎

Example 2. The regular language $\{ a^m b^n a^\ell \mid m, n, \ell \geq 1 \}$ is generated by an SAS.

3   SAS with Less Derivation Control

The derivation of an SAS allows two control mechanisms. On the one hand, the units are arranged in three sets, such that initial units have to be taken from one set, ending units from another, and in between only units from the third set are allowed. On the other hand, whenever the current strands are extended, the last symbol is glued on top of the first symbol of the extending substring. This section is devoted to study the generative capacity gained from these mechanisms.

3.1   Free String Assembling Systems

The first restricted variant are so-called *free* assembling systems, where the control mechanism derived from the fact that the assembled substrings have to overlap the last symbol of the current strand is relaxed.

An SAS $S = \langle \Sigma, A, T, E \rangle$ is said to be free, if $A, T, E \subset \Sigma^* \times \Sigma^*$, and its units are assembled according to the derivation relation $\overset{f}{\Rightarrow}$ by

1. $(uv, u) \overset{f}{\Rightarrow} (uvx, uy)$ if
   (i) $(x, y) \in T \cup E$, for $x, y \in \Sigma^*$, and
   (ii) $vx = yz$ or $vxz = y$, for $z \in \Sigma^*$.
2. $(u, uv) \overset{f}{\Rightarrow} (uy, uvx)$ if
   (i) $(y, x) \in T \cup E$, for $x, y \in \Sigma^*$, and
   (ii) $vx = yz$ or $vxz = y$, for $z \in \Sigma^*$.

Example 3. Let $h\colon \{a_1, b_1\} \to \{a_2, b_2\}$ be a homomorphism with $h(a_1) = a_2$ and $h(b_1) = b_2$. The language $\{\$_0 w_1 \$_1 h(w_1) \$_2 \mid w_1 \in \{a_1, b_1\}^+\}$ is not context free but generated by the free SAS $S = \langle \{a_1, a_2, b_1, b_2, \$_0, \$_1, \$_2\}, A, T, E \rangle$, where all following units are defined for all $x, y, z \in \{a, b\}$.

1. $(\$_0 x_1, \lambda) \in A$	5. $(x_2 y_2, x_1 y_1) \in T$	9. $(\lambda, \$_2) \in E$
2. $(x_1 y_1, \lambda) \in T$	6. $(x_2 \$_2, x_1 \$_1 z_2) \in T$	10. $(\lambda, x_2 \$_2) \in E$
3. $(\$_1, \$_0) \in T$	7. $(x_2 y_2 \$_2, x_1 y_1 \$_1 z_2) \in T$	
4. $(x_1 \$_1, \$_0) \in T$	8. $(\lambda, x_2 y_2) \in T$	

There are three basic ideas of the construction of S. First, the axiom (1) has an empty lower string. This ensures that subsequently only units (2) can be assembled until the derivation of the upper strand $\$_0 w_1 \$_1$ is completed by one of the units (3) or (4). Second, since the concluding $\$_2$ in the lower strand is only defined in the ending units (9) and (10), it is impossible to generate anything after $\$_2$. Third, the units assembling the upper w_1 extend the current strand at even positions and have length two, while units assembling w_1 in the lower strand extend the current strand at odd positions. Thus, they overlap, which ensures that the format of the generated words is correct, and that there are no symbols of $\{a_1, b_1\}$ and $\{a_2, b_2\}$ mixed up. These ideas are similarly applied to the construction of the units generating the substring w_2 between the symbols $\$_1$

and $\$_2$. Here the units in the upper strand start at an odd position of w_2 and at an even position in w_2 in the lower strand.

The units (6) and (7) complete the derivation of the upper strand. Both place $\$_1$ in the lower strand, which ensures the equality of $h(w_1)$ and w_2. The generation of the lower strand and the whole derivation is completed by the units (8) and (9) or (10).   ∎

In order to show that the loss of the control mechanism that requires overlapping may weaken the generative capacity of SAS, we first show that witness languages cannot be generated by free string assembling systems.

Lemma 4.   *Neither the language $L = \{a^n b^n \$ a^m \mid m, n \geq 1\}$ nor its iterated version $L_+ = \{a\}L_0^*$ with $L_0 = \{a^{n-1} b^n \$ a^m \mid m, n \geq 1\}$ can be generated by any free SAS.*

Proof. In contrast to the assertion assume that L or L_+ is generated by some free SAS $S = \langle \{a, b, \$\}, A, T, E \rangle$. First, it is shown that there must exist units of both forms (a^i, a^j), $i > j \geq 0$ and $(a^{i'}, a^{j'})$, $j' > i' \geq 0$, or a unit of the form (a^l, a^l), $l \geq 1$.

Consider the derivation of a word $w = ab\$ a^m$ with m large enough. At some point in the derivation the generated strands must have the form (u, v), where one of the two strands, say u, is of the form $ab\$ a^p$. If v is of the form $ab\$ a^q$ as well, we may assume that $p \geq q$. In order to extend p and q to the large m, both strands can be extended by applying units of the form (a^l, a^l), $l \geq 1$, or units of both forms (a^i, a^j), $i > j \geq 0$ and $(a^{i'}, a^{j'})$, $j' > i' \geq 0$, can be used. Now assume that $|v| < 3$. Then a unit of the form (a^i, λ), $i \geq 1$ can be applied which yields generated strands of the same form (u, v), or units (a^i, x), $i \geq 0$, $|x| \geq 1$, can be applied at most three times. Afterwards the generated strands are again of the same form (u, v). It follows that there must exist units of both forms (a^i, a^j), $i > j \geq 0$ and $(a^{i'}, a^{j'})$, $j' > i' \geq 0$, or a unit of the form (a^l, a^l), $l \geq 1$.

Next, consider the derivation of a word $w = a^n b^n \$ a^m$ with m, n large enough. After an appropriate axiom has been chosen, the generated strands are of the form (u, v) with $u, v \in \{a\}^*$. Applying the unit (a^l, a^l), $l \geq 1$, shows that $a^{n+l} b^n \$ a^m$ is generated by S as well, a contradiction. The same contradiction is obtained when units (a^l, a^l) do not exist but units of both forms (a^i, a^j), $i > j \geq 0$ and $(a^{i'}, a^{j'})$, $j' > i' \geq 0$. In this case applying $j' - i'$ times the unit (a^i, a^j) and $i - j$ times the unit $(a^{i'}, a^{j'})$ shows that $a^{n+(i-j)(j'-i')} b^n \$ a^m$ is also generated. So, we conclude that neither L nor L_+ can be generated by any free SAS.   □

The proof of the next theorem uses the witness language L_+ from Lemma 4.

Theorem 5.   *There is a language generated by some SAS that cannot be generated by any free SAS.*

It is currently an open problem whether there is a strict inclusion or incomparability between the language families generated by free SAS and SAS. However, the differences in the generative capacities disappear for unary languages.

In order to show that SAS and free SAS are equally powerful with respect to unary languages the next lemma is useful.

Lemma 6. *For each unary free SAS an equivalent free SAS can be constructed whose sole ending unit is* (λ, λ).

Proposition 7. *A unary language can be generated by an SAS if and only if it can be generated by a free SAS.*

Proof. First, we show how a free SAS can simulate a given unary SAS $S = \langle \{a\}, A, T, E \rangle$. To this end, a free SAS $S' = \langle \{a\}, A, T', E' \rangle$ is constructed as follows. For every unit $(a^i, a^j) \in T$, $i, j \geq 1$ the unit $(a^{i-1}, a^{j-1}) \in T'$ is defined, and similarly for E and E'. In this way, clearly, each derivation step $(a^u, a^v) \Rightarrow (a^{u+i-1}, a^{v+j-1})$ in S using the unit (a^i, a^j) from T or E is simulated by a derivation step $(a^u, a^v) \overset{f}{\Rightarrow} (a^{u+i-1}, a^{v+j-1})$ in S' using the unit (a^{i-1}, a^{j-1}) from T' or E', and vice versa.

Second, it has to be shown how an SAS can simulate a given unary free SAS $S = \langle \{a\}, A, T, E \rangle$. By Lemma 6 we may assume that $E = \{(\lambda, \lambda)\}$. Now, an SAS $S' = \langle \{a\}, A', T', E' \rangle$ is constructed as follows. In order to overcome the problem that the units in A may have empty substrings but the units in A' may not, some units have to be merged. This can be done, since unary units always fit to the current double strand. The set of axioms is defined as $A' = A_0' \cup A_1' \cup A_2' \cup A_3' \cup A_4'$, where

$$
\begin{aligned}
A_0' &= \{(a^i, a^j) \mid (a^i, a^j) \in A, \text{ for } i, j \geq 1\}, \\
A_1' &= \{(a^{i_1 + i_2}, a^j) \mid (a^{i_1}, \lambda) \in A \text{ and } (a^{i_2}, a^j) \in T, \text{ for } i_1, j \geq 1\}, \\
A_2' &= \{(a^i, a^{j_1 + j_2}) \mid (\lambda, a^{j_1}) \in A \text{ and } (a^i, a^{j_2}) \in T, \text{ for } i, j_1 \geq 1\}, \\
A_3' &= \{(a^i, a^j) \mid (\lambda, \lambda) \in A \text{ and } (a^i, a^j) \in T, \text{ for } i, j \geq 1\}, \\
A_4' &= \{(a^i, a^j) \mid (\lambda, \lambda) \in A \text{ and } (a^i, \lambda) \in T, (\lambda, a^j) \in T, \text{ for } i, j \geq 1\}.
\end{aligned}
$$

So, any axiom in A that have at least one empty substring is replaced by an axiom without empty substrings (unless the axiom does not appear in any successful derivation and is useless). The set of ending units is defined as $E' = \{(a, a)\}$, and the set T' as $T' = \{(a^{i+1}, a^{j+1}) \mid (a^i, a^j) \in T\}$.

Now, for a successful derivation generating a non-empty word in S that starts with axiom u_0, assembles the units $u_1, u_2, \ldots, u_x$, and ends with the sole ending unit (λ, λ) there is a successful derivation in S' as follows. If u_0 does not contain an empty substring then the derivation starting with axiom $u_0' = u_0 \in A_0'$, assembling the units $u_1', u_2', \ldots, u_x'$, where $u_k' = (a^{i+1}, a^{j+1})$ if $u_i = (a^i, a^j)$, $1 \leq k \leq x$, and ending with $(a, a) \in E'$ generates the same word in S', and vice versa.

If u_0 contains one or two empty substrings then there is one unit or there are two units in the sequence such that the empty substring is or the empty substrings are extended, say there is one unit u_l. Now the derivation starting with the axiom that merges u_0 and u_l, assembling the units $u_1', u_2', \ldots, u_{l-1}', u_{l+1}', \ldots, u_x'$ and ending with $(a, a) \in E'$ generates the same word in S', and vice versa. So, we conclude that S and S' generate the same unary language. □

3.2   One-Set String Assembling Systems

The second restricted variant are so-called *one-set* string assembling systems, where the control mechanism derived from the fact that the units are arranged in the three sets of axioms, assembling units, and ending units is relaxed. So, in particular, a derivation can end at any point in a possibly infinite derivation. On the other hand, if there is no unit whose strings overlap with the last symbols of the current strands, then the derivation necessarily ends.

A string assembling system is said to be one set, if the sets A, T, and E are merged into one set $T \subset \Sigma^+ \times \Sigma^+$. Accordingly we write $S = \langle \Sigma, T \rangle$. The units are assembled according to the derivation relation $\Rightarrow$. Now every derivation that begins with a single unit from T and ends with both strands identical is *successful*, and the *language* $L(S)$ *generated* by S is as before defined to be the set $L(S) = \{w \in \Sigma^+ \mid (p, q) \Rightarrow^* (w, w) \text{ is a successful derivation}\}$.

Example 8. The language $L = \{a^m b^n \mid m + n \geq 2\}$ is generated by the one-set SAS $S = \langle \{a, b\}, T \rangle$, where the units are defined as follows.

1. $(aa, aa) \in T$ 2. $(ab, ab) \in T$ 3. $(bb, bb) \in T$ ∎

The next lemma is helpful for showing that certain languages cannot be generated by one-set SAS.

Lemma 9. *Let S be a one-set SAS with symbols from Σ, $w_1, w_2 \in \Sigma^*$, and $x \in \Sigma$. If $w_1 x$ and $x w_2$ are generated by S then $w_1 x w_2$ is generated by S as well.*

Theorem 10. *The family of languages generated by one-set SAS is strictly included in the family of languages generated by SAS.*

Proof. A one-set SAS $\langle \Sigma, T \rangle$ can directly be simulated by an SAS $\langle \Sigma, A, T, E \rangle$, where $A = T$ and $E = T$. Therefore, the family of languages generated by one-set SAS is included in the family of languages generated by SAS.

By Example 2 the language $L = \{a^m b^n a^\ell \mid m, n, \ell \geq 1\}$ is generated by some SAS. Assume that it is also generated by some one-set SAS. The words aba and $aaba$ do belong to L. So, Lemma 9 implies that $abaaba$ belongs to L as well, a contradiction.   □

In order to study the unary case we first utilize the fact that in one-set SAS there are no explicit ending units. This allows to characterize the unary one-set SAS languages. A unary language L is said to be *expanded* from language L_0 by $z \geq 1$ if $L = \{a^n \mid n = z \cdot m + 1, \text{ for } a^m \in L_0\}$.

The proof of the following proposition relies on a useful fact which is related to number theory and Frobenius numbers (see, for example, [12] for a survey).

Proposition 11. *Every unary language generated by a one-set SAS is either empty or $\{a\}$ or expanded from a cofinite language.*

The converse of Proposition 11 does not hold. For example, the language $\{a^n \mid n \in \{2,3\}$ or $n \geq 42\}$ cannot be generated by any one-set SAS but is expanded from the cofinite language $\{a^n \mid n \in \{1,2\}$ or $n \geq 41\}$ by $z = 1$.

Proposition 11 reveals that, for example, the finite singleton language $\{aa\}$ can not be generated by any one-set SAS. On the other hand they are able to generate infinite languages.

Corollary 12. *The family of finite languages and the family of languages generated by one-set SAS are incomparable.*

It turns out that the two possibilities to relax one of the two control mechanisms studied and to keep the other yields incomparable generative capacities.

Theorem 13. *The families of languages generated by free SAS and by one-set SAS are incomparable.*

Proof. By Proposition 11 the singleton language $\{aa\}$ can not be generated by any one-set SAS. On the other hand, it is generated by the free SAS

$$\langle\{a\}, \{(aa, aa)\}, \{(\lambda, \lambda)\}, \{(\lambda, \lambda)\}\rangle.$$

Conversely, Lemma 4 shows that the language

$$L_+ = \{a\}L_0^* \text{ with } L_0 = \{a^{n-1}b^n\$a^m \mid m, n \geq 1\}$$

cannot be generated by any free SAS. On the other hand, the SAS generating L_+ constructed in the proof of Theorem 5 is actually a one-set SAS. The axiom (a, a) can safely be removed since any successful derivation has to continue with unit (2) or unit (3). The ending unit (a, a) just terminates the derivation without extending the strands.   □

3.3   Pure String Assembling Systems

The last restriction considered in this section is a combination of the both restrictions studied above. For so-called *pure* string assembling systems neither the control mechanism derived from the fact that the assembled substrings have to overlap the last symbol of the current strand nor the mechanism derived from the fact that the units are arranged in the three sets of axioms, assembling units, and ending units is available.

A one-set SAS $S = \langle \Sigma, T \rangle$ is said to be pure if $T \subset \Sigma^* \times \Sigma^*$ and its units are assembled according to the derivation relation $\overset{f}{\Rightarrow}$.

Example 14. Let $S = \langle\{a, b, \bar{a}, \bar{b}\}, T\rangle$ be the pure SAS where the following units are defined for the homomorphism $h(a) = \bar{a}$ and $h(b) = \bar{b}$ and all $x \in \{a, b\}$.

1. $(x, \lambda) \in T$ 2. $(h(x), x) \in T$ 3. $(\lambda, h(x)) \in T$.

Since the context-free languages are closed under intersection with regular sets, and the intersection $L(S) \cap \{a, b\}^+ \{h(a), h(b)\}^+$ is the non-context-free language $\{wh(w) \mid w \in \{a, b\}^+\}$, the language $L(S)$ is not context free.

In order to generate words from $L(S) \cap \{a, b\}^+ \{h(a), h(b)\}^+$ the derivation has to start with units (1). After assembling repeatedly units (1), the only possibility to obtain a matching lower string is to continue with a unit (2). Since the word generated has to belong to the regular set $\{a, b\}^+ \{h(a), h(b)\}^+$, units (2) have to be assembled until strands of the form $(wh(w), w)$ are derived. Again, the only possibility to obtain a matching lower string is to continue with units (3) until a word of the desired form is derived. ∎

In general, we obtain the following property of pure SAS languages.

Proposition 15. *Every language L generated by a pure SAS is Kleene plus closed, that is, $L = L^+$.*

For unary languages, the difference between one-set SAS and pure SAS is subtle. Following [6] a unary language L is said to be *stretched* from language L_0 by $z \geq 1$ if $L = \{a^n \mid n = z \cdot m, \text{ for } a^m \in L_0\}$. So, the difference between the properties of being expanded and being stretched is the addition of one to the word lengths for expanded languages.

Proposition 16. *Every unary language generated by a pure SAS is either empty or a stretched cofinite language.*

As for Proposition 11, the converse of Proposition 16 does not hold.

Corollary 17. *The family of finite languages and the family of languages generated by pure SAS are incomparable.*

In particular, the subtle difference between being stretched or being expanded from a cofinite language makes both language families incomparable.

Theorem 18. *The families of languages generated by (unary) one-set SAS and (unary) pure SAS are incomparable.*

Proof. The unary language $L_e = \{a^n \mid n \geq 2 \text{ and } n \text{ even}\}$ is generated by the pure SAS $\langle \{a\}, \{(aa, aa)\} \rangle$. Assume L_e is generated by some one-set SAS S. Since a^{2x} and a^{2y} belong to L_e for some $x, y \geq 1$, the fact that S is one-set yields that $a^{2x+2y-1}$ is generated by S as well. But $a^{2x+2y-1}$ does not belong to L_e.

Conversely, the unary language $L_o = \{a^n \mid n \geq 3 \text{ and } n \text{ odd}\}$ is generated by the one-set SAS $\langle \{a\}, \{(aaa, aaa)\} \rangle$. Assume L_o is generated by some pure SAS S'. Since a^{2x+1} and a^{2y+1} belong to L_o for some $x, y \geq 1$, the fact that S' is pure yields that $a^{2x+2y+2}$ is generated by S' as well. But $a^{2x+2y+2}$ does not belong to L_o. □

On the other hand, the family of languages generated by pure SAS are strictly included in the family of languages generated by free SAS.

Theorem 19. *The family of languages generated by pure SAS is strictly included in the family of languages generated by free SAS.*

The relations between the variants of string assembling systems studied so far are summarized in Fig. 1. We conclude the section by the relations with the language families of the Chomsky hierarchy. While string assembling systems where the units are arranged in three sets, that is SAS and free SAS, can generate all finite languages by using corresponding axioms and a trivial ending unit, the absence of this control mechanism yields incomparability with the family of finite languages (see Corollaries 12 and 17).

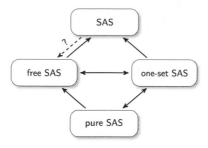

Fig. 1. Inclusion structure of the language families. A single arrow means strict inclusion, a double arrow means incomparability, and the dashed line together with the adjacent solid line indicates the open problem whether there is a strict inclusion or incomparability.

Proposition 20. *The families of languages generated by SAS, free SAS, one-set SAS, and pure SAS are incomparable with the families of regular and (deterministic) (linear) context-free languages.*

Proof. The unary regular language $\{a\} \cup \{a^{2n} \mid n \geq 2\}$ is not generated by any SAS [4]. So, from the results above we conclude that it is not generated by any of the three remaining variants of SAS.

On the other hand, non-context-free languages generated by SAS, free SAS, and pure SAS are given in Examples 1, 3, and 14. A slight modification of the construction of Example 14 shows that one-set SAS can generate non-context-free languages as well. □

A result in [4] reveals that any unary language generated by some SAS is semilinear and, thus, regular. So, in the unary case the families of languages generated by SAS, free SAS, one-set SAS, and pure SAS are strict subsets of the regular languages.

Another result in [4] shows the strict inclusion of the family of languages generated by SAS in the complexity class NL. Since, in turn, NL is strictly included in $\text{NSPACE}(n)$ (see, for example, [8]), which is equal to the family of context-sensitive languages, we obtain the following corollary.

Corollary 21. *The families of languages generated by SAS, free SAS, one-set SAS, and pure SAS are strictly included in* NL *and, thus, in the family of context-sensitive languages.*

4 Length-Restricted SAS

In this section we turn to a structural limitation of string assembling systems. Since the length difference of the subwords in units can be seen as a very basic kind of memory, we consider SAS where the length of the subwords in units are restricted.

Now we turn to SAS where the lengths of the subwords in units is limited by a constant and explore the generative capacity gained in the lengths of the subwords.

Let $k \geq 1$ be an integer. An SAS $S = \langle \Sigma, A, T, E \rangle$ is said to be k-*length-restricted*, if $|u|, |v| \leq k$ for each unit $(u, v) \in A \cup T \cup E$.

First we consider unary languages and assume that the words are ordered according to their lengths. The question is, how large can the gaps between two consecutive words be if the language is generated by some k-length-restricted SAS. The following example gives a quadratic lower bound.

Example 22. Let $k \geq 1$ be an integer. The language $L_k = a(a^{(k-1)^2})^*$ is generated by the k-length-restricted string assembling system $S = \langle \{a\}, A, T, E \rangle$ with the following units.

1. $(a, a) \in A$ 2. $(a^k, a) \in T$ 3. $(a^2, a^k) \in T$ 4. $(a, a) \in E$

Assembling the sole axiom and the sole ending unit results in the word a. So, the assembling of units from T has to result in equally long upper and lower strands. The length difference between upper and lower substring is $k - 1$ in unit (2) and $k - 2$ in unit (3). Since for $k \geq 3$ the numbers $k - 1$ and $k - 2$ are relatively prime, each $k - 1$ units (3) and $k - 2$ units (2) have to be assembled in order to obtain equally long upper and lower strands. Assembling $k - 1$ units (3) extends the upper strand by $k - 1$ and the lower strand by $(k-1)(k-1)$ symbols. Assembling $k - 2$ units (2) extends the upper strand by $(k - 2)(k - 1)$ and the lower strand by 0 symbols. So, the current strands can be extended by blocks of length $(k - 1) + (k - 2)(k - 1)$ or equivalently $(k - 1)(k - 1)$. Adding the initial symbol a shows that S generates L_k, for $k \geq 3$. For $k = 1$, unit (2) does not extend the current strands and, thus, unit (3) cannot contribute to a successful derivation. Therefore, the initial word a is the only one that can be derived. Since $L_1 = \{a\}$, the SAS S generates L_k for $k = 1$ as well. Finally, if $k = 2$ then unit (3) extends the current strands by 1, which shows that $a^+ = L_2$ is generated. ∎

The next lemma shows that the lower bound for the gaps presented in Example 22 is tight.

Lemma 23. *Let $k \geq 1$ and L be a unary language generated by some k-length-restricted SAS. Assume the words of L are ordered according to their lengths. Then the length difference between two consecutive words is at most $(k-1)^2$.*

The previous Lemma and Example 22 yield an infinite and tight hierarchy dependent on the length restrictions.

Theorem 24. *Let $k \geq 1$ be an integer. The family of languages generated by k-length-restricted string assembling systems is strictly included in the family of languages generated by $(k+1)$-length-restricted string assembling systems.*

Proof. By definition a k-length-restricted SAS is a $(k+1)$-length-restricted SAS. Thus it remains to be shown that the inclusion is strict.

Example 22 shows that the language $L_{k+1} = a(a^{(k)^2})^*$ is generated by a $(k+1)$-length-restricted SAS. But by Lemma 23 it can not be generated by any k-length-restricted SAS. □

References

1. Bordihn, H., Kutrib, M., Wendlandt, M.: Nonterminal controlled string assembling systems. J. Autom. Lang. Comb. **19**, 33–44 (2014)
2. Freund, R., Păun, G., Rozenberg, G., Salomaa, A.: Bidirectional sticker systems. In: Pacific Symposium on Biocomputing (PSB 1998), pp. 535–546. World Scientific, Singapore (1998)
3. Kari, L., Păun, G., Rozenberg, G., Salomaa, A., Yu, S.: DNA computing, sticker systems, and universality. Acta Inform. **35**, 401–420 (1998)
4. Kutrib, M., Wendlandt, M.: String assembling systems. RAIRO Inform. Théor. **46**, 593–613 (2012)
5. Kutrib, M., Wendlandt, M.: Bidirectional string assembling systems. RAIRO Inform. Théor. **48**, 39–59 (2014)
6. Kutrib, M., Wendlandt, M.: Expressive capacity of subregular expressions. In: Bordihn, H., Freund, R., Nagy, B., Vaszil, G. (eds.) Non-Classical Models of Automata and Applications (NCMA 2016), books@ocg.at, vol. 321, pp. 227–242. Austrian Computer Society (2016).
7. Moore, G.E.: Cramming more components onto integrated circuits. Electronics **38**, 114–117 (1965)
8. Papadimitriou, C.H.: Computational Complexity. Addison-Wesley, Reading (1994)
9. Păun, G., Rozenberg, G.: Sticker systems. Theoret. Comput. Sci. **204**, 183–203 (1998)
10. Păun, G., Rozenberg, G., Salomaa, A.: DNA Computing: New Computing Paradigms. Texts in Theoretical Computer Science. Springer, Heidelberg (1998). https://doi.org/10.1007/978-3-662-03563-4
11. Rozenberg, G., Salomaa, A.: The Mathematical Theory of L Systems. Academic Press, New York (1980)
12. Shallit, J.: The Frobenius problem and its generalizations. In: Ito, M., Toyama, M. (eds.) DLT 2008. LNCS, vol. 5257, pp. 72–83. Springer, Heidelberg (2008). https://doi.org/10.1007/978-3-540-85780-8_5

Two Routes to Automata Minimization and the Ways to Reach It Efficiently

Sylvain Lombardy[1][(✉)] and Jacques Sakarovitch[2]

[1] LaBRI - UMR 5800 - Bordeaux INP - Bordeaux University - CNRS,
Bordeaux, France
Sylvain.Lombardy@labri.fr
[2] IRIF - UMR 8243 - CNRS/Paris Diderot University and Telecom ParisTech,
Paris, France

Abstract. This paper reports on the work done for the implementation of the algorithms for the computation of the minimal quotient of an automaton in the AWALI platform. In the case of non-deterministic or of weighted automata, the minimal quotient of an automaton is obtained by merging all states *in bisimulation*. Two strategies are explored for the computation of the coarsest bisimulation equivalence. The first one is an extension of the Moore algorithm for the computation of the minimal quotient of a DFA; the second one is inspired by the Hopcroft algorithm for the same problem. These two strategies yield algorithms with the same quadratic complexity and we study the cases where the second strategy can be improved in order to achieve a complexity similar to the one of Hopcroft algorithm.

1 Introduction

This paper reports on the work done for the implementation of the algorithms for the computation of the minimal quotient of an automaton in the AWALI platform [12]. It amounts to a thorough analysis of procedures that perform an iterative partition refinement and the ways to implement them.

The *existence* of a minimal deterministic finite automaton, canonically associated with every regular language is one of the basic and fundamental results in the theory of finite automata [7]. The problem of the *computation* of this minimal (deterministic) automaton has given rise to an extensive literature, due to the importance of the problem, from both a theoretical and practical point of view. A rich account of it is to be found in the chapter written by Jean Berstel and his colleagues for the yet unpublished *Handbook on Automata* [3].

In contrast, the problem of the definition and the computation of the minimal quotient of nondeterministic Boolean, or of weighted, automata is much less documented. It can be nevertheless considered as folklore or common knowledge that such a minimal quotient is obtained by merging states that are *in bisimulation* and that, exactly as in the case of deterministic Boolan automata, the coarsest bisimulation relation is obtained by partition refinements.

© Springer International Publishing AG, part of Springer Nature 2018
C. Câmpeanu (Ed.): CIAA 2018, LNCS 10977, pp. 248–260, 2018.
https://doi.org/10.1007/978-3-319-94812-6_21

An algorithm for computing the coarsest bisimulation relation then goes as follows: at a given step of the procedure, a partition $\mathcal{P}$ of the state set Q of an automaton, and a class I of $\mathcal{P}$ are considered. Then there are two possible strategies for determining a refinement of $\mathcal{P}$. In the first one, the class I itself is split, by considering the labels of the *outgoing transitions* from the different states in I. This is an extension of the Moore algorithm for the computation of the minimal quotient of a deterministic automaton and we call it the 'Forward Algorithm'. The second policy is an adaptation of the algorithm due to Hopcroft for the same problem. The class I determines the splitting of classes that contain the origins of the transitions incoming to the states of I and we call it the 'Backward Algorithm'.

Although the two strategies yield distinct orderings in the splitting of classes, the two algorithms have many similarities that we describe in this paper. Not only do they have the same time complexity, in $O(nm)$, where n is the number of states of the automaton and m its number of transitions, but the criterium for distinguishing states — the splitting process — is based on the same state function that we call *signature*. And in both cases, achieving the above mentioned complexity implies that signatures are managed through the same efficient data structure that implements a *weak sort*.

It is also well-known that the Hopcroft algorithm achieves a better time complexity than the Moore algorithm, in $O(n \log n)$. Our analysis allows to describe a condition — which we call *simplifiable signatures* — under which an analogous handling of the partition refinement yields a time complexity in $O(m \log n)$ (in complete DFAs, $m = \alpha n$, where α is the size of the alphabet).

The paper is organized as follows: after a few words on the implementation of automata at Sect. 2, we recall at Sect. 3 the definition and the characterization of the minimal quotient of a finite automaton, in full generality, nondeterministic Boolean automata, or weighted automata. At Sect. 4, we describe a general procedure for the partition refinement, the signature, and the way to implement weak sort. Sect. 5 details the *Forward Algorithm* and its complexity, Sect. 6 the *Backward Algorithm* and its complexity. Some experiments presented at Sect. 8 show that the algorithms behave with their theoretical complexity. Some more experiments, and the detailed algorithms are given in the appendix for sake of completeness.

2   Implementation of Weighted Automata

In this paper, we deal with (finite) automata over a free monoid A^* with weight in a semiring $\mathbb{K}$, also called $\mathbb{K}$-automata. Classical automata are $\mathbb{B}$-automata where $\mathbb{B}$ is the Boolean semiring.

Indeed, all what follows will apply as well to automata over a monoid M which is non necessarily free, for instance to transducers that are automata over $A^* \times B^*$. Such automata are considered as automata over a free monoid C^*, where C is the set of labels on the transitions of the automaton. Remark that there exists no theory of quotient that takes into account non trivial relations between labels.

We essentially follow the definitions and notation of [10]. The model of weighted automaton used in this paper is more restricted though, for both theoretical and computational efficiency. An automaton $\mathcal{A}$ is a directed graph whose *transitions* are labelled by a letter in A and a weight in $\mathbb{K}$, together with an *initial function* and a *final function*. The states in the support of the initial function are called initial states, those in the support of the final function are called final states. Figure 1(a) shows such an automaton $\mathcal{A}_1$.

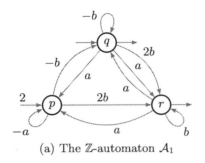

$\rightarrow$	p	q	r	t
i	$2\$$	$\$$		
p	$-a$	$-b$	$2b$	
q	a	$-b$	$a+2b$	$\$$
r	a	a	b	$\$$

(a) The $\mathbb{Z}$-automaton $\mathcal{A}_1$ (b) The incidence matrix of $\mathcal{A}_{1\,\$}$

Fig. 1. Two representations of the same automaton

An automaton $\mathcal{A}$ with set of states Q is denoted by a triple $\mathcal{A} = \langle\, I, E, T \,\rangle$ where I and T are vectors of dimension Q that denote the initial function and the final functions and E is the incidence matrix of the graph, that is, a $Q \times Q$-matrix whose (p,q) entry is the sum of the weighted labels of the transitions from p to q. We say that Q is the *dimension* of $\mathcal{A}$ and we denote by $E(p,a,q)$ the weight of the transition labeled by a that go form p to q.

In order to deal computationally in the same way with the initial and final functions and with the transitions, it is convenient to consider that the alphabet A is equipped with a *supplementary letter* $\$$, which will be used as a left and right marker, and that A is equiped with two *supplementary states* i and t and with transitions that go from i to every initial state p with label $\$$ and with weight I_p and transitions that go from every final state q to t with label $\$$ and with weight T_q. We write $A_\$$ for $A_\$ = A \cup \{\$\}$ and $\mathcal{A}_\$$ for this augmented automaton over $A_\$^*$. Finally, the only initial state of $\mathcal{A}_\$$ is i, with weight $1_\mathbb{K}$, and its only final state is t, also with weight $1_\mathbb{K}$.

If w is in A^*, there is a 1–1 correspondence between the successful computations with label w in $\mathcal{A}$ and the computations with label $\$w\$$ in $\mathcal{A}_\$$, hence they are given the same weight by the two automata.

Example 1. The incidence matrix of the $\mathbb{Z}$-automaton $\mathcal{A}_{1\,\$}$ is shown on Fig. 1(b). It is interpreted as follows. For instance, on line q and column r, $2b$ means that there is a transition from q to r with label b and weight 2, hence, if E_1 is the transition function of $\mathcal{A}_{1\,\$}$, $E_1(q,b,r) = 2$; likewise, $E_1(q,a,r) = 1$; in contrast, there is no transition from r to q with label b: $E_1(r,b,q) = 0$. There is no column i

nor row t in the table for there is no transitions incoming to i nor transitions outgoing from t.

We write $\mathcal{A}_\$ = \langle Q, i, E_\$, t \rangle$ if $\mathcal{A} = \langle I, E, T \rangle$ is a $\mathbb{K}$-automaton of dimension Q, and more often, simply $\mathcal{A} = \langle Q, i, E, t \rangle$ when it is clear by the context that we deal with an augmented automaton.

3   The Minimal Quotient of a (Weighted) Automaton

A $\mathbb{K}$-automaton $\mathcal{B} = \langle J, F, U \rangle$ is a *quotient* of a $\mathbb{K}$-automaton $\mathcal{A} = \langle I, E, T \rangle$ if there exists a surjective map $\varphi \colon Q \to R$ which is a *morphism*. In [10] or [2], we have defined mophisms — *Out-morphisms* to be more precise — via the notion of *conjugacy* of ($\mathbb{K}$-)automata. What makes a map φ an Out-morphism are conditions on the *map equivalence* of φ which we can take as *definition* of an Out-morphism. We first take some definitions and notation to deal with equivalences. An *equivalence* on a set Q is a *partition* of Q, that is, a set of disjoint nonempty subsets of Q, called *classes*, whose union is equal to Q. If $\mathcal{P}$ is an equivalence on Q, for every pair (p, q) of elements of Q, we denote $p \, \mathcal{P} \, q$ if and only if there exists a class C in $\mathcal{P}$ such that both p and q belong to C.

Definition 1. *Let $\mathcal{A} = \langle Q, i, E, t \rangle$ be a $\mathbb{K}$-automaton. An equivalence $\mathcal{P}$ on Q is an Out-morphism, also called* congruence on $\mathcal{A}$, *if:*

$$\{i\} \in \mathcal{P}, \qquad \{t\} \in \mathcal{P}, \qquad and \qquad (1)$$

$$\forall p, q \quad p \, \mathcal{P} \, q \quad \Longrightarrow \quad \forall a \in A_\$, \forall C \in \mathcal{P} \quad \sum_{r \in C} E(p, a, r) = \sum_{r \in C} E(q, a, r). \quad (2)$$

It is a classical result that two states p and q in the same class of a congruence are in *bisimulation*: for every word w, the $\mathbb{K}$-automaton behaves identically when it reads w from state p or from state q.

If $\mathcal{P}$ is a congruence, then equivalent states can be merged and this merging defines the quotient automaton $\mathcal{A}_\mathcal{P} = \langle \mathcal{P}, i, E_\mathcal{P}, t \rangle$ where $E_\mathcal{P}$ is defined by:

$$\forall C, D \in \mathcal{P}, \, \forall a \in A_\$, \, \forall p \in C \qquad E_\mathcal{P}(C, a, D) = \sum_{q \in D} E(p, a, q). \quad (3)$$

It follows from (2) that the sum in (3) is independent from the choice of p in C and from Definition 1 that $\mathcal{A}_\mathcal{P}$ is equivalent to $\mathcal{A}$.

An equivalence $\mathcal{R}$ is *coarser* than an equivalence $\mathcal{P}$ if, for every C in $\mathcal{P}$, there exists D in $\mathcal{R}$ such that $C \subseteq D$. The equivalences on a set Q, ordered by this inclusion relation, form a lattice, with the identity — where every class is a singleton — at the top and the universal relation — with only one class that contains all elements of Q — at the bottom.

The *proof of the existence* of a coarsest congruence goes downward, so to speak, whereas the *computation* of the coarsest congruence goes upward.

Proposition 1. *Every automaton $\mathcal{A}$ admits a unique coarsest congruence.*

The coarsest congruence is an extension of the Myhill-Nerode equivalence.

Definition 2. *The quotient of a $\mathbb{K}$-automaton $\mathcal{A}$ by its coarsest congruence is the* minimal quotient *of $\mathcal{A}$.*

The minimal quotient of $\mathcal{A}$ is not necessary the smallest $\mathbb{K}$-automaton equivalent to $\mathcal{A}$ nor a canonical automaton associated with the series realized by $\mathcal{A}$.

4   The Common Trunk

Both Forward and Backward algorithms that compute partition refinements are instantiation of a common general procedure, which we call a *proto-algorithm*. For efficiency, both algorithms use *weak sort*, which is a method to gather similar values in linear time.

4.1   The Proto-Algorithm

The computation of the coarsest congruence of an automaton $\mathcal{A} = \langle Q, i, E, t \rangle$ *goes upward.* It starts with $\mathcal{P}_0 = \{\{i\}, Q, \{t\}\}$, the coarsest possible equivalence. Every step of the algorithm splits some classes of the current partition, yielding an equivalence which is *higher* in the lattice of equivalences of $Q \cup \{i, t\}$.

In order to split classes, we use a criterion on states of $\mathcal{A}$, which we call *signature*, and which, given a partition, tells if two states in a same class should be separated in a congruence of $\mathcal{A}$. It has been used in [1] for the minimization of *incomplete* DFAs, the 'first' example for which the classical minimization algorithms for complete DFA have to be adapted.

Definition 3. *The* signature *of a state p of a $\mathbb{K}$-automaton $\mathcal{A} = \langle Q, i, E, t \rangle$ with respect to a subset D of Q is the map from $A_\$$ to $\mathbb{K}$, defined by:*

$$sig[p, D](a) = \sum_{q \in D} E(p, a, q).$$

It follows from (2) that a partition $\mathcal{P}$ is a congruence if and only if

$$\forall C \in \mathcal{P}, \ \forall p, q \in C, \ \forall D \in \mathcal{P} \qquad sig[p, D] = sig[q, D].$$

Thus $\mathcal{P}$ is a congruence if and only if, for every pair (C, D) of classes of $\mathcal{P}$, all states p in C have the same signature with respect to D. A pair (C, D) for which this property is not satisfied is called a *splitting pair*. The equivalence on C induced by the signature with respect to D, called *the split of C by D* and denoted by $split[C, D]$, can be computed:

$$\forall p, q \in C \qquad split[C, D](p) = split[C, D](q) \quad \Longleftrightarrow \quad sig[p, D] = sig[q, D].$$

The split of the class C by the class D of $\mathcal{P}$ leads to a new equivalence on Q: $\mathcal{P} \wedge split[C, D]$, and the proto-algorithm runs as follows:

$\mathcal{P} := \mathcal{P}_0$
while there exists a splitting pair (C, D) in $\mathcal{P}$
    $\mathcal{P} := \mathcal{P} \wedge split[C, D]$

When there are no more splitting pairs, the current equivalence is a congruence; it is an invariant of the algorithm that the current equivalence is coarser than any congruence, hence the final equivalence is the coarsest congruence.

This procedure is not a true algorithm, in particular, it does not tell how to find a splitting pair, nor how to implement *split* to make it efficient. The main difference between Forward and Backward algorithms is the classes partition $\mathcal{P}$ they split when then iterate over the classes of that partition:

- the Forward Algorithm iterates over classes C and computes how C can be split with respect to the signatures of its states, that is, with respect to the classes that can be reached by transitions *outgoing from states of C*.
- the Backward Algorithm iterates over classes D and computes which classes are split with respect to D, that is, classes that contain states that are the origin of transitions *incoming to states in D*.

4.2   The Weak Sort

A key to efficient implementation is avoiding to sort letters or states, as every sort would have a logarithmic overhead on top of the cost of other operations. Nevertheless, the computation of signatures requires that the transitions arriving in the same class are gathered. Moreover, comparing signatures of states (implemented as lists) in linear time requires that the signatures are described by the same lists. This is allowed by the *weak sort* introduced in [8].

Let f be a function from a set X to a set Y. We say that a *list* of elements of X are *weakly sorted* (with respect to f) if the elements with the same image by f are *contiguous*. An algorithm that weakly sorts elements of X readily improves to directly return classes of equivalent elements (under the map equivalence of f).

Both Forward and Backward algorithms are based on a weak sort of signature lists. In a first step, and for every state, transitions outgoing from that state with the same label and destinations in the same class must be gathered. Moreover, for two states with the same signature, the list of pairs (label, weight) that form the signature must appear in the same ordering, in such a way the equality test is made efficient. In a second step, the weak sort is used to gather states with the same signature and to form the new classes.

A *bucket sort algorithm* realizes a weak sort with linear complexity. Once the values in Y are coded by integers, an 'enhanced' array indexed by integers can be used: for every n, a pointer to the sublist of elements with value n is stored in the array element of index n. The size of the array hence depends on the maximal value of $f(X)$. Under the assumption that memory allocation without initialization can be made with constant complexity, *sparse lists* allow to implement the weak sort in linear time. However, *hash maps* are more suitable than sparse lists to deal with the blowing up of memory due to this maximal value. Since we need to efficiently iterate over the elements of $f(X)$, we use *linked hash maps*, that is, hash maps where keys are stored in a linked list.

5   Forward Algorithm

The Forward Algorithm is an extension of the Moore algorithm for the minimization of DFAs. At each iteration, a class C is considered; the global signature of all states p in C is computed and C is split accordingly. The *global signature* of a state p is the aggregation of all signatures of p:

$$GSig[p](a) = \bigcup_{D \text{ class of } \varphi, \, sig[p,D](a) \neq 0_\mathbb{X}} (sig[p, D](a), D).$$

In this algorithm, a partition is an array *class* of lists of states, so a class is an index in this array. A queue contains all classes that can potentially be split.

The signature $GSig[p]$ of p in the current class C is a list of triples (a, k, D); such a triple means that the sum of the weights of all transitions with label a that go from p to some state in D is equal to k. This signature is weakly sorted: if the signatures of two states contain the same set of triples, the triples appear in the same ordering. The computation of $GSig[p]$ requires two steps.

First, for every state p and for every transition $p \xrightarrow{a|k} q$, the pair (p, k) is inserted in a list *meet[a,D]*, where D is the class of q. This insertion is special in the case where *meet[a,D]* is not empty and its last element is a pair (p', k') with $p' = p$: k' is then updated to $k' + k$; if $k' + k$ is zero, the pair is removed from the list. The second step iterates over the keys of *meet*, and for every (p, k) in *meet[a,D]*, inserts (a, k, D) into *GSig[p]*.

The split of a class with respect to a signature is a weak sort. At each round, the states in the same subclass with a signature that begins with the same triple are gathered and this triple is removed from the signature.

When the class with index C is split, the first subclass inherits the index, the other ones are indexed with fresh integers. Singletons are not inserted in the queue (they can not be split).

Example 2. On the automaton $\mathcal{A}_1$, the equivalence is initialized with $D_0 = \{i\}$, $D_1 = \{t\}$, $D_2 = \{p, q, r\}$. Class D_2 is put in the queue (the other classes are singletons and cannot be split). The signature of states in D_2 is computed as follows. For every state of D_2, every outgoing transition is considered to fill the *meet* table, then the *GSig* table is filed based on the *meet* table.

$$
\begin{aligned}
meet : \; &a, D_2 \mapsto (p, -1)(q, 2)(r, 2) \qquad GSig : p \mapsto (a, -1, D_2)(b, 1, D_2) \\
&b, D_2 \mapsto (p, 1)(q, 1)(r, 1) \qquad\qquad\quad q \mapsto (a, 2, D_2)(b, 1, D_2)(\$, 1, D_1) \\
&\$, D_1 \mapsto (q, 1)(r, 1) \qquad\qquad\qquad\;\; r \mapsto (a, 2, D_2)(b, 1, D_2)(\$, 1, D_1)
\end{aligned}
$$

State p differs from q and r on the first triple of the signature; hence p is separated from q and r; q and r coincide on the second and the third triple, thus they stay in the same class. The class D_2 is then split and the new partition is $\{\{i\}, \{t\}, \{p\}, \{q, r\}\}$. The new class which is not a singleton is put in the queue.

Building the new classes from the signature can be computed in linear time in the size of the signature (that is the number of triples which appear in the signatures of all the states of the current part), which is at most as large as the number of transitions outgoing from states of the current class.

If a class is not split, it must be reinserted in the queue because it may be split later if a class which contains some successors is split. To ensure termination of the algorithm, some *rounds* are defined. A round ends when all classes that were in the queue at the beginning of the round have been dequeued. If no split has occurred during the round, the algorithm has actually checked that the current equivalence is a congruence and stops; otherwise, a new round begins.

Complexity. The evaluation of the complexity is made under the assumption that operations in the semiring (addition, comparison to 0) can be performed in constant time and that there exists a constant time hash function on the semiring in order to weakly sort states with respect to their signatures. If these conditions are not met, a more refined evaluation should be made.

For every class C, the computation of *GSig[p]* for all states in C is in $O(|C| + m_C)$, where $|C|$ is the number of states in C and m_C is the maximal number of transitions outgoing from a state of this class. The total number of triples in the signature is at most m_C.

The complexity of the computation of the new classes is in $O(|C| + m_C)$, as well as the insertion of classes in the queue. Moreover, at the beginning of each round, the queue contains a subset of a partition of Q, hence, the global cost of the computation of *GSig* and class splitting is in $O(n + m)$ at each round, where n is the number of states of the automaton and m is the number of transitions. At each round (except the last one), the partition is refined. It can only be refined at most n times, hence the following statement.

Theorem 1. *The Forward Algorithm computes the minimal quotient of a $\mathbb{K}$-automaton with n states and m transitions in time $O(n(m + n))$.*

6   Backward Algorithm

The Backward Algorithm is inspired by the Hopcroft algorithm for the minimization of DFAs. At each iteration, a class D is considered and for every predecessor p of some state of D, $sig[p, D]$ is computed; then all the classes containing some predecessors of D are split according to the computed signatures.

The computation of $sig[p, D]$ is similar to the computation of the signature in the Forward Algorithm. For each q in D, for every transition $p \xrightarrow{a|k} q$, (p, k) is inserted in a list $meet[a]$. Then, for every key a of $meet$, for every (p, k) in $meet[a]$, (a, k) is inserted in $sigD[p]$ with the same special insertion used in the Forward Algorithm.

Example 3. On the automaton $\mathcal{A}_1$, the equivalence is initialized with $D_0 = \{i\}$, $D_1 = \{t\}$, $D_2 = \{p, q, r\}$. Classes D_1 and D_2 are put in the queue (i has no predecessor, thus D_0 can not split any class). Assume that D_2 is considered first. The signature of predecessors of states in D_2 is computed as follows. For every state of D_2, every incoming transition is considered to fill the $meet$ table, then the $sigD$ table is filled, based on the $meet$ table.

$$meet : \$ \mapsto (i, 2)(i, 1) \qquad\qquad sigD : i \mapsto (\$, 3)$$
$$a \mapsto (p, -1)(q, 1)(r, 1)(r, 1)(q, 1) \qquad p \mapsto (a, -1)(b, 1)$$
$$b \mapsto (p, -1)(q, -1)(p, 2)(q, 2)(r, 1) \qquad q \mapsto (a, 2)(b, 1)$$
$$r \mapsto (a, 2)(b, 1)$$

In fact, i is not considered since D_0 is a singleton. State p differs from q and r on the first pair of the signature; hence p is separated from q and r; q and r also coincide on the second pair, thus they stay in the same class. Class D_2 is then broken and the new partition is $\{\{i\}, \{t\}, \{p\}, \{q, r\}\}$. The new classes are put in the queue.

The computation of the new classes requires some care in order to keep it linear in the number of the incoming transitions on the splitting part, and not in the sum of the sizes of the split parts (which may be larger). In particular, each class is implemented as a list, and the location of a state in the class is recorded in an array in order to remove a state from a class in constant time. And when a class C is split with respect to a class D, if there are states in C which are not predecessors of D, all the predecessors of D are removed from C to form new classes. The cost of this operation is independant from the size of C.

After considering class D as splitter, D is not reinserted in the queue. Classes are inserted in the queue only when they are split (and when their identifier is not already in the queue).

Complexity. The computation of $sigD$ is in $O(|D| + m'_D)$, where m'_D is the number of transitions incoming to states of D. The total number of triples in the signature is at most m'_D. The complexity of gathering states with the same signature is in $O(m'_D)$, as well as the creation of new classes and the insertion of these classes in the queue.

If in the course of the computation, a state p belongs to a class D_1 and then to a class D_2, then D_2 derives from a split of D_1. Hence, any state p appears at most n times in $class[D]$ along all iterations, and it holds:

Theorem 2. *The Backward Algorithm computes the minimal quotient of a $\mathbb{K}$-automaton with n states and m transitions in time $\mathrm{O}(n(m+n))$.*

7   The Fast Backward Algorithm

Hopcroft's algorithm can be seen as an improvement of the Backward Algorithm for complete DFA. Its time complexity is $\mathrm{O}(\alpha n \log n)$ (*cf.* for instance [4,6]), where α is the size of the alphabet (for complete DFA, $m = \alpha n$); this algorithm has been extended to incomplete DFA [1,11] with complexity $\mathrm{O}(m \log n)$.

The strategy: "All but the largest", introduced in [9], can be applied to improve the Backward Algorithm in some cases that we now study.

The signatures are equipped with the pointwise addition: for every a in $A_{\$}$, $\big(sig[p, D] + sig[p, D'] \big)(a) = sig[p, D](a) + sig[p, D'](a)$, and if D is a subset of Q and ψ a partition of D, then it holds:

$$sig[p, D] = \sum_{D' \text{ class of } \psi} sig[p, D'].$$

We say that an automaton has *simplifiable signatures* if, for every subset D and every C subset of D, and for every pair of states p, q, it holds

$$sig[p, D] = sig[q, D] \ \text{ and } \ sig[p, C] = sig[q, C] \implies sig[p, D \setminus C] = sig[q, D \setminus C].$$

If the additive monoid $(\mathbb{K}, +)$ is a cancellative monoid, that is, for every a, b, and c in $\mathbb{K}$, $a + b = a + c$ implies $b = c$, then every $\mathbb{K}$-automaton has simplifiable signatures. This is in particular the case when $\mathbb{K}$ is a ring.

For other weight semirings, the simplifiability of signatures depends on the automaton. If $\mathcal{A}$ is a deterministic[1] $\mathbb{K}$-automaton, that is, if for every state p and every letter a, there is at most one transition outgoing from p with label a, then the signatures are simplifiable, independantly of $\mathbb{K}$, since it holds:

$$\forall p \in Q, \ \forall a \in A_{\$} \quad sig[p, D \setminus C](a) = \begin{cases} sig[p, D](a) & \text{if } sig[p, C](a) = 0_{\mathbb{K}}, \\ 0_{\mathbb{K}} & \text{otherwise.} \end{cases}$$

Example 4. Assume $\mathbb{K}$ is the Boolean semiring. Let $\mathcal{A}_2$ be the NFA of Fig. 2. It holds:

$$sig[p, \{r, s\}](a) = 1 \qquad sig[q, \{r, s\}](a) = 1$$
$$sig[p, \{s\}](a) = 1 \qquad sig[q, \{s\}](a) = 1$$
$$sig[p, \{r\}](a) = 1 \qquad sig[q, \{r\}](a) = 0.$$

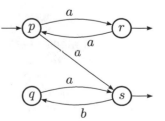

Fig. 2. The NFA $\mathcal{A}_2$

---

[1] Called *sequential* in [10].

Hence, $\mathcal{A}_2$ has not simplifiable signatures.

Let $\mathcal{A}$ be an automaton with simplifiable signatures. In this case, the algorithm can be modified in the following way: for every class C which is split with respect to a partition ψ, if C is not already in the queue, all the classes in ψ except one of the largest are put in the queue.

Actually, since C is not in the queue, the splitting of classes with respect to C has already be considered: for every D in the current partition, $sig[p, C]$ is the same for all p in D. Let C_1 be some subclass of C; if (D, C_1) is a splitting pair for some class D, then, since signatures are simplifiable, there exists some other class C_2 in ψ such that (D, C_2) is also a splitting pair.

Let $c(k)$ be the maximal number of times that a state p which belongs to a class D of size k that is removed from the queue will appear again in classes removed from the queue. A class D' containing p will be inserted only if D' results from a split of D. If D is split into r subclasses, since one of the largest class is not inserted, the size of D' is at most $(k-r+2)/2$ (if all the other classes but the largest have size 1). Finally $c(k) \leqslant 1 + c(k/2)$, and, since a singleton class will not be split, $c(1) = 0$; therefore $c(k)$ is in $\mathrm{O}(\log k)$. Thus, the complexity of the algorithm is in $\mathrm{O}((m + n) \log n)$ which is the complexity of the Hopcroft algorithm.

Theorem 3. *If $\mathcal{A}$ is a $\mathbb{K}$-automaton with simplifiable signatures, the Fast Backward algorithm computes the minimal quotient of $\mathcal{A}$ in time $\mathrm{O}((m + n) \log n)$.*

If the signatures of $\mathcal{A}$ are not simplifiable, for instance for NFA or automata over a $(\min, +)$-semiring, the Backward Algorithm cannot be improved in this way, and it is an open problem to know whether there exists an algorithm in $\mathrm{O}(m \log n)$.

8   Benchmarks

The Forward, Backward and Fast Backward algorithms are implemented in the AWALI library [12]. We present here a few benchmarks to compare their respective performances and to check that their execution time is consistent with their asserted complexity. Benchmarks have been run on an iMac Intel Core i5 3,4GHz, compiled with Clang 9.0.0.

The first family of automata is an adaptation of a family used in [5] to show that the Hopcroft algorithm requires $\Theta(n \log n)$ operations.

Let φ be the morphism defined on $\{a, b\}^*$ by $\varphi(a) = a\,b$ and $\varphi(b) = a$; for instance $\varphi(a\,b\,a\,a\,b) = a\,b\,a\,a\,b\,a\,b\,a$. The k-th Fibonacci word is $\varphi^k(a)$; its length is equal to the k-th Fibonacci number F_k, hence it is in $\Theta\!\left(\left(\frac{1+\sqrt{5}}{2}\right)^k\right)$. Let $\mathcal{F}_k$ be the automaton with one initial state and a simple circuit around this initial state with label $\varphi^k(a)$ (all states are final).

We observe on the benchmarks of Table 1 that the running time of the Forward Algorithm is quadratic, while the running time of both the Backward and the Fast Backward algorithms are in $\Theta(k\,F_k)$ (*i.e.* $\Theta(F_k \log F_k)$), where F_k is the number of states).

Table 1. Minimization of $\mathcal{F}_k$

	k	14	17	20	23	26	30
	F_k	987	4181	17711	75025	317811	2178309
Forward	t (s)	0.42	7.37	139	-		
	$10^{-7}t/F_k^2$	4.3	4.2	4.4			
Backward	t (s)	0.010	0.045	0.257	1.36	73	257
	$10^{-7}t/kF_k$	7.2	6.3	7.3	7.6	6.7	7.5
Fast	t (s)	0.006	0.025	0.140	0.70	41	139
Backward	$10^{-7}t/kF_k$	4.2	3.5	3.9	3.8	3.5	3.7

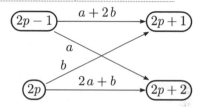

The second family is an example where the Backward and the Fast Backward algorithms have not the same complexity. Notice that these automata are acyclic and there may exist faster algorithms (*cf.* [3] for specific algorithms for acyclic DFA), but this is out of the scope of this paper. Table 2 shows the minimization of the

Fig. 3. A railroad $\mathbb{Z}$-automaton

"railroad" automaton with states in $[1; 2n]$: state 1 is initial, states $n-1$ and n are final, and for every p in $[1; n-1]$, the transitions are described by Fig. 3. In the minimization, every pair of states $(2p+1, 2p+2)$ is merged.

Table 2. Minimization of Railroad(n)

	n	2^{10}	2^{12}	2^{13}	2^{14}	2^{15}	2^{22}
Forward	t (s)	3.29	53.2	214	-		
	$10^{-6}t/n^2$	3.1	3.2	3.2			
Backward	t (s)	0.31	4.92	20.5	86.1	346	-
	$10^{-7}t/n^2$	3.0	2.9	3.1	3.2	3.2	
Fast	t (s)	0.008	0.030	0.061	0.12	0.24	30.8
Backward	$10^{-6}t/n$	7.8	7.3	7.4	7.3	7.3	7.3

Analysis. On these railroad automata, if a temporary class contains all states between 1 and $2k$, it is split into one class $[1; 2k-2]$ and one class $\{2k-1, 2k\}$: the size of the classes lowers slowly. On these examples, Forward and Backward algorithms are therefore quadratic. In the Fast Backward algorithm, when this splitting occur, the largest class $([1; 2k-2])$ is not put in the queue for further splittings; therefore, except at the first round, all splitters are pairs of states and the algorithm is linear.

References

1. Béal, M.P., Crochemore, M.: Minimizing incomplete automata. In: Finite-State Methods and Natural Language Processing FSMNLP 2008, pp. 9–16 (2008)
2. Béal, M.-P., Lombardy, S., Sakarovitch, J.: Conjugacy and equivalence of weighted automata and functional transducers. In: Grigoriev, D., Harrison, J., Hirsch, E.A. (eds.) CSR 2006. LNCS, vol. 3967, pp. 58–69. Springer, Heidelberg (2006). https://doi.org/10.1007/11753728_9
3. Berstel, J., Boasson, L., Carton, O., Fagnot, I.: Minimization of automata. In: Pin, J.E. (ed.) Automata: From Mathematics to Applications (to appear). arXiv:1010.5318v3
4. Berstel, J., Carton, O.: On the complexity of Hopcroft's state minimization algorithm. In: Domaratzki, M., Okhotin, A., Salomaa, K., Yu, S. (eds.) CIAA 2004. LNCS, vol. 3317, pp. 35–44. Springer, Heidelberg (2005). https://doi.org/10.1007/978-3-540-30500-2_4
5. Castiglione, G., Restivo, A., Sciortino, M.: On extremal cases of Hopcroft's algorithm. Theor. Comput. Sci. **411**(38–39), 3414–3422 (2010)
6. Gries, D.: Describing an algorithm by Hopcroft. Acta Informatica **2**, 97–109 (1973)
7. Hopcroft, J.E., Motwani, R., Ullman, J.D.: Introduction to Automata Theory, Languages and Computation, 3rd edn. Addison-Wesley, Boston (2006)
8. Paige, R.: Efficient translation of external input in a dynamically typed language. In: Technology and Foundations - Information Processing IFIP 1994, IFIP Transactions, vol. A-51, pp. 603–608. North-Holland (1994)
9. Paige, R., Tarjan, R.E.: Three partition refinement algorithms. SIAM J. Comput. **16**(6), 973–989 (1987)
10. Sakarovitch, J.: Elements of Automata Theory. Cambridge University Press, New York (2009)
11. Valmari, A., Lehtinen, P.: Efficient minimization of DFAs with partial transition. In: STACS 2008, LIPIcs, vol. 1, pp. 645–656. Schloss Dagstuhl (2008)
12. AWALI: Another Weighted Automata LIbrary. vaucanson-project.org/AWALI

Towards the Algorithmic Molecular Self-assembly of Fractals by Cotranscriptional Folding

Yusei Masuda, Shinnosuke Seki[(⊠)], and Yuki Ubukata

Department of Computer and Network Engineering,
The University of Electro-Communications, 1-5-1, Chofugaoka,
Chofu, Tokyo 1828585, Japan
s.seki@uec.ac.jp

Abstract. RNA cotranscriptional folding has been just experimentally proven capable of self-assembling a rectangular tile at nanoscale *in vivo* (RNA origami). We initiate the theoretical study on the algorithmic self-assembly of shapes by cotranscriptional folding using a novel computational model called the oritatami system. We propose an oritatami system that folds into an arbitrary finite portion of the Heighway dragon fractal, also-known as the paperfolding sequence $P = \text{RRLRRLLR} \cdots$. The i-th element of P can be obtained by feeding i in binary to a 4-state DFA with output (DFAO). We implement this DFAO and a bit-sequence bifurcator as modules of oritatami system. Combining them with a known binary counter yields the proposed system.

1 Introduction

An RNA sequence, over nucleotides of four kinds A, C, G, U, is synthesized (*transcribed*) from its template DNA sequence over A, C, G, T nucleotide by nucleotide by an RNA polymerase (RNAP) enzyme according to the one-to-one mapping A → U, C → G, G → C, and T → A (for details, see, e.g., [2]). The yield, called *transcript*, starts folding immediately after it emerges from RNAP. This is the *cotranscriptional folding* (see Fig. 1). Geary, Rothemund, and Andersen have recently demonstrated the capability of cotranscriptional folding to self-assemble an RNA molecule of an intended shape at nano-scale [7]. They actually proposed an architecture of a DNA sequence whose transcript folds cotranscriptionally into an RNA tile of specific rectangular shape highly likely *in vitro*.

Algorithms and computation are fundamental to molecular self-assembly as illustrated in an enormous success of their use in DNA tile self-assembly (see, e.g., [4,12,15] and references therein). Finite portions of the Sierpinski triangle fractal

---

This work is in part supported by JST Program to Disseminate Tenure Tracking System, MEXT, Japan, No. 6F36, by JSPS KAKENHI Grant-in-Aid for Young Scientists (A) No. 16H05854, and by JSPS and NRF under the Japan-Korea Basic Scientific Cooperation Program No. YB29004.

C. Câmpeanu (Ed.): CIAA 2018, LNCS 10977, pp. 261–273, 2018.
https://doi.org/10.1007/978-3-319-94812-6_22

Fig. 1. RNA cotranscriptional folding. An RNA polymerase attaches to a template DNA sequence (double-spiral), scans it through, and synthesizes its RNA copy. The RNA sequence begins to fold upon itself immediately as it emerges from polymerase.

was algorithmically self-assembled even *in vitro* from coalescence of DNA tiles that compute XOR [13]. Cotranscriptional folding exhibits highly sophisticated computational and algorithmic behaviors as well. Indeed, fluoride riboswitches in *Bacillus cereus* bacteria cotranscriptionally fold into a terminator stem or do not, in order to regulate gene expression [14]. This is just one example but should be enough to signify both the context-sensitivity of cotranscriptional folding and shapes thus self-assembled. Geary et al. have proved the capability of context-sensitivity to count in binary using a novel mathematical model of cotranscriptional folding called *oritatami system* (abbreviated as OS) [6].

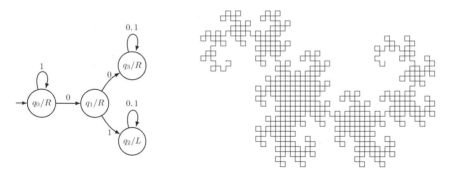

Fig. 2. (Left) DFAO to output the direction (L/R) of i-th turn of the Heighway dragon given $i \geq 0$ in binary from the LSB. (Right) The first $2^{10}-1$ turns of the dragon.

We shall initiate theoretical study on algorithmic self-assembly of shapes by cotranscriptional folding using oritatami system. Sierpinski triangle would allow our study to borrow rich insights from the DNA tile self-assembly. However, in order to cut directly to the heart of algorithmic self-assembly by cotranscriptional folding, shapes of choice should be traversable somehow algorithmically. One such way is to feed a turtle program (see [1]) with an *automatic sequence* as commands (drawing a line segment, rotation, etc.), whose i-th bit can be obtained by giving i in binary from the least significant bit (LSB) to one DFA with output (DFAO) [3]. Shapes thus describable include the Heighway dragon [3] and von Koch curve [10]. A DFAO for the Heighway dragon is illustrated in

Fig. 2. It outputs the following sequence, given $i = 0, 1, 2, \ldots$ in binary:

$$P = \text{RRLRRLLRRRLLRLLRRRLRRLLLRRLLRLL} \cdots .$$

(The notation P is after its appellative *paperfolding sequence* [3].) For instance, given $i = 2$ in binary from the LSB as 01, the DFAO transitions as $q_0 \rightarrow q_1 \rightarrow q_2$ and hence $P[2] = \text{L}$. A turtle should interpret an L (resp. R) as "move forward by unit distance and turn left (resp. right) 90 degrees." Any portion of the dragon can be represented by a factor of P; for instance, Fig. 2 (Right) depicts the portion $P[0..1022]$, i.e., the first $2^{10} - 1$ turns of the dragon.

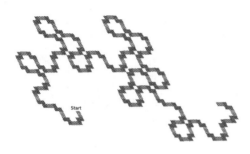

Fig. 3. The portion $P[0..62]$ of the Heighway dragon folded by the proposed OS.

In this paper, we propose a generic design of oritatami system for the algorithmic cotranscriptional folding of an arbitrary finite portion of the Heighway dragon. Figure 3 shows the portion $P[0..62]$ thus folded (the dragon is slanted but this is because the OS operates on the triangular grid rather than on the square grid). The OS transcribes three modules: counter module, DFAO module, and turning module, in this order repeatedly. The counter module is a technical modification of the binary counter proposed in [6] so that it increments a given count i exactly by 1 while folding into a line segment. At the end of the segment comes a DFAO module, which computes the turn direction $P[i]$ and propagates it along with the count i to the next module for turn. An L-shaped block is the turning module. It is a concatenation of three bit-sequence bifurcators, each of which folds into a rhombus, bifurcates i leftward as well as rightward, and guides further folding according to the turning direction. The next counter module then again increments one of the bifurcated i and folds into the next line segment, and so on.

The generic design proves the next theorem (for terminologies, see Sect. 2).

Theorem 1. *For any finite portion $P[i..j]$ of the Heighway dragon, there exist a scaling factor $c \in \mathbb{N}^+$ and a cyclic deterministic oritatami system of delay 3 and arity 3 that weakly folds into the c-rhombus scaling of $P[i..j]$.*

A JavaScript program to run this OS is available at https://wolves13.github.io.

2   Preliminaries

Let Σ be a set of types of abstract molecules, or *beads*, and Σ^* be the set of finite sequences of beads. A bead of type $a \in \Sigma$ is called an a-bead. Let $w = b_1 b_2 \cdots b_n \in \Sigma^*$ be a string of length n for some integer n and bead types $b_1, \ldots, b_n \in \Sigma$. The *length* of w is denoted by $|w|$, that is, $|w| = n$. For two indices i, j with $1 \leq i \leq j \leq n$, we let $w[i..j]$ refer to the subsequence $b_i b_{i+1} \cdots b_{j-1} b_j$; if $i = j$, then we simplify $w[i..i]$ as $w[i]$. For $k \geq 1$, $w[1..k]$ is called a *prefix* of w.

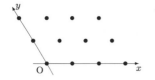

Fig. 4. Triangular grid graph $\mathbb{T}$ with the (x, y)-coordinate and the origin.

Oritatami systems fold their transcript, a sequence of beads, over the triangular grid graph $\mathbb{T} = (V, E)$ (see Figs. 4 and 5) cotranscriptionally based on hydrogen-bond-based interactions (*h-interactions* for short) which the system allow for between adjacent beads of particular types. When beads form an h-interaction, informally we say they are bound. For two points $p_1 = (x_1, y_1), p_2 = (x_2, y_2) \in V$, $\{p_1, p_2\} \in E$ if $|x_1 - x_2| = 1$ and $y_1 = y_2$ or $x_1 = x_2$ and $|y_1 - y_2| = 1$. A directed path $P = p_1 p_2 \cdots p_n$ in $\mathbb{T}$ is a sequence of *pairwise-distinct* points $p_1, p_2, \ldots, p_n \in V$ such that $\{p_i, p_{i+1}\} \in E$ for all $1 \le i < n$. Its i-th point is referred to as $P[i]$. A *conformation* C is a triple (P, w, H) of a directed path P in $\mathbb{T}$, $w \in \Sigma^*$ of the same length as P, and a set of h-interactions $H \subseteq \{\{i, j\} \mid 1 \le i, i + 2 \le j, \{P[i], P[j]\} \in E\}$. This is to be interpreted as the sequence w being folded in such a manner that its i-th bead $w[i]$ is placed on the i-th point $P[i]$ along the path and the i-th and j-th beads are bound if and only if $\{i, j\} \in H$. The condition $i + 2 \le j$ represents the topological restriction that two consecutive beads along the path cannot be bound. A *rule set* $\mathcal{H} \subseteq \Sigma \times \Sigma$ is a symmetric relation over the set of pairs of bead types, that is, for all bead types $a, b \in \Sigma$, $(a, b) \in \mathcal{H}$ implies $(b, a) \in \mathcal{H}$. An h-interaction $\{i, j\} \in H$ is *valid with respect to* $\mathcal{H}$, or simply $\mathcal{H}$-*valid*, if $(w[i], w[j]) \in \mathcal{H}$. This conformation C is $\mathcal{H}$-valid if all of its h-interactions are $\mathcal{H}$-valid. For an integer $\alpha \ge 1$, C is *of arity* α if it contains a bead that forms α h-interactions and no bead of C forms more. By $\mathcal{C}_{\le \alpha}$, we denote the set of all conformations of arity at most α.

Oritatami systems grow conformations by elongating them under their own rule set. Given a rule set $\mathcal{H}$ and an $\mathcal{H}$-valid finite conformation $C_1 = (P, w, H)$, we say that another conformation C_2 is an *elongation of* C_1 *by a bead* $b \in \Sigma$, written as $C_1 \xrightarrow{\mathcal{H}}_b C_2$, if $C_2 = (Pp, wb, H \cup H')$ for some point p not along the path P and set of h-interactions $H' \subseteq \{\{i, |w| + 1\} \mid 1 \le i < |w|, \{P[i], p\} \in E, (w[i], b) \in \mathcal{H}\}$, which can be empty. Note that C_2 is also $\mathcal{H}$-valid. This operation is recursively extended to the elongation by a finite sequence of beads as: for any conformation C, $C \xrightarrow{\mathcal{H}}{}^*_\lambda C$; and for a finite sequence of beads $w \in \Sigma^*$ and a bead $b \in \Sigma$, a conformation C_1 is elongated to a conformation C_2 by wb, written as $C_1 \xrightarrow{\mathcal{H}}{}^*_{wb} C_2$, if there is a conformation C' that satisfies $C_1 \xrightarrow{\mathcal{H}}{}^*_w C'$ and $C' \xrightarrow{\mathcal{H}}_b C_2$.

A finite *oritatami system* (OS) is a 5-tuple $\Xi = (\mathcal{H}, \alpha, \delta, \sigma, w)$, where $\mathcal{H}$ is a rule set, α is an arity, $\delta \ge 1$ is a parameter called the *delay*, σ is an initial $\mathcal{H}$-valid conformation of arity α called the *seed*, upon which its finite *transcript* $w \in \Sigma^*$ is to be folded by stabilizing beads of w one at a time so as to minimize energy collaboratively with the succeeding $\delta - 1$ nascent beads. The energy of a conformation $C = (P, w, H)$, denoted by $\Delta G(C)$, is defined to be $-|H|$; the more h-interactions a conformation has, the more stable it gets. The set $\mathcal{F}(\Xi)$ of conformations *foldable* by this system is recursively defined as: the seed σ is in

$\mathcal{F}(\Xi)$; and provided that an elongation C_i of σ by the prefix $w[1..i]$ be foldable (i.e., $C_0 = \sigma$), its further elongation C_{i+1} by the next bead $w[i+1]$ is foldable if

$$C_{i+1} \in \underset{\substack{C \in \mathcal{C}_{\leq \alpha} s.t. \\ C_i \xrightarrow{\mathcal{H}}_{w[i+1]} C}}{\arg\min} \min \left\{ \Delta G(C') \mid C \xrightarrow{\mathcal{H}}^{*}_{w[i+2...i+k]} C', k \leq \delta, C' \in \mathcal{C}_{\leq \alpha} \right\}. \quad (1)$$

We say that the bead $w[i+1]$ and the h-interactions it forms are *stabilized* according to C_{i+1}. Note that an arity-α OS cannot fold any conformation of arity larger than α. A conformation foldable by Ξ is *terminal* if none of its elongations is foldable by Ξ. The OS Ξ is *deterministic* if for all $i \geq 0$, there exists at most one C_{i+1} that satisfies (1). The deterministic OS is abbreviated as DOS. Thus, a DOS folds into a unique terminal conformation. An OS is *cyclic* if its transcript is of the form $u^i u_p$ for some $i \geq 2$ and a prefix u_p of u. The cyclic OS is considered to be one of the practical classes of OS because a periodic RNA transcript is likely to be transcribed out of a circular DNA sequence [5].

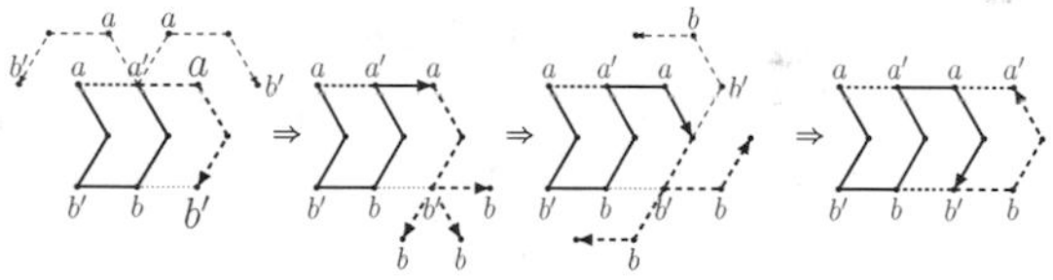

Let us provide an example of cyclic DOS that folds into a useful *glider* motif. Consider a delay-3 OS whose transcript w is a repetition of $a \bullet b' b \bullet a'$ and whose rule set is $\mathcal{H} = \{(a, a'), (b, b')\}$, making $\bullet$-beads inert. Its seed, bold in Fig. 5 (left), can

Fig. 5. Progression of a glider by distance 1.

be elongated by the first three beads $w[1..3] = a \bullet b'$ in various ways, only three of which are shown as a dashed arrow. Only $w[3] = b'$ can form a new h-interaction (dotted line), with the b in the seed (according to $\mathcal{H}$, the first a is also capable of binding, with a', but the sole a' around is just "too close"). For the b–b' binding, $w[1..3]$ must be folded as the bold dashed arrow. According to this most stable "bolded" elongation, the bead $w[1] = a$ is stabilized to the east of the previous bead. Then $w[4] = b$ is transcribed. We can easily check that no matter how $w[2..4]$ is folded, b'-beads around are either too far or too close for $w[4]$ to bind to. Hence, $w[4]$ cannot override the previous "decision" so that $w[2]$ is stabilized as bolded. $w[5]$ cannot override it, either, simply because it is inert. It is easily induced inductively that gliders of arbitrary "flight distance" can be folded.

Gliders also provide a medium to propagate 1-bit arbitrarily far as the position of their last beads, which is determined by the height (top or bottom) of the first bead and a propagating distance. For instance, the glider in Fig. 5 launches top and thus its last bead (the a') also comes top after traveling the distance 2. The OS we shall propose exploits this information-carrying capability.

Assume the (x, y)-coordinate over $\mathbb{T} = (V, E)$ as shown in Fig. 4. A *shape* S is a set of points in V. For an integer $c \geq 1$, let $Rhomb_c = \{(x, y) \in V \mid x, y \leq c\}$. Let $S' = \{(cx, cy) \mid (x, y) \in S\}$. The *c-rhombus scaling* of S, denoted by $\Diamond_c(S)$, is the union over all $\boldsymbol{p} \in S'$ of sets of points $Rhomb_c + \boldsymbol{p} = \{\boldsymbol{v} \in V \mid \boldsymbol{v} = \boldsymbol{r} + \boldsymbol{p} \text{ for some } \boldsymbol{r} \in Rhomb_c\}$. We say that an OS Ξ *weakly folds* (or "self-assembles") $\Diamond_c(S)$ if every terminal assembly of $\varXi$ puts at least one bead in $Rhomb_c + \boldsymbol{p}$ for all $\boldsymbol{p} \in S'$ and no bead in $Rhomb_c + \boldsymbol{q}$ for all $\boldsymbol{q} \notin S'$.

3   Folding the n-bit Heighway Dragon

We propose a generic design of DOS that allows us to fold an arbitrary finite portion $P[j_1..j_2]$ of the slanted Heighway dragon. Independently of j_1, j_2, both delay and arity are set to 3 and 567 bead types[1] 1, 2, ..., 567 with a fixed rule set $\mathcal{H}$ are employed. The design also challenges to make the resulting DOS cyclic. Otherwise, one could simply implement left and right-turn modules and concatenate their copies according to the (non-periodic) sequence P. However, it is highly unlikely that an OS for the infinite Heighway dragon, if any, could adopt this approach in order to be describable by a finite mean. Such a "hardcoding" also runs counter to the spirit of algorithmic self-assembly.

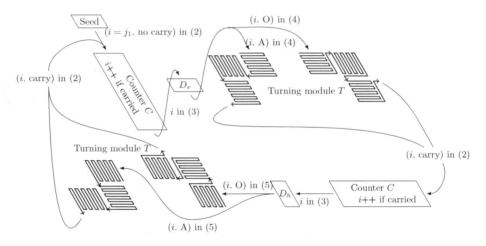

Fig. 6. Module automaton for the Heighway dragon $P[j_1..j_2]$. Transitions are labeled with the information propagated with its format.

Modularization is a semantic factorization of transcript into functional units. Functions of modules and transitions from one module to another are described in the form of module automaton. The generic design employs the module automaton in Fig. 6. This automaton yields the periodic transcript which repeats six modules of the following four types as CD_vTCD_hT:

– C is a *counter module*; it increments the count i (index of P), which is "initialized" to j_1 on the seed, by 1 and propagates it;
– D_v and D_h are a *DFAO module*; they compute $P[i]$ and interpret it properly (this issue of interpretation shall be discussed shortly);

---

[1] Some of the bead types might be saved but not easily due to the NP-hardness of minimizing the number of bead types without changing the behavior [8].

– T is a *turning module*; it makes a turn according to the interpretation.

The first C and D_v modules fold into a vertical line segment, while the second C and D_h fold into the next line segment, which is guaranteed to be horizontal since vertical and horizontal segments alternate on the Heighway dragon. The DFAO modules D_v, D_h differ from each other only in their way to interpret their intermediate outcome $P[i]$. The slanted Heighway dragon involves two types of left turn as well as two types of right turn: acute and obtuse. Observe that after (slanted) vertical line segments, the dragon turns left obtusely and right acutely, whereas after horizontal ones, it turns left acutely and right obtusely. Therefore, it suffices for D_v and D_h to compute $P[i] \in \{L, R\}$ in the same way and D_v interprets L as O and R as A, while D_h interprets L as A and R as O.

One issue intrinsic to the folding by OS rises when the dragon makes a turn where it has already turned before. The OS is, by definition, not allowed to put a bead anywhere occupied by another bead. Hence, the dragon must be scaled-up somehow. We employ the c-rhombus scaling for c so large that a rhombus corresponding to a point affords two turning modules, which otherwise collide, as long as they fold into an L-shape (see Figs. 3, 6, and 7). The turning module

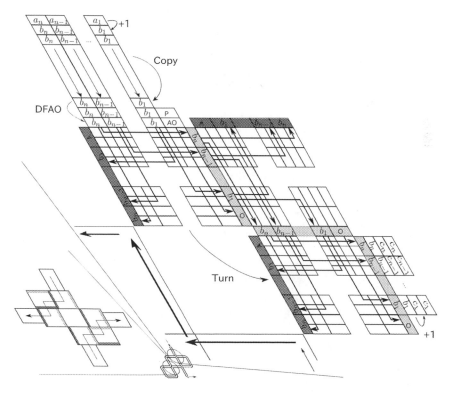

Fig. 7. Folding of one segment plus turn of the Heighway dragon, flow of information through it, and the two ways of collision avoidance between two turns.

consists of three copies of a functional subunit that bifurcates i while folding into a $c/3 \times c/3$ rhombus and guides the further folding in a way specified by the A/O signal fed by the previous DFAO module; acutely by A or obtusely by O as shown in Fig. 7 (also refer Figs. 11 and 14).

Having outlined the generic design, now we explain how the design implements an OS for a specific target portion $P[j_1..j_2]$, or more precisely, how the modules C, D_v, D_h, T and their submodules are implemented, interlocked with each other, and collaborate. Let $n = \min\{m \mid j_2 < 2^m\}$. Each of the modules consists of submodules which are small, say, with several dozens of beads. Submodules implement various "functions" each of which is "called" in proper *environments*, i.e., the beads already placed around the tip of the transcript acting as the memory in the computation. The conformation that a submodule folds deterministically in a "valid" environment corresponds to the function to be called then. These "functional" conformations are called *bricks*, upon which the whole folding is built. *Brick automata* describe the OS' behavior at submodule level by enumerating all the pairs of an environment to be encountered and the brick to be folded there as well as transitions among them. Once verified, all the brick automata for C (resp. D_v, D_h, and T) guarantee that the module outputs in the expected format (3) (resp. (4), (5), and (2)), and hence we can say that the DOS behaves as described in the module automaton and folds into $P[j_1..j_2]$. Using a simulator developed for [9], we have verified all the brick automata. This amounts to the proof of Theorem 1.

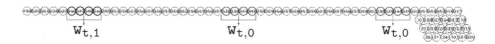

Fig. 8. The seed for the 3-bit Heighway dragon that starts at $j_1 = 100_2$.

Seed (Fig. 8) encodes the initial count $i = j_1$ in its binary representation $b_n b_{n-1} \cdots b_1$ as the following sequence of bead types:

$$499 \to 500 \to 501 \to 506 \to 507 \to \bigodot_{k=n}^{2}(\mathtt{w}_{\mathtt{t},\mathtt{b}_k} \to 350 \to 351 \to (356 \to 357 \to)^6)\mathtt{w}_{\mathtt{t},\mathtt{b}_1} \tag{2}$$

where $\mathtt{w}_{\mathtt{t},0} = 338 \to 339 \to 344 \to 345$ and $\mathtt{w}_{\mathtt{t},1} = 346 \to 347 \to 348 \to 349$.

Counter module C is borrowed from [6] with technical modification to let it operate in the dynamics (1), which is more prevailing [8,9,11] though less tractable. It takes the current count i formatted as (2), which is fed by the seed or by the previous turning module, increments the count by 1 unless it is preceded by the seed, and outputs the resulting count in its binary representation $a_n a_{n-1} \cdots a_1$ in the following format:

$$44 \to 45 \to 46 \to 51 \to 52 \to \bigodot_{k=n}^{2}(\mathtt{w}_{\mathtt{c},\mathtt{a}_k} \to (75 \to 76 \to)^5 51 \to 52 \to)\mathtt{w}_{\mathtt{c},\mathtt{a}_1} \tag{3}$$

where $\mathtt{w}_{\mathtt{c},0} = 57 \to 58 \to 63 \to 64 \to 69 \to 70$ and $\mathtt{w}_{\mathtt{c},1} = 65 \to 66 \to 67 \to 68 \to 69 \to 70$.

DFAO modules D_v, D_h receive the current count i in the format (3) from the previous counter module, compute $P[i]$, and interpret it as A or O properly. The modules D_v and D_h then output the interpretation along with the count i in the following formats, respectively:

$$\bigodot_{k=n}^{2}\left(\mathtt{w}_{\mathtt{d,a_k}}\to(52\to51\to)^7\right)\mathtt{w}_{\mathtt{d,a_1}}\to52\to51\to200\to199\to\mathtt{w}_{\mathtt{dv,P[i]}} \qquad (4)$$

$$\bigodot_{k=n}^{2}\left(\mathtt{w}_{\mathtt{d,a_k}}\to(52\to51\to)^7\right)\mathtt{w}_{\mathtt{d,a_1}}\to52\to51\to311\to310\to\mathtt{w}_{\mathtt{dh,P[i]}} \qquad (5)$$

where $\mathtt{w}_{\mathtt{dv,L}} = 198\to197,$ $\mathtt{w}_{\mathtt{dv,R}} = 194\to193,$ $\mathtt{w}_{\mathtt{dh,L}} = 305\to304,$ and $\mathtt{w}_{\mathtt{dh,R}} = 309\to308.$

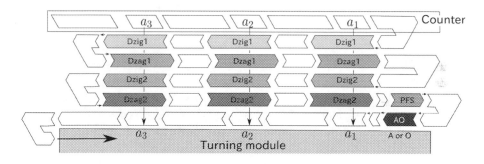

Fig. 9. Submodule-level abstraction of the folding of DFAO module.

What the DFAO in Fig. 2 really does for computing $P[i]$ is to search for the first 0 from the LSB and check if it is followed by 0 ($P[i] = $ R) or by 1 ($P[i] = $ L). See Fig. 9. D_v (resp. D_h) employs the six submodules: Dzig1, Dzag1, Dzig2, Dzag2, PFS, and $\mathtt{AO}_v$ (resp. $\mathtt{AO}_h$), which are interleaved by spacers, as well as those that guide the transcript into two zigzags and one more zig (throughout the paper, zigs are to go leftward while zags are to go rightward). The first zigzag is for the search, the second is for the check and computation of $P[i]$, and the third zig is for the interpretation of $P[i]$ as A/O. While performing these tasks, these zigs and zags also propagate the count i to the next turning module.

In the first zig, n copies of Dzig1 detect the first 0 collaboratively in two phases. See Fig. 10 for all the bricks of Dzig1 with the corresponding environments. Phase 1 is to copy all the 1's prior to the first 0 and Phase 2 is to copy all the bits after the 0. Dzig1 knows which phase it is in by the relative position to start folding to the input above (top in Phase 1, bottom in Phase 2). In Phase 1, Dzig1s certainly fold into the brick Dzig1-1. At the first 0, a Dzig1 rather folds into Dzig1-f0 brick, ending at the top in order to transition to Phase 2. Each of the remaining Dzig1 folds into either Dzig1-20 or Dzig1-21, copying all the remaining bits. Interleaving spacers are implemented as a glider (see Sect. 2), hence capable of propagating 1bit (top/bottom) on which phase the system is in. In the first zag, n copies of Dzag1 reformat and propagate 0's, 1's, and the first 0 using three bricks.

In the second zig, n copies of `Dzig2` check whether the first 0 is followed (being read from LSB) by 0 or 1, in a similar manner to the search in the first zig. They usually take one of the two bricks Dzig2-0 and Dzig2-1 to copy 1's and 0's, which start and end at the bottom. At the encounter to the first

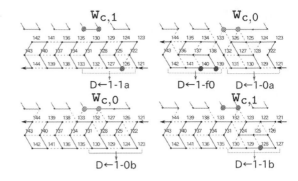

Fig. 10. The four bricks of `Dzig1`: (top) Dzig1-1 and Dzig1-f0; (bottom) Dzig1-20 and Dzig1-21.

0, a `Dzig2` folds into a special brick Dzig2-f0 and ends rather at the top. The next `Dzig2`, if any, starts folding at the top so that it takes the special brick Dzig2-1f0 if it is followed by 1 or Dzig2-0f0 otherwise. Recall the reading 1 here is a necessary and sufficient condition for $P[i] = L$. Dzig2-1f0 exposes a marker q_2 downward. These bricks end at the bottom so that the remaining bits are copied by the ordinary bricks Dzig2-0 and -1. The second zag starts at the bottom and copy 0's and 1's by two bricks of `Dzag2` until a `Dzag2` encounters the 1 marked by q_2, if any. At the encounter, the `Dzag2` folds into the special brick Dzag2-T1 and changes the ending position to the top, letting the remaining `Dzag2` rather fold into the bricks Dzag2-L0 and -L1 for copying, which end at the top. As such, the second zag can feed $P[i]$ to `PFS` as the position of its first bead.

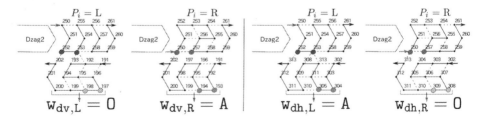

Fig. 11. The two bricks of `PFS` above and the corresponding two bricks of (left) AO_v and (right) those of AO_h.

At the beginning of the third zig, D_v employs AO_v to convert $P[i]$ into $w_{dv,P[i]}$ while D_h employs rather AO_h to convert $P[i]$ into $w_{dh,P[i]}$. The turning module interprets $w_{dv,L}$ and $w_{dh,R}$ as turning obtusely while $w_{dv,R}$ and $w_{dh,L}$ as turning acutely. As a part of effort to save bead types, the submodule AO_v is also diverted in order for both D_v and D_h to propagate i in the rest of this zig.

Turning module T consists of 3 copies of the pair of two functional units called *bit-bifurcator* and *steering arm*. See Fig. 13. The bit-bifurcator forks the count $i = a_n a_{n-1} \cdots a_1$ left and rightward while folding into zigzags. It consists of 10 submodules, which handle the following tasks:

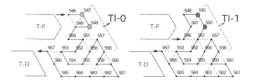

Fig. 12. The two bricks of `turn-rgp`.

1. Propagate 1-bit vertically: `body-rpx1`, `body-rpx2`, `body-lpx1`, `body-lpx2`;
2. Let 1-bit propagating vertically cross another 1-bit propagating horizontally: `body-gx1`, `body-gx2`;
3. Fork 1-bit vertically and horizontally: `body-rgy`, `body-lgy`;
4. Undergo transition between a zig and a zag and exposes 1-bit outside: `turn-rgp`, `turn-lgp`.

Submodules to handle the first two types of tasks have already been implemented (see, e.g., [9]). The submodule `body-rgy` is implemented by recycling the first half of `Dzag2`. Starting from the bottom, it can take two conformations that end at different heights and expose sequences bead types distinct enough downward. The 1-bit thus forked transfers till the end of a zag and is converted into a sequence of bead types by `turn-rgp` (Fig. 12). The submodules `body-lgy` and `turn-lgp` are the zig-counterparts of them.

The bifurcator also propagates the 1-bit A/O signal, output by the previous DFAO module, to let the steering arm know which way to go. Specifically, the signal has the `change-route` submodule of the steering arm take one of the two bricks shown in Fig. 14, guiding the rest of the arm towards the specified direction. The rest of the arm is a catenation of `move` submodules, which is capable of letting the bifurcated bit sequence through. Note that the turning module does not have to bifurcate the A/O signal. Indeed, the second and third pairs of bifurcator and steering arm are supposed to turn in the same manner as the first. It hence suffices to append A and O to the bifurcated bit sequences on the acute and obtuse sides, respectively.

272   Y. Masuda et al.

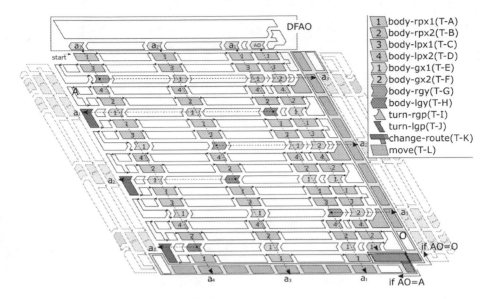

Fig. 13. Submodule-level abstraction of the whole folding of the pair of a bifurcator and steering arm. All the white submodules are spacers, some of which are implemented in the shape of parallelogram instead of glider.

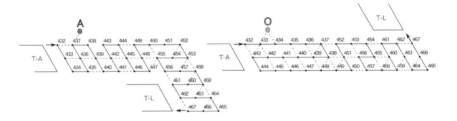

Fig. 14. The two bricks of `change-route`.

4   Conclusion

In this paper, we proposed a generic design of oritatami systems for an arbitrary finite portion of Heighway dragon. One down side is that the scaling factor depends on the length of the portion, though just logarithmically. It is hence of significant interest whether the dependency is necessary. Should it not be, we could implement an OS that folds into the real (infinite) Heighway dragon.

Acknowledgements. We would like to thank Hwee Kim for valuable discussions.

References

1. Abelson, H., diSessa, A.: Turtle Geometry The Computer as a Medium for Exploring Mathematics. The MIT Press, London (1981)
2. Alberts, B., Johnson, A., Lewis, J., Morgan, D., Raff, M., Roberts, K., Walter, P.: Molecular Biology of the Cell, 6th edn. Garland Science, New York and Abingdon (2014)
3. Allouche, J.P., Shallit, J.: Automatic Sequences: Theory, Applications, Generalizations. Cambridge University Press, Cambridge (2003)
4. Doty, D.: Theory of algorithmic self-assembly. Commun. ACM **55**(12), 78–88 (2012)
5. Geary, C.W., Andersen, E.S.: Design principles for single-stranded RNA origami structures. In: Murata, S., Kobayashi, S. (eds.) DNA 2014. LNCS, vol. 8727, pp. 1–19. Springer, Cham (2014). https://doi.org/10.1007/978-3-319-11295-4_1
6. Geary, C., Meunier, P.E., Schabanel, N., Seki, S.: Programming biomolecules that fold greedily during transcription. In: MFCS2016, pp. 43:1–43:14. LIPIcs 58 (2016)
7. Geary, C., Rothemund, P.W.K., Andersen, E.S.: A single-stranded architecture for cotranscriptional folding of RNA nanostructures. Science **345**(6198), 799–804 (2014)
8. Han, Y.-S., Kim, H.: Ruleset optimization on isomorphic oritatami systems. In: Brijder, R., Qian, L. (eds.) DNA 2017. LNCS, vol. 10467, pp. 33–45. Springer, Cham (2017). https://doi.org/10.1007/978-3-319-66799-7_3
9. Han, Y.-S., Kim, H., Ota, M., Seki, S.: Nondeterministic seedless oritatami systems and hardness of testing their equivalence. In: Rondelez, Y., Woods, D. (eds.) DNA 2016. LNCS, vol. 9818, pp. 19–34. Springer, Cham (2016). https://doi.org/10.1007/978-3-319-43994-5_2
10. Ma, J., Holdener, J.: When Thue-Morse meets Koch. Fractals **13**, 191–206 (2005)
11. Ota, M., Seki, S.: Ruleset design problems for oritatami systems. Theor. Comput. Sci. **671**, 26–35 (2017)
12. Patitz, M.J.: Self-assembly of fractals. In: Kao, M.Y. (ed.) Encyclopedia of Algorithms, pp. 1918–1922. Springer, Heidelberg (2016). https://doi.org/10.1007/978-3-642-27848-8
13. Rothemund, P.W.K., Papadakis, N., Winfree, E.: Algorithmic self-assembly of DNA Sierpinski triangle. PLoS Biol. **2**(12), e424 (2004)
14. Watters, K.E., Strobel, E.J., Yu, A.M., Lis, J.T., Lucks, J.B.: Cotranscriptional folding of a riboswitch at nucleotide resolution. Nat. Struct. Mol. Biol. **23**(12), 1124–1133 (2016)
15. Winfree, E.: Algorithmic self-assembly of DNA. Ph.D. thesis, California Institute of Technology, June 1998

On the Values for Factor Complexity

Birzhan Moldagaliyev[1], Ludwig Staiger[2], and Frank Stephan[1,3](✉)

[1] Department of Mathematics, National University of Singapore,
10 Lower Kent Ridge Road, Singapore 119076, Republic of Singapore
birzhanm@gmail.com
[2] Martin-Luther-Universität Institut für Informatik, Von-Seckendorff-Platz 1,
06120 Halle, Federal Republic of Germany
ludwig.staiger@informatik.uni-halle.de
[3] School of Computing, National University of Singapore,
Singapore 117417, Republic of Singapore
fstephan@comp.nus.edu.sg

Abstract. In this paper, we consider factor complexity/topological entropy of infinite binary sequences. In particular, we show that for any real number α with $0 \leqslant \alpha \leqslant 1$, there is a subset of the Cantor space with Hausdorff dimension α, such that each one of its elements has factor complexity α. This result partially generalises to the multidimensional case where sequences are replaced by their d-dimensional analogs.

1 Introduction

There are many connections between computability, automata theory and symbolic dynamics. For example, Hochman and Meyerovitch [11] have shown that a real number is in the range of a multidimensional shift of finite type if and only if it is recursively enumerable from the right, that is, has a descending approximation by a recursive sequence of rational numbers. Another example of such interplay is the work of Simpson [22], where it was shown that topological entropy, Hausdorff dimension and effective dimension coincide in the case of subshifts under some conditions. Staiger [24] showed, in the one-dimensional case, the corresponding result for subsets of the Cantor space definable by finite automata. There are also investigations on connections between subshifts and appropriate topologies for Cantor Space [12]. As for the multidimensional setting, Frisch and Tamuz [8] have shown that for any real α with $0 \leqslant \alpha \leqslant \log_2(|\Sigma|)$ there is a weakly mixing subshift of A^G with entropy α. The methods employed in the given paper are said to be nonconstructive, and the objects under consideration are shifts, rather than single sequences.

In this paper we provide an algorithm for direct construction of sequences of the given factor complexity. In the case of dimension one, for any α with

This work is partially supported by the Singapore Ministry of Education Academic Research Fund Tier 2 Grant MOE2016-T2-1-019/R146-000-234-112 (PI Frank Stephan).

C. Câmpeanu (Ed.): CIAA 2018, LNCS 10977, pp. 274–285, 2018.
https://doi.org/10.1007/978-3-319-94812-6_23

$0 \leqslant \alpha \leqslant 1$, we present an algorithmic procedure, which uses α as oracle, to construct a subset of the Cantor space $\mathcal{A}$ satisfying the following conditions:

- The classical Hausdorff dimension of $\mathcal{A}$ is α;
- The constructive Hausdorff dimension of $\mathcal{A}$ relative to α is α;
- For any $\xi \in \mathcal{A}$, the factor complexity of ξ equals to α;
- There is $\xi \in \mathcal{A}$ such that the constructive dimension of ξ relative to α is α.

As for the multidimensional case with dimension d, for every α with $0 \leqslant \alpha \leqslant 1$, we present an algorithmic procedure using α as an oracle to construct a nonempty collection of d-dimensional sequences, each having factor complexity α.

2   Background

Since this work covers multiple domains, it might be worthwhile to provide a brief overview of the ingredients that make up the final results. For this purpose, this section offers a brief overview of the factor complexity, classical and constructive Hausdorff dimensions. We refer the readers to the textbooks of Calude [1], Downey and Hirschfeldt [4], Hopcroft et al. [13], Li and Vitányi [14] and Nies [19] for more complete introductions to the given topics.

2.1   Factor Complexity

We work in a multidimensional case with dimension d, as the usual one-dimensional version of factor complexity follows from it. Let Σ be a finite alphabet, which is assumed to be binary throughout the paper, that is, $\Sigma = \{0, 1\}$. Consider a d-dimensional sequence of symbols from Σ, which can be viewed as a function $\xi : \mathbb{N}^d \to \Sigma$.

The collection of such sequences form a space denoted as $\mathcal{C}_d$. It can be given a metric similar to the original Cantor Space, with the exception that intervals starting at 0 are replaced with d-dimensional hypercubes starting at 0^d. A d-dimensional hypercube of size n can be viewed as a function: $x : \{0, \ldots, n-1\}^d \to \Sigma$. Let us denote the domain $\{0, \ldots, n-1\}^d$ of x as B_n, the d-dimensional grid of size n. A term *volume* of B_n refers to its cardinality as a set, i.e. n^d. A hypercube x is said to be a *factor* or a *subword* of d-dimensional sequence ξ if ξ contains x. More formally,

$$\exists p \in \mathbb{N}^d \, \forall q \in B_n \, [\xi(p+q) = x(q)].$$

Let $F_n(\xi)$ denote the collection of factors of ξ with size n. Consider the quantity

$$\tau_n(\xi) = \frac{\log_2(|F_n(\xi)|)}{n^d}$$

and its limit is then the factor complexity of ξ:

$$\tau(\xi) = \lim_n \tau_n(\xi).$$

The above limit is known to exist [22]. The above limiting value is known as *factor complexity* or *subword complexity* in automata theory and *topological entropy* in symbolic dynamics. One studies both this limit number [22–24] and the order of growth of the above function F_n itself [2,3,5,6]. The intuition behind factor complexity in dimension one can be described as follows. Given an infinite sequence, we can study the language of its finite factors. Intuitively, we expect that "simple" sequences will also have a "simple" language of factors. One way to quantify this is to just count factors of each length. In doing so, we associate a function with the infinite sequence which counts the number of factors per length. This function was introduced in 1938 by Morse and Hedlund [18] under the name block growth, as a tool to study symbolic dynamics. The name subword complexity, as the one-dimensional version of factor complexity, was given in 1975 by Ehrenfeucht et al. [5].

2.2 Hausdorff Dimension

Given any metric space X, Hausdorff [10] introduced a notion of dimension of a subset Y of X which is now known as its *Hausdorff dimension*, $\dim_H(Y)$; Falconer [7] provides an overview and introduction to this now widely studied dimension. In the case of the Cantor space $\mathcal{C} = \{0,1\}^\omega$, Lutz [15] has found an equivalent definition of Hausdorff dimension via generalisations of martingales. By imposing some algorithmic conditions on these generalised martingales, it is then possible to define the constructive Hausdorff dimension, $cdim(X)$. Furthermore, by allowing access to an oracle, say ζ, one could define the relative constructive dimension, $cdim(X|\zeta)$, with respect to the given oracle. Ryabko and also Lutz have observed that the constructive Hausdorff dimension of a class is the supremum of the constructive Hausdorff dimension of its members [15,20,21]. Zvonkin and Levin [29, Theorem 3.4] provide a convenient formula for computing the constructive dimension of sequences, see also Mayordomo [17] or Staiger [25],

$$cdim(\xi) = \liminf_n \frac{K(\xi[n])}{n}. \tag{1}$$

Here K stands for the prefix-free Kolmogorov complexity and $\xi[n]$ denotes a prefix of ξ of length n. The above formula can be relativised given any sequence ζ as an oracle. So one has following relativised version

$$cdim(\xi|\zeta) = \liminf_n \frac{K(\xi[n]|\zeta)}{n}. \tag{2}$$

We refer the interested reader also to [26,28] for more details on this connection and the historic background and use the above formulas of Zvonkin and Levin as a definition for constructive Hausdorff dimension.

2.3 Computing the Hausdorff Dimension

Even in the case of the Cantor space, computing the Hausdorff dimension of an arbitrary subset of the Cantor space is rather difficult. This is mainly due to the hardness of providing accurate lower bounds for the Hausdorff dimension. However, there is a convenient formula for computing the Hausdorff dimension for subsets generated by special kinds of infinite trees. Let us then introduce some terminology for working with trees. Given a binary tree T, let T_n denote the nodes located at a distance n from the tree's root. Given a sequence of $\{T_n\}$ one could define *lower* and *upper growth rates*

$$\underline{gr}T = \liminf_{n \to \infty} |T_n|^{\frac{1}{n}} \quad \text{and} \quad \overline{gr}T = \limsup_{n \to \infty} |T_n|^{\frac{1}{n}}.$$

If these two quantities coincide, then they give us the *growth rate*

$$grT = \lim_{n \to \infty} |T_n|^{\frac{1}{n}}.$$

Another important notion is that of a *branching number* for trees. Let $\lambda \geqslant 1$, and assume that T is such that every finite branch can be extended to an infinite branch. A flow through T is a measure on the set of all infinite branches of T such that for every node x on T of length n, the measure of the sequences extending x is at most λ^{-n}. Here we say that a sequence ξ is an *infinite branch* of T if for all n, $\xi[n] \in T$; for simplicity we ignore finite branches and therefore call the infinite branches just branches. The collection of all branches of the tree T is called the class generated by T, and denoted ∂T. In the case of the full binary tree, for any $\lambda \leqslant 2$, such a flow exists. However, as soon as $\lambda > 2$, there is no flow for this λ. This idea gives rise to the following definition of the branching number of T:

$$brT = \sup\{\lambda \mid \text{There is a flow on } T \text{ for } \lambda\}.$$

Furstenberg [9] has shown that $brT = exp(\dim_H(\partial T))$. This result gives us a link between brT and the Hausdorff dimension of the class generated by T. When it comes to spherically symmetric trees, we have the following well-known property, given as an exercise by Lyons and Peres [16].

Proposition 1. *If T is an infinite spherically symmetric tree, then*

$$brT = \underline{gr}T.$$

Recall that a tree is called *spherically symmetric* if for any n, the out-degree of the elements of T_n are equal. Combining it with the result by Furstenberg, for a spherically symmetric tree T we have

$$2^{(\dim_H(\partial T))} = \underline{gr}T. \tag{3}$$

This relation gives us a convenient mechanism for computing the Hausdorff dimension of boundaries of spherically symmetric trees. We are going to use this formula for computing the Hausdorff dimension of corresponding classes in the one-dimensional case.

3   The One-Dimensional Case

In this section, we consider the usual one-dimensional sequences. The following theorem solves an open problem which was mentioned recently in [27].

Theorem 2. *For any real number α with $0 \leqslant \alpha \leqslant 1$ there is an algorithm using α as an oracle which constructs a subset $\mathcal{A}$ of $\mathcal{C}$ such that the following conditions hold:*

- *$\dim_H(\mathcal{A}) = cdim(\mathcal{A}) = cdim(\mathcal{A}|\alpha) = \alpha$;*
- *For all $\xi \in \mathcal{A}$, $\tau(\xi) = \alpha$;*
- *There is $x \in \mathcal{A}$ such that $cdim(\{x\}|\alpha) = \alpha$.*

Proof. Let us address the cases $\alpha \in \{0, 1\}$ first. If $\alpha = 0$, then take $\mathcal{A} = \{0^\omega\}$. The given choice of $\mathcal{A}$ ensures that the above conditions are satisfied. For the case $\alpha = 1$, let $\mathcal{A} = MLR$, the collection of Martin-Löf random sequences. Since the Lebesgue measure of MLR is 1, we have $\dim_H(\mathcal{A}) = cdim(\mathcal{A}) = 1$. Since each Martin-Löf random sequence contains any word as a factor, $\tau(\xi) = 1$ for all $\xi \in \mathcal{A}$. Finally, for any Martin-Löf random ξ, $K(\xi[n]) \geqslant n - c$ for some c. Using Eq. (1) we have that $cdim(\{\xi\}) = 1$ for any $\xi \in MLR$. Thus, all conditions are satisfied. Next we consider the main case where $0 < \alpha < 1$.

Basic Idea. The idea is to construct a spherically symmetric infinite binary tree T such that $\dim_H(\partial T) = \alpha$ and for any $\xi \in \partial T$, $\tau(\xi) = \alpha$. Then one could exhibit an existence of a branch $x \in \partial T$ such that $cdim(\{x\}|\alpha) = \alpha$. The construction of T proceeds in a step-by-step fashion. At each stage k, we build a finite spherically symmetric tree T_k of depth n_k so that T is a limit of the trees T_k. For the Hausdorff dimension and the factor complexity, convergence to α is reached from above. Let $\{q_n\}_{n=0}^\infty$ be a strictly decreasing sequence of rational numbers below 1 which converges to α from above and which furthermore can be computed using the oracle α. Given this approximating sequence $\{q_n\}$, the construction ensures that

$$q_k \leqslant z_k = \frac{\log_2(|X_k|)}{n_k} \leqslant q_{k-1} \text{ for all } k \geqslant 1, \text{ where } X_k \text{ denotes the leaves of } T_k.$$

The whole construction can be carried out recursively relative to the oracle α. All recursion-theoretic notions involved are to be interpreted relative to α. For simplicity we are going to omit dependence to α so that $K(\xi|\alpha)$ and $cdim(\xi|\alpha)$ become $K(\xi)$ and $cdim(\xi)$, respectively. Let us now proceed to the construction itself.

Stage 0. Let T_0 be a tree of depth 1 containing both strings of unit length. Clearly, T_0 is spherically symmetric.

Stage $k+1$. Given a finite tree T_k we are going to construct a tree T_{k+1}. Let $r(T_k)$ denote the number of branching levels in T_k out of n_k levels it has. Letting X_k denote the set of leaves of T_k, one has $|X_k| = 2^{r(T_k)}$. Our construction ensures that

$$z_k = \frac{\log_2(|X_k|)}{n_k} = \frac{r(T_k)}{n_k} \geqslant q_k.$$

Observe that this condition holds for $k = 0$, since the left-hand side is simply 1. Let η_k denote the concatenation of elements of X_k in some order, say lexicographic. It is possible then to choose natural numbers i and j so that

$$q_{k+1} \leqslant \frac{r(T_k) \cdot i}{n_k \cdot i + |\eta_k| \cdot j} < q_k.$$

To clarify how these i, j could be chosen, one could start by dividing both numerator and denominator of the above fraction by i, obtaining

$$\frac{r(T_k)}{n_k + |\eta_k|(j/i)}.$$

Now consider ϕ defined as

$$\phi(x) = \frac{r(T_k)}{n_k + |\eta_k|x}$$

which maps non-negative reals to non-negative reals. Clearly this function is continuous, $\phi(0) = z_k$ and $\lim_{x \to \infty} \phi(x) = 0$. By the intermediate value theorem, there is $x \in \mathbb{R}$ such that $q_{k+1} < \phi(x) < q_k$. By the density of rational numbers and continuity of ϕ, there is $q \in \mathbb{Q}$ with $q_{k+1} \leqslant \phi(q) < q_k$. The numbers j and i can be taken as the numerator and the denominator of q. Let $\Gamma_k = (T_k)^i \cdot (\eta_k)^j$; this tree extends T_k. Here a product of finite trees T_1 and T_2 correspond to gluing the root of a copy of T_2 to each of the leaves of T_1. Furthermore, for a finite tree T, T^ω corresponds to an infinite product of T with itself. Clearly, Γ_k is still spherically symmetric. Let Y_k denote the collection of leaves of Γ_k and m_k denote the depth of Γ_k. We can now estimate the desired quantity $\frac{\log_2(\cdot)}{|\cdot|}$ as follows:

$$q_{k+1} \leqslant \frac{\log_2(|Y_k|)}{m_k} = \frac{r(T_k) \cdot i}{n_k \cdot i + |\eta_k| \cdot j} < q_k.$$

The tree Γ_k serves as an intermediate step in construction of T_{k+1}. Consider a tree Γ_k^ω and one of its branches, say ξ. Since ξ contains all elements of X_k, we have

$$\tau_{n_k}(\xi) \geqslant \frac{\log_2(|X_k|)}{n_k} \geqslant q_k \geqslant \alpha.$$

This inequality gives us a lower bound. As for a meaningful upper bound, $\tau_{n_k}(\xi)$ will not work because of possible overlaps and emergence of new factors. The idea is that if we consider much longer factors, then the relative ratio of overlaps will go to zero. Formally, let $n_{k+1} = lm_k$ and consider factors of length lm_k.

Since $\xi \in \Gamma_k^\omega$ such factors can be fully characterised by a word in Γ_k^{l+1} and an initial position p with $0 \leqslant p < m_k$. Thus, $|F_{lm_k}(\xi)| \leqslant |Y_K|^{l+1} \times m_k$. So we have

$$\tau_{lm_k}(\xi) = \frac{\log_2(F_{lm_k}(\xi))}{lm_k} \leqslant \left(\frac{l+1}{l}\right)\frac{\log_2(|Y_k|)}{m_k} + \frac{\log_2(m_k)}{lm_k}.$$

By choosing large enough l one can ensure that the above expression is strictly less than q_k. We finally let $T_{k+1} = (\Gamma_k)^l$.

Finalisation. Let $T = \bigcap_k T_k^\omega$ and $\mathcal{A} = \partial T$. We claim that the given class $\mathcal{A}$ satisfies all required conditions. Let us go through the conditions one by one. Prior to that, however, we need to show that $\mathcal{A}$ is nonempty. In other words, we need to show that T is a valid infinite binary tree. Firstly, T is a binary tree being an intersection of binary trees. Furthermore, the construction ensures that the elements at level n_k will no longer change after stage $k+1$. This shows that at each level T has a member, which shows that T is an infinite tree. Thus, nonemptiness of $\mathcal{A}$ follows.

Hausdorff Dimension. Given the final tree T, let $r_n(T)$ denote the number of branching levels in T up to the level n. By the construction, T and T_k coincide up to the level n_k. Thus, we have $r_n(T) = r_n(T_k)$, for all $n \leqslant n_k$. Furthermore, the construction ensures that for any tree T_k used in the construction, $r_n(T_k) \geqslant \alpha n$ for all $n \leq n_k$. These two facts imply that

$$\forall n\, [r_n(T) \geqslant \alpha n].$$

As $T \subseteq T_k^\omega$, for all n which are multiples of n_k, we have $\frac{r_n(T)}{n} \leqslant q_{k-1}$. Combining these facts we conclude that $\liminf_n \frac{r_n(T)}{n} = \alpha$. Using the formula for computing the Hausdorff dimension Eq. (3) one arrives at $\dim_H(\partial T) = \alpha$. As for the constructive dimension relative to α, by default we have $\alpha = \dim_H(\mathcal{A}) \leqslant cdim(\mathcal{A}|\alpha) \leqslant cdim(\mathcal{A})$. The other inequality $cdim(\mathcal{A}) \leqslant \alpha$ follows from

$$cdim(\mathcal{A}) \leqslant \sup\{\tau(\xi) : \xi \in \mathcal{A}\}$$

(cf. Staiger [24,26]) and $\tau(\xi) = \alpha$, for $\xi \in \mathcal{A}$, which will be proven next.

Factor Complexities. Since it is known that $\lim_n \tau_n(\xi) = \tau(\xi)$ for all ξ, it suffices to exhibit a strictly increasing subsequence $\{t_k\}_{k=0}^\infty$ such that for any $\xi \in \mathcal{A}$, we have $\lim_k \tau_{t_k}(\xi) = \alpha$. Set $t_k = n_k$ for the n_k used in the construction and observe that for any $\xi \in \mathcal{A}$, $\xi \in \partial T_{k+1}^\omega$ for any k. From the construction, it is known that

- $\tau_{n_k}(\xi) \geqslant \alpha$;
- $\tau_{n_{k+1}}(\xi) \leqslant q_k$.

Combining the above inequalities, one concludes that $\lim_k \tau_{n_k}(\xi) = \alpha$. Thus, the factor complexity of each element of $\mathcal{A}$ is exactly α.

Existence of an Element of Given Constructive Dimension. In order to show the existence of an element of a given relative constructive dimension, we use an argument based on the encoding of a Martin-Löf random sequence as a branch of T; this method is also known as dilution [15,24,28]. Let us take a Martin-Löf random sequence ζ relative to α. We wish to encode this sequence into a branch of T. Each level of tree T is either branching or nonbranching. It is possible to encode ζ as the branching directions in T. As for the nonbranching levels of T they are already taken by some fixed symbols. Let $\chi(T)$ denote a $\{0, 1\}$-valued sequence corresponding to the branching behaviour of T, where 1 denotes a branching level and 0 denotes a nonbranching level. Furthermore, let $\rho(T)$ denote a sequence consisting of symbols located at nonbranching levels of T with brackets located at the branching levels. For instance, $\chi(T)$ and $\rho(T)$ might look like $\chi(T) = 1011000\ldots$ and $\rho(T) = []0[][]101\ldots$ and one could then place bits of ζ into the positions corresponding to the bracket symbols in $\rho(T)$. This operation of placement can be viewed as a transformation of one infinite sequence to another. More formally, we consider a map $\phi : \mathcal{C} \to \mathcal{C}$ such that it places bits of an input sequence ξ into the bracket positions in $\rho(T)$. For example, taking the above $\rho(T)$ and $\xi = \mathbf{010}\ldots$, then $\mathbf{0010101}\ldots$ is the resulting sequence $\phi(\xi)$. Since the tree T is recursive in α, both ϕ and its inverse can be viewed as partial functions recursive in α. Now we let $x = \phi(\zeta)$ and observe that knowledge of x up to length n ensures knowledge of ζ up to length at least αn, as we have verified in the paragraph on the Hausdorff dimension above that $r_n(T) \geqslant \alpha \cdot n$ for all n. Thus $K(x[n]|\alpha) \geqslant \alpha \cdot n - c$ for some fixed c and for all n. This ensures that $x \in \partial T$ and $cdim(x) \geqslant \alpha$ using the relativised version Eq. (2). As $cdim(\mathcal{A}) \leqslant \alpha$, it follows that $cdim(x) = \alpha$ by the result of Ryabko [20,21] and Lutz [15, Theorem 4.1]. □

4   The Higher Dimensional Case

Here we state the partial generalisation of Theorem 2 to the multidimensional case.

Theorem 3. *For every real number α with $0 \leqslant \alpha \leqslant 1$, there is an algorithm using α as an oracle which constructs a nonempty subset $\mathcal{A}$ of C_d such that for all $\xi \in \mathcal{A}$, $\tau(\xi) = \alpha$.*

Proof. The boundary cases of $\alpha \in \{0, 1\}$ are considered first. If $\alpha = 0$, then the d-dimensional sequence consisting of a single symbol 0 fulfills the condition. In the case of $\alpha = 1$, any standard d-dimensional arrangement of a Martin-Löf random sequence meets the criterion. For values α with $0 < \alpha < 1$, we present the construction based on the ideas used in the proof of the one-dimensional case.

Basic Idea. The main feature of this construction is manipulations with hypercubes, rather than strings. Let $\{q_n\}_{n=0}^{\infty}$ be a strictly decreasing sequence of rational numbers below 1 which converge to α from above. We choose the sequence such that the map $n \mapsto q_n$ is recursive relative to α. The construction proceeds in stages so that at each stage k we construct a collection X_k of hypercubes of size n_k such that

$$q_k \leqslant z_k = \frac{\log_2(|X_k|)}{n_k^d} \leqslant q_{k-1}.$$

Since the limit $\lim_{n \to \infty} \tau_n(\xi) = \tau(\xi)$ exists, it suffices to show that $\lim_k \tau_{n_k}(\xi) = \alpha$ for some strictly increasing sequence $\{n_k\}$, given any $\xi \in \mathcal{A}$. Let us now proceed to the actual construction.

Stage 0. We let $n_0 = 1$ and $X_0 = \Sigma$ (so that X_0 represents a set of hypercubes of size 1). Observe that the induction hypothesis holds, namely $q_0 \leqslant \frac{\log_2(|X_0|)}{n_0^d}$.

Stage $k + 1$. Given a collection X_k of hypercubes of size n_k we need to construct a subsequent collection X_{k+1} of hypercubes. Recall that in the one-dimensional case we have constructed $X_{k+1} = Y_k^l$, where $Y_k = X_k^i \cdot \eta_k^j$ with η_k being the concatenation of elements of X_k and the constants i, j, l were chosen to satisfy the corresponding inequalities. In the d-dimensional case a simple product X_k^i is going to be replaced with a *grid product* and the η_k^j part is going to be replaced with an operation of *periodic filling*. Let us elaborate on these terms.

Grid Products. Given some d-dimensional grid $B_r \subset \mathbb{N}^d$ of size r and the collection of hypercubes X_k, each being of size n_k, $X_k^{B_r}$ denotes the collection of all hypercubes of size rn_k obtained by placing elements of X_k on the nodes of the grid B_r. Observe that the cardinality of $X_k^{B_r}$ as a set can be computed as $|X_k^{B_r}| = |X_k|^{r^d}$. Furthermore, one could also allow the underlying grid to be infinite. In particular, $X_k^{\mathbb{N}^d}$ refers to the grid product of X_k over the infinite grid $\mathbb{N}^d$.

Periodic Fillings. Suppose that we are given a finite grid $F \subset \mathbb{N}^d$ of cardinality or volume at least $|X_k|$. Note that F is not necessarily a regular grid, it might have any kind of shape and be disconnected. There are many possible ways to place elements of X_k into the nodes F so that each element of X_k appears at least once. However, we wish to define some canonical way of placing elements of X_k along any finite subset F. Moreover, it is desirable for such a procedure to be effective and well-defined. Note that there is an effective procedure that allows enumeration of elements of F given by the map $h(F) : F \to \{0, \ldots, |F| - 1\}$. By composing this map with a modulo by $|X_k|$, we obtain a surjective map from F to $\{0, \ldots, |X_k| - 1\}$. Let $g(X_k) : \{0, \ldots, |X_k| - 1\} \to X_k$ be a bijective enumeration of elements of X_k. Finally, by composing the earlier map with $g(X_K)$, we obtain an effective periodic filling map $f_k(F) : F \to X_k$. This map allows us to fill any finite subset of sufficient size with elements of X_k so that each element of X_k appears. Furthermore the above map is well-defined and effective in the algorithmic sense.

Construction of New Hypercubes. Let a hypercube B_n serve as a grid for placement of elements of X_k. The hypercube B_n is then divided into two parts, the first of which is used for the grid product operation, while the second one is periodically filled with elements of X_k. The first part is a subgrid of size i with

$1 < i < n$ nearest to the origin. The complement of the first part constitutes the second part. Observe that the first part has a volume of i^d, while the second part has a volume of $n^d - i^d$. The second part could be periodically filled with the elements of X_k whenever $|X_k| \leqslant n^d - i^d$. Given an arbitrary pair (n, i), the given inequality can always be achieved by multiplying both n and i by some large enough constant c. Let Y_k denote the collection of hypercubes obtained by applying the operation of grid product over the first part of B_n and the operation of periodic filling over the second part of B_n. Observe that each element of Y_k has size $m_k = nn_k$, while the cardinality of Y_k as a set is $|X_k|^{i^d}$. We now compute the desired quantity $\frac{\log_2(\cdot)}{|\cdot|}$ using the following formula:

$$\frac{\log_2(|Y_k|)}{(m_k)^d} = \left(\frac{i}{n}\right)^d \frac{\log_2(|X_k|)}{n_k^d}. \tag{4}$$

Observe that the above expression is invariant under multiplications of n and i with a constant, i.e. it does not change by multiplying both n and i with a positive constant c. We claim that one could choose a pair (n, i) so that the value of Eq. (4) lies in the open interval from q_{k+1} to q_k. This condition can be written as

$$q_{k+1} < \left(\frac{i}{n}\right)^d z_k < q_k \quad \text{which is equivalent to} \quad \frac{q_{k+1}}{z_k} < \left(\frac{i}{n}\right)^d < \frac{q_k}{z_k}.$$

Recall that by the induction hypothesis $q_k \leqslant z_k \leqslant q_{k-1}$ and thus $0 < \frac{q_{k+1}}{z_k} < \frac{q_k}{z_k} \leqslant 1$. As the function $x \to x^d$ is continuous and increasing, and maps 0 to 0 and 1 to 1, and as the rationals are dense in the reals, one can find a rational $\frac{i}{n}$ with $1 \leqslant i \leqslant n$ such that $(\frac{i}{n})^d$ lies inside the given open interval. By multiplying the resulting pair (n, i) with a large enough integer c, we can ensure that the second part of B_n has a large enough volume. Consider a grid product $Y_k^{\mathbb{N}^d}$ and its arbitrary element ξ. Since ξ contains all elements of X_k as factors, we conclude that

$$\tau_{n_k}(\xi) = \frac{\log_2(F_{n_k}(\xi))}{n_k^d} \geqslant q_k \geqslant \alpha.$$

Having a lower bound to work with, we now look for meaningful upper bounds. As in the one-dimensional case, factors of size n_k will not work because of possible overlaps. The idea is to consider much larger factors so that the relative ratio of overlaps goes to zero. Formally, let $n_{k+1} = lm_k$ and consider factors of size lm_k. For any $\xi \in Y_k^{\mathbb{N}^d}$, its factors of a given size can be fully characterised by a hypercube in $Y_k^{B_{l+1}}$ and some initial position $p \in B_{m_k}$. Thus, $F_{lm_k}(\xi) \leqslant |Y_k|^{(l+1)^d} \times m_k^d$. So we have

$$\tau_{lm_k}(\xi) \leqslant \frac{\log_2(m_k^d |Y_k|^{(l+1)^d})}{(lm_k)^d} = \left(\frac{(l+1)}{l}\right)^d \frac{\log_2(|Y_k|)}{m_k^d} + \frac{d \log_2(m_k)}{l^d m_k^d}.$$

By choosing l large enough, one could ensure that the above quantity is strictly less than q_k. Finally, let $X_{k+1} = Y_k^{B_l}$.

Finalisation. Observe that for any k, $X_{k+1}^{\mathbb{N}^d}$ is a compact subset of $X_k^{\mathbb{N}^d}$. This means that $\mathcal{A} = \bigcap_k X_k^{\mathbb{N}^d}$ is nonempty and compact. For every $\xi \in \mathcal{A}$ and every k, it holds that $\xi \in X_{k+1}^{\mathbb{N}^d}$, $\tau_{n_k}(\xi) \geqslant \alpha$ and $\tau_{n_{k+1}}(\xi) \leqslant q_k$. Combining the last two inequalities, we conclude that $\lim_k \tau_{n_k}(\xi) = \alpha$. As $\lim_n \tau_n(\xi)$ exists for every ξ [22], $\lim_n \tau_n(\xi)[3] = \alpha$. $\qquad\square$

5   Conclusion

This paper explored an interplay between different notions such as factor complexity, Hausdorff dimension and relative constructive dimension. In the one-dimensional case, for any real α with $0 \leqslant \alpha \leqslant 1$, we have constructed a subset of the Cantor space consisting of sequences with factor complexity α such that both Hausdorff and constructive dimension of this subset is α. Moreover, the same subset contains a sequence of constructive dimension α. This provides a positive answer to a question which was raised e.g. in the talk "Finite automata and randomness" [27]. As for the multidimensional case, we have constructed a nonempty subset of the d-dimensional Cantor space consisting of elements of factor complexity α.

If one views sequences over an alphabet of size 2^k as k-tuples of binary sequences, then our results generalise to all α with $0 \leqslant \alpha \leqslant k$ in a natural way; however, if one views such sequences as 2^k-ary presentations of single reals, then one would have to introduce some corrective terms in above equations which would again restrict the values of α to the interval from 0 to 1 [24,26,28].

Acknowledgments. The authors would like to thank the anonyomous referees of CIAA 2018 and Hugh Anderson for very helpful comments on the mathematics and the English of this paper.

References

1. Calude, C.S.: Information and Randomness - An Algorithmic Perspective, 2nd (edn.). Springer, Heidelberg (2002). https://doi.org/10.1007/978-3-662-04978-5
2. Cassaigne, J.: Special factors of sequences with linear subword complexity. In: Developments in Language Theory, DLT 1995, pp. 25–34. World Scientific Publishing, Singapore (1996)
3. Cassaigne, J., Frid, A.E., Puzynina, S., Zamboni, L.Q.: Subword complexity and decomposition of the set of factors. In: Csuhaj-Varjú, E., Dietzfelbinger, M., Ésik, Z. (eds.) MFCS 2014, Part I. LNCS, vol. 8634, pp. 147–158. Springer, Heidelberg (2014). https://doi.org/10.1007/978-3-662-44522-8_13
4. Downey, R.G., Hirschfeldt, D.R.: Algorithmic Randomness and Complexity. Springer, New York (2010). https://doi.org/10.1007/978-0-387-68441-3
5. Ehrenfeucht, A., Lee, K.P., Rozenberg, G.: Subword complexities of various classes of deterministic developmental languages without interactions. Theor. Comput. Sci. **1**, 59–75 (1975)
6. Ehrenfeucht, A., Rozenberg, G.: On the subword complexity of square-free D0L languages. Theor. Comput. Sci. **16**, 25–32 (1981)

7. Falconer, K.: Fractal Geometry - Mathematical Foundations and Applications, 2nd edn. Wiley, Hoboken (2003)
8. Frisch, J., Tamuz, O.: Symbolic dynamics on amenable groups: the entropy of generic shifts. Ergodic Theory Dyn. Syst. **37**(4), 1187–1210 (2017)
9. Furstenberg, H.: Intersections of cantor sets and transversality of semigroups. In: Problems in Analysis: a Symposium in Honor of Salomon Bochner, pp. 41–59 (1970)
10. Hausdorff, F.: Dimension und äußeres Maß (Dimension and outer measure). Mathematische Annalen **79**(1–2), 157–179 (1919)
11. Hochman, M., Meyerovitch, T.: A characterization of the entropies of multidimensional shifts of finite type. Ann. Math. **171**(3), 2011–2038 (2010)
12. Hoffmann, S., Schwarz, S., Staiger, L.: Shift-invariant topologies for the Cantor Space X^ω. Theor. Comput. Sci. **679**, 145–161 (2017)
13. Hopcroft, J.E., Motwani, R., Ullman, J.D.: Introduction to Automata Theory, Languages, and Computation, 2nd edn. Addison-Wesley, Reading (2001)
14. Li, M., Vitányi, P.: An Introduction to Kolmogorov Complexity and Its Applications, 3rd edn. Springer, Berlin (2008). https://doi.org/10.1007/978-0-387-49820-1
15. Lutz, J.H.: The dimensions of individual strings and sequences. Inf. Comput. **187**, 49–79 (2003)
16. Lyons, R., Peres, Y.: Probability on Trees and Networks. Cambridge Series in Statistical and Probabilistic Mathematics. Cambridge University Press, Cambridge (2017)
17. Mayordomo, E.: A Kolmogorov complexity characterization of constructive Hausdorff dimension. Inf. Process. Lett. **84**(1), 1–3 (2002)
18. Morse, M., Hedlund, G.A.: Symbolic dynamics. Am. J. Math. **60**(4), 815–866 (1938)
19. Nies, A.: Computability and Randomness. Oxford University Press, New York (2009)
20. Ryabko, B.Ya.: Coding of combinatorial sources and Hausdorff dimension. Soviet Mathematics - Doklady **30**(1), 219–222 (1984)
21. Ryabko, B.Ya.: Noiseless coding of combinatorial sources, Hausdorff dimension and Kolmogorov complexity. Problemy Peredachi Informatsii **22**(3), 16–26 (1986)
22. Simpson, S.G.: Symbolic dynamics: Entropy = Dimension = Complexity. Theory Comput. Syst. **56**(3), 527–543 (2015)
23. Sinai, Y.G.: On the notion of entropy of a dynamical system. Doklady Russ. Acad. Sci. **124**, 768–771 (1959)
24. Staiger, L.: Kolmogorov complexity and Hausdorff dimension. Inf. Comput. **103**(2), 159–194 (1993)
25. Staiger, L.: Constructive dimension equals Kolmogorov complexity. Inf. Process. Lett. **93**(3), 149–153 (2005)
26. Staiger, L.: The Kolmogorov complexity of infinite words. Theor. Comput. Sci. **381**(1–3), 187–199 (2007)
27. Staiger, L.: Finite automata and randomness. Invited Talk (without proceedings) at Jewels of Automata: from Mathematics to Applications, Leipzig, 6–9 May 2015. http://www.automatha.uni-leipzig.de/
28. Staiger, L.: Exact constructive and computable dimensions. Theory Comput. Syst. **61**(4), 1288–1314 (2017)
29. Zvonkin, A.K., Levin, L.A.: The complexity of finite objects and the development of the concepts of information and randomness by means of the theory of algorithms. Russ. Math. Surv. **25**, 83–124 (1970)

Enumeration of Cryptarithms
Using Deterministic Finite Automata

Yuki Nozaki, Diptarama Hendrian, Ryo Yoshinaka$^{(\boxtimes)}$, and Ayumi Shinohara

Graduate School of Information Sciences,
Tohoku University, 6-6-05 Aramaki Aza Aoba, Aoba-ku, Sendai, Japan
yuki_nozaki@shino.ecei.tohoku.ac.jp,
{diptarama,ryoshinaka,ayumis}@tohoku.ac.jp

Abstract. A cryptarithm is a mathematical puzzle where given an arithmetic equation written with letters rather than numerals, a player must discover an assignment of numerals on letters that makes the equation hold true. In this paper, we propose a method to construct a DFA that accepts cryptarithms that admit (unique) solutions for each base. We implemented the method and constructed a DFA for bases $k \leq 7$. Those DFAs can be used as complete catalogues of cryptarithms, whose applications include enumeration of and counting the exact numbers $G_k(n)$ of cryptarithm instances with n digits that admit base-k solutions. Moreover, explicit formulas for $G_2(n)$ and $G_3(n)$ are given.

Keywords: Cryptartihms · Alphametics · Automaton · DFA
Enumeration

1 Introduction

A cryptarithm is a mathematical puzzle where a given arithmetic formula consisting of letters rather than numerals, players try to find an injective substitution of numerals for letters that makes the formula hold true. Figure 1 shows a well-known example of a cryptarithm and its solution. To solve a cryptarithm is, in principle, not quite hard. One can find a solution (if any) by trying at most 10! assignments of numerals on letters, i.e., cryptarithms are solvable by brute force in linear time. Nevertheless, cryptarithms have been an interesting topic of computer science [7] and different methods for solving cryptarithms have been proposed [1,8] including a number of online solvers on the web [2,9]. In fact, although cryptarithms can be solved in linear time under the decimal system, Eppstein [6] showed that to decide whether a given cryptarithm has a solution under the base-k system is strongly NP-complete when k is not fixed. His discussions involve only arithmetic formulas with just one addition, like the one in Fig. 1. Following Eppstein, this paper focuses on such formulas only. A cryptarithm example that has a binary solution but no decimal solution is shown in Fig. 2.

© Springer International Publishing AG, part of Springer Nature 2018
C. Câmpeanu (Ed.): CIAA 2018, LNCS 10977, pp. 286–298, 2018.
https://doi.org/10.1007/978-3-319-94812-6_24

```
    s e n d          9 5 6 7                    P          1
  + m o r e        + 1 0 8 5                  + P        + 1
  ─────────        ─────────                  ─────      ─────
  m o n e y        1 0 6 5 2                  P A        1 0
```

Fig. 1. Example of a cryptarithm and its solution [3]

Fig. 2. Cryptarithm solvable under the binary system

Our goal is not only to provide a cryptarithm solver but to propose a method to enumerate cryptarithms for different base systems. Towards the same goal, Endoh et al. [5] presented a method for constructing a deterministic finite automaton (DFA) that accepts cryptarithms solvable under the k-base system for $k = 2, 3, 4$. Their method constructs the goal DFA as the product of several auxiliary DFAs corresponding to different conditions that solvable cryptarithms must satisfy. On the other hand, our proposed method constructs the objective DFA directly. This approach enabled us to construct the goal DFAs for $k \leq 7$.

Those DFAs can be seen as complete catalogues of cryptarithms for different bases. Once the cryptarithm DFA for base-k arithmetics is constructed, this can be used as a cryptarithm solver using the information added to its states that runs in linear time in the size of the input with no huge coefficient. Moreover, different types of analyses on cryptarithms are possible with standard techniques on edge-labeled graphs. For example, one can enumerate all the solvable cryptarithms one by one in the length-lexicographic order. It is also possible to compute the mth solvable cryptarithm quickly without enumerating the first $m - 1$ cryptarithms. Counting the number of solvable cryptarithms of n digits is also easy. In particular, we derived explicit formulas for the number $G_k(n)$ of cryptarithms of n digits solvable under the base-k system for $k = 2, 3$ as $G_2(n) = 6 \times 4^{n-2} - 3 \times 2^{n-2}$ and $G_3(n) = 4 \times 9^{n-1} - 2 \times 5^{n-1} - 3^{n-1}$, respectively.

2   Preliminaries

For an alphabet Σ, Σ^* and Σ^+ denote the sets of strings and non-empty strings, respectively. For a map θ from an alphabet Σ to another Δ, its homomorphic extension from Σ^* to Δ^* is denoted by $\hat{\theta}$. For a string or a tuple of strings w over Δ, $\Sigma \lceil w$ denotes the subset of Σ consisting of letters occurring in w. An *extension* of a function $f \colon A \to B$ is a function $g \colon A' \to B'$ such that $A \subseteq A'$ and $g(x) = f(x)$ for all $x \in A$. The cardinality of a set A is denoted by $|A|$. The length of a string w is also denoted by $|w|$. We let N_k denote the alphabet of numerals $0, \ldots, k - 1$.

2.1   Cryptarithms

A *cryptarithm* is a triple $\boldsymbol{w} = \langle w_1, w_2, w_3 \rangle$ of non-empty strings over an alphabet Σ. Each w_i is called the ith *term*. The *size* of $\boldsymbol{w}$ is defined to be $\max\{|w_1|, |w_2|, |w_3|\}$. Any injection from $\Sigma\!\upharpoonright\!\boldsymbol{w}$ to N_k is called a *base-k assignment* for $\boldsymbol{w}$. Moreover it is a *base-k solution* if it makes the equation $\hat{\theta}(w_1) + \hat{\theta}(w_2) = \hat{\theta}(w_3)$ true when interpreting strings over N_k as numerals in the base-k system: that is, for $w_i = w_{i,|w_i|} \ldots w_{i,1}$ with $w_{i,j} \in \Sigma$, it holds $\sum_{j=1}^{|w_1|} \theta(w_{1,j}) k^{j-1} + \sum_{j=1}^{|w_2|} \theta(w_{2,j}) k^{j-1} = \sum_{j=1}^{|w_3|} \theta(w_{3,j}) k^{j-1}$ and $\theta(w_{i,|w_i|}) \neq 0$ for each $i = 1, 2, 3$. A cryptarithm that admits a solution is said to be *base-k solvable*.

Following Endoh et al. [5], in order for DFAs to treat cryptarithms, we convert cryptarithms into single strings over $\Sigma \cup \{\$\}$ with $\$ \notin \Sigma$ by

$$\psi(\langle w_1, w_2, w_3 \rangle) = w_{1,1}w_{2,1}w_{3,1}\, w_{1,2}w_{2,2}w_{3,2} \,\cdots\, w_{1,n}w_{2,n}w_{3,n}\,\$\$\$$$

where $w_i = w_{i,|w_i|} \ldots w_{i,1}$, $n = \max\{|w_1|, |w_2|, |w_3|\}$, and $w_{i,j} = \$$ for $|w_i| < j \leq n$. Such a string $\psi(\boldsymbol{w})$ is called a *cryptarithm sequence*.

Example 1. Let $\boldsymbol{w} = \langle \texttt{send}, \texttt{more}, \texttt{money} \rangle$. This admits a unique base-10 solution $\theta = \{\texttt{d} \mapsto 7, \texttt{e} \mapsto 5, \texttt{y} \mapsto 2, \texttt{n} \mapsto 6, \texttt{r} \mapsto 8, \texttt{o} \mapsto 0, \texttt{s} \mapsto 9, \texttt{m} \mapsto 1\}$. The sequential form of $\boldsymbol{w}$ is $\psi(\boldsymbol{w}) = \texttt{dey nre eon smo \$\$m \$\$\$}$.[1]

We say that two instances $\boldsymbol{w}$ and $\boldsymbol{v}$ are *equivalent* if there is a bijection γ from $\Sigma\!\upharpoonright\!\boldsymbol{w}$ to $\Sigma\!\upharpoonright\!\boldsymbol{v}$ such that $\hat{\gamma}(\boldsymbol{w}) = \boldsymbol{v}$. In such a case, an injection $\theta \colon \Sigma\!\upharpoonright\!\boldsymbol{v} \to N_k$ is a k-base solution for $\boldsymbol{v}$ if and only if so is $\theta \circ \gamma$ for $\boldsymbol{w}$. Fixing the alphabet to be $\Sigma_k = \{\texttt{a}_1, \ldots, \texttt{a}_k\}$, we define the canonical form among equivalent instances. A base-k cryptarithm $\boldsymbol{w} \in (\Sigma_k^*)^3$ is said to be *canonical* if

- wherever $\texttt{a}_{i+1}$ occurs in the sequential form $\psi(\boldsymbol{w})$ of $\boldsymbol{w}$, it is after the first occurrence of $\texttt{a}_i$ for any $i \geq 1$.

Identifying a cryptarithm and its sequential form, we adapt terminology on cryptarithms for cryptarithm sequences as well. For example, the sequential form of a canonical cryptarithm is also called canonical. A solution of a cryptarithm instance is also said to be a solution of its sequential form.

For the ease of presentation, we use Latin letters $\texttt{a}, \texttt{b}, \texttt{c}, \ldots$ instead of $\texttt{a}_1, \texttt{a}_2, \texttt{a}_3, \ldots$ when k is relatively small: $k \leq 26$.

Example 2. The cryptarithm $\boldsymbol{w} = \langle \texttt{send}, \texttt{more}, \texttt{money} \rangle$ in Example 1 is not canonical. Its canonical form is $\boldsymbol{v} = \langle \texttt{gbda}, \texttt{hfeb}, \texttt{hfdbc} \rangle$, whose sequential form is $\psi(\boldsymbol{v}) = \texttt{abc deb bfd ghf \$\$h \$\$\$}$.

3   Cryptarithm DFAs

3.1   Naive Cryptarithm DFA

We will define a DFA M_k that accepts all and only canonical cryptarithms that admit solutions. Our DFA is slightly different from the standard ones. First, each edge is labeled by a trigram so that letters belonging to the same place

---

[1] For readability a small space is inserted in every three letters.

will be read at once. Second, it has two distinguishable accepting states f_1 and f_2 where cryptarithm sequences with unique and multiple solutions shall be accepted at f_1 and at f_2, respectively. Accordingly, our DFA is a sextuple $M_k = \langle Q, \Sigma_k, \delta, q_0, f_1, f_2 \rangle$ where Q_k is the state set, $\delta \colon Q \times (\Sigma_k \cup \{\$\})^3 \rightharpoonup Q$ is the transition partial function, and f_1 and f_2 are accepting states, which define two languages

$$L_{k,\mathrm{uniq}} = \{ w \in (\Sigma_k \cup \{\$\})^+ \mid \hat{\delta}(q_0, w) = f_1 \}$$
$$= \{ \psi(\boldsymbol{w}) \in (\Sigma_k \cup \{\$\})^+ \mid \boldsymbol{w} \text{ admits exactly one solution} \}, \qquad (1)$$
$$L_{k,\mathrm{multi}} = \{ w \in (\Sigma_k \cup \{\$\})^+ \mid \hat{\delta}(q_0, w) = f_2 \}$$
$$= \{ \psi(\boldsymbol{w}) \in (\Sigma_k \cup \{\$\})^+ \mid \boldsymbol{w} \text{ admits at least two solutions} \}, \qquad (2)$$

where $\hat{\delta}$ is the usual extension of δ for domain $((\Sigma_k \cup \{\$\})^3)^*$. We call a string $w \in ((\Sigma_k \cup \{\$\})^3)^*$ *valid* if it is a prefix of some canonical cryptarithm sequence with at least one solution. We say that an assignment $\theta \colon \Sigma_k \restriction w \to N_k$ is *consistent with* w if there is an extension of θ which is a solution of a cryptarithm sequence of which w is a prefix. When $\Sigma_k \restriction w = \Sigma_{k-1}$, each consistent assignment on Σ_{k-1} has just one trivial proper extension injection with domain Σ_k. Therefore, we "promote" consistent assignments on Σ_{k-1} to their extensions on Σ_k. We let $\Theta(w)$ denote the set of consistent assignments, possibly with promotion:

$$\Theta(w) = \begin{cases} \{\, \theta \colon \Sigma_k \to N_k \mid \theta \text{ is consistent with } w \,\} & \text{if } \Sigma_k \restriction w = \Sigma_{k-1}, \\ \{\, \theta \colon \Sigma_k \restriction w \to N_k \mid \theta \text{ is consistent with } w \,\} & \text{otherwise.} \end{cases}$$

For a valid sequence w, one can characterize succeeding sequences v that will make wv a solvable canonical cryptarithm sequence with $\Theta(w)$ and other parameters. The parameters the DFA M_k maintains in its states have the form $\langle d_1, d_2, \ell, P \rangle$, which we will call a *configuration*. Every state except accepting ones has a unique configuration. Among those parameters, $d_1, d_2 \in \{0,1\}$ are used to ensure that a sequence may be extended to a cryptarithm sequence and $\ell \in \{1, \ldots, k\}$ is used to ensure that a sequence may be extended to a canonical one. The last parameter P is a non-empty set that remembers possible assignments on letters together with auxiliary information. Suppose that the configuration of the state q reached from q_0 by reading a valid sequence w in M_k is $\langle d_1, d_2, \ell, P \rangle$ and let $w = w' x_1 x_2 x_3$ with $x_1, x_2, x_3 \in \Sigma_k \cup \{\$\}$ and $\psi^{-1}(w) = \langle w_1, w_2, w_3 \rangle$. Then,

- $d_i = 1$ if $x_i = \$$ and $d_i = 0$ otherwise for $i = 1, 2$,
- $\ell = \min\{k, |\Sigma \restriction w| + 1\}$,
- P consists of $[\theta, c, b_1, b_2] \in \Theta(w) \times \{0,1\}^3$ where
  - $\theta \in \Theta(w)$,
  - $\hat{\theta}(w_1) + \hat{\theta}(w_2) = \hat{\theta}(w_3) + c k^{|w_3|}$,
  - $b_i = 0$ if $x_i \neq \$$ and $\theta(x_i) = 0$, and $b_i = 1$ otherwise, for $i = 1, 2$.

One can see P as a function from $\Theta(w)$ to $\{0,1\}^3$. For $[\theta, c, b_1, b_2] \in P$, when $c = 1$, we have a carry under the assignment θ. When $b_i = 0$, the ith term must be extended to have a more significant digit since the current most significant digit is 0 under θ.

Now let us define $M_k = \langle Q, \Sigma_k, \delta, q_0, f_1, f_2 \rangle$ so that M_k satisfies the above. We identify a state and its configuration, since no distinct states have the same configuration: in case two states happen to have the same configuration, they must be merged. The initial state is the configuration $\langle 0, 0, 1, \{[\varnothing, 0, 0, 0]\}\rangle$, where $\varnothing$ is the empty assignment.

The transition function δ is defined as follows. For $x_1, x_2, x_3 \in \Sigma_k \cup \{\$\}$, let us write $\langle d_1, d_2, \ell, P \rangle \xrightarrow{x_1 x_2 x_3} \langle d_1', d_2', \ell', P' \rangle$ if

- $x_3 = \$$ implies $x_1 = x_2 = \$$,
- $d_i = 1$ implies $x_i = \$$ for $i = 1, 2$,
- $d_i' = 1$ if $x_i = \$$, and $d_i' = 0$ otherwise, for $i = 1, 2$,
- $x_1 \in \Sigma_\ell \cup \{\$\}$, $x_2 \in \Sigma_{\ell_1} \cup \{\$\}$, $x_3 \in \Sigma_{\ell_2} \cup \{\$\}$, where $\ell_1 = \ell$ if $x_1 \in \Sigma_\ell$ and $\ell_1 = \min\{k, \ell + 1\}$ otherwise, and ℓ_2 is defined from ℓ_1 and x_2 in the same manner,
- ℓ' is defined from ℓ_2 and x_3 in the same manner,
- $P' = \{ p' \mid p \xrightarrow{x_1 x_2 x_3} p' \text{ for some } p \in P \}$ is not empty,

where we write $[\theta, c, b_1, b_2] \xrightarrow{x_1 x_2 x_3} [\theta', c', b_1', b_2']$ if

- $b_i = 0$ implies $x_i \neq \$$ for $i = 1, 2$,
- $\theta' \colon \Sigma' \to N_k$ is an extension of θ where $\Sigma' = \Sigma_k$ if $\ell' = k$, and $\Sigma' = \Sigma_{\ell'-1}$ otherwise,
- $c + \tilde{\theta}'(x_1) + \tilde{\theta}'(x_2) = c'k + \tilde{\theta}'(x_3)$ where $\tilde{\theta}'$ extends θ' by $\tilde{\theta}'(\$) = 0$,
- $b_i' = 0$ if $x_i \neq \$$ and $\theta'(x_i) = 0$, and $b_i' = 1$ otherwise, for $i = 1, 2$.

If $x_1 x_2 x_3 \neq \$\$\$$, then we define $\delta(q, x_1 x_2 x_3) = q'$ for $q \xrightarrow{x_1 x_2 x_3} q'$. When $x_1 x_2 x_3 = \$\$\$$, this means the end of the input sequence, if it is a cryptarithm sequence. For $q' = \langle d_1', d_2', \ell', P' \rangle$ with $q \xrightarrow{\$\$\$} q'$, we define $\delta(q, \$\$\$) = f_1$ if $|P'| = 1$, and $\delta(q, \$\$\$) = f_2$ if $|P'| \geq 2$.

The state set Q is defined to consist of the states reachable from the initial state according to δ.

Example 3. Let $k = 3$. Suppose that a state q in M_3 has a configuration $\langle d_1, d_2, \ell, P \rangle = \langle 0, 0, 2, P \rangle$ with

$$P = \{[\{\mathsf{a} \mapsto 0\}, c, b_1, b_2]\} = \{[\{\mathsf{a} \mapsto 0\}, 0, 0, 0]\} \,.$$

In fact, this state is reached by reading aaa from the initial state, where we did not yet find $\$$ (so $d_1 = d_2 = 0$), the second letter b may appear in the nearest future (so $\ell = 2$), and the only consistent assignment θ maps a to 0 (otherwise $\theta(\mathsf{a}) + \theta(\mathsf{a}) \neq \theta(\mathsf{a})$), under which we have no carry ($c = 0$), but each term must not finish ($b_1 = b_2 = 0$). Therefore, this state q has no outgoing transition edge labeled with a trigram including $\$$. When reading aaa again from this state, the situation does not change. So we have $\delta(q, \mathsf{aaa}) = q$. If we read abb, where b is a new letter, we reach a new state q'. Although the last letter c in Σ_3 has not appeared yet, it is ready to come. The domain of the assignments in the configuration of q' is now Σ_3. We have two consistent assignments extending the one $\{a \mapsto 0\}$ in q. One maps b to 1 and the other maps b to 2. In both cases, we have no carry and the second term may finish. Thus, the configuration of q' is $\langle 0, 0, 3, P' \rangle$ with

$$P' = \{[\{a \mapsto 0,\, b \mapsto 1,\, c \mapsto 2\}, 0, 0, 1],\ [\{a \mapsto 0,\, b \mapsto 2,\, c \mapsto 1\}, 0, 0, 1]\}\,.$$

On the other hand, it is not hard to see that there is no p'' such that $[\{a \mapsto 0\}, 0, 0, 0] \xrightarrow{\text{abc}} p''$. Hence q has no edge labeled with abc. In this way, we decide whether a state has an outgoing edge labeled with a trigram over $\Sigma_k \cup \{\$\}$ and the configuration of the reached state.

We now have established Eqs. (1) and (2). An assignment θ is a solution of a cryptarithm sequence $w\$\$\$$ if and only if $[\theta, 0, 1, 1] \in P$ of the configuration $\langle d_1, d_2, \ell, P \rangle$ of the state $\delta(q_0, w)$. In other words, one can regard our DFA as a Mealy machine that outputs solutions when reading $\$\$\$$.

We remark that the constructed DFA is minimum as a Mealy machine but is not necessarily minimum if we ignore output solutions. For example, let us consider the states reached by $\text{abc}\$\text{ab}$ and $\text{abc}\$\text{ba}$ from the initial state in M_3. They have different configurations $\langle 1, 0, 3, P_1 \rangle$ and $\langle 1, 0, 3, P_2 \rangle$ where $P_i = \{[\{a \mapsto i,\, b \mapsto (3-i),\, c \mapsto 0\}, 0, 1, 1]\}$ for $i = 1, 2$. Those states are not merged but the strings that will lead us to the accepting state f_1 from those states coincide: namely, they have the form $\$x_1 x_1 \ldots \$x_n x_n \$\$\$$ where $x_i \in \{a, b, c\}$ for $i < n$, $x_n \in \{a, b\}$ and $n \geq 0$.

The number of states of M_k is bounded by the number of possible configurations. A trivial and loose upper bound on it is $2^{O(k!)}$. If one is interested only in cryptarithms with a unique solution, one can remove the state f_2. If uniqueness of a solution does not matter, two accepting states f_1 and f_2 can be merged.

Figure 3 shows the finally obtained automaton for $k = 2$. This automaton M_2 misses the accepting state f_2, because no cryptarithm has two distinct base-2 solutions.

3.2   Compressed Cryptarithm DFA

By observing Fig. 3, one may realize that the DFA has isomorphic substructures. Namely, the sub-automaton M_2^2 whose initial state is set to be 2 is isomorphic to M_2^{15} with initial state 15 by swapping a and b on the edge labels. There exist just 2 base-2 assignments, $\{a \mapsto 0, b \mapsto 1\}$ and $\{a \mapsto 1, b \mapsto 0\}$. The first trigram of any cryptarithm sequence uniquely determines one of the two as a consistent assignment. The former assignment corresponds to M_2^2 and the latter to M_2^{15}. We say that two configurations $\langle d_1, d_2, \ell, P \rangle$ and $\langle d_1', d_2', \ell', P' \rangle$ are *permutative variants* if $d_1 = d_1'$, $d_2 = d_2'$, $\ell = \ell'$, and there is a bijection π on Σ_m with $m = k$ if $\ell = k$ and $m = \ell - 1$ otherwise such that

$$P' = \pi(P) = \{[\theta \circ \pi, c, b_1, b_2] \mid [\theta, c, b_1, b_2] \in P\}\,.$$

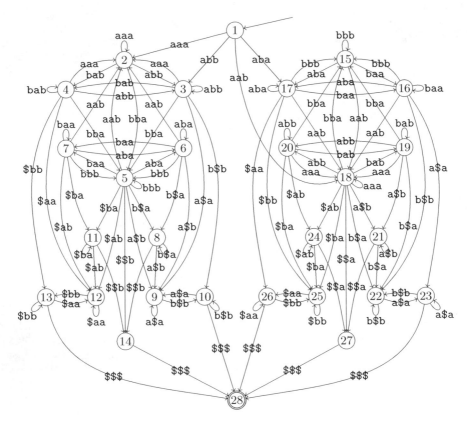

Fig. 3. DFA M_2 that accepts base-2 solvable canonical cryptarithm sequences. The initial state is $q_0 = 1$ and the accepting state is $f_1 = 28$. The other accepting state f_2 is missing in M_2.

Clearly if the configurations of two states are permutative variants, the subautomata consisting of reachable states from those states are isomorphic under the permutation. This allows us to reduce the size of the automaton by merging those states. In our new DFA $\widetilde{M_k}$, each transition edge has two labels: one is a trigram as before and the other is a permutation on Σ_k. After passing a transition edge labeled with a permutation π, we will follow transition edges by replacing each letter in accordance with π. Figure 4 shows a fragment of $\widetilde{M_2}$.

We formally define this new kind of DFAs with edges labeled with a letter and a permutation. A *DFA with permutation edges* is a sextuple $M = \langle Q, \Sigma, \delta, \gamma, q_0, F \rangle$, where δ and γ are partial functions $Q \times \Sigma \rightharpoonup Q$ and $Q \times \Sigma \rightharpoonup \Pi_\Sigma$, respectively, where Π_Σ is the set of all permutations over Σ, such that the domains of δ and γ coincide. For $x \in \Sigma$, $w \in \Sigma^*$ and $q \in Q$, define

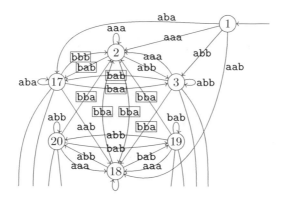

Fig. 4. Fragment of $\widetilde{M}_2$, where boxed trigram labels are with the permutation $\{\mathtt{a} \mapsto \mathtt{b},$ $\mathtt{b} \mapsto \mathtt{a}\}$, while the others are with the identity ι. States with the same name in Figs. 3 and 4 have the same configuration.

$\hat{\delta} \colon Q \times \Sigma^* \rightharpoonup Q$ and $\hat{\gamma} \colon Q \times \Sigma^* \rightharpoonup \Pi_\Sigma$ by

$$\hat{\delta}(q, \varepsilon) = q,$$
$$\hat{\gamma}(q, \varepsilon) = \iota,$$
$$\hat{\delta}(q, wx) = \delta(\hat{\delta}(q, w), \hat{\gamma}(q, w)(x)),$$
$$\hat{\gamma}(q, wx) = \gamma(\hat{\delta}(q, w), \hat{\gamma}(q, w)(x)) \circ \hat{\gamma}(q, w),$$

where ι is the identity. The strings that the automaton M accepts are those $w \in \Sigma^*$ such that $\hat{\delta}(q_0, w) \in F$. Mealy machines with permutation edges can also be defined, where outputs may depend on the current state, permutation and next input letter.

We modify M_k to $\widetilde{M}_k$ by merging states that are permutative variants and adding appropriate permutation labels to edges. In our cryptarithm DFAs with permutation edges, permutation labels are defined on letters in Σ_k and homomorphically extended to trigrams on $\Sigma_k \cup \{\$\}$, where $\$$ is always mapped to $\$$ itself. Algorithm 1 shows the pseudo code for constructing $\widetilde{M}_k$. An assignment $\theta \circ \hat{\gamma}(q_0, w)$ is a solution of a cryptarithm sequence $w\$\$\$$ if and only if $[\theta, 0, 1, 1] \in P$ for the configuration $\langle d_1, d_2, \ell, P \rangle$ of the state $\hat{\delta}(q_0, w)$.

On Line 13 of Algorithm 1, we check whether a configuration $q' = \langle d'_1, d'_2, \ell', P' \rangle$ is a permutative variant of an existing state $q'' \in Q$. In the actual implementation, we do not try all the possible combinations of $q'' \in Q$ and $\pi \in \Pi_k$. Applying a hash function to q', we compare it with only configurations $q'' - \langle d'_1, d'_2, \ell', P'' \rangle \in Q$ such that $|P'_{c,b_1,b_2}| = |P''_{c,b_1,b_2}|$ for all $(c, b_1, b_2) \in \{0,1\}^3$ where P_{c,b_1,b_2} is the subset of P whose elements have the form $[\theta, c, b_1, b_2]$ for some θ. Let $[\theta, c, b_1, b_2]$ and $[\theta_i, c_i, b_{1i}, b_{2i}]$ be the first element of P'' and the ith element of P', respectively. For each $i \in \{1, \ldots, |P'|\}$, we compare P'' and $\pi_i(P')$ where $\pi_i \in \Pi_{\Sigma_k}$ satisfies $\pi_i(\theta_i) = \theta$. If P'' and $\pi_i(P')$ coincide exactly, q' and q'' are permutative variants.

Algorithm 1. Constructing $\widetilde{M}_k$

```
1: let q₀ := ⟨0, 0, 1, {[∅, 0, 0, 0]}⟩ and Q := {q₀, f₁, f₂};
2: push q₀ to the stack;
3: while the stack is not empty do
4:     pop the top element q from the stack;
5:     for each trigram u on Σₖ ∪ {$} do
6:         if there is a configuration q′ such that q ⇒ᵘ q′ then
7:             if u = $$$ then
8:                 if q′ = ⟨d₁, d₂, ℓ, P⟩ with |P| = 1 then
9:                     add an edge from q to f₁ with label ⟨u, ι⟩;
10:                else
11:                    add an edge from q to f₂ with label ⟨u, ι⟩;
12:                end if
13:            else if there are q″ ∈ Q and π ∈ Π_{Σₖ} such that q′ = π(q″) then
14:                add an edge from q to q″ with label ⟨u, π⟩;
15:            else
16:                add q′ to Q and push q′ to the stack;
17:                add an edge from q to q′ with label ⟨u, ι⟩;
18:            end if
19:        end if
20:    end for
21: end while
22: return ⟨Q, Σₖ, δ, γ, q₀, f₁, f₂⟩;
```

3.3   Comparison of Naive and Compressed Cryptarithm DFAs

Table 1 compares the numbers of states of M_k and $\widetilde{M}_k$. We succeeded in calculating the automata for $k \leq 7$ but gave up for $k \geq 8$ due to the long time calculation and big memory consumption. For the purpose of reference, we also show the number of states of $\min(M_k)$, the minimized version of M_k. Note that minimization loses the information of possible solutions for cryptarithm sequences and therefore $\min(M_k)$ cannot be used as a solver. Our compression technique achieves a more compact representation than the classical state minimization technique for solvable cryptarithm sequences, while keeping the solver function.

Table 1. Number of states and edges of cryptarithm automata

Base k		2	3	4	5	6	7
States	M_k	28	110	859	10267	370719	30909627
	$\widetilde{M}_k$	15	27	163	1061	17805	472518
	$\min(M_k)$	27	93	607	6589	248192	–
Edges	M_k	112	1032	17662	350019	23508141	3017993409
	$\widetilde{M}_k$	58	233	3860	40042	1214972	48635469
	$\min(M_k)$	111	985	16602	330297	22673144	–

Table 2. Used computational resources for constructing cryptarithm automata

	Base k	2	3	4	5	6	7
Time (s)	M_k	<0.01	<0.01	0.03	0.59	35 s	85 min
	$\widetilde{M_k}$	<0.01	<0.01	0.01	0.18	23 s	264 min
Space (MB)	M_k	<2	2.1	4.5	18	1.0 GB	90 GB
	$\widetilde{M_k}$	<2	<2	2.8	6.5	92 MB	3.7 GB

Table 2 compares the time and space used to construct M_k and $\widetilde{M_k}$. Our implementation was compiled with Go 1.10 on Ubuntu 14.04 LTS with CPU Xeon E5-2609 2.4 GHz and 256 GB memory. To construct $\widetilde{M_k}$ was quicker than M_k for $k \leq 6$ but it was reversed for $k = 7$. Nonetheless, $\widetilde{M_k}$ requires much smaller memory than M_k for all k.

3.4   Cryptarithms with Limited Number of Letters

As we have observed in the previous subsection, we were unable to compute M_k and $\widetilde{M_k}$ for $k \geq 8$. On the other hand, there are many interesting base-10 cryptarithms in the real world that do not involve all the 10 numerals. It is still interesting to construct a DFA $\widetilde{M_{k,s}}$ that accepts all and only base-k solvable cryptarithm sequences over Σ_s for $s \leq k$. This can be achieved by a slight modification on Algorithm 1, where we refrain from making transition edges whose label includes forbidden letters not in Σ_s. In addition, when $s = k - 1$, we need to give up "promotion" of an assignment with domain Σ_{k-1} to its extension with domain Σ_k. This results actually in a simpler construction algorithm.

Tables 3 and 4 show the numbers of states and the computation times of the construction of $\widetilde{M_{k,s}}$ for $8 \leq k \leq 10$ and $2 \leq s \leq 5$.

Table 3. Number of states of $\widetilde{M_{k,s}}$

$k \backslash s$	2	3	4	5
8	23	302	5623	133385
9	20	313	6688	220255
10	19	320	7507	328959

Table 4. Construction time of $\widetilde{M_{k,s}}$ (sec. except for $s = 5$)

$k \backslash s$	2	3	4	5
8	<0.01	0.01	1.6	10 min
9	<0.01	0.01	2.3	34 min
10	<0.01	0.01	2.6	76 min

4   Analysis of Cryptarithms

Cryptarithm automata M_k, $\widetilde{M_k}$ and $\widetilde{M_{k,s}}$ can be used as cryptarithm puzzle solvers as we have described in the previous section. Moreover, they can be used as complete catalogues of solvable cryptarithms. For example, one can count the number of base-k solvable cryptarithms of size n and one can enumerate the base-k solvable cryptarithm sequences by the length-lexicographic order.

4.1   Counting Solvable Cryptarithms

The number $F_k(n)$ of base-k uniquely solvable cryptarithms of size n is the number of the paths of length $n+1$ from the initial states to the accepting state f_1 in $\widetilde{M_k}$. The number $G_k(n)$ of (not necessarily uniquely) solvable cryptarithms is obtained by adding the number of paths to the accepting state f_2 to this number. Those numbers can be calculated by the standard technique using the adjacency matrix A_k of the automaton in $O(m_k^3 \log n)$ time, where m_k is the number of states of the automaton (i.e., m_k is the number of rows (columns) of A_k). Table 5 summarizes the numbers of uniquely and not necessarily uniquely solvable cryptarithms. Although we have computed $\widetilde{M_7}$, we were unable to calculate $F_7(n)$ and $G_7(n)$ even for small numbers n by multiplying the adjacency matrices due to the size of the matrices. Moreover, for $k = 2, 3$, we obtain $F_k(n)$ and $G_k(n)$ as explicit formulas of n using Mathematica^{TM}. Unfortunately, Mathematica^{TM} returned no answers for bigger $k \geq 4$ within 3 days on our environment.

Table 5. The numbers $F_k(n)$ and $G_k(n)$ of uniquely and not necessarily uniquely solvable cryptarithms, respectively. Among those, numbers shown with bold figures were not known in [4].

$F_k(n)$:

$k \backslash n$	1	2	3	4	5	6	7	8	...	n
2	0	3	18	84	360	1488	6048	24384	...	$6 \times 4^{n-2} - 3 \times 2^{n-2}$
3	1	19	233	2443	23825	223939	2063993	**18821563**	...	$4 \times 9^{n-1} - 4 \times 5^{n-1} - 3^{n-1}$
4	1	46	1200	24094	431424	7326008	121032266	**1970599868**	...	-
5	0	42	3190	125940	3866438	106663574	2797440502	**71604333066**	...	-
6	0	10	3470	336367	18978996	**847469530**	**33983003374**	**1292957034805**	...	-

$G_k(n)$:

$k \backslash n$	1	2	3	4	5	6	7	8	...	n
2	0	3	18	84	360	1488	6048	24384	...	$6 \times 4^{n-2} - 3 \times 2^{n-2}$
3	1	23	265	2639	24913	229703	2093785	**18973439**	...	$4 \times 9^{n-1} - 2 \times 5^{n-1} - 3^{n-1}$
4	2	69	1463	26716	456639	7561377	123194460	**1990281467**	...	-
5	2	115	4622	148483	4184478	110899540	**2852251360**	**72299094358**	...	-
6	2	123	8650	498307	22931188	**933488391**	**35745728867**	**1327783229135**	...	-

4.2   Enumerating and Indexing Cryptarithms

By depth-first search on a cryptarithm automaton, one can enumerate all the base-k (uniquely) solvable cryptarithm sequences by length-lexicographic order. Moreover, from an index number i, one can efficiently give the ith (uniquely) solvable cryptarithm sequence. This can be computed in $O(m_k^3 n \log n)$ time, where n is the length of the ith cryptarithm, using powers of the adjacency matrix A_k. Conversely, from a solvable cryptarithm of length n, the indexing number of it can be computed in $O(m_k^3 n \log n)$ time as well. As examples, the first 30 base-3 solvable cryptarithm sequences are given below.

aab\$\$\$,   aaabbc\$\$\$,   aab\$\$b\$\$\$,   aab\$aa\$\$\$,   aab\$ba\$\$\$,

aab\$bb\$\$\$,   aaba\$a\$\$\$,   aabaab\$\$\$,   aabb\$a\$\$\$,   aabb\$b\$\$\$,

aba\$aa\$\$\$,   aba\$cc\$\$\$,   abaaac\$\$\$,   abacca\$\$\$,   abbb\$b\$\$\$,

abbbbc\$\$\$,   abbc\$c\$\$\$,   abbccb\$\$\$,   abc\$\$a\$\$\$,   abc\$\$b\$\$\$,

abc\$ab\$\$\$,   abc\$ba\$\$\$,   abca\$b\$\$\$,   abcb\$a\$\$\$, aaaaaabbc\$\$\$,

aaaabbb\$b\$\$\$, aaaabbbbc\$\$\$, aaaabbc\$c\$\$\$, aaaabbccb\$\$\$, aaabab\$bb\$\$\$,

5   Conclusions and Discussions

This paper proposed an algorithm to construct a DFA that accepts solvable cryptarithms under the base-k numeral system. Our construction method involves a technique to reduce the number of states more significantly than the classical minimization of DFAs by enriching transition edge labels. Using those automata, we demonstrated that the numbers of base-k solvable cryptarithms of n digits are computable for $2 \le k \le 6$.

Our compression technique is based on the symmetry among assignments. We could not define a canonical representative among permutative variants. If one could efficiently compute such a canonical form, the computation time would be shortened. Another type of symmetry is found between the first and second summand terms. It is future work to take advantage of this type of symmetry to reduce the size of cryptarithm DFAs. We are also interested in applying our DFAs for generating alphametics, which are cryptarithms with meaningful words.

Acknowledgments. We thank to Kaizaburo Chubachi for assisting us in some of the experiments. We also appreciate anonymous reviewers' helpful comments. The work is supported in part by KAKENHI 15H05706.

References

1. Abbasian, R., Mazloom, M.: Solving cryptarithmetic problems using parallel genetic algorithm. In: Second International Conference on Computer and Electrical Engineering, pp. 308–312 (2009)
2. Collins, T.: Alphametic puzzle solver. http://www.tkcs-collins.com/truman/alphamet/alpha_solve.shtml. Accessed 01 May 2018
3. Dudeney, H.E.: Strand Magazine, vol. 68, pp. 97–214. George Newnes, London (1924)
4. Endoh, H.: Automata-theoretic approaches to puzzle analysis. Master's thesis, Graduate School of Information Sciences, Tohoku University (2013). (in Japanese)
5. Endoh, H., Narisawa, K., Shinohara, A.: An automaton theory approach for analyzing alphametic. In: Proceedings of the 16th Game Programming Workshop, pp. 54–61 (2011). (in Japanese)
6. Eppstein, D.: On the NP-completeness of cryptarithms. ACM SIGACT News **18**(3), 38–40 (1987)
7. Knuth, D.E.: The Art of Computer Programming, vol. 4A. Addison-Wesley, Reading (2017)

8. Luoma, K.: Cryptarithms: a non-programming approach using excel. Spreadsh. Educ. (eJSiE) **9**(2), 6 (2016)
9. Tamura, N.: Cryptarithmetic puzzle solver. http://bach.istc.kobe-u.ac.jp/llp/crypt. html. Accessed 01 May 2018

One-Counter Automata for Parsing and Language Approximation

Alexander Sakharov$^{(\boxtimes)}$

Synstretch, Framingham, MA, USA
mail@sakharov.net

Abstract. A grammar characterization of partially blind one-counter languages is presented. One-counter automata are used to build parse trees of the respective grammars. One-counter automata are also used to find the most probable derivations for the stochastic versions of these grammars. Both these tasks are executed in quadratic time in the size of the input. Regular expressions are extended with one-counter language capabilities. Context-free languages are approximated with one-counter languages.

1 Introduction

The time complexity of parsing context-free (CF) languages is cubic in the size of the input in a general case, which includes the majority of ambiguous languages. See the CYK and Earley algorithms [1]. This time complexity is prohibitive for some applications. Sub-cubic parsing algorithms do exist but they are not practical [2].

CF grammars are often ambiguous. Natural language grammars are almost always ambiguous [1]. Ambiguous grammars are widely used in bioinformatics [3]. Selecting better derivations is an additional parsing challenge for these languages. Stochastic (aka probabilistic) grammars are an instrument for dealing with ambiguity. They associate probabilities with productions. Stochastic parsing amounts to finding the most probable derivations for given input strings [1]. Due to grammar splitting methods, stochastic parsing can be highly accurate, including natural language parsing [4].

Finding the most probable derivation is solved by dynamic programming algorithms such as the CYK algorithm for stochastic CF grammars [1]. The stochastic CYK algorithm also has a cubic time complexity in the size of the input. Enhanced algorithms for parsing stochastic CF languages execute much faster than the CYK algorithm in practice, but still exhibit a cubic asymptotic time complexity [5].

As opposed to CF languages, regular languages can be parsed in linear time by finite automata (FA). The task of finding the most probable derivation can be solved in linear time of the size of the input by the Viterbi algorithm [1]. The Viterbi algorithm finds the most probable sequence of automaton transitions (path) accepting the input for stochastic FAs. It can be applied to the

© Springer International Publishing AG, part of Springer Nature 2018
C. Câmpeanu (Ed.): CIAA 2018, LNCS 10977, pp. 299–311, 2018.
https://doi.org/10.1007/978-3-319-94812-6_25

automata recognizing right-linear, i.e. regular, grammars. The most probable path is also the most probable derivation in the respective right-linear grammar. Its time complexity makes the Viterbi algorithm the tool of choice for numerous applications, since many of them require a real-time result. Unfortunately, regular languages constitute a very limited subclass of CF languages. Having faster parsing algorithms for supersets of regular languages including algorithms for finding the most probable derivations is crucial.

One-counter (OC) automata are FAs extended with a non-negative counter [6]. The languages recognized by OC automata are a proper subset of CF languages and a proper superset of regular languages. OC automata have plenty of applications [7,8], and so do stochastic OC automata [9,10]. Stochastic OC automata are equivalent to discrete-time quasi-birth death processes [11].

Partially blind one-counter (PBOC) automata are OC automata without counter tests [12]. They are also known as restricted one-counter automata [13] and one-counter nets [14]. PBOC automata are equivalent to B-automata [15]. The languages recognized by PBOC automata are a proper superset of regular languages and a proper subset of OC languages. The properties of OC and PBOC languages have been extensively studied [6,13,14,16].

OC automata, including stochastic ones, have not been used much for parsing. Grammar characterization of OC and PBOC languages has been an open issue for decades [6,8]. We specify a class of grammars characterizing PBOC languages. We describe how to build matching PBOC automata from these grammars and vice versa. The time complexity of parsing the characterizing languages, including stochastic parsing, is quadratic in the size of the input. We augment regular expressions (RE) with OC capabilities. These extended REs give another characterization of PBOC languages.

The approximation of CF languages has recently caught much attention. CF languages are usually approximated with regular languages [17]. Fast parsing is one of the reasons of this approximation. Some advanced approximation methods have been developed [18].

We introduce a technique for approximating CF languages by OC automata. OC automata are more adequate for handling parenthesis constructs than FAs. This technique enables the generation of approximate parse trees. The languages accepted by the approximating automata include the source CF languages. We present a sufficient decidable condition for a CF grammar to be recognizable by a OC automaton. We describe a method for approximating automaton transition probabilities from grammar production probabilities.

2   One-Counter Automata

Definition 1. *A (nondeterministic) OC automaton is a tuple* (S, R, s, F, T) *where S is a finite set of states, R is a set of input symbols (alphabet), $s \in S$ is the start state, $F \subset S$ is a set of final states, T is a set of transitions. The transitions have the form: $s, t, c \to r, n$ where s and r are states, t is an input symbol, $c \in \{0, +\}$ is a counter test, $n \in \{+1, -1, 0\}$ is a counter operation.*

Transitions with $c = 0$ apply when the counter is zero, and transitions with $c = +$ apply when the counter is positive. The transition adds n to the counter value. Transitions with $c = 0$ and $n = -1$ are disallowed. The value of the counter is zero at the start. An input is accepted if the automaton is in a final state and the counter is zero. Transitions are classified as incrementing ($n = +1$), decrementing ($n = -1$), and internal ($n = 0$).

Some definitions of OC automata allow ϵ-transitions, i.e. transitions without input symbols. Alternatively, OC automata can be defined as pushdown automata with a single stack symbol and a special bottom symbol [11].

Definition 2. *A transition sequence is called balanced if the counter value at the beginning equals its value at the end, and the counter value at other states is not less than that.*

In the case of stochastic OC automata, probability p is associated with every transition [11]. It is assumed that transition probabilities satisfy the following conditions for any non-final state s:

$$\sum_{t,r,n} p(s,t,0 \to r,n) = 1 \qquad \sum_{t,r,n} p(s,t,+ \to r,n) = 1$$

For any final state, these sums are less than one by the final state probability. Some definitions of stochastic OC automata include start state probabilities.

The probability of an automaton path is defined as the product of the probabilities of its transitions. The Viterbi algorithm from [19] outputs the most probable path accepting the input of a stochastic OC automaton. Its time complexity is quadratic in the size of the input. This algorithm can be used to output acceptance paths for non-stochastic OC automata if we assign $p(s,t,c \to r,n) = 1$ instead of probabilities for all transitions.

Trees can be generated from acceptance paths of OC automata [19]. These trees play the role of parse trees. Input symbols are leaf nodes of these trees. The source states of incrementing and internal transitions label non-leaf nodes. The source states of decrementing transitions could be leaf nodes, or these states could have one child. Both interpretations are based on the intuitive assumption that any incrementing transition opens a construct, and a matching decrementing transition closes it.

In order to build a tree, we iterate over transitions in an acceptance path and maintain the stack of states. For any transition $A, u, c \to B, 0$, u and B are the children of A. For any transition $A, u, c \to B, +1$, u and B are the first two children of A. A is pushed onto the stack. For any transition $C, v, + \to D, -1$, the top state is popped from the stack. Under the first interpretation, C has no child nodes, v and D are added as children of the node popped from the stack. Under the second interpretation, v becomes the sole child of C, and D is added as a child of the node popped from the stack.

Definition 3. *A OC automaton is called PBOC if the following holds for any s, t, r, h: the automaton has transition $s,t,0 \to r,h$ iff it has transition $s,t,+ \to r,h$ (cf. [12]).*

Usually, PBOC automata are defined by transitions without the counter test, and the automata halt when the counter becomes negative. Following this tradition, we drop the counter test from the notation of PBOC automaton transitions. PBOC automata can also be defined as pushdown automata with a single stack symbol and without bottom symbol transitions [13].

3 Counting Regular Expressions

REs are regarded as a simpler notation than CF grammars. REs are also more widely used [20]. The notion of a counter can be incorporated into REs without affecting their simplicity but enhancing the expressiveness. OC automata can be used to parse these extended REs, which will be called counting regular expressions (CRE), and to generate trees. Let $\mathcal{L}$ denote the language defined by a RE, grammar, or automaton.

CREs are defined as REs in which some terminals may be annotated with plus or minus, for instance, a^+ or a^- for terminal a. A string matches a CRE if the following three conditions are met. First, the string matches this CRE with the annotations ignored. Second, the number of input symbols matching the plus terminals should be greater or equal to the number of input symbols matching the minus terminals for any partial input, i.e. for any substring $n_1...n_k$ of input $n_1...n_m$. Third, these two numbers should be equal for the entire input.

For example, the following CRE specifies additive expressions (terminals are underlined, terminal $\underline{id}$ represents identifiers):

$$((\underline{(}^+)^* \; \underline{id} \; \underline{()}^-)^* \; ((\underline{\pm} \mid \underline{\mp}) \; ((\underline{(}^+)^* \; \underline{id} \; \underline{()}^-)^*)^*$$

Theorem 1. *The sets of languages defined by CREs and PBOC automata are identical.*

Proof. We can view any CRE X as a RE in which a, a^+, a^- are treated as distinct terminals even though they match the same input. Let us convert this RE to its recognizing nondeterministic FA without ϵ-transitions X' [21]. Now we can transform X' transitions into transitions of PBOC automaton X'' as follows:

$$s, x \to t \qquad \Rightarrow \qquad s, x \to t, 0$$
$$s, x^+ \to t \qquad \Rightarrow \qquad s, x \to t, +1$$
$$s, x^- \to t \qquad \Rightarrow \qquad s, x \to t, -1$$

The start and final states remain unchanged. Any string $s \in \mathcal{L}(X)$ is accepted by X'. Using the above rules, we can transform any X' acceptance path into a X'' path. It is also an acceptance path for X'' because it is balanced, and the counter is zero at the end. Now suppose string u is accepted by X''. It is also accepted by X'. Since the input symbols matching annotated terminals of X satisfy the CRE conditions, $u \in \mathcal{L}(X)$.

These transformations can be reverted to transform any PBOC automaton to a FA with annotated terminals. Any FA can be transformed to an equivalent RE. Annotations are carried from the FA to this RE which is treated as a CRE. We can use the same arguments as before to show that this CRE and the source PBOC automaton define the same language. □

Using the Viterbi algorithm for OC automata and the first interpretation of acceptance paths, we can build parse trees for the strings matching CRE.

4 Compartmentalized Grammars

Without loss of generality, we can assume that CF grammar productions are in the quadratic Greibach normal form (QGNF), i.e. every production is $A \to bB_1...B_k$ where $0 \leq k \leq 2$ [6]. As usual, $=>^*$ denotes grammar derivation. Let $\mathcal{R}(A)$ be the set consisting of nonterminal A and all such nonterminals B that $A =>^* \alpha B$ where α is a string of terminals and/or nonterminals. A simple iterative procedure can calculate $\mathcal{R}(A)$ for all nonterminals A of any CF grammar. Let $\mathcal{I}$ be the set of nonterminals D such that there is production $A \to bB_1B_2$, and $D \in \mathcal{R}(B_1)$.

Consider a OC automaton whose states are grammar nonterminals. Additionally, there is one and only final state Z that does not map to any nonterminal. Start nonterminal S is the start state. Transitions are constructed as follows:

For every production $A \to bB_1$:
$$A, b, 0 \to B_1, 0 \quad \text{if } A \in \mathcal{R}(S)$$
$$A, b, + \to B_1, 0 \quad \text{if } A \in \mathcal{I}$$
For every production $A \to bB_1B_2$:
$$A, b, 0 \to B_1, +1 \quad \text{if } A \in \mathcal{R}(S)$$
$$A, b, + \to B_1, +1 \quad \text{if } A \in \mathcal{I}$$
For every production $A \to bB_1B_2$ and production $D \to d$ such that $D \in \mathcal{R}(B_1)$:
$$D, d, + \to B_2, -1$$
For every production $D \to d$ such that $D \in \mathcal{R}(S)$:
$$D, d, 0 \to Z, 0$$

Theorem 2. *If OC automaton Ω is built by the above rules from CF grammar Γ in QGNF, then $\mathcal{L}(\Gamma) \subseteq \mathcal{L}(\Omega)$.*

Proof. Consider the parse tree of an input string from $\mathcal{L}(\Gamma)$. Let us traverse this parse tree in pre-order. Nonterminals and terminals alternate in the traversal sequence. Every triple A, b, C in the sequence (where b is a terminal) corresponds to a transition of the automaton generated from the grammar. Triples originating from productions $A \to tB$ map to transitions $A, t, n \to B, 0$ where $n = 0$ or $n = +$ depending on the counter value. Productions $A \to uBC$ are the source of transitions $A, u, n \to B, +1$. Along with productions $D \to c$ where $D \in \mathcal{R}(B)$, they are also the source of transitions $D, c, + \to C, -1$. In both cases, $A \in \mathcal{R}(S)$ if $n = 0$, and $A \in \mathcal{I}$ if $n > 0$.

The destination state of every transition in the traversal sequence equals to the source state of the next one. Incrementing and decrementing transitions are paired according to parse tree nodes for productions $A \to uBC$. Therefore, the counter value is always non-negative and equals zero at the end. The counter is always positive at the source states of decrementing transitions. If A, b is the last pair in the traversal sequence, then $A \in \mathcal{R}(S)$, and this pair maps to transition $A, b, 0 \to Z, 0$. Therefore, the input is accepted by Ω. ☐

We also can construct a PBOC automaton from productions of any grammar in QGNF. Let both $A, u, 0 \rightarrow B, h$ and $A, u, + \rightarrow B, h$ be generated regardless of whether $A \in \mathcal{R}(S)$, $A \in \mathcal{I}$, or not. Clearly, Theorem 2 holds after this change.

Definition 4. *Grammar Γ in QGNF is called compartmentalized quadratic Greibach (CQG) if for any two productions $A \rightarrow bBC$ and $E \rightarrow fFG$, $\mathcal{R}(B) \cap \mathcal{R}(F) = \emptyset$. If for any such productions, either $\mathcal{R}(B) \cap \mathcal{R}(F) = \emptyset$ or the grammar includes productions $A \rightarrow bBG$ and $E \rightarrow fFC$ as well, then Γ is called semi-compartmentalized (SCQG).*

For example, the following grammar is CQG:

$$S \rightarrow id \qquad S \rightarrow id\, S \qquad S \rightarrow (SR \qquad R \rightarrow) \qquad R \rightarrow)S$$

Here is the PBOC automaton constructed from this grammar:

$$S, id \rightarrow S, 0 \qquad R,) \rightarrow S, 0 \qquad S, (\rightarrow S, +1$$
$$S, id \rightarrow R, -1 \qquad R,) \rightarrow R, -1 \qquad S, id \rightarrow Z, 0 \qquad R,) \rightarrow Z, 0$$

Theorem 3. *If OC automaton Ω is built by the above rules from SCQG grammar Γ, then $\mathcal{L}(\Gamma) = \mathcal{L}(\Omega)$.*

Proof. Let $\overleftarrow{t}$ and $\overrightarrow{t}$ denote the source and destination state of transition t, respectively. We prove by induction on the number of incrementing transitions that if $t_1...t_n$ is a balanced sequence of transitions of Ω for input string $s_1...s_n$ and $\overrightarrow{t_n} \neq Z$, then $\overleftarrow{t_1} \Rightarrow^* s_1...s_n \overleftarrow{t_n}$ is a valid derivation in Γ, and $\overrightarrow{t_n} \in \mathcal{R}(\overleftarrow{t_1})$.

Base: Clearly, this proposition holds for balanced sequences without incrementing transitions.

Induction step: Suppose the proposition holds for sequences with not more than m incrementing transitions. Consider the first incrementing transition t_i in sequence $t_1...t_n$ with $m + 1$ incrementing transitions. Let t_j be its balancing decrementing transition.

Suppose t_i corresponds to production $A \rightarrow s_i B_1 B_2$, and t_j corresponds to production pair $E \rightarrow s_j$, $C \rightarrow dD_1 D_2$ such that $E \in \mathcal{R}(D_1)$. By the induction assumption, transition sequence $t_{i+1}...t_{j-1}$ maps to derivation $B_1 \Rightarrow^*$ $s_{i+1}...s_{j-1}E$, and $E \in \mathcal{R}(B_1)$. Since $E \in \mathcal{R}(D_1)$, Γ contains production $A \rightarrow s_i B_1 D_2$ as well. Transition t_i is identical to the transition generated from production $A \rightarrow s_i B_1 D_2$, and t_j is identical to the transition generated from production pair $E \rightarrow s_j$, $A \rightarrow s_i B_1 D_2$, and hence, $A \Rightarrow^* s_i...s_j D_2$.

By the induction assumption, $D_2 \Rightarrow^* s_{j+1}...s_n \overleftarrow{t_n}$ is a valid derivation, and $\overrightarrow{t_n} \in \mathcal{R}(D_2)$. Transitions $s_1...s_{i-1}$ are all internal, and thus, $\overleftarrow{t_1} \Rightarrow^* s_1...s_{i-1}A$, $A \in \mathcal{R}(\overleftarrow{t_1})$. Combining the three derivations, we get $\overleftarrow{t_1} \Rightarrow^* s_1...s_n \overleftarrow{t_n}$, and $\overrightarrow{t_n} \in \mathcal{R}(\overleftarrow{t_1})$.

If $t_1...t_k$ is an acceptance path, then $t_1...t_{k-1}$ is balanced, $S \Rightarrow^* s_1...s_{k-1} \overrightarrow{t_{k-1}}$ is a valid derivation in Γ, and $\overrightarrow{t_{k-1}} \in \mathcal{R}(S)$. Γ has production $\overrightarrow{t_{k-1}} \rightarrow s_k$ because $\overrightarrow{t_k} = Z$. Hence, $S \Rightarrow^* s_1...s_k$. □

Theorem 3 also holds for the PBOC automata built from SCQG grammars. Using the second interpretation of OC automaton acceptance paths, we can build trees from acceptance paths for the OC automata built from CF grammars in QGNF. These trees contain relevant syntactic information even if they do not exactly match productions of the source grammar. As the proof of Theorem 3 shows, the trees constructed from acceptance paths can be converted to the parse trees of the source SCQG grammars.

5   Stochastic Parsing

Any proper CQG grammar has no more than one distinct production $A \to bBC$ for any triple A, b, B. For any production $D \to c$ from a CQG grammar, there is no more than one such production $A \to bBC$ that $D \in \mathcal{R}(B)$.

Transition probabilities of the OC automata built from stochastic CQG grammars are expressed via grammar production probabilities:

$$p(A, b, 0 \to B, 0) = p(A, b, + \to B, 0) = p(A \to bB)$$
$$p(A, b, 0 \to B, +1) = p(A, b, + \to B, +1) = p(A \to bBC)$$
$$p(A, b, + \to B, -1) = p(A \to b) \qquad p(A, b, 0 \to Z, 0) = p(A \to b)$$

In stochastic grammars, the sum of probabilities of the productions $A \to \dots$ equals one for every nonterminal A [1]. For every state A except Z, the sum of $p(A, b, + \to B, n)$ for all b, B, n equals one because the sum of the respective production probabilities equals one. The same is true about the sum of $p(A, b, 0 \to B, n)$ for all b, B, n.

If a grammar undergoes a transformation, then the probabilities of new productions usually cannot be expressed via the probabilities of original productions. The following theorem guarantees that the Viterbi algorithm from [19] can be used to find the most probable derivations for stochastic CQG grammars.

Theorem 4. *Suppose stochastic OC automaton Ω is built from stochastic CQG grammar Γ, and their probabilities satisfy the above equations. A derivation in Γ is the most probable iff the respective Ω acceptance path is the most probable.*

Proof. The probability of a grammar derivation is calculated as the product of the probabilities of the productions in the respective parse tree. The probability of an acceptance path is the product of the probabilities of its transitions. There is one-to-one mapping between nonterminal nodes of Γ parse trees and transitions of Ω acceptance paths. The probabilities of the Γ productions associated with parse tree nodes and the probabilities of the respective Ω transitions equal each other. The most probable derivations corresponds to the most probable acceptance paths for CQG grammars and their counterpart stochastic OC automata because the probabilities of the derivations and acceptance paths are calculated as the products of the same values.   □

6   Grammar Characterization

We can transform any PBOC automaton into a CF grammar. Let us assign a unique positive number (identifier) to every distinct transition pair

$(A, b \rightarrow B, +1, \ D, c \rightarrow C, -1)$. We define nonterminal $[B, r]$ for every state B and every transition pair identifier r. Also, we define nonterminal $[B, 0]$ for every state B where 0 is a dummy identifier. If S is the start state, then $[S, 0]$ is the start nonterminal. The following rules define grammar productions. ϵ denotes the empty string.

1. $[A, r] \rightarrow b\,[B, r]$ for every transition $A, b \rightarrow B, 0$ and every identifier r
2. $[A, r] \rightarrow b\,[B, u]\,c\,[C, r]$ for every identifier $u = (A, b \rightarrow B, +1, \ D, c \rightarrow C, -1)$ and every identifier r
3. $[D, u] \rightarrow \epsilon$ for every identifier $u = (A, b \rightarrow B, +1, \ D, c \rightarrow C, -1)$
4. $[A, 0] \rightarrow \epsilon$ for every final state A

Lemma 1. *If grammar Γ is built from PBOC automaton Ω by the above rules, then $\mathcal{L}(\Gamma) = \mathcal{L}(\Omega)$.*

Proof. 1. $\mathcal{L}(\Gamma) \subseteq \mathcal{L}(\Omega)$

Consider an arbitrary parse tree for Γ and traverse it in pre-order. Every triple $[A, r], b, [B, r]$ in the traversal string corresponding to production $[A, r] \rightarrow b\,[B, r]$ has source transition $A, b \rightarrow B, 0$. Let $[A, r], b, [B, u]$ and $[E, v], c, [C, r]$ be the first and the last triple corresponding to production $[A, r] \rightarrow b\,[B, u]\,c\,[C, r]$ in the parse tree. This production is induced by transition pair $u = (A, b \rightarrow B, +1, \ D, c \rightarrow C, -1)$. $u = v$ because $[E, v] \in \mathcal{R}([B, u])$, and all elements of $\mathcal{R}([B, u])$ share the same identifier. Hence, $E = D$.

Every triple maps to an Ω transition. The destination state of every transition in the traversal sequence equals to the source state of the next one. Incrementing and decrementing transitions are paired according to parse tree nodes for productions $[A, r] \rightarrow b\,[B, u]\,c\,[C, r]$. Therefore, the counter value is always nonnegative, and it equals zero at the end. The counter value is always positive at nodes $[D, u]$ corresponding to the source states of decrementing transitions. If $[C, s]$ is the last node in the traversal sequence, then $s = 0$, and hence, C is a final state. Therefore, the sequence of triples from the traversal maps to an Ω acceptance path.

2. $\mathcal{L}(\Omega) \subseteq \mathcal{L}(\Gamma)$

We can prove by induction on the number of incrementing transitions that if $t_1 ... t_n$ is a balanced sequence of transitions of Ω for input string $s_1 ... s_n$, and r is an identifier, then $[\overleftarrow{t_1}, r] \Rightarrow^* s_1 ... s_n [\overrightarrow{t_n}, r]$ is a valid derivation in Γ. The fact that the input string of any Ω acceptance path is derivable in Γ is a corollary of that because the last state is final, and we can pick $r = 0$.

The proof is similar to the proof of Theorem 3. The difference is the following. If t_i is the first incrementing transition, and t_j is its balancing decrementing transition, then production $[\overrightarrow{t_j}, u] \rightarrow \epsilon$ is generated for transition pair $u = (t_i, t_j)$. Productions $[\overleftarrow{t_i}, v] \rightarrow s_i\,[\overleftarrow{t_{i+1}}, u]\,s_j\,[\overrightarrow{t_j}, v]$ are generated for $u = (t_i, t_j)$ and for every v. Combining these productions with derivation $[\overleftarrow{t_{i+1}}, u] \Rightarrow^* s_{i+1} ... s_{j-1} [\overrightarrow{t_{j-1}}, u]$, we get $[\overleftarrow{t_i}, v] \Rightarrow^* s_i ... s_j [\overrightarrow{t_j}, v]$. $\qquad\square$

Theorem 5. *The sets of languages defined by CQG grammars, SCQG grammars, and PBOC automata are identical.*

Proof. The Theorems 2 and 3 reformulated for PBOC automata show that an equivalent PBOC automaton, i.e. defining the same language, can be constructed for any SCQG grammar. Lemma 1 shows that an equivalent CF grammar can be constructed for any PBOC automaton. Consider any two productions $[A, r] \rightarrow b\,[B, u]\,c\,[C, r]$ and $[E, s] \rightarrow f\,[F, v]\,g\,[G, s]$ of the grammar built from a PBOC automaton. If $u = v$, then these productions are identical. If the two productions are distinct, then $\mathcal{R}([B, u]) \cap \mathcal{R}([F, v]) = \emptyset$ because all elements of $\mathcal{R}([X, z])$ share the same identifier z.

The grammars built from PBOC automata can be easily transformed into equivalent grammars in QGNF. First, every production $A \rightarrow bBcC$ is transformed into pair $A \rightarrow bBC'$, $C' \rightarrow cC$ where C' is a new nonterminal. Second, productions $A \rightarrow b$ and $A \rightarrow bB$ are added in lieu of productions $D \rightarrow \epsilon$. These additional productions are the result of removing D from the right-hand sides of productions. The resulting grammar defines the same language, it is CQG, and thus, SCQG as well. □

Any CQG grammar can be converted to an equivalent PBOC automaton and vice versa. The same is true about CREs and PBOC automata. Hence, any CRE can be converted to an equivalent CQG grammar and vice versa.

7   Approximation of Context-Free Languages

Theorem 3 gives an indication that OC automata better approximate grammars with fewer productions $A \rightarrow bB_1B_2$. We call them long productions. For instance, grammars having one long production are recognizable by OC automata.

Definition 5. *Nonterminal A from a CF grammar in QGNF is called regular if no $E \in \mathcal{R}(A)$ has long productions or if all nonterminals from the right-hand side of every A production are regular.*

Regular nonterminals can be effectively identified. If the start nonterminal is regular, then the grammar is regular. The following grammar transformation may boost the accuracy of the approximation by OC automata.

If B_1 is a regular nonterminal, then productions $A \rightarrow bB_1B_2$ can be eliminated at the expense of newly introduced nonterminals and productions of the form $C \rightarrow dD$. Let us start with such B_1 that no $D \in \mathcal{R}(B_1)$ has long productions. First, we replicate all these D along with all their productions and replace all replicas $E \rightarrow c$ with productions $E \rightarrow cB_2$. Second, we replace $A \rightarrow bB_1B_2$ with $A \rightarrow bB'$ where B' is the replica of B_1. By applying the above transformation iteratively, we eliminate all long productions with regular nonterminals B_1. This transformation does not introduce new long productions and does not change the language defined by the grammar.

Any proper CF grammar can be effectively converted to QGNF [6]. After that, the aforementioned transformation can be applied. Finally, we check if the transformed grammar is SCQG. Therefore, we have a sufficient condition for CF languages to be recognizable by PBOC automata. This condition can be effectively verified for an arbitrary CF grammar, and the recognizing automaton can be built when the condition is met.

Now we outline an approach to approximating transition probabilities of stochastic OC automata generated from stochastic CF grammars in QGNF. The transition probabilities can be learned from grammar production probabilities. Describing implementation details and estimating the accuracy of this approximation is beyond the scope of this paper.

A training set can be easily created. Strings belonging to the language are generated by constructing random derivations from the start nonterminal. For this purpose, productions are randomly applied by taking into account their probabilities. We calculate the probabilities of the generated strings from their parse trees. We generate acceptance paths of the approximating OC automaton from the parse trees as it is done in the proof of Theorem 2.

Let us build a model for the approximation of the probabilities of transitions. w_i will denote the probability of transition i. If there is only one transition t for source state a and counter test c, then $w_t = 1$. Otherwise, let us pick one transition among all transitions for given a and c. Note that a is not final. Let X be the set of these picked transitions, Y be its complement, and $C(i)$ denote the set of complementary transitions for transition $i \in X$. The probabilities of transitions from Y are model parameters.

The model equation is:

$$z = \prod_{i \in Y} w_i^{m_i} \prod_{i \in X} (1 - \sum_{j \in C(i)} w_j)^{m_i}$$

where m_i is the number of occurrences of transition i in the acceptance path, z is the probability of the corresponding grammar derivation. This model also has the following box constraints: $0 \leq w_i \leq 1$ for $i \in Y$.

We can symbolically calculate $\frac{\partial z}{\partial w_i}$ for $i \in Y$. Therefore, the model parameters w_i can be learned by gradient descent methods, e.g. stochastic gradient descent with square loss or another loss function [22]. Projections onto sets defined by box constraints are trivial. It is well-known that stochastic gradient descent gives robust results for a variety of optimization problems like this [22].

8   Related Work

The author is unaware of any previous work investigating the relationship between OC automata and grammars except for XML grammars. PBOC automata are used to validate XML documents against certain recursive DTDs in [8].

Recursive REs aim to incorporate CF features into REs [20]. They extend and complicate the notation of REs. Recursive REs disallow backtracking within recursive calls [20], i.e. recursive REs are not declarative unlike REs and CF grammars. Our extension, i.e. CREs, is less ambitious, but it adds the power of

OC languages while preserving the simplicity of REs and retaining their declarative nature.

RE parsers usually produce parse trees on the basis of the structure of a given RE [23]. CRE parsing employs annotated terminals as opening and closing markers for parse tree nodes.

Regular approximation of CF languages usually leads to the loss of syntactic information. A grammar defining arithmetic expressions is used as an illustrating example in [17]. Its approximating FA has only two states, and thus, its acceptance paths do not carry much syntactic information.

It is claimed in [17] that the approximating FAs can be used for parsing, but the parse trees reconstructed from acceptance paths of the approximating automaton differ from the parse trees of the source language. Another method for reconstructing parse trees from acceptance paths of the approximating automata was proposed in [24]. The problem with this method is that the reconstruction requires cubic time, which defeats the purpose of language approximation.

A method of learning transitions probabilities of stochastic FAs was proposed in [25]. This method works only for unambiguous FAs, while stochastic automata and grammars are expected to be ambiguous. In general, unambiguous automata do not need stochastic methods.

9   Conclusion

The characterization of PBOC languages by CREs and CQG grammars is an indication of relevance of PBOC automata to parsing. However, the approximation of CF languages could potentially be more accurate if it involves all OC automata. CQG languages is a new addition to the sparse collection of subclasses of ambiguous or stochastic CF languages that can be parsed in quadratic time or faster.

The approximation of CF languages by OC automata has the potential to be more realistic than the approximation by regular languages. The latter is inhibited by the limitations of regular languages. Our approximation applies to stochastic CF grammars as well. Language approximation makes more sense for stochastic languages because stochastic parsing is inherently approximate.

References

1. Jurafsky, D., Martin, J.H.: Speech and Language Processing, 2nd edn. Prentice-Hall Inc., Upper Saddle River (2009)
2. Lee, L.: Fast context-free grammar parsing requires fast boolean matrix multiplication. J. ACM **49**(1), 1–15 (2002)
3. Dowell, R.D., Eddy, S.R.: Evaluation of several lightweight stochastic context-free grammars for RNA secondary structure prediction. BMC Bioinformatics **5**(1), 71 (2004)
4. Petrov, S., Barrett, L., Thibaux, R., Klein, D.: Learning accurate, compact, and interpretable tree annotation. In: Proceedings of the 21st International Conference on Computational Linguistics, pp. 433–440 (2006)

5. Klein, D., Manning, C.D.: A* parsing: fast exact Viterbi parse selection. In: Proceedings of the 2003 Conference of the North American Chapter of the Association for Computational Linguistics on Human Language Technology - Volume 1, pp. 40–47 (2003)
6. Autebert, J., Berstel, J., Boasson, L.: Context-free languages and push-down automata. In: Rozenberg, G., Salomaa, A. (eds.) Handbook of Formal Languages. Springer, Heidelberg (1997). https://doi.org/10.1007/978-3-642-59136-5_3
7. Bouajjani, A., Bozga, M., Habermehl, P., Iosif, R., Moro, P., Vojnar, T.: Programs with lists are counter automata. Formal Methods Syst. Des. **38**(2), 158–192 (2011)
8. Chitic, C., Rosu, D.: On validation of XML streams using finite state machines. In: Proceedings of the 7th International Workshop on the Web and Databases, pp. 85–90 (2004)
9. Brázdil, T., Brozek, V., Etessami, K., Kucera, A., Wojtczak, D.: One-counter Markov decision processes. In: Proceedings of the 21st Annual ACM-SIAM Symposium on Discrete Algorithms, pp. 863–874 (2010)
10. Brázdil, T., Brozek, V., Etessami, K.: One-counter stochastic games. In: IARCS Annual Conference on Foundations of Software Technology and Theoretical Computer Science, pp. 108–119 (2010)
11. Etessami, K., Wojtczak, D., Yannakakis, M.: Quasi-birth-death processes, tree-like QBDs, probabilistic 1-counter automata, and pushdown systems. In: 5th International Conference on the Quantitative Evaluation of Systems, pp. 243–253 (2008)
12. Greibach, S.A.: Remarks on blind and partially blind one-way multicounter machines. Theoret. Comput. Sci. **7**, 311–324 (1978)
13. Berstel, J.: Transductions and Context-Free Languages. Leitfäden der angewandten Mathematik und Mechanik. Teubner (1979)
14. Czerwinski, W., Lasota, S.: Regular separability of one counter automata. In: 32nd Annual ACM/IEEE Symposium on Logic in Computer Science, pp. 1–12 (2017)
15. Render, E., Kambites, M.: Polycyclic and bicyclic valence automata. In: Martín-Vide, C., Otto, F., Fernau, H. (eds.) LATA 2008. LNCS, vol. 5196, pp. 464–475. Springer, Heidelberg (2008). https://doi.org/10.1007/978-3-540-88282-4_42
16. Brandenburg, F.J.: On the intersection of stacks and queues. Theoret. Comput. Sci. **58**(1), 69–80 (1988)
17. Mohri, M., Nederhof, M.J.: Regular approximation of context-free grammars through transformation. In: Junqua, J.C., van Noord, G. (eds.) Robustness in Language and Speech Technology. Text, Speech and Language Technology, pp. 153–163. Springer, Dordrecht (2001). https://doi.org/10.1007/978-94-015-9719-7_6
18. Eğecioğlu, Ö.: Strongly regular grammars and regular approximation of context-free languages. In: Developments in Language Theory: 13th International Conference, pp. 207–220 (2009)
19. Sakharov, A., Sakharov, T.: The Viterbi algorithm for subsets of stochastic context-free languages. Inf. Process. Lett. **135**, 68–72 (2018)
20. Friedl, J.E.F.: Mastering Regular Expressions. O'Reilly & Associates Inc., Sebastopol (2002)
21. Hromkovič, J., Seibert, S., Wilke, T.: Translating regular expressions into small ε-free nondeterministic finite automata. J. Comput. Syst. Sci. **62**(4), 565–588 (2001)
22. Cotter, A., Gupta, M.R., Pfeifer, J.: A light touch for heavily constrained SGD. In: Proceedings of the 29th Conference on Learning Theory, pp. 729–771 (2016)
23. Grathwohl, N.B.B., Henglein, F., Rasmussen, U.T.: Optimally streaming greedy regular expression parsing. In: International Conference on Theoretical Aspects of Computing, pp. 224–240 (2014)

24. Nederhof, M.J.: Context-free parsing through regular approximation. In: Proceedings of the International Workshop on Finite State Methods in Natural Language Processing, pp. 13–24 (1998)
25. Nederhof, M.J.: A general technique to train language models on language models. Comput. Linguist. **31**(2), 173–186 (2005)

On Syntactic Complexity of Circular Semi-flower Automata

Shubh N. Singh[1] and K. V. Krishna[2]([✉])

[1] Central University of South Bihar, Patna, India
shubh@cub.ac.in
[2] Indian Institute of Technology Guwahati, Guwahati, India
kvk@iitg.ac.in

Abstract. We investigate the syntactic complexity of a class of circular semi-flower automata (CSFA) classified by their bpi(s) – branch point(s) going in. In this work we obtain the syntactic complexity of CSFA with at most two bpis. In particular, we show that the syntactic complexity of the class of n-state CSFA with a unique bpi is linear. Further, for $n \geq 3$, we prove that the syntactic complexity of the class of n-state CSFA with two bpis over a binary alphabet is $2n(n + 1)$.

Keywords: Syntactic complexity · Transition monoids
Semi-flower automata

1 Introduction

The syntactic complexity of a recognizable language is the cardinality of its syntactic monoid. Further, the syntactic complexity of a class of recognizable languages is the maximal syntactic complexity of languages in that class, taken as a function of the state complexity of the languages. The syntactic complexity of a class of automata is considered to be the syntactic complexity of the class of languages accepted by the automata in that class.

Investigation on syntactic complexity of recognizable languages has received more attention in recent years. While Brzozowski et al. have pioneering contributions in obtaining syntactic complexity of various classes of recognizable languages (cf. [4–8]), syntactic complexity has been a topic of interest for many others (e.g., see [1,13,19,20]).

In [16], Maslov observed that n^n is the tight upper bound on the size of the transition monoid of n-state automata. Holzer and König [12] studied the unary and binary recognizable languages. For instance, they showed that the syntactic complexity of unary recognizable languages is linear. If the size of alphabet is at least three, they proved that the syntactic complexity is reached to the maximal size n^n. It turns out that the most crucial case is to determine the syntactic complexity of binary recognizable languages. Krawetz et al. [14], also studied the unary and binary recognizable languages.

© Springer International Publishing AG, part of Springer Nature 2018
C. Câmpeanu (Ed.): CIAA 2018, LNCS 10977, pp. 312–323, 2018.
https://doi.org/10.1007/978-3-319-94812-6_26

This paper investigates the syntactic complexity of certain classes of sub-monoids accepted by circular semi-flower automata (in short, CSFA). We consider CSFA classified by their bpi(s) – branch point(s) going in. Circular automata have been studied in various contexts. The Černý conjecture has been verified for synchronizing circular automata [9,17]. Semi-flower automata have been introduced to study the finitely generated submonoids of a free monoid [10,21]. Using semi-flower automata, the rank and intersection problem of certain submonoids of a free monoid have been investigated [11,22,24]. Semi-flower automata with at most one bpi are exactly automata of Huffman codes, and their synchronization properties were studied in [3]. Semi-flower automata have also been studied in various contexts [18,23].

In the next section, we present various fundamental notions and state a number of facts that are required in this paper. In Sect. 3, we obtain some necessary properties of CSFA and determine the syntactic complexity of the class of CSFA with a unique bpi. The syntactic complexity of CSFA with two bpis is determined in Sect. 4.

2   Preliminaries

This section provides necessary background material from [2,15,21]. Let P and Q be nonempty finite sets. The cardinality of P is denoted by $|P|$. By $P \setminus Q$, we mean the set of elements of P which are not in Q. Let α be an arbitrary function on P. We use $p\alpha$ to denote the image of $p \in P$ under α. The image set of α is denoted by $\mathrm{im}(\alpha)$. The *rank* of α, denoted by $\mathrm{rank}(\alpha)$, is defined as $\mathrm{rank}(\alpha) = |\mathrm{im}(\alpha)|$. A composition of functions on P is read from left to right: for example, $p\alpha\beta = (p\alpha)\beta$. The set of all functions on P forms a monoid under the composition of functions. For $n \in \mathbb{N}$, the function α^n denotes the composition of α with itself for n times. A function α is called an *idempotent* if $\alpha^2 = \alpha$. In fact, α is an idempotent if and only if its restriction to $\mathrm{im}(\alpha)$ is the identity. The set of all idempotents in a monoid M is denoted by $E(M)$. Let $P = \{p_1, p_2, \ldots, p_m\}$; we say that α is *circular permutation* if there is an ordering, say $p_{i_1}, \ldots, p_{i_m}$, of elements in P such that $p_{i_j}\alpha = p_{i_{j+1}}$ for $1 \le j < m$, and $p_{i_m}\alpha = p_{i_1}$.

An *alphabet* is a nonempty finite set, whose elements are called *symbols*. The free monoid over an alphabet A is denoted by A^*. The elements of A^* are called *words*, and ε denotes *empty* word – the identity element of A^*. A *language* is a subset of A^*. An *automaton* $\mathcal{A}$ is a quintuple (Q, A, δ, q_0, F), where Q is a nonempty finite set of *states*, A is an alphabet, $q_0 \in Q$ is the *initial* state, $F \subseteq Q$ is a nonempty set of *final* states, and δ is a *transition* function $\delta : Q \times A \to Q$. The domain of δ can be extended from $Q \times A$ to $Q \times A^*$. Let $x \in A^*$ and $q \in Q$; we write qx instead of $\delta(q, x)$. Clearly, by denoting the states as vertices and the transitions as labeled edges, an automaton can be represented by a digraph in which the initial state and final states shall be distinguished appropriately. A *path* in an automaton is a path in its digraph. For $p_i \in Q$ $(0 \le i \le k)$ and $a_j \in A$ $(1 \le j \le k)$, let $p_0 \xrightarrow{a_1} p_1 \xrightarrow{a_2} \cdots p_{k-1} \xrightarrow{a_k} p_k$ be a path in $\mathcal{A}$. The word $a_1 \cdots a_k \in A^*$ is called the *label* of the path. A *null* path is a path from a state to itself labeled by ε. A path that starts and ends at the same state is called a *cycle*, if it is not a null path. A state q is called a *branch point going in* (in short, bpi) if the indegree of q in the digraph of $\mathcal{A}$ is at least two. We denote by $BPI(\mathcal{A})$ the set of all bpis of $\mathcal{A}$. A state q is *accessible* (respectively, *coaccessible*) if there is a path from q_0 to q (respectively, a path from q to a final state). An automaton is called a *semi-flower automaton* (in short, SFA) if its set of final states is $\{q_0\}$, every state is accessible as well as coaccessible, and all cycles in the automaton visit the initial-final state q_0.

Let $\mathcal{A}$ be an automaton. $\mathcal{A}$ is called *minimal* if its each state is accessible and the equivalence relation on Q given by $p \equiv q$ if and only if $\forall x \in A^*(px \in F \iff qx \in F)$ is diagonal. The language *accepted* by $\mathcal{A}$, denoted $L(\mathcal{A})$, is the set of words that are labels of paths from q_0 to a final state. A language L is *recognizable* if $L = L(\mathcal{A})$ for some automaton $\mathcal{A}$. The *state complexity* of a recognizable language is the number of states in the minimal automaton accepting the language. For $x \in A^*$, there is a function $\overline{x} : Q \to Q$ defined as $q\overline{x} = qx$ for all $q \in Q$. An automaton is called *circular* if there is a symbol which induces a circular permutation on its state set. The set $M(\mathcal{A}) = \{\overline{x} \mid x \in A^*\}$ forms a monoid under the composition of functions, called the *transition* monoid of $\mathcal{A}$. Clearly, $M(\mathcal{A})$ is generated by functions induced by the symbols of $\mathcal{A}$, and $\overline{xy} = \overline{x}\,\overline{y}$ for all $x, y \in A^*$.

The *syntactic monoid* of a language L is the quotient monoid $A^*/_{\sim_L}$, where the congruence $\sim_L$ is given by $u \sim_L v$ if and only if $\forall x, y \in A^*(xuy \in L \iff xvy \in L)$. The *syntactic complexity* of a recognizable language is the size of its syntactic monoid. Further, the syntactic complexity of a class of recognizable languages is defined as the maximal syntactic complexity of languages in that class, taken as a function of state complexity of these languages. It is known that the syntactic complexity of a recognizable language is the same as the cardinality of the transition monoid of the minimal automaton accepting the language. Thus, in order to determine the syntactic complexity of a recognizable language, it is convenient to consider the transition monoid of its minimal automaton.

The *group of units* of a finite monoid M is the subgroup of M containing all invertible elements in M. Let G be a finite group with identity e and X a nonempty finite set. An *action* of G on X is a function $X \times G \to X$ denoted $(x, g) \mapsto xg$ such that $(xg)g' = x(gg')$, and $xe = x$ for all $x \in X$ and $g, g' \in G$. Given an action of G on X, the *orbit* of an element $x \in X$, denoted as $\mathcal{O}(x)$, is the equivalence class containing x of the equivalence relation $\sim$ on X defined as $y \sim x$ if and only if $y = xg$ for some $g \in G$. Note that the orbits partition X. The *stabilizer* of an element $x \in X$ is the subgroup $G_x = \{g \in G \mid xg = x\}$ of G. Clearly, $|\mathcal{O}(x)| = \dfrac{|G|}{|G_x|}$.

3   Circular Semi-flower Automata

In this section we prove certain properties of circular semi-flower automata (in short, CSFA) which are useful in determining its syntactic complexity. We also determine the syntactic complexity of the class of CSFA with a unique bpi. We first recall the necessary results from [23].

Theorem 1. *([23]). Let $\mathcal{A}$ be an SFA.*

(i) *For $a \in A$, if $\bar{a}$ is a permutation, then $\bar{a}$ is a circular permutation.*
(ii) *For $a, b \in A$, if $\bar{a}$ and $\bar{b}$ are permutations, then $\bar{a} = \bar{b}$.*
(iii) *$BPI(\mathcal{A}) = \varnothing$ if and only if $|A| = 1$.*

Unless otherwise stated, in what follows, $\mathcal{A}$ denotes an n-state CSFA. In view of Theorem 1, there is a unique circular permutation induced by symbols. For the rest of paper, we fix the following regarding $\mathcal{A}$. Assume that the symbol $a \in A$ induces the circular permutation $\bar{a}$, and accordingly $q_0, q_1, \ldots, q_{n-1}$ is the cyclic ordering of Q with respect to $\bar{a}$.

Theorem 2. *([23]). If $|BPI(\mathcal{A})| = k$ for some integer $k \geq 1$, then*

(i) *$q_0 \in BPI(\mathcal{A})$, and*
(ii) *any non-permutation in $M(\mathcal{A})$ has rank at most k.*

Hence, if $k = 1$, then $Q\bar{b} = \{q_0\}$ for all $b \in A \setminus \{a\}$.

We denote by G the cyclic subgroup of $M(\mathcal{A})$ generated by $\bar{a}$. Clearly, $|G| = n$. Moreover, G is the group of units of $M(\mathcal{A})$. For instance, for $x \in A^*$, let $\bar{x} \in M(\mathcal{A})$ be a permutation. Then

$$\bar{x} = \overline{a_1 a_2 \cdots a_m} = \bar{a}_1 \bar{a}_2 \cdots \bar{a}_m,$$

where $x = a_1 a_2 \cdots a_m$, $a_i \in A (1 \leq i \leq m)$. Since $\bar{x}$ is permutation, each $\bar{a}_i$ is a permutation. By Theorem 1(ii), we get $\bar{a} = \bar{a}_i$ for all i ($1 \leq i \leq m$). Hence, $\bar{x} = \bar{a}^m$ so that $\bar{x} \in G$.

Remark 1. For any two states p and q of $\mathcal{A}$, there exists $\bar{x} \in G$ such that $p\bar{x} = q$. Indeed, if $p = q_i$ and $q = q_j$ for some integers i, j ($0 \leq i \leq j < n$), then $\bar{x} = a^{j-i}$ will serve the purpose.

Proposition 1. $\mathcal{A}$ *is a minimal automaton.*

Proof. Since every state of $\mathcal{A}$ is accessible, it is sufficient to prove that the relation $\equiv$ on Q is diagonal. Let p and q be arbitrary states such that $p \equiv q$. By Remark 1, there exists $\bar{x} \in G$ such that $p\bar{x} = q_0$. Since $p \equiv q$, we get $q\bar{x} = q_0$. Now

$$p\bar{x} = q_0 = q\bar{x} \implies p\bar{x} = q\bar{x} \implies p = q \text{ (since } \bar{x} \in G).$$

Hence the relation $\equiv$ is diagonal. □

Since the function $M(\mathcal{A}) \times G \to M(\mathcal{A})$, defined by the composition of functions, is a group action, $M(\mathcal{A})$ is the union of disjoint orbits. Thus, in view of the following proposition, we focus on counting the number of disjoint orbits in $M(\mathcal{A})$ to determine the syntactic complexity of $\mathcal{A}$.

Lemma 1. $|\mathcal{O}(\overline{x})| = n$ *for all* $\overline{x} \in M(\mathcal{A})$.

Proof. Since $|\mathcal{O}(\overline{x})| = \frac{|G|}{|G_{\overline{x}}|}$ for all $\overline{x} \in M(\mathcal{A})$ and $|G| = n$, it is sufficient to prove that $G_{\overline{x}} = \{\overline{\varepsilon}\}$. Let $\overline{y} \in G_{\overline{x}}$ be arbitrary. Then

$$\overline{x}\,\overline{y} = \overline{x} \implies q(\overline{x}\,\overline{y}) = q\overline{x} \text{ for all } q \in Q \implies (q\overline{x})\overline{y} = q\overline{x}.$$

Let $p \in Q$ be arbitrary. By Remark 1, there exists $\overline{z} \in G$ such that $p = (q\overline{x})\overline{z}$. Now

$$p = (q\overline{x})\overline{z} \implies p\overline{y} = ((q\overline{x})\overline{z})\overline{y} \implies p\overline{y} = ((q\overline{x})\overline{y})\overline{z} \text{ (since } \overline{y}, \overline{z} \in G)$$
$$\implies p\overline{y} = (q\overline{x})\overline{z} \text{ (since } (q\overline{x})\overline{y} = q\overline{x}) \implies p\overline{y} = p \text{ (since } p = (q\overline{x})\overline{z}).$$

Therefore $\overline{y} = \overline{\varepsilon}$, as required. $\qquad\square$

We now determine the syntactic complexity of the class of n-state CSFA with a unique bpi. By Theorem 1(iii), we have $|A| \geq 2$. If $n = 1$, then all the functions induced by symbols are constant and equal, and therefore its syntactic complexity is $n = 1$. For $n \geq 2$, we find its syntactic complexity in the following theorem.

Theorem 3. *For* $n \geq 2$, *the syntactic complexity of the class of* n-*state CSFA with a unique bpi is* $2n$.

Proof. Let $\mathcal{A}$ be an n-state CSFA with a unique bpi. By Theorem 2, we have $Q\overline{b} = \{q_0\}$ for all $b \in A \setminus \{a\}$. Then $\overline{b} = \overline{c}$ for all $b, c \in A \setminus \{a\}$. Let $b \in A \setminus \{a\}$ be arbitrary. Notice that $\mathcal{O}(\overline{b}) = \{\overline{ba^i} \mid 0 \leq i < n\}$.

We claim that $\mathcal{O}(\overline{b}) = M(\mathcal{A}) \setminus G$. Clearly $\mathcal{O}(\overline{b}) \subseteq M(\mathcal{A}) \setminus G$. Let $\overline{x} \in M(\mathcal{A}) \setminus G$ be arbitrary. By Theorem 2(ii), we get $Q\overline{x} = \{q_k\}$ for some k ($0 \leq k < n$). Also $Q\overline{ba^k} = \{q_k\}$. Therefore $\overline{x} = \overline{ba^k} \in \mathcal{O}(\overline{b})$.

Thus, there are exactly two distinct orbits $\mathcal{O}(\overline{a}) = G$ and $\mathcal{O}(\overline{b}) = M(\mathcal{A}) \setminus G$. By Lemma 1, we get $|M(\mathcal{A})| = 2n$. Since $\mathcal{A}$ is arbitrary, the syntactic complexity of the class of n-state CSFA with a unique bpi is $2n$. $\qquad\square$

4   CSFA with Two Bpis

In this section we determine the syntactic complexity of the class of n-state CSFA with two bpis over a binary alphabet. If $n = 2$, then its syntactic complexity is $n = 2$. For $n \geq 3$, we prove the following main theorem.

Theorem 4. *For* $n \geq 3$, *the syntactic complexity of the class of* n-*state CSFA with two bpis over a binary alphabet is* $2n(n + 1)$.

We fix the following notation for the rest of this section. For $n \geq 3$, let $\mathcal{A}$ be an n-state CSFA with two bpis over the alphabet $A = \{a, b\}$. As earlier, $\overline{a}$ is the circular permutation. Notice that $Q\overline{b} = BPI(\mathcal{A})$ for non-permutation $\overline{b}$. By Theorem 2(i), the state q_0 is a bpi. Let q_m ($1 \leq m < n$) be the other bpi of $\mathcal{A}$, and so $Q\overline{b} = BPI(\mathcal{A}) = \{q_0, q_m\}$. We now establish some results for proving Theorem 4 in the following subsections.

4.1   Idempotents in $M(\mathcal{A})$

In this subsection we obtain idempotents in $M(\mathcal{A})$ which will be useful to give a representation of functions in $M(\mathcal{A})$. In view of Theorem 2(ii), notice that rank$(\overline{x}) \in \{1, 2, n\}$ for all $\overline{x} \in M(\mathcal{A})$. The identity is only function of rank n in $E(M(\mathcal{A}))$. Each function of rank one is in $E(M(\mathcal{A}))$, provided that it exists. We now estimate the functions of rank two in $E(M(\mathcal{A}))$. For that we prove the following results.

Remark 2. If $\overline{x} \in E(M(\mathcal{A}))$, then $\overline{a^i x a^{n-i}} \in E(M(\mathcal{A}))$ for all integer i ($1 \leq i \leq n$). For instance, $(\overline{a^i x a^{n-i}})^2 = (\overline{a^i x a^{n-i}})(\overline{a^i x a^{n-i}}) = \overline{a^i x^2 a^{n-i}} = \overline{a^i x a^{n-i}}$.

Proposition 2. *If n, m, t are nonnegative integers such that $t < m < n$, then there exists a positive integer k such that $m \leq t + k(n - m) < n$.*

Proof. Since $n - m > 0$, there exists an increasing sequence $\{t + i(n-m)\}_{i=1,2,\dots}$. Let k be the least integer such that $m \leq t + k(n-m)$. We show that $t + k(n-m) < n$. Since k is the least integer, it follows that

$$t + (k-1)(n-m) < m \Longrightarrow t + (k-1)n - km < 0$$
$$\Longrightarrow t + (k-1)n - km + n < n \Longrightarrow t + k(n-m) < n.$$

Hence $m \leq t + k(n-m) < n$.   □

Lemma 2. *There exists an integer r ($1 \leq r < n$) such that $\overline{a^r b}$ is an idempotent of rank two in $M(\mathcal{A})$.*

Proof. Note that $q_m \overline{b} = q_0$ and $Q\overline{a^i b} = \{q_0, q_m\}$ for $i \in \mathbb{N}$. Since $q_m \in BPI(\mathcal{A})$, we get some integer j ($0 \leq j < m$) such that $q_j \overline{b} = q_m$. Let t ($0 \leq t < m$) be the least integer such that $q_t \overline{b} = q_m$. Then $q_0 \overline{a^t b} = q_m$, and so

$$q_m \overline{a^{n-m+t} b} = (q_m \overline{a^{n-m}}) \overline{a^t b} = q_0 \overline{a^t b} = q_m.$$

If $q_0 \overline{a^{n-m+t} b} = q_0$, then choose integer $r = n - m + t$ which will serve the purpose. Otherwise $q_0 \overline{a^{n-m+t} b} = q_m$. Then

$$q_m \overline{a^{2(n-m)+t} b} = (q_m \overline{a^{n-m}}) \overline{a^{(n-m)+t} b} = q_0 \overline{a^{(n-m)+t} b} = q_m.$$

If $q_0 \overline{a^{2(n-m)+t} b} = q_0$, then choose integer $r = 2(n-m) + t$ which will serve the purpose. Otherwise $q_0 \overline{a^{2(n-m)+t} b} = q_m$. Then

$$q_m \overline{a^{3(n-m)+t} b} = (q_m \overline{a^{n-m}}) \overline{a^{2(n-m)+t} b} = q_0 \overline{a^{2(n-m)+t} b} = q_m.$$

As long as we continue this process, we get $q_m \overline{a^{i(n-m)+t} b} = q_m$ at each ith step. By Proposition 2, there exists an integer k such that $m \leq k(n-m) + t < n$. If above process terminates before k^{th} step, then we are through. Otherwise $q_m \overline{a^{k(n-m)+t} b} = q_m$ at the kth step.

Since $m \leq k(n-m) + t < n$, we have $q_0 \overline{a^{k(n-m)+t} b} = q_0$. Therefore, choose $r = k(n-m) + t$, and consequently $\overline{a^r b}$ is an idempotent of rank two in $M(\mathcal{A})$.   □

Notation 5. *We denote by κ the integer $k(n-m)+t$ obtained in Lemma 2.*

Lemma 3. (i) *If $q_0\overline{b} = q_m$, then $\overline{b^2}$ is an idempotent of rank two in $M(\mathcal{A})$.*
(ii) *If $q_0\overline{b} = q_0$, then there exists an integer t ($1 \le t < m$) such that $(\overline{a^t b})^2$ is an idempotent of rank two in $M(\mathcal{A})$.*

Proof. Note that $q_m\overline{b} = q_0$.

(i) Given $q_0\overline{b} = q_m$. Consider $Q\overline{b^2} = (Q\overline{b})\overline{b} = \{q_0, q_m\}\overline{b} = \{q_0, q_m\}$. Also $q_0\overline{b^2} = (q_0\overline{b})\overline{b} = q_m\overline{b} = q_0$, and $q_m\overline{b^2} = (q_m\overline{b})\overline{b} = q_0\overline{b} = q_m$. Hence $\overline{b^2}$ is an idempotent of rank two in $M(\mathcal{A})$.

(ii) Since q_m is a bpi, there exists an integer j ($1 \le j < m$) such that $q_j\overline{b} = q_m$. Let t be the least integer such that $q_t\overline{b} = q_m$. Then $q_0\overline{a^t b} = (q_0\overline{a^t})\overline{b} = q_t\overline{b} = q_m$. We claim that $q_m\overline{a^t b} = q_0$.

On the contrary, let us assume that $q_m\overline{a^t b} = q_m$. Then there is cycle from q_m to q_m labeled by the word $a^t b$. Since $\mathcal{A}$ is SFA, the cycle labeled by the word $a^t b$ should pass through q_0. Now $q_0\overline{b} = q_0$, there exist integers t_1 and t_2 ($1 \le t_1, t_2 < t$) with $t_1 + t_2 = t$ such that $q_m\overline{a^{t_1}} = q_0$ and $q_0\overline{a^{t_2}b} = q_m$. But $q_0\overline{a^{t_2}b} = q_{t_2}\overline{b} = q_m$. This contradicts the choice of t, as $t_2 < t$. Therefore $q_m\overline{a^t b} = q_0$. Now note that

$$Q(\overline{a^t b})^2 = (Q\overline{a^t b})\overline{a^t b} = \{q_0, q_m\}\overline{a^t b} = \{q_0, q_m\}.$$

Also $q_0(\overline{a^t b})^2 = (q_0\overline{a^t b})\overline{a^t b} = q_m\overline{a^t b} = q_0$, and $q_m(\overline{a^t b})^2 = (q_m\overline{a^t b})\overline{a^t b} = q_0\overline{a^t b} = q_m$. Hence $(\overline{a^t b})^2$ is an idempotent of rank two in $M(\mathcal{A})$. $\square$

Notation 6. *We denote by τ the least integer obtained in Lemma 3(ii). That is, if $q_0\overline{b} = q_0$ and τ ($1 \le \tau < m$) is the least integer such that $q_\tau\overline{b} = q_m$, then $(\overline{a^\tau b})^2$ is an idempotent of rank two in $M(\mathcal{A})$.*

In view of Remark 2, we obtain the following corollary of Lemmas 2 and 3.

Corollary 1. *For each integer i ($1 \le i \le n$), the following are idempotents of rank two in $M(\mathcal{A})$.*

(i) $\overline{a^i(a^\kappa b)a^{n-i}}$
(ii) *If $q_0\overline{b} = q_m$, then $\overline{a^i b^2 a^{n-i}}$.*
(iii) *If $q_0\overline{b} = q_0$, then $\overline{a^i(a^\tau b)^2 a^{n-i}}$.*

Definition 1. *We call the following list of $2(n+1)$ idempotents in $M(\mathcal{A})$, if they exist, as the* basic idempotents. *We denote by $\mathfrak{B}$ the set of all basic idempotents.*

(i) *The identity function $\overline{\varepsilon}$.*
(ii) *The constant function whose image set is $\{q_0\}$, denoted by $\overline{\nu}$.*
(iii) *For each integer i ($1 \le i \le n$), the idempotent $\overline{a^i(a^\kappa b)a^{n-i}}$.*
(iv) *For each integer i ($1 \le i \le n$), if $q_0\overline{b} \ne q_0$, then the idempotent $\overline{a^i b^2 a^{n-i}}$; else, the idempotent $\overline{a^i(a^\tau b)^2 a^{n-i}}$.*

Remark 3. $|\mathfrak{B}| \leq 2(n+1)$.

The following example shows that the cardinality of $\mathfrak{B}$ is not necessarily $2(n+1)$.

Example 1. Consider the 4-state CSFA $\mathcal{A}$ over the binary alphabet $A = \{a, b\}$ given in the righthand side. Here $BPI(\mathcal{A}) = \{q_0, q_2\}$. We observe that the transition monoid $M(\mathcal{A})$ does not contain any constant functions. Hence $|\mathfrak{B}| < 10\ (=2(4+1))$.

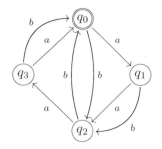

4.2   Functions of Rank Two in $M(\mathcal{A})$

In this subsection we obtain a representation of functions of rank two in $M(\mathcal{A})$. We recall the definition of the complement of a function of rank two from [14].

Definition 2. *Let X be a nonempty finite set and $\alpha : X \to X$ a function such that $X\alpha = \{i, j\}$. The complement of α is the function $\alpha^{\#} : X \to X$ defined by, for $k \in X$,*

$$k\alpha^{\#} = \begin{cases} i & \text{if } k\alpha = j; \\ j & \text{if } k\alpha = i. \end{cases}$$

The following lemma is useful in the sequel.

Lemma 4. (i) *If $q_0\bar{b} = q_m$, then $\bar{b}^{\#} = \bar{b^2}$.*
(ii) *If $q_0\bar{b} = q_0$, then $\bar{b}^{\#} = \overline{ba^\tau b}$.*

Proof. Recall that $q_m\bar{b} = q_0$ and $Q\bar{b} = \{q_0, q_m\}$. Let $q \in Q$ be arbitrary. Then either $q\bar{b} = q_0$ or $q\bar{b} = q_m$.

(i) Given $q_0\bar{b} = q_m$. If $q\bar{b} = q_0$, then $q\bar{b^2} = (q\bar{b})\bar{b} = q_0\bar{b} = q_m$. Otherwise $q\bar{b} = q_m$. Then $q\bar{b^2} = (q\bar{b})\bar{b} = q_m\bar{b} = q_0$. Hence $\bar{b}^{\#} = \bar{b^2}$.
(ii) Given $q_0\bar{b} = q_0$. If $q\bar{b} = q_0$, then $q\overline{ba^\tau b} = (q\bar{b})\overline{a^\tau b} = q_0\overline{a^\tau b} = q_m$. Otherwise $q\bar{b} = q_m$. Then $q\overline{ba^\tau b} = (q\bar{b})\overline{a^\tau b} = q_m\overline{a^\tau b} = q_0$. Hence $\bar{b}^{\#} = \overline{ba^\tau b}$.

$\square$

Theorem 7. *Every function of rank two in $M(\mathcal{A})$ has one of the following forms. For $i, j \in \{1, \dots, n\}$,*

(β) $\overline{a^i b a^j}$
(γ) $\overline{a^i b^2 a^j}$
(δ) $\overline{a^i b a^\tau b a^j}$

Proof. Let $\overline{w} \in M(\mathcal{A})$ be an arbitrary function of rank two. Then

$$w = a^{i_1} b a^{i_2} b \dots b a^{i_{k-1}} b a^{i_k},$$

where $i_t \geq 0$ $(t \in \{1, \dots, k\})$. Write $w = a^{i_1} buba^{i_k}$, where $u = a^{i_2} b \dots b a^{i_{k-1}}$. Notice that $\overline{bub}$ has rank two with its image set $\{q_0, q_m\}$. We consider the following two possibilities separately.

Case ($\overline{bub} = \overline{b}$). Then $\overline{w} = \overline{a^{i_1}buba^{i_k}} = \overline{a^{i_1}ba^{i_k}}$, which is of the form (β).

Case ($\overline{bub} \neq \overline{b}$). We first show that $\overline{bub} = \overline{b}^{\#}$. Since $\overline{bub} \neq \overline{b}$, there exists $p \in Q$ such that $p\overline{bub} \neq p\overline{b}$. We proceed by considering the following two subcases.

Subcase ($p\overline{b} = q_0$). Since $p\overline{bub} \neq p\overline{b}$, we have $p\overline{bub} = q_m$. This gives $(p\overline{b})\overline{ub} = q_m \implies q_0\overline{ub} = q_m$. Now rank($\overline{bub}$) = 2, it follows that $q_m\overline{ub} = q_0$. Let $q \in Q$ be arbitrary. Then either $q\overline{b} = q_0$ or $q\overline{b} = q_m$. If $q\overline{b} = q_0$, then $q\overline{bub} = (q\overline{b})\overline{ub} = q_0\overline{ub} = q_m$. Otherwise $q\overline{b} = q_m$. Then $q\overline{bub} = (q\overline{b})\overline{ub} = q_m\overline{ub} = q_0$. Hence $\overline{bub} = \overline{b}^{\#}$.

Subcase ($p\overline{b} = q_m$). Since $p\overline{bub} \neq p\overline{b}$, we have $p\overline{bub} = q_0$. This gives $(p\overline{b})\overline{ub} = q_0 \implies q_m\overline{ub} = q_0$. Now rank($\overline{bub}$) = 2, it follows that $q_0\overline{ub} = q_m$. Let $q \in Q$ be arbitrary. Then either $q\overline{b} = q_0$ or $q\overline{b} = q_m$. If $q\overline{b} = q_0$, then $q\overline{bub} = (q\overline{b})\overline{ub} = q_0\overline{ub} = q_m$. Otherwise $q\overline{b} = q_m$. Then $q\overline{bub} = (q\overline{b})\overline{ub} = q_m\overline{ub} = q_0$. Hence $\overline{bub} = \overline{b}^{\#}$.

Now we know that either $q_0\overline{b} = q_m$ or $q_0\overline{b} = q_0$. If $q_0\overline{b} = q_m$, then by Lemma 4(i), we have $\overline{b}^{\#} = \overline{b^2}$ and therefore $\overline{w} = \overline{a^{i_1}buba^{i_k}} = \overline{a^{i_1}b^2a^{i_k}}$, which is of the form (γ). If $q_0\overline{b} = q_0$, then by Lemma 4(ii), we have $\overline{b}^{\#} = \overline{ba^\tau b}$ and therefore $\overline{w} = \overline{a^{i_1}buba^{i_k}} = \overline{a^{i_1}ba^\tau ba^{i_k}}$, which is of the form (δ).   □

4.3   Representation of $M(\mathcal{A})$

In this subsection we give a canonical representation of the elements in $M(\mathcal{A})$ in terms of basic idempotents and permutations.

Theorem 8. *Every element in $M(\mathcal{A})$ can be written as a composition of a basic idempotent and a permutation, i.e.,*

$$M(\mathcal{A}) = \mathfrak{B}G = \{\overline{e}\,\overline{g} \mid \overline{e} \in \mathfrak{B} \text{ and } \overline{g} \in G\}.$$

Proof. By Theorem 2(ii), we have rank($\overline{x}$) $\in \{1, 2, n\}$ for all $\overline{x} \in M(\mathcal{A})$.

Case (rank($\overline{x}$) = 1). Then $Q\overline{x} = \{q_k\}$ for some integer k ($0 \leq k \leq n-1$). Also $Q\overline{v}a^k = (Q\overline{v})a^k = \{q_0\}\overline{a^k} = \{q_k\}$. Hence $\overline{x} = \overline{v}\,\overline{a^k} \in \mathfrak{B}G$.

Case (rank($\overline{x}$) = n). Then $\overline{x} \in G$, and so $\overline{x} = \overline{\varepsilon}\,\overline{x} \in \mathfrak{B}G$.

Case (rank($\overline{x}$) = 2). By Theorem 7, either $\overline{x} = \overline{a^iba^j}$ or $\overline{x} = \overline{a^ib^2a^j}$ or $\overline{x} = \overline{a^iba^\tau ba^j}$ for some integers $i, j \in \{1, \ldots, n\}$. In this case, we find the required in the following three subcases.

Subcase ($\overline{x} = \overline{a^iba^j}$). Then $\overline{x}$ can be written as $\overline{x} = \overline{a^{i-\kappa}(a^\kappa b)a^j} = \overline{a^{i-\kappa}(a^\kappa b)a^{n-(i-\kappa)}}\,\overline{a^{j+(i-\kappa)}} = \overline{a^{i'}(a^\kappa b)a^{n-i'}}\,\overline{a^{j'}} \in \mathfrak{B}G$, where i' and j' are, respectively, residues of $(i - \kappa)$ and $(j + i - \kappa)$ mod n.

Subcase ($\overline{x} = \overline{a^ib^2a^j}$). Then $\overline{x}$ can be written as $\overline{x} = \overline{a^ib^2a^{n-i}}\,\overline{a^{j-(n-i)}} = \overline{a^ib^2a^{n-i}}\,\overline{a^{j'}} \in \mathfrak{B}G$, where j' is residue of $(j + i - n)$ mod n.

Subcase ($\overline{x} = \overline{a^iba^\tau ba^j}$). Then $\overline{x}$ can be written as $\overline{x} = \overline{a^{i-\tau}(a^\tau b)^2a^j} = \overline{a^{i-\tau}(a^\tau b)^2a^{n-(i-\tau)}}\,\overline{a^{j-n+(i-\tau)}} = \overline{a^{i'}(a^\tau b)^2a^{n-i'}}\,\overline{a^{j'}} \in \mathfrak{B}G$, where i' and j' are, respectively, residues of $(i - \tau)$ and $(j + i - \tau - n)$ mod n.

Thus, in all cases, each function in $M(\mathcal{A})$ can be written as a composition of a basic idempotent and a permutation, and consequently $M(\mathcal{A}) = \mathfrak{B}G$.   □

4.4   An Example

For $n \geq 3$, let us consider the n-state CSFA $\mathcal{A} = (Q, \{a, b\}, \delta, 1, \{1\})$, where $Q = \{1, 2, 3, \ldots, n\}$ and δ is given in the following transition table.

$$
\begin{array}{c|ccccc}
\delta & 1 & 2 & 3 & \cdots & n-1 & n \\
\hline
a & 2 & 3 & 4 & \cdots & n & 1 \\
b & 2 & 1 & 1 & \cdots & 1 & 1
\end{array}
$$

Clearly $BPI(\mathcal{A}) = \{1, 2\}$ and the functions $\overline{a}$ and $\overline{b}$, written in two-row notation, are as follows.

$$
\overline{a} = \begin{pmatrix} 1 & 2 & 3 & \cdots & n-1 & n \\ 2 & 3 & 4 & \cdots & n & 1 \end{pmatrix}, \quad \overline{b} = \begin{pmatrix} 1 & 2 & 3 & \cdots & n-1 & n \\ 2 & 1 & 1 & \cdots & 1 & 1 \end{pmatrix}.
$$

Note that $\overline{bab} = \overline{\nu}$ and $\overline{a^r b} \neq \overline{b}$ for any integer r $(1 \leq r < n)$. Further, we observe $\kappa = n - 1$, and the following distinct functions are idempotents of rank two.

$$
\overline{b^2} = \begin{pmatrix} 1 & 2 & 3 & \cdots & n-1 & n \\ 1 & 2 & 2 & \cdots & 2 & 2 \end{pmatrix}, \quad \overline{a^\kappa b} = \begin{pmatrix} 1 & 2 & 3 & \cdots & n-1 & n \\ 1 & 2 & 1 & \cdots & 1 & 1 \end{pmatrix}.
$$

By Remark 2, for any integer i $(1 \leq i \leq n)$, the functions $\overline{a^i b^2 a^{n-i}}$ and $\overline{a^i (a^\kappa b) a^{n-i}}$ are basic idempotents of rank two in $M(\mathcal{A})$. For integer r $(1 < r < n)$, notice that $\overline{a^r b^2} \neq \overline{b^2}$ and $\overline{a^r b^2} \neq \overline{a^\kappa b}$, where

$$
\overline{a^r b^2} = \begin{pmatrix} 1 & 2 & \cdots & n-r & n-r+1 & n-r+2 & \cdots & n-1 & n \\ 2 & 2 & \cdots & 2 & 1 & 2 & \cdots & 2 & 2 \end{pmatrix}.
$$

We now claim that the orbits of any two basic idempotents of rank two are disjoint. We prove our claim in three cases.

Case-1. Suppose that $\mathcal{O}(\overline{a^i b^2 a^{n-i}}) \cap \mathcal{O}(\overline{a^j b^2 a^{n-j}}) \neq \varnothing$ for some integers i, j $(1 \leq j < i \leq n)$. Then

$$
\overline{a^j b^2 a^{n-j}} \; \overline{a^t} = \overline{a^i b^2 a^{n-i}} \implies \overline{b^2 a^{i-j+t}} = \overline{a^{i-j} b^2}
$$

for some integer t $(1 \leq t \leq n)$. If $i - j + t \neq 0 \pmod{n}$, then $Q\overline{b^2 a^{i-j+t}} \neq \{1, 2\}$. This is a contradiction since $Q\overline{a^{i-j} b^2} = \{1, 2\}$. Otherwise $i - j + t = 0 \pmod{n}$. Recall that $\overline{a^r b^2} \neq \overline{b^2}$ for any integer r $(1 \leq r < n)$. It follows that $\overline{a^{i-j} b^2} \neq \overline{b^2}$, a contradiction. Hence $\mathcal{O}(\overline{a^i b^2 a^{n-i}}) \cap \mathcal{O}(\overline{a^j b^2 a^{n-j}}) = \varnothing$ for i, j $(1 \leq j < i \leq n)$.

Case-2. Suppose that $\mathcal{O}(\overline{a^i (a^\kappa b) a^{n-i}}) \cap \mathcal{O}(\overline{a^j (a^\kappa b) a^{n-j}}) \neq \varnothing$ for some integers i, j $(1 \leq j < i \leq n)$. Then

$$
\overline{a^j (a^\kappa b) a^{n-j}} \; \overline{a^t} = \overline{a^i (a^\kappa b) a^{n-i}} \implies \overline{(a^\kappa b) a^{i-j+t}} = \overline{a^{i-j} (a^\kappa b)}
$$

for some integer t $(1 \leq t \leq n)$. If $i - j + t \neq 0 \pmod{n}$, then $Q\overline{(a^\kappa b) a^{i-j+t}} \neq \{1, 2\}$, which is a contradiction since $Q\overline{a^{i-j} (a^\kappa b)} = \{1, 2\}$. Otherwise $i - j + t = 0 \pmod{n}$. Note that $\overline{a^r b} \neq \overline{b}$ for any integer r $(1 \leq r < n)$. This gives

322   S. N. Singh and K. V. Krishna

$\overline{a^{i-j}(a^\kappa b)} \neq \overline{(a^\kappa b)}$, a contradiction. Hence $\mathcal{O}(\overline{a^i(a^\kappa b)a^{n-i}}) \cap \mathcal{O}(\overline{a^j(a^\kappa b)a^{n-j}}) = \varnothing$ for i, j $(1 \leq j < i \leq n)$.

Case-3. Suppose that $\mathcal{O}(\overline{a^i b^2 a^{n-i}}) \cap \mathcal{O}(\overline{a^j(a^\kappa b)a^{n-j}}) \neq \varnothing$ for some integers i, j $(1 \leq j < i \leq n)$. Then

$$\overline{a^j(a^\kappa b)a^{n-j}}\ \overline{a^t} = \overline{a^i b^2 a^{n-i}} \implies \overline{(a^\kappa b)a^{i-j+t}} = \overline{a^{i-j}b^2}$$

for some integer t $(1 \leq t \leq n)$. If $i - j + t \neq 0(\mathrm{mod}\ n)$, then $Q\overline{(a^\kappa b)a^{i-j+t}} \neq \{1, 2\}$, which gives a contradiction since $Q\overline{a^{i-j}b^2} = \{1, 2\}$. Otherwise $i - j + t = 0(\mathrm{mod}\ n)$. Since $\overline{a^\kappa b} \neq \overline{a^r b^2}$ for any integer r $(1 \leq r < n)$, $\overline{a^\kappa b} \neq \overline{a^{i-j}b^2}$, a contradiction. Hence, for i, j $(1 \leq j < i \leq n)$, $\mathcal{O}(\overline{a^i b^2 a^{n-i}}) \cap \mathcal{O}(\overline{a^j(a^\kappa b)a^{n-j}}) = \varnothing$.

Thus, the orbits of basic idempotents of rank two are disjoint. Therefore the basic idempotents of rank two are distinct, and consequently $|\mathfrak{B}| = 2(n + 1)$. Hence the syntactic complexity of $\mathcal{A}$ is $|M(\mathcal{A})| = |\mathfrak{B}G| = 2n(n + 1)$.

4.5   Proof of Theorem 8

We now summarize the proof of the main result in the following: We know that

$$M(\mathcal{A}) = \bigcup_{\overline{x} \in M(\mathcal{A})} \mathcal{O}(\overline{x}) = \bigcup_{\overline{x} \in \mathfrak{B}G} \mathcal{O}(\overline{x}) \text{ by using Theorem 8}$$

$$= \bigcup_{\overline{x} \in \mathfrak{B}} \mathcal{O}(\overline{x}).$$

Therefore, by Lemma 1 and Remark 3,

$$|M(\mathcal{A})| \leq |\mathfrak{B}||\mathcal{O}(\overline{x})| \leq 2n(n + 1).$$

Thus, the sizes of syntactic monoids of the languages accepted by n-state CSFA with two bpis are bounded by $2n(n + 1)$. Since the syntactic monoid size of the n-state CSFA that is presented in Subsect. 4.4 is exactly $2n(n+1)$, the syntactic complexity of the class of n-state CSFA with two bpis is $2n(n + 1)$.

References

1. Beaudry, M., Holzer, M.: On the size of inverse semigroups given by generators. Theor. Comput. Sci. **412**(8–10), 765–772 (2011)
2. Berstel, J., Perrin, D.: Theory of Codes. Pure and Applied Mathematics, vol. 117. Academic Press Inc., Orlando (1985)
3. Biskup, M.T., Plandowski, W.: Shortest synchronizing strings for Huffman codes. Theor. Comput. Sci. **410**(38–40), 3925–3941 (2009)
4. Brzozowski, J., Ye, Y.: Syntactic complexity of ideal and closed languages. In: Mauri, G., Leporati, A. (eds.) DLT 2011. LNCS, vol. 6795, pp. 117–128. Springer, Heidelberg (2011). https://doi.org/10.1007/978-3-642-22321-1_11
5. Brzozowski, J., Li, B., Ye, Y.: Syntactic complexity of prefix-, suffix-, bifix-, and factor-free regular languages. Theor. Comput. Sci. **449**, 37–53 (2012)

6. Brzozowski, J., Li, B., Liu, D.: Syntactic complexities of six classes of star-free languages. J. Autom. Lang. Comb. **17**(2–4), 83–105 (2012)
7. Brzozowski, J., Li, B.: Syntactic complexity of R- and J-trivial regular languages. Int. J. Found. Comput. Sci. **25**(7), 807–821 (2014)
8. Brzozowski, J., Szykula, M., Ye, Y.: Syntactic complexity of regular ideals (2015). http://arxiv.org/abs/1509.06032
9. Dubuc, L.: Sur les automates circulaires et la conjecture de Černý. RAIRO Inform. Théor. Appl. **32**(1–3), 21–34 (1998)
10. Giambruno, L.: Automata-theoretic methods in free monoids and free groups. Ph.D. thesis, Università degli Studi di Palermo, Palermo, Italy (2007)
11. Giambruno, L., Restivo, A.: An automata-theoretic approach to the study of the intersection of two submonoids of a free monoid. Theor. Inform. Appl. **42**(3), 503–524 (2008)
12. Holzer, M., König, B.: On deterministic finite automata and syntactic monoid size. Theor. Comput. Sci. **327**(3), 319–347 (2004)
13. Iván, S., Nagy-György, J.: On nonpermutational transformation semigroups with an application to syntactic complexity. Acta Cybernet. **22**(3), 687–701 (2016)
14. Krawetz, B., Lawrence, J., Shallit, J.: State complexity and the monoid of transformations of a finite set. Int. J. Found. Comput. Sci. **16**(3), 547–563 (2005)
15. Lawson, M.V.: Finite Automata. Chapman & Hall/CRC, Boca Raton (2004)
16. Maslov, A.N.: Estimates of the number of states of finite automata. Dokl. Akad. Nauk SSSR **194**, 1266–1268 (1970)
17. Pin, J.E.: Sur un cas particulier de la conjecture de Černý. In: Ausiello, G., Böhm, C. (eds.) ICALP 1978. LNCS, vol. 62, pp. 345–352. Springer, Heidelberg (1978). https://doi.org/10.1007/3-540-08860-1_25
18. Pribavkina, E.V.: Slowly synchronizing automata with zero and noncomplete sets. Math. Notes **90**, 411–417 (2011)
19. Rigo, M., Vandomme, É.: Syntactic complexity of ultimately periodic sets of integers. In: LATA, pp. 477–488 (2011)
20. Lacroix, A., Rampersad, N., Rigo, M., Vandomme, É.: Syntactic complexity of ultimately periodic sets of integers and application to a decision procedure. Fundam. Inform. **116**(1–4), 175–187 (2012)
21. Singh, S.N.: Semi-flower automata. Ph.D. thesis, IIT Guwahati, India (2012)
22. Singh, S.N., Krishna, K.V.: The rank and Hanna Neumann property of some submonoids of a free monoid. Ann. Math. Inform. **40**, 113–123 (2012)
23. Singh, S.N., Krishna, K.V.: The holonomy decomposition of some circular semi-flower automata. Acta Cybernet. **22**, 791–805 (2016)
24. Singh, S.N., Krishna, K.V.: A sufficient condition for the Hanna Neumann property of submonoids of a free monoid. Semigroup Forum **86**(3), 537–554 (2013)

Complexity of Proper Suffix-Convex Regular Languages

Corwin Sinnamon$^{(\boxtimes)}$

David R. Cheriton School of Computer Science,
University of Waterloo, Waterloo, ON N2L 3G1, Canada
sinncore@gmail.com

Abstract. A language L is suffix-convex if for any words u, v, w, whenever w and uvw are in L, vw is in L as well. Suffix-convex languages include left ideals, suffix-closed languages, and suffix-free languages, which were studied previously. In this paper, we concentrate on suffix-convex languages that do not belong to any one of these classes; we call such languages *proper*. In order to study this language class, we define a structure called a *suffix-convex triple system* that characterizes the automata recognizing suffix-convex languages. We find tight upper bounds for reversal, star, product, and boolean operations of proper suffix-convex languages, and we conjecture on the size of the largest syntactic semigroup. We also prove that three witness streams are required to meet all these bounds.

Keywords: Atom · Most complex · Suffix-convex · Proper
Quotient complexity · Regular language · State complexity
Syntactic semigroup

1 Introduction

Suffix-Convex Languages: Convex languages were introduced in 1973 by Thierrin [18], and revisited in 2009 by Ang and Brzozowski [1]. Convexity can be defined with respect to several binary relations on words, but in this paper we concentrate only on suffix-convex regular languages. If a word $w \in \Sigma^*$ can be written as $w = xy$ for $x, y \in \Sigma^*$, then y is a *suffix* of w. A language L is *suffix-convex* if whenever w and uvw are in L, then vw is also in L, for all $u, v, w \in \Sigma^*$. The class of suffix-convex languages includes three well-known subclasses: left ideals, suffix-closed languages, and suffix-free languages.

A language L over an alphabet Σ is a *left ideal* if it is non-empty and $L = \Sigma^* L$. In other words, if L contains a word $w \in \Sigma^*$, then it also contains every word in Σ^* that has w as a suffix. Left ideals play a role in pattern matching: If

---

This work was supported by the Natural Sciences and Engineering Research Council of Canada grant No. OGP0000871, NSERC Discovery grant No. 8237-2012, and the Canada Research Chairs Program.

C. Câmpeanu (Ed.): CIAA 2018, LNCS 10977, pp. 324–338, 2018.
https://doi.org/10.1007/978-3-319-94812-6_27

one is searching for all words ending with words in some language L in a given text, then one is looking for words in $\Sigma^* L$. Left ideals also constitute a basic concept in semigroup theory.

A language L is *suffix-closed* if every suffix of every word in L is also in L. The complement of every suffix-closed language (other than Σ^*) is a left ideal.

A language is *suffix-free* if no word in the language is a suffix of another word in the language. Suffix-free languages are suffix codes (with the exception of $\{\varepsilon\}$, where ε is the empty word). They play an important role in coding theory and have been studied extensively; see [2] for example.

Contributions: In this paper, we focus on the remaining suffix-languages that do not fall into any of these subclasses; we call these languages *proper*. These languages are wide-ranging in structure and appearance, and difficult to reason about using conventional methods. In order to approach the complexity properties of proper languages, we develop a theory of suffix-convex regular languages based on a new object we call a suffix-convex triple system. We use this theory to discover and prove tight upper bounds for reversal, star, product, and boolean operations of proper languages. We describe a proper language that we conjecture to have the largest possible syntactic semigroup. Finally, we prove that three different language streams are required to meet all of these bounds.

Omitted proofs can be found in [17].

2   Background

Quotient/State Complexity: If L is a language over an alphabet Σ^*, such that every letter of Σ appears in a word of L, then the *(left) quotient* of L by a word $w \in \Sigma^*$ is $w^{-1}L = \{x \mid wx \in L\}$. A language is regular if and only if the set of distinct quotients is finite. For this reason the number of quotients of L is a natural measure of complexity for L; this number is called the *quotient complexity* [3] of L. A equivalent concept is the *state complexity* [19] of L, which is the number of states in a complete minimal deterministic finite automaton (DFA) over alphabet Σ recognizing L. We refer to quotient/state complexity simply as *complexity* and we denote it by $\kappa(L)$.

If $\circ$ is a unary operation on languages, then the *quotient/state complexity of* $\circ$ is the maximal value of $\kappa(L_n^\circ)$, expressed as a function of n, as L_n ranges over all regular languages of complexity n or less. Similarly, if $\circ$ is a binary operation on languages, then the *quotient/state complexity of* $\circ$ is the maximal value of $\kappa(L'_m \circ L_n)$, expressed as a function of m and n, as L'_m and L_n range over all regular languages of complexity m and n, respectively. We assume in this paper that L'_m and L_n are over a common alphabet Σ, however the *unrestricted* complexity of binary operations, where the two languages may use different alphabets, has recently been studied as well [5,10]. The complexity of an operation gives a worst-case bound on the time and space complexity of the operation, and it has been studied extensively (see [3,4,11,12,19]).

Witness Streams: To find the complexity of a unary operation one proves an upper bound on this complexity and then exhibits languages that meet this bound. Since a bound is given as a function of n, we require a sequence of languages $(L_k, L_{k+1}, \dots)$ called a language *stream*; here k is usually a small integer because the bound may not hold for a few small values of n. Usually the languages in a stream have the same basic structure and differ only in the parameter n. For example, $((a^n)^* \mid n \geqslant 2)$ is a stream. Two streams are required for a binary operation. Sometimes the same stream can be used for both arguments, however this is not the case in general.

Dialects: It has been shown in [4] that for all common binary operations on regular languages the second stream can be a "dialect" of the first. Let $\Sigma = \{a_1, \dots, a_k\}$ be an alphabet ordered as shown; if $L \subseteq \Sigma^*$, we denote it by $L(a_1, \dots, a_k)$. A *dialect* of L is obtained by changing or deleting letters of Σ in the words of L. More precisely, if Σ' is an alphabet, a dialect of $L(a_1, \dots, a_k)$ is obtained from an injective partial map $\pi \colon \Sigma \mapsto \Sigma'$ by replacing each letter $a \in \Sigma$ by $\pi(a)$ in every word of L, or deleting the word entirely if $\pi(a)$ is undefined. We write $L(\pi(a_1), \dots, \pi(a_k))$ to denote the dialect of $L(a_1, \dots, a_k)$ given by π, and we denote undefined values of π by "$-$". Undefined values for letters at the end of the alphabet are omitted; for example, $L(a, c, -, -)$ is written as $L(a, c)$.

Automata: A *deterministic finite automaton (DFA)* is a quintuple $\mathcal{D} = (Q, \Sigma, \delta, q_0, F)$, where Q is a finite non-empty set of *states*, Σ is a finite non-empty *alphabet*, $\delta \colon Q \times \Sigma \to Q$ is the *transition function*, $q_0 \in Q$ is the *initial* state, and $F \subseteq Q$ is the set of *final* states. We extend δ to a function $\delta \colon Q \times \Sigma^* \to Q$ as usual. A DFA $\mathcal{D}$ *accepts* a word $w \in \Sigma^*$ if and only if $\delta(q_0, w) \in F$. The language of all words accepted by $\mathcal{D}$ is denoted $L(\mathcal{D})$. If q is a state of $\mathcal{D}$, then the language of q is the language accepted by the DFA $(Q, \Sigma, \delta, q, F)$. The language of q is a quotient of $L(\mathcal{D})$, and we often denote it K_q. A state is *empty* or a *sink state* if its language is empty. Two states p and q of $\mathcal{D}$ are *equivalent* if $K_p = K_q$; otherwise they are *distinguishable*. A state q is *reachable* if there exists $w \in \Sigma^*$ such that $\delta(q_0, w) = q$. A DFA is *minimal* if all of its states are reachable and no two states are equivalent. Usually DFAs are used to establish upper bounds on the complexity of operations and also as witnesses that meet these bounds. For convenience, say that a DFA is (proper) suffix-convex if the language it accepts is (proper) suffix-convex.

A *nondeterministic finite automaton (NFA)* is a quintuple $\mathcal{D} = (Q, \Sigma, \delta, I, F)$, where Q, Σ and F are defined as in a DFA, $\delta \colon Q \times \Sigma \to 2^Q$ is the *transition function*, and $I \subseteq Q$ is the *set of initial states*. An *ε-NFA* is an NFA in which transitions under the empty word ε are also permitted.

Transformations: Without loss of generality we take $Q_n = \{0, \dots, n-1\}$ to be the states set of every DFA with n states. A *transformation* of Q_n is a function $t \colon Q_n \mapsto Q_n$. We treat a transformation t as an operator acting on Q_n from the right, so that qt denotes the *image* of $q \in Q_n$ under t. If s, t are transformations of Q_n, their composition is denoted by $s \circ t$, or more commonly just st, and defined by $q(st) = (qs)t$. In any DFA, each letter $a \in \Sigma$ induces a transformation δ_a of the set Q_n defined by $q\delta_a = \delta(q, a)$. By a slight abuse of notation, we use the letter a to denote the transformation it induces; thus we write qa instead of $q\delta_a$.

We also extend the notation to sets of states: if $P \subseteq Q_n$, then $Pa = \{pa \mid p \in P\}$. Alternatively, we write $P \xrightarrow{a} P'$ to indicate that the image of P under a is P'.

For $k \geqslant 2$, a transformation t of a set $P = \{q_0, q_1, \ldots, q_{k-1}\} \subseteq Q_n$ is called a k-cycle if $q_0 t = q_1, q_1 t = q_2, \ldots, q_{k-2} t = q_{k-1}, q_{k-1} t = q_0$, and we denote such a cycle by $(q_0, q_1, \ldots, q_{k-1})$. A 2-cycle (q_0, q_1) is called a *transposition*. A transformation is a called a *permutation* if it is bijective, or equivalently, if it can be written as a composition of cycles. A transformation that sends all the states of P to q and acts as the identity on the remaining states is denoted by $(P \to q)$. If $P = \{p\}$ we write $p \to q$ for $(\{p\} \to q)$. The identity transformation is denoted by $\mathbb{1}$. The notation $(^j_i\, q \to q+1)$ denotes a transformation that sends q to $q+1$ for $i \leqslant q \leqslant j$ and acts as the identity for the remaining states. The notation $(^j_i\, q \to q-1)$ is defined similarly. Using composition, the notation introduced here lets us succinctly describe many different transformations.

Semigroups: Let $\mathcal{D} = (Q_n, \Sigma, \delta, q_0, F)$ be a DFA. For each word $w \in \Sigma^*$, the transition function induces a transformation δ_w of Q_n by w: for all $q \in Q_n$, $q\delta_w = \delta(q, w)$. The set $T_\mathcal{D}$ of all such transformations by non-empty words forms a semigroup of transformations called the *transition semigroup* of $\mathcal{D}$ [16]. Conversely, we may define δ by describing δ_a for each $a \in \Sigma$. We write $a\colon t$, where t is a transformation of Q, to mean that the transformation δ_a induced by a is t.

The *Myhill congruence* [15] $\approx_L$ of a language $L \subseteq \Sigma^*$ is defined on Σ^+ as follows: For $x, y \in \Sigma^+$, $x \approx_L y$ if and only if $wxz \in L \iff wyz \in L$ for all $w, z \in \Sigma^*$. This relation is also known as the *syntactic congruence* of L. The quotient set $\Sigma^+/\approx_L$ of equivalence classes of the relation $\approx_L$ is a semigroup called the *syntactic semigroup* of L. If $\mathcal{D}$ is a minimal DFA for L, then $T_\mathcal{D}$ is isomorphic to the syntactic semigroup T_L of L [16], and we represent elements of T_L by transformations in $T_\mathcal{D}$. The *syntactic complexity* of a language is the size of its syntactic semigroup [4,9,13].

Atoms: Atoms are defined by the congruence in which two words x and y are equivalent if $ux \in L$ if and only if $uy \in L$ for all $u \in \Sigma^*$. In other words, x and y are equivalent if $x \in u^{-1}L$ if and only if $y \in u^{-1}L$. An equivalence class of this congruence is called an *atom* of L [8]. Thus, an atom is a non-empty intersection of complemented and uncomplemented quotients of L, written $A_S = \bigcap_{i \in S} K_i \cap \bigcap_{i \notin S} \overline{K_i}$ for $S \subseteq Q_n$, where $K_0, K_1, \ldots, K_{n-1}$ are the quotients of L. The number of atoms and the complexities of the atoms were suggested as measures of complexity of regular languages [4]. For more information about atoms and their complexity, see [7,8,14].

3   Suffix-Convex Triple Systems

Suffix-convex languages are difficult to reason about through the common representations of regular languages. To alleviate this, we introduce a structure called a *suffix-convex triple system* (or just "triple system"). A triple system is a set of 3-tuples of states in Q_n that satisfy some structural conditions. For every triple system, there is a nonempty family of DFAs on the state set Q_n that are said to *respect* the system. Triple systems have the following properties:

1. Every DFA that respects any triple system is suffix-convex.
2. For every suffix-convex DFA, there is at least one triple system that it respects.
3. For any triple system, among the transition semigroups of DFAs that respect the system, there is a unique maximal semigroup that contains all others.

Through properties 1 and 2, triple systems effectively characterize suffix-convex regular languages. However, as suggested by 2, the correspondence between triple systems and suffix-convex DFAs is not a bijection; most suffix-convex DFAs respect a number of different triple systems, and most triple systems are respected by many different DFAs. Property 3 helps to identify DFAs of suffix-convex languages whose transition semigroups are particularly complex, which is useful both for discovering and reasoning about complex suffix-convex languages.

The inspiration for the triple system framework lies in the following reformulation of the definition of suffix-convexity. A regular language L is suffix-convex if and only if, for all $u, v, w \in \Sigma^*$,

$$w^{-1}L \cap (uvw)^{-1}L \subseteq (vw)^{-1}L.$$

This statement is more usefully expressed in terms of the states of a DFA. Let $\mathcal{D} = (Q_n, \Sigma, \delta, 0, F)$ be a DFA, and let K_q denote the language accepted by $(Q_n, \Sigma, \delta, q, F)$. Setting $p = 0w$, $q = 0uvw$, and $r = 0vw$, the statement above becomes $K_p \cap K_q \subseteq K_r$. This relationship between quotients satisfies some nice properties: If $p, q, r, s \in Q_n$, then

- $K_p \cap K_q \subseteq K_p$,
- $K_p \cap K_q \subseteq K_r \iff K_q \cap K_p \subseteq K_r$,
- $K_p \cap K_q \subseteq K_r$ and $K_q \cap K_r \subseteq K_s \implies K_p \cap K_q \subseteq K_s$, and
- $K_p \cap K_q \subseteq K_r$ and $p, q \in F \implies r \in F$.

All four properties are trivial to prove, yet it turns out that they capture the essential character of suffix-convex DFAs. We can now make a formal definition, in which these four properties appear in a more abstract way.

Definition 1. *A suffix-convex triple system is a tuple* $\mathcal{S} = (Q, q_0, F, \mathcal{R})$, *where* $q_0 \in Q$ *is the* initial *state,* $F \subseteq Q$ *is a set of* final *states, and* $\mathcal{R} \subseteq Q \times Q \times Q$ *is a relation* such that, *for all* $p, q, r, s \in Q$,

(A) $(p, q, p) \in \mathcal{R}$,
(B) $(p, q, r) \in \mathcal{R} \iff (q, p, r) \in \mathcal{R}$,
(C) $(p, q, r) \in \mathcal{R}$ *and* $(q, r, s) \in \mathcal{R} \implies (p, q, s) \in \mathcal{R}$, *and*
(D) $(p, q, r) \in \mathcal{R}$ *and* $p, q \in F \implies r \in F$.

Definition 2. *A DFA* $\mathcal{D} = (Q, \Sigma, \delta, q_0, F)$ *is said to* respect *a triple system* $\mathcal{S} = (Q, q_0, F, \mathcal{R})$ *if, for all transformations* $t \in T_\mathcal{D}$ *and states* $p, q, r \in Q$, *it satisfies both*

Condition 1: $(p, q, r) \in \mathcal{R} \implies (pt, qt, rt) \in \mathcal{R}$.
Condition 2: $(q_0, q, r) \in \mathcal{R} \implies (q_0, qt, rt) \in \mathcal{R}$.

Also say a transformation $t\colon Q \to Q$ *respects* $\mathcal{S}$ *if it satisfies Conditions 1 and 2 for* $\mathcal{S}$.

We frequently refer back to these definitions. Henceforth, let (A), (B), (C), (D), Condition 1, and Condition 2 denote the properties in these two definitions.

Notice that if a DFA $\mathcal{D}$ respects a triple system $\mathcal{S}$, then they must have the same state set, initial state, and final states. As shorthand, we sometimes refer to a triple system $\mathcal{S} = (Q, q_0, F, \mathcal{R})$ only by $\mathcal{R}$ when the other parameters are clear from context. In particular, it suffices to say that a DFA $\mathcal{D} = (Q, \Sigma, \delta, q_0, F)$ respects $\mathcal{R}$, since the other pieces of the triple system must be Q, q_0, and F. In all future DFAs and triple systems, we use Q_n as the state set and 0 as the initial state.

Although the motivation for the triples in $\mathcal{R}$ are those satisfying $K_p \cap K_q \subseteq K_r$ in some DFA that respects the system, it is not generally the case that $(p, q, r) \in \mathcal{R} \iff K_p \cap K_q \subseteq K_r$. We can only guarantee that $(p, q, r) \in \mathcal{R} \implies K_p \cap K_q \subseteq K_r$; the proof of this is an easy exercise using (D) and Condition 1. Let us now prove the essential properties of triple systems that we mentioned at the beginning of this section.

Proposition 1. *If a DFA* $\mathcal{D} = (Q_n, \Sigma, \delta, 0, F)$ *respects a triple system* $\mathcal{R}$ *then* $\mathcal{D}$ *is suffix-convex.*

Proof. Let $u, v, w \in \Sigma^*$ such that $w, uvw \in L(\mathcal{D})$. To prove suffix-convexity, we show that $vw \in L(\mathcal{D})$. Observe the following:

- $(0, 0u, 0) \in \mathcal{R}$ by (A),
- $(0, 0uv, 0v) \in \mathcal{R}$ by Condition 2,
- $(0w, 0uvw, 0vw) \in \mathcal{R}$ by Condition 1,
- $0w, 0uvw \in F$ since $w, uvw \in L(\mathcal{D})$,
- $0vw \in F$ by (D).

Hence $vw \in L(\mathcal{D})$. □

Proposition 2. *If a minimal DFA* $\mathcal{D} = (Q_n, \Sigma, \delta, 0, F)$ *is suffix-convex, then it respects the triple system* $(Q_n, 0, F, \mathcal{R})$ *where*

$$\mathcal{R} = \{(p, q, r) \mid K_p \cap K_q \subseteq K_r\}.$$

Proof. It is easy to verify that $(Q_n, 0, F, \mathcal{R})$ is a triple system when $\mathcal{D}$ is minimal. We must check that every transformation in $T_{\mathcal{D}}$ satisfies Condition 1 and Condition 2.

Condition 1: Let $t \in T_{\mathcal{D}}$ and suppose $(p, q, r) \in \mathcal{R}$. We wish to show that $(pt, qt, rt) \in \mathcal{R}$, or equivalently, $K_{pt} \cap K_{qt} \subseteq K_{rt}$. Choose a word $w \in \Sigma^*$ that induces t in $\mathcal{D}$. Since $K_p \cap K_q \subseteq K_r$, we have $w^{-1}(K_p \cap K_q) \subseteq w^{-1}K_r$. Notice

$w^{-1}(K_p \cap K_q) = w^{-1}K_p \cap w^{-1}K_q = K_{pt} \cap K_{qt}$ and $w^{-1}K_r = K_{rt}$. Therefore $K_{pt} \cap K_{qt} \subseteq K_{rt}$.

Condition 2: Let $t \in T_{\mathcal{D}}$ and suppose $(0, q, r) \in \mathcal{R}$. Then $K_0 \cap K_q \subseteq K_r$, and we wish to show $K_0 \cap K_{qt} \subseteq K_{rt}$. To a contradiction, suppose there exists a word $w \in (K_0 \cap K_{qt}) \setminus K_{rt}$. Choose words $u, v \in \Sigma^*$ such that $0u = q$ and v induces t in $\mathcal{D}$. Since $w \in K_0 \cap K_{pt}$, both w and uvw must be in L. But by Condition 1, $K_{0t} \cap K_{qt} \subseteq K_{rt}$, and since $w \in K_{qt}$ and $w \notin K_{rt}$, it follows that $w \notin K_{0t}$. As $K_{0t} = K_{0v} = v^{-1}L$, we have $vw \notin L$, contradicting the suffix-convexity of $L(\mathcal{D})$. $\qquad\square$

Proposition 3. *Let $\mathcal{S} = (Q_n, 0, F, \mathcal{R})$ be a triple system and define*

$$T^* := \{t \colon Q_n \to Q_n \mid t \text{ respects } \mathcal{S}\}.$$

If a DFA $\mathcal{D}$ respects $\mathcal{S}$ then $T_{\mathcal{D}} \subseteq T^*$. Moreover, there is a DFA $\mathcal{D}'$ respecting $\mathcal{S}$ with $T_{\mathcal{D}'} = T^*$.

Proof. The first claim is obvious, since every transformation in $T_{\mathcal{D}}$ must respect $\mathcal{S}$. For the second claim, we may simply choose $\mathcal{D}' = (Q_n, \Sigma, \delta, 0, F)$ where Σ and δ are defined by $\Sigma = \{a_t \mid t \in T^*\}$ and $\delta(p, a_t) = pt$ for all $t \in T^*$. Since T^* is a semigroup under composition, $T_{\mathcal{D}'} = T^*$. $\qquad\square$

While a triple system gives a ternary relation between states, it also yields an interesting binary relation that is very useful in describing triple systems and reasoning about them. As suggested by the asymmetry in Condition 2, the initial state q_0 plays a special role in a triple system.

Definition 3. *Given a triple system $\mathcal{S} = (Q, q_0, F, \mathcal{R})$, define $\trianglelefteq_R$, a binary relation on Q, by*

$$p \trianglelefteq_R q \iff (q_0, p, q) \in \mathcal{R}.$$

When $\mathcal{R}$ is clear from context, we will simply write $\trianglelefteq$ instead of $\trianglelefteq_R$. It turns out that $\trianglelefteq$ is a kind of order relation called a *preorder* (also called a *quasiorder*).

Proposition 4. *For any triple system $\mathcal{S} = (Q_n, 0, F, \mathcal{R})$, $\trianglelefteq_R$ is a preorder on Q_n; that is, it satisfies*

1. $p \trianglelefteq_R p,$ *(Reflexivity)*
2. $p \trianglelefteq_R q$ *and* $q \trianglelefteq_R r \implies p \trianglelefteq_R r.$ *(Transitivity)*

Proof. Reflexivity follows by (A) and (B). To prove transitivity, suppose $p \trianglelefteq_R q$ and $q \trianglelefteq_R r$. Then

- $(0, p, q) \in \mathcal{R}$ by assumption,
- $(p, 0, q) \in \mathcal{R}$ by (B),
- $(0, q, r) \in \mathcal{R}$ by assumption,

- $(p, 0, r) \in \mathcal{R}$ by (C),
- $(0, p, r) \in \mathcal{R}$ by (B).

Hence $p \trianglelefteq_{\mathcal{R}} r$.   □

A preorder is similar to a partial order, except that it does not require the antisymmetry property ($p \trianglelefteq q$ and $q \trianglelefteq p \implies p = q$). It is not true that $\trianglelefteq$ is always a partial order, since there may be states p and q where $p \trianglelefteq q$ and $q \trianglelefteq p$, but $p \neq q$; such elements are called *symmetric* and we write $p \sim q$. We also write $p \triangleleft q$ to indicate $p \trianglelefteq q$ but $q \ntrianglelefteq p$.

We will find $\trianglelefteq$ useful because triple systems can be complicated and varied, whereas $\trianglelefteq$ has a more restricted structure. Besides being a preorder, $\trianglelefteq$ has the interesting property that $p \trianglelefteq 0$ for all $p \in Q_n$ (since $(0, p, 0) \in \mathcal{R}$ for all $p \in Q_n$ by (A)). Thus, 0 is always a maximum element of $\trianglelefteq$. Note that there could be other elements, symmetric with 0, which are also maximum elements with respect to $\trianglelefteq$.

The most pleasing feature of $\trianglelefteq$ is that it gives us an intuitive way of restating Condition 2.

Condition 2: t is monotone with respect to $\trianglelefteq$.

In this context, t being *monotone* means that $p \trianglelefteq q \implies pt \trianglelefteq qt$. We frequently use this property and the structure of $\trianglelefteq$ as an entry point to reasoning about triple systems. It is sometimes sufficient to consider only $\trianglelefteq$ in proofs, ignoring the finer details of the triple system entirely. As demonstrated by the next theorem, when $\trianglelefteq$ is a partial order we can effectively ignore the rest of the triple system because every monotone transformation can be included in the transition semigroup without breaking suffix-convexity. Since it is never harmful to have a larger semigroup for proving complexity properties, the cases where $\trianglelefteq$ is a partial order are the simplest and most natural.

Theorem 1. *Fix any partial order $\preceq$ on Q_n in which 0 is the maximum element. Let $f \in Q_n$ and consider the triple system $\mathcal{S} = (Q_n, 0, \{f\}, \mathcal{R})$, where*

$$\mathcal{R} = \{(p, q, r) \mid p \preceq r \preceq q \text{ or } q \preceq r \preceq p\}.$$

There exists a minimal suffix-convex DFA $\mathcal{D} = (Q_n, \Sigma, \delta, 0, F)$ respecting $\mathcal{S}$ such that

$$T_{\mathcal{D}} = \{t \colon Q_n \to Q_n \mid t \text{ is monotone with respect to } \preceq\}.$$

Furthermore, $\trianglelefteq_{\mathcal{R}} = \preceq$, i.e. $p \trianglelefteq_{\mathcal{R}} q$ if and only if $p \preceq q$.

Proof. It is easy to check that $\mathcal{S}$ satisfies (A), (B), (C), and (D). By construction, $(0, p, q) \in \mathcal{R}$ if and only if $p \preceq q \preceq 0$. Since 0 is the maximum element in $\preceq$, this implies $\trianglelefteq_{\mathcal{R}} = \preceq$. We construct a minimal DFA respecting $\mathcal{S}$ with every monotone function in its transition semigroup.

Let $\mathcal{M}$ denote the set of monotone transformations on Q_n with respect to $\preceq$. Since monotonicity is preserved under composition, $\mathcal{M}$ is a semigroup under composition. Let $\mathcal{D} = (Q_n, \Sigma, \delta, 0, \{f\})$ where $\Sigma = \{a_t \mid t \in \mathcal{M}\}$ and

$\delta(p, a_t) = pt$ for all $t \in \mathcal{M}$ (in other words, include a dedicated letter in Σ for each monotone transformation). Clearly $T_\mathcal{D} = \mathcal{M}$.

It is easy to show that $\mathcal{D}$ is minimal: State p is reached by the transformation $(Q_n \to p)$, and two states p and q, $q \not\preceq p$, are distinguished by the monotone transformation t defined by

$$rt = \begin{cases} f & \text{if } r \preceq p, \text{ and} \\ 0 & \text{otherwise.} \end{cases}$$

To prove suffix-convexity, we show that every transformation in $\mathcal{M}$ respects $\mathcal{S}$. Condition 2 is trivial, since $\preceq = \trianglelefteq_\mathcal{R}$. For Condition 1, observe that if $p \preceq r \preceq q$ then $pt \preceq rt \preceq qt$ for all $t \in \mathcal{M}$. Hence $(p, q, r) \in \mathcal{R}$ implies $(pt, qt, rt) \in \mathcal{R}$ for all $t \in \mathcal{M}$. $\qquad\square$

Remark 1. The set of final states in Theorem 1 need not be a singleton. We only require that $\emptyset \subsetneq F \subsetneq Q_n$ and that F is *convex* with respect to $\preceq$; that is, there cannot be states $f \preceq g \preceq h$ where $f, h \in F$ and $g \notin F$.

4   Star, Product, and Boolean Operations

This section has our first application of the triple system framework. We present a proper suffix-convex witness stream $(L_n \mid n \geqslant 3)$ that meets the regular language upper bound for (Kleene) star. With a dialect stream, it also meets the regular language upper bound for product and boolean operations. Upper bounds for all of these operations on regular languages are well known (e.g. [4,19]): If L' and L are regular languages of complexity m and n, respectively, then $\kappa(L^*) \leqslant 2^{n-1} + 2^{n-2}$, $\kappa(L'L) \leqslant (m-1)2^n + 2^{n-1}$, and $\kappa(L' \circ L) \leqslant mn$ for $\circ \in \{\cup, \oplus, \backslash, \cap\}$.

The witness DFA we introduce respects a triple system such that $\trianglelefteq_\mathcal{R}$ is a total order on Q_n. We define the triple system such that $0 \triangleright 1 \triangleright \cdots \triangleright n-2 \triangleright n-1$ (Fig. 1).

Definition 4. *For $n \geqslant 3$, define $\mathcal{S}_n = (Q_n, 0, \{n-2\}, \mathcal{R}_n)$ where*

$$\mathcal{R}_n = \{(p, q, r) \mid p \geqslant r \geqslant q \text{ or } q \geqslant r \geqslant p\}.$$

Note that $\mathcal{R}_n$ is exactly the triple system from Theorem 1 if "$\preceq$" is replaced with "$\geqslant$". Therefore, by Theorem 1, any monotone transformation can be included in the transition semigroup of the witness DFA without violating suffix-convexity. For simplicity, we use a small alphabet that generates a non-maximal semigroup since it is sufficient for our purposes (Fig. 2).

Definition 5. *For $n \geqslant 3$, let $L_n(\Sigma)$ be the language recognized by the DFA $\mathcal{D}_n = (Q_n, \Sigma, \delta_n, 0, \{n-2\})$, where $\Sigma = \{a, b, c, d, e, f\}$ and δ_n is given by the transformations a: $\binom{n-2}{0}i \to i+1$, b: $\binom{n-1}{1}i \to i-1$, c: $(\{n-3, n-2\} \to n-1)$, d: $(n-2 \to n-1)$, and $e = f = \mathbb{1}$.*

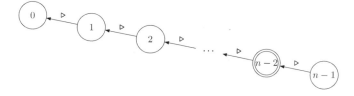

Fig. 1. The order relation $\unlhd_{\mathcal{R}_n}$ of Definition 4 used in the complex witness stream for star and product.

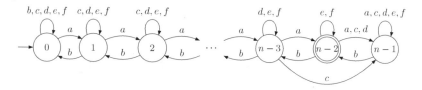

Fig. 2. DFA $\mathcal{D}_n$ of Definition 5.

Proposition 5. *For $n \geqslant 3$, $L_n(\Sigma)$ of Definition 5 is proper and $\kappa(L_n) = n$.*

Theorem 2. *The language stream $(L_n(a,b,c,d) \mid n \geqslant 3)$ of Definition 5 meets the upper bound for star. That is, for $n \geqslant 3$, $\kappa(L_n^*) = 2^{n-1} + 2^{n-2}$.*

One may wonder what is required of a suffix-convex language to meet the bound for star. It turns out that the triple system it respects must be somewhat similar to that of Definition 4.

Lemma 1. *Suppose L is a suffix-convex language with $\kappa(L) = n \geqslant 3$ and $\kappa(L^*) = 2^{n-1} + 2^{n-2}$. Let $\mathcal{D} = (Q_n, \Sigma, \delta, 0, F)$ be a minimal DFA for L and assume that $\mathcal{D}$ respects a triple system $\mathcal{R}$. Then $\unlhd_\mathcal{R}$ must admit a comparison between every pair of states in Q_n, i.e. for all $p, q \in Q_n$, either $p \unlhd q$ or $q \unlhd p$.*

This lemma does not imply that $\unlhd$ must be a total order on the states because it could have symmetric elements.

Theorem 3. *The dialect streams $(L_m(a,b,c,-,e,f) \mid m \geqslant 3)$ and $(L_n(e,f,-,-,a,b) \mid n \geqslant 3)$ of Definition 5 meet the upper bound for product of proper suffix-convex languages. Specifically, for $m, n \geqslant 3$, $\kappa(L_m(a,b,c,-,e,f)L_n(e,f,-,-,a,b)) = (m-1)2^n + 2^{n-1}$.*

Theorem 4. *The dialect streams $(L_m(a,b,-,-,e,f) \mid m \geqslant 3)$ and $(L_n(e,f,-,-,a,b) \mid n \geqslant 3)$ of Definition 5 meet the upper bounds for boolean operations on proper suffix-convex languages. Specifically, for $m, n \geqslant 3$ and $\circ \in \{\cup, \oplus, \backslash, \cap\}$, $\kappa(L_m(a,b,-,-,e,f) \circ L_n(e,f,-,-,a,b)) = mn$.*

5   Reversal

We first prove an upper bound for the complexity of reversal in suffix-convex languages (not necessarily proper), and then give a proper suffix-convex witness stream that meets the bound for $n \geqslant 3$.

Theorem 5. *If L is a suffix-convex language with $\kappa(L) = n$, then $\kappa(L^R) \leqslant 2^n - 2^{n-3}$.*

The proof of Theorem 5 actually tells us a great deal about what a complex witness must look like. Extending the proof slightly, we obtain an important corollary.

Corollary 1. *Suppose L is a suffix-convex language with $\kappa(L) = n \geqslant 3$ and $\kappa(L^R) = 2^n - 2^{n-3}$. Let $\mathcal{D} = (Q_n, \Sigma, \delta, 0, F)$ be a minimal DFA for L and assume that $\mathcal{D}$ respects a triple system $\mathcal{R}$. Then there are exactly two non-zero states p and q such that $p \trianglelefteq_\mathcal{R} q$. Furthermore, $\trianglelefteq_\mathcal{R}$ is a partial order, i.e. no states are symmetric with respect to $\trianglelefteq_\mathcal{R}$.*

Simply put, this corollary says that the triple system of a witness for reversal must look something like Fig. 3. We use this triple system to create our witness for reversal.

Definition 6. *For $n \geqslant 3$, define $\mathcal{S}_n = (Q_n, 0, \{1\}, \mathcal{R}_n)$ where*

$$\mathcal{R}_n = \{(p, q, p) \mid p, q \in Q_n\} \cup \{(p, q, q) \mid p, q \in Q_n\} \cup \{(0, 2, 1), (2, 0, 1)\}.$$

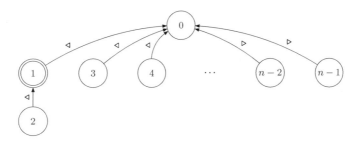

Fig. 3. The order relation $\trianglelefteq_{\mathcal{R}_n}$ of Definition 6 used in the complex witness stream for reversal.

Notice that $\trianglelefteq_{\mathcal{R}_n}$ is a partial order and $\mathcal{R}_n$ is the relation defined in Theorem 1. Hence there exists a DFA respecting $\mathcal{S}_n$ whose transition semigroup contains every transformation of Q_n that is monotone with respect to $\trianglelefteq_{\mathcal{R}_n}$. However, the DFA defined in that theorem has an enormous alphabet, with one letter for each monotone function. Instead, we define a trimmed-down version with a smaller transition semigroup to be our witness for reversal (Fig. 4).

Definition 7. *For $n \geqslant 3$, let $L_n(\Sigma)$ be the language recognized by the DFA $\mathcal{D}_n = (Q_n, \Sigma, \delta_n, 0, \{1\})$, where $\Sigma = \{a, b, c, d, e, f, g, h\}$ and δ_n is given by the transformations*

$$
\begin{aligned}
a &: (3, 4, \ldots, n-1) & e &: (1 \to 2) \\
b &: (3 \to 1) & f &: (2 \to 1) \\
c &: (3 \to 2) & g &: (Q_n \to 3) \\
d &: (1 \to 0) & h &: (Q_n \setminus \{0\} \to 2)(0 \to 1)
\end{aligned}
$$

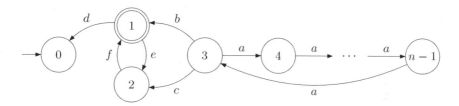

Fig. 4. DFA $\mathcal{D}_n$ of Definition 7. Missing transitions are self-loops. Letters g and h not shown.

Proposition 6. *For $n \geqslant 3$, $L_n(\Sigma)$ of Definition 7 is proper suffix-convex and $\kappa(L_n) = n$.*

Theorem 6. *The language stream $(L_n(\Sigma) \mid n \geqslant 3)$ of Definition 7 meets the upper bound for reversal of proper suffix-convex languages. That is, for $n \geqslant 3$, $\kappa(L_n^R) = 2^n - 2^{n-3}$.*

6 Syntactic Semigroup

The final complexity measure we consider is *syntactic complexity*, the size of the syntactic semigroup. The size and nature of the most complex semigroup in the class of proper suffix-convex languages is an interesting and difficult open question. We describe a stream that we conjecture to be maximal in this respect (Fig. 5).

Definition 8. *For $n \geqslant 3$, define $\mathcal{S}_n = (Q_n, 0, \{n-2\}, \mathcal{R}_n)$ where*

$$
\begin{aligned}
\mathcal{R}_n = {} & \{(p, q, p) \mid p, q \in Q_n\} \cup \{(p, q, q) \mid p, q \in Q_n\} \\
& \cup \{(0, p, q) \mid 0 \leqslant p, q \leqslant n-2\} \cup \{(p, 0, q) \mid 0 \leqslant p, q \leqslant n-2\} \\
& \cup \{(0, n-1, q) \mid q \leqslant n-2\} \cup \{(n-1, 0, q) \mid q \leqslant n-2\}.
\end{aligned}
$$

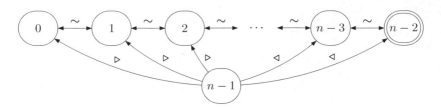

Fig. 5. The order relation $\unlhd_\mathcal{R}$ used in the conjectured witness for syntactic semigroup.

We can compute a bound on the number of transformations that respect $\mathcal{R}_n$. Observe that:

1. If 0 is fixed by t, then $pt \neq n-1$ for all $p \leqslant n-2$ by monotonicity.
2. If $0t \in \{1, 2, \ldots, n-2\}$ then $\{1, 2, \ldots, n-2\}t = 0t$ since $(0t, 0t, pt)$ must be in $\mathcal{R}$ for all $p \in Q_n \setminus \{n-1\}$, and this fails unless $pt = 0t$.
3. If $0t = n-1$ then $Q_n t = n-1$ by monotonicity.

By 1, the number of transformations satisfying $0t = 0$ is at most $n(n-1)^{n-2}$. By 2, the number of transformations satisfying $0t \in \{1, 2, \ldots, n-2\}$ is at most $n(n-2)$. By 3, there is only one transformation where $0t = n-1$. Thus, the size of the transition semigroup is at most $n(n-1)^{n-2} + (n-1)^2$. A more careful analysis reveals that every transformation counted by this argument satisfies Conditions 1 and 2, and thus they all may be added to the transition semigroup.[1] There is a fairly simple DFA that respects $\mathcal{S}$ and has this semigroup:

Definition 9. *For $n \geqslant 3$, let $L_n(\Sigma)$ be the language recognized by the DFA $\mathcal{D}_n = (Q_n, \Sigma, \delta_n, 0, \{n-2\})$, where $\Sigma = \{a, b, c, d, e, f, g, h\}$ and δ_n is given by the transformations*

$$a: (1, \ldots n-2), \qquad\qquad e: (Q_n \setminus \{n-1\} \to 1),$$
$$b: (1, 2), \qquad\qquad\qquad f: (n-1 \to 0),$$
$$c: (n-2 \to 1), \qquad\qquad g: (n-1 \to 1),$$
$$d: (n-2 \to 0), \qquad\qquad h: (Q_n \to n-1).$$

The transition semigroup of $\mathcal{D}_n$ contains every transformation satisfying Condition 1 and Condition 2 with respect to $\mathcal{S}_n$ of Definition 9. Hence the size of the syntactic semigroup of L_n is $n(n-1)^{n-2} + (n-1)^2$. We conjecture that this is optimal.

Conjecture 1. For $n \geqslant 3$, the syntactic complexity of any proper suffix-convex language of complexity at most n is at most $n(n-1)^{n-2} + (n-1)^2$.

Note that the conjectured bound does not hold for general suffix-convex languages, as there is a left ideal stream with syntactic complexity $n^{n-1} + n - 1$ [9].

---

[1] This fact is offered without proof, but it is not difficult to verify.

This witness is known to have maximal syntactic complexity among left ideals and suffix-closed languages. If Conjecture 1 holds, it would imply that the left ideal witness has the largest syntactic complexity over all suffix-convex languages, since suffix-free languages are known to have smaller syntactic complexity [6].

7 Most Complex Streams

A *most complex* language stream is required to meet all the operational bounds for reversal, star, product, and boolean operations, as well as the bound for syntactic complexity.[2] Using results already stated in this paper, we can easily show that there is no most complex proper stream.

Lemma 2. *For $n \geqslant 4$, there does not exist a proper suffix-convex language of complexity n that meets the complexity bounds for both reversal and star.*

Proof. Suppose L is a proper suffix-convex language of complexity n with $\kappa(L^R) = 2^n - 2^{n-3}$ and $\kappa(L^*) = 2^{n-1} + 2^{n-2}$. Let $\mathcal{D} = (Q_n, \Sigma, \delta, 0, F)$ be a minimal DFA for L. By Corollary 1, any triple system $\mathcal{R}$ respected by $\mathcal{D}$ must have only two states (besides 0) that are comparable by $\trianglelefteq_\mathcal{R}$. Yet by Lemma 1, every pair of states (p, q) must have some comparison in $\trianglelefteq_\mathcal{R}$ (either $p \trianglelefteq q$ or $q \trianglelefteq p$). This is impossible for $n \geqslant 4$. $\qquad\square$

Surprisingly, even though the true upper bound for syntactic complexity is not known with certainty, we can still prove that a third stream, different from those for reversal and star, is needed to meet this bound. Thus, at least three streams are needed to meet all the bounds.

Theorem 7. *For $n \geqslant 4$, there does not exist a proper suffix-convex language of complexity n that meets the upper bounds for any two of reversal, star, and syntactic complexity.*

8 Conclusion

We have exhibited several new tight upper bounds for proper suffix-convex languages, some of which apply to all suffix-convex languages. The introduction of triple systems was an essential tool in this endeavour, so perhaps variant triple systems can be developed for other difficult classes of regular languages. The question of determining the maximal syntactic complexity of proper languages remains open. A more involved argument using triple systems may be required.

---

[2] Additionally, it is usually required that the atoms of the language are as complex as possible [4], but this measure is not discussed here.

References

1. Ang, T., Brzozowski, J.: Languages convex with respect to binary relations, and their closure properties. Acta Cybernet. **19**(2), 445–464 (2009)
2. Berstel, J., Perrin, D., Reutenauer, C.: Codes and Automata (Encyclopedia of Mathematics and its Applications). Cambridge University Press, New York (2010)
3. Brzozowski, J.: Quotient complexity of regular languages. J. Autom. Lang. Comb. **15**(1/2), 71–89 (2010)
4. Brzozowski, J.: In search of the most complex regular languages. Int. J. Found. Comput. Sci. **24**(6), 691–708 (2013)
5. Brzozowski, J.: Unrestricted state complexity of binary operations on regular languages. In: Câmpeanu, C., Manea, F., Shallit, J. (eds.) DCFS 2016. LNCS, vol. 9777, pp. 60–72. Springer, Cham (2016). https://doi.org/10.1007/978-3-319-41114-9_5
6. Brzozowski, J., Szykuła, M.: Complexity of suffix-free regular languages. In: Kosowski, A., Walukiewicz, I. (eds.) FCT 2015. LNCS, vol. 9210, pp. 146–159. Springer, Cham (2015). https://doi.org/10.1007/978-3-319-22177-9_12
7. Brzozowski, J., Tamm, H.: Quotient complexities of atoms of regular languages. Int. J. Found. Comput. Sci. **24**(7), 1009–1027 (2013)
8. Brzozowski, J., Tamm, H.: Theory of átomata. Theor. Comput. Sci. **539**, 13–27 (2014)
9. Brzozowski, J., Ye, Y.: Syntactic complexity of ideal and closed languages. In: Mauri, G., Leporati, A. (eds.) DLT 2011. LNCS, vol. 6795, pp. 117–128. Springer, Heidelberg (2011). https://doi.org/10.1007/978-3-642-22321-1_11
10. Brzozowski, J.A., Sinnamon, C.: Complexity of left-ideal, suffix-closed and suffix-free regular languages. In: Drewes, F., Martín-Vide, C., Truthe, B. (eds.) LATA 2017. LNCS, vol. 10168, pp. 171–182. Springer, Cham (2017). https://doi.org/10.1007/978-3-319-53733-7_12
11. Gao, Y., Moreira, N., Reis, R., Yu, S.: A survey on operational state complexity. J. Autom. Lang. Comb. **21**(4), 251–310 (2016)
12. Holzer, M., Kutrib, M.: Descriptional and computational complexity of finite automata-a survey. Inf. Comput. **209**(3), 456–470 (2011)
13. Holzer, M., König, B.: On deterministic finite automata and syntactic monoid size. Theor. Comput. Sci. **327**(3), 319–347 (2004)
14. Iván, S.: Complexity of atoms, combinatorially. Inform. Process. Lett. **116**(5), 356–360 (2016)
15. Myhill, J.: Finite automata and representation of events. Wright Air Development Center Technical report 57–624 (1957)
16. Pin, J.E.: Syntactic semigroups. In: Rozenberg, G., Salomaa, A. (eds.) Handbook of Formal Languages, vol. 1: Word, Language, Grammar, pp. 679–746. Springer, New York (1997)
17. Sinnamon, C.: Complexity of proper suffix-convex regular languages (2018). http://arxiv.org/abs/1805.03375
18. Thierrin, G.: Convex languages. In: Nivat, M. (ed.) Automata, Languages and Programming, pp. 481–492. North-Holland (1973)
19. Yu, S.: State complexity of regular languages. J. Autom. Lang. Comb. **6**, 221–234 (2001)

Author Index

Printed in the United States
By Bookmasters